June 1986

Israel in the Middle East

ISRAEL
IN THE
MIDDLE EAST

Documents and Readings on Society, Politics, and Foreign Relations 1948–present

Edited by

ITAMAR RABINOVICH   JEHUDA REINHARZ
Tel Aviv University   Brandeis University

New York   Oxford
OXFORD UNIVERSITY PRESS
1984

Library of Congress Cataloging in Publication Data
Main entry under title:
Israel in the Middle East.
Bibliography: p.
Includes index.
1. Israel—History—Sources.   I. Rabinovich, Itamar,
1942–   . II. Reinharz, Jehuda.
DS126.5.I784   1984   956.94'05   83-6297
ISBN 0-19-503362-0
ISBN 0-19-503363-9 (pbk.)

Printing (last digit): 9 8 7 6 5 4 3 2

Printed in the United States of America

For Efrat and Shulamit

in brackets; all interpolations appearing in the original documents are in parentheses. Transliterations of Hebrew and Arabic names and terms have been standardized throughout; where events such as wars are known by several names, we have sought in our editorial material to use the least polemical. Some of the documents were written originally in English; about one-fourth were translated from Hebrew and Arabic especially for this volume.

We wish to thank Professors Yonathan Shapiro and David Vital of Tel Aviv University for their advice and help in the preparation of this book. Many of our colleagues and friends in academic and public life generously gave their permission to reprint articles or chapters from their books. In two instances, as no written material was available, they prepared original contributions for this book. All of these individuals are acknowledged in source notes.

We also wish to acknowledge the help of our research assistants, Eliezer Yemini and Gita Yaffe of Tel Aviv University, Steven Heydemann formerly of The University of Michigan and Harvey Sukenic of Brandeis University. We are grateful to Sandra Fine, Dr. Max M. Rothschild, and Batsheva Taube for their competent translations and to Mrs. Lidya Gareh who typed the manuscript. Professor Charles Tilly of the University of Michigan generously provided access to the resources of the Center for Research on Social Organization during the final preparation of the manuscript. Amira Margalith of the Shiloah Center of Tel Aviv University was indispensable in all the technical aspects of the work. Professor Jacob Neusner of Brown University assisted in securing a grant from the D. S. and R. H. Gottesman Foundation. We particularly appreciate the intelligent and resourceful assistance of Benjamin M. Ben-Baruch of the University of Michigan, who helped in the final revisions of the scholarly apparatus of the manuscript. Specifically, the tables and charts in the appendix reflect his ingenuity and perseverance in tracking down the necessary information. Ann Hofstra Grogg is a masterful copyeditor; her comments and suggestions are reflected on every page of this book.

Tel Aviv   I. R.
Waltham, Mass.   J. R.
August 1983

Preface

The purpose of this volume is to provide the English-speaking public with convenient access to the most significant documents of Israel's domestic politics and foreign policies between 1948 and 1983. Numerous books and articles have analyzed these subjects, but there has been no accurate or complete documentary collection that would provide the reader with the basic materials by which to weigh these analyses.

Several criteria determined the editors' selection of materials. Whenever possible a primary source was chosen, such as memoirs, treaties, legal texts, exchanges of letters, parliamentary debates, diaries, speeches, and the like. For a number of issues a single primary source could not by itself illuminate the matter under consideration. In such cases a secondary source—scholarly or journalistic—was chosen.

A special effort was made to diversify the nature and scope of the sources. Thus materials were selected from Israeli, Arab, American, and Soviet records, including government archives as well as journalistic accounts. The range of materials has not been limited to political and diplomatic history but includes economic, cultural, legal, and social material as well.

The volume consists of four chronological divisions, 1948 to 1983. The appendix includes tables on demographic trends and government structure; maps in the text have been prepared especially for this volume. Each document in the book is annotated and is preceded by an explanatory headnote. Major figures, events, and organizations are usually identified at first mention; the page number on which the identification appears is indicated in the index by italics. Consequently cross-references have been kept to a minimum. Our interpolations in the documents appear

Contents

I 1948–56

DOMESTIC ISSUES

FOREIGN POLICY ISSUES

II   1956–67

DOMESTIC ISSUES

FOREIGN POLICY ISSUES

III   1967–73

DOMESTIC ISSUES

FOREIGN POLICY ISSUES

IV   1973–83

DOMESTIC ISSUES

FOREIGN POLICY ISSUES

Appendix   Demography and Government in Israel

Index, 391

List of Maps

Israel in the Middle East

Introduction

Scholars characteristically demarcate Israel's history by its wars. These wars are turning points not only in Israel's foreign policy but also in the country's internal development. Following this practice, the chronological framework of this book's treatment of Israel's domestic and foreign issues is based on a division into four phases.

1948–56

This phase begins with the first full-scale Arab-Israeli war (the War of Independence, from Israel's perspective) and ends with the Sinai Campaign of 1956. During these years the State of Israel was proclaimed, established, and recognized, the institutions of the state and a governmental structure were formed or transformed from their prestate versions, social and economic patterns were set, and great numbers of immigrants from Europe and the Islamic world arrived and settled. The enormity and pace of these changes made the early years of Israel's statehood highly turbulent. In addition, the period was characterized by debates over the nature of the political system, the relation of state and religion, the need for a constitution, the question of reparations from Germany, and others.

Israel's international position during this period, as in later years, was determined primarily by the severity and salience of the Arab-Israeli conflict. This relation was not immediately apparent. The First Arab-Israeli War ended with armistice agreements and attempts at reconciliation and peacemaking. But by 1950 it became clear that the conflict between the Arabs and the Israelis was deep and complex and intertwined with numerous regional and international political issues.

During this period Israel gradually drew away from the Soviet Union and became increasingly tied to and dependent on the West. The Western powers, however, were interested in tying the Arab world to a pro-Western alliance, and Israel found itself in the early 1950s at the height of its international isolation. This isolation diminished in 1955 with the emergence of the French-Israeli alliance. The rise of Nasserism, the radicalization of Arab politics, and the Soviet-Western rivalry all contributed to the exacerbation of the Arab-Israeli conflict, which culminated in the second Arab-Israeli war, the Sinai Campaign of 1956.

1956–67

The years that followed the war saw a gradual improvement in the economic condition and standard of living in Israel. The austerity regimen of the early 1950s ended, and a variety of development schemes were inaugurated. The early 1960s were years of sound economic growth and relative prosperity, which ended with the recession of 1965–67.

In the country's domestic politics the most important development of the period was the demise of David Ben-Gurion's leadership. Ben-Gurion had dominated the Jewish community in Palestine since the late 1920s, but his power and influence began to decline in the mid-1950s. He retired in 1963 but continued to affect the politics of the state and his party under his successor, Levi Eshkol. Ben-Gurion's conflict with his own party's leadership reflected a changing of the guard in Mapai, the major political force in Israel. The changes within Mapai and the Labor movement were in turn related to a diminution of the chief dichotomy of Israeli public life: the Labor movement and Mapai on the one hand, and the nationalist Right, led by the Herut movement, on the other.

The social and economic stabilization within Israel during these years was matched by the consolidation of Israel's regional and international position. First, the international isolation that characterized the early 1950s gave way to a virtual alliance with France and improved relations with Britain and the United States. This development, however, came at the cost of growing friction in Israel's relationship with the Soviet Union. Second, while Israel's cooperation with Britain and France in the Sinai Campaign damaged its relationship with the Third World, it also endowed it with a new stature. Ben-Gurion was able to convert this prestige into an improved regional position through the development of the "periphery orientation"—a semialliance with other non-Arab, anti-Soviet states such as Turkey, Iran, and Ethiopia. Finally, Israel's military success in the Sinai Campaign and the security arrangements made in its aftermath served as a deterrent and helped stabilize Arab-Israeli relations for approximately ten years.

This stability diminished in the mid-1960s as the Arab-Israeli conflict and the international conflict in the region were once more exacerbated. Among the issues at stake were the waters of the Jordan, the reemergence of an autonomous Palestinian national movement, border clashes with Syria, and conflicts between moderate and radical Arab states and their respective superpower patrons. These culminated in the crisis of May 1967 and the June 1967 War, also called the Six-Day War.

1967–73

The events of May–June 1967—the May crisis, the decisive military victory, the capture of territories from Syria, Jordan, and Egypt—constitute a watershed in the domestic and external history of Israel.

Domestically, the formation of the National Unity government as a result of the May crisis brought the Herut movement for the first time into the realm of national leadership and power. Previously Ben-Gurion had deliberately and successfully kept the Herut movement outside the pale. The movement's participation in the government (June 1967–August 1970) was an important aspect of the process that enhanced the nationalist Right's power, legitimacy, and respectability and culminated in its electoral victory ten years later.

Israel's postwar control over all of Palestine west of the Jordan, all of the Sinai, and a major portion of the Golan Heights turned the debate over the future of these territories and Jerusalem into the major issue of Israel's domestic and foreign politics. The debate has not been confined to the narrower questions of control and final disposition of these territories, but addresses a myriad of related issues such as the essence of Zionism, the allocation of resources, and the transformation of religious Zionism.

The June 1967 War terminated the economic recession of the mid-1960s and ushered in a phase marked by an economic boom, an accelerated inflationary pace, and growing political tensions between ethnic, social, and economic groups. The partial overlapping of socioeconomic disparities and communal ethnic differences led to occasional outbursts of frustration, particularly by Israelis of North African extraction. In the 1970s such tensions were aggravated by the increased immigration from the Soviet Union. The special privileges extended to this group as well as to new immigrants from other countries who came in the 1970s irritated underprivileged groups who had arrived in the 1950s and were absorbed in the austere conditions of those years.

Externally, the Arab-Israeli conflict came to assume a progressively central place in Israel's policies. In the early 1960s the development of Israel's relations with Africa and Latin America was an important concern of Israel's foreign policy. After 1967 this, as well as other interests, were submerged by the special considerations arising as a consequence of the war. The Israeli government sought to use its military victory and control of former Arab territories to achieve a settlement of the Arab-Israeli conflict. Over time an interest in returning at least some of these territories developed. The Arab states, as a rule, sought to regain the lost territories without giving up their pre-1967 stance in the conflict. All Arab efforts to dislodge

Israel from the territories, first through the United Nations and then through the War of Attrition, proved futile, and a stalemate ensued until 1973.

With this stalemate Israel found it increasingly difficult to obtain international support for its position. The Soviet Union and the Eastern bloc countries severed diplomatic relations with Israel immediately after the June 1967 War. Later the Arab and particularly Palestinian position received increasing support in Third World and then Western countries. The initially favorable reception accorded to Israel's benign rule in the West Bank and Gaza was gradually replaced by criticism of what was termed Israel's intransigence and suppression of a Palestinian national movement.

Israel's ability to withstand Arab and Soviet pressures during this period can be explained largely by American backing and support. Washington did not agree with all aspects of Israeli policy but accepted its fundamental premise, that unlike the situation following the Sinai Campaign, Israel should not relinquish the captured territories without a solid and proper settlement of the Arab-Israeli conflict. Also, as Soviet-American rivalry in the Middle East stiffened in the late 1960s, Israel played an important role as a powerful and reliable American ally.

This sense of American-Israeli partnership was particularly strong in the years 1970–73 following the two countries' successful cooperation during the Jordanian crisis of September 1970. But by 1973 a reassessment of U.S. policies in the Middle East was under way. Cairo's turn toward the West in 1972 and the oil crisis—of both supply and cost—created new opportunities and new constraints for Washington, but their full impact was felt only after the October 1973 War.

1973–83

The October 1973 War, also called the Yom Kippur War, ended ambiguously. A cease-fire was imposed by the United States as Israel was about to defeat the Egyptian army, was firmly lodged on the Egyptian side of the Suez Canal, and had already advanced well into newly captured Syrian territory. Yet Egypt controlled most of the Suez Canal. The Egyptians and Syrians had enjoyed military success at the outset of the surprise war. Israel had suffered heavy casualties and loss of matériel and had to resort to an American airlift.

These failures expedited the Labor movement's decline, and in the elections of 1977 Yitzhak Rabin, Golda Meir's successor, was defeated by Menahem Begin and the Likud alignment. The new government encountered difficult problems. The lack of cohesiveness in the ruling coalition, the prime minister's poor health, the extreme polarization of public opinion over the question of the West Bank administration, the economic crisis (inflation, trade balance deficit, etc.), and the domestic impact of the peace treaty with Egypt eventually produced a process of disintegration.

The Egyptian-Israeli peace treaty of March 1979, which implemented the Camp David Agreements, was the high point of the rapprochement process that began in the immediate aftermath of the October 1973 War. Paradoxically, though, the peace treaty—the chief goal of Israeli policy since independence—met with little enthusiasm, internationally or regionally, and produced domestic difficulties in both Israel and Egypt. Of the major difficulties that confronted Israel as a result of the peace treaty several should be mentioned.

1. The linkage between the Egyptian-Israeli peace agreement and other dimensions of the Arab-Israeli conflict, particularly the Palestinian dimension, was unwieldy.

2. Israel remained uncertain about Egypt's true long-range intentions.

3. The peace had a heavy economic and military price. The uncertain nature of the new relationship with Egypt and the fact that in its other aspects the Arab-Israeli conflict remained unresolved meant that the arms race and military buildup continued. At the same time Israel had made significant concessions such as handing over the airfields and oilfields in Sinai.

4. The benefits expected by Israelis in return for such concessions materialized only in part: trade between the two countries has thus far been nonexistent, there is no cultural exchange, and tourism has been one-sided. While Egypt lived up at least to the letter of its commitments, Israel's regional and international position did not improve. Rather, the peace treaty was criticized for its partial nature, and pressure was exercised to reach a comprehensive settlement of the Arab-Israeli conflict.

5. Israel continued to be concerned with Sadat's (and after his assassination, with Husni Mubarak's) support base within Egypt.

6. Nationalist Israeli groups attempted to undermine the treaty, which in their view threatened Israeli security.

7. Other Arab parties to the conflict were unwilling to come forward as negotiating partners.

By the fall of 1980 the government of Menahem Begin seemed to have lost its momentum for making decisions. Support in the Knesset was being further eroded, and two of the government's most prominent members—Ezer Weizman and Moshe Dayan—resigned. In the economic sphere the inflationary spiral continued to rise, and the autonomy negotiations concerning the Palestinians both with the United States and with Egypt came to a halt. These events were punctuated by scandals. Under these circumstances pressures mounted to call for elections prior to November 1981, their scheduled date. A compromise date of June 30 was finally agreed on by the Knesset.

When these decisions were made in early 1981, public opinion polls and other political indexes showed that the Labor alignment would win a sweeping majority.

But during the next few months this prediction changed as the Likud alignment, dominated by Begin and the Herut movement, regained the support it had lost during the previous two years. Begin won a slim victory in the elections, and his close relationship with the religious parties enabled him to form a new government relying on a small parliamentary majority.

The political recovery of Begin and the Likud alignment during the first six months of 1981 was a remarkable phenomenon based on a number of simultaneous developments.

1. Begin regained political credibility through his adroitness in controlling the pace and direction of domestic politics during these months. His health seemed to be improving, and the electorate regained faith in his ability to continue in office.

2. The Likud successfully portrayed itself as antiestablishment despite its control of the government, and Labor failed to discard its image as an establishment party. This labeling fed into the communal image and interests of the Oriental Jews, primarily those of North African extraction, who lent their support to the Likud and more precisely to Begin.

3. The economic policies launched shortly before the elections by the new minister of finance were successful, at least for the short term.

4. A configuration of events provided Israel respite in its foreign relations. In the United States the administration of Ronald Reagan, which took office in January 1981, sought to minimize friction with Begin. Similarly Egypt maintained a low-profile stance and even seemed to support Begin, as exemplified by Sadat's public meeting with Begin immediately preceding the Israeli elections. The war between Iran and Iraq deflected world attention from Israel and its immediate neighbors. The domestic problems of the Ba'ath regime in Syria and the temporary disorganization within the ranks of the Palestine Liberation Organization (PLO) created a regional situation that was particularly favorable from the point of view of the Israeli government and public.

5. At the same time there occurred a number of crises that clearly enhanced Begin's stature as an assertive and fearless leader. First was his strong stance when the Syrians moved anti-aircraft missiles in areas agreed to be off limits to such armaments. More dramatic was the Israeli pinpoint destruction of Iraqi nuclear facilities near Baghdad. Even the unprecedented American condemnation of this action in the United Nations did not alter the Israeli public's general approval.

Several important trends were demonstrated and established by the elections of June 1981. The currents transforming the Israeli political system in the 1970s were still in full swing. Many of the structures, doctrines, and myths were failing under the impact of new forces and challenges. The change of administrations in 1977 from Labor to Likud proved to be a phenomenon more durable than observers believed possible. The political system continued its "rightward" shift, and the dividing line between Ashkenazi and Sephardi voters assumed an alarming significance. On the other hand, the shift by Israeli Arab voters from their former Communist party protest vote to the Labor party could mark the beginning of an important integration of the Israeli Arab population into the mainstream of Israeli politics. The decline of several smaller parties and electoral lists could, in turn, indicate a trend toward the formation of two large political blocs, with the religious parties enjoying inflated power as the decisive element in coalition forming.

The events of the two years following the July 1981 elections were governed by the War in Lebanon in the summer of 1982. The year between the elections and the war seems, in retrospect, as the prelude to the war. It lasted the whole summer of 1982, and, even if September 1982 is seen as its terminal point, it has dominated Israeli and Middle Eastern politics since then.

The war was launched in June by an Israeli government that sought first and foremost to solve Israel's security problem in southern Lebanon. But the government, moved primarily by the defense minister, Ariel Sharon, tried at the same time to solve other problems and to achieve additional objectives. These proved too ambitious. Israel could not restructure the Lebanese state or sustain its ally, Bashir Jumayyil, as Lebanon's president. A year after the war a large Israeli army was still stationed in Lebanon; Syria—after a temporary decline—held the key to a settlement in Lebanon; and another Lebanese president, Amine Jumayyil, was trying to build an effective central government.

One significant outcome of the war was the PLO's forced evacuation of Beirut. Combined with Syria's decision to bring the organization under its firm authority, this resulted in a serious decline in the PLO's standing and influence. Concomitantly the position of other contenders for representing the Palestinian cause—Jordan and local leaders in the West Bank—improved. But the failure of the Reagan administration to promote its plan and the Israeli government's own difficulties prevented any new ideas on addressing the broader Palestinian issue from taking effect.

The Israeli government's difficulties were to a great extent a direct result of the War in Lebanon. The government of Menahem Begin and Ariel Sharon, which launched the war, was at the height of its power. But the complications during the summer of 1982 began to cast shadows on the government. From mid-September until February 1983, when the Commission of Inquiry into Israel's potential responsibilities for the massacres in Sabra and Shatila completed its work, the government lived under a threat of its expected verdict. The findings indeed forced Sharon's resignation as minister of defense. In subsequent months it became more and more clear that despite a very heavy price, Israel effected few desirable changes in Lebanon despite the signing of a peace agreement with Lebanon on May 17, 1983. This treaty has affected neither the internal conflicts within Lebanon nor Israel's ability to extricate itself from southern Lebanon because its implementation is conditional upon the simultaneous withdrawal of Israeli, Syrian and PLO troops; yet Syria and the PLO have refused to withdraw. There was a marked decline in the government's performance and its standing in public opinion polls. Toward the end of 1983 many Israelis felt that a chapter in the country's domestic history was coming to an end. This was symbolized by Prime Minister Begin's resignation on September 15, 1983 following several weeks of ill health. On October 10, 1983 a third Likud government was formed by Yizhak Shamir. That government must tackle the unresolved Arab-Israeli conflict, now complicated by the Lebanese conflicts, while facing Israel's most serious economic crisis since the early 1950s.

I

1948–56
Domestic Issues

1. The Proclamation of the State of Israel

Theodor Herzl (1860–1904) was the father of political Zionism and founder of the World Zionist Organization. An assimilated Jew of minimal Jewish commitment, he was aroused by the growing anti-Semitism he witnessed as the Paris correspondent for the *Neue Freie Presse* of Vienna, 1890–95. He concluded that the only feasible solution to the Jewish problem was a mass exodus of the Jews from the countries of their birth and a resettlement in the Land of Israel, and he devoted the rest of his life to realizing this idea. His book *The Jew's State: An Attempt at a Modern Solution of the Jewish Question* (1896) set forth his basic ideas and program.

The World Zionist Organization (WZO) was established in 1897 primarily as a result of Herzl's efforts. It encompassed virtually every Zionist organization in the world and coordinated programs to establish a national Jewish homeland. Policies were set by Zionist congresses, to which each Zionist organization sent delegates in proportion to its membership. In order to broaden its support among world Jewry, the WZO established the Jewish Agency in 1929.

The WZO achieved international recognition of its major political goal with the Balfour Declaration of November 2, 1917. This "declaration" was a letter approved by the British cabinet, signed by Foreign Secretary Arthur James Balfour, and sent to Lionel Walter Rothschild, honorary president of the Zionist Federation of Great Britain and Ireland, who was asked to convey it to the World Zionist Organization.

It stated in part: "His Majesty's Government view with favour the establishment in Palestine of a national home for the Jewish people, and will use their best endeavours to facilitate the achievement of this object, it being clearly understood that nothing shall be done which may prejudice the civil and religious rights of existing non-Jewish communities in Palestine, or the rights and political status enjoyed by Jews in any other country."

The declaration was included in the text of the Mandate for Palestine issued to Britain by the League of Nations on July 24, 1922, and was the basis for British rule in this area until, on November 29, 1947, the U.N. General Assembly voted (33–13–10) to partition Palestine into an independent Jewish state and an independent Arab state, with Jerusalem having a unique international status as a *corpus separatum*. This Partition Plan (see map 1) was to be implemented upon the termination of British rule.

On May 14, 1948, British rule over Palestine ended. At 8:00 A.M. the British lowered the Union Jack in Jerusalem. By midafternoon the neighboring Arab states had launched a full-scale attack. At 4:00 P.M., despite great pressure from the United States and the doubts of many of his colleagues, David Ben-Gurion, chairman of the Jewish Agency Executive, read the Proclamation of the State of Israel. The Jewish population of Palestine—except for Jerusalem, which was without electricity—heard the proclamation ceremonies as they were broadcast from the Tel Aviv Museum.

The Land of Israel was the birthplace of the Jewish people. Here their spiritual, religious and national identity was formed. Here they achieved independence and created a culture of national and universal significance. Here they wrote and gave the Bible to the world.

Exiled from Palestine, the Jewish people

Source: Palestine Post, May 16, 1948, pp. 1–2.

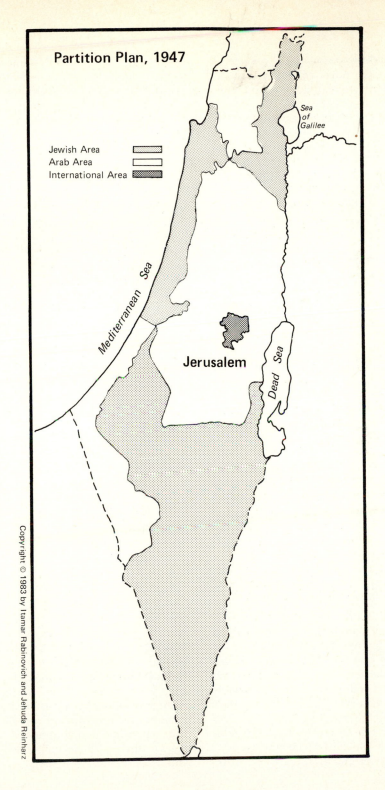

Partition Plan, 1947

Jewish Area
Arab Area
International Area

Sea of Galilee

Mediterranean Sea

Jerusalem

Dead Sea

13

remained faithful to it in all the countries of their dispersion, never ceasing to pray and hope for their return and the restoration of their national freedom.

Impelled by this historic association, Jews strove throughout the centuries to go back to the land of their fathers and regain their Statehood. In recent decades they returned in their masses. They reclaimed the wilderness, revived their language, built cities and villages, and established a vigorous and ever-growing community, with its own economic and cultural life. They sought peace yet were prepared to defend themselves. They brought the blessings of progress to all inhabitants of the country.

In the year 1897 the First Zionist Congress, inspired by Theodor Herzl's vision of the Jewish State, proclaimed the right of the Jewish people to national revival in their own country.

This right was acknowledged by the Balfour Declaration of November 2, 1917, and reaffirmed by the Mandate of the League of Nations, which gave explicit international recognition to the historic connection of the Jewish people with Palestine and their right to reconstitute their national home.

The Nazi holocaust, which engulfed millions of Jews in Europe, proved anew the urgency of the reestablishment of the Jewish State, which would solve the problem of Jewish homelessness by opening the gates to all Jews and lifting the Jewish people to equality in the family of nations.

The survivors of the European catastrophe, as well as Jews from other lands, proclaiming their right to a life of dignity, freedom and labor, and undeterred by hazards, hardships and obstacles, have tried unceasingly to enter Palestine.

In the Second World War the Jewish people in Palestine made a full contribution in the struggle of the freedom-loving nations against the Nazi evil. The sacrifices of their soldiers and the efforts of their workers gained them title to rank with the peoples who founded the United Nations.

On November 29, 1947, the General Assembly of the United Nations adopted a Resolution for the establishment of an independent Jewish State in Palestine, and called upon inhabitants of the country to take such steps as may be necessary on their part to put the plan into effect.

This recognition by the United Nations of the right of the Jewish people to establish their independent state may not be revoked. It is, moreover, the self-evident right of the Jewish people to be a nation, like all other nations, in its own sovereign state.

Accordingly, we, the members of the National Council, representing the Jewish people in Palestine and the Zionist movement of the world, met together in solemn assembly today, the day of the termination of the British Mandate for Palestine, and by virtue of the natural and historic right of the Jewish people and of the resolution of the General Assembly of the United Nations, hereby proclaim the establishment of the Jewish State in Palestine, to be called Israel.

We hereby declare that as from the termination of the Mandate at midnight, this night of the fourteenth to the fifteenth of May, 1948, and until the setting up of the duly elected bodies of the State in accordance with a Constitution, to be drawn up by a Constituent Assembly not later than the first day of October 1948, the present National Council shall act as the Provisional State Council, and its executive organ, the National Administration, shall constitute the Provisional Government of the State of Israel.

The State of Israel will be open to the immigration of Jews from all countries of their dispersion, will promote the development of the country for the benefit of all its inhabitants; will be based on the precepts of liberty, justice and peace taught by the Hebrew Prophets; will uphold the full social and political equality of all its citizens, without distinction of race, creed or sex; will guarantee full freedom of conscience, worship, education and culture; will safeguard the sanctity and inviolability of the shrines and Holy Places of all religions; and will dedicate itself to the principles of the Charter of the United Nations.

The State of Israel will be ready to cooperate with the organs and representatives of the United Nations in the implementation of the Resolution of the Assembly of November 29, 1947, and will take steps to bring about the Economic Union over the whole of Palestine.

We appeal to the United Nations to assist the Jewish people in the building of its State and to admit Israel into the family of nations.

In the midst of wanton aggression, we yet call upon the Arab inhabitants of the State of Israel to return to the ways of peace and play their part in the development of the State, with full and equal citizenship and the representation in all its bodies and institutions, provisional or permanent.

We offer peace and amity to all the neighboring states and their peoples, and invite them to cooperate with the independent Jewish nation for the common good of all. The State of Israel is ready to contribute its full share to the peaceful progress and development of the Middle East.

Our call goes out to the Jewish people all over the world to rally to our side in the task of immigration and development and to stand by us in the great struggle for the fulfillment of the dream of generations—the redemption of Israel.

With trust in the Rock of Israel, we set our hand to this Declaration, at this Session of the Provisional State Council, in the city of Tel Aviv, on this Sabbath eve, the fifth of Iyar, 5708, the fourteenth day of May, 1948.

DAVID BEN-GURION
2. The First Arab-Israeli War

David Ben-Gurion was the single most important personality in Israel's early history. As leader of the largest political party, Mapai, he was elected in 1935 to chair the Jewish Agency Executive in Palestine and thus became head of the semiautonomous government of the Yishuv (the organized Jewish community in Palestine). When the state was proclaimed, he became prime minister, a position he held (with a brief interruption) until June 1963. By that time his personal political influence began to wane; he left Mapai and formed a splinter party, Rafi.

The following reading is from his reflections during the First Arab-Israeli War (called the War of Independence by the Israelis), which lasted from May 14, 1948, until January 7, 1949. Even before the British left Palestine, the Arab League[1] undertook military preparations to negate the Partition Plan and began intermittent attacks on Jewish settlements and institutions. Simultaneously, the military forces attached to various Jewish parties[2] were also preparing for the inevitable clash. As soon as the British left, Israel was invaded by five Arab states— Egypt, Syria, Iraq, Transjordan (soon to be called Jordan), and Lebanon. Saudi Arabia sent a military contingent that operated under Egyptian command. Yemen declared war on Israel but did not take any military actions.

The war began with an Egyptian air attack

Source: David Ben-Gurion, *Israel: A Personal History* (New York and Tel Aviv: Funk and Wagnalls, Inc. and Sabra Books, 1971), pp. 111–21. Reprinted by permission.

on Tel Aviv. When a temporary truce was declared (lasting from June 11 to July 7), Israel was cut off from the Negev (in the south) by the Egyptians; the Syrians had a foothold west of the Jordan River; Iraq controlled the headwaters of the Yarkon River (whose mouth is just north of Tel Aviv), and the Lebanese army and Qawuqji's Arab Liberation Army[3] consolidated themselves in much of the Galilee in the north. The Israelis had established a tenuous supply link to besieged Jerusalem.

Fighting flared up again immediately after the first truce. The turning point occurred during the ten days of July 9–18. Israel made major gains in the central region and in the Galilee. A second truce lasted from July 18 (July 17 in Jerusalem) until October 15. After fighting resumed, Israel made further gains. On January 7, 1949, the final cease-fire took effect (see map 2).

The war involved virtually the entire Jewish population of the new state, as Ben-Gurion's memoirs, excerpted here, show. The professional armies of the Arab states were fought by ill-equipped military forces originally operating under separate commands (see doc. 4) and by untrained civilians. The Jewish population of about 750,000 suffered heavy casualties.

May 16, 1948

At 11 A.M. Israel Galili[4] and Shkolnik[5] were called to Menahem Begin.[6] He proposed that their (Ezel's) ship be purchased for a quarter of a million, and that the money be used to buy arms.

The Carmeli Brigade reached Rosh Hanikrah, where it blew up houses and bridges. Bridges on the northern road leading to Malkiya were blown up at Hanita as well. Acre is ready to surrender, but the situation in the eastern section of upper Galilee is quite bad. The battle for Malkiya was hard fought, with both sides suffering heavy losses. We have a hundred and fifty wounded in a battalion of five hundred men. An enemy unit holds the police station at Nebi Yusha. All the Arabs have left Safed. Two hundred men of the Carmeli Brigade have gone from the west to the east. Seventy men have reached there from Tel Aviv to replace the wounded. The first artillery pieces are now being unloaded. Among the immigrants was a French (Jewish) officer.

The Jordan Valley is under bombardment. They are asking for ammunition. The Syrians have descended from the hills. One of our planes is operating there with great effectiveness. The Alexandroni Brigade is facing an attack from Kalkilya, where some of Kaukji's men are now located. The morale of the field units is very low, as a result of the losses they have suffered. Nahum [Sarig] in the Negev, demands that a high-ranking person be sent to discuss the situation in the area. Yigael Yadin[7] is not certain about the situation there himself. Yesterday there were heavy attacks, led by tanks, on Nir Am, Nirim, and Kfar Darom. Our people don't think that they will be able to hold out. There are also reports of Egyptian columns along the coast, between Gaza and Mijdal. A large force of Abdullah's[8] men have entered Beersheba. Nahum has only two and a half companies that are not tied down. The south is wide open, Stone (Marcus)[9] visited the Jerusalem road. Stone and Mundik (Moshe Ben Tikvah-Pasternak) have agreed on a plan of operations. Latrun was to have been attacked tonight, but I have not yet received a report about what happened. The Givati Brigade has established a Home Guard battalion of five or six hundred men. They are in Gedera digging trenches. We are holding all of our Jerusalem outposts, except in the Old City. We captured Allenby Barracks and Sheikh Jarrah. We are about to capture Su'afat. David Shaltiel says that if he is given piats,[10] artillery, and other equipment, he will be able to stand firm against the Arab Legion.[11]

Yizhak Sadeh[12] feels that we should evacuate all settlements below Nir Am. In my opinion, there is no rush. Whatever time

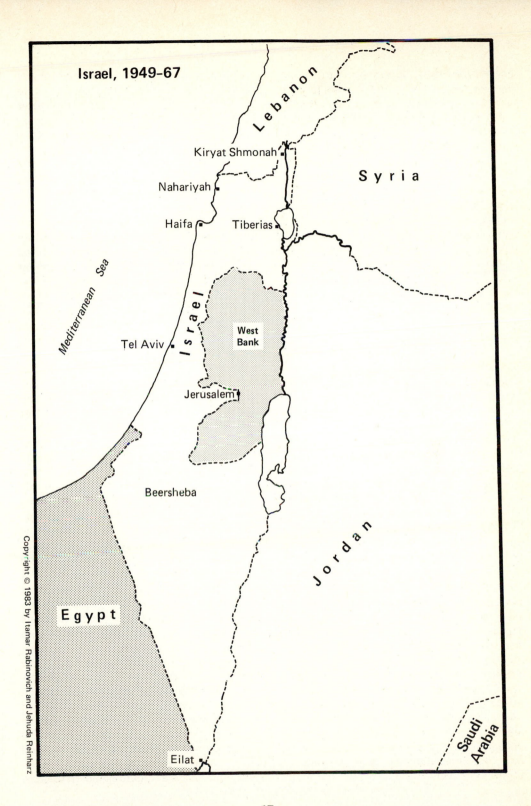

Israel, 1949–67

Lebanon

Kiryat Shmonah

Syria

Nahariyah

Haifa   Tiberias

Mediterranean Sea

Israel

West Bank

Tel Aviv

Jerusalem

Beersheba

Jordan

Egypt

Saudi Arabia

Eilat

can be gained is important. Perhaps by Thursday units will be ready for offensive action in the Negev. An engineer has gone to the south to deal with fortifications and tank traps.

Yohanan Ratner is afraid that the Arabs are planning to seize the Akir airbase and says it is necessary to fortify it. We have one Sherman tank to operate against all enemy tanks. In the course of the week our brigades will suffer losses and we must establish new units. People should be taken from the settlements. We lose an average of one brigade per week, and need a brigade to hold in reserve. We should also send replacements to units suffering casualties.

Operating procedures for the Air Force have been worked out with Aharon Remez.[13]

A delegation consisting of Yaakov Haft, Zekser, and Eli Bahir (Geller), has come from the Jordan Valley. Iraqi troops are attacking the Jordan Valley settlements. The attack on Ein Gev has ceased. Armored cars, and perhaps tanks as well, lead the way, followed by Iraqi infantry.

We must immediately dispatch machine guns, piats, and mortars to the Jordan Valley. Mordekhai Makleff[14] should be sent there.

Tel Aviv was bombed again at 11:30.

Stone presented his plan for gaining control of the Tel Aviv–Jerusalem road. (1) Two battalions should entrench themselves along the ridges in order to prevent the enemy from reaching the road. (2) The enemy has four 75-mm field guns and we need similar weapons (65-mm) for operations in the Negev. Each company should be supplied with four mortars and four piats. The road must be kept in good condition. An engineering platoon and four armored cars should be ready to deal with problems arising out of air attacks, road blocks, or enemy ground action. (3) There should be a strong, motorized striking force at Shaar Hagai to defend convoys should they be attacked. The convoys should travel only at night. The General Staff accepted the Stone plan. The convoys will be organized tonight and tomorrow.

May 17, 1948

An attempt was made to bomb us again at 5 A.M., but our antiaircraft batteries drove off the "brave" pilots.

Tonight twenty-eight trucks are being loaded with supplies for the Harel and Ezioni Brigades.

Yigael Yadin reports: There is fighting within the Old City. Who started it? Yigael says the Arabs violated the cease-fire. The convoy carrying supplies to the Negev has been held up because the Arab Legion had entered the Iraq-Sudan police station. Stone flew to the Negev today. The Arab Legion has entered the Triangle with airplanes and armored vehicles. There is a report that Nebi Yusha has been conquered. Legion units at Sarafand attacked Rishon LeZion yesterday. The Ezel attack at Ramle is not going well. There is much Arab activity at the Lydda airfield. We are getting ready to bomb Lydda.

Beit Yosef in the Jordan Valley is under artillery bombardment. Radio Cairo announces that one Egyptian plane is missing. Radio Damascus announces that three Syrian planes have been shot down. An immigrant ship arrived this morning. An ammunition ship has been unloaded. Three cargo planes have arrived so far. Four piats, dynamite, and other matériel have been sent to the Jordan Valley.

Weapons are being collected from the settlements. Givati has already gathered 350 rifles, while Alexandroni expects to obtain 600. There are no reports yet from the Valley of Jezreel or from Galilee.

I asked Yigael whether we can fight on for another two weeks even without additional weapons from abroad. He is not certain. It will depend on the speed with which we can mobilize our own resources. Ratner reports: Kaukji's forces have been strengthened by the Arab Legion. If they are successful, local Arabs will join them. A commando operation must be carried out behind Arab lines.

Moshe Dayan[15] has been given responsibility for organizing a commando group in the central region. Ratner doubts whether we can hold out if we do not receive additional airplanes within two weeks. We are struggling against a coalition of states, which is a different matter from fighting a single nation. One side or the other will be knocked out.

Berl Repetur and Ben-Aharon came to see me; they quote Moshe Sneh[16] and Israel Barzilai to the effect that airplanes can be obtained from Czechoslovakia and Poland if these countries are approached by the Provisional Government. When were Sneh and Barzilai there? Ten days ago—I asked Sneh to come and see me. Speaking on behalf of Berman (one of the heads of Left Poalei Zion[17]), he told me that Poland would supply us with food (wheat from Danzig) for dollars or for goods that she needs. We will be able to receive full assistance from Yugoslavia and Czechoslovakia only if Russia approves. Sneh met with a Polish (Jewish) general, who told him: Poland's arms production is very small; everything was destroyed by the Germans and there is nothing much we can promise in the way of weapons. I asked: Were you there together with Barzilai? No, Barzilai was there before me. Did they promise Barzilai more? No, Sneh told Barzilai what he had been told and Barzilai had nothing to add. Sneh was also in Czechoslovakia, but he did not deal with these matters.

There was refreshing news in the evening: Molotov[18] answered Moshe Shertok's[19] message by according us recognition (de jure). Austin, in the Security Council, demanded at a Council meeting that the Arabs cease their attacks on Israel for thirty-six hours. Air raids have begun again.

May 18, 1948

Twenty trucks with supplies for the army went to Jerusalem during the night. A twenty-five truck convoy to the Negev arrived safely. Armored cars accompanying Givati came back from the Negev without losses. The situation in the Old City is critical. But in the Jordan Valley it remains stable; the Arabs have retreated and are digging in. They are also digging in upper Galilee. Moshe Dayan has been appointed commander of the Jordan Valley front. The late-afternoon bombing of Tel Aviv wrecked the Central Bus Station: dozens of people were killed and more than a hundred were wounded.

Aryeh Bahir, a member of Afikim, called me from Haifa in the evening. He told me that the situation in the Jordan Valley is getting worse all the time. The settlements are under artillery fire. A great deal of assistance is necessary. A Palmah company from upper Galilee has arrived, but this is not sufficient.

Apparently David Namiri of Ashdot Yaakov has arrived from America. Good opportunities exist for purchases in Mexico, but only in lots of at least $1 million. Al Shwimmer, who is very capable, has gone into action. We must obtain two-engine bombers, single-engine fighters, cannon, and other equipment.

May 19, 1948

Ephraim Visnitski wired that we had taken all of western Galilee.

Bahir came from Haifa. He had been in contact during the night with all the Jordan Valley settlements. A bridge over the Jordan was built opposite Kinneret. A Palmah company arrived from the Galilee. Our counterattack began at midnight. It was made in an attempt to take the Zemah police station. The members of Massadah abandoned their settlement and went to Afikim. The members of Shaar Hagolan left theirs and went to Bet Zera. In both cases the settlers acted on their own initiative, without orders. They said that they had only eighteen rifles, which just was not enough.

May 20, 1948

There are 5000 members of the Arab Legion in action: 1500 between Jerusalem and Bet Gubrin, 300 near Latrun, 1500 to 2000 in the Triangle, 300 to 400 in the Jordan Valley and 400 to 500 in the Ramle-Lydda area.

We have a battalion of 500 ex-soldiers in Ein Shemer. They have 460 rifles, 460 Sten guns, 8 2-inch mortars (each one with 96 shells), 2 3-inch mortars, 20 machine guns, 560 Mills hand grenades, 140 mines, 3 piats, and 46 shells. There is also an armored battalion at Ein-Shemer composed of 9 half-tracks and 360 men, half of them trained. Their weapons are included in the previous list. Laskov[20] is at Ein Shemer.

At Tel Litvinsky, there are a unit of armored cars, 60 people, the battalion of Zvika Horowitz, 700 trainees, the heads of the Training Branch, 250 rifles, 15 machine guns, and 6 mortars.

The situation in Jerusalem: one column of the Arab Legion has reached Sheikh Jarrah. The Ezel unit there has fled. A second column has reached the Mount of Olives, and a third is at the Damascus Gate. Our forces are in control of Mount Zion. We have sufficient men and weapons there. Harel has 4 infantry companies and a heavy weapons company, altogether 700 men, but they are exhausted. On their return from Mount Zion they had an accident in which a truck overturned and 40 men were injured. They have 2 Davidkas,[21] 4 machine guns, 2-inch mortars, heavy machine guns, and 18 armored cars. All the outposts west of Latrun are in our hands, Kiryati has 250 men there, and Givati has a reserve unit.

I have discovered that the orders I gave Israel Galili about the appointment of commanders were not carried out.

May 21, 1948

The first Messerschmitt, a German plane built in Czechoslovakia, has arrived. Our planes tonight bombed Su'afat, as well as Gaza and Dir-Sunid in the Negev. All our pilots returned safely.

Four artillery pieces were sent to the Jordan Valley, where they raised the morale of the settlers. Gad (Mahnes), Jacobson, and Chizik (the Governor of Jaffa) complain about theft and anarchy in Jaffa.

May 22, 1948

A heavy attack was made yesterday on the Deganyah settlements. Six enemy tanks were put out of action. One of them is in our hands.

Eleven men have gone to Czechoslovakia to participate in a pilots' course. They are dressed in Czech Air Force uniforms: They have been given English-speaking instructors.

A ship is scheduled to arrive with weapons purchased by Ehud Avriel[22] under the terms of Contract B: 10,000 rifles, 1421 machine guns, 16 million rounds of ammunition—altogether 800 tons of material costing $2,528,000.

In the evening a second Messerschmitt and a cargo plane arrived.

I was shown an urgent cable announcing that the Arab Legion had surrounded the Hadassah Hospital. Negotiations with the consuls and the Legion are under way. The Legion demands that the Haganah surrender, turn over its weapons, and allow its men to be sent as prisoners to Amman. I refuse to accept the Legion's conditions. I have cabled Yadin to mobilize a larger force and go on fighting.

May 23, 1948

A messenger arrived with a report from Stone (Marcus): The situation is critical, but there is no reason to panic. Yad Mordekhai, defended by 80 settlers and 25 other people, has suffered 50 casualties: 20 killed and 30 wounded. An Egyptian battalion is attacking. A motorized Egyptian brigade is operating in the Negev, where it has renewed its attacks on Bet Eshel and Nirim. Egyptians, not Arab Legionnaires, are in Beersheba. The Arab Legion has gone to Bet Gubrin. Heavy attacks were made on Kfar Darom (where we have 50 people). Our men went on the offensive and inflicted heavy losses on the Egyptians, who sustained about 100 casualties: several of their tanks were damaged. They retreated.

An emissary reports that the Iraq-Sudan police station has not been captured. It is held by Egyptians and not by the Arab Legion.

The Arabs of the Negev are not active; a few of them are working for us.

Two hundred children were evacuated from the Negev tonight. Only in Dorot and Ruhama (with a total population of 350) have youngsters remained. Stone demands 300 rifles, 150 Sten guns, 30 to 40 heavy light machine guns, 15 heavy machine guns, 7 mortars, 50 piats, 100 flamethrowers, and smoke and tear-gas grenades. 250 Palmahniks have gone to the Negev; they have had a little training, and 70 percent of them are armed.

Yigael Yadin: After I left my office in the evening, a message was received from the Harel Brigade. Two companies have remained in outposts. We were asked to bomb Sheikh Jarrah at midnight. The message arrived late, but two planes nevertheless went out at midnight, by way of the university, and returned safely. Our forces were unable to break through into the Old City, or to reach the university. The Arabs are in control of Mount Zion.

Benny Dunkelman (a Canadian) volunteered to deal with the production of 6-inch mortars. I gave him the necessary authorization to undertake the project.

Israel (apparently referring to Israel Amir-Zovlotsky) reported from Ramat David that four Egyptian Spitfires had attacked the British airfield there, thinking we had taken it over. All four were shot down. Perhaps two can be salvaged.

I asked Nahum Kirschner to cable Cecil Margo in South Africa and request that he come to serve as an adviser on aviation to the Provisional Government.

8 P.M.: The situation at Yad Mordekhai is extremely grave. A column comprising dozens of Egyptian tanks and armored cars has arrived at Iraq-Sudan. Givati has sent another company to the Negev. Givoni cables that the Arab Legion has conquered Ramat Rahel and is entrenching itself in Sur Bahur. The Arab Legion has also moved into Ein Kerem, Bet Safata, and El Malha.

I have demanded that men under the command of Shlomo Shamir and Eliyahu Ben-Hur, who are trained and armed, be sent to Jerusalem. Those who are not trained should be dispatched to the Alexandroni Brigade and replaced with experienced men. These battalions should be provided with all available weapons: twenty-five guns, three hundred Molotov cocktails, ten piats, eighteen mortars, etc. The armored cars should be transferred immediately from Ein Shemer to Hulda. Latrun and all the villages in the vicinity should be taken and the road to Jerusalem opened up.

Our forces presently are distributed as follows: five thousand in service units, two thousand in the Central District, two thousand in Tel Aviv, twenty-five thousand in Givati, fifteen hundred in the Negev, three thousand in Jerusalem, twelve hundred in Harel, two thousand under the command of Shlomo, a thousand under the command of Eliyahu, three thousand in Golani, fifteen hundred in Carmeli, and two thousand in Galilee Palmah units.

May 23, 1948

Shaul Avigur cabled: Ehud Avriel has begun negotiations with the Czechs for the purchase of airplanes, tanks, and artillery on credit. But $1 million must be paid immediately and $5 million more in six months.

Another Messerschmitt arrived tonight; now we have three. Each plane has two cannons, two heavy machine guns, and bombs. Two of our planes attacked Napoleon Hill and Kfar Azariya tonight. The pilots returned safely.

The English are leaving Ramat David tomorrow. Our men will move in immediately. Engineers are already there. Vivian Herzog came from Jerusalem. He reports that the Arab Legion is in Sheikh Jarrah, the Police School, Mount Scopus, and has reached as far as the Damascus Gate. How many men do they have? We don't know. Both the Legion and the Iraqis are in the Old City. Rabbis Meisenberg and Hazan cabled the following message 3 o'clock yesterday afternoon to Rabbi Isaac Herzog[23] and Yitz-hak Ben-Zvi:[24] "The community faces total annihilation. This is a desperate call for help. Synagogues—Or Haim, Sukat Shalom, Bet Hillel, Tiferet Israel, Nissan Beck, Porat Yosef, the Brisk Yeshivah, Ohel Moshe, etc.—have been destroyed and Torah scrolls burned. Misgav Ladah is under heavy fire. Bring our desperate plea to the attention of the entire world. Save us."

Two platoons of the Field Forces captured Ramat Rahel yesterday. We lost twelve men. Arab losses ran into the dozens. Six enemy armored cars were put out of action. We control all of Jerusalem except the Old City, Musrarah, the American Colony, Sheikh Jarrah, Wadi Joz, Bab El-Sahara, and Augusta Victoria. An attempt is now being made to penetrate the Old City by using flamethrowers. Mount Zion is in our hands. The enemy is bombarding Jerusalem day and night with shells falling everywhere. Morale is very low. People find it impossible to sleep and have practically nothing to eat. There is enough bread only for another two weeks, and no other food at all. Water is being distributed in the streets: a half tin per person every two days. There are plenty of seekers of peace, namely people willing to surrender. They are putting pressure on Rabbi Herzog.

We tapped a telephone conversation between Williams, the British Consul, and a BBC reporter. Williams said: "Amman doesn't make a move without first receiving orders from the Foreign Office." Dov Joseph[25] is doing an excellent job. If there is any food at all, it is thanks to Dov Joseph. Our bombing raids have encouraged the population. All the members of Kfar Ezion were killed; settlers from other villages were taken prisoner. The Arab Legion has treated them very decently.

Almogi reports from Haifa: 250 immigrants arrived and disembarked on Friday. The (British) Army then ordered them to return to their ship. Abba Hushi [Mapai leader and Mayor of Haifa] responded by calling a strike in the port. The stevedores surrounded the British Army units and told them to shoot. The British backed down and allowed the immigrants to leave the port. The next day another ship, the *Providence,* arrived with 960 immigrants of military age. The British Army did not interfere.

There was a meeting of the Provisional Government from 4 to 9 P.M.

I fell into bed dead tired, after forty-eight hours of constant strain.

May 24, 1948

Yesterday's experiment with 6-inch mortars was a success. Three have already been made, and two more are manufactured every day. They have a range of three and a half kilometers.

Yesterday an airplane arrived loaded with bombs.

Pressure on the Negev is very heavy. Dorot was shelled yesterday—its arsenal was hit. Yad Mordekhai is still holding out. An airplane of ours bombed Iraq-Sudan and Mijdal. Egyptian armored cars advanced on Bet Mahsir but were repulsed.

The enemy bombardment of Jerusalem continues day and night. Our pressure on the Old City goes on. Ratner has returned from the central region and lower Galilee. We have taken Tantura, which has a good port. The Alexandroni Brigade has eleven hundred men from the Home Guards and eighteen hundred from the Field Forces.

There is no defense worthy of the name on the Jordan front. Kinneret miraculously holds out.

I met with a Mapam[26] delegation on Israel Galili's role in defense matters. Ben-Aharon demanded that Israel have the right to issue orders to the General Staff. I replied that while I would not oppose Galili's being given the Defense portfolio, if I were to be responsible for defense, it was on condition that I alone give orders to the General Staff. Ben-Aharon argued that Israel would in fact be giving orders in accordance with my instructions. I rejected this approach, after which Israel announced that there was nothing more for him to do in the circumstances.

A freighter is being unloaded. Tomorrow we will have forty-five more artillery pieces and five thousand rifles—an important landmark.

Mikunis came to see me in the afternoon. He immigrated to this country in 1921, and became a communist in 1936. He has just returned from a visit to Rumania, Yugoslavia, Czechoslovakia, Poland, and Bulgaria. While there he discussed arms supplies. In Bulgaria he spoke to Dimitrov (they have no weapons themselves). In Yugoslavia he met Ramkovitch, in Rumania Luka, in Czechoslovakia Clementis, and in Poland Berman and Modolsky (both of them Jews). He asked whether we were unwilling to turn to the East for assistance, as *Al Hamishmar*[27] had reported. I told him the report was untrue. We had asked for and received assistance from the East even before the establishment of the State.

May 25, 1948

The commander of Yad Mordekhai came out of the settlement with eighteen wounded men in armored cars. Yad Mordekhai is surrounded by Arab villages. According to kibbutz members who also fought in Stalingrad, there is no comparison between that struggle and the present one.

May 26, 1948

Two Messerschmitts arrived last night. I asked the members of the General Staff whether a truce would be to our advantage. All of them (Yigael, Sadeh, Ratner, Zvi Ayalon, Lehrer) agreed that it would.

Yaakov Hazan[28] came to me to speak about Galili. He said it was imperative that I should continue to handle defense matters, and have all the necessary authority to do so, but I could not handle everything myself. I should therefore have Galili coordinate matters under my direction. I would retain control of appointments. He believed that Mapai[29] has been discriminated against in the High Command (almost all our commanders are Mapam members). I told him that I wasn't worried about discrimination

and didn't care to which party the commanders belonged. It was my firm conviction, I added, that the Army should be absolutely nonpolitical. I told Hazan I would not agree to Israel's giving orders to the Army. I was unable to complete the discussion because of the pressure of other matters. We decided to meet again the next day. After four Cabinet meetings, the Israel Defense Forces Ordinance I drafted was approved [see doc. 4].

Large Arab forces are concentrating around Kiryat Anavim and Maale Hahamishah. It appears they want to conquer Jerusalem at all costs.

Simhah Blass, one of the heads of our arms industry, is producing seven piats and five to seven hundred shells per day. He fears that the 6-inch mortars may not be effective.

May 27, 1948

Ratner inspected fortifications in the south and found them satisfactory. However, they are not properly camouflaged, and can be detected easily.

Yehudah (Prihar-Friedberg) has come from Prague. Our representatives there are about to purchase another thirty Messerschmitts, thirty Spitfires, and nine Mosquitos. The Mosquitos are capable of flying directly to this country without refueling. The Czechs are also willing to sell us thirty sixteen-ton tanks now and thirty at the end of June, as well as twenty nine-ton tanks. Perhaps they will give us a $10 million credit for six months, if we pay 20 percent of what we owe them in cash.

Shmurak (a former British Army officer) came from Jerusalem this morning with a message from Dov Joseph. All the outposts that were in our hands, including Ramat Rahel, are still being held. Sheikh Jarrah and the Police School are under Arab control. Yesterday the Arabs delivered an ultimatum to the Jews in the Old City to surrender within twelve hours or the Hurva Synagogue would be bombarded. The Arabs are at Mar Elias. There is bread, sugar, and tea for another ten days and enough water for another three months. Our soldiers are waiting for ammunition; they think they will be able to hold out. The civilian population displays great courage. Rudi Klein (special operations officer in the General Staff) came to me from Sodom. All the members of Bet Haaravah and the North have been transferred to Sodom. They took all their weapons with them. The seven hundred people in Sodom have food for a month. There are sixty Arab Legionnaires in Safa, and a hundred or so in Mizra. There are four hundred rifles, eleven Lewis guns, three machine guns, one Spandau, three 311 mortars, six 211 mortars, four piats, and a great deal of ammunition.

Dov Joseph cabled from Jerusalem: each week the population requires a hundred and forty tons of bread, three tons of powdered eggs, ten tons of powdered milk, ten tons of dried fish, ten tons of lentils, ten tons of barley, five tons of yellow cheese, and five tons of jam.

May 28, 1948

Beit Susin has been captured. A large transport plane arrived last night with bombs and propellers. Only 20 percent of the goods on the ship have been unloaded; the process goes forward very slowly. There is no news from the Negev.

Stone came. We raided Gaza. We destroyed the Egyptian artillery. With fifteen hundred men we could have captured the town. Our army is excellent. The Egyptians have weapons, which we must seize. I sent Stone to Latrun to speed up the capture of the town and the liberation of Jerusalem. With Yigael's approval, I have appointed Stone as commander of the Jerusalem Front. He will be in charge of the Harel Brigade, plus the troops serving under David Shaltiel and Shlomo Shamir.

May 29, 1948

At 10:30 I attended a meeting of the Mapai Central Committee for the first time since the establishment of the State. I gave a report on internal arrangements and on the security situation. I proposed that we halt negotiations with other parties about the appointment of government officials, as this was not a subject for interparty haggling.

Yitzhak Rabin[30] came to see me. Seven hundred Old City Jews were freed by the Arabs and allowed to cross over to the New City. The Arab Legion occupied the Jewish Quarter on May 28, 1948, after its leaders decided there was no alternative to surrender. The conditions of surrender were: (1) weapons, ammunition, and military equipment to be turned in; (2) all men capable of bearing arms to be imprisoned; (3) all other residents, women, children, and wounded, to be transferred, under the supervision of a U.N. representative, from the Old City to the New City; (4) the officer signing the agreement on behalf of King Abdullah to be responsible, together with other Legion officers, for the safety of the civilians and wounded being evacuated from the Old City; (5) the Arab Legion to be given absolute control of the Quarter.

The Jewish Quarter was ablaze in the morning. The Legion treated the Haganah men and the prisoners very well. There is now tremendous pressure on Kiryat Anavim and Maale Hahamishah. Women, children, and cows have been evacuated from the settlements. The New City is under heavy bombardment. One hundred and fifty trained men will join the Harel Brigade tonight. The bombing of Ramallah was successful; 75 percent of the men in one Harel Company and 50 percent in another have been put out of action. Three hundred soldiers remain, not counting those in outposts. According to Rabin, the Arab forces are concentrated at Bet Nuba, Imans, Yalu, and Latrun. Dir Ayub is almost empty.

I have drafted an oath of allegiance for the Israel Defense Forces.

Nahum Sarig arrived by plane from the Negev. I asked him whether it would be possible to conquer Beersheba. His answer: if we can leave the west undefended and concentrate all our forces on that objective, Beersheba can be taken. But he must have a decision by tomorrow if he is to carry out the operation.

May 31, 1948

Haim Laskov penetrated into Latrun with his armored force, killing some hundred and fifty Arab soldiers. But the two companies of Brigade Seven ordered to support him were frightened by the enemy bombardment and failed to move. Thus Haim was forced to abandon Latrun. Our losses were moderate: some twenty killed and thirty wounded.

Harel reports: The enemy is using poisoned mortar shells: two men who were scratched by shell fragments died of poisoning six hours later.

I was visited at 6 P.M. by Count Folke Bernadotte[31] accompanied by Dr. Ralph Bunche.[32] If an armistice is arranged, peace talks will be possible. During a cease-fire the Arab forces would be prohibited from moving from their positions. Food would be brought to Jerusalem by the Red Cross. Bernadotte realizes the problems involved in preventing the movement of arms across the borders, but hopes to overcome them after a period of time. Abdullah's entrance into Jerusalem after a cease-fire would be considered a violation of the cease-fire.

At 8 o'clock Haim Laskov and Shlomo Shamir came from Latrun. Yigal Allon[33] came in from Galilee. If there is no cease-fire, we will prepare an operation to free Jerusalem. We have decided to bomb Amman and Cairo.

Laskov, who hadn't slept for eight days, reported on the Latrun operation. According to the battle plan, Prulov's battalion was to take Yalu, while Laskov's unit advanced toward the village of Latrun, the monastery, and the police station. In doing so, Haim lost about one hundred men killed, wounded, or missing. Four of his halftracks remained inside the police station; most of his drivers were killed or wounded. One of Zvika's companies went up with Prulov to the hills.

Two hundred men remain in the armored battalion, but they are in no condition to go into action immediately. Five hundred shells were pumped into Latrun in the course of the night. Had infantrymen from Brigade Seven advanced as they were ordered, the town would have been taken. Two companies occupy Beit Jis and Beit Susin, which permits us to open a new road to Jerusalem.

NOTES

1. League of Arab States (Arab League), an association of Arab states formed at a conference in Alexandria, Egypt, in 1944. The Covenant, signed in 1945, aims to strengthen ties among Arab states and to coordinate policies on issues of mutual concern. The original members were Egypt, Iraq, Syria, Saudi Arabia, Lebanon, Jordan, and Yemen. Libya joined in 1953; Sudan in 1956; Morocco and Tunisia in 1958; Kuwait in 1961; Algeria in 1962; South Yemen in 1968; Qatar, Bahrein, Oman, and the United Arab Emirates in 1971; Mauritania in 1973; Somalia in 1974; and Djibouti in 1977. The Arab League has officially recognized the Palestine Liberation Organization (PLO) as the representative of the Palestinians and invites the PLO to its deliberations. In 1976 the PLO's status was raised from observer to full member.

2. The military forces in the Jewish sector included the Haganah and Palmah as the official forces of the Yishuv, and Ezel and Lehi as independent "secessionist" forces.

Haganah (lit., Defense), semiunderground military force established in 1920 under the authority of the Jewish Agency and in prestate years dominated by the Labor movement. With independence the Haganah became the organizational core of the Israel Defense Forces.

Palmah (acronym for Plugot Mahaz; lit., Strike Companies, or Shock Force) elite unit of the Haganah comprised of well-trained soldiers ready to carry out special assignments, including commando operations. Founded in 1941, it was headed by Yigal Allon during the First Arab-Israeli War and always retained very close relations with the left wing of the Labor movement; it drew its recruits from Hakibbutz Hameuhad. In 1948 Ben-Gurion disbanded the Palmah and integrated it into the Israel Defense Forces, thereby protecting the new state against the politicization of an important section of its armed forces and protecting Mapai's hegemony over the Labor movement. The left wing of the Labor movement (e.g., Hakibbutz Hameuhad and Mapam) opposed this action.

Ezel (acronym for Irgun Zvai Leumi; lit., National Military Organization; also referred to as the Irgun and IZL), military arm of the Revisionist movement, the political and ideological opponent of the dominant trends of Zionism. Ezel was formed in April 1937 when its precursor, the Haganah Bet, split from the Haganah and the Jewish Agency over the issue of independence. Members of Ezel asserted the right to retaliate against Arab attacks on Jews, which were increasing in the late 1930s. In 1944 Ezel began to use terrorist tactics, usually directed against British military installations, in order to force the British out of Palestine. Ezel's activities on behalf of the Revisionist program brought it into conflict with the Haganah, the Jewish Agency, and after May 14, even the State of Israel itself. Ben-Gurion insisted that Ezel disban and join the Israel Defense Forces, while Menahem Begin and Ezel desired to retain at least a certain measure of autonomy. This conflict was the basis of the *Altalena* affair, in which on June 20, 1948, a cargo ship carrying arms for Ezel (which refused to allow the state's army to control arms supplies) was sunk by the Haganah acting on Ben-Gurion's orders. Ben-Gurion saw the issue as the new state's authority over the entire population and control of all armed forces, but Begin and others saw Ben-Gurion's actions as partisan and foolish, since Ezel was willing to allow the government to share in the arms delivered in the *Altalena*. Two former commanders of Ezel are prominent in the present Likud government, Menahem Begin (see n. 6 below) and Yaakov Meridor (b. 1913), the commander in chief of Ezel, 1941–43. When Begin assumed command, Meridor became the second in command, 1943–48, and the political and personal relationship between the two has remained close. Meridor, as founder and chairman of the board of directors of the Maritime Fruit Carriers, Ltd., is one of Israel's leading businessmen. In 1981 he joined Begin's government as economic coordinator, a new portfolio created for him.

Lehi (acronym for Lohamei Herut Israel; lit., Freedom Fighters of Israel; also referred to as FFI and the Stern Gang), underground military organization formed in 1940 by Avraham Stern, a student at the Hebrew University, after a split in Ezel. Lehi formed the Fighters' list, headed by Natan Friedmann-Yellin (Yelin-Mor), during the elections to the First Knesset.

3. Fawzi al-Qawuqji (Kaukji) (b. 1897 in Tripoli in Ottoman Syria), Arab political and military leader. Qawuqji served in the Ottoman army and gained fame in the anti-French rebellion of 1925. In August 1936 he was recruited to make a cohesive force out of Arab bands engaged in terror during the Arab Revolt of 1936. During the First Arab-Israeli War he retained a force of troops, loyal to himself, called the Arab Liberation Army. It was defeated in Operation Hiram in October 1948.

4. Israel Galili (b. 1910 or 1911), deputy minister of defense in the Israeli Provisional government. Galili began his political career at age fourteen when he founded Hanoar Haoved, a Labor youth movement, and its first agricultural settlement. Later he became a leading member of Ahdut Haavodah, the Socialist Zionist party, and deputy commander in chief of the Haganah. Since the establishment of the state he has served in several governments.

5. Levi Eshkol (Shkolnik) (1895–1969), a Socialist Zionist since his youth in Russia and a founder of both Mapai and the Histadrut, the trade union federation. Eshkol served in several early governments, becoming prime minister and defense minister in June 1963. The events of June 1967 forced him to give up the defense portfolio. He remained prime minister until his death in March 1969.

6. Menahem Begin (b. 1913), Israeli prime minister, 1977–83, and leader of the Herut movement. Begin joined the Revisionist youth movement, Beitar, in interbellum Poland and quickly became one of the leaders of the Revisionist movement in Europe. He was imprisoned in the Soviet Union for his activities and spent time in a Soviet labor camp. Upon his release, he left for Israel and in December 1943 became the commander of Ezel. With the formation of the state, Begin reorganized the Revisionists into a political party—the Herut movement—and thus he has remained the leader of the Israeli Labor movement's chief political rival. As such he was given a position in the National Unity cabinet of June

1967. Following the 1977 elections Begin became prime minister.

7. Yigael (Yigal) Yadin (Sukenik) (b. 1917), Israeli chief of operations during the First Arab-Israeli War and the country's second chief of staff, 1949–52. In 1953 Yadin joined the faculty of the Hebrew University's archeology department. His work as an archeologist, particularly on the Dead Sea Scrolls, Hazor, and Massadah, sustained his prominence as a national figure. In 1977 he formed the Democratic movement, which merged with the Movement for Change in a successful election campaign. The movement's disintegration was largely caused by Yadin's decision to join Begin's Likud-led coalition. Yadin became deputy prime minister in Begin's first government. In 1981 he did not run on any list.

8. Abdullah Ibn Hussein (Abdullah I) (1882–1951), emir and king of Transjordan from 1921 until his assassination in 1951. Personally, and as a contender on behalf of the Hashemite family, Abdullah sought to extend his rule into Syria and western Palestine. This led to a complex involvement in Palestinian affairs, sometimes in cooperation with the Zionists and sometimes as an exacerbater of conflict.

9. David Marcus (1902–48), American Jewish colonel who was recruited to advise the Israeli army during the First Arab-Israeli War. Marcus was smuggled into Palestine in January 1948 under the name Michael Stone. Two weeks after independence he became supreme commander of the Jerusalem front. On June 10, 1948, he was accidentally killed by an Israeli watchman.

10. Piat (acronym for projector infantry antitank), short-range antitank weapon.

11. Arab Legion, the Jordanian army. It was created by Abdullah as the armed forces of Transjordan and was developed into a modern army by John Bagot Glubb (Pasha) during World War II.

12. Yizhak Sadeh (Landsberg) (1890–1952), founder of the Palmah. Sadeh began his military career in the Russian army during World War I and then, as a company commander, in the Red Army. A Socialist Zionist, he went to Palestine in 1921 and became a leader of the Haganah. He commanded the Palmah from its beginning in 1941 until 1945. During the First Arab-Israeli War he commanded the Eighth Armored Brigade. After the war he left the army and assumed a leading role in Mapam.

13. Aharon Remez (b. 1919), first commander of the Israel Air Force. Remez later served in the Ministry of Foreign Affairs, 1960–68, and was ambassador to Great Britain. Over the past decade he has been chairman of the Ports Authority and chairman of the Airports Authority.

14. Mordekhai Makleff (1920–78), Israeli chief of staff, 1952–53. Makleff's prestate military experience was with the Jewish police and in the British army. He was a member of the Israeli delegation to the Rhodes armistice negotiations, indirect talks between the U.N. mediator and the belligerents that led to the 1949 armistice agreements.

15. Moshe Dayan (1915–81), Israeli military and political leader. Dayan received his early military experience in the Haganah and British forces. During the First Arab-Israeli War he held several different commands. In 1949 he was a member of the Israeli delegation to the Rhodes armistice negotiations. From 1953 to 1957 he was chief of staff. In 1957 he became active in Mapai. As one of Ben-Gurion's young protégés being groomed for future leadership, Dayan was appointed minister of agriculture in 1959. Dayan resigned in October 1964 as a result of his conflict with Prime Minister Eshkol, and the next year he left Mapai to join Ben-Gurion in Rafi. During the May 1967 crisis Dayan was asked to serve as defense minister. After that his political career was uneven. He was elected to the Knesset in 1977 on the Labor party list. After the elections he left the Labor party and joined Begin's government. Then he left Begin's government because he was denied the role of chief negotiator for Israel in the autonomy talks relating to policy in the West Bank. In the 1981 elections he gained a seat in the Knesset by forming his own new party, Telem.

16. Moshe Sneh (Kleinbaum) (1909–72), leader of Maki, the Israeli Communist party. Sneh began his political career in Europe as a member of the liberal-centrist General Zionists. He was chief of staff of the Haganah, 1940–46. In 1947 he joined the Marxist Mapam party and was avowedly pro-Soviet. In 1953 he formed a small splinter party, Mifleget Hasmol Hasozialisti (lit., Socialist Left Party), which soon merged with Maki. In 1965 Maki split into two factions. Sneh's faction, which retained the name Maki, became independent and critical of Moscow.

17. Left Poalei Zion, early Marxist Zionist party that opposed cooperation with "bourgeois Zionism." Based in Eastern Europe, it had a negligible

impact on Palestinian affairs. In 1946 it merged with Ahdut Haavodah.

18. Vyacheslav Mikhaylovich Molotov (b. 1890), Soviet foreign minister, 1939–49, 1953–56.

19. Moshe Sharett (Shertok) (1894–1965), the most important figure in Israel's early foreign relations. Sharett was active in Ahdut Haavodah, the Histadrut, and the Jewish Agency from the early 1920s. From 1930 on he was a member of Mapai. In 1947 Sharett, as head of the Jewish Agency's Political Department, was its representative to the United Nations. He then became foreign minister, May 1948–June 1956. His advocacy of political work and diplomacy, as opposed to reliance on military strength, brought him into conflict with David Ben-Gurion (see doc. 19). When Ben-Gurion temporarily resigned, Sharett took over as prime minister, January 1954–November 1955.

20. Haim Laskov (1919–82), leading Israeli military figure and chief of staff, 1958–61. Laskov was a member of the Agranat Commission (see doc. 60), which investigated the military's lack of preparedness following the October 1973 War. He has served for many years as the army's chief ombudsman.

21. Davidka, crude mortar developed and produced by the fledgling Israeli arms industry to meet the emergency situation of 1948. It was an effective noisemaker but, because of its inaccuracy and lack of firepower, an ineffective mortar.

22. Ehud Avriel (1917–80), leading figure in the Israeli Ministry of Foreign Affairs. As minister to Czechoslovakia and Hungary in 1948, Avriel was involved in arms procurement. As deputy director general in charge of African affairs and international cooperation and ambassador to Ghana in the 1960s, he was one of the architects of Israel's African policy.

23. Yizhak (Isaac) Halevi Herzog (1888–1959), founder of the Religious Zionist Mizrahi movement in England. In 1936 Herzog became the chief rabbi of the Ashkenazi community in Palestine. He is the father of Chaim and Yaacov Herzog.

24. Yitzhak Ben-Zvi (Shimshelevitz) (1884–1963), second president of the State of Israel, 1952–1963. Ben-Zvi was an early leader of the Socialist Zionist movement in Russia and Palestine and a cofounder of the Hashomer movement.

25. Dov Joseph (Bernard) (1899–1980), early leader of Mapai. In prestate years Joseph worked closely with Moshe Sharett in the Jewish Agency's Political Department. He was military governor of Jerusalem, 1948–49, and from March 1949 until January 1966 he held various cabinet positions.

26. Mapam (acronym for Mifleget Hapoalim Hameuhedet; lit., United Workers' party), Marxist Zionist party with roots in the pioneer Zionist youth movement Hashomer Hazair (lit., Young Guard). Hashomer Hazair was formed in Europe during World War I. Beginning in the 1920s its members founded collective settlements, which formed the federation Hakibbutz Haarzi. Eventually the Hashomer Hazair became a Marxist Zionist party stressing the role of kibbutzim in the building of the national Jewish homeland and in the class struggle of the workers in that new society. Mapam was formed in 1947 and formally established in early 1948 as a merger of Ahdut Haavodah and Hashomer Hazair. Both groups desired the merger prior to independence in order to challenge Mapai's hegemony over the Labor movement. In 1954 most members of Ahdut Haavodah left to reorganize their party. In January 1969 Mapam joined the Labor party in an electoral coalition, thus forming the second Maarakh, or Labor alignment.

27. *Al Hamishmar* (lit., On Guard), daily newspaper of Mapam.

28. Yaakov Hazan (Jacob Chasan) (b. 1899), leader of Hashomer Hazair and Mapam, founder of Hakibbutz Haarzi, and one of the major proponents within Mapam of joining the second Maarakh.

29. Mapai (acronym for Mifleget Poalei Erez Israel; lit., Israeli Workers' party), major political party of the Labor movement and the dominant political party in Israel until May 1977. Mapai was formed in 1930 as a merger of Ahdut Haavodah and Hapoel Hazair. In 1944 a leftist faction split to form a new party with the old name of Ahdut Haavodah. In 1965 Ben-Gurion led a faction away to form Rafi. In January 1968 these three parties reunited to form the Israel Labor party. In its early years Mapai was social-democratic; in recent years it has encompassed factions with more liberal-centrist ideological orientations but has remained nominally social-democratic.

30. Yitzhak Rabin (b. 1922), Israeli prime minister, 1974–77. Rabin joined the Palmah in 1941. Just before the First Arab-Israeli War he took command of the Second Brigade and shortly thereafter of the Palmah force defending Jerusalem. After the war he continued his military career, becoming chief of staff of the Israel Defense Forces, 1964–68. He then entered politics and was

ambassador to the United States 1968–73. Throughout the 1970s Rabin was involved in a struggle for leadership of the Labor party with Yigal Allon and Shimon Peres. Initially Rabin was successful and succeeded Golda Meir as prime minister. Then Peres gained the party's nomination for coalition leader and prospective prime minister in the party convention preceding the 1981 elections. Toward the end of that campaign, however, Peres was forced to promise publicly that if Labor emerged victorious he would appoint Rabin to the defense ministry.

31. Folke Bernadotte (1895–1948), Swedish diplomat appointed by the U.N. General Assembly on May 20, 1948, as the mediator in the First Arab-Israeli War. His solutions to the conflict were unacceptable to Israel, and the Israelis felt he was exceeding his mandate by offering them. On September 17, 1948, he and his assistant were assassinated in Jerusalem by members of Lehi.

32. Ralph Johnson Bunche (1904–71), American diplomat who accompanied Bernadotte on his mission to the Middle East and succeeded him as mediator. Bunche was successful in arranging a cease-fire and the following Rhodes armistice negotiations. For this work he was awarded the 1950 Nobel Peace Prize, the first of several individuals to receive the award for peace efforts in this still war-ravaged area. After the Suez crisis Bunche directed U.N. operations, including the U.N. Emergency Force, in the Middle East.

33. Yigael (Yigal) Allon (Feikovitz) (1918–80), leader of Ahdut Haavodah and the Labor party. Allon was commander in chief of the Palmah from 1946 until its dissolution in 1948. He entered the government for the first time in 1961. After the formation of the Labor party he emerged as one of the major political figures in Israel, serving as deputy prime minister and minister of foreign affairs.

PROVISIONAL STATE COUNCIL
3. The First Ordinance of the State of Israel

In Mandatory Palestine the Yishuv (the organized Jewish community) enjoyed a considerable degree of autonomy and developed a network of political and administrative institutions. It elected the Representative Assembly (Asefat Hanivharim), which in turn elected the National Council (Vaad Leumi, or, as referred to by the British, the General Council). The National Council met between the infrequent sessions of the Representative Assembly and conducted most of the legislative business of the Yishuv.

In April 1948, in preparation for statehood, the government of the Yishuv was restructured. The National Administration (Minhelet Haam; lit., People's Administration) was the new executive council; after May 14 it was called the Provisional government. A legislative assembly, the Constitu-

ent Assembly, was elected by universal adult suffrage in January 1949. This assembly was transformed into the Knesset.

The authority and functions of the Jewish Agency prior to the establishment of the state were outlined in Article 4 of the British Mandate for Palestine, which provided that "an appropriate Jewish agency shall be recognized as a public body for the purpose of advising and cooperating with the administration of Palestine in such matters as may affect the establishment of the Jewish National Home and the interests of the Jewish population in Palestine," and that "the Zionist Organization . . . shall be recognized as such agency." Desiring to increase the scope of support of world Jewry for the Zionist program, the World Zionist Organization created the Jewish Agency to act as

Source: David Ben-Gurion, *Israel: A Personal History* (New York and Tel Aviv: Funk and Wagnalls, Inc. and Sabra Books, 1971), p. 98. Reprinted by permission.

an organ of all Jews (and not only of the Zionists) in furthering this goal. With the establishment of the State of Israel the Jewish Agency automatically ceased to be the spokesman for the interests of the Jewish population in that country. It continues as an international nongovernmental body that coordinates all Jewish overseas efforts for Israel.

At the second meeting of the Provisional State Council, on May 19, 1948, the following Law and Administration Ordinance (1–1948) was adopted after a brief debate. The texts of this and the following document demonstrate the fashion in which the new state coped with the formidable task of transforming the institutions of the Yishuv into governmental institutions of a sovereign state.

By virtue of the power conferred upon the Provisional Council of State by the Declaration of the Establishment of the State of Israel, of the 5th Iyar 5708 (May 14, 1948), and by the Proclamation of that date, the Provisional Council of State hereby enacts as follows:

Chapter 1: The Administration
The Provisional Council of State

1. (a) The Provisional Council of State consists of the persons whose names are set out in the Schedule to this Ordinance. Representatives of Arabs being residents of the State who recognize the State of Israel will be coopted on the Provisional Council of State, as may be decided by the Council; their non-participation in the Council shall not derogate from its power. (b) The Provisional Council of State itself prescribes the procedure for its meetings and business.

The Provisional Government

2. (a) The Provisional Government consists of the persons whose names are set out in the Schedule to this Ordinance. Representatives of Arabs being residents of the State who recognize the State of Israel will be coopted on the Provisional Government, as may be decided by the Provisional Council of State; their non-participation in the Provisional Government shall not derogate from its power. (b) The Provisional Government shall act in accordance with the policy laid down by the Provisional Council of State, shall carry out its decisions, shall report to it on its activities, and shall be answerable to it for its activities. (c) The Provisional Government shall elect one of its members to be Prime Minister, and shall prescribe the functions of each of its members. A member of the Provisional Government shall be called "Minister." (d) The Provisional Government may confer any of its powers upon the Prime Minister and upon any of the Ministers, insofar as that is not repugnant to any of the Ordinances of the Provisional Council of State. (e) Decisions of the Provisional Government in respect of the division of Powers among the Ministers shall be published in the *Official Gazette*. (f) The Provisional Government itself prescribes the procedure for its meetings and business.

District Administration

3. The Provisional Government may divide the area of the State into districts and subdistricts and shall demarcate their boundaries.

Local Authorities

4. The municipal corporations, local councils, and other local authorities shall continue to act within the areas of their jurisdiction and scope of their authority.

DAVID BEN-GURION
4. The Formation of the Israel Defense Forces

Prior to statehood and independence, the underground or semi underground military forces in the Yishuv sometimes clashed with each other. During the First Arab-Israeli War the Haganah, as the military arm of the political establishment, had to transform itself into a regular army of the newly proclaimed state and to establish for itself and the new state a monopoly over military power.

David Ben-Gurion designed this ordinance, adopted May 26, 1948, to regulate and centralize the various military forces under a single command, the Israel Defense Forces (a direct translation of the Hebrew, Zva Haganah LeIsrael; also frequently referred to by its acronym Zahal, or in English

IDF). Ezel and Lehi agreed to discontinue independent activities except in Jerusalem. By September an IDF ultimatum forced them to place their forces under the central command as well. Nevertheless, the political nature of these forces and of their leadership meant that they were not fully integrated until after victory and independence were assured. Ben-Gurion also disbanded the Palmah as a separate unit of the IDF, thereby removing that arm of the former Haganah which was almost totally dominated by one political faction. His account of the adoption of the IDF ordinance by the Provisional State Council, and the ordinance itself, are reprinted here.

At a meeting of the Provisional Government on May 23, 1948, Prime Minister Ben-Gurion presented the draft of an Ordinance on the Israel Defense Forces. Shapira[1] opposed the insertion of the word "haganah" (defense), but no one supported him. In accordance with the request of several members, a final decision on the Ordinance was postponed until May 26, 1948. On that date it was approved. The Ordinance reads:

In accordance with Section 18 of the Law and Administration Ordinance No. 1–1948 [see doc. 3], the following Ordinance is issued:

1. Herewith are established the Israel Defense Forces, consisting of ground, air, and naval units.

2. In times of emergency, conscription will be enacted for all formations and services of the IDF, with ages of those liable for conscription to be determined by the Provisional Government.

3. Every person serving in the ranks of the IDF

will take an oath of allegiance to the State of Israel, its laws, and its lawful authorities.

4. The establishment or maintenance of any other armed force outside the IDF is hereby prohibited.

5. All orders, declarations, and regulations in regard to national service promulgated between November 29, 1947, and the date of this Ordinance by the Jewish Agency, the National Council for Palestinian Jews, the National Administration, the Provisional Government or one of its departments, will remain in effect until such time as they are changed, amended, or canceled.

6. All actions carried out in accordance with this Ordinance will be considered legal, even if they are in conflict with another section of an existing law.

7. The Ministry of Defense is responsible for carrying out this Ordinance.

8. This will be known as the Israel Defense Forces Ordinance—1948.

Source: David Ben-Gurion, *Israel: A Personal History* (New York and Tel Aviv: Funk and Wagnalls, Inc. and Sabra Books, 1971), p. 109. Reprinted by permission.

NOTE

1. Haim Moshe Shapira (1902–70), early leader of Mizrahi and Hapoel Hamizrahi, the Religious Zionist movement and its Labor wing. Shapira was a member of the prestate Jewish Agency Executive and early cabinets.

ZEEV SHAREF

5. Negotiations with King Abdullah and the Formation of a Governmental Structure

Zeev Sharef (b. 1906) began his public career and service in the Political Department of the Jewish Agency. Prior to independence he was close to the negotiations with King Abdullah of Jordan. As the first secretary of the cabinet, he was uniquely placed to observe the formation of the Israeli government. His career in public service was distinguished; he was later a member of the Knesset (Labor party), minister of housing, and minister of commerce and industry.

As the first part of this reading from Sharef's memoirs shows, Israel made early and persistent attempts to avoid a clash with the Arabs living in Mandatory Palestine. The history of such negotiations dates back to the meeting of Chaim Weizmann with Faisal in 1919. Before the British withdrawal and the inevitable war with the neighboring Arab states, Israeli negotiators sought a political solution to what has since become known as the Palestinian problem. Negotiations with Jordan (see also docs. 15, 56, 77) are a recurring part of Israel's continuing efforts.

The term "Minister" for a member of Government had not yet been introduced and the title "Government" was being reserved for future use; but from the standpoint of responsibility for affairs and procedures, the actual existence of "Ministers" preceded the fact of the "Government," and the Government of Israel became a substantial fact on that day, the 12th of May. The meeting of Minhelet Haam, the National Administration, began at ten o' clock that morning and lasted—with intervals—until eleven o'clock that night, forty-nine hours before the expiration of the British Mandate. It may well be that upon dispersing to their homes after the meeting, the members of the National Administration felt that the body which would administer the State-to-be had been ushered in that day.

Neither the subject-matter nor the agenda of the meeting had been determined in advance—the agenda developed out of the proceedings; and the events within the territory of Palestine and along its circumambient frontiers, and the occurrences overseas, within the United Nations agencies, were the determinants of those proceedings. Half of the time was devoted by those present to hearing information about the threatened dangers from the

Source: Zeev Sharef, *Three Days* (London: W. H. Allen and Co., 1962), pp. 69–76, 154–57. Reprinted by permission of Zeev Sharef.

neighboring countries, the position in the interior of the country and the fate of Jerusalem, and the attitudes of the Big Powers, both of those sympathizing with and those hostile to the Jewish cause, as well as the implications arising therefrom.

At the meeting also were Mrs. Golda Meyerson (now Meir),[1] director of the Jewish Agency's Political Department, and for part of the proceedings her two advisers on Arab affairs, Ezra Danin[2] of Hadera and Eliyahu Sasson[3] of Jerusalem.

The negotiations with King Abdullah of Jordan, on which Golda Meyerson reported, were in the nature of a last attempt to prevent an invasion by the Arab armies generally, or at least to forestall the entry of the Arab Legion into the arena of war. True, Arthur Creech-Jones, the British Colonial Secretary, had promised that the Arab Legion would leave Palestine before the 15th of May. Only four weeks previously, on the 16th of April 1948, the chief United Kingdom delegate at the United Nations, Sir Alexander Cadogan, had stated clearly and specifically in reply to a direct question by Moshe Shertok [Sharett]: "As regards the Arab Legion, we announced some time ago that Arab Legion units would be withdrawn from Palestine before the Mandate ended." It was now evident that not even this British assurance would be fulfilled. Only that morning Legion troops had stormed the positions of the isolated Ezion bloc[4] of settlements in the Hebron hills and it was patent to anyone that they would later be deployed against Jewish Jerusalem.

Moshe Shertok had only just returned from New York and a few days before his departure he had conferred with the U.S. Secretary of State, General George C. Marshall. His review at the meeting was intended to clarify the problem of whether the United States of America meant to interfere with the proclaiming of the State, and if so, the extent to which it would succeed in enlisting U.N. personnel for this purpose.

Part of the meeting was attended by Israel Galili ("Hillel"), Chief of the "Haganah" Command, and Yigael Sukenik ("Yadin"), its Chief of Operations Staff. Their reports were brief, penetrating and comprehensive, and left no room for illusion or misapprehension of the military position and of the possible upheavals within it one way or the other.

Eliezer Kaplan and Moshe Shapira, who had returned the previous day from Jerusalem, brought with them an impression of the feeling in the besieged city and the anxiety of its leaders. The meeting would have to decide on a reply to the British High Commissioner's proposal for a truce in Jerusalem, the supervision of which was to be in the hands of the Committee of Consuls (representing the United States of America, France and Belgium) set up by Security Council decision at the end of April, or of the Red Cross.

Zero hour had been fixed by the British Government when it announced that the Mandate would end at midnight of the 14th of May. But not all clocks were set to Greenwich time on the British plan. At Lake Success desperate efforts were being made to defer this zero hour by proclaiming a truce, the real significance of which would be to postpone the declaration of the Jewish State.

It was the accepted notion before that date that the regular Arab armies would launch their invasion only after the termination of the Mandate, but the attack launched by the Jordan Arab Legion against the Jewish settlements of the Ezion area was an anticipation of the British zero hour, and it was uncertain whether the other Arab armies might not behave similarly.

The duty which lay before the meeting was to assess all the complex information and to retain in Jewish hands the initiative in determining the course of events. Its chairman, David Ben-Gurion, defined its function in the following terms at the outset of the meeting: "Time is of the essence; it is pressing for two reasons: (1) Because of the danger of invasion which is liable to occur at any moment. It may already have started to a certain extent. The Legion's attack on the Ezion bloc may be called an invasion. The danger necessitates action, and not only by the security people. (2) Because of the date of 14th May. Ernest Bevin[5] anticipated the date and something is bound to happen on Friday night. Whatever happens, action is necessary."

The meeting continued, with a short interval, for thirteen hours. The lack of clarity at its outset had been dissipated by the time the meeting ended. The barque of Jewish history was no longer to be tossed about on the waves, driven by alien winds. Its sails had been unfurled, its course was set. "Jerusalem Time" had replaced "Greenwich Time."

Golda Meyerson told of her dramatic encounter with King Abdullah. It was her second meeting with him. The first had taken place in the middle of November 1947 in the Rutenberg house at the power-station on the River Jordan at Naharayim. That conversation had been friendly and had been conducted on the assumption that there would be no collision between the Jews and himself. If the U.N. Assembly decided upon the partition of Palestine into two States, Jewish and Arab, he wanted, he said, to annex the Arab area to his kingdom. The reply given was that the Jews would not lend a hand to a breach of the U.N. Assembly's resolution. But it was no business of theirs as to what would happen in the Arab area. Obviously, if the Arabs attacked the Jews, then force would be met by force.

Abdullah rejoined that he understood this and promised that his friendship for the Jews remained. He spoke in derogatory terms of the strength of the neighboring states. The conversation concluded with an agreement that, after the U.N. decision, a second meeting would be arranged.

Two points during the colloquy aroused some doubts. Once he asked as to what the Jewish attitude would be to including their state (he called it "the Jewish republic")

within his kingdom. When the response was a negative one, he did not pursue that line. Another time he remarked that he did not want Partition to be disappointing from the standpoint of the area which the Arabs would receive. He told the Palestinian Arab leaders that he would stand aside and give them no support whatever unless they submitted the Palestine case to his exclusive handling.

No further meeting had been held with him since then although contact was maintained through someone who had visited him twice. A little while earlier, Mrs. Meyerson said, this person had come from Abdullah with a query as to whether the Jews were ready to offer concessions in the area designated as the Jewish State in the Partition plan, so that he could appear before the Arab world showing a territorial gain in comparison with what had been allotted by the United Nations. The answer via the emissary was that the Jews would make no concessions whatever in its area. Generally, he must know that the frontier proposed by the United Nations was a peace-time one and it would be honored so long as conditions of peace were observed. But if hostilities broke out, then each side would take what it could. No more news was received from him after that, as the disturbances which began at the end of November 1947 suspended all communications.

But contact was re-established a week ago and a meeting had been arranged, she said. This time Abdullah refused to come to the boundary of Jewish territory and they were compelled to go to him. While the previous meeting had been successfully kept secret, news about the second one filtered through to the public and even to the press before it took place, and consequently extraordinary precautions had to be taken for the journey. Owing to bad weather, Eliyahu Sasson's aircraft did not arrive from Jerusalem in time, and she was accompanied only by Ezra Danin. She drove in the car belonging to one of the King's faithful henchmen and was dressed as a Moslem woman. Ezra Danin wore Arab headgear.

The journey took several hours. They left from Naharayim, and after their identity was checked about ten times en route, they arrived in Amman and were taken straight to the meeting-place. The King received them in the presence of one of his confidants; he gave them a friendly welcome, but in general he seemed to be a different man—depressed, preoccupied, tense.

The go-between had conveyed Abdullah's proposals in advance: the country must remain undivided, and within it the Jews would have autonomy in the areas inhabited by them. This arrangement would be effective for one year, and at the end of that period the country would be amalgamated with Jordan. A joint Parliament would be set up, with fifty per cent Jewish membership; there might also be a government consisting of one-half Jews and one-half Arabs, but this was not clearly stated.

At the outset of the conversation the King asked whether his proposal had been transmitted, and Mrs. Meyerson answered affirmatively, adding that she had deemed it necessary to meet with him although his proposal was wholly unacceptable as a basis for negotiation. He repeated that he desired peace and did not want to see the destruction of agriculture and industry. But if his proposal were not accepted, then war became inevitable. Generally, he asked, why were the Jews in such a hurry to proclaim an independent and sovereign state?

Did he believe that expectation going back two thousand years could be called "haste"? Mrs. Meyerson countered. To our regret, we had lingered and delayed too long. There had been mutual understanding and friendship between the Jews and himself for years, she went on, and the friendship was also founded on the fact that they had common enemies. During the past five months the Jews had hit hard at those enemies. The Mufti's[6] strength had diminished as a result

of the Jewish military successes. The foreign mercenaries who had invaded the country had been beaten. As a result of our exertions the way had been cleared for him as well. If he returned to the previous plan and concentrated solely within the area set aside for the Arabs, then it was possible to establish an understanding. The Jewish strength today was nothing like that of four or five months ago, she asserted. If there had to be war, then we would fight with all our powers and would have no mercy upon any enemy.

The King said that he understood "you will have to repel any attack." While he desired to carry out the previous plan, several events had occurred in the meantime to prevent it. There was the massacre at Deir-Yassin (the Arab village west of Jerusalem attacked by men of the Irgun Zvai Leumi [Ezel]). He went on: "I was then alone but now I am one among five. I have no alternative and I cannot act otherwise."

Mrs. Meyerson declared that we were ready to honor the frontiers so long as there was peace. But if war came, we would fight wherever we could reach and so long as our strength lasted, and he must know, she repeated, that our strength was far greater than it was four or five months ago.

To this the monarch reiterated his warning, although in friendly tones, that he was sorry but had no alternative. He deplored the havoc and the blood of the young people which would have to be spilled as water. He offered to invite the Palestinian Arab leaders connected with him and several of his moderate followers, and suggested that the Jews should also send "moderate representatives" to such a meeting, at which the matter could be settled. He further said there would be no Jew-hating Arab extremists in government, but only Arab moderates.

When Mrs. Meyerson referred to the fact that he must remember that we were his only friends, among all those around him, who showed him friendly faces but were in reality seeking to do him evil, he replied the same as at previous meetings: I know it and I have no illusions on that score. I know them and their "good intentions." I firmly believe that Divine Providence has restored you, a Semite people who were banished to Europe and have benefited by its progress, to the Semite East, which needs your knowledge and initiative. It is only through your help and guidance that the Semitic peoples will be able to regain their lost glory. The Christians will not do this because of their aloof and contemptuous attitude towards the Semites. If we do not help ourselves by our joint efforts, then we shall not be helped. All this I know and I have a profound belief in what I have said. But the situation is grave, and we must not err through hasty action. Consequently I beg of you again to be patient.

"We do not wish to delude you," she retorted, "but we cannot consider your proposal at all. It would not only be rejected by the responsible institutions, but there are not even ten responsible Jews who will be ready to support such a plan. The answer can be given at once: it is unacceptable. If you give up the agreement and want war, then we shall meet *after* the war."

King Abdullah stated he had heard that Shertok was in France, and perhaps one of his men could meet with him there. He added, "We don't need America and Europe. We, the people of the East, ought to show this miracle to the world. Let us sit down at one table and secure peace among us."

Finally, he turned to Ezra Danin and in a paternal tone asked why he, Ezra, a son of the East, had not helped him out in the conversation. Danin pointed out to him his fatal error. He had no friends in the Arab world and he relied on the armored cars of the Legion just as the French had relied on the Maginot Line. We shall smash these armored vehicles, Danin said. It was a pity that he stood to lose all that he had built up with such great effort. It was still not too late.

"I am very sorry," the King replied. "I deplore the coming blood-shed and destruction. Let us hope we shall meet again and will not sever our relations. If you find it necessary to meet me during the actual fighting, do not hesitate and come to see me. I shall always be glad to have such a meeting."

Before they parted Ezra Danin remarked that he, the King, would have to alter his gracious custom of allowing his flock to approach and greet him by kissing his hand or the hem of his robe. Townsmen were not the same as Bedouin tribesmen, and the guard upon him must be increased so as to avert the evil plotted by scoundrels, sons of Belial, against him.

"*Habibi*, my dear, I shall not change the customs of my fathers," King Abdullah rejoined. "I am a Bedouin and I shall not become the prisoner of my bodyguards. Let whatever happen, I shall not prevent my subjects from expressing their affection for me."

The impression gained from the conversation was that he did not contemplate the prospect of battle gladly or with self-confidence, and actually did not want it, as he feared defeat and was even afraid of his comrades-in-arms, the Arab States and the British together. But he had become entangled in complications, or the British had entangled him, and he could no longer extricate himself.

On their way back to Naharayim, Mrs. Meyerson and her companion saw at a distance the invading Iraqi Army moving toward the front with its heavy equipment and extensive field artillery.

Such was the account of that historic meeting, the last diplomatic effort with an Arab leader on the eve of the invasion. . . .

The Ministries of Agriculture, Public Works and Labor existed only on paper. Their high officials were in Jerusalem. Aharon Zisling, who had taken the portfolio of Agriculture, and Mordecai Ben-Tov, who held Labor and Public Works, made every effort to organize nucleus staffs and enlisted people close to these fields of activity in various institutions quartered in Tel Aviv. Their prospective offices in Sharonah had not been handed over to them, and Zisling began work in the headquarters of Mapam, the United Workers Party (which then federated the Mapam of today and the Ahdut Haavodah-Poalei Zion party).[7] Mordecai Ben-Tov functioned in the editorial offices of the daily *Al Hamishmar*, where he was at home—he had been its editor-in-chief from the day it first appeared.

The other members of the National Administration occupied their former offices. Felix Rosenblueth[8] superintended the initial legislative work of the State at his law office. The personnel and records of other units scheduled to become part of the Ministry of Justice were in Jerusalem. Behor S. Shitrit,[9] who had been a Magistrate until then, did his work in the Law Courts building; he was in charge of Arab affairs and Police. Arab affairs were then handled by local Emergency Committees, some of which were connected with Municipalities and others of which operated separately. Behor Shitrit, with the help of several advisers, tried to introduce some orderly procedure and unity into the administration of these matters. Most of the Arabs were displaced, far away from their homes and without means of livelihood, and it was necessary in some way to give them housing and support. His particular concern was with the Arab inhabitants who had remained in Haifa and those of Jaffa which was due to surrender in a few hours.

His other Ministerial responsibility was the Police. Its organization had been prepared by Yehezkel Saharoff (now Sahar) and Yosef Nahmias,[10] who had been liaison officers of the Jewish Agency's Political Department in matters concerning the "legitimate" Jewish police formations, such as the Jewish Settlement Police and Auxiliary Constabulary. When the central Emergency Committee was set up and services began to be organized, they were invited to draft the scheme of police reorganization. Later on, Saharoff received his appointment from the "Haganah's" affiliates.

Registration for officers' courses was announced and several candidates were approved. But Saharoff failed to get the full quota of men he required to set up the force. The demand for combat troops was insatiable, and kept on growing. Both Saharoff and Nahmias had literally to struggle for the men they needed in each area.

Meanwhile they had to cope with a grave situation. The Irgun Zvai Leumi and Fighters for the Freedom of Israel [Lehi] took anything that came to hand, and there were even instances of "Haganah" units which did not exactly behave virtuously or with restraint. They needed, and commandeered, everything: autos, typewriters, tables, telephone instruments. Units were being formed, commanding officers set up offices, they required equipment and accessories. As there was no Quartermaster-General, they did their own foraging as they saw fit.

The IZL and FFI, former underground dissident groups, legitimized their position by the act of public appearance, and capitalized this putative legitimacy by undertaking confiscations without any centralized control, even by their own commands. We therefore asked the commanders of the incipient police to post guards over the offices of the outgoing British government, of which we regarded ourselves as the successor authority. The combatant forces treated them as natural prey—the offices of a hostile government in disbandment; we saw them as our own future premises, upon which we had focused our past planning. But the fledgling police force had to decline the assignment as it was under-manned. The Jewish Agency also had its own worries over safety precautions. It used armed watchmen to guard valuable property and even called in the Military Police on special occasions. The latter were an entirely new phenomenon for the Jewish population: their smart uniformed appearance set them apart from other "Haganah" men, who generally wore an assortment of garments and were none too meticulous about the way they looked.

Very little was left of the vaunted Palestine Police. It had been methodically destroyed by the outgoing Government. Only a small number of officers and constables remained in the police stations under Jewish control. Vehicles in good condition were taken away, records were destroyed, laboratory paraphernalia and the Port Police motorlaunches were removed. The new Police H.Q. did its utmost to re-create the framework of organization with the aid of Jewish officers and men who had served in Mandate days. New men were taken on through the central military recruiting bureaux, but— as I remarked earlier—front-line drafts took precedence over the rear echelons. Yet in spite of the handicaps, the building-up of the force went ahead according to plan and along clear-cut, purposeful lines.

The Health sector was organized by the late Dr. Avraham Katznelson (later Nissan), director of the *Vaad Leumi* Health Department. Moshe Shapira later took over this responsibility. Immigration was handled by the Agency's Immigration Department. Plans were readied for all other spheres of activity, but they were not put into effect owing to the truncation of Jerusalem.

Briefly, then, we were able to include on our table of organization a not inconsiderable number of active administrative components, part of which were housed in the seat of the future Government at Sharonah. Among them were the Controllers of Food and Stockpiles in the Ministry of Trade and Industry; the Public Works Department, which had already mustered the few Jewish workers in the districts but occupied itself mostly with getting the seat of Government ready for its tenants; Police Headquarters; the directorates of Posts and the Broadcasting Service; Immigration; and Transport.

But now the day and hour for the inauguration of governmental operations had been determined it was evident that demand outstripped supply in providing accommodation, and the pace of the last-minute preparations had to be stepped up. It was by no means a simple matter at the time. Normally a few groups of artisans and workmen would have been organized and set to work simultaneously on various parallel jobs. But men were being called up day after day by age-groups or categories. Only the day before, Emergency Order No. 17 published by the "Central Command for National Service" had summoned forthwith to the Colors all men aged twenty to thirty-five years, irrespective of family status, who had served in any foreign army in the Second World War. The Order further proclaimed that all soldiers in these classes who had previously received deferment or release for personal or economic reasons were now liable for immediate conscription, and *all previous decisions* (emphasis in the original) were suspended for a period of sixty days.

The Order drew the attention of all institutions and industrial establishments to the following regulations: (1) The Central Command for National Service would not entertain any appeal against the Order except by the Palestine Electric Corporation, ports, hospitals, and waterworks. (2) Persons wishing to appeal against their conscription could do so only when they were on active service.

The watchword which had once been "We will do and be obedient" now became "Join Up and Appeal." The effect was that workmen and engineers, clerks and laborers, who had begun work on a certain day had to quit almost precipitately, leaving papers on their desks and tools at their jobs—and did not report for duty on the morrow. They vanished into thin air. During the evening or late at night they were called to arms and went; or the Military Police came to their homes and took the laggards. Pleas and excuses were unavailing: they had to go.

NOTES

1. Golda Meir (Meyerson) (1898–1979), Israeli prime minister, 1969–74. During the course of her long political career, most of which as a leader in Mapai, Meir headed the Political Department of the Jewish Agency, was Israel's first envoy to the Soviet Union, and served in several ministerial posts.

2. Ezra Danin (b. 1903), leading Arab affairs expert in the Jewish Agency's Political Department. After independence, Danin served for twenty years as a senior official in the Ministry of Foreign Affairs.

3. Eliyahu Sasson (1902–78; a native of Damascus), head of the Arab Department of the Jewish Agency, 1933–48. With the establishment of the state, Sasson became head of the Middle East Department of the Ministry of Foreign Affairs. He held various ambassadorial and diplomatic positions until 1961, when he joined the cabinet.

4. Ezion bloc (Gush Ezion), group of four Jewish settlements southeast of Jerusalem that were captured by the Arab Legion in May 1948. This area came under Israeli rule in 1967, and the settlements were reestablished.

5. Ernest Bevin (1881–1951), British foreign secretary, 1945–51. Bevin was a chief formulator of British Middle East policy, which during this period tried to court Arab favor.

6. Hajj Amin Al-Husayni (c. 1895–1974) prominent leader of Palestinian Arab nationalism. Al-Husayni was appointed mufti (Muslim religious leader) of Jerusalem by the British in 1921 and was dismissed by them in 1937. A religious fundamentalist who wanted Palestine to be an Arab state governed by Islamic laws, he militantly opposed both Zionism and Abdullah. His influence was felt in Palestine even from his exile in Cairo and Beirut. The Muslim Brotherhood, established in 1929 and based in Egypt, was a network of local fundamentalist Islamic societies devoted to intensifying devotion to Islam and desiring to impose Islamic laws on society.

7. Ahdut Haavodah (lit., Unity of Labor), Socialist Zionist party. Actually, this name is used to refer to two separate political parties.

Ahdut Haavodah was founded in 1919. In 1930 it merged with Hapoel Hazair to form Mapai. Hapoel Hazair (lit., Young Worker; full name Histadrut Hapoalim Hazeirim Beerez Israel; lit., Organization of Young Workers in Erez Israel) was a Zionist social-democratic party active in Palestine, 1919–30.

In the 1930s Siah Bet (lit., Faction B), a leftist faction within Mapai, opposed many of Ben-Gurion's compromises with the Revisionists and with the non-Socialist Zionists. This faction was based in the settlements of Hakibbutz Hameuhad, which had been politically aligned with the previous Ahdut Haavodah party, and in the Tel Aviv Labor Council. In 1942 Mapai decided to prohibit organized factions within the party. In 1944 Siah Bet left Mapai and formed a new party, Hatnuah Leahdut Haavodah (lit., Movement for the Unity of Labor).

In 1946 Hapoel Hazion Smol (lit., Leftist Labor Zionists) joined this party to form Hatnuah Leahdut Haavodah-Poel Zion. In 1947–48 Hatnuah Leahdut Haavodah-Poel Zion merged with Hashomer Hazair to form Mapam, but this merger lasted only until 1954, when Ahdut Haavodah reconstituted itself as a separate party. In 1968 Ahdut Haavodah joined in the formation of the Labor party.

8. Pinhas Rosen (Felix Rosenblueth) (1887–1978), early leader of the German Zionist movement. In 1948 Rosen helped found the centrist Progressive party. He was a member of the Provisional government and early cabinets.

9. Behor Shitrit (1895–1967), Israeli minister of police, 1949–66. Shitrit began his career in the Mandatory police force, becoming head of the Tel Aviv police in 1927 and chief magistrate of Tel Aviv in 1945. He contributed to the building of the Israeli national police force. He was one of the few leaders from the Sephardi community in Mapai.

10. Yosef Nahmias (b. 1901), assistant director general of the Israeli Ministry of Foreign Affairs in 1958.

6. The Law of Return

On July 5, 1950, the Knesset unanimously passed the Hok Hashvut (lit., Law of Return). This law reflects the messianic hope of the Jewish people for the "ingathering of the exiles" and the political goal of the Zionist movement to repatriate the "exiled" Jewish people into their ancestral homeland. But its significance is much more than symbolic. Following the experience of Jews attempting to flee Nazi persecution and massacres only to find the doors of all countries of refuge closed to them—(including the gates to Palestine, which were closed by the British)—this law assured all Jews throughout the world that there would always be at least one country whose gates would be perpetually open.

This open immigration policy had been impossible during the latter years of the Mandate period. Following the outbreak of the Arab Revolt in 1936, the British Mandatory government limited Jewish immigration and land ownership. In response, the Haganah and Ezel organized illegal immigration, which continued up to independence in 1948. Stories of this period have become "mythified" and are now part of the folklore glorifying the early *haluzim* (sing., *haluz;* lit., pioneers).

The Law of Return, based on the Zionist tenet of the centrality of Israel to Jewish life, continues to have political significance, particularly in terms of Israel's relations to the Diaspora (i.e., Jews living outside of Israel). From the late 1960s it has served as the legal basis for Israel's policy of encouraging immigration from Western nations and the Soviet Union. Moreover, it has forced the state into legally defining "who is a Jew" (see doc. 34).

---

1. Every Jew has the right to immigrate to the country.

2. (a) Immigration shall be on the basis of an immigrant's visa. (b) An immigrant's visa shall be granted to every Jew who has expressed his desire to settle in Israel, unless the minister of immigration is convinced that the applicant (1) is acting against the Jewish People, (2) is likely to endanger public health or the security of the state.

3. (a) A Jew who comes to Israel and after his arrival expresses his desire to settle there, is entitled, while he is still in Israel, to obtain an immigrant certificate. (b) The reservations detailed in section 2(b) will also be in force regarding the granting of an immigrant certificate, but a person will not be considered as endangering the public health as a result of an illness contracted after arrival in Israel.

4. Every Jew who immigrated to Israel before this law entered into effect, and every Jew born in the country, whether before or after this law entered into effect, shall be considered as having immigrated according to this law.

5. The minister of immigration is responsible for the enforcement of this law, and he is empowered to enact regulations in all matters concerning its implementation as well as the granting of immigrant visas and immigrant papers to minors under the age of eighteen.

Source: Reshumot (Official Record of the Laws of the State of Israel) (Jerusalem: Government Printer, 1951), 51:159.

7. The Debate on a Constitution

Several of the chief problems confronting the State of Israel during the first years of independence are addressed in this and the following documents. The issue of a constitution reveals the depth of the ideological cleavage in the Israeli body politic at that time. Despite repeated attempts to draft such a document, fundamental differences could not be reconciled, and the idea of a constitution was eventually dropped. The minutes of the Knesset's debates in this matter present the full spectrum of opinion over the basic issues of life and politics in Israel: religious and antireligious parties, socialist and antisocialist parties, parties committed to the institutions that evolved from the Yishuv and parties opposed to the institutions of the Yishuv and the WZO. The inability to agree on the principles that should be embedded in a constitution reflect historical differences within the Zionist movement regarding the type of state and society that should be created. In the absence of a constitution, the Knesset has the formal power to legislate all laws.

At the end of the debate, Yizhar Harari (1908–78), a lawyer and cofounder of the Progressive party, proposed a compromise that was approved by the Knesset on June 13, 1950, by a majority of 50 to 38. The proposal, which is part of the following reading, established the basis for formulating what are known as Basic Laws that could become chapters of a future constitution. Seven Basic Laws have been enacted: they deal with the Knesset (1958); Israel lands (1960); the president (1964); the government (i.e., cabinet) (1968); the state economy (i.e. taxes and the budget) (1975); the army (1976); and the Jerusalem Law (formally establishing Jerusalem as the capital) (1980). Although the Law of Return is not a Basic Law because it was not drafted according to the procedures outlined in Harari's proposal, it is generally agreed that in the (at present unlikely) event that a constitution is drafted, this law will be treated as if it were a Basic Law.

Debate on the Report of the Constitution, Legislative, and Judicial Committee regarding the Question of a State Constitution, February 1, 1950

NAHUM NIR[1] (chairman): Until the conclusion of the Provisional State Council's term of office, there was no doubt that we were electing the Constituent Assembly—that was its title—and each of us included, within his party's platform, the content of the constitution as he saw it. However, as early as January 1949 the mood of the Provisional State Council had already shifted slightly, and when we met to adopt the Transition Ordinance, the majority of the Constitution Committee proposed the inclusion of a paragraph stating that the function of the Constituent Assembly is to draft a constitution, and that, until it does this, it serves as an ordinary House of Legislature. The debate began, then and immediately, and the first opinions opposing the need to prepare a constitution were voiced. But the arguments we heard in the Constitution Committee were not presented there. There only one point was made: Why

Source: February 1, June 13, 1950, *Divrei Haknesset* (Knesset Minutes) (Jerusalem: Government Printer, 1950), 4:714–828; 5:1257–1722.

should we obligate the Constituent Assembly? It is a sovereign body and will decide when it is elected; why then, should the Provisional State Council obligate it? We thought that if the Provisional State Council adopts an ordinance, it does not obligate the Constituent Assembly because the Constituent Assembly can nullify the ordinance, just as it can nullify any law. . . .

. . . It is said that there is no need to adopt a basic constitution but only basic laws. Dr. Warhaftig[2] said, in the Constitution Committee, that the only difference between a basic constitution and basic laws is that a constitution is adopted ceremoniously, which is not the case with basic laws. This is not quite correct. There is another important difference. A constitution provides principles of the state's character, whereas basic laws are more like pieces of patchwork, such as we are accustomed to; and not only do the patches not always match, they sometimes clash dangerously.

I once gave this example in the Constitution Committee and I beg, in advance, the government's forgiveness. I don't think our government will do that. I speak only of the juridical circumstances. Our situation is such that, according to the basic constitution, the present government has the right to dissolve the Knesset. It need only refer to paragraph 9 of the Law and Administration Ordinance [see doc. 3], which states that the government can pass emergency regulations which alter, or even nullify, an existing law, and are then brought before the Knesset for approval, for up to three months. I beg of you not to think that I suspect anyone, but this is the juridical situation, even though I am certain that the government would never take advantage of this possibility.

YOHANAN BADER[3] (Herut movement):[4] Don't trust it.

NAHUM NIR: The juridical situation is such that it is possible to produce emergency regulations today that nullify last year's Elections Law, to dissolve the Knesset, to produce a new Elections Law, to hold new elections—all this within three months, and the new Knesset will approve the emergency regulations. And once again, I do not suspect anyone of such actions, but such a situation could occur in our circumstances, when we are without a constitution; for this reason, we must formulate a basic constitution—in order to set limits. . . .

Y. BAR RAV HAI (Mapai): . . . There is one more point to which I would like to draw the House's attention. To the best of my knowledge, one does not create a constitution at the beginning of a revolution, but when it is completed. All constitutions are an attempt to "freeze" certain principles, to preserve them, inasmuch as it is possible to preserve any particular thing in the life of a nation. A state, or a people, which has arrived at a certain level and achieved certain principles, by revolutionary means or by casting off foreign rule, tries, by means of a constitution, to preserve and stabilize this development. Therefore all those constitutions that were created apropos the revolutionary process were nullified, exchanged, or altered as the revolution progressed. It is necessary to achieve a more or less stable situation that will enable the casting of a mold expressing the development level of a people or state at a particular stage. . . .

The constitution is created for that population which was in existence within the borders of the state. Ours is a different situation. Our population is fluid. We are not at the end of a revolutionary process but at its beginning. For our revolution is not the establishment of the state—that is only one of its stages. Our revolution is the ingathering of the exiles; it is the maximum concentration of Jewry within Erez Israel. The question is, Can we, today, in these fluid circumstances, cast the decisive molds that will determine the permanent framework of the State of Israel?

. . . It is clear that this state needs laws, and we establish laws from time to time. Also, insofar as reality demands, insofar as it allows, we attempt to solve each problem without entering into meaningless, abstract debate about meaningless, abstract principles. . . .

. . . Therefore, in conclusion, I should like to propose to this House that it charge the Constitution, Legislative, and Judicial Committee with the duty of preparing a list of laws necessary to ensure the efficient administration of the state and that will regulate the most pressing problems, on the basis of the principles established in the Proclamation of the State of Israel [see doc. 1]. This committee will not only prepare the list of these necessary laws; it will also prepare— and I am confident that in this it will have the government's cooperation—the individual bills and will present them to this Supreme House. Then there will be a pointed debate on the proposals in this House—a debate about the fundamentals of our state, not about principles, not rhetoric, but rather about our real problems of living. This is the only way to guarantee us a basic constitution. I am not one of those who believe that states can usually exist indefinitely without a basic constitution. The unique spectacle of England does not repeat itself in history. I also reject the conventional notion that England has no written constitution. In the committee I attempted to quote the list of laws that, to all intents and purposes, determine the constitutional structure of England. I reject the view that a constitution is an immediate necessity; I merely state that it can be achieved stage by stage, and that only in this way will we draw closer to the objective. . . .

ZERAH WARHAFTIG (National Religious front):[5] It is my opinion that the Proclamation of the State of Israel does not obligate us in any way to adopt a constitution—not on October 1, 1948, and not on any other date. The Proclamation of the State of Israel is a document connected with the political system and can only be explained in relation to that system's development.

As for the second question, Have we already a constitution? I think we do have one, according to that commitment that is contained in the Proclamation of the State of Israel. This commitment is not to the United Nations. We have undertaken such a commitment independently of the U.N. General Assembly decision, and we do not have to promise conditions that cannot be altered. We already have such a constitution, having adopted the Law and Administration Ordinance, the Transition Law, and the Knesset Elections Law, on the basis of which elections were held. A constitution is a system of laws that regulate the matters of government and law in the state. Such a system exists in our state, therefore we have a constitution.

To the extent that we know the difference between a written and an unwritten constitution, it may be said that we have no written constitution. But when one speaks of a constitution in the general sense, it includes both the written and the unwritten types. The study of constitutions distinguishes several types of constitutions, among them the written and the unwritten, although both are known as constitutions. If it says in the Proclamation of the State of Israel that we are committed to adopting a constitution, that means that we must make those arrangements which will enable the existence of a regulated government in the state. This we have done. Mind you, we did not do so on October 1, 1948, because the Knesset elections did not take place until January, but we have regulated the process of government in the country, though it can and must be improved. But it cannot be said that we have no constitution. . . .

. . . The Provisional State Council rejected by a majority vote the proposal of the committee majority to obligate the Constituent Assembly to adopt a constitution. It took the stand that the Constituent Assembly is under no obligation to adopt a constitution. I have no idea why Mr. Nir did not, at that time, use the Proclamation of the State of Israel as an argument, nor do I know why other members did not use that argument.

But in any case, the Proclamation of the State of Israel already existed then, and the Provisional State Council, the same council that issued the proclamation, ruled that we are not obligated to adopt a constitution. . . .

. . . A constitution consists of two sections: the executive section and the declarative. In our case, the executive section already exists—in the form of basic laws, which we have yet to complete. In concluding I will mention those basic laws we still lack and will have to adopt.

The declarative section of a constitution consists of an introduction and of vague principles that, lacking the executive section, without laws of implementation, have no practical value. Mr. Nir suggests deleting the introduction from the declarative section, for the reason that in the introduction, one may mention the "Rock of Israel," and of this he is afraid. . . .

. . . If the intention is to draw up a constitution based on some other constitutions, then it is unnecessary; not only that, it is actually harmful. Perhaps it is easy for MK [Member of the Knesset] Nir to draw up a constitution; to me it seems that the work demands inspiration, and that the Spirit of God must guide those who engage in such a project. Any who think that the granting of a constitution is nothing more than the drawing up of a number of superficial principles, a few platitudes, is mistaken. Take, for example, the collection of constitutions of the South and Central American countries, which was recently translated into English and published—I'm willing to wager any one of you that if you erase the names of the countries whose constitutions are included in this book, you won't be able to distinguish between that of Haiti and that of the Honduras, between that of Nicaragua and that of Costa Rica. If you want to adopt this sort of a constitution, it's possible, but it won't add anything to Israel's stature—not in our own opinion and not in that of other nations. Also, such a constitution will not have any educational value, either in Israel or in the Diaspora.

Gentlemen, what is a constitution? A constitution must have educational value for the youth of Israel and for the Jewry of the Diaspora. The constitution is very important as an educational and cultural factor in the whole world. It must be a sort of calling card, an indicator of the character of this nation and of this state. The constitution that is being, or will be proposed, cannot serve these two functions. We are known in the world as the People of the Bible. We have no need of a second calling card. It will not add to our stature; on the contrary, it will detract from it.

YISRAEL BAR-YEHUDAH (Mapam): . . . The very opposing of the legislation of a basic constitution is a continuation of the system that I mentioned—a constant legislative irresponsibility, with all depending on the moment, the doer, or the circumstances. We must legislate permanent and stable basic elements that will obligate all. I want to remind all of you, my learned friends, who quote from all types of constitutions: You always mention three things that must be established in such basic laws—you mention that the constitution must determine the rights of the legislative authority, the executive authority, and the judicial authority. In my opinion, there is also a fourth very important point. Not only, What are the rights of those who are handed the job of governing the citizen-resident, but also, What are the rights of the citizen with regard to the government? What is the minimum beyond which the legislative, executive, and judicial powers must not go? We feel that in a state like ours this is one of the most important factors, and for this reason the drafting of a constitution is an urgent matter. There are some special circumstances that make the matter one of particular urgency in our case. I need only mention three such points. I could bring many examples, but in order to save time, I will concentrate on the main ones.

Don't forget that here we are the majority people, and that at our side there is a minority people—this after a bitter war—

and coexistence will not be achieved so easily. Perhaps in this matter we should not depend only on the freedom to use emergency measures and various ordinances; rather, basic rules should be formulated, which will obligate everyone. I would like to continue and explain that principle which, in my opinion, should be first in importance and about which there is seemingly no debate or conflict of opinion among us. We live in this country, in the peculiar circumstances of the ingathering of the exiles, of different communities, coming from the four corners of the earth, with different habits, and—as Mr. Warhaftig mentioned—having all sorts of strange unwritten constitutions that sometimes contradict and oppose one another. Our goal is to create one nation out of this mixed multitude. To achieve this goal, we must act on all possible fronts: the educational, the organizational, in short, in all aspects of our lives, in order to live together and not as we do now—apart. This trend must find its expression in legislation as well—in the education toward a common legislation for all and in our taking account of each person and his needs when we legislate laws. This period of our history in our country is certainly not the end of our national revolution; it is the middle of it, perhaps only its beginnings. The expulsion of the British from this country did not conclude our national revolution; it simply initiated a new stage. After all, the ingathering of the exiles—the process of transferring masses of Jews to Erez Israel, and that not only from the geographical aspect but also with the intention of turning them into citizens and workers in our country—this is one of the supreme commands of the continuation of our national revolution. Has this command already been fulfilled? . . .

MENAHEM BEGIN (Herut movement): There is one thing you wish to prevent: the existence of a law of freedom, of justice, that will take precedence over all other laws and that you will not be able to nullify one fine morning by a mechanical majority. Look, gentlemen. When liberal thought flourished

it was said of the state's authority that it ought to be limited to the role of "night watchman." That period is past, and every free man prays that we will not be forced to admit that it has gone forever. But in the meantime, generations have passed, and all of humanity is searching for the golden mean between the freedom of the individual and the aspiration for a world of justice. No nation has yet discovered that golden mean. Yet we, here, seem to have found the final answer to the question of the type of living regime we should establish in our state. Not only will we extend the authority of the government apparatus to all aspects of our life, but we will turn the state into a sort of "night thief." The citizen—surrounded by detectives, superintendents, policemen, clerks; the rule—suspicion; the exception to the rule—trust. The rule is that the citizen is a criminal; the exception to that rule is that he is law abiding. Therefore one must even enter private homes and search the refrigerator; one must pile supervision on supervision and carry out personal searches. . . .

. . . You have repudiated the mandate granted by the people in the elections. You have the right to make a change but on one condition—that you ask the people. The nation chose the Constituent Assembly; that is, it charged us all with the duty of legislating a constitution for the State of Israel. For whatever reason, impulsive or calculated, you do not wish to legislate a constitution. Go to the nation and tell it, We have no need of a constitution, we lack the inspiration, we hesitate to bind the coming generations, etc. Let the nation decide. (An interruption from the Mapai benches: The Constituent Assembly is the nation!). You are mistaken. The Constituent Assembly is merely the instrument of the nation, and in the event that it repudiates the will of the nation, the nation has the right to demand new elections. That is your philosophy— that your majority is superior to the nation, and that is why you oppose the constitution. If the Constituent Assembly legislates a constitution, then the government will not be free to do as it likes. At present, the government is superior to the law—the majority in the House does not control the government or guide it; on the contrary, the government imposes its will on the majority. Does the government want a particular law? Then, that law is adopted. Does it want to nullify a particular law? Then, that law is nullified. And so, you really are situated above the law. That's how it is in our state. We have a ruling sect, superior to the law, because there is no constitution to restrain it. You want to preserve this status quo; *that*'s the real reason for your objection to a constitution, and *that* you do not reveal to the nation. Not only are you violating the law of the State, as I quoted from the Transition Law, 1949; you are ignoring the will of the people as it was expressed in the general elections. All of you ran for elections to the Constituent Assembly, each and every one of you; not one of you let the nation know that there would be no constitution. Therefore we demand of you one of the following: Either you fulfill the duty with which the nation has charged you and that is to legislate a constitution; or you hold a referendum, in which all the voters in the state will participate, and you will act according to their decision on the question of a constitution. Your first obligation is to enact a constitution. You do not have the authority to change your mandate.

The question is most grave. He who wants the public to respect the laws of the government is duty bound to make sure that the government respects the law of the state. If you violate the nation's will, if you repudiate the voters' mandate, there will be no law in Israel and no respect for the law. . . . I don't believe that the citizens of the State are obligated to expose their files for Dov Joseph. It is contrary to the natural right of the citizen and the man. But if you have decided to install such laws in Israel, then ask the nation if it releases you from your principal duty—to enact a basic constitution for the State of Israel. When the nation replies yes, then you can continue to legislate laws with a mechanical majority and from your position of supremacy vis-à-vis the law. As long as the nation does not speak thus, you have no right to decide for yourselves, no matter what your arguments.

Therefore, honored chairman, in order to conclude the debate on the constitution I wish to present two proposals, as follows: "The First Knesset, which is the Constituent Assembly, has decided to legislate a constitution for the State of Israel, in accordance with the duty with which the nation has charged the Constituent Assembly in the general elections." . . .

Knesset Decision regarding a State Constitution, June 13, 1950

The proposal of MK Y. Harari supported by Mapai, the Progressive party,[6] the Sephardim,[7] and WIZO:[8] "The First Knesset charges the Constitution, Legislative, and Judicial Committee with the duty of preparing a draft constitution for the state. The constitution will be constructed chapter by chapter in such a way that each chapter in itself will constitute a basic law. The chapters will be brought before the Knesset as the committee completes its work, and all the chapters together will form the state constitution."

NOTES

1. Nahum Yaakov Nir (Rafalkes) (1884–1968), leader of the prestate Socialist Zionist movement and a member of the Provisional State Council. Nir represented Mapam (and later Ahdut Haavodah) in the Knesset.

2. Zerah Warhaftig (b. 1906), leader of Hapoel Hamizrahi and the National Religious party (see n. 5). Warhaftig has served in many cabinets and has been one of the major figures in the Religious Zionist movement in Israel. He retired from the Knesset following the 1981 elections.

3. Yohanan Bader (b. 1901), one of the chief

leaders of the Herut movement and a longtime active member of the Knesset. Bader is an economist and a lawyer by profession.

4. Herut (lit., Freedom) movement, political arm and organizational successor to Ezel, formed in June 1948 under Begin's leadership. Although the Revisionists had refused to accept the legitimacy of the Labor-dominated Jewish Agency Executive, independence forced them to participate in the elections to the First Knesset.

5. National Religious front, coalition formed in 1948 of Mizrahi, the Religious Zionist organization, and its Labor wing Hapoel Hamizrahi. In the elections to the First Knesset the National Religious front joined with the two other religious parties, Agudat Israel and Poalei Agudat Israel, to form the United Religious front. Since that time Hamizrahi and Hapoel Hamizrahi have run on their own joint list. In 1956 the two organizations merged to form the National Religious party (also called Mafdal, acronym for Miflagah Datit Leumit; in English, NRP). The party and its predecessors have participated in all Israeli governments. In the 1950s and 1960s the NRP was primarily interested in the relationship between religion and state and in securing state-controlled resources so as to provide better services to its constituents.

6. Progressive party, a small party, formed in 1948, that was antisocialist but willing to cooperate with Mapai and joined some of the early coalition governments. In 1961 the Progressives and General Zionist party merged to form the Liberal party. In 1965 the Liberal party split. The minority, led by Yizhar Harari and coming largely from the former Progressive party, created the Independent Liberal party (IL). In 1981 the Independent Liberal party failed to receive enough votes to receive representation in the Knesset and subsequently joined the Israel Labor party in October 1982.

7. Sephardi Jews generally come from Mediterranean and Middle Eastern countries, while Ashkenazi Jews generally come from Europe or the United States; their different histories have led to somewhat different religious and cultural traditions. The traditional Sephardi community in Israel (as opposed to the Sephardim who entered the state during the years of mass immigration) organized a political party that was active in the early years.

8. Womens' International Zionist Organization (WIZO), worldwide Zionist service organization established in London in 1920. Its Israeli branch, particularly since the establishment of the state, has been responsible for administering an extensive range of services and institutions that serve women, their children and families, particularly in development areas. Its candidate, Rachel Kagan, was elected to the First Knesset.

GIORA JOSEPHTAL
8. The Absorption of Immigrants

Giora Josephtal (1912–62) was born in Germany where he was active in social work and the Haluz movement in the years prior to World War II. He went to Palestine in 1938, where he helped establish Kibbutz Gal-Ed in 1945. After the war he began organizing the Jewish Agency's Absorption Department (Misrad Haklitah) and was successively its director and treasurer of the Jewish Agency Executive. In 1959 he became Israeli minister of labor, in which capacity he continued the work of absorption through the building of housing projects. His last post before his death was that of minister of housing and development.

Josephtal's report in August 1951 to the

Source: Ben Halpern and Shalom Wurm, eds., The Responsible Attitude: Life and Opinions of Giora Josephtal (New York: Schocken Books, 1961), pp. 101–4. Reprinted by permission of Schocken Books, Inc.

Twenty-third Zionist Congress, reproduced here, sheds light on a central aspect of Israeli life in the early 1950s—the absorption of hundreds of thousands of Jewish refugees and the regimen of austerity that this effort imposed upon the whole society. After the Arab-Israeli hostilities were brought to a close by the armistice agreements, most of the difficulties facing the new state revolved around the great number of immigrants. Josephtal's official duties brought him into direct contact with the emergencies that arose in every field connected with the absorption. Housing was the major problem. Immigrants were settled in abandoned Arab houses and former British army camps. Finally, beginning in January 1950 *maabarot* (sing., *maabarah*; lit., transit camps) were established to provide immediate temporary housing. The buildings were generally small prefabricated structures without central heating. By 1954 the *maabarot* were being steadily emptied as new methods of absorption were introduced, particularly the attempt to place newcomers directly in homes in new settlements, or development towns. Nevertheless, many *maabarot* eventually became permanent low-income residential areas.

─────────────────────

The slogans "ingathering of the exiles" and "communal integration" have been so overworked by Israel and world Jewry that their precise meaning has begun to be vague.

During the three years since Israel's establishment, the bodies responsible for absorbing the immigrants have waged a constant battle with material, organizational, and spiritual problems in order to enable the mass immigration to continue. Even if the local Jewish community is showing certain signs of fatigue under the strain of taking in so many immigrants in such a short time, we are duty-bound to do everything possible before the gates of potential sources of immigration are closed, and not to wait for pogroms in countries where the Jewish community's political situation is today clearly unstable. This must constantly be borne in mind in doing our day-to-day work.

The most immediate task is to rescue the Jews living in the Arab lands. Two-thirds of them are already in Israel. We must save the remaining third as well. Only someone who regards the ingathering of exiles as an urgent rescue operation can possibly put up with some of the methods we are forced to use in settling the immigrants.

The Jewish people left us in a state of poverty at the decisive moment when Israel had to be saved. We are continuing to take in the waves of mass immigration and to conduct a desperate campaign against a shortage of raw materials and means of production, a shortage of funds, and a shortage of trained personnel.

What does every new arrival need the moment he reaches Israel? A roof over his head, a place of work, a bed, a mattress, blankets, cooking utensils, medical supplies, a doctor to look after him, a nurse, a place in a hospital, a kindergarten for his children, a school, a kindergarten teacher, a school teacher, an instructor, vocational training, and food (which the country is not yet producing). He also needs a warm and cordial atmosphere, because everyone who transplants himself from one country to another undergoes a spiritual crisis of some kind. We supply only some of these needs. We cannot supply all of them, because the Jewish people have given us only 20 percent of the means we need to integrate the immigrants fully.

Our greatest achievement has been the provision of employment for virtually all the new settlers, despite inadequate investments. We have arranged jobs for the immigrants and set them on the road to a productive future; we have freed them from a life of idleness and decay; but we have not yet fully exploited their productive potential, and we have not been able to instill in them the approach to work which they must adopt if this country is going to be built up. It will take years before we see the full fruit of the investments we have made in all branches of the economy. In agriculture this may take many years.

There are large areas of the country—such as Galilee and the Negev—where nature does not make intensive agriculture possible. Work villages, which prepare the ground for full-time farming, are a prerequisite for the expansion of the area under cultivation. And if we want to ensure a minimal supply of home-grown produce, we will have to prepare large tracts of land for cultivation for a long time to come.

We cannot live in the plains and valleys. If we want to safeguard Israel's security and provide food for its population, we will need a better appreciation of the importance of soil amelioration, we will have to understand its intrinsic value and not consider it a mere waste of man power and money.

We have begun to adapt the form of the new agricultural settlements to the social structure of the immigrant families. Even if this means that the moshav (and not the kibbutz)[1] holds a leading place among the newly established settlements, can we forget that we are engaged in eliminating Diaspora patterns? Three generations come to Israel together: grandfather, son, and grandchild. All these have to be fitted into an appropriate framework for easy integration, and all these have to be helped to make a pioneering effort,[2] in accordance with the outlook on life accessible to each one. If 20 percent of the immigrants are working on the land, this can rightly be considered a tremendous revolution. Before the recent waves of mass immigration the number of Jewish wage earners working in agriculture was never as high as 20 percent.

After every unselective wave of immigration we find that some of the initial attempts at absorption do not succeed. Such trends as

the flight from the villages to the town and the drift from manual labor to commerce are perfectly natural under the circumstances.

The most important factor in our efforts to ensure jobs for all the new arrivals was the immigrants themselves. If the immigrants had not shown initiative in finding work for themselves, in creating jobs for one another and for others, all our efforts would have been in vain. Anyone who visits the immigrant centers and sees what they have done to improve their situation by using their own resources, comes away with a deep feeling of confidence in the future of this nation and a conviction that its life force, powers of ingenuity, and common sense are no less important than all the efforts by all the organizations and the entire country. Of course, there are limits to the immigrants' ability to help themselves: and without the means of production and adequate capital no great and lasting enterprise can be established. We are still short of both. . . .

Second in the order of priority for immigrant services comes housing. However, it is obvious to us that the meager foreign currency at our disposal should first be placed in basic, productive investments, and only later invested in housing and services. We must spread the large sums of money needed for immigrant housing over many years. Rather than trying to build a small number of high-quality housing units, we should concentrate on giving every immigrant a roof over his head, even in the most primitive way. Here too we must avoid giving everything to a few people. A minimum must be provided for everyone. If we use wood, then every wooden unit takes the place of two canvas units; if we build with concrete, then every two concrete units take the place of three wooden units. We will be able to erect better-quality housing if the immigration rate declines or if our foreign currency income increases. As long as neither of these two conditions has been fulfilled, we must continue following our present policy: as much as possible, as quickly as possible, as cheaply as possible.

Our greatest concern at present is the situation in the services, and social integration. A fundamental condition for successful communal integration is a change in the way of life of settlers from the more backward countries. One of the ways of achieving this is to support the weaker and underprivileged members of the family cell: the children and the women.

NOTES

1. Moshav, cooperative agricultural settlement based on privately owned farms, as opposed to a kibbutz, which is a collective settlement with an agricultural base. In recent years kibbutzim have established many industrial enterprises as well. During the years of mass immigration immediately after the establishment of the state, many immigrants were settled in newly established moshavim, as the socialist ideology and collective way of life of the kibbutzim made them unsuitable for absorbing large numbers of these new immigrants.

2. The concept of *haluziut* (lit., pioneering) was central to the Zionist ideology of the Labor movement. It had several important components, including self-fulfillment through labor (especially agricultural labor) and sacrificing for the common good and the realization of Zionist goals. Each member of the Zionist movement was expected to become a *haluz* in Erez Israel.

ISAAC OLSHAN
9. Jewish Religion and Israeli Democracy

Israel's history is marked by several deep political and ideological rifts that have their origins in the early Zionist movements of Europe and in the prestate Jewish community in Palestine. In a very rough way, three corners of a triangular "continuum" can be delineated, each characterizing a particular vision of the ideal Jewish state. Socialist Zionists envision a state organized along socialist, egalitarian, and democratic principles in which the economy is dominated by publicly owned and cooperative enterprises affording a high degree of workplace democracy and in which Jewish secular culture flourishes while religious institutions and culture are fully protected. The Revisionist Zionists envision an economically and militarily strong state that can provide a homeland and haven for Jews. They envision a state-directed or regulated capitalist economy able to compete favorably in international markets and ensure the state's economic prosperity and security. They also envision a state militarily strong enough to advance and defend the national interests of the state and of world Jewry. The Religious Zionists envision a theocratic state in the land given to the Jewish people by God where Jews can and do live complete religious lives, guided by religious leaders with the political power to ensure the theocratic integrity of the state and society.

Source: Isaac Olshan, *Din Udvarim* (Memoirs) (Jerusalem: Schocken Books, 1979), pp. 325–28. Reprinted by permission of Schocken Books, Tel Aviv.

One aspect of this ideological and political competition was the struggle between the military units of various political movements for control of the emerging state (see docs. 2, 4). In the following reading, the efforts of the religious parties to establish political influence within the state apparatus are discussed by Isaac Olshan (1895–1983), whose roots were in Socialist Zionist organizations. Olshan was one of the original five members of the Israeli Supreme Court and its second president, 1954–65. His position, personality, and long tenure of office enabled him to enrich his memoirs of cases and events with insightful comments.

Immediately after the establishment of the state, the religious politicians began their efforts to secure strongholds with the intent of establishing life in the state on a firm halakhic[1] basis, and in this way they tried to fortify positions in the various government offices by giving preference to members of religious parties in the bureaucratic apparatus. It must be admitted that politicians of other parties, too, as soon as they reached ministerial status, followed the same path. The only difference was that in the latter case these things were done out of a sense of obligation toward their own party members, whereas in the former case it grew out of an effort to create facts and customs, and by these means to achieve the penetration of halakhah in the management of the affairs of state and, in a roundabout way, in the life of the individual as well. To that end the leaders of the religious parties were most eager to widen the power and the authority of the rabbis. In the wake of a defective electoral system that actually corrupted the principles of democracy in the state and led to the fragmentation and multiplication of political parties, there arose the need to run the state by means of coalition governments. In those coalition governments, Mapai was the strongest party according to the number of representatives in the Knesset, but it never succeeded in achieving a majority in the elections.

Since it was the strongest party in the Knesset, Mapai always felt that it had the responsibility to form the governments in Israel during the entire period since the foundation of the state. Therefore it had to arrive, after each and every round of elections, at agreements with small factions. Here then was the possibility for the small parties to make conditions, which derived ostensibly from principles they professed but which were actually nothing but combinations of attempts to gain seats in the government. The negotiations about those conditions and the agreements concerning them were termed the "ground rules" of the coalition. Despite the fact that in the party newspapers as well as in public the politicians professed to be democratic in a general way, and despite the fact that in every interparty discussion the opponents pretended to base their viewpoints on principles of democracy—each according to a sophisticated reasoning all his own—when it came to determining those ground rules very little attention was paid to the needs of the community. The leaders cared little about whether they actually had received a mandate from the majority of the voting public to establish particular ground rules.

It would stand to reason that before the elections a number of parties would be forced to join together in order to form a coalition government on the basis of agreed-upon ground rules, and that each and every party entering into a coalition of this sort would present itself to the voter with its program, the principles of which were to be based on agreed-upon ground rules. But, instead of this procedure being followed before the elections, it was actually done after them, without giving the voters a chance to express their assent or opposition to the ground rules. What is called by the Israeli politicians in the area of legislation "the democratic system" was in actuality a party regimentation that allowed no choice but required compromise agreements and even conspiracies contrived by coalition members after the fact, i.e., after the elections. This situation was the cause of all kinds of mishaps in the public administration. The lion's share of the public service apparatus was party based, and even if this was not intended, at least the impression was created among the public at large that the affairs of such-and-such a department were in the area of such-and-such a party, and the affairs of another office lay in the power of a certain other party, and so forth.

Even in the government itself, it was impossible to create the efficient intermeshing between the different ministries because the relationships among them were most tenuous and every minister was careful not to intrude upon the territory of his colleague. As opposed to a government composed of the members of one single party, here every attempt by the head of the government, or the minister of one party, to respond to a subject under the jurisdiction of the leader of another party, was considered as impairing that leader's "sovereignty," and this could well lead to a government crisis because the injured party might throw down the gauntlet. It even happened that a particular minister or several of the ministers were opposed to the conduct of another minister, and although the majority of the ministers might be of the opinion that that opposition was justified, they hesitated to take measures in order to change the situation lest the stability of the government be undermined.

During the process of consolidation of the parties for the purpose of forming a coalition government, the parties "more fit" from the standpoint of the ruling party (Mapai) were the religious ones. It seemed that those parties represented only those aspirations that aimed at the penetration of religious laws into the life of the state, but that they knew very well that the promises, or most of them, would not be kept. Thus the formula of the status quo was created in the area of religious affairs. However, when they were given such ministries as Religious Affairs, Interior, and Welfare, they were able to support, or defend, various institutions in keeping with their efforts to impose matters of religious interest on the nonreligious citizen as well. Parties such as Mapam and to a lesser extent Ahdut Haavodah appeared on the political stage with obsolete slogans of the kind used in the nineteenth century. These slogans were appropriate in that particular period, and at that time they really contributed to the growth and the progress of the socialist movement and to the protection of the working people from the exploiting classes. But now, in the second half of the twentieth century, during the period of the creation and the growth of the welfare state, when the government was forced to penetrate into all areas of individual life because of the responsibility placed on it for the livelihood and sustenance of every individual, these parties lost their vitality.

For example, in the nineteenth century the strike was an efficient and just instrument in the war of the workers against their unlimited exploitation by their employers. However, in the welfare state, as the government's responsibility to provide a livelihood for the masses has grown steadily, and with it the responsibility for the national economy, the unjustified use of the strike can increasingly be harmful, particularly when wildcat strikes at one enterprise threaten the economic viability of other enterprises. In such cases the strike weapon actually limits workers' power, especially if the national federation has lost influence over its local organizations. These observations apply particularly to a state that is forced to seek an opening into foreign markets and to compete there against the exports from other states with regimes not considered progressive in social policies. The prohibition against strikes in Soviet Russia is inevitable, and it can serve as proof as to the extent to which the doctrines of the previous century have become obsolete. The religious parties have been more reluctant than any others to profess socialist models for society or for anything connected with the economy of the state. For this reason, then, it was more convenient for the ruling party to ally itself through coalitions with the religious parties, in exchange for the preservation of existing affairs. In actuality, this alliance led to religious suppression, in many cases to halakhic decisions that had become totally obsolete, such as personal status laws (*ishut*) and others. In short, Mapai was able to make arrangements quite easily with the religious parties, as they did not demand doctrines that had a bearing on the economy of the state. On the other hand, the leftist parties that stood for anachronistic doctrines shut their eyes to the existing situation and did not recognize the danger lurking in the militant religious establishment.

For these reasons compromises, concessions, and intrigues occurred in the religious camp without consideration for the fact that the State of Israel had been established as a secular state on the basic principle of the rule of law.

As we said, the religious parties began as early as the first years after the establishment of the state to conquer strongholds in the direction of religious coercion of the broad secular public. This occurred at a very slow pace, in order not to arouse instinctive reactions on the part of those wide circles that, although they were ready to grant all religious needs to those who required them, still were not ready to agree to a conversion of the state to one based on religious laws, many of which had been created under the force and conditions of life during the period in which they originated but were no longer suited for life and its conditions in our own era.

As already recounted, as early as the end of 1948 there arose, right after the declaration of the establishment of the state, the demand for a widening of the jurisdiction of the rabbinical courts. At that time, on the heels of the establishment of the Supreme Court, the religious parties demanded that among the five judges there should be named at least one religious judge, i.e., a rabbi. The matter was discussed by the Provisional government, and in spite of the fact that there were members of Mapam within the government, who of course did not ask the opinion of their membership and did not get their approval to agree to this imposition by the religious parties, the demand was accepted without opposition. At that time, Rabbi Simhah Assaf was named, and his nomination was confirmed by the Provisional State Council (Moezet Hamedinah), which functioned on a temporary basis. That nomination was even against the law, according to which the conditions for the jurisdiction of the judges of the state were still anchored in the law of the Mandate, which had not yet been changed following the establishment of the state and was thus still in force.

The pill was sweetened by the fact that Rabbi Assaf—although he had no juridical training—was still an exalted personality, bright, progressive in his outlook, pleasant to deal with and not fanatical in his orthodoxy. He was easy to work with. All these qualities compensated in a large measure for the additional burden placed upon us—the four other judges—as we had to guide him along in connection with the application of various laws in cases brought before us. Cases that had a bearing upon questions of personal status, falling under the purview of religious rules, were decided in the religious courts; the instances in which we in the Supreme Court had anything to do with them were few. With respect to the majority of the cases, we had to explain to Rabbi Assaf the secular law.

In connection with the illegality of the nomination, a special law was afterward passed in the Knesset in order to make his nomination as judge legal. Wisecracks of that time termed it "Assaf's Law." In the years 1952–53 two of the judges of the Supreme Court resigned: Dr. [Menaham] Dunkleblum and Rabbi Assaf.

After the resignation of Rabbi Assaf there

were those among the religious parties who demanded, on the basis of an established claim (*hazakah*), that another rabbi be named in place of Rabbi Assaf. Mr. Eliyahu Elyashar[2] even began to lobby for the appointment of a Sephardi judge to the Supreme Court. This time around, however, because it was well known beforehand that

we as judges of the Supreme Court would take an unwavering stand that any nomination be made solely and entirely according to the qualifications of the candidates without religious considerations, the question was removed from the agenda of the various busybodies.

NOTES

1. Halakhah, Jewish religious law based upon the Pentateuch, Talmud, and other traditional rabbinic teachings.

2. Eliyahu (Elihu) Elyashar (c. 1899–1981),

president of the Sephardi community in Jerusalem. Elyashar came from a long line of respected rabbinic leaders who have been in Palestine for centuries.

NAHUM GOLDMANN
10. The German Reparations

Following the reconstruction of Germany after World War II, the West German government agreed, in principle, to pay reparations to those Jews who were victimized by the Nazi government. The Conference on Jewish Material Claims was established in October 1951 by world Jewish organizations to represent world Jewry in the negotiations, and an agreement was signed in Luxembourg on September 10, 1952. West Germany agreed to pay DM 3 billion ($750 million) in goods to Israel to offset the cost of absorbing the refugees, DM 450 million ($107 million) to Israel to be transferred to the Jewish Claims Conference for the rehabilitation of victims outside of Israel, and additional direct payments to the Jewish Claims Conference for individual compensation. These payments were to be made over a period of fourteen years. In addition, Bonn's Federal Indemnity Law of 1954,

which provided for restitution to individuals oppressed by the Nazis, led to an influx of an additional DM 7 billion ($1.7 billion) into the Israeli economy over ten years.

It is now widely agreed that the decision to accept the reparations was correct and that the reparations money played an important role in consolidating Israel's economic foundations during a period in which the state was virtually bankrupt. At the time the agreement was negotiated, however, it was one of the most controversial issues of Israeli life. The experience of the Holocaust has affected much of Menahem Begin's political thinking, and Herut, under his leadership, opposed the negotiations, arguing that accepting reparations was tantamount to pardoning Germany for unpardonable crimes; the movement threatened to cause widespread violence during the massive demonstrations it organized.

Source: Nahum Goldmann, *Memories: The Autobiography of Nahum Goldmann. The Story of a Lifelong Battle by World Jewry's Ambassador at Large,* trans. Helen Sebba (London: Weidenfeld and Nicolson, 1970), pp. 259–63. Reprinted by permission of Nahum Goldmann.

Dr. Nahum Goldmann (1895–1982), a longtime Zionist leader and activist within the World Zionist Organization, was instrumental in establishing contact with the West German chancellor, Konrad Adenauer, and in facilitating the negotiations that led to the Luxembourg Agreement. Goldmann, who headed the World Jewish Congress, 1953–77, had considered joining Israel's political system but made his home and political base in the Jewish Diaspora. In 1962 he left the United States (to which he had emigrated shortly after the outbreak of World War II) and became a citizen of Israel, spending part of his time there and part in Europe. In 1968 he became a Swiss citizen and made Geneva his home base. His insistence on emphasizing the distinction between Israel and the Jewish people as well as some of his policies embittered his relations with successive Israeli prime ministers (see, e.g., docs. 35, 49). In the following excerpt from his memoirs, Goldmann not only describes the delicate reparations negotiations but also presents the position taken by the majority of Israeli and Jewish institutions.

Next morning [December 6, 1951] at eleven o'clock, when I went with Dr. Barou[1] to see the chancellor at Claridge's Hotel, taking every precaution to avoid the press, I sensed that the coming conversation was going to be a momentous one. I asked Adenauer to allow me fifteen or twenty minutes to state my case and pointed out how significant it was that for the first time since Hitler, a representative of Jewry should be confronting a German chancellor. I told him of the heated, not to say passionate controversy in the Jewish world and of the violent attacks I myself had been subjected to for months, but said that my confidence in his statement to the Bundestag [West German legislature] had led me to arrange this conversation. I explained how important it was morally to atone for the crimes of the Nazi era, at least materially, by a great gesture of good will, and said that from the perspective of history, a contribution to the development of the Jewish state was an honor for Germany. The Jewish people would never forget what the Nazis had done to them, and no one should ever expect them to forget it, but a conspicuous symbol of atonement would show the Jews and the world that a new Germany had arisen. The form and extent of the restitution this Germany would make to the Jewish people would demonstrate, perhaps more clearly than anything else, the extent of Germany's breach with National Socialism.

At the same time I emphasized that whatever Germany did, could be no more than a gesture. Nothing could call the dead to life again; nothing could obliterate those crimes; but a symbolic gesture would have a deep meaning. The coming negotiations, I said, were unique in nature. They had no legal basis; they were backed by no political power; their meaning was purely an ethical one. If there was to be any haggling, it would be better not to begin the talks at all. If the negotiations were not to be conducted on the basis of an acknowledged moral claim, if they were not to be begun and ended in a spirit of magnanimity, then I, the sponsor of this claim, would advise the chancellor and Israel not to engage in them at all. Conducted under the wrong conditions, they would only poison relations between the Jews and the Germans still more.

I told the chancellor that I understood how difficult it must be for him to accept Israel's demands as they stood as the basis for negotiation and mentioned my talk with Blankenhorn[2] of the day before. On the other hand, I assured him that unless they were accepted, neither the Israeli parliament nor the Claims Conference would authorize the opening of negotiations and postponement would jeopardize the whole undertaking. Finally, I told him that I knew I was asking something unusual, something that by conventional standards might be considered incorrect. "But this is a unique case," I concluded. "Until now, Chancellor, I did not know you, but in the twenty-five minutes I have been sitting here opposite you, you have impressed me as a man of such stature that I can expect you override conventional regulations. I ask you to take upon yourself the responsibility of approving the undertaking I have requested, not merely verbally, as I suggested to Blankenhorn, but in the form of a letter."

Chancellor Adenauer was visibly moved and replied: "Dr. Goldmann, those who know me know that I am a man of few words and that I detest high-flown talks. But I must tell you that while you were speaking I felt the wings of world history beating in this room. My desire for restitution is sincere. I regard it as a great moral problem and a debt of honour for the new Germany. You have sized me up correctly. I am prepared to approve the undertaking you request on my own responsibility. If you will give me the draft of such a letter after our talk, I will sign it in the course of the day." As a matter of fact, I dictated a text to his secretary in his apartment and, in the afternoon, on the occasion of an address the chancellor gave at Chatham House, Dr. Barou received the letter addressed to me . . .

In Israel a majority of the coalition parties authorized the government to negotiate, after a stormy debate in parliament accompanied by tumultuous demonstrations from outside. The Claims Conference deliberately waited for Israel's decision, but after the resolution had been passed in the Knesset, I called a meeting in New York for January 20, 1952. That produced another very heated debate, although this time it ended in endorsement of the negotiations by a much larger majority. An executive committee, of which I was elected chairman, was appointed to direct the negotiations; its members included Jacob Blaustein of the American Jewish Committee, Frank Goldmann of the B'nai B'rith, Israel Goldstein of the American Jewish Congress, and Adolph Held of the Jewish Labor Committee, all of

them from New York. Two European representatives were later co-opted: Barnett Janner of the British Board of Deputies and Jules Braunschvig of the Alliance Israélite Universelle.[3]

We worked out a set of procedural directives. The main thing was to get the West German government to pass legislation applicable to all of the Federal Republic, so that claims for restitution and compensation could be handled uniformly. Up until then there had been great discrepancies in individual German states' handling of claims. Measures would also be required to make the Federal Republic responsible for enforcing this legislation, especially its financial provisions, since practice had shown how difficult it would be for several of the poorer states to meet legitimate claims. Finally, in addition to the individual claims, we demanded restitution of heirless Jewish property. A team of experts was asked to produce a detailed plan for implementing these directives and it did an excellent job.

In a joint session of the executive committee and the Israeli delegation, held in Paris on February 11, 1952, and attended by Sharett, the global claim of the Claims Conference was set at five hundred million German marks. This completed the necessary preliminaries on the Jewish side; the only thing that remained to be settled before negotiations could begin were some technical details of form and place, and I had already spoken to Adenauer in London on February 4 about these. During that talk, in which German Secretary of State for Foreign Affairs, Walter Hallstein, and Assistant Secretary Blankenhorn joined, we had agreed that the discussions should be held in Belgium or Holland in mid-March and that there should be two parallel negotiations, one between the Israeli delegation and the Germans and a second between representatives of the Claims Conference and Germany.

On March 16, 17, and 18 the executive committee of the Claims Conference held further meetings in London to appoint our team. We decided on Moses Leavitt of the American Jewish Joint Distribution Committee as leader of the delegation and Alex Easterman of the WJC,[4] Seymour Ruben of the American Jewish Committee, and Maurice Boukstein of the Jewish Agency for Palestine as its members. They were to be assisted by a number of experts, notably Dr. Nehemiah Robinson. . . .

On March 20, 1952, negotiations began in Wassenaar near The Hague. I deliberately took no part. I could not afford to spend months in Wassenaar and in any case I thought it better to remain in the background during the complicated and protracted discussions of detail, so that I could more effectively intervene in a crisis. It was only to be expected that difficulties would arise. In a great courageous gesture Chancellor Adenauer had accepted the Israeli claims of a billion dollars as the basis of discussions, but I knew that this gigantic sum was firmly opposed within his cabinet and by the party leaders, as well as by banking and industrial interests. I had been told by various sources that there was no hope of anything approaching that amount. I remained optimistic, trusting to the chancellor's word and his way of accomplishing what he desired, even in the face of opposition.

NOTES

1. Noah Barou (1889–1955), economist and Labor Zionist who settled in Britain and became chairman of the British and European sections of the World Jewish Congress.

2. Herbert Blankenhorn (b. 1904), political director of the West German Ministry of Foreign Affairs, 1950–55.

3. American Jewish Committee (est. 1906), oldest Jewish defense organization in the United States. Originally an elitist organization of prominent Jews, it has broadened its membership and organizational base. In the early 1950s it cooperated, to a limited extent, with other Jewish organizations.

B'nai B'rith (est. 1843), world's oldest and largest Jewish service and fraternal organization.

American Jewish Congress (est. 1922), organization with a broad membership base and a democratic structure that seeks to act on behalf of the desires and interests of American Jewry.

Jewish Labor Committee (est. 1934), organization founded by American Socialist Zionist organizations and Jewish trade unions. At first it existed to coordinate their efforts to help Jewish labor organizations in Europe. Today it coordinates political activities on issues of mutual concern to its constituent organizational members.

Board of Deputies of British Jews (est. 1760), representative organization of British Jewry.

Alliance Israélite Universelle (est. 1860), first modern international Jewish organization, centered in Paris. Among its most significant activities was the establishment of many schools for Jewish children in the French colonies, which facilitated their "modernization."

4. American Joint Jewish Distribution Committee (frequently called "The Joint"; est. November 27, 1914, as the Joint Distribution Committee of American Funds for the Relief of Jewish War Sufferers), major relief organization of American Jewry, which coordinated American Jewish philanthropic efforts to aid European Jewry during and after the Holocaust.

World Jewish Congress (WJC; est. 1936), umbrella organization representing communal Jewish organizations throughout the world. Its greatest achievement is the role it played in bringing about the Luxembourg Agreement.

BENYAMIN GIVLI
11. The Mishap in Egypt

In July 1954 eleven Egyptian Jews organized by Unit 131[1] exploded bombs at an Alexandria post office and the American information center in Cairo. A third action was supposedly planned, and other targets were considered. The bombings, which caused minor property damage and an injury to the fingers of one postal clerk, were apparently meant to strain America's relations with the Arab world at a time when the United States was increasing its arms sales to Arab countries.

Following this ill-conceived act of Israeli intelligence warfare, the Egyptian government arrested and tried eight Egyptian Jews. Two were sentenced to death and executed; the others received prison terms. Three of the participants in the bombings escaped arrest. This so-called Mishap (*esek bish*) subsequently developed into a serious political scandal that shook the Israeli political system in the early 1960s (see doc. 29). Serious questions were raised about the Mishap: Who gave the order to carry out the operation? Who was responsible for the operation? Was it the defense minister, Pinhas Lavon, or the chief of the IDF's Intelligence Branch, Benyamin Givli?

Pinhas Lavon (Lubianiker) (1904–76), Israeli defense minister from 1953 to 1955, was at the center of this controversy. Despite his position as Ben-Gurion's heir apparent, he was forced to resign his cabinet position. Givli was also dismissed.

The document reproduced here—a top secret memorandum of October 1954 from Givli to the General Staff—is one of the original documents around which the controversy has raged. It was printed in an account of the Mishap and its consequences by Haggai Eshed, an Israeli journalist commissioned by Ben-Gurion to research and document the event. Eshed's version is obviously only one among several.

Pursuant to your request, I am listing herewith the details in connection with the operations [of Unit] 131 in Egypt and the mishap that occurred there:

1. For prior reference, see: (a) report on operations in Egypt, July 1954, dated 8/8 of this year, (b) arrest of IDF officer in Egypt of 9/24 of this year, (c) report on events in Egypt July–September dated 10/5 of this year.

2. On 7/16/54 a discussion took place in the home of the defense minister on the topic "Significance of British evacuation of Suez"; the participants were the defense minister, Brigadier (Aluf) Avidar,[2] Lieutenant Colonel Yuval Neeman,[3] Mr. Ephraim Evron,[4] and myself.

During the discussion I was asked about the possibility of putting Unit 131 into action against British targets and my reply was affirmative from the operational point of view.

After the conclusion of the meeting, I was requested by the defense minister to stay on. In the conversation between us the subject of the operations [of Unit] 131 against British targets was again raised.

The targets that seemed acceptable to me were British missions and vehicles as well as other British institutions and personnel.

Source: Haggai Eshed, *Mi Natan et Hahoraah?* (Who Issued the Order?) (Jerusalem: Edanim Books, 1979), pp. 258–59. Reprinted by permission of Haggai Eshed.

British soldiers were not designated as such because of the assumption that they would not move beyond the area of the canal zone, in view of the prevailing tension there.

Thereafter the defense minister told me that I should issue instructions to 131 to operate against British elements. In that conversation, we talked about two additional matters that have no connection with the present subject. After the meeting, I invited to my home the commander of Unit 131 and another commander.

The commander of 131 informed me that he hoped the men would be in a position to act, since during the last meeting the need for a state of readiness was emphasized in view of the unsatisfactory situation in the ranks, and I instructed him to transmit operational directions by way of proper communication channels.

The other officer was unable to make any concrete suggestions and informed me that he would examine the matter and let me know. Several days later the press published stories of arrests and operations in Cairo and Alexandria, taken from broadcasts by Radio Damascus and Radio Cairo.

The officer on location received the instructions transmitted by Kol Israel[5] in a garbled and unclear form, and operated according to his best judgment.

From reports that reached us afterward it became clear that operations in the post office and in the American information offices were carried out by the men on location, according to their best judgment and based upon the instructions that had been issued for planning purposes only.

NOTES

1. Unit 131, special operations unit of the IDF's Intelligence Branch, which at that time was under the command of Isser Harel, head of the Mossad. The Mossad is Israel's agency for intelligence and special operations. At the time of the October 1973 War the Mossad was under the direction of the Office of the Prime Minister.

2. Yosef Avidar (b. 1906), prominent figure in Mapai and the Labor movement. Avidar joined the Haganah in the late 1920s and worked his way up through the defense establishment and later into the leading circles of the Ministry of Foreign Affairs. He was ambassador to the Soviet Union, 1955–58, and to Argentina, 1961–65. He was also director general of the ministry of labor, 1959–60, and comptroller of the Histadrut, 1968–71.

3. Yuval Neeman (b. 1925), prominent figure in Israeli defense and intelligence establishments, also a well-known physicist and professor. Neeman was deputy commander of the Givati Brigade in 1948. He then became deputy director of the Operations Section of the General Staff and director of the Planning Section. In 1958 he was the military attaché to London. He was an active member of the Likud in the 1970s, but in 1979 he left the Likud and formed a new party. In 1982 he reentered the Likud coalition and, as a member of Hatehiyah, the new party he helped form, became minister of science—a position created for him.

4. Efraim Evron (b. 1921), leading member of the Israeli foreign service for many years. In 1954–55 Evron was head of the Defense Minister's Office. Later, after the Likud came to power, he became ambassador to the United States, succeeding Simha Dinitz in 1978. He stepped down from this post in January 1982 and was succeeded by Moshe Arens.

5. Kol Israel (lit., Voice of Israel), Israeli government broadcasting service. Immediately before independence, Kol Israel was established as the illegal radio station of the Haganah. After independence, control of the broadcasting service was maintained by the Ministry of the Interior and later by the Office of the Prime Minister. In 1965 the independent Israel Broadcasting Authority (IBA) was established by the government in order to ensure greater freedom in broadcasting. The extent of the IBA's autonomy has become a political issue on several occasions.

MOSHE DAYAN
12. The Transformation of the Israeli Army

Moshe Dayan, one of the central figures of Israeli public life, was chief of staff of the Israeli army before entering the political arena. The following excerpt from his autobiography describes the reshaping of the Israeli army in the early 1950s as well as some of the major problems of Israeli defense policy.

On December 7, 1952, I was appointed head of the Operations Branch of the General Staff, and I held this post for one year until my appointment as chief of staff on December 6, 1953. During that year I applied myself to developing the operational capability of the army—the sole purpose of an army's existence—and sharpening the tools for doing that job—organizing the appropriate combat units and raising the standards of the individual fighting man.

My predecessor in Operations was Lt. Gen. Mordekhai Makleff, who moved up to become chief of staff upon the resignation of Lt. Gen. Yigael Yadin. Our appointments came during a difficult financial period for the army. The War of Independence was behind us, and the country's priorities were the reception, absorption and settlement of the several hundred thousand new immigrants who had reached our shores in the few years since statehood. The treasury coffers had to be channelled to essential immigrant services and civilian development projects, and the budgets of other ministries, including defense, had to be drastically cut.

Makleff and I agreed in principle that the fighting units of the army had to be strengthened at the expense of the service units, and this principle was indeed reflected in the three-year program decided upon by the General Staff at sessions devoted to the reorganization of the army within the framework of our restricted budget. It was generally agreed that we had to change the character of the combat units. They were not what they had been in the War of Independence. Many officers had left. The best of the recruits doing their national service elected to join the Air Force or the Navy. Many of the new immigrants, without experience of the life and temper of beleaguered Israel, required longer training. Units were understrength and ill equipped.

We had seen the effects of lowered fighting standards in our infantry units reflected in the minor border actions that had taken place in the period since the War of Independence. At the beginning of 1953, the incidence of infiltration for sabotage and murder had increased, and several small-scale reprisal raids had been undertaken against terrorist bases in or near Arab villages just across the border. The results were unsatisfactory. In some cases our detachments returned after one or two men were killed and a few wounded without having fulfilled their mission.

I considered it my job to change all this and to fashion fighting units that could always be relied upon to attain their objectives. This, I felt, should be the sole concern of the head of Operations. I was aware of the great importance of effecting the necessary organizational changes in the structure of the army. Abolishing military laundries, using civilian hospital services for army

Source: Moshe Dayan, *Story of My Life* (London: Weidenfeld and Nicolson, 1976), pp. 139–47. Reprinted by permission of Weidenfeld and Nicolson.

personnel, or reducing the number of field kitchens would make more funds available for armaments. But these changes could be made without anyone having to crawl on his belly through an enemy fence and risk getting a bullet in his back. It was the fighting man I was concerned with, for he was the cutting edge of the army's tool, and a soldier in the army of Israel, under constant threat from its neighbors, had always to be ready for battle. If we failed in minor border actions, as we had in the previous year, how would we stand up to the Arab armies on the battlefield? No amount of reorganization would alter the basic function of the Israel Defense Forces— to be fit for battle at all times.

It seemed to me that the recent failures were due to altered attitudes since the War of Independence in three spheres: the degree of the soldier's readiness to risk his life in fulfillment of his mission; the place and duties of the officer in battle; and the basic approach of the General Staff to casualty rates in a period of restricted hostilities.

It was not difficult to change the approach of the General Staff, and I accordingly met with the Operations officers of all the commands. I told them that in the future, if any unit commander reported that he failed to carry out his mission because he could not overcome the enemy force, his explanation would not be accepted unless he had suffered 50 percent casualties. The term "could not" was relative, and the question was how much effort was put into meeting enemy resistance in order to complete the mission. As long as the unit had not lost its combat power, it had to go on attacking. What I left unsaid when I spoke to the officers was transmitted by the expression on my face. They were left in no doubt that if they failed to carry out their assignment, they would have to face a detailed debriefing; and if their explanations did not satisfy me, there would be little future for them in the army.

The factors that helped to bring about a practical change in combat standards during the year when Makleff was chief of staff and

I was head of Operations were the channelling of the better-educated national service recruits to the fighting units and, above all, the establishment of a special unit known as Force 101. This was a volunteer unit which undertook special operations across the border. The commander was the daring and combat-wise Maj. Ariel Sharon,[1] whom I had admired and known well since he had been my Intelligence officer at Northern Command. Arik, as everyone called him, gathered to his unit picked men, most of them reservists. I confess that when the proposal to establish this unit was brought before the General Staff in May 1953, I did not support it. I felt that our primary problem was not what to do to the Arab terrorists in reprisal, but how to improve the fighting capacity of our army. In fact, however, it was the practical influence of this unit which brought about the very aim I sought—raising combat standards. Force 101 operated with such brilliance that its achievements set an example to all the other formations in the army. It proved the feasibility of successfully carrying out the kind of mission at which other units had failed.

In January 1954, a few weeks after I became chief of staff, Force 101 was merged with the paratroops, and Arik became commander of the Paratroop Battalion. For some time thereafter, this unit alone undertook all the reprisal actions against Arab terrorists and raids across the border. Later, there was a growing recognition that such assignments should also be given to other units. The paratroops ceased to be solely an army formation and became a concept and a symbol—the symbol of courageous combat—that other formations in the army tried to live up to. Through the paratroops, the army recovered its self-confidence, and it was now rare indeed that a unit commander returned from action having to explain the failure of his mission.

My appointment as chief of staff placed me at the top of the army pyramid, and I knew that I had to safeguard the image of the Israel Defense Forces. But I also knew that I had to carry out those changes I thought essential and to mold the army into the shape I wanted. I recognized that I would now have to deal with matters which I had managed to steer clear of up to now. A chief of staff, particularly in times of comparative quiet, is occupied with administrative and technical problems—manpower, budget, armament, equipment, maintenance—and he is further away from the combat units in the field. As I rose in the military hierarchy, the gap between battle and me widened. Instead of fighting, I would tell others what to do. I would issue directives, give oral and written orders, but in the field, in battle, matters would be decided by the combatants. Sitting at General Staff headquarters, it would be difficult for me to determine, and at times even influence, the character of the fighting by our units in the distant Negev or on the Jordan border. I would have to live through them and their reports. It would be the commanders in the field who would tell me what could and what could not be done.

I felt an understandable pride in becoming the number one soldier in the Israel Defense Forces. But even at the height of the ceremony, when Ben-Gurion pinned on my badges of rank and I received the standard of the chief of staff, I had no sense of elation. I realized the weight of the responsibility, and I was ready to shoulder it faithfully and with devotion.

At the end of the ceremony, the secretary of the Cabinet came over to me and casually observed that I would now have to change my partisan character, be circumspect in my ways, become more respectable. I would have to "fashion a new Moshe Dayan," he said. I told him he was wide of the mark. It was not I who would change; the image of the chief of staff would change. It was not I who had made myself a new suit of clothes; it was the army that had acquired a new chief. I intended to change the style and content of the army, abolish the gap between the chief of staff and the private soldier, cut down on ceremonial, introduce

more simplicity in the work habits of the army brass, and fill the higher echelon posts with talented and battle-hardened young officers who had fought in the War of Independence.

I started the change of style in my own office. I abolished the post of aide-de-camp to the chief of staff and I took over his room as my office. I brought in the field table covered by a khaki blanket and a glass top which I had used when I was head of Operations. I turned the large, well-furnished room which had been the office of the chief of staff, with its massive table and upholstered chairs, into a conference room. I wanted the field commanders who came to see me to feel that they had come to the headquarters of a higher command which was not very different and not cut off from their own. When I inspected units in the field, I wore fatigues, sat on the ground with the troops, got dirty and dusty together with them.

I paid a lot of surprise visits at night, mostly driving alone. I wanted to check whether units were in a constant state of readiness; ensure that there was always a responsible senior officer in every command headquarters; and talk to the soldiers returning from a night exercise or from guard duty at an outpost. Whenever there was an operational problem, I would see the head of the Operations Branch, the unit commander, and his junior platoon commanders. I wanted to hear what had happened, if it was after an action, or what special problems were envisaged, if it was before an operation. I wanted to hear things from them at first hand, without intermediaries, and I wanted the young officers to hear what I had to say directly from me, in my own words and in my own style. . . .

Since it was through the young officers that we could shape the kind of army we wanted, I would use the occasion of a graduation parade at an Officers' Course whenever I had something special to say. I remember one such occasion at the end of May 1955, and also what I said when I addressed the cadets on whom I had just pinned officer's insignia. A few days earlier, I had had the unpleasant duty of terminating the service of a young career officer who had ordered a soldier to proceed on a dangerous action while he himself sat in safety. A vehicle of ours was struck close to the border of the Gaza Strip and was under heavy fire from the Egyptians. The officer in charge sent a driver to retrieve it, while he himself lay behind cover and issued directions from there. I told the cadets: "I would not have dismissed this officer if he had decided that the danger was too great and it was better to abandon the vehicle rather than endanger lives. But if he decided to take daring action and save the vehicle, he should have advanced with his troops and laid his own life on the line together with theirs. Officers of the Israeli army do not send their men into battle. They lead them into battle."

Forging an army, however, requires more than talk, and officers require more than courage and moral leadership. They should also be well educated and of rounded intellect. Most of our officers at that time had fought in the War of Independence and stayed on, having had no opportunity before that war or since of attending the university. I thought that should be corrected, and we accordingly introduced a system of sending officers to the university at the army's expense. They could take a degree in any subject that interested them, from economics and Middle Eastern studies, to history and literature. One officer who later became commander of the Armored Corps studied philosophy. At the same time, we also started sending officers in the technical services, such as ordnance and engineering, to the Haifa Technion (Institute of Technology) to study subjects related to their work.

In mid-1955 we sent a detachment of volunteers on a daring reconnaissance mission through Sinai to find a land route to Sharm el-Sheikh, at the southern tip of the peninsula. Sharm el-Sheikh commanded the narrow Straits of Tiran at the entrance to the Gulf of Aqaba. The Egyptians had blockaded this waterway to Israeli shipping, thereby closing our sea lane to East Africa and the Far East and stifling Eilat port, as well as the development of its hinterland, the Negev. Egypt also closed the direct air route over the gulf for our civilian planes. The reconnaissance was part of our planning preparation for the capture of Sharm el-Sheikh if the Egyptians failed to lift the blockade. The results of the survey would make possible the extraordinary trek of one of our brigades in the Sinai Campaign a year and a half later.

On September 27, 1955, Gamal Abdul Nasser[2] of Egypt opened a military exhibition in Cairo and announced that the week before, "we signed a commercial agreement with Czechoslovakia whereby that country will supply us with arms in exchange for cotton and rice." This was Nasser's innocent-sounding announcement of what was to mark a turning point in Middle Eastern affairs, for his "commercial agreement," which would soon be known as the Czech arms deal, revolutionized the scale and quality of arms supplies to the region, planted a Soviet foot firmly in an area which had been closed to her, opened a second front for the United States in the Cold War, and gravely threatened the existence of Israel.

Under this arms agreement, Egypt would be receiving from the Soviet bloc some 300 medium and heavy tanks of the latest Soviet type, 200 armored personnel carriers, 100 armored self-propelled guns, several hundred field howitzers, medium guns, and anti-tank guns, 134 anti-aircraft guns, and 200 MIG-15 jet fighters and 50 Ilyushin bombers, in addition to transport planes, radar systems, 2 destroyers, 4 mine-sweepers, 12 torpedo boats, ammunition, spare parts, ground equipment for aircraft, and hundreds of battle vehicles of various types. All small arms and light weapons were to be replaced by huge quantities of the Russian semi-automatic rifle.

These arms, types and quantities, may not seem startling by today's standards. But at that time, they represented a stunning acceleration of the pace of rearmament in the

Middle East. In quantity alone, they tipped the arms balance drastically against Israel; in quality, the tilt was even more drastic. We had never imagined that we could ever match the size of the arsenals possessed by the Arab states. But we believed we could bridge the gap by the superior fighting capacity of our troops, as long as we could match the quality of their weaponry. In modern warfare, however, the elements of range, speed and fire power in technologically advanced aircraft, naval vessels, and armor can be so superior that inferior weapons are simply unable to stand up to them. For every rise in standards of an enemy's arms, there must be a minimum means of reply. Without it, no amount of courage can get the better of objective technical superiority. A brilliant pilot in a propeller aircraft has no chance against mediocrity in a jet. A daring tank gunner in an obsolete Sherman, which is the tank we had, would find his shells bouncing off the armor of a Stalin-3 tank, which was what the Egyptians were about to receive. The Czech arms deal placed in doubt the capability of the Israeli army to give expression to its qualitative human advantages.

It was clear to us in Israel that the primary purpose of this massive Egyptian rearmament was to prepare Egypt for a decisive confrontation with Israel in the near future. The Egyptian blockade, Egyptian planning and direction of mounting Palestinian guer-rilla activity against Israel, Nasser's own declarations, and now the Czech arms deal left no doubt in our minds that Egypt's purpose was to wipe us out, or at least win a decisive military victory which would leave us in helpless subjugation.

The Soviet arms began flowing into Egypt at the beginning of November 1955, and at meetings of the General Staff we considered that it would take the Egyptian army from 6 to 8 months to absorb and digest most of its new weapons and equipment. We therefore had to expect an Egyptian attack at any time from late spring to late summer. In that time, we had to acquire at least some planes and tanks which could match their Russian counterparts. The problem for us was that our sources were limited. The United States and Britain produced quality planes and tanks, but at that time they were refusing to sell us arms. There was talk that America might change her policy and consider letting us have defensive weapons, but even that was dubious. The only possible source for new tanks was France, but she produced only the light AMX tank. We would try to get that and make do with it, and also to recondition some obsolete American tanks which we had acquired from World War Two surplus stores in Europe. On planes, the only European manufacturers, apart from Britain, were Sweden and France. We would try to get them quickly from France.

NOTES

1. Ariel (Arik) Sharon (b. 1918), prominent Israeli general and politician. Sharon made his mark as an outstanding and unconventional strategist and field commander. His successes in the October 1973 War helped launch his political career. Although he had nominally belonged to Mapai, he left that party when he entered national politics. In 1977 he formed the Shlomzion party and joined Begin's government as minister of agriculture. He was placed in charge of the government's controversial settlement policy. Sharon is an advocate of increasing Jewish settlement in the West Bank. In 1981 he ran on the Likud list and became defense minister. In the aftermath of the 1982 War in Lebanon, the Kahan Commission of Inquiry recommended that he resign his ministerial post (see doc. 79). In 1983 he resigned as defense minister and became minister without portfolio.

2. Gamal Abdul Nasser (1918–70), president of Egypt, 1954–70. A key member of the conspiratorial group of officers that overthrew King Farouk, Nasser soon emerged as the leader of the new regime, and generated a new movement—Nasserism—that swept most of the Arab world. He emerged as a leader of the Third World bloc at the 1955 Bandung Conference.

1948–56
Foreign Policy Issues

13. The Syrian-Israeli Armistice Agreement

The First Arab-Israeli War ended with a series of armistice agreements, secured through the mediation of the United Nations (see doc. 14), that were to have been replaced by peace treaties. Since they were not, they had to regulate a complex and hostile set of relationships for eighteen years, despite the fact that negotiations continued through various channels to reach a broader Arab-Israeli peace.

The Syrian-Israeli Armistice Agreement was signed on July 20, 1949. Israel had already signed armistice agreements with Egypt on February 24, Lebanon on March 23, and Jordan on April 3, 1949. Iraq did not become a party to these agreements. Map 2 shows the 1949 armistice lines, which were the same as the cease-fire lines.

The following excerpt from the Syrian-Israeli Armistice Agreement exemplifies both the complexities and the provisional nature of these agreements.

Preamble

The Parties to the present Agreement,

Responding to the Security Council resolution of 16 November 1948,[1] calling upon them, as a further provisional measure under Article 40 of the Charter of the United Nations[2] and in order to facilitate the transition from the present truce to permanent peace in Palestine, to negotiate an armistice;

Having decided to enter into negotiations under United Nations Chairmanship concerning the implementation of the Security Council resolution of 16 November 1948; and having appointed representatives empowered to negotiate and conclude an Armistice Agreement;

The undersigned representatives, having exchanged their full powers found to be in good and proper form, have agreed upon the following provisions:

Article 1

With a view to promoting the return of permanent peace in Palestine and in recognition of the importance in this regard of mutual assurances concerning the future military operations of the Parties, the following principles, which shall be fully observed by both Parties during the armistice, are hereby affirmed:

1. The injunction of the Security Council against resort to military force in the settlement of the Palestine question shall henceforth be scrupulously respected by both Parties. The establishment of an armistice between their armed forces is accepted as an indispensable step toward the liquidation of armed conflict and the restoration of peace in Palestine.

2. No aggressive action by the armed forces—land, sea or air—of either Party shall be undertaken, planned or threatened against the people or the armed forces of the other; it being understood that the use of the term "planned" in this context has no bearing on normal staff planning as generally practised in military organizations.

3. The right of each Party to its security and freedom from fear of attack by the armed forces of the other shall be fully respected.

Article 2

With a specific view to the implementa-

Source: Meron Medzini, ed., *Israel's Foreign Relations: Selected Documents, 1947–1974* (Jerusalem: Ministry of Foreign Affairs, 1976), 1:192–97, 202–3, 205–7. Reprinted by permission of the Director General, Ministry of Foreign Affairs, Jerusalem.

tion of the resolution of the Security Council of 16 November 1948, the following principles and purposes are affirmed:

1. The principle that no military or political advantage should be gained under the truce ordered by the Security Council is recognized.

2. It is also recognized that no provision of this Agreement shall in any way prejudice the rights, claims and positions of either Party hereto in the ultimate peaceful settlement of the Palestine question, the provision of this Agreement being dictated exclusively by military, and not by political, considerations.

Article 3

1. In pursuance of the foregoing principles and of the resolution of the Security Council of 16 November 1948, a general armistice between the armed forces of the two Parties—land, sea and air—is hereby established.

2. No element of the land, sea or air, military or para-military, forces of either Party, including non-regular forces, shall commit any warlike or hostile act against the military or para-military forces of the other Party, or against civilians in territory under the control of that Party; or shall advance beyond or pass over for any purpose whatsoever the Armistice Demarcation Line set forth in Article 5 of this Agreement; or enter into or pass through the air space of the other Party or through the waters within three miles of the coastline of the other Party.

3. No warlike act or act of hostility shall be conducted from territory controlled by one of the Parties to this Agreement against the other Party or against civilians in territory under control of that Party.

Article 4

1. The line described in Article 5 of this Agreement shall be designated as the Armistice Demarcation Line and is delineated in pursuance of the purpose and intent of the resolution of the Security Council of 16 November 1948.

2. The basic purpose of the Armistice Demarcation Line is to delineate the line beyond which the armed forces of the respective Parties shall not move.

3. Rules and regulations of the armed forces of the Parties, which prohibit civilians from crossing the fighting lines or entering the area between the lines, shall remain in effect after the signing of this Agreement, with application to the Armistice Demarcation Line defined in Article 5, subject to the provisions of paragraph 5 of that Article.

Article 5

1. It is emphasized that the following arrangements for the Armistice Demarcation Line between the Israeli and Syrian armed forces and for the Demilitarized Zone are not to be interpreted as having any relation whatsoever to ultimate territorial arrangements affecting the two Parties to this Agreement.

2. In pursuance of the spirit of the Security Council resolution of 16 November 1948, the Armistice Demarcation Line and the Demilitarized Zone have been defined with a view toward separating the armed forces of the two Parties in such manner as to minimize the possibility of friction and incident, while providing for the gradual restoration of normal civilian life in the area of the Demilitarized Zone, without prejudice to the ultimate settlement.

3. The Armistice Demarcation Line shall be as delineated on the map attached to this Agreement as Annex 1. The Armistice Demarcation Line shall follow a line midway between the existing truce lines, as certified by the United Nations Truce Supervision Organization for the Israeli and Syrian forces. Where the existing truce lines run along the international boundary between Syria and Palestine, the Armistice Demarcation Line shall follow the boundary line.

4. The armed forces of the two Parties shall nowhere advance beyond the Armistice Demarcation Line.

5. (a) Where the Armistice Demarcation Line does not correspond to the interna-

tional boundary between Syria and Palestine, the area between the Armistice Demarcation Line and the boundary, pending final territorial settlement between the Parties, shall be established as a Demilitarized Zone from which the armed forces of both Parties shall be totally excluded, and in which no activities by military or para-military forces shall be permitted. This provision applies to the Ein Gev and Dardara sectors which shall form part of the Demilitarized Zone. (b) Any advance by the armed forces, military or para-military, of either Party into any part of the Demilitarized Zone, when confirmed by the United Nations representative referred to in the following sub-paragraph, shall constitute a flagrant violation of this Agreement. (c) The Chairman of the Mixed Armistice Commission established in Article VII of this Agreement and United Nations Observers attached to the Commission shall be responsible for ensuring the full implementation of this Article. (d) The withdrawal of such armed forces as are now found in the Demilitarized Zone shall be in accordance with the schedule of withdrawal annexed to this Agreement (Annex 2). (e) The Chairman of the Mixed Armistice Commission shall be empowered to authorize the return of civilians to villages and settlements in the Demilitarized Zone and for internal security purposes, and shall be guided in this regard by the schedule of withdrawal referred to in subparagraph (d) of this Article.

6. On each side of the Demilitarized Zone there shall be areas, as defined in Annex 3 to this Agreement, in which defensive forces only shall be maintained, in accordance with the definition of defensive forces set forth in Annex 4 to this Agreement.

Article 6

All prisoners of war detained by either Party to this Agreement and belonging to the armed forces, regular or irregular, of the other Party, shall be exchanged as follows:

1. The exchange of prisoners of war shall be under United Nations supervision and control throughout. The exchange shall take place at the site of the Armistice Conference within twenty-four hours of the signing of this Agreement.

2. Prisoners of War against whom a penal prosecution may be pending, as well as those sentenced for crime or other offence, shall be included in this exchange of prisoners.

3. All articles of personal use, valuables, letters, documents, identification marks, and other personal effects of whatever nature, belonging to prisoners of war who are being exchanged, shall be returned to them, or, if they have escaped or died, to the Party to whose armed forces they belonged.

All matters not specifically regulated in this Agreement shall be decided in accordance with the principles laid down in the International Convention Relating to the Treatment of Prisoners of War, signed at Geneva on 17 July 1929.

5. The Mixed Armistice Commission established in Article 7 of this Agreement shall assume responsibility for locating missing persons, whether military or civilian, within the areas controlled by each Party, to facilitate their expeditious exchange. Each Party undertakes to extend to the Commission full co-operation and assistance in the discharge of this function.

NOTES

1. Resolution 62 adopted by the Security Council on November 16, 1948, states:

The Security Council, . . .
Decides that in order to eliminate the threat to the peace in Palestine and to facilitate the transition from the present truce to permanent peace . . . an armistice shall be established in all sectors of Palestine;

Calls upon the parties directly involved in the conflict in Palestine, as a further provisional measure under Article 40 of the Charter, to seek agreement forthwith, by negotiations conducted either directly or through the Acting Mediator on Palestine, with a view to the immediate establishment of the armistice including: (a) the delineation of permanent armistice demarcation lines . . . ; (b) such withdrawal and reduction of their armed forces as will ensure the maintenance of the armistice during the transition to permanent peace in Palestine.

2. Article 40 of the U.N. Charter states: "In order to prevent an aggravation of the situation, the Security Council may . . . call upon the parties concerned to comply with such provisional measures as it deems necessary or desirable."

PALESTINE CONCILIATION COMMISSION
14. Conclusions, 1951

The Palestine Conciliation Commission was formed by the United Nations in December 1948 to assist in a final settlement of the Palestine question.[1] It included representatives of the United States, France, and Turkey. The commission's report, published in 1951, marked not only the termination of its work but also the realization by the international community of the complexity of the Arab-Israeli conflict. The report also revealed the gap between the Arab and Israeli positions on the fundamental issues of the conflict, as the conclusions printed here demonstrate. Although the commission suspended its activities after three years, it has never been officially dissolved.

In its work during the past year—and indeed during the three years of its existence—the Conciliation Commission has been unable to make substantial progress on the task given to it by the General Assembly of assisting the parties to the Palestine dispute towards a final settlement of all questions outstanding between them.

In the course of its efforts to accomplish that task, the Commission has successively employed all the procedures which were at its disposal under the relevant General Assembly resolutions. At Lausanne, in the spring of 1949, it tried to render that assistance in the role of an intermediary between the parties; at Geneva, in 1950, the Commission attempted to bring about direct negotiations between the parties through the medium of Mixed Committees; and, finally, at its recent conference in Paris, the Commission assumed the function of a mediator and, in that role, submitted to the parties for their consideration a comprehensive pattern of concrete proposals towards a solution of the Palestine question.

This pattern of proposals comprised practical arrangements for a solution of the refugee question, and a method of revising or amending the Armistice Agreements concluded between Israel and her neighbours with a view to promoting the return to peace in Palestine.

In linking those two issues together in a comprehensive pattern of proposals the Commission took account of two factors: (a) that the Armistice Agreements, although of a military character, were designed as a means of transition from war to peace and

Source: Meron Medzini, ed., *Israel's Foreign Relations: Selected Documents, 1947–1974* (Jerusalem: Ministry of Foreign Affairs, 1976), 2:279–80. Reprinted by permission of the Director General, Ministry of Foreign Affairs, Jerusalem.

provided for procedures by which that aim could be attained; and (b) that positive progress in the transition from war to peace in Palestine is impossible if the refugee problem remains unsolved.

This final effort at the Paris conference was no more successful than the prior attempts by the Commission during the past three years. Despite that lack of progress, the Commission recognizes that both sides have expressed their desire to co-operate with the United Nations towards the achievement of stability in Palestine; but the Commission believes that neither side is now ready to seek that aim through full implementation of the General Assembly resolutions under which the Commission is operating.

In particular, the Government of Israel is not prepared to implement the part of paragraph 11 of the General Assembly resolution of 11 December 1948 which resolves that the refugees wishing to return to their homes and live at peace with their neighbours should be permitted to do so at the earliest practicable date.

The Arab Governments, on the other hand, are not prepared fully to implement paragraph 5 of the said resolution, which calls for the final settlement of all questions outstanding between them and Israel. The Arab Governments in their contacts with the Commission have evinced no readiness to arrive at such a peace settlement with the Government of Israel.

The Commission considers that further efforts towards settling the Palestine question could yet be usefully based on the principles underlying the comprehensive pattern of proposals which the Commission submitted to the parties at the Paris Conference. The Commission continues to believe that if and when the parties are ready to accept these principles, general agreement or partial agreement could be sought through direct negotiations with United Nations assistance or mediation.

The Commission is of the opinion, however, that the present unwillingness of the parties fully to implement the General Assembly resolutions under which the Commission is operating, as well as the changes which have occurred in Palestine during the past three years, have made it impossible for the Commission to carry out its mandate, and this fact should be taken into consideration in any further approach to the Palestine problem.

Finally, in view of its firm conviction that the aspects of the Palestine problem are interrelated, the Commission is of the opinion that in any further approach to the problem it is desirable that consideration be given to the need for coordinating all United Nations efforts aimed at promotion of stability, security and peace in Palestine.

NOTE

1. The key operative sections of U.N. General Assembly Resolution 194 (III), adopted on December 11, 1948 are:

The General Assembly, . . .

2. *Establishes* a Conciliation Commission; . . .

5. *Calls upon* the Government and authorities concerned to extend the scope of negotiations provided for in the Security Council's resolution of 16 November 1948 [see doc. 13] and to seek agreement by negotiations conducted either with the Conciliation Commission or directly, with a view to the final settlement of all questions outstanding between them; . . .

7. *Resolves* that the Holy Places—including Nazareth— . . . should be protected and free access to them assured, in accordance with existing rights and historical practice; . . . that the . . . Conciliation Commission, in presenting . . . its detailed proposals for a permanent international regime for the territory of Jerusalem, should include recommendations concerning the Holy Places in that territory; . . .

8. *Resolves* that, in view of its association with three world religions, the Jerusalem area, including the present municipality of Jerusalem *plus* the surrounding villages and towns . . . should be accorded special and separate treatment from the

rest of Palestine and should be placed under effective United Nations control; . . .

11. *Resolves* that the refugees wishing to return to their homes and live at peace with their neighbors should be permitted to do so at the earliest practicable date, and that compensation should be paid for the property of those choosing not to return and for loss of or damage to property which, under principles of international law or in equity, should be made good by the Governments or authorities responsible.

ABDULLAH AL-TAL
15. The Jordanian-Israeli Negotiations

The Jordanian-Israeli negotiations in 1949 differed from the other armistice negotiations in two important respects. There were prior contacts and "feelers" between Jordan and Israel. Perhaps more important, the armistice lines between Israel and Jordan affected numerous civilians, both Jewish and Arab, and village boundaries.

The following discussion of the negotiations that led to the armistice agreement between Jordan and Israel on April 3, 1949, is from the memoirs of Abdullah al-Tal.

Al-Tal was a Jordanian officer who, as lieutenant colonel, became commander of Jordanian Jerusalem. As an anti-British and anti-Hashemite Arab nationalist, he tried to obstruct all attempts at Jordanian-Israeli understanding. Nevertheless, his memoirs of the Jordanian-Israeli negotiations reflect the special relationship between King Abdullah and the Israeli government as well as the centrality of negotiations with Jordan to Israeli peacemaking efforts (see doc. 5).

In the evening of March 22–23, 1949, at precisely eight o'clock, the Jewish delegation arrived at El-Shuneh. They were received at the palace by the protocol officials, who escorted them into the parlor, and there they awaited the king's arrival. After a short while, His Royal Highness entered and shook hands with the members of the delegation, which included Eytan,[1] Yadin, Dayan, and Harkabi,[2] i.e., those men who participated in the meeting with the Jordanian governmental mission in Jerusalem. On behalf of the government were present at this time Said Al-Mufti the acting prime minister, Fallah al Madadkha, Muhammad al-Shunkeiti, and Hussein Saraj, and for the army Major Cooker, head of the Operations Branch of the Arab Legion, and Lieutenant

Abdal Rakham Rassas representing the cartographic division. The stay in the reception hall was not long, since the king invited all present to follow him into the dining room. There he placed each of the guests into the seat prepared for him.

At the table the discussions were mostly carried on between the king and Eytan. The king entertained the guests by speaking about the universities in Britain and about living languages. After that, His Royal Highness proceeded to talk about Ben-Gurion and asked Eytan about the fields of knowledge in which Ben-Gurion had shown a special interest.

Eytan replied that Ben-Gurion was interested in philosophy and that he was also a great scholar in the field of history. Follow-

Source: Abdullah al-Tal, *Zikhronot Abdullah al-Tal* (Memoirs of Abdullah al-Tal) (Tel Aviv: Maarakhot Publishing House, 1960), pp. 366–77. Reprinted by permission.

ing that, the king turned to Dayan and asked him why his knowledge of Arabic was so weak, despite the fact that he was born in Palestine. Dayan replied that the reason was a lack of contact with the Arabs.

At the conclusion of the meal, His Royal Highness rose and proceeded to the meeting room, with the guests and government representatives following him in his steps. . . .

In addition to those mentioned above, Doctor Shaukat al-Sati and Hashem al-Dabas, one of the king's entourage, also participated in this meeting. The king opened the session by directing his remarks to Dr. Eytan and expanding upon the problem of Palestine and how it had developed. His Royal Highness spoke to the Jews as if he were addressing members of his own government, without paying attention to the results of his frankness, which revealed to the Jews his entire way of thinking. He did not hesitate to reveal and explain to the Jews that the Arab Legion was not fighting against the Jews and that it had no such aim. Among other things the king said:

The Jews are a progressive and cohesive nation, and the Arabs a weak and backward nation. The West is against us and I swear to God that we did not receive even one single bullet from abroad in this war. The foreigners support you and give you every possible assistance. The Arabs had hoped for victory, but exactly the opposite happened. Our intention was not to fight; but we were forced to enter this war against our will, since they refused to accept our advice. I personally am not afraid, and I am ready to accept all the responsibility to bring this problem to a conclusion and to come to an understanding with you. That is my goal, and you know that I am a frank person.

Following this, His Royal Highness reviewed his trip for a meeting with the regent of Iraq at "H3" and the results of that meeting. . . .

The king spoke for about an hour and concluded with the warm request that the Jews should make his task easier by not exaggerating their demands, since that would have a negative influence upon his own standing in the Arab world—some-

thing, according to his estimate, even the Jews would not want. Then the king stated that he would name the same commission, with the addition of Major Cooker, in place of Abdullah al-Tal, who did not want to participate in this commission since he was now out of the army.

The king concluded his remarks with these words: "And now I would like you to tell me a thing or two, so that I might find out to what extent my words have influenced you."

Major Harkabi translated the king's remarks to Eytan in Hebrew, and after that Hussein Saraj translated Eytan's words, which had been spoken in English, into Arabic.

Eytan began by conveying to His Royal Highness the greetings of Ben-Gurion and his appreciation for the honor with which he received the Jews who had come to meet with him. Then Eytan proceeded to the main topic and said that he was in full agreement with regard to most of the points the king had raised during his remarks and that he was interested that a final peace between Israel and His Royal Highness be reached as soon as possible. Eytan continued by stating that in the past the Arabs had neither understood nor believed that the Jews wanted to live, both in Palestine and in the rest of the Arab states, in peace and harmony with the Arabs. But now this is what we are hoping for. The emergence of Israel and its becoming a reality will not be merely a historic event but an event of importance to the entire Middle East. Eytan said further that friendship and the understanding would have to be founded on a firm basis and that therefore the Jews were asking for certain territorial changes in the Triangle sector[3] as a fundamental factor in the mutual understanding with His Royal Highness.

In explaining the factors that prompted Israel to demand certain changes in the Triangle as a condition for its agreement to the occupation of that area by the Arab Legion, Eytan stated that Israel was suffering great difficulties because of the shape of the state in that particular sector and that every day men and women were slain as the result of constant clashes originating in that abnormal situation in the sector that threatens Israel's peace and its very existence. Following that, Eytan said frankly that if King Abdullah's government were to refuse to accede to Israel's demands, he would suggest that Transjordan should cease to interfere between the two sides—i.e., between the Jews and the Iraqis—but that it should be left to those two sides to arrange matters among themselves in a way suitable to Israel. Eytan continued by promising that the demands of his government would be realized if the matter would be left to direct negotiations with Jordan or with Iraq, since these demands were, in his eyes, justified and would secure for Israel peace and quiet and would strengthen the link between North and South.

When Eytan finished his talk the king replied by stating that he agreed the demands of the Jews were indeed vital to them but that he would ask them to give up several villages, such as Umm El Faham, Baqa al-Gharbiyya, and El-Taybeh, in order that the refugee problem not become even more complicated. When the hour of eleven at night approached, the king said, "Let us leave the study of the problem to the two delegations, and I promise you that I shall not retire to bed and shall not sleep until I am informed of the success of the meeting."

NOTES

1. Walter Eytan (b. 1910), leading member of Israel's foreign service. Eytan was a member of the Israeli delegation to the Rhodes armistice negotiations. He was director general of the Ministry of Foreign Affairs, 1948–59, and ambassador to France, 1960–70.

2. Yehoshafat Harkabi (b. 1921), Israeli general and academic. Harkabi was also a member of the delegation to the Rhodes armistice negotiations. He later became head of Israel's military intelligence. In his second career he became a professor of Middle Eastern studies and international relations at the Hebrew University of Jerusalem. His major areas of research include Arab positions regarding Israel and Zionism, and terrorism and guerrilla warfare.

3. The Triangle, three triangular areas of Palestine, inhabited almost exclusively by Arabs. The Arab or Large Triangle is the northern section of the West Bank, roughly bounded by the villages of Tulkharm, Jenin, and Nablus (Shekhem). The Israeli Triangle borders the Large Triangle in the western Sharon district and includes the villages of Baqa al-Gharbiyya, Kfar Kasem, and Taybeh. It has been under continuous Israeli control since 1949. The Little Triangle is near Haifa in the Carmel Mountain range and extends to the seacoast. It was conquered by Israel in Operation Hashoter (lit., Policeman). The area discussed in this document includes the Little Triangle and the Israeli Triangle, which are contiguous.

NEW TIMES
16. The Period of Soviet-Israeli Cooperation

The Soviet Union extended vital support to Israel in the late 1940s and early 1950s. It was an important factor in the success of the U.N. resolution on the partition of Palestine and promoted Israel's admission to the United Nations. Likewise, Soviet aid during

Source: "Palestine and the United Nations," *New Times*, no. 24 (June 9, 1948), pp. 1–2.

the First Arab-Israeli War proved crucial to Israel's victory. This phase of the Soviet-Israeli relationship is reflected in the following editorial from the English-language Soviet weekly *New Times*, published in Moscow.

For over a year the Palestine problem has been almost continuously under consideration in the United Nations, in particular at two special sessions of the General Assembly. The discussions clearly revealed what forces prevented the U.N. from performing its direct function of safeguarding international security.

The decision to partition Palestine was adopted in November 1947, after six months' discussion at a special session of the General Assembly. The majority of the countries, including the United States, voted for this decision. However, three months had scarcely passed before the Palestine question was up again for discussion in the Security Council, where only two delegations—the Soviet and the Ukrainian—insisted that the General Assembly's decision to divide Palestine into two states should be carried out.

Undoubtedly, the best solution for the Palestine problem would be to set up an independent democratic Jewish-Arab State. On the basis of its own successful experience the Soviet Union always believed that the peoples of Palestine could live and work peacefully side by side and not interfere with each other. But thanks to the efforts of uninvited guardians, relations between the two peoples of Palestine have become so bad that it is practically impossible at the present juncture to create a joint Arab-Jewish State. Under these circumstances, the creation of two separate, independent states is a reasonable solution. It is a fair solution, because it conforms to the national interests of both peoples, each of which has a right to independent statehood, and would promote tranquility in the Middle East, and hence international security.

It was these considerations that guided the United Nations when it approved the partition of Palestine. The speedier this plan were carried out, the less would be the sacrifices borne by Arabs and Jews, the less blood would be shed in this country, and the less destruction would there be to material wealth.

The Soviet Union took up a firm stand from the very beginning and insisted upon the speedy and precise implementation of the General Assembly's decision. The Soviet delegation held the view that the Security Council was formally responsible for the carrying out of the decision to partition Palestine. At the various stages of the discussion of the Palestine question it persistently parried the attempts of the British and American delegations to evade or retard the carrying out of the decision.

When, in April 1948, the Palestine question again figured in the agenda of the United Nations, the Soviet delegation insistently demanded that the Security Council take effective measures to facilitate the carrying out of the Assembly's decision. By this time it became perfectly clear that the United States and Great Britain were endeavouring to prevent partition, that for them the Palestine question was not one involving the destinies of the peoples inhabiting the country, but a question of Middle Eastern oil, of bases and strategical positions in the Eastern Mediterranean, and that it suited their plans to turn Palestine into an arena of unintermitting conflict between Arabs and Jews.

The Soviet delegation made two proposals, representing the very minimum that had to be done in the situation which had arisen. The first proposal was for the withdrawal of armed groups which had invaded Palestine with the purpose of preventing by force of arms the partition decided on by the General Assembly. The second proposal was to stop any further invasion of armed groups. Although it was patent to everyone that there could be no truce so long as there were armed detachments on Palestine territory which had come there with the special purpose of resisting the General Assembly's decision, the Soviet proposals were not accepted, and the Security Council confined itself to passing a resolution, on April 17, which contained not a single point capable of alleviating the situation in Palestine.

Thanks to the firm and consistent stand taken by the Soviet delegation at the second special session of the General Assembly called to discuss the Palestine question in April and May of this year, the United States failed to put through its plan to place Palestine under trusteeship. This plan ran counter to one of the cardinal principles of the U.N. Charter—the right of self-determination of nations, their right to exist independently within their own states.

At the meetings of the Security Council in May, the Soviet Union again submitted a proposal which would have guaranteed peace in Palestine: it recommended that the situation in the country be regarded as a violation of peace and coming within the provisions of Article 39 of the U.N. Charter.

This proposal was rejected by those who were not willing to have the Security Council perform its direct function. The result is that blood is flowing in Palestine.

Instead of taking effective measures to expel the invading troops from Palestine and to prevent their return, the Security Council engages in endless debates, which are often only a mask for the machinations of the powers who are fanning the Palestine conflict.

These machinations are cynical in the extreme. The invading Arab armies are actually financed by the British taxpayer, whether he wants it or not. That oil interests are behind the war in Palestine is known to everyone who reads any newspaper in any part of the globe. Jewish settlements are being destroyed by bombs dropped from British Spitfires supplied to the Arab countries. Arab troops are armed and trained by British officers dozens of whom are taking part in the hostilities.

The whole course of developments shows why every proposal made by the Soviet delegation to prevent the decision to create two independent states in Palestine from being rescinded or weakened is so stubbornly rejected. It is quite obvious that if this decision, backed by the authority of the United Nations, were carried out it would put an end to the bloodshed and would create normal conditions in the Middle East which would render ineffective the intrigues of those powers which are determined at any price to perpetuate the colonial regime and to establish their domination in Palestine.

The Soviet Union is consistent in its policy, considering the partition of Palestine into two states the most just and correct solution in the given circumstances; it has recognized the State of Israel, proclaimed in accordance with the decision of the United Nations.

The elements who are fanning conflict in Palestine are assiduously spreading the allegation in the Arab countries that the Soviet Union is not willing to defend the national interests of the Arab peoples. Everyone knows that the Soviet Union has always stood and still stands in favour of the independence of the Arab people. But in their armed attack undertaken at outside instigation, on the state of Israel the Arab countries are not fighting in defence of their national interests or their independence.

The Soviet public, which has always expressed its sympathy with the national liberation movement of all peoples, including Arabs, emphatically condemns the aggression of the Arab states against Israel and the efforts forcibly to prevent the Jews from forming their own state in accordance with the General Assembly's decision.

The Soviet people wholeheartedly support the efforts of their Government to get the United Nations to adopt effective measures to stop the bloodshed and to bridle the states which engineered the military invasion of Palestine and which are brazenly violating the decision of the General Assembly.

17. The Deterioration of Soviet-Israeli Relations

The deterioration of Soviet-Israeli relations in the early 1950s, which followed the brief period of cooperation, was dramatically manifested by the Soviet Union's decision in February 1953 to sever diplomatic relations with Israel. The action was presented as a response to a bombing at the Soviet embassy in Tel Aviv by an Israeli citizen protesting Soviet policies. The real reasons, however, were more complex. Among the issues contributing to Soviet-Israeli tension was the Jewish problem in the Soviet Union (see doc. 26). In addition, the Soviets were shifting support from Israel to the Arab states while at the same time resenting Israel's increasing reliance on the West. In the following article from *New Times*, the Soviet view is briefly presented.

A terrorist act was committed against the Soviet Legation in Tel Aviv, capital of Israel, on February 9, when, with the obvious connivance of the police, a bomb was exploded in the precincts of the Legation, resulting in injuries to K. V. Yershova, wife of the Minister, A. P. Sysoyeva, wife of a Legation official, and I. G. Grishin, a Legation employee. Part of the building was wrecked.

The next day the President and Foreign Ministry of Israel sent letters to the Soviet Legation expressing condemnation of the crime and conveying the apologies of the Israeli government.

But the statement and apology are in flat contradiction to generally known and undeniable facts indicative of the complicity of representatives of the Israeli government in stirring up hatred and enmity towards the Soviet Union and inciting to hostile acts against it.

The unbridled campaign of slander conducted by the press of the Israeli government parties against the Soviet Union and the People's Democracies has lately been greatly intensified. It was reinforced by infamous anti-Soviet attacks by members of the government, notably Foreign Minister Sharett, whose statement of January 19 was an open incitement to hostile actions against the Soviet Union.

Recent revelations—at the trial of Slansky and his gang of conspirators in Prague and in the exposure of a group of medical assassins in the Soviet Union,[1] for instance—testify that agents of international Zionism are used by the American imperialists for the commission of the most abominable crimes, for espionage and sabotage activities in the countries of the democratic camp. Zionists holding leading positions in the Israeli government are also implicated in these vile acts. It was revealed at the Prague trial that in 1947 Ben-Gurion, the present Prime Minister of Israel, and Sharett, now Foreign Minister, had a secret conference with Truman, Acheson and Morgenthau in Washington, where they accepted the so-called "Morgenthau-Acheson plan," the object of which was to undermine the building of socialism into a Mediterranean base of American aggressive policy.[2]

The exposure of these facts aroused consternation in the imperialist camp, and the malignant campaign against the Soviet Union was intensified. The explosion of the bomb in the Soviet Legation, a terrorist act

Source: "The Tel Aviv Crime," *New Times*, no. 8 (February 18, 1953), p. 4.

committed with the obvious connivance of the police, was the outcome of this campaign.

In its note to the Israeli government of February 11, the Soviet government qualified the latter's statement and apologies as a piece of hypocrisy, and announced its decision to break off diplomatic relations with the Israeli government.

Israeli government circles cannot escape responsibility for the situation that has arisen. The Tel Aviv crime exposes them as enemies of peace and international cooperation, as supporters of the American warmongers.

NOTES

1. The Slansky trial and the Doctors' Plot trial were two of the most infamous "show trials" accompanying the wave of Soviet anti-Semitic purges by Stalin in the early 1950s. These purges were not limited to the Soviet Union.

In 1952 Rudolf Slansky, former secretary general of the Czech Communist party and vice-premier of Czechoslovakia, and thirteen other high-ranking state and party officials were tried for "Trotskyite-Titoist-Zionist" activities. Slansky and ten of the others were ethnically Jewish but had been opposed to Zionism and Jewish nationalism. Most were executed, and three were sentenced to life imprisonment.

In January 1953 nine eminent doctors, including six Jews, were arrested for the murder of Soviet leaders who had died in the 1940s and for conspiracy to murder leading Soviet military leaders. *Pravda* stated "Most of the participants in the terrorist group were connected with the international Jewish bourgeois nationalist organization, the 'Joint' . . . established by American intelligence" (*Encyclopaedia Judaica*, 6:144–45). Apparently the plot was hatched as part of Stalin's attempt to purge L. P. Beria, who headed the security services. After Stalin's death the doctors were freed.

2. Harry S. Truman (1884–1972), president of the United States, 1945–53. Despite much advice to the contrary, Truman personally decided to recognize Israel almost immediately after the Proclamation of the State.

Dean Acheson (1893–1971), U.S. undersecretary of state, 1945–47, and secretary of state, 1949–53.

Henry Morgenthau, Jr. (1891–1967), U.S. secretary of the treasury under Franklin D. Roosevelt and Truman, 1939–45. During his service in government Morgenthau remained active on behalf of Jewish and Zionist causes.

Morgenthau-Acheson Plan, proposal to forge a pact between Israel and the Arab states to keep communism out of the area. Part of the "containment" policy that dominated U.S. strategic considerations during these years—a policy to "contain," or limit the Soviet sphere of influence—the plan was never more than an idea, and no serious diplomatic attempt was made to pursue it.

EHUD YAARI
18. The Challenge of the Fedayeen

In the years following the establishment of the State of Israel the political dimensions of the Arab-Israeli conflict were superseded by escalating violence. Arab infiltration (both spontaneous and organized) from across the borders and Israeli retaliation led to a deepening cycle of conflict. This cycle was reinforced by numerous border and armistice problems and by violent fallout from the frequent political contests between Israel

Source: Ehud Yaari, *Mizraim ve-ha-Fedayun 1953–1956* (Egypt and the Fedayeen, 1953–1956) (Givat Havivah: Center for Arab and Afro-Asian Studies, 1975), pp. 18–23. Reprinted by permission.

and its Arab neighbors, such as Arab resistance to Israel's diversion of Jordan River waters. Internationally, Israel was feeling threatened and isolated. The United States was increasing arms sales to Arab countries, and some of its State Department officials were publicly critical of Israel. Soviet-Egyptian relations were growing closer, and more weapons were being supplied to Egypt from the Soviet bloc. In 1955 what became known as the Czech arms deal was negotiated between Egypt and the Soviet Union, and Egypt began receiving the latest Soviet military equipment from Czechoslovakia. Within Israel there was considerable debate on Israel's policies: Was it wise to retaliate for Arab acts of aggression, or should remedies be sought through diplomatic channels? In a somewhat simplistic fashion the two sides of this debate in the 1950s and early 1960s have been identified with David

Ben-Gurion and Moshe Sharett respectively (see docs. 19, 22).

Ehud Yaari, an Israeli journalist specializing in Arab affairs, uses Egyptian military and intelligence documents captured in Gaza to shed interesting light both on the conduct of the anti-Israeli irregular warfare in the 1950s and on Israel's policy of retaliation. He recounts the turning point in Egyptian policy toward Palestinian commands raids from Gaza and Jordan into Israel. These terrorists came to be known as fedayeen (sing., fedayi), from the Islamic term meaning martyrs. On February 28, 1955, an Israeli paratroop unit attacked an Egyptian base near Gaza in retaliation for acts of sabotage and murder committed by fedayeen from bases there. Thirty-eight Egyptian soldiers and two civilians were killed, and many were wounded.

The raid of the Israel Defense Forces into Gaza on February 28, 1955, was, in the opinion of everyone, an important milestone in Egyptian-Israeli relations. Nasser and a number of Western diplomats and researchers have for many years suggested that it represents the turning point in Cairo's policy. Nasser himself declared on numerous occasions that this was the hour of truth and that only then did he realize the futility of continuing his previous policy and grasp the extent of the Israeli problem, and on this basis turned to accept Soviet arms. This is not the place to discuss the complications or the principles involved in that action and its results, although it is clear that Nasser's explanation is much too simplistic and one-sided even if we supposed that there is a grain of truth in it. But it is difficult to connect the Israeli raid with the activity of infiltration, because the Israeli action came precisely during a period of relative calm in that area and in the wake of major efforts on the part of the Egyptian regime to stop infiltrations in the Gaza Strip. Hence it is necessary to look in another direction for an

explanation for Ben-Gurion's decision to call for the raid a few days after his return from Sdeh Boker to the Ministry of Foreign Affairs.

Immediately after the raid into Gaza, which raised a great commotion in the entire world, several large demonstrations occurred throughout the Gaza Strip that raised questions about the achievements of the Egyptians in stabilizing their rule there. In the town of Gaza itself the Egyptian army opened fire and killed four demonstrators when the ruling governor Abdullah Rif'at was wounded by a stone thrown at him. Two U.N. vehicles went up in flames. In Dir Al-Balakh demonstrators smashed windows in the police building, and Egyptian soldiers were beaten in the streets. In Khan Yunis a food warehouse was burned. And there were many other incidents. Demonstrators demanded that weapons be distributed to civilians and that the border be fortified against Israeli incursions. There were also slogans condemning Egypt and its army in particular. Order was restored only after widespread arrests among the demonstrators and those responsible for inciting the people and after extended patrols by vehicles with loudspeakers declaring that the army would disperse further demonstrations with an iron hand.

The list of those arrested reveals the opposition to Egyptian policy among important and influential portions of the local Palestinian establishment at that period. Among the names: Munir Al-Rayyes, shortly to become head of the Gaza municipality; his grandson Zvheir Al-Rayyes, a lawyer and publisher of the local paper *Akhbar Falastin;* Gamal Al-Surani, son of the well-known Sheikh Moussa Al-Surani, for some time member of the executive committee of the Palestine Liberation Organization;[1] Faisal Al-Husayni, a pillar of an old family in Gaza; Muhammad Yusuf Al-Najjar, an official of the UNRWA[2] who was among the founders of the PLO; and others.

The very fact that these men openly stood up against the Egyptian regime is significant and shows the difficulties Cairo had in imposing a strict rule and harnessing the old local leadership in its direction. The Egyptian regime was able to overcome the opposition on the fringes: the cells of the Communist party were by and large destroyed around the time of the court case of Hassan Makki and his men at the end of 1952, and the circles of the Muslim Brotherhood were already no longer a security threat, as we learn from the plentiful reports of the secret police. Egypt's problem was how to handle the old members of the Mufti movement and the local leadership.[3]

Nasser announced on March 1 that his country was "not going to take a quick revenge," but late in May there occurred a sharp turnabout within the regime regarding the problem of infiltration, and the change is evident from the official correspondence. The term *fedayeen*, with a positive connotation, now comes in place of the term *infiltrators*. Reinforcements of the Egyptian army are brought into the Gaza Strip, and instead of expressions of condemnation and worry about the penetrations into Israel,

the secret documents now speak in terms of glorification and encouragement. On May 8 the intelligence office of the army command in Sinai even issued a circular describing the crisis in Israeli border kibbutzim as the result of the infiltrations.

According to Moshe Dayan, the Egyptians began to form the fedayeen units in April 1955 in order to carry out terrorist operations against Israel. But actually, when the Egyptians activated the fedayeen for the first time according to their plan—at the end of August—the job was given to the men of the national guard. In other words, the arm that had been established to stop the infiltration movement and to preserve order and control in the refugee camps was now mobilized for fedayeen operations. This arrangement indicates a change of policy from relying on professional infiltrators to relying on new groups, subject to the discipline of the Egyptian command. The old infiltrators were apparently considered of doubtful loyalty, and some of them were identified with anti-Egyptian political factors.

The succession of fedayeen operations at the end of August came in the wake of the occupation by the IDF of widespread areas and the gun battle at Kilometer 90 in the course of which one Egyptian officer and two volunteers were killed. A classified official circular, distributed in all army units, states clearly that the activization of the fedayeen was in retaliation for those clashes: it had been decided "to carry out revenge operations against the Jews by the forces of the Egyptian national guard and the national Palestinian guard."

The national guard of Egypt carried out four encounters on the border of the Gaza Strip on the night of August 25–26, but the main assignments were given to four groups of the Palestinian national guard, one of which was able to penetrate up to eighteen kilometers from Tel Aviv. On August 31 the IDF responded to the Fedayeen incursions with the large-scale attack on the Khan Yunis police station.

The Egyptian press published at length—

and for the first time—a number of glowing reports about the feats of the fedayeen, complete with maps and exaggerated descriptions about their success. (By the way, two of the fedayeen who had participated in these activities were taken captive.)

Beginning with these events toward the end of August, the fedayeen entered upon the Arab-Israeli scene. Their first operation characterizes in large measure their future activities: the Egyptians established firm control over the activities of the Palestine national guard, and those men became fedayeen only at the orders of Egypt. Orders were issued at the discretion of the higher echelons, first and foremost—as we shall see further—as military instruments within the framework of military encounters with Israel in order to increase the element of surprise and the Egyptian army's ability to inflict damage.

The Egyptians succeeded, thus, in doing away with the infiltrators, and in their place came the fedayeen who had demonstrated back in August that they were an efficient and sharp weapon in the struggle against Israel. From the series of the first fedayeen operations, the Egyptians learned to look on them as an extreme and drastic instrument that could not be utilized for uninterrupted action. Therefore the Egyptians attempted to widen the scope of the national guard as a reservoir for the fedayeen in times of need and also to set a limit to their operations, and even to divert part of them to actions from the direction of the Jordanian border.

In any event, there is not the slightest doubt that the appearance of the fedayeen under Egyptian guidance belongs to the period subsequent to the incursion of the IDF into Gaza. This was one of the clearest indications of a developing change in the Middle East, whether it came as a direct result or was evident only in its wake.

NOTES

1. Palestine Liberation Organization (PLO), organization committed to destroying the State of Israel and establishing a Palestinian state under its leadership. The PLO was founded in 1964 by the First Arab Summit Conference. At that time it was headed by Ahmad Shuqeiri and was an instrument of the Arab states rather than a genuine Palestinian organization. In 1969 Palestinian groups led by al-Fatah, the terrorist party headed by Yasir Arafat, took over the PLO, and since that time the PLO has been an umbrella organization based on a coalition of constituent organizations but actually dominated by Fatah. Various Arab states—e.g., Syria, Iraq, and Libya—still influence PLO policies and activities by establishing and supporting constituent organizations.

2. United Nations Relief and Works Agency (UNRWA), agency established by the United Nations on December 8, 1949 (U.N. General Assembly Resolution 312 [IV]) to provide assistance and relief to Palestinian refugees and administer refugee camps. UNRWA was not mandated to deal with the political problem per se.

3. After deposing King Farouk in 1952, the Egyptian officers almost immediately neutralized all possible opposition to their political hegemony except for the Muslim Brotherhood. During 1953–54 there was a struggle between the new regime and the brotherhood, which wanted a full partnership in the government. General Muhammed Naguib, who led the junta in its first years, was more sympathetic to the brotherhood than was Nasser, and this was one of the internal conflicts connected with Nasser's seizure of power from Naguib.

19. The Ben-Gurion–Sharett Clash over Defense Policies

The Egyptian Officers' Revolt deposed King Farouk in 1952, and by 1954 Gamal Abdul Nasser had emerged as the dominant figure in Egyptian politics. These events were crucial in the development of the Arab-Israeli conflict. Nasser espoused a militant philosophy of Arab unity that included the call for a military, as opposed to political, solution to the conflict with Israel. As a result, his popularity and influence rose within the Arab world while Egyptian-Israeli relations deteriorated, culminating in the Sinai Campaign. The following selection records the process from an Israeli perspective.

Moshe Sharett kept a personal diary from 1953 to 1957, meticulously recording the events in which he participated and his reflections on them. The diaries illuminate numerous issues as well as the workings of the innermost circles of Israel's political system. The following excerpts dated July 31, 1955, when Sharett was prime minister, describe two Israeli attempts to negotiate with Arab leaders in search of accommodation and then the difference of opinion between himself and Ben-Gurion over the very foundations of Israel's foreign and defense policies (see also doc. 22).

The meeting ended early so that I was able to spend some two hours in the Foreign Ministry.

I listened to the first chapter of the report by Gideon Raphael,[1] who had returned about a week before me from a trip to Europe. He informed me about two interesting meetings—one with the ex-prime minister of Syria, Husni Barazi, and with one of the idols of Egyptian capitalism, Aboud Pasha.

Husni's aim was to return to power, and to this end he was willing to accept the assistance of whoever was at hand—Turkey, in exchange for a promise to join the Ankara-Baghdad axis;[2] the United States, in order to identify himself with the West; Israel, with whom he was willing to make a peace treaty. It was clear that just a hint from Turkey against the liaison with us, lest it interfere with her pact with Iraq, would be sufficient to make him betray us. In the meantime he wanted things from us: money for newspapers, money to buy people, money to buy political parties. Gideon tried to infuse him with ideals—here he was himself a large landowner, and he should get together a group of estate owners and should initiate a large program of resettling refugees, including draining swamps and utilizing water from the Orontes for irrigation, for this would gain him merit in the opinion of the United States, he would be the recipient of extensive funding and genuine political support. Husni lent a willing ear, said that these were the words of the living God but that these matters would receive his attention after he had returned to power; but until such time, he needed an advance on the account.

Aboud turned out to be Nasser's confidant. He was evidently able not only to maintain his position and entrench himself under the new regime of hostility toward big capital but to make himself a pillar of support for this regime, which he cleverly

Source: Moshe Sharett, *Yoman Ishi* (Personal Diary), ed. Yaakov Sharett (Tel Aviv: Maariv, 1978), pp. 1100–1102. Reprinted by permission of Yaakov Sharett.

used for his own purposes. A serious person, who carefully considered his words. Nasser once told him that he saw two dangerous elements in Israel that prevented him from making peace with her: the danger of economic competition and the danger of expansionism. Aboud responded that the danger of competition was nonsense, but as far as the expansion was concerned, he was not qualified to pass an opinion. He asked Gideon for proof to contradict this claim, and the explanations he received satisfied him. He expressed his willingness to act to achieve a mitigation of the Suez embargo—free passage for all cargoes including fuel in non-Israeli ships. He reminded us that immediately after the cease-fire he had proposed that we renew permission for the Khedive ships [belonging to the Egyptian State Company] to anchor in the ports of Haifa and Jaffa. We replied that we would agree to this only on a reciprocal basis. To this day he was still amazed at our short-sightedness. If we had accepted his proposition, we would have thereby knocked the blocks out from under the Arab embargo.

According to Aboud's description, Nasser's position among his own supporters was shaky. He was subject to perpetual nervousness and was at a loss with whom to begin reconciliation. The top echelons of his faction were in discord, and the officers, each of whom derived his support from one of the forces—infantry, navy, and air force— were at odds with one another. The setup was completely out of equilibrium, and there was no telling what would happen. In short, there was no peace in the Land of the Nile. . . .

. . . At three o'clock in the afternoon a meeting of our "friends" was held at Ben-Gurion's request. The nine ministers were present, as well as Teddy[3] and Zeev Sharef. I was of the opinion, and had also heard this from someone, that it was Ben-Gurion's intention to clarify the moves toward forming a coalition, but he had not been candid about his position. He arrived tense and taut as a violin string, in quite a state. He

announced that I had demanded a policy clarification in the pertinent party institution. He had called this meeting in order to state his position and was not willing to participate in any discussion held under any other auspices, for experience had shown that anything said in a larger circle was leaked to the press. At the behest of Golda [Meir] and [Mordekhai] Namir, who had appealed to him at Sdeh Boker, he had returned to accept the defense portfolio upon Lavon's resignation and he explained why he had complied at the time—solely out of a concern for the Israel Defense Forces. When I had approached him later, he informed me that in his opinion cease-fire matters should return to the Defense Ministry, simply "because these are matters of defense." I had disagreed, and we had not settled our differences. Later he had written me that only on this condition would he return to the government, but he had found out—I don't know when or from whom— that I had not managed to read his letter before I put the changes before the Knesset. And so cease-fire matters had remained under the control of the Foreign Ministry, and he had accepted the verdict and had fallen in with my decision as prime minister. Here I thought he was going to say what he had said to the government—that since these affairs had been transferred to the Foreign Ministry, great steps forward had been made—but he did not say it this time and left the impression that he held the same opinion: Nevertheless he did add that, ultimately, the question of which ministry was in charge of cease-fire affairs was an administrative matter and not a matter of principle. As far as the principle was concerned, he wished to clarify his position beyond all shadow of doubt. Here he began to read from a detailed written declaration the main contents of which were: he was in favor of peace, and opposed to initiating any war, and considered it obligatory to keep the cease-fire agreements faithfully, but if the opponent broke them and the United Nations was unable to prevent this, the response should be force, regardless of the consequences. He would only be a member of a government that acted in this way. He would not participate in a government that acted in any other way either as prime minister or as minister of defense or in any other capacity, and he would not only not be a minister in such a government but would also not support that government from outside it (this was a softening of the version he had expressed to Nahum Goldmann, in which he stated that he would fight against such a government to the bitter end).

The extreme tension prevailing was not dispersed by my words. I said that it was no secret to the opposition members that things had come to a head in the last few months between myself and Ben-Gurion regarding national security. Had it not been for the imminent elections and anxiety for the fate of the party—and by implication the fate of the country—I would not have hesitated to tender my resignation since I remained in the minority in my party faction in the government concerning several momentous decisions. In the future I was not prepared to give in or to swing the balance against Ben-Gurion and the majority of party members by means of the minority together with members of other factions [in the government]. For that reason I had come to the conclusion that it was better for me to resign now while at the same time preserving the good name of the government, rather than to resign over a specific matter that was liable to weaken the status of the government. In the meantime, however, the results of the election were publicized. The party had been dealt a death blow [Mapai lost five seats—dropping from forty-five to forty seats], and I was reluctant to heap yet another calamity upon it. But my position remained unchanged—I was certainly, and with no personal difficulty, to become once

more the foreign minister in a government headed by Ben-Gurion as prime minister, but as foreign minister I would not undertake to implement a foreign policy to which I was totally opposed and that all my confidants, from within and without, know I negate completely. I would not betray my soul—and no one would ask it of me—and so, if such a conflict were to arise, I would leave and Ben-Gurion would have to find himself a new foreign minister. But I felt that first of all, policy should be thrashed out in the competent institutions of the party so that a clear stand could be decided upon. I added that I did not rule out a preliminary discussion in the present circle, although I knew the opinions of all the members. But I was not willing to make do with this. And in any case, I was not prepared for such a discussion at present—Ben-Gurion had arrived ready for it but I had had no idea that he was going to present this problem for discussion and I was also in a hurry to go to Tel Aviv to [Shmuel] Elyashiv's memorial service.

Ben-Gurion reiterated that there would be leaks from any larger forum. Eshkol and Golda supported me—for some time no discussion had been held in the party on this penetrating question and a framework should be found that would be able to maintain the secrecy.

I did not state before that Ben-Gurion also spoke about coalition problems in general and proposed convening the Histadrut[4] Committee for a public debate with the left-wing factions on the subject of the status of the laborer in Israel; his spirit compelled him to settle his account with Tabenkin,[5] to reply to those who were decrying the leadership of Ahdut Haavodah, and to vent his wrath on Mapam. The discussion moved to this subject, and before it had come to an end I left the meeting.

NOTES

1. Gideon Raphael (b. 1913), high ranking Israeli foreign service official. Raphael headed the Political Department of the Jewish Agency, 1943–47. After independence he was a member of

Israel's permanent delegation to the United Nations, 1948–53. He rose to become the director general of the Ministry of Foreign Affairs. Since then he has been the senior political adviser to the foreign minister, 1972–73, and ambassador to the United Kingdom, 1973–78.

2. Ankara-Baghdad axis, unofficial name for the alliance based on the defense treaty of February 24, 1955, between Iraq and Turkey, sometimes called the Baghdad Pact. This treaty was to be the cornerstone of U.S. plans for a comprehensive Middle East defense treaty to include the United States, Britain, and the Northern Tier of friendly Middle Eastern states; it was part of U.S. attempts to "contain" Soviet expansionism in the area. Britain, Pakistan, and Iran joined the pact in 1955. Egypt and other states denounced it as "imperialist" and turned to the Soviet Union. With the fall of the Iraqi monarchy in 1958, the Baghdad Pact collapsed, although there were later attempts to resuscitate it as the Central Nations Treaty Organization (CENTO).

3. Theodore (Teddy) Kollek (b. 1911), mayor of Jerusalem since 1965 and formerly director general of the Office of the Prime Minister, 1952–64. Kollek began his career in Mapai, followed Ben-Gurion to Rafi, and rejoined the Labor party.

4. Histadrut (short for Hahistadrut Haklalit Shel Haovdim Beerez Israel; lit., General Federation of Workers in Erez Israel; subsequently renamed Histadrut Haovdim Beerez Israel; lit., Federation of Workers in Israel), workers' organization and trade union federation. In addition to its union activities, it operates a health insurance program (Kupat Holim) covering the majority of Israel's residents, a bank, and several large industrial enterprises.

5. Yizhak Tabenkin (1887–1971), ideological leader of Ahdut Haavodah in the 1920s and leader of the Siah Bet faction in the 1930s and 1940s. After the June 1967 War Tabenkin became one of the leaders of the Greater Land of Israel movement.

SHIMON PERES
20. The Quest for Arms

The early 1950s were difficult years for Israel's foreign policy. Shortly after the establishment of the state, Israel drew away from the Soviet Union but was not willingly accepted by the Western powers, which were bent on preserving or obtaining the goodwill of the major Arab states. Shimon Peres,[1] one of Ben-Gurion's closest aides, was director general of the Ministry of Defense from 1953 to 1959. In that capacity he played a major role in developing the French-Israeli alliance in the mid-1950s and in procuring French and other weapons for the Israeli army, which was still being transformed into a military organization that could meet the young state's security needs (see doc. 12). In the following excerpt from his memoirs, Peres discusses some of the ways in which Israel dealt with two of its most persistent and crucial foreign policy problems: overcoming international isolation and procuring arms for its defense needs.

What water is to agriculture, armaments are to security. Israel suffers from a shortage of both. Revolutionary efforts to utilize every drop of water have led to revolutionary achievements in an arid land. Similar efforts in the field of local arms manufacture

---

Source: Shimon Peres, *David's Sling* (London: Weidenfeld and Nicolson, 1970), pp. 31–64. Reprinted by permission of Shimon Peres.

have also produced significant gains. But there were basic weapons like warplanes, tanks and heavy guns, vital in modern warfare, for which Israel had to rely—and to a great extent has still to rely—on outside sources. It is difficult to exaggerate the importance of such armaments for the establishment and maintenance of an effective defence and deterrent force for Israel. Without them, Israel would have been in a calamitous situation.

Getting arms has thus been one of the central tasks of Israel's leadership. At times it has given rise to their sharpest anxiety; for while Israelis feel the urgency, it has been excessively difficult to get outsiders to feel the same. At times, such as the arrival of a clandestine arms shipment at a critical moment in battle, it has excited their deepest sense of relief.

If there was a genocide in Biafra—irrespective of the political issues involved—it was because the Biafrans failed to secure the arms they needed, while the Nigerians received planes and guns from Russia and Egypt. Israel was saved from this fate because she managed to acquire some of the armaments she needed. Israelis were naturally sensitive to this problem, with the memory still fresh of the six million unarmed Jews who were crushed and murdered by the Nazis in Europe.

The need to secure arms for a regular army was born with Israel's birth, since she came under attack by the regular armies of six neighbouring Arab States within hours of her proclamation of independence. The majority of the members of the United Nations had voted for the establishment of the Jewish State; but they refused to supply even the elementary types of arms she required for her defence. They followed a curiously paradoxical policy of political amiability coupled with an arms embargo, though it was evident that a formal signature on a piece of paper was not sufficient to create a State. A country under attack cannot defend itself with a verbal decision alone, even if the words come from members of the United Nations.

The open declaration of war by seven Arab States—and no-one disputes who was the aggressor in Israel's war of independence—did not alter the policy on arms supply of those countries who supported the establishment of Israel. Israel had to face the invaders alone, and with her hands tied by an arms embargo; the invaders already enjoyed a preponderance of arms, and could get virtually unlimited additional supplies. The world certainly knew what had happened to the Jews of Europe, and knew, too, that many of Israel's inhabitants were among the few survivors of the holocaust. Despite it, beleaguered Israel had the utmost difficulty in securing even simple rifles, to say nothing of tanks and planes.

The United States refused arms. Britain refused. So did Russia. (Russia, incidentally, had also voted for the U.N. resolution calling for a Jewish State.)

The arms which nevertheless reached the Israel Army during the War of Independence came through "illegal" channels, in small quantities, and always at the last moment.

Some came from Czechoslovakia, which at that time was still governed by a coalition of communists and non-communists. . . .

The rifles from Czechoslovakia arrived just in time to be distributed to the units who were about to go into action to break the siege of Jerusalem. They were issued to some of the troops who were actually en route to the front.

Czechoslovakia also sold us some old Messerschmitts, the German fighter planes of World War Two. (Even though the price for these second-hand craft was sky high at that time—$200,000 a piece—some of them were found to suffer from a serious technical defect. The plane was equipped with machine-guns which fired through the propeller space, but the synchronization device did not always work, so that at times the burst hit the propeller and shattered it.) They sold us some heavy machine-guns which were very useful in both ground and anti-aircraft defence. The Czechs also helped us in training, and they put an airfield at our disposal.

Until then, Israel's General Staff had had the most trying time deciding on how, when and where to allocate the four guns they possessed, the total artillery force in Israel's arsenal. These were four old 65 mm weapons which had somehow survived, and still managed to work, from World War ONE!

One of the historic decisions of the General Staff was to send one of these guns to the northern front, to save Degania, Israel's first kibbutz, which was under pressure from a formidable force of Syrian tanks. The gun arrived without sights and the gunners had to test its range and workability by firing across the Sea of Galilee. To its credit—and to that of its operators—it must be said that age had not weakened its powers, and it fulfilled its task with efficiency and honour.

Small quantities of arms, including planes, were brought to Israel under ingenious circumstances which today evoke the image of a James Bond tale rather than that of a young country fighting for its life. For instance, some of our arms procurement people set up a film company in England and the first sequence of the script of the first film, which was of course a war film, called for shooting an air battle. They went out on location, the cameras were in place, and the planes took off. The cameras went on whirring and the planes went on flying— all the way to Israel, where the actions in which they were subsequently engaged were rather more realistic than those envisaged in the script.

Other arms were acquired in France and Italy, and three American Flying Fortresses made the long flight, filled with incident, via the Caribbean to Israel. Most of these planes were flown by non-Israel Jewish pilots who had volunteered to fight in Israel's War of Independence.

Despite delays, defects and meagre quantities, these overseas weapons enabled the Israel Army to hold out for a year, to beat off their enemies and ultimately to chase them from Israel soil.

The end of the War of Independence did not bring an end to the arms embargo. For the next seven years, this ban remained in operation, whether official or unofficial, complete or partial. Israel followed with an anxious heart the steady accumulation by the Arab States of heavy and sophisticated weapons of war.

In 1951, America, France and Britain publicly announced their tripartite agreement on an arms policy for the Middle East.[2] After some obscure references to the need to maintain the status quo in the area, the three signatories undertook to co-ordinate their individual supplies of weapons to the Middle Eastern States. This meant the continued denial to Israel of supplies from any of the three powers. The Arab States suffered no such restrictions with the signatories; and other sources were also open to them. The British, for example, under the Anglo-Jordanian Treaty, supplied weapons to Jordan's Army and officers to train and command it. Saudi Arabia continued to receive arms under its treaty with the United States. Egypt acquired arms from France and Italy— additions to the not inconsiderable supplies which had been left behind after World War Two.

This policy was due largely to inertia. The British continued to be sensitive about routes to India—even after they lost India. The French clung to their "Levant Policy" even when they had lost their position in the Levant. The United States faithfully supported these two countries who could not seem to make up their minds whether to maintain the posture of great powers or resign themselves to the status of middle-ranking States. They conducted their affairs with indolence, hesitancy, and the pusillanimity of closed minds.

The vacuum in the Middle East created by the gradual departure of Britain and France began to be filled by powers who had had no major historic associations with the region and whose diplomatic representatives scorned both the table manners of the British and the subtlety of the French.

Soviet Russia appeared on the scene in the spring of 1955 in the form of a handsome, outgoing, middle-aged man, quite unlike his reserved predecessors. Indeed, he seemed to live in the eye of the camera, and pictures of him feeding the pigeons in Cairo squares soon appeared on the pages of the world press. Mr. [Dimitri] Shepilov, soon to become the Soviet Foreign Minister, was welcomed with open arms—and he did not disappoint his hosts. He seemed uninhibited by the cautiousness that characterized the experienced Middle East representatives of the former world powers. He did not argue with the Egyptians over their requests, did not bargain with them over each detail in the long shopping list of armaments which, in quality and quantity, were quite new to the region. The demands were wholesale; so was the response.

What followed Shepilov's visit was the "Czech Arms Deal." Within a short time, jet planes, tanks, guns, destroyers and submarines began to reach Egypt from Czechoslovakia. All were of the latest type, and they arrived in quantities which seemed fanciful. Up to then, the normal arsenals of the Middle Eastern States had been made up of obsolescent weapons (by western standards), and even those in comparatively small quantities.

The Czech arms deal thus violently upset the arms balance, and with it the security of Israel. To Egypt's great new military strength, Israel had no answer. The menace grew more grave as Egypt grew more confident—her threats now had a bite. Nasser charged that King Farouk[3] had armed the army with "rotten weapons" and that was why Egypt had lost the 1948 war with Israel; but now Egypt had acquired great supplies of spanking new armaments and equipment, and would know what to do with them.

Israel again had to cast about for even minimal quantities of arms to safeguard her existence. The entire nation well understood that its fate depended on the results of that quest.

Arms procurement thus became the principal aim of Israel's foreign policy (and it has remained one of the central purposes to this day).

Constant technical advances in the development of weaponry have turned the supply of arms into a complicated issue. Highly sophisticated armaments can no longer be manufactured and sold within the commercial framework. The enormous investment required in research and development, and the need for co-ordination between numerous plants (often, plants in different countries), have led more and more to the transfer of arms production from private to governmental control. . . .

When jets started to become the bread and butter of the air force, the sources of supply were extremely limited. Whereas the prop plane had long been manufactured by numerous countries and stocks were available all over the world, from Japan to Canada, the basic production of jets was confined to five countries alone: the United States, the Soviet Union, Britain, France and Sweden. The governments themselves were involved in their development and manufacture, and kept scrupulous supervision and control over their disposal. No country could acquire them from any one of the five in a simple commercial transaction. The considerations were almost wholly political. Indeed, the sale of jets was a marked expression of political friendship.

From 1955 onwards, Egypt, Syria and Iraq were able to buy these planes from Soviet Russia, and since the political rather than the economic factor was the prime ingredient the terms were unusually favourable. The Russian price tag for a MIG was $400,000 (as against more than a million dollars for the comparable French jet, the Mirage); and long term credits were granted at the remarkably low interest rate of 1½ percent.

The reasons prompting Russian generosity in its arms dealings with the Arab States were also the reasons for the deterioration in Russia's relations with Israel—frigid in times of relative quiet, downright hostile in periods of tension. It is largely with the coin of Israel that Russia has tried to buy the Arabs, wean them away from the western world, and pursue her historic ambition of penetrating into the Middle East. Her cold-shouldering of Israel undoubtedly increased the spread of her influence in the region.

It was quite clear, therefore, that Israel could expect no supply of jets from Russia. She was thus left with four possible sources of supply, at least theoretically. Sweden had to be excluded from the start. Sweden follows a policy of scrupulous neutrality, and she does not sell arms to "areas of tension." . . .

American would appear to have been the most likely country from which to get them. But United States' policy during the 1950s was expressed by President Eisenhower:[4] "We are not prepared to become the major supplier of arms to the Middle East." The reasons for this ran the range of the spectrum. The cold war was at its height. The world was divided into blocs, and the countries of each were bound by military treaties. NATO and SEATO[5] had just been launched, and they were treated by their creators with a reverence that was almost holy. The United States supplied the armaments of their members, and this was America's great contribution to strengthening these two treaty organizations. But Israel was a member of neither. She was bound by no treaty, either bilateral or multilateral, with the United States. Moreover, this was a period in which Congress was reluctant to approve the supply of arms unless the American Government could exercise supervision. Such supervision, however, again involved agreements with conditions which excluded Israel. For Israel's enemy was not communist, and only countries "favoured" with an enemy recognized as belonging to the communist camp were able to receive American military help. . . .

As for Great Britain, she was still very much a power in the Arab Middle East right up to 1955, and was heavily involved in Egypt, Jordan, Iraq and the Emirates and principalities of the Arabian peninsula. She had an army in Suez. Her officers commanded the Arab Legion. Nuri Sa'id, Prime Minister of Iraq, was the pampered favourite of the Foreign Office, who regarded him as the wisest statesman in the Middle East and the most faithful ally of the British Crown. British administration of the Arabian principalities was backed by the Royal Navy. The wealthy sheikhs of Kuwait and Bahrein kept their vast deposits in British banks. Marked friendship for Israel would have endangered this British presence in the Arabian world. So Britain could be eliminated as a supplier of jets to Israel.

There remained France. France at that time was not yet out of the military mess in Indo-China; she was conducting independence negotiations with the exiled leaders of Tunisia and Morocco; and she was almost wholly concerned with the grave situation in Algeria and the more than a million French *colons*, the "pieds noirs,"[6] whose fate rested on the outcome of the growing Algerian rebellion. The France of the Fourth Republic, split as it was, was forced to determine anew her international status in the postwar world, to re-establish her shattered and obsolete economy. She was faced by the powerful challenge of an advancing technology which could lead to a regarding in the status of countries, great and small, old and young.

In Israel's search for weapons to match those of her enemies, the cardinal question was whether or not there was a chance of getting jets from France. . . .

Many of the new leaders of the Fourth Republic had spent terms in Nazi concentration camps. There they had seen what was done to the Jews; they had seen the gas chambers, seen the ovens, smelt the smoke. For many, therefore, the Jewish tragedy was felt as a personal experience. . . .

The emergence of Nasser on the Egyptian scene was also viewed differently by these new French leaders. To them, he was no romantic new Pharaoh who had suddenly been unwrapped from a 4,000 year old mummy, but a pale shadow of the dictators whose lives had ended in Germany and Italy only ten years earlier. Guy Mollet,[7] leader of the Labour Party, termed him "an apprentice dictator" who aroused instinctive revulsion.

They did not regard Nasser's intervention in the Algerian rebellion—his supply of arms and instructors to the FLN[8]—as revolutionary altruism, but as an ingredient in a new "Pan" movement—Pan-Arabism—which was as distasteful to them as Pan-Germanism or Pan-Slavism.

Israel, on the other hand, stirred their imagination. It was a democratic country, a haven for the survivors, the persecuted and the dispossessed, a challenge to young Jewish pioneers from the lands of comfort, a country of social equality, whose people sought to bring life to the desert and to create a new society and who were determined to fight to defend their independence and their future.

This did not mean that these new men of France favoured an attitude of friendship towards Israel without any of the reservations of traditional French diplomacy which the Quai d'Orsay [French Foreign Ministry] expressed so skilfully. Because the territory had been administered by a British Mandate, Israel was widely regarded as belonging to the English-speaking world, and it was the French feeling that her problems should be tackled by the "Anglo-Saxons," whose centre had shifted from London to Washington. "Where is the logic," I was once asked by Couve de Murville when I was on an arms shopping expedition, "in the proposal that France should turn itself into the "lone knight of the Middle East" when Britain, who once governed you, and the United States, who is so friendly to you, refuse your requests with such stubbornness?"

Another reservation stemmed from the traditional competition for influence in the Middle East between France and Britain. The competition was still there, but it had already been overtaken by history. The new competitors were the United States and Soviet Russia, whose eyes were on its warm-water ports. Nevertheless, France tried its utmost to hold on to its positions in Syria and Lebanon whose political leaders, military commanders and professional classes spoke French, who had cultural and economic ties with France, and whose currencies were based on the French franc. A closer French relationship with Israel was likely to endanger French influence in these two Arab States, an influence which France believed was being seriously undermined by British agents.

There were divided opinions as to the effect of French policy in the Middle East on the Algerian revolt. Some leaders, notably those responsible for defence matters, held that clipping Nasser's wings would limit his ambitions and impact on the Algerian front. Others, particularly those in charge of French diplomacy, believed that closer friendship with the Arab world would induce it to stay out of what was an exclusively French issue, even though the site of the conflict was Arab.

France's foreign policy had thus to take into account contradictory considerations: a natural feeling of warmth towards Israel, and the need to strengthen France's weakened status in the Arab States; a conflict over interests with Britain, and the need to join in partnership with Britain and America to provide the basic core of NATO; anger over Nasser's intervention in Algeria, and the prospect of nullifying it by drawing closer to Egypt.

Each view had its partisans in the governments of the Fourth Republic, coalition regimes made up of statesmen of different schools, several of whom exercised considerable individual influence on decisions when they were in power. But they were not always in power. Change of government was frequent—there were twenty-two in twenty years. Any one of those twenty-two might have favoured a policy of friendship with Israel only to find the position reversed by any one of its successors. Conversely, a hostile attitude by one of these governments was also not necessarily immutable. . . .

At the end of 1954, I went to Paris with a personal letter in my pocket from Ben-Gurion to General Pierre Koenig, France's Defence Minister. I arrived on a Friday evening after all offices were closed, and so it was only next morning that I could telephone for a meeting. It was promptly arranged for an unlikely day and hour—4 P.M. next day, Sunday. I teemed up together with our Defence Ministry representative in France, Yosef Nahmias. General Koenig, hero of Bir Hakim, with a reputation both as a great fighting commander and as a man of few words, knew quite a lot about Israel and the fate of the Jews, and he had met our units during the war in the Libyan desert. He listened to our arms requests, asked some pertinent questions, and then gave his decision on the spot with characteristic brevity: "I agree. Give me your list."

I promised to let him have our requirements by about 10 o'clock next morning. Never will I forget the telephone call I received at precisely that hour. Koenig was on the line, and his tone was impatient: "It's already ten. Where's your list?" That was the start of a long and deep friendship between the General and Israel, a friendship which saw us through many critical situations and called for considerable personal courage on his part.

It was, indeed, as a result of this meeting that the first practical moves were made to supply us with tanks and guns. The tanks were the AMX-13, a fast and light tank which was to prove its worth in the Sinai Campaign. The gun was the 155 mm, and we got this first. . . .

Throughout 1955, and particularly in the final months, the situation in Israel became steadily worse. The first shipments of Soviet-bloc arms began to reach Egyptian ports, and the scale of these supplies shocked the Israel public and its leaders. The Arab States, notably Egypt, sent in more and more infiltrators to carry out acts of terror and sabotage. The mounting actions of these Arab fedayeen called forth counter-operations from Israel along three borders—her borders with Syria, Jordan and the Gaza Strip (which drew down upon her American pressure to exercise restraint).

The Czech arms deal with Egypt produced a "backs to the wall" feeling in Israel. She possessed no weapons sufficient in quality and numbers to meet the new situation. In the absence of a better immediate alternative, the Israel Government announced an interim "Israel deal"—to strengthen the fortifications of the land. Israel became a nation of volunteers as young and old, workers and professional men, shopkeepers and housewives, the Prime Minister and secondary school pupils, took up picks and spades and went out to build fieldworks. . . .

As France's election day approached, in the final month of 1955, we could sum up the results of our year's activities with a certain measure of satisfaction but also with one clear disappointment. We had established direct contact with many of France's leaders; we had broken through the arms-supply barrier; and we had already received some guns and tanks. But as far as jet planes were concerned, apart from a few Ouregans which we had been allowed to buy, the obstacles were still there. We now had to prepare for the future, for the new year and for the new Government that would come into power. . . .

The results of the French elections became known at the beginning of 1956. With the left and right wing blocs fairly evenly matched, the balance was held by the Socialist Party, and contrary to all political expectations, Guy Mollet became Prime Minister. Maurice Bourgès-Maunoury got the Ministry of Defence. Shortly after his assumption of office, Guy Mollet invited us to Paris. When we arrived at his official residence at the Hotel Matignon for dinner on our first evening, he put forth his hand and, before I had a chance to congratulate him, he smiled and said: "Now you will see that I will not be a Bevin." We found the new chief of government a man of his word, the word he had given us on election eve when he was still only chief of a party.

It was the start of a new era in Franco-Israel relations, an era that was to last without interruption for twelve years, enabling Israel to overcome most of her security problems during this period, and having the vital international impact of changing the balance of forces in the Middle East. This was a friendship almost unexampled in the history of international relationships. Being utterly informal—there was no official treaty, no formal alliance—it blossomed on a degree of mutual trust and mutual understanding rare among governments. . . .

With the landing of the planes, something else happened. Our close relationship with France had started, after all, through the somewhat circumscribed fields of arms procurement, and that had been carried through almost as an underground operation. But the news spread very quickly, and was greeted with extraordinary enthusiasm by the people of both countries. There was, indeed, a spontaneous fusion of friendship between the two nations, and this mood suddenly took on a life of its own, going far beyond the bounds of anything envisaged in the preliminary cooperation between the two administrations. Frenchmen and Israelis found themselves personally involved, each moved by this common bond which had just been created. Its expression was everywhere apparent in the two countries. Israelis arriving in France found it in the warmth of their reception from the moment they stepped off the plane, and it was echoed in parliament and the press. Frenchmen found the same on visits to Israel. This deep and wide-spread feeling of mutual affection was a rare phenomenon in international relationships—the spontaneous coming together of two nations.

The basis of this relationship was mutual interest. But it would be utterly false to the very nature of this bond to conceive of it in terms of interest alone. It had about it a romantic quality—a strange manifestation in a cynical world—the kind of quality that at times lifts man from the prosaic greyness of a calculating pragmatism and gives him the inspiration to gaze anew at human values.

Official France and official Israel were also seized by this intangible new dimension of friendship. At no time did France seek to dictate conditions, request supervision over the arms we acquired, or demand that she be consulted over their use—or non-use. France's specific and prescribed aim was to help, not to control. Her purpose was to strengthen our army without encroaching on our independence. Her behaviour was that of an equal, not of a patron to one in need. This attitude was hailed by most Frenchmen, proud that their Government was helping "courageous little Israel" to defend herself. Israelis on their part were profoundly grateful to "the centre of civilization" for coming to their aid at a critical moment. The new Franco-Israel relationship showed that traditional policies of "what's in it for me," based on self-interest, could give way to policies informed by generosity, understanding and comradeship.

This association between the two countries was to stand the test of the Sinai Campaign a year later, and also to yield fruit eleven years later. In 1959 we started negotiating for Mirage jets, and in the summer of 1960, Isser Penn, our representative in Paris, and I signed the first agreement on their supply. In the Six Day War, June 1967, Israel pilots flying these Mirages played a key part in overcoming the air forces of the enemy and thus stifling the new danger that threatened to engulf the nation.

NOTES

1. Shimon Peres (b. 1923), leader of the Labor party since 1977. Like Dayan, Peres's public and political career developed through his close association with Ben-Gurion. Considered a superb technocrat, Peres forged the alliance with France and helped shape the defense establishment.

After serving as director general of the Defense Ministry, he became deputy minister of defense, 1959–65. Peres's influence declined in the mid-1960s as Ben-Gurion's influence waned. With Ben-Gurion and Dayan, Peres formed the Rafi party in 1965. Following the creation of the Labor alignment, Peres's influence began to rise again, and throughout much of the 1970s Peres struggled against Rabin and Allon for its leadership. At first he had to settle for being Rabin's minister of defense, 1974–77, instead of prime minister. In 1981 he led the Labor party in the election campaign, having defeated Rabin for the leadership position in the party convention.

2. Tripartite Declaration, statement of policy for the Middle East issued by the United States, Britain, and France in 1950. It stated in part: "The three Governments take this opportunity of declaring their deep interest in and their desire to promote the establishment and maintenance of peace and stability in the area and their unalterable opposition to the use of force or threat of force between any of the states in that area. The three Governments, should they find that any of these states was preparing to violate frontiers or armistice lines, would, consistent with their obligations as members of the United Nations, immediately take action, both within and outside the United Nations, to prevent such violation" (U.S. *Department of State Bulletin* 22, no. 570 [June 5, 1950]: 886).

3. Farouk (1920–65), king of Egypt, 1936–52. Farouk was forced to abdicate in July 1952 after the successful Officers' Revolt.

4. Dwight David Eisenhower (1890–1969), president of the United States, 1953–61.

5. North Atlantic Treaty Organization (NATO), mutual defense pact of the United States, Canada, and most of Western Europe. Established in 1949, NATO is the cornerstone of the Western bloc's defense policies and strategies. Southeast Asia Treaty Organization (SEATO), mutual defense pact between the United States, Great Britain, France, Australia, New Zealand, Pakistan, Thailand, and the Philippines, established in Manila in September 1954. It was part of the U.S. policy of containment and formally extended the U.S. sphere of influence in Asia.

6. *Colons*, the French who went from the metropole to the colonies. The *pieds noirs* were the *colons* who returned to mainland France.

7. Guy Alcide Mollet (1905–75), secretary general of the French Socialist party and prime minister of France, January 1956–May 1957. His was the longest lasting government of the Fourth Republic.

8. Front de Liberation Nationale (FLN), national liberation movement in Algeria fighting for independence from France, which was achieved in 1962.

MOSHE SHARETT
21. The Soviet Union and the Czech Arms Deal

In October 1955 Moshe Sharett traveled to Paris and Geneva to meet with the foreign ministers of the four major powers—the United States, the Soviet Union, Britain, and France. His mission underlined Israel's diplomatic difficulties and isolation during this period. This excerpt from his diaries records his meeting on October 31, 1955, with the Soviet foreign minister, Vyacheslav Mikhaylovich Molotov, when Soviet-Israeli relations were deteriorating and Soviet-Egyptian relations growing closer.

Finally, at almost eight o'clock, they called from the Soviet delegation to say that Molotov had just returned and was ready to receive me. We went immediately; I was

Source: Moshe Sharett, *Yoman Ishi* (Personal Diary), ed. Yaakov Sharett (Tel Aviv: Maariv, 1978), pp. 1272–74. Reprinted by permission of Yaakov Sharett.

tense, anticipating the coming battle of words.

And it was, indeed, a stormy debate—unique among the series of talks I have experienced. Molotov's countenance justified [Harold] Nicholson's pointed definition. He was polite and cold as ice. Gromyko[i] and an anonymous fellow who recorded the meeting sat with him. I greeted Gromyko as an old acquaintance—I could tell by his face that he was a sick man.

I began by thanking the Soviet Union for 1947 [see doc. 16]—"Our people is graced with an excellent historical memory, and this support by the Soviet Union during such a crucial hour will never be forgotten"—and I gave a short description of the country's development since then: immigration, building, the regimen of national development. I said that our country possessed the highest development coefficient in the world, relative to area and population. At this point I noticed an inimical glint in the icy eyes. What nerve! To suggest that a country existed which exceeded the Soviet Union in its speed of development! However, he made no reaction to this part of my speech; his face showed no sign of interest, as if the matter made no difference. I mentioned the financial sources of our development project—Jewish appeals, an American grant, reparations from West Germany. I emphasized that there were no political strings attached to the grant; it imposed no limitations upon us. No reaction.

When, however, I switched to a description of our unique security situation—the siege, the animosity, the arms superiority of our enemies, the hostile intentions of the entire Arab world and Egypt in particular, he cut in, saying, "But here you are, threatening a preventive war," and out of his pocket he pulled a newspaper containing a statement by Dov Joseph in New York. As of that moment, he didn't stop interrupting me, until I began to do the same to him, and the conversation became very "lively," with the tone on both sides becoming ever more sharp.

Despite all this, I succeeded in explaining the matter of a *security treaty*—what it included (Israel's defense) and what it excluded (defense of the area); that it was not yet more than an idea, albeit a good one, but still far from the implementation stage. I had the impression that this explanation was duly received. Overcoming the interruptions, I concluded my introduction with a statement of the danger threatening our security from Egypt's direction, compounded tenfold as it would be by the new weapons; I requested, officially and ceremoniously, that the Soviet Union exert its influence on Prague to retract the deal, which would endanger the peace. I said that should a war break out, it would involve the entire Middle East and start a conflagration, the sparks of which would reach vast areas of the world.

Though in his interruptions and in his reply he denied all my assumptions, this was due neither to deep analysis of the matter, nor to questions about my analyses and conclusions. Rather, he related to the problem superficially and dogmatically, by means of general formulas: "You are strong; after all, you have received plenty of weapons. Egypt has no intention of attacking; it is a small, weak country, dependent on weapons in order to secure its independence, and that's all there is to it. You have important friends. Macmillan[2] stands up for you, Dulles[3] speaks in your favor, and if they are not rushing to help you, it means that they too are convinced that you are not in danger, etc. The main point is, Why should you talk of war? What we need is to strive for peaceful relations, to appeal to the Egyptians, to find a common language, etc."

I pressed him to the wall with two lines of attack, without crushing him: (a) "Egypt had an advantage over us in all types of heavy weapons on land, sea and air even before the Czech arms deal—now its advantage will be significantly greater." He stood his ground: "Egypt needs weapons to strengthen itself." At one point, when I listed jet planes, tanks, submarines, etc., he said, "Do you believe everything that is written in the newspapers?" I replied, "Would you state unequivocally that this is not true? That we are talking about pistols for the police force and a few machine guns?" He was silent. (b) "We are prepared and willing to enter into peace negotiations at any time, and they declare that they will never make peace and that their aspiration is to wipe Israel off the face of the earth. Why do you arm a country which does not strive for peace, but rather lays obstacles in its path?" There was no reply. Regarding the danger of an offensive war by Egypt, and my referring to the 1948 invasion, his reply was that "now the world situation is entirely different. Anyone who initiates a war now will arouse the anger of the whole world."

The argument—it would be more correct to call it a quarrel—was heated throughout. We did not go beyond the bounds of verbal politeness, but there were nasty jibes from both sides. On my side, when he claimed that Egypt had no aggressive intentions: "On what do you base your statement? How do you know? We are there, we are involved and we know better than you. You are shouldering a very heavy responsibility." On his part: "Your words to the effect that we are obstructing peace are not only incorrect, they are also insulting (oskorbitelni). There is no world power as desirous of peace as the Soviet Union, and all its actions are directed only to peace."

Some statements were conspicuous by their absence: (a) He did not once present this as a "trade deal"; it was presented specifically as a political step. (b) He didn't use the insipid excuse that it was Czechoslovakia, an independent state over which the Soviet Union had no control, that had sold the weapons, but always spoke in terms of "we." (c) He made not the slightest hint of an offer to supply us with weapons.

And his words included some salient political points: (a) I already mentioned the claim that the intention was to strengthen Egypt's independence—on this point he expounded for some time, mentioning that

England had not yet vacated the canal zone completely. (b) He stated explicitly; that the Baghdad-Ankara Pact "obligated us to enter": (c) At the end, he said, "If there really is a danger to security, methods exist for dealing with such a situation—we will be prepared for that," or something to that effect. In any case, it was clear from the gestures of his hands that his intention was to hint at the Soviet Union's readiness for a comprehensive agreement in which it, too, would participate. (d) He said, "If a small country feels itself threatened, it is up to a great power to take note of that, and I am prepared to review the question once again." This would seem to have been an important declaration of positive intent toward us, and it was worth holding on to; however, he added a "but" and reiterated his claim that in actual fact there is no danger and that the most important thing is to arrive at a settlement. The intimation was very strong that this is our responsibility.

At about a quarter to nine he mentioned that he was having guests for dinner—Dulles and his aides, whom he had first invited for eight o'clock and had then postponed until nine. At nine exactly the secretary entered and announced that Mr. Dulles had arrived. Gromyko, who had sat in silence all the time, nervously tapping his fingers, and who had only once blurted out, "But they are afraid of you," rose and announced that he was going out to take care of Dulles in the meantime. A few minutes after he left we also got up, but Molotov continued with his argument—the Soviet Union aspires to peace, etc. He added, "We are very anxious to be on friendly terms with both Israel and the Arab countries." "We, too, are most interested in friendly relations with the Soviet Union," I replied. The answer to this was, "Oh, if you were really interested in friendship with us, the relations would be entirely different."

Thus we descended the stairs, Molotov talking all the while, and so he stood and talked in the hall while I donned my coat—no helping hand, heaven forbid—until he came outside to accompany me, asking his servants, "Where is the prime minister's car?" I said to him, "It's cold outside, don't catch cold." "Don't worry," he replied, not

moving until our car was on its way, and waving good-bye to us.

Avidar was agitated by the storminess and sharpness of the talk.

NOTES

1. Andrei Gromyko (b. 1909), Soviet minister of foreign affairs since 1957. From 1953 to 1957 Gromyko was the Soviet first deputy minister of foreign affairs.

2. Harold Macmillan (b. 1894), British prime minister, January 1957–1963, and leader of the Labour party.

3. John Foster Dulles (1888–1959), U.S. secretary of state, 1953–59. Dulles believed in the cold war policy of containment, and so he opposed neutralism on the part of the Third World bloc.

MOSHE SHARETT
22. Israel's Foreign and Middle Eastern Policy

In 1955 Moshe Sharett prepared this review of Israel's foreign affairs and policies and presented it to a senior forum in the Ministry of Foreign Affairs. Of particular interest are his statements on Israel's "retaliations policy" in response to the irregular warfare conducted against it from across the Jordanian and Egyptian borders.

In the evening [May 28, 1955], the final meeting for consultations with the ambassadors. The invitation was extended not only to the limited circle but also to all heads of departments at the Ministry of Foreign Affairs. Teddy [Kollek] and Isser [Harel], who in any case participated in all the meetings, were also there. There were close to twenty people. I spoke for over an hour. I explained to those who were displeased with the timing of the briefing that if we had not convened now our meeting would have had to have been deferred until after the meeting of the General Assembly, that is until the beginning of 1956 owing to U Nu[1] and Johnston's[2] continued schedule of visits in May and June, the U.N. Convention in

San Francisco at the end of June, the election campaign in July, the trials and tribulations of forming a new government in August, which would bring us to the opening of the General Assembly in New York in September continuing until December. I refrained from adding that had we not held our briefing now, it is doubtful whether I would have participated in it.

Following an analysis of the situation and policy of the United States, on the one hand, and England on the other, I stated that our aim of achieving a defense treaty with the United States was a central tenet of our policy. It was not improbable that we would succeed in signing a treaty with the United States only, because of an agreement be-

Source: Moshe Sharett, Yoman Ishi (Personal Diary), ed. Yaakov Sharett (Tel Aviv: Maariv, 1978), pp. 1024–25. Reprinted by permission of Yaakov Sharett.

tween her and England concerning the Baghdad Pact, to which England had become a party while the United States had not. It is not clear what the prospects are of achieving this goal, but it is worth investing every effort. Its advantages: it would guarantee our security through a mutual pact; it would strengthen us in relation to the Arab states; it would assist peace; it would increase our worth in the eyes of the world; it would provide an incentive for capital investment; it would constitute a message to Jewry. The treaty should be explained to the Soviet bloc and the Asian states as arising exclusively out of our concern for security in the face of Arab hostility and as a conclusion drawn from the Bandung Conference.[3] We did not see that Yugoslavia's ties with the Balkan Alliance[4] were damaging to her relations with the Soviet Union. On the contrary. On the other hand, Yugoslavia cannot be a model for us in its independent maneuvering owing to the Arab peril, the Jewish link, and the necessity of economic assistance, all of which differentiate us from her. In the final analysis, she also has more armed divisions than we do. We do not request a defense treaty merely because we are exposed to danger from the Arab countries on account of their ongoing hostility toward us. Our request derives from the formation of alignments that the policy of the Western powers has generated in the structure of the Middle East. In other words, we are not sounding the alarm, nor are we pleading to be saved; we are merely stating the responsibility of the powers and leaving them to draw their conclusions, to respond or not. We are not asking them for favors, but we are asking them to accept the responsibility for the change in the situation against us, which was brought about through their initiative. I warned that in the discussion the supporters of the treaty had not indicated any concern for the intrigues of U.S. policy toward us. Since the absence of peace in the Middle East obstructs its inclusion in the defense setup, there is likely to be an attempt to achieve peace by putting

pressure on us to give in on the issues of territory and refugees. I also warned against any thought of returning tens of thousands of people even as a price for peace, and on this question I adopted a firmly negative position. I also warned against talking lightly of adjusting the borders as an intermediate stage. It would be a distortion of the facts to assume that the strange state of the Jordanian border is the cause of infiltration. When the [Arab] Legion does what it is supposed to, there is no infiltration even when the border divides villagers from their lands. On the other hand, if the Jordanian authorities become careless or neglect their job, there will be large-scale armed infiltration even if the border is as it should be. In any event, no straightening of the borders is possible unless they are fixed once and for all, and that is not possible except within the framework of a peace treaty. A different kind of border adjustment is possible only as an amendment in cease-fire treaties. Are the Arabs ready for this? How long will negotiations take, and who knows how they will end? For all these reasons, it would be better to put our efforts, not into clarifying possibilities of altering the borders as a precondition for a defense treaty, but rather into striking this problem completely off the agenda of our negotiations over the treaty— particularly in view of the fact that the slogan of adjusting the borders camouflages a trend to extract much more from us than they would be willing to give to us. The direction for advancing in a practical manner toward achieving an intermission in the tension between us and our neighbors (as an interim step toward signing a defense treaty) lies in compensation for refugees in exchange for lifting the hostile embargo and boycott, an agreement with Johnston concerning water affairs, and stabilizing the peace on the border. All three matters depend on the attitude of the opponent.

At the end of my talk I devoted some time to the issue of retaliations. I opposed the facile charge brought by ambassadors and other members against the policy adopted by the government. I claimed that this was not merely a question of pure political reason, and the problem should not be viewed only as a reflection of foreign affairs of the state. The representatives should state their opinion about the internal affairs of the country. At the core of the question lie deep-rooted ideas that could not be eradicated by persuasion alone. The soul of the nation, the youth, and the army are subject to waves of depression and disequilibrium that create serious crises; not releasing this tension at the appropriate time would be perilous. I described the growth of Revisionism[5] in the 1920s and 1930s and told them that Weizmann[6] and his system could not be absolved from responsibility for this pestilence. He [Weizmann] also had political reason on his side, but his fault lay in not understanding the soul of the movement. The disease of dissent might be revived in the state if we attempt to pull the string too taut. The machinations of Kibbutz Beitar on the one hand and the vengeance wreaked by the young men of Ein Harod and Deganyah Bet on the other give an indication of what awaits us. Practically speaking, the account cannot be set straight so simply either. The assumption that incidents can be prevented from occurring simply by being on guard is absolutely superficial. On the other hand, it is a fact that the Kibiyah and Nahlin [opera-

tions] brought the Legion to the front line of border protection and thus obstructed murderous infiltration.[7] Kibiyah was a political and moral disaster because of the slaughter of women and children, but a distinction must be drawn between the vigorous retaliatory action in itself and the cruel, ugly character it had in this case, which was by no means mandatory. Verdicts of Jordanian courts and articles in the Jordanian press indicate an understanding there of the fact that murderous attacks by gangs ultimately result in disasters befalling peaceful villages, and for this reason they should be viewed as a national crime that ought to be eradicated. All in all, a bitter, determined struggle is being waged, sometimes even a desperate one, against the desire for reprisal, and for every action that is given approval, several much more drastic ones are forbidden or prevented. I expressed my grievance at the fact that the criticisms and complaints leveled against me had not taken into account the fact I had stated, that with much effort we had been saved from the greatest calamities to the state. In conclusion, I pointed out in a positive light Teddy's criticism of the low level of the Ministry of Foreign Affairs' activity in the field of internal propaganda among our people both concerning the problems confronting foreign policy and relating to its achievement.

NOTES

1. U Nu (b. 1907), prime minister of Burma from its independence until he was deposed by a coup (with two minor interruptions), 1948–62.

2. Eric Johnston (1896–1963), American businessman sent by President Eisenhower to seek an Arab-Israeli agreement regarding the distribution and utilization of the waters of the Jordan River. His mission lasted from 1953 to 1955 and successfully laid the groundwork for a de facto agreement between Israel and Jordan.

3. Bandung Conference, first conference of African and Asian states, held in Bandung, Indonesia, April 18–24, 1955. It provided the setting for the organization of a Third World bloc

in international relations and for the spread of nonalignment as a conscious collective strategy of these states. Israel did not attend. Nasser emerged from the conference as a major leader and spokesman for this bloc.

4. Balkan Alliance, alliance between nonaligned communist Yugoslavia and Turkey and Greece (both of which are members of NATO), signed in 1953 at the height of Joseph Stalin's hostility to Yugoslavia's independent policies. This pact had a silent birth and death.

5. The World Union of Zionist Revisionists was established in Paris in 1925 by Zeev Jabotinsky. Jabotinsky wanted to organize a parallel set

of institutions to oppose the "official Zionism" of the World Zionist Organization and its "organic" approach, advocated by Chaim Weizmann, for slowly building the Jewish national home. Jabotinsky demanded a radical revision of this policy and called upon the Zionist movement to set as its unequivocal objective the immediate establishment of a sovereign "Jewish State within its historic boundaries" and to prepare for the evacuation of the Jewish masses to the state. Ezel and the Herut movement emerged from the Revisionist organizations. Today Menahem Begin and Herut are the political and ideological practitioners of this faction that had, until recently, been at the periphery of the Zionist movement.

6. Chaim Weizmann (1874–1952), most prominent figure in the Zionist movement since the end of World War I. Weizmann was president of the World Zionist Organization, 1920–31, 1935–46, and the president of the State of Israel from 1949 until his death.

7. During this period fedayeen attacks on Israeli settlements were common, and Israel responded with reprisal raids. One was led by Meir Har-Zion and his friends, young men of Ein Harod and Deganyah Bet, who undertook a private revenge against a Bedouin whose men murdered Har-Zion's sister and her friend while they were on a trip to Petra. In 1953 and 1954, Unit 101 retaliated against two Jordanian villages, Kibiyah and Nahlin, whose inhabitants had committed acts of murder. Many civilians were killed in the raids. All these incidents aroused Israeli public opinion.

YAACOV HERZOG
23. The Background to the Sinai Campaign

Yaacov David Herzog (1921–72) was active at the highest levels of Zionist politics prior to the founding of the State of Israel and until his death. Under the British Mandatory government he was a member of the clandestine Jewish intelligence network in Palestine. After Israel was established he quickly became one of the most influential members of Israel's foreign policy–making elite and served as ambassador to Canada, assistant director general of the Ministry of Foreign Affairs in charge of economic affairs, and director general of the Office of the Prime Minister under Eshkol and Meir. He is the son of Rabbi Yizhak Halevi Herzog and the brother of Chaim Herzog. In the following interview published November 11, 1966, on the tenth anniversary of the second major war of the Arab-Israeli conflict, he discusses the background to the Sinai Campaign.

Following the Czech arms deal, Egypt instituted a blockade against Israeli shipping, confiscating Israeli ships in international waters and imprisoning Israeli sailors. Then, on July 27, 1956, Nasser nationalized the Suez Canal, canceling the Anglo-Egyptian agreement under which it was to be operated by Egypt. Britain and France vehemently opposed this step, and undertook a joint military venture to regain control of the canal.

Yaacov Herzog explains how and why Israel became involved in this operation. Most immediately, Israel was concerned about fedayeen attacks (see doc. 18), but the rise of Nasserism (see doc. 19) and Egypt's recent acquisition of large quantities of Soviet weapons convinced Ben-Gurion and Moshe Dayan, chief of staff, that a preemptive strike against Egypt was a necessity. Britain and France attacked Egyptian airfields and began moving their fleets in the Mediterranean toward Egypt. For Israel the Sinai Campaign (code name Operation Kad-

Source: Yaacov Herzog, *A People That Dwells Alone: Speeches and Writings of Yaacov Herzog*, ed. Misha Louvish (New York: Sanhedrin Press, 1975), pp. 229–36. Reprinted by permission of Pnina Herzog.

esh) lasted from October 29 to November 11, 1956. Israeli forces swept through the Sinai Peninsula and reached the Suez Canal. From Israel's standpoint, its three major goals— the eradication of the fedayeen bases in Gaza and Sinai border areas, the prevention of an Egyptian attack by the destruction of Sinai airfields, and the opening of the Gulf of Eilat to Israeli shipping—were all achieved. Pressure from the international community brought the joint operations to a halt in two weeks.

An important element in the background to the Sinai Campaign was the personal rivalry between Nasser and Prime Minister Nuri Sa'id, which reflected the national rivalry between Egypt and Iraq. The efforts to integrate Egypt into the Western defence system had failed. After the conclusion of the Baghdad Pact in 1955, Nasser went to Bandung. According to one account, it was Chou En-Lai[1] who advised Nasser at Bandung to approach the Soviet bloc for arms. In the summer of 1955, Dimitri Shepilov, then editor of *Pravda*, visited Cairo; he was followed by the Soviet Foreign Minister. And in December 1955, the Czech-Egyptian arms deal was signed.

Anyone who follows international developments can perceive that Nasser was already moving away from the West in the autumn of 1954, after the signature of the agreement for the evacuation of the Canal zone by the British forces. Nasser wanted American arms without an accompanying American military delegation, but, in keeping with their policy, the Americans insisted on a delegation going with their armaments, as they did with other countries in the Middle East. The Soviets, on the other hand, supplied Nasser with arms "unconditionally." With his approach to the Soviet bloc, Nasser began his political game. Although he had failed in every one of his external efforts in the Middle East (with Syria, Lebanon, Jordan, Iraq, Yemen, etc.), he succeeded in strengthening his international position by playing East and West against each other. At one and the same time, he convinced the West that if his regime fell it would be replaced by a Communist one, and the East that an extreme rightist regime would emerge from the ruins of his own.

In view of these developments, little importance should be attached to the Israeli raid on Gaza at the beginning of 1955, . . . despite the views of those, including some Israelis, who regard it as the main reason for Nasser's appeal for arms to the Soviet bloc [see doc. 18]. The Gaza raid may have somewhat stimulated the process, but it may be assumed that, even without it, Nasser would have made the same change in his policy.

If Nasser had only asked for defensive arms against Israel, the Americans would probably have been prepared to supply them. In fact, the United States was very eager to establish the Western defence system with a base in Egypt, or at least with her participation, and this aroused serious anxiety in Israel. Against the background of Nasser's inter-Arab activity and the international position he adopted for reasons that have no particular connection with Israel, Israel was the touchstone in the inter-Arab struggle. Each side wanted to prove that its international policy would serve Arab interests against Israel. The more Nasser denounced Nuri Sa'id as an agent of Western imperialism, the greater was Nuri's pressure on his partners in the Baghdad Pact— especially Britain and the United States—to reduce their support for Israel.

The Western attempt to establish a defence system in both the north and the south of the Middle East aroused the Soviet Union to look for a way to penetrate into the region. The Czech-Egyptian deal was signed as a counter-balance to the Baghdad Pact and a "prize" for Nasser's non-adhesion to the Western defence system, and not in order to give him arms superiority over Israel—although this was the inevitable result.

It is possible that Nasser aspired from the beginning to neutralism as he understood it, a fact that was not perceived in 1953–54 by the Americans, who had great hopes for him. This trend facilitated the growth of Indian influence, especially in view of the establishment of the Baghdad Pact. Nehru's[2] influence was considerable at the time and the Indian Ambassador in Cairo influenced Nasser to adopt the neutralist position in the inter-bloc struggle.

On the Israeli side, a main feature of the background to the Sinai Campaign was concern at any strengthening of Egypt, whether by plans that did not come to fruition—such as MEDO (Middle East Defence Organization) and Dulles' plan to base the Western defence system on Egypt—or though the Czech arms deal. Foreign Minister Moshe Sharett's journey to Geneva (where the first Summit Conference was taking place) at the end of 1955 was meant to bring home to the Powers the gravity of Israel's position as a result of the upsetting of the balance of forces. Later, Sharett and Eban (then Israeli Ambassador to the U.S.)[3] had talks in Washington with Dulles about the supply of arms—especially planes—to Israel. If the Secretary of State had responded to Israel's request in December 1955, it is highly possible that the Sinai Campaign would not have taken place. Ultimately, he agreed to arrange to have Israel supplied with planes by other countries.

Why was U.S. action in this regard delayed for several months more? Sharett believed that the Kinneret Operation at the end of 1956 was the reason. (On 11 December 1956 Israeli forces attacked Syrian army posts east of Lake Kinneret, from which Israeli farmers and fishermen had been harrassed.) True, the operation did not make Washington's efforts any easier, but there can be no certainty on this subject. In the U.S. State Department there was a conflict between various evaluations. Some took the Czech arms deal as proof that Nasser had fallen victim to Soviet influence, while others—headed by Henry Byroade, the American Ambassador in Cairo—argued that the deal was a one-time event and that Nasser had made it in despair. Byroade claimed that Nasser could still be saved from Soviet influence.

In November 1955, shortly before the Geneva Summit Conference, Dulles summoned Byroade and the late Edward Lawson, then U.S. Ambassador in Israel, to Paris. He agreed to wait six months to test Byroade's view that Nasser could still be won over for the West. As part of the effort to repair relations with Egypt, negotiations continued during the following months for American aid for the building of the Aswan Dam. Dulles did not believe that Israel was in any immediate danger. He apparently thought that from Israel's point of view action on aircraft supply could be put off, thus avoiding a step that might have interfered with the process of testing relations with Nasser. At the same time, Washington did not give up the hope, which it had cherished since 1954, that somehow or other it would be possible to prevent a deterioration on the Egyptian-Israeli borders and perhaps to improve relations between Cairo and Jerusalem. In fact, during the first few months of 1956 there was some American activity to this end. President Eisenhower sent a special envoy to the area, who met several times with Ben-Gurion and Sharett in Jerusalem and Nasser in Cairo [see doc. 24].

During the critical period of early 1956, the United States was thus operating on three levels at one and the same time: examining the possibilities of improving her diplomatic relations with Egypt, including continued talks on an American grant for the building of the Aswan Dam; attempting to persuade Israel that she was in no immediate danger, while promising to work for the satisfaction of her immediate requirements in aircraft through France and Canada, but without taking energetic steps to speed up these supplies; and a last and supreme effort to find out whether it was possible, despite the growing tension, to arrive at a reconciliation between Egypt and Israel. If I am not mistaken, the question of the agreements for the supply of planes from France and Canada—twenty-four Mysteres (for which American approval was necessary) from the former and twenty-four F84s from the latter—was on the way to settlement between March and May 1956. During the same period it became clear that there was no hope of an improvement in Cairo's attitude to Israel.

In July 1956, two successive crises broke out: the first over the Aswan Dam and the second over the Suez Canal. Various accounts have been published of the reasons for America's ultimate withdrawal from the Aswan project. According to one version, it was doubtful whether Congress was prepared to budget the enormous sum required; according to another, the United States found out that the Egyptian Government was conducting parallel negotiations with the Soviet Union to finance the dam. In any case, it may be assumed that by this time Washington had come to the conclusion that Ambassador Byroade had been mistaken in his evaluation of the situation. During that summer, tension in Israel grew. In the face of the threat to our security, France agreed (after negotiations in which Shimon Peres, then Director-General of the Ministry of Defence, played a major role) to supply Israel with arms [see doc. 20]. The nationalization of the Suez Canal and the failure of the efforts to reach a political settlement that would satisfy France and Britain intensified the crisis in relations between these two countries and Egypt.

Israel felt that she was engaged in a race with time. The operations of the fedayeen (terrorists based in Egypt, Gaza and Jordan who raided Israeli territory) intensified and there was growing concern at the unknown dimensions of Egyptian power and the pace at which new Soviet arms were being absorbed by the Egyptian Army. In addition, the situation deteriorated in Jordan: on the one hand, pro-Naserist forces were attempting to overthrow Hussein's regime and, on the other hand, the Iraqi Army stood ready to enter the country. In October, pro-Naserist elements gained a majority in the Jordanian parliament, and the unification of the Egyptian, Jordanian and Syrian armies under Egyptian command was proclaimed. Jordanian-Israeli relations were extremely tense, and Britain warned Israel against any military action in case of the entry of Iraqi forces into Jordan. It was clear in Jerusalem, however, that the real focus was in Cairo.

The Sinai Campaign, which began on 29 October, and the accompanying events were no mere episode. They were of historic significance for Israel, the Middle East and the world as a whole. From Israel's point of view, the campaign led to a fundamental change in her regional and world position, as well as in political and military thinking both in Israel and in the Arab States. For the Middle East as a whole, the campaign strengthened the trend towards greater independence of the countries of the region as against the doctrine of Nasserist hegemony under the mask of Arab unity. For the Great Powers, the campaign emphasized the consequences of a local outbreak in the Middle East for the relations between them. From the international point of view, the events of 1956 were followed by a transformation in the system of external influences over the area.

In the United Nations, 1956 marked the beginning of the appearance of the Afro-Asian bloc, which was then relatively small, as a force of great international importance. In the maelstrom of the 1956 crisis, the United Nations international police force (United Nations Emergency Force),[4] which has since played its part in foci of international tension in Africa and elsewhere, was born.

The direct results of the Sinai Campaign—the crushing of the threatening Egyptian force, the stoppage of fedayeen activities and the opening of the Straits of Tiran to free navigation—were perceptible immediately, but in the course of the years it transpired that the campaign also had demonstrated that Israel is a permanent factor in the Middle East. This recognition has since struck roots in the international consciousness and has also begun to penetrate the Arab consciousness. At the end of the War of Independence, it was believed that the armistice agreements would be a preface to peace in a few years, but it became clear that Arab hostility had not only not declined, but was steadily growing, and peace was still far away. Israel suffered from isolation and discrimination. In the various proposals for international military arrangements in the region, there was no place for her. She found it difficult to get defensive arms in face of the growing threats from the Arab countries. From the international point of view, the solution to the Israel-Arab problem appeared to involve concessions by Israel, including border revisions to which Israel could on no account agree. In the eyes of the Powers, Israel was regarded, in a way, as a nuisance.

The Sinai Campaign was a turning-point in the relations between Israel and the Powers. When, a few months later, the Eisenhower Doctrine[5] for the Middle East was enunciated, Israel was recognized equally with the Arab countries. Until a few months before the Sinai Campaign, the tripartite declaration by the Powers, issued in 1950, calling for the maintenance of the balance of forces in the Middle East, was still on record, but it was never carried out in practice. Before the campaign, the arms embargo was broken in regard to France. During the succeeding years, diplomatic struggles were needed to ensure the opening of significant sources of arms in other Western countries. Today it is generally agreed that a careful balance of forces is the most effective guarantee against war in the region. Without such a balance, Israel is liable, whenever the Arabs received large quantities of arms, to find it necessary to take action in self-defence. Since the Sinai Campaign, the voices that called for Israeli territorial concessions have died down.

True, the Israeli Army returned to the armistice lines, but since its return it has made them permanent, and none of the Western Powers has expressed any reservations regarding them.

It is also true that the Sinai Campaign exacerbated the relations between Israel and the Soviet Union, but against the background of Soviet activity in the region, which was then in its earliest stages, it is doubtful whether the relations would have improved very much even had the campaign never taken place. Today, ten years later, it appears that it is not the memory of the campaign that is the major reason for the lack of progress in improving relations between Israel and the Great Powers.

It is a fact that since 1956 Israel's relations with the non-Arab countries in and around the Middle East have improved. It seems that the campaign has been followed by a growing recognition in these countries that Israel is strong and her position in the area is firm. Against the background of the serious clash in the United Nations between Israel and the Afro-Asian bloc, many were anxious lest the campaign and the charges that were flung against Israel might in the future raise a barrier between ourselves and the peoples of Africa and Asia, many of which were then on the threshold of independence. In reality, the African and Asian peoples were not influenced for long by Arab propaganda about Israel's motives in the Sinai Campaign. Friendship and real understanding between them and Israel continued to develop and was strengthened on the practical plane by the opening of the sea routes from Israel to these two continents.

Most critical of Israel's moral position in connection with the campaign was the Government of India, and for many years Prime Minister Nehru continued to rebuke Israel for her reaction. He saw the campaign against the background of his fundamental prejudice, regarding Israel as a foreign body in the region, and even without the campaign it is doubtful whether his attitude would have been any different.

According to Zionist political thinking during the decades preceding the establishment of Israel's independence, Arab hostility to the Zionist enterprise was not fundamental, but was the consequence of Arab social structure, local interests, a temporary failure to understand the Zionist contribution to the progress of the entire area and continual mischief-making by external factors. A historian who studies the history of the Zionist effort may reach the conclusion that a more accurate and comprehensive perception by the Jews and world public opinion might have made greater difficulties for the realization of the Zionist idea.

In any case, it is very doubtful whether many people could have foreseen in 1947 that, after almost twenty years, Israel-Arab relations would be as they are today. With the signature of the armistice agreements it was believed that peace was around the corner, though this faith was gradually undermined as the years went by. However, the alternative, the continuation of a prolonged state of war, was in such glaring contradiction to the original assumptions that it seems there were psychological barriers to its acceptance in Israeli consciousness.

From 1954 to 1965 there were, therefore, two schools of thought about the prospect of settlement with the Arabs. After the Sinai Campaign, out of a feeling of strength, it was easier to absorb the idea that we should have to stand firm for many years to come with our deterrent force in the hope that historical processes would have their effect on Arab consciousness. It transpired that even the shattering of a threatening Arab military force does not necessarily mean peace. The hope, which was born after the military victory in the first week of the campaign, that we might get direct negotiations for peace in return for the evacuation of Sinai, was not realized. Nor were the Great Powers ready to sacrifice world interests on the altar of Israeli-Arab relations. Israel, therefore, adapted herself to the thought that peace would be the result of a slow and gradual process, which must be carefully watched and stimulated whenever possible. In the meantime, Israel must protect her security and prevent war by strengthening her deterrent force.

Arab hostility to Israel is founded on a failure to understand the true nature of Israel and the spiritual and historical roots that bind the Jewish people for all eternity to its homeland. Just as the Jews did not understand the Muslims, so they did not understand us. This lack of understanding still dominates Arab consciousness, but Arab thinking today is not the same as it was ten years ago. The change was emphasized after the Summit Conference [see doc. 42], which was convened in 1964 under the same banner of hostility that was brandished in 1948 and in the framework of the same crude thinking that called for the immediate crushing of Israel by force. If this were so at the beginning of the Summit Conference, however, three main trends were apparent in Arab thinking during the course of it. The first trend, for which Syria was the spokesman, called for the launching of war against Israel without delay and with no concern to the relations between the forces. This trend recalled the Arab thinking that was dominant to the eve of Israel's independence and that was revived during the years 1954–56. The second trend, which was expressed by Nasser, might be called "Arab Zionism." It called upon the Arabs to continue to cherish the ardent conviction that Israel is a foreign growth in the area. In order to uproot her, the Arab world must first achieve unity, strengthen its military forces, improve the international position of the Arab countries and consolidate the Arab economics. In the course of time, all these endeavours would endow the Arab countries with superiority over Israel and at the same time tighten the siege against her. Time and logic would inevitably have their effect. This trend, then, calls for patience and the long view. The third trend is publicly represented by President [Habib] Bourguiba of Tunisia. It argues that the Arabs have lost the opportunity to solve the problem of Israel by war. Hence they must try to realize their claims, or part of them, by negotiations and international pressure. (The Tunisian President's ultimate goal is still wrapped in obscurity.)

We cannot exclude the possibility that the changes and differences in the Arab approach during the past few years are ultimately due to the shock caused by the Sinai Campaign. The campaign proved that there was no basis for oversimplified Arab thinking about the prospect of overwhelming Israel by force, which reigned previously. The fruitless efforts to achieve Arab unity and Nasser's attempt to dominate the Arab world continued, in stages, also after the Sinai Campaign. The fact that the other countries did not rush to give Egypt military aid during the campaign did not remain without effect on the Arab consciousness. Though this cannot be stated with certainty, it may be assumed that the shattering of the legend of Egyptian power dwarfed Nasser's image to some extent in the eyes of the masses, at least outside Egypt, and released the other Arab rulers from the complex of Nasser's exclusive supremacy in the region. It is possible, therefore, that the Sinai Campaign made an important contribution to the inculcation of the principle that the Middle East is a pluralistic region, in which there is room for various peoples, each with its own political character and its sovereign independence.

The events of 1956 also shook international public opinion. Rightly or wrongly, the conviction grew that the grave tension among the Middle East countries involved the danger of an international conflagration.

There is the impression that the Powers are interested in preventing a major outbreak in the region: but if there is some contradiction between the desire to prevent war and the Powers' acts of commission or omission that lead to an increase in tension, it is due to the fact that the Powers are more influenced by global considerations than by the interests of the peoples in the region.

In 1956, the United States took vigorous action to stop the fighting. In the political struggle that followed, it pressed relentlessly for the evacuation of the Israeli forces from Sinai, thus perhaps saving Nasser's regime. This intervention not only aroused among Americans the feeling that perhaps the United States had not given fair consideration to Israel's situation before the campaign, but also led to the conclusion that, just as America had not allowed Nasser's regime to be overthrown by force, so it should not allow Nasser to overthrow other regimes by force. Only a year and a half after the events of 1956, American marines landed in Lebanon to protect Camille Chamoun's[6] regime against pro-Nasserist forces, and British troops, with American encouragement, were sent to Jordan to save Hussein's regime from Nasserist subversion. Anyone who was intimately familiar with the situation in the Middle East during the period before the Sinai Campaign will find it difficult to imagine any such American action at that time. This development was not only a paradoxical result of 1956; it also symbolized the appearance of the United States as the major Western factor in the Middle East.

NOTES

1. Chou En-Lai (1898–1976), first prime minister of the People's Republic of China, from 1949 until his death. Chou was also minister of foreign affairs. He played a major role in the Bandung Conference and in early efforts to promote Third World interests, especially opposition to the two great powers, the United States and the Soviet Union.

2. Jawaharlal Nehru (1889–1964), prime minister of India, 1957–64, and a leader of the Bandung Conference. Nehru was a leading advocate of Third World neutralism. As India's minister of defense, 1953–57, he supported the withdrawal of Western troops from Suez in 1956.

3. Abba Eban (b. 1915), member of Israel's foreign policy–making elite from 1948 to 1974.

Eban was deputy prime minister, 1964–65, and foreign minister, 1966–74. From 1950 to 1959 he served as ambassador to the United States and chief Israeli delegate to the United Nations. He was a member of Mapai and then of the Labor party.

4. United Nations Emergency Force (UNEF), U.N. military force established in late 1956 and early 1957 to promote a rapid withdrawal of English, French, and Israeli troops from the Sinai Peninsula and Gaza. The UNEF remained a buffer between Israel and Egypt until Nasser requested its removal in 1967.

5. Eisenhower Doctrine, U.S. policy statement on the Middle East issued by President Eisenhower on January 5, 1957. It granted military and economic assistance to Middle Eastern states requesting aid and promised the use of U.S. military forces to protect the territorial integrity of any state threatened by communist aggression (see doc. 37).

6. Camille Chamoun (b. 1900), Christian president of Lebanon, 1952–58, and leader of the National Liberal party. In the 1950s Chamoun advocated close relations with the United States. His attempt to run for another term in 1958 was one of the precipitants of U.S. military intervention in Lebanon that year. Today he opposes Syria's presence in Lebanon, and his party and forces have a secondary role within Lebanon's Christian community.

YAACOV HERZOG
24. The Anderson Mission

The exacerbation of tensions between Israel and the Arab states, especially Egypt, and the growing estrangement of Egypt, prompted President Eisenhower to send Robert Anderson, secretary of the treasury, on a mission to Egypt and Israel. Anderson visited both countries twice in January 1956 and once at the beginning of March. At his first meeting in Jerusalem he met with Prime Minister David Ben-Gurion, Foreign Minister Moshe Sharett, and their two aides, Teddy Kollek, director general of the Prime Minister's Office, and Yaacov Herzog, director of the United States Division of the Foreign Ministry.

From the historical perspective of over a decade later, Herzog recalled this mission and its relationship to U.S. and Soviet diplomacy in the Middle East. His reflections in the following interview provide his analysis of how the events of this period became a critical turning point for Israel in Middle East and global arenas.

My impression at the time—and it is not contradicted by anything I have learned since—was that the mission was doomed to failure from the beginning. It came a year and a quarter after the beginning of the deterioration in the relations between the Egyptian revolutionary regime and Israel. At that time, Nasser was starting his efforts to undermine Arab regimes that, in his view, were anti-revolutionary and pro-Western, and he appeared to be advancing towards the realization of his dream of Egyptian hegemony throughout the Middle East. At the same period, Nasser also embarked on his policy of "neutrality" leaning to the Soviet Union, and, after the Czech-Egyptian arms deal of September 1955, extensive Soviet arms supplies began to flow into Egypt.

Source: Yaacov Herzog, A People That Dwells Alone: Speeches and Writings of Yaacov Herzog, ed. Misha Louvish (New York: Sanhedrin Press, 1975), pp. 237–42. Reprinted by permission of Pnina Herzog.

His first aim was absolutely fundamental to the Egyptian revolutionary outlook on the place of the Land of the Nile in the Arab world. Nasser's attitude towards the Cold War—the chilly winds of which had started to blow in our region before the Egyptian revolution—was either the result of his world outlook, a reaction to the inclusion of Baghdad in a Western defence treaty (in January 1955), or an expression of his quest for status, prestige and the international and regional advantages involved in manoeuvring between the two blocs. Possibly a combination of all these considerations made up Nasser's motives.

From 1953 (when the American Secretary of State, John Foster Dulles, visited the area) until the beginning of 1955, the United States hoped to base a Western defence treaty on Egypt, and it was this consideration that led it to press Britain to respond to the Egyptian revolutionary regime's demand for the withdrawal of the British forces from the Suez Canal zone. When America despaired of this possibility, she started to work for the "Northern Tier" treaty, in which she included Baghdad in response to the demands of the British. The Soviet Union wanted to outflank the Baghdad Treaty by jumping over the Northern Tier into our region. It met with a response from Nasser, who had already started to draw inspiration from the neutralist policies of Nehru and Tito[1] and saw himself as a potential partner in the leadership of the "non-identified" world bloc. The feelers between the Soviet Union and Egypt over the arms deal started, apparently, in the spring of 1955 at the Bandung Conference, with Chou En-Lai—strangely enough—as the go-between. In September 1955 the Czech-Egyptian deal was born, opening a new chapter in the history of the Middle East. Into this new situation President Eisenhower's emissary made his entry at the beginning of 1956.

The struggle between pan-Arabism, or Arab unity under Nasser's leadership, and the independence of the Arab states, became intertwined with the Cold War, each struggle influencing the other, with the focal points of the combined struggle at Baghdad on the one side and Cairo on the other. An outstanding example of the combination of the two tensions was the violent outbreak in Jordan in November 1955, when the visit of the British Chief of the General Imperial Staff, who came to discuss the inclusion of Jordan in the Baghdad Pact, ended in failure. Five months later, early in 1956, Glubb Pasha, the British Commander of the Jordanian Arab Legion, was dismissed.

While he was still struggling for supremacy in the Arab world as the chief spokesman and leading representative of the region on the international scene, it is difficult to see how Nasser could have let go of the Israel-Arab problem, even had he so wished, especially as the problem was connected with the two other struggles in the Arab world. Nor are there any grounds for the assumption that at the time of the mission, at the beginning of 1956, he really had any such intention. Had he wished, even without taking the risk of direct contact with Israel, he could have discussed proposals for a settlement in the region as put forward by (John) Foster Dulles in the summer of 1955 and Anthony Eden, the British Prime Minister, in his Guildhall speech towards the end of that year. Both involved an Israeli withdrawal from part of the Negev to enable a direct link to be established between Egypt and Jordan. It seems, therefore, that even the political isolation of Israel was not so important in Nasser's eyes as his dream of subduing her by force. It is clear, at any rate, that the emissary himself, at the end of his mission, did not have the impression that there was any sense in continuing to attempt to arrive at a settlement, and his opinion was shared by his superiors in Washington. In any case, we have never heard any accusation that Israel was to blame for the failure of the mission.

Although the emissary concentrated on Egyptian-Israeli and Arab-Israeli relations during his discussion with us, it may be stated with confidence that with Nasser he also tried to clarify all the aspects of U.S.-Egyptian relations after the Czech-Egyptian deal. It was my impression that the emissary made no greater progress in this matter than he had in connection with an Israeli-Arab settlement. In any case, a few months after the end of the mission, the United States announced the withdrawal of her financial support for the building of the Aswan Dam and informed Egypt accordingly in quite an offensive fashion. Even on the limited question of border pacification, with which the emissary dealt, together with his quest for a fundamental settlement, he did not receive satisfactory replies from Nasser.

The Secretary-General of the United Nations[2] visited the Middle East during the same period and came again in April 1956 for the purpose of finding some arrangement, even a temporary one, to stop the killing on the borders. His attempt also ended in failure. The argument that Nasser repeated to various visitors, including the emissary, that it was very difficult for him to impose his authority on the fedayeen in the Gaza Strip, was proven baseless after the Sinai Campaign: between 1957 and 1967 he was perfectly capable of preventing the murderous infiltration.

To sum up, during that period Nasser was trying at one and the same time to undermine the pro-Western regimes in the region, to gain advantages from the Cold War in the Middle East and to appear as the standard-bearer of "the liberation of Palestine," first through the fedayeen and later by all-out war. When we come to analyse Nasser's attitude during his talks with the emissary, it should be remembered that at the time of the mission—from January to March 1956—Nasser still hoped to get American finance for the Aswan Dam project. He was apprehensive of the increasing influence of Nuri Sa'id, the Iraqi Prime Minister, through Western support. He also wanted to convince the United States that the Czech-Egyp-

tian deal, which had been born four months previously, did not mean that he was sliding into the Soviet sphere of influence. Nasser's policy was based on the desire to balance—if only in appearance—his relationships with the Great Powers.

His great success in this regard was the support he received from both the United States and the Soviet Union after the Sinai Campaign. The break came in the summer of 1958, when the U.S. Government landed marines in Lebanon, and Britain sent troops to Jordan to prevent Nasser from gaining control over both countries. From 1958 to 1960, Nasser was out of favour with Washington. But when Kennedy[3] became President, Nasser renewed his hopes to balance his relations with the Powers and indeed gained American recognition for the revolutionary government in Yemen. The failure to achieve a solution in Yemen over a period of five years again disturbed his relations with Washington, though not completely. Even in our own period, the quest for balanced relations, if only outwardly, continues to be an element in Egyptian policy.

This is not the place for an extensive analysis of Nasser's place in the Israel-Arab dispute, but anyone who follows the course of events cannot escape the impression that he added to the conflict a new historic dimension in that it was his contention that so long as Israel existed there could be no complete success for Arab nationalism. During the entire period of Nasser's rule, some argued that he was the only man who was capable of making peace with Israel. This view has evaporated, I believe, since his death.

It was not only to the emissary, but to Western visitors in general, that Nasser alleged that the Gaza raid was the turning-point in the prospects of a settlement with Israel and even hinted that this was what compelled him to appeal for arms to the Soviet Union in order to wipe out the stain on the honour of the Egyptian Army. This story gained currency in the Western literature of the period. Without belittling the shock that the operation caused to the Egyptian Army, and without analysing the political situation at the time, it is difficult to regard this argument of Nasser's as sincere. Nasser was a master of calculated moves. He was perfectly capable of restraining his emotions and refraining from changes in basic policy under the impact of emotional impulse (until May 1967). His numerous failures were due rather to mistaken evaluation of the effectiveness of his military strength than to lack of planning and cold calculation. It is hardly conceivable that because of the Gaza raid—which the Egyptian people did not even hear about—he decided overnight to change Egyptian policy if, indeed, he sincerely wanted a settlement with Israel (especially as the Israeli-Egyptian border had already been in a ferment for many months). Moreover, in considering his allegation that it was the Gaza raid that drove him to contact the Soviet Union, it is impossible to ignore the fact that the same month in which the raid took place also saw the signature of the Baghdad Pact which Nasser regarded as a fundamental Western challenge to the prospects of his leadership in the Middle East. The rivalry between Egypt and the Northern Tier countries over the fate of the Middle East goes back to the beginning of its history.

The Arab world at the time was convinced of two fundamental axioms: that time was on their side and that Israel's doom would be sealed in a much shorter period than that of the Crusaders. Moreover, many of the world's capitals had grave doubts about the long-term survival of Israel. In my opinion, the Arab world lived on this plane of thought until after the shock it received in the Six Day War. True, the axiom has not been abandoned, but it is burdened with doubts, which have even been uttered in public by Arab spokesmen. In 1956 no Arab leader dared use the name of Israel expressly in public. It was as if Israel were a leper among nations, or some kind of nightmare that would soon vanish. To talk of peace with Israel was certainly impossible, if only

for emotional reasons; and, with the exception of a remark by President Bourguiba of Tunisia, this situation continued until 1967.

In 1956 Israel was faced by a multi-dimensional siege: the attacks of the fedayeen; the Egyptian blockage of the Straits of Tiran and the Suez Canal; Egypt's military preparations for war; the West's wholehearted support for part of the Arab world and the Soviet Union's for the other part, with no one favouring Israel; the danger of Nasserism gaining control over the Middle East; the American and British plans for a settlement, which would have weakened Israel's prospects of independent survival and, above all, the lack of response to Israel's desperate requests for defensive arms. In 1955 and 1956 Israel felt more isolated than at any other period since the establishment of her independence. Without underestimating the dangers of today, it is hard to see how anyone can argue that time has worked to Israel's disadvantage. Despite the more extensive Russian support, the Arabs themselves are not sure that time has been and still is on their side. Our great challenge today is to protect our security while seeking every crack in Arab consciousness that may lead to peace.

At the beginning of 1956, Washington believed—or wanted to believe—that there was still some possibility of an Israeli-Egyptian settlement. Not only had Jerusalem stopped believing in such a possibility at that stage, but it was afraid that the pursuit of a settlement would have only one result: namely, a prolonged delay in meeting Israel's urgent demand for defensive arms. On the one hand the emissary was busy for a few months shuttling between Cairo and Jerusalem. On the other, the hands of the clock moved on: the Czech arms were being absorbed into the Egyptian Army, and the threat of an unannounced air attack on Israel's cities cast a lengthening shadow. The late Moshe Sharett, then Foreign Minister, believed that but for the Kinneret Operation, which was carried out in December when he himself was in Washington for talks on the supply of arms, our request would have met with a positive response at the time. I believe there was no solid basis for this view, though the operation undoubtedly served as an excuse for delay. For fear of injuring her position in the Middle East, the United States did not want to become a supplier of arms to Israel, but after the failure of the 1956 mission she tried, for lack of any alternative, to help us get arms from Canada and France. Her efforts in this direction were not totally effective; in a few months we concluded an extensive arms agreement directly with France.

If the United States had responded in time to our demands, the history of the Middle East might have been different. In the course of time, it appears that the lesson that Israel must not be left defenceless—both for fear that she might be driven to take desperate action and because her deterrent power is a central factor in the prevention of war— began to make an impression on the American consciousness. The process was gradual and passed through several stages. The principle won full recognition in President Johnson's[4] public statement in 1968 about America's responsibility for the preservation of the balance of forces in the region, and the measures that President Nixon[5] took with this end in view.

The mission of the U.S. President's emissary to Jerusalem and Cairo between January and March 1956 was indeed one of the most unsuccessful attempts to break the fifty-year deadlock in Arab-Israeli relations, but I believe the historian will have to designate it as one of the central events and turning-points in the development of the Middle East in our time.

NOTES

1. Joseph Broz Tito (1892–1980), prime minister of Yugoslavia 1945–53, and president from 1953 until his death. Tito was a leader of the Bandung Conference and an advocate of neutralism. Although he emerged as a leading European communist in the Yugoslavian underground during World War II, Tito pursued policies independent of Moscow.

2. Dag Hammarskjold (1905–61), Swedish diplomat who was secretary general of the United Nations, 1953–61. Hammarskjold won the 1961 Nobel Peace Prize posthumously for his long years of service to the United Nations.

3. John Fitzgerald Kennedy (1917–63), president of the United States, 1961–63. Kennedy was assassinated in November 1963.

4. Lyndon Baines Johnson (1908–73), president of the United States, 1963–69. As vice-president, Johnson assumed the presidency when Kennedy was assassinated. He was elected in 1964 and served during a turbulent period in U.S. history that saw domestic violence, the civil rights struggle, dissent over the War in Vietnam, and the June 1967 Arab-Israeli War.

5. Richard Milhous Nixon (b. 1913), president of the United States, 1969–73. Nixon resigned in disgrace in August 1974 following the Watergate scandal. Nixon had served as Eisenhower's vice-president, 1953–61.

WALTER EYTAN
25. Israel and the Jewish Diaspora

The establishment of a Jewish state inhabited by a small portion of the Jewish people created a complex relationship between Israel and the Jewish Diaspora. What did the creation of Jewish sovereignty mean for the public position of the major Jewish communities in the world? What were the repercussions on Jewish life and political Zionism in the Diaspora? How dependent was Israel on Jewish help from abroad? Was Israel to become the political and spiritual center of Jewish life? How were Israel's relations with the Diaspora to be regulated? These were just some of the questions that had to be answered. Even the use of the term Diaspora (*galut*) seemed to imply support of the central Zionist tenets of the "abnormality" of a Jewish people without a sovereign state and of the centrality of Israel to the Jewish people.

An Israeli outlook on these issues is presented through an article by Walter Eytan. Like many other leading Israeli diplomats, Eytan began his public career in the Political Department of the Jewish Agency. He was Israel's first director general of the Ministry of Foreign Affairs, a position he held until 1959.

It is a commonplace of our Foreign Service that every Envoy Extraordinary and Minister Plenipotentiary of Israel has a dual function. He is Minister Plenipotentiary to the country to which he is accredited—and Envoy Extraordinary to its Jews. This has come to be accepted generally—by other governments in the "free" world, by the Jews of the diaspora, and by everyone in Israel. It is, in fact, a natural enough situation. King George VI once startled the Chief Rabbi of the Commonwealth by mentioning to him, at a Buckingham Palace reception, that he had the day before received "your ambassador," meaning the ambassador of Israel in London.

In each country the foreign residents constitute what in their circles and in the diplomatic corps is known as a "colony." There is a French colony in Italy, a Swedish colony in Japan, a British colony in Peru. The Jewish community in many countries is seen by gentiles as the Israeli colony. In September 1955, at a climax of the Cyprus crisis, when Jewish property in Istanbul was plundered by anti-Greek rioters, the Turkish Government thought it perfectly natural to instruct its representative at Tel Aviv to express its regrets to the Government of Israel and to assure it that there existed in Turkey "no intention or inclination to prejudice in any way the security or the rights of the Jews of Turkey." The Swiss minister to Brazil once envied his Israeli colleague on the size of his colony; he himself had only 12,000 fellow countrymen—and there were ten times as many Jews.

These colonies can be extremely helpful to their country of origin, and it is one of the duties of every ambassador, minister and consul to keep in close touch with them. The Jews are exceptional, however, and nowhere form a colony in the accepted sense. Members of a Danish colony, for example, are Danish citizens or they may at most, if their own and the local laws allow it, have dual nationality—their Danish nationality of origin and the nationality of the country in which they reside and perhaps were born.

Source: Walter Eytan, *The First Ten Years: A Diplomatic History of Israel* (London: Weidenfeld and Nicolson, 1958), pp. 192–200. Reprinted by permission of Walter Eytan.

Jews in general do not have Israeli nationality; the only Israelis are those who are or have been domiciled in Israel—and the overwhelming majority of Jews in the world have never been to Israel even on a visit. Yet the ties which bind Jews everywhere to Israel are very strong, and Jewish communities abroad are often "colonies" in at least as real a sense as the Germans or Danes or Swiss. Israel does not claim their political allegiance. The Jews are citizens of their own countries, and the question of double loyalty does not arise. But they are bound to Israel by sentiment, and to some extent by self-interest. Exposed as they often are to discrimination, and in many countries fearful for their future, they have felt more secure since Israel came into existence. Just as Americans of Swedish, Irish, English or Italian origin have a "home country" in which they take a pride and an interest even after many generations, Jews all over the world can take a pride and an interest in Israel; and just as Irish Americans and Greek Americans support their "home country," its institutions and villages and their own families, so Jews support Israel, materially and morally.

When Herzl first gave the dream of Jewish independence political shape, he did so in a pamphlet entitled *Der Judenstaat*, "The State of the Jews." He did not call it *Der Jüdische Staat*, "The Jewish State." The difference may seem subtle, but it is real enough. Israel is not merely a state predominantly Jewish in the race, religion or way of life of its people. It is a state for all Jews. The principle was laid down in its Declaration of Independence [doc. 1] "The State of Israel will be open to the immigration of Jews from all countries of their dispersion." Legislative effect was given to this in the Law of Return [doc. 6], passed unanimously by the Knesset on July 5, 1950. Israel is the only country in the world which confers citizenship on an immigrant automatically at the moment he steps off the boat or plane. Every Jew knows that he can migrate to Israel whenever he feels like it. The gates are always open. At the same time, Israel places no Jew under compulsion to exercise this birthright of his. He is perfectly free, as far as Israel is concerned, to stay where he is. But inevitably a special relationship has sprung up between Israel and Jews everywhere who share the age-old attachment to the Land of Israel. Even if they are unwilling or unable to link their personal lives with it by coming as immigrants, they are animated by a powerful sentiment of solidarity and love. Mr. Ben-Gurion, in an Independence Day message in 1957, defined succinctly the links which join Israel and the Jews all over the world: "The unity of the Jewish people, its sense of common responsibility for its fate, its attachment to its spiritual heritage, and its love for the nation's ancient homeland, have become more and more intense as a result of the rise of the Third Commonwealth. The ingathering of Israel's exiled and scattered sons is the common task of all sections of the Jewish people wherever they may live. Everything that has been created in this country is the common possession of the Jews of all lands."

Few would quarrel with this definition; it reflects indisputable fact. But it has not been easy to adjust the relationship between Israel and the Jewish communities abroad, particularly in the United States. Before Israel attained political independence, a Jew could either be a Zionist or not. If he was, he believed in Jewish statehood as a political ideal and goal and did his best to help achieve it. If he was not, he would be either indifferent or hostile to the idea, believing it not worth striving for or incapable of realization or, in extreme cases, positively harmful. With the rise of Israel, there had to be a reorientation of attitudes and action. The Zionist's goal was achieved—what was there left for him to do? The non-Zionist and anti-Zionist found themselves faced with a fait accompli—Israel existed, whether they were interested or pleased or not, and they were forced to think again.

The adjustment of Jews outside Israel to the reality of Israel has not yet been completed. It is now less a problem of action than of ideas. It was not simply for the sake of talking that as late as August 1957 an "ideological conference" was called at Jerusalem and attended by Jewish leaders and thinkers from all over the world. There is genuine confusion, even distress. The classical concept of Jewish "exile" presents itself in a new form. In traditional Jewish thought, reflected in Mr. Ben-Gurion's Independence Day message, the Jewish people had been in exile since the destruction of the Second Commonwealth in the year 70. The concept of "exile" applied in some measure even to those who lived in Palestine, for they were living there under foreign rule. With the establishment of the Third Commonwealth, Israel, the exile came to an end—in the sense, at least, that there was again a Jewish state and that any Jew who wished to return to it was free to do so. It became natural to distinguish, if not always explicitly, between those Jews who were "at home" or "in their own country"—that is, in Israel as Israeli citizens—and those who continued to live "in exile," anywhere outside Israel. Instinctively, the majority of Jews accepted this distinction, though no undue stress was laid on it either in Israel or abroad; the essential unity of the Jewish people, in terms of race, tradition and faith, was too strong to brook differentiation along hard and fast lines of any kind.

An ideological crisis arose in the United States, however, where Jews resented any suggestion that they were living in "exile." America was their home, Americanism their creed, the American way of life their heritage. This denial of an American "exile" implied a break with almost two thousand years of Jewish thought and teaching. Israeli leaders, steeped in Jewish tradition, found it difficult to adjust themselves to the idea that America was excluded from the "exile," and they continued to think, and sometimes speak, in terms of two Jewish worlds—Israel and the rest. Each time such a thought found expression in speech there would be a protest from American Jewish leaders, deeply sympathetic though they were by nature

to Israel and her aspirations. In the end, a modus vivendi was achieved. The problem was aired exhaustively in June 1957, when a delegation of the American Jewish Committee, an influential "non-Zionist" group, visited Israel. After much discussion, Mr. Ben-Gurion, as Prime Minister of Israel, defined his position in terms which proved acceptable to the Committee's leaders:

While Israel is open for all Jews who desire or need to come and live in it . . . the State of Israel represents and speaks only on behalf of its own citizens and in no way represents or speaks on behalf of Jews of any other country. The attachment of Jews throughout the world to Israel is based on a joint spiritual and cultural heritage, and on a historical sentiment toward the land which was the birthplace of the Jewish people and of the Book, and which today as the Third Commonwealth of Israel enshrines the regeneration of a people in its ancient homeland and revival of its civilization. Jews throughout the world give expression to this attachment and dedication in various ways. But these, in whatever form they may be expressed, carry no political connotation whatsoever.

This was taken to mean that in Israel's official view American Jews were American citizens, no more and no less, and that they were not necessarily looked upon as children of Israel in exile. Anything they did to express their "attachment and dedication" to Israel, they did as Americans, and not as the detached limb of a foreign state.

Events have robbed the term "Zionism" of much of its original meaning and the old "Zionist movement" of much of its strength. Mr. Ben-Gurion, in his personal capacity, has in recent years made a point of declaring that he is not a Zionist—he is a Jew first, an Israeli second, and that is all. Jews who live outside Israel cannot, in his conception, be partners in Israel's cause, but only "helpers." His attitude has caused some resentment on the part of veteran Zionists who, having devoted their lives to this cause, find they can no longer claim a monopoly of support for Israel. All they can do, differently from others, is to take pride in having been right all along. Support for Israel is now universal among Jews everywhere, apart from a handful of eccentrics. (Here and there one may find a Jew who gives comfort to Abdul Nasser, propagandizing for him actively against Israel, impelled by a form of self-hate which borders on the abnormal.) The fact that so many "Zionists" continue to live in the diaspora has served to blur the distinction between them and other Jews; logic would dictate that Zionists come to Israel to live, but not everyone acts logically. For Israel it is important, indeed vital, that support for her be not confined to any single group. The Jews who in their thousands close their shops and line the streets of Buenos Aires cheering when the ambassador of Israel drives to the Casa Rosada [Brazilian president's house] to present his letters of credence may not all have been "Zionists" ten years ago, and the term "Zionist" hardly applies to them now. It is sufficient that today every single one of them takes a pride in Israel, glories in her achievements, worries when things go wrong for her and feels a personal obligation to do whatever he can, financially or otherwise, to help.

Israel has received massive financial support from the Jews of the diaspora. It came to be agreed that the Israeli taxpayer would bear all the normal burden of government expenditure, including defense, thus making Israel responsible for her own budget, like any other state. On the other hand, the costs of immigration would be borne primarily by the diaspora, which had a long tradition of succoring Jews and had for generations financed Jewish rescue and relief work and Jewish migration to every part of the world. In practice, the division of responsibility has worked out rather differently. Israel herself has had to carry an increasing share of the cost of immigration, and particularly of settlement and integration. At the same time, the diaspora has invested large sums in Israel, either directly in industrial enterprises and the like, or through successive bond issues launched in the United States and in countries of Latin America and Western Europe. These loans have gone a long way toward financing Israel's development budgets; the larger the income from them has been, the more Israel herself has been able to divert from development to defense and other urgent domestic needs.

The two-way relationship between Israel and the Jews of the world has a profound significance, politically, materially and morally. It takes up much of the time of all Israel's diplomatic representatives abroad, and most of the time of some. They do their best not to get involved in the internal controversies of local Jewish communities, but they cannot avoid being asked for advice or, when necessary, giving it. At all costs they must refrain from taking sides. In particular, they are careful not to interfere in matters at issue between the Jewish community and the government of the country in which they serve. A Jewish community will sometimes look to them for help of this kind, but it would clearly create an impossible position if the representative of Israel appeared as the protagonist of local Jews in dealings with their governments. Generally speaking, the limitations of an Israeli ambassador in this field are understood and respected, but the latitude he can allow himself in practice will vary. It has happened more than once that a government, on its own initiative, has discussed with the representative of Israel some problem concerning the local Jewish community. He will normally report to his own Government on important Jewish affairs, particularly when they may affect Israel's interests. He and his staff will be in demand as speakers at Jewish functions and will concern themselves with cultural and educational work. Jews planning investments in Israel will look to the embassy or legation for advice; others will have problems connected with Israeli relatives. All this, with the normal duties of diplomacy, leaves Israel's representatives little time for idling.

ARIE L. ELIAV
26. Israel and Soviet Jewry

Israel's relations with Diaspora Jewry have been particularly problematic regarding Jews in the Soviet Union. In the 1950s the estimated 3 million Soviet Jews constituted the world's second largest Jewish community (next to the United States). Even today, with an estimated 2–2.5 million Jews in the Soviet Union, only the United States and Israel have larger Jewish communities. On the one hand, the State of Israel has to deal with a hostile and anti-Semitic Soviet regime that is a major world power. On the other hand, Israel and world Jewry have a special concern for their brethren there who face various forms of discrimination and persecution. In this reading, Arie L. Eliav,[1] who served as first secretary in the Israeli embassy in Moscow from 1958 to 1960, offers both an analysis of the Jewish problem in the Soviet Union and a vivid description of the encounter between Soviet Jewry and an Israeli emissary.

It need not surprise us that dormant national feelings were aroused in many Soviet Jews, possibly stimulated at times by the government which allowed the Jewish Anti-Fascist Committee[2] to proceed with its propaganda. Further, the Soviet Jews interpreted their government's support of the Jews of Israel and its favorable vote at the United Nations as permission to identify themselves more closely with Israel in its fight for existence. It must also be remembered that many tens of thousands of Jews, most of whom had been raised on Zionism and the Hebrew language, were added all at once to the population of Russia as a result of the annexations that took place after the war.[3]

All of this accounts for the rising tide of excitement among Soviet Jews in the years 1947–48. The crest of this excitement was reached during the spontaneous demonstration that took place near the Moscow synagogue (during Stalin's darkest days!) when thousands of Jews came to greet Golda Meir, the new Ambassador of Israel, and the "Hatikvah"[4] burst out from the throng, and the cry "The people of Israel is alive" echoed through the air. We know that some naive Jews even went so far as to petition the authorities to let them join the Israel Defense Forces as gunners, tank drivers, sailors, and pilots.

The dictator was made aware of these extraordinary events, and his dark suspicions were intensified. Now, after thirty years of communist rule, the regime had not succeeded in severing the Jews, spiritually and psychologically, from their ethnic and national roots and from the course of dramatic developments in the Jewish world outside the land of the Soviets. The dictator then decided that in order to put out the flame that had begun to blaze again from the dormant Jewish embers, he would have to extinguish their cultural and national feelings with "freezing water."

First, it was necessary to cut off all contact with Western Jewry. Those concerned had to be made aware that the maintenance of contacts would be regarded by the authorities as an act of conspiracy and espionage directed against the regime. This accounts

Source: Ben-Ami [Arie L. Eliav], *Between Hammer and Sickle* (New York: Signet Books, New American Library, 1969), pp. 33–40. Copyright © The Jewish Publication Society of America. Reprinted by permission.

for the numerous articles that appeared in the Soviet press on the subject of Zionism, the American Joint Distribution Committee, and other international Jewish organizations, all exposed as enemies of the Soviet Union. They were dubbed as agents of the imperialist powers and as the spearhead of the dark forces that were attempting to undermine the Soviet Union and destroy its foundations. But that was not enough. In order to make certain that such demonstrations of Jewish solidarity would not recur, it was imperative to drain the morass, called Jewish culture, which had bred the mosquitoes that generated the sudden fever which seized the Jews. It was necessary to dry up the mainsprings of Jewish culture—language, education, and literature—and leave its adherents absolutely naked and sterile, so that they could be taken in hand again and made into faithful citizens of the Soviet Union.

These decisions were quickly enforced in the manner and style typical of Stalin. All Yiddish schools were shut; the newspapers were discontinued; the few theaters still performing in Yiddish were closed and their personnel scattered; writers and poets were at first silenced, and then taken away. For in order to make doubly sure, Stalin had decided to have the flag bearers of the communist Jewish culture liquidated.

Many thousands of leading figures of the Jewish intelligentsia were thus arrested and deported to concentration camps. Many were leaders of the autonomous Jewish region of Birobidzhan;[5] others were theatrical people, journalists, authors, poets, active members of the Jewish Anti-Fascist Committee, or simply important Jews. The best of them were executed—Markish, Pfeffer, Bergelson, Der Nister, and a host of other gifted and capable personalities. They all paid with their lives for their only sin: the writing of stories and songs, some even praising the regime and the dictator, in a language that read from right to left.[6]

This insane treatment of Jews and their culture had a logical sequel. It was not enough to frighten the Jews away from maintaining any contact with their brethren or to block all the streams of their culture; they also had to be exposed to the eyes of all Soviet peoples as dangerous and obnoxious elements, as bearers of the sign of Cain. This explains the attacks against Jews as cosmopolitan parasites battening on the healthy Soviet society. This was only one step away from the next phase initiated by Stalin in the last months of his life: the staging of the "doctors' plot," as a result of which some of the leading physicians in the Soviet Union—all of them Jews—were charged with plotting the murder of top Soviet government officials [see doc. 17].

By dint of such logic Stalin sought to sterilize the Jews spiritually, to remove their fangs, and at the same time to prevent them from assimilating completely with the peoples of the Soviet Union—to make it difficult for them to disappear into the masses—for who knew what they might be capable of if they hid and became anonymous inside Soviet society. It was therefore seen to be essential to bar their way to complete assimilation and to prevent them from erasing the sign of Jewish nationality that was stamped on their identity cards. Stalin's Jewish policy during his last years may be characterized as cultural blood-letting. He created a shadow people who had no territory of their own, no culture or language, and no organization with which to identify themselves.

Thus the Jews of the Soviet Union were plunged into the seven years they describe as "the black years" (*die schvartse yoren*). You can still hear to this day, from Jews in every corner of the land and from every class of society, that had "the mustached fellow" (many do not dare breathe the name Stalin even today) lived and ruled a few more years, he would undoubtedly have followed this policy to the end. He intended to turn the trial of the doctors into a show trial to end all show trials, and then to start banishing thousands of Jews to forced labor in Siberia and to physical annihilation.

Stalin died and the people of the Soviet Union, especially the Jews, awoke from the long night of terror. After the initial shock, the Russian people hoped that the new rulers, especially Khrushchev,[7] who was the leading figure in the hierarchy, would bring about a change. And indeed "the great thaw" began. The stream did not always flow in one direction. It took a crooked course with sharp angles, and, at times, stopped and froze over. Nevertheless, hundreds of thousands were liberated from the concentration camps; the reputations of thousands, alive or dead, were rehabilitated. Whole peoples and regions were favored with rehabilitation, and the hand of death placed over their heads by Stalin was removed.

The Jews—individually, of course, for they did not have any representative organization or any organs of expression—began hoping secretly, within their own four walls, if not for deliverance or a miracle (they were too down-trodden and pessimistic to expect miracles), at least for a return to conditions that had prevailed before "the black years." They hoped that a school would be opened here or there; a few newspapers published; an occasional theater created; that some contact would be established with Jews outside Russia and with Israel; that they would, in short, be given an opportunity to identify themselves once again with their Jewish nationality. But nothing of the sort happened.

Khrushchev, who had inherited Stalin's scorched earth policy in relation to the Jewish problem, gave the Jews no sign or indication that they would be permitted to cultivate this burnt land, seed it, uncover new springs of spiritual life, irrigate it, and develop on it, once again, their language and culture. In the absence of such an indication, or, more accurately, in the presence of signs that clearly said, "Do not touch," the Jews of Russia did not dare, and still do not dare, to do a thing.

It is true that some Jewish singers are now touring the Soviet Union and are appearing at Yiddish concerts before packed halls. It is true that about half a dozen Yiddish books and pamphlets have appeared since Khrushchev's advent to power. It is true that two Yiddish periodicals (*Birobidzhaner Stern* and *Sovietish Heimland*) are now being published. We will deal further with the causes and motives behind these phenomena. We shall at this point merely state that these are not even oases in the wilderness, but only mirages toward which the thirsty person runs and finds nothing, while his soul dies all the more quickly from disillusion.

. . . While on the subject of the Jews of today who live as a nation in the Soviet Union, it must be emphasized that despite their lack of connection with their people's past, they managed to create a culture and value system of their own during the thirty to forty years they participated actively in Soviet society. They fought in the Second World War and shed their blood not only as the slaughtered victims of the Nazis and their followers but also as partisans fighting in the forests and as soldiers in all units of the Red Army. Even if one were to assume that the Soviet disregard of all the Russian Jewish history that occurred up to the Bolshevik revolution is "natural"—that history is officially looked upon as totally reactionary, growing out of an obscurantist religion and steeped in the narrow horizons of Zionism and nationalism—even so, what of the three generations of Jewish history that have taken place in the Soviet Union itself? Actually, according to the cruel logic of Stalin and his heirs, it was necessary to eradicate this history as well; it too was suspect. That is to say, it was not enough to shut down the Jewish schools, theaters, and periodicals, it must also never be mentioned that they even once existed. It was not enough to arrest and exile to the camps some of the bravest Jewish soldiers, it must also not even be acknowledged that they had once lived. Moreover, it must not be said openly that Jews perished as Jews at the front. Russians, Ukrainians, Latvians, Lithuanians, Belorussians, Moldavians, and others—all of them fell in the war against the fascist invaders as faithful sons of their respective peoples. Monuments were erected in their honor throughout the land. But let no mention ever be made of the Jews. Is it surprising that to this very day no memorial has been erected to the victims of Babi Yar, the slaughter field near Kiev, where eighty thousand Jews were liquidated all at one time?[8] And even now that the bold poem of Yevtushenko[9] has been heard, and in spite of it, Babi Yar remains desolate while residential buildings rise around it. Soon it will be blotted out. Western tourists may still nag the Intourist guides and ask where Babi Yar is, but the latter will evade the question. Only a taxi driver will perhaps take the determined tourist to the place of slaughter, and then will watch as he leaves the cab and stands in silence and sheds tears by the deserted and desolate spot.

And what of Fonar, the collective grave of Vilna's Jews? When the huge monument to the murdered thousands was erected, the Jews of Vilna engraved on it an epitaph written both in Russian and Yiddish. Shortly thereafter, the local authorities began urging the heads of the Vilna community to obliterate the Hebrew letters. When they refused, the authorities sent workmen who poured cement over the epitaph, then engraved on the monument a new inscription in Russian which does not indicate even by a word that the victims were Jews. This is only one step removed from defamation of the Jews and their share in the war: it is claimed that not only did the Jews fight poorly against the Nazi foe, they also tried to evade combat and fled from the front. Soviet Jews repeatedly confess, with pain and shame, that when they wear their medals, they are mocked with, "Did you buy these medals in the Tashkent market place?" These "medals of the Tashkent market place" are a taunting accusation that most Jews fled to Central Asia far away from the dangers of war, and there, in the bazaar, purchased the military medals and decorations which they now dare to wear on their chests.

I visited the city of Bobruisk in Belorussia. The Intourist people arranged a meeting with the mayor. I told him that his city is famous in my country, as some of the founders of the State of Israel were born and raised there. I mentioned the names of Berl Katznelson[10] ("a great labor leader"), David Shimonovich ("a great national poet in my country"), Kadish Luz ("the Speaker of our Parliament") and others. The mayor listened, even took down the names, without moving an eyelid. I asked how many Jews lived in Bobruisk. He answered: "There are Jews but we have no specific statistics." I asked if there was a synagogue in town. "No," he answered. "The Jews have no synagogue because they do not need one." Led by a guide who was no doubt a Jew, I visited the city museum. I went with him from room to room until we came to a display of pictures, drawings, and documents which illustrated the participation of the people of Bobruisk and its surroundings in the Second World War. In this entire display there was not a single word about the Jews. I remarked: "Both of us know there was once a large Jewish community here with a proud past; we both know that there were thousands of Jews among the soldiers and partisans who died here: and we know that several thousand Jews still live here. Why isn't any of this mentioned in the display?" The guide looked at me sadly (he himself limped on one leg as a result of war injuries) but said nothing.

Next day I visited a neighboring town and, together with an Israeli family, rowed across the famous Berezina River, which flows through the town, to the public beach on the opposite bank. When we came ashore, a man of about forty-five got out of the water. The upper part of his body was muscular, handsome, and athletic, but his legs were disfigured as a result of surgery and he waddled like a duck. He identified us at once as Israelis and in front of everyone fell on our necks, shouting: "Take me away with you, let me join the Israeli Army and die in its ranks. Look at me. I was wounded three times in battle and kept on fighting. I am now a building workman and I can hardly climb the scaffolding; and whenever the workmen taunt me about the Tashkent medals, the blood rises to my head and I hit anyone who says it, and get beaten in return. I have no more strength! Take me with you!" Other Jews who were nearby tried to pacify him because he was getting more and more excited as he went on. He pushed them aside and cried: "What have I to fear? From whom? Go to hell!" When he calmed down somewhat and we had moved on, the others said to me: "You have to forgive him. After everything that had happened to him, his young son was murdered, and he had a nervous breakdown."

This is what happened to the son. Handsome and very talented, he had succeeded in becoming a teacher and sports instructor in the city school. He was very much liked by his pupils. One day, some two years before, he went out of the school building to the main street and saw a policeman stop one of his pupils, a non-Jew, who was riding a bicycle, for a traffic offense. The young instructor went over and asked the policeman what was wrong. The latter answered rudely that it was none of his business and told him to leave. The teacher said that he wanted to go with them to the police station and testify to the boy's good character. The policeman told him to get out of there at once, and added a foul remark. As the teacher argued with him, the policeman suddenly cursed: "Dirty Jew!" Losing his temper, the instructor approached the policeman threateningly. The policeman took out his pistol and shot him dead on the spot. He was sentenced to two years in prison but was released a few months later for good behavior. "You must understand the father's feelings," said the Jews, "and overlook his outburst."

NOTES

1. Arie (Lyova) Eliav (b. 1921), Israeli political leader. After serving as first secretary in the Israeli embassy in Moscow, 1958–60, Eliav served as deputy minister of industry and commerce and of immigration and absorption and was appointed secretary general of the Labor party, 1969–71. After the June 1967 War, Eliav became increasingly critical of the Labor party and its leaders, particularly regarding policies toward the Arab population. He finally split from the Labor party and formed the Independent Socialists, which merged with other leftist groups in 1977 to form Shelli. In January 1979, when the Shelli electoral alignment became a unified party, Eliav resigned from the Knesset, where he had served for thirteen years.

2. Jewish Anti-Fascist Committee, organization established in 1941–42 as part of the war effort of the Soviet Bureau of Information. Its secretary wrote that the "basic activity of the . . . Committee was directed towards enlightening the Jewish popular masses in all countries about the great historical accomplishments with which Soviet reality is replete" (quoted in S. W. Baron, *The Russian Jew under Tsars and Soviets* [New York: Macmillan, 1978], p. 262). It was abolished in late 1948 after years of tension with Soviet authorities regarding its Zionist and nationalist tendencies. Many of its members were executed during and after its short life.

3. Baron (ibid., p. 251) estimates that the annexations following the Molotov-Ribbentrop Treaty in August 1939 increased the Jewish population from 3 million to 5 million. Many of these Jews were able to flee into the interior of Russia and so escape the Nazi genocide. This new Jewish population had not been subjected to a generation of communist attempts to destroy traditional cultural and religious institutions.

4. "Hatikvah" (lit., Hope), Israel's national anthem, written by Naftali Herz Imber and sung at early Zionist congresses. Historical developments have led to slight changes in wording from the original nineteenth-century text.

5. Birobidzhan, region in eastern Siberia designated by the Soviet Union in 1928 as an area for Jewish settlement and granted national autonomy in 1934. It reflects the ambivalence of early Soviet policy toward its Jewish minority. On the one hand, the Soviets encouraged the revival and

development of certain aspects of secular Yiddish culture; on the other, they tried to contain and isolate Jewish nationalism and solidarity. Birobidzhan, geographically remote from the historical areas of Jewish settlement and cultural life, attracted very few Jews and was unsuccessful.

6. In April 1949 five leading Yiddish writers—Peretz Markish (1895–1952), Itzik Pfeffer (1900–52), David Bergelson (1884–1952), Der Nister (pseud. of Pinkhes Kahanovich) (1884–1950), and Samuel Halkin (1897–1960)—were arrested. Bergelson was accused of pro-Israel tendencies, the charges against the others were vague. This was the beginning of a wave of arrests that culminated on August 12, 1952, when most of the Jewish writers were tried and executed in one day.

7. Nikita S. Khrushchev (1894–1971), Soviet premier, 1958–64. Following Stalin's death in March 1953, Khrushchev became the first secretary of the Communist party. He consolidated his power in 1958.

8. Babi Yar, ravine outside of Kiev where the Nazis murdered 33,771 Jews by lining them up before a mass grave and shooting them on September 29–30, 1941. Although all of the victims were Jewish, the Soviet-erected memorial at the site ignores this fact.

9. Yvgeny Yevtushenko (b. 1933), modern Soviet poet. As a young man in the early post-Stalin years, Yevtushenko wrote a poem, "Babi Yar," in which he criticized his countrymen for anti-Semitic tendencies, concluding that the true Russian is not anti-Semitic and desires to recognize Babi Yar as the grave of Jews.

10. Berl Katznelson (1887–1944), leader of the Socialist Zionist movement and one of the founders of the Histadrut. Katznelson was perhaps the most influential figure in the establishment of the central institutions of the Labor movement in Palestine.

II

1956–67
Domestic Issues

27. The Transition from Ben-Gurion to Eshkol

The Israeli political system and its constituent parties underwent considerable changes during the late 1950s and the first half of the 1960s. One major development was David Ben-Gurion's political decline. Aspects of this process—the antagonism between Ben-Gurion and his chosen successor Levi Eshkol, the conflict between "veterans" and "youngsters" within Mapai, Ben-Gurion's insistence on a thorough investigation of the 1954 Mishap (see docs. 11, 29)—are described in Teddy Kollek's autobiography and in the documents that follow.

Teddy Kollek is presently the mayor of Jerusalem. As director general of the Office of the Prime Minister, he was particularly well placed to observe the transition from Ben-Gurion to Eshkol.

On June 15, 1963, the Saturday night before Ben-Gurion resigned, I brought Golda [Meir] to Ben-Gurion's home. The conversation was about the German scientists in Egypt and other aspects of our relationship with Germany. I didn't think that Ben-Gurion would make the decision to resign that night, but I saw his despair at not being able to convince Golda about that matter. The conflict over the subject was probably so sharp because there was already a rift anyway, not because this particular problem was insurmountable. Their conversation didn't end with an explosion. It was more like an estrangement, an abyss in their thinking. Ben-Gurion did not accept the appraisal he was given on the matter. He didn't think the situation was dangerous, and he didn't believe the scientists—if, indeed, there were any—were working with the backing and approval of the German government. Ben-Gurion had met with Carlo Schmidt, the chairman of the German parliament and a key figure in the Social Democratic Party, who had always been a friend. When he came to Jerusalem bearing a message from Adenauer and swore there was no truth in the accusations, Ben-Gurion knew he could believe him. But a whole campaign had been organized by Ben-Gurion's adversaries through the Press Office. It included sending reporters all over the world to speak out against Germany and the scientists, and that made Ben-Gurion furious.

The morning following that meeting with Golda, Uri Lubrani[1] (who had temporarily replaced Yizhak Navon)[2] came into my office very alarmed and said Ben-Gurion was about to gather the party leadership and announce his resignation. I was dumbfounded. Of course, I knew Ben-Gurion was unhappy, but I hadn't thought he was actually planning to leave. During the day I tried to persuade him to reconsider—as did many others—but to no avail. He would not be moved from his decision.

Perhaps a great many people in Israel and all over the world, common citizens and statesmen alike, were relieved that the stubborn old man was leaving and now there would be an easier regime. They may have hoped that some badly needed young blood would be injected into Israeli politics. But being well acquainted with Eshkol and the group surrounding him, I knew this would not happen. Israel was losing a great leader, and there was no one to take his place. The next generation of leadership—Eshkol, Pin-

Source: Teddy Kollek, For Jerusalem: A Life, with Amos Kollek (London: Weidenfeld and Nicolson, 1978), pp. 152–61. Reprinted by permission of Weidenfeld and Nicolson.

has Sapir,[3] Zalman Aranne[4]—none of them "young blood," had no real understanding of what statehood was about. They still acted as though they were living in an enlarged shtetl[5] and dwelled on the old concepts they had brought with them from Eastern Europe. Perhaps if Ben-Gurion had stayed on for a few more years, the third generation—Dayan, Peres, and their contemporaries—politically more sophisticated men—would have taken over. But by the time that generation finally did take over, things had already become much worse.

I don't know to what extent the people in Israel realize even today that the battle Ben-Gurion fought over the Lavon Affair was for a principle no democracy can exist without. With all the attention focused on corruption now, I doubt that if a similar incident occurred it would be treated any differently. I am afraid that most of the people in this country have not yet grasped the importance of Ben-Gurion's stand. Basically, it is the same principle that I invoked in my long battle against what I call "Sapirism.". . .

Sapir had been director-general of the treasury, then minister of trade and industry, and later minister of finance and the Labor Party secretary, the two jobs which made him a tremendously powerful political figure. His last appointment was as chairman of the Jewish Agency. He was a big, tall, bald-headed man who looked a lot like Kojak.[6] I, on the whole, rather liked him. Furthermore, it is quite rightly said that there was practically no development town, no development scheme, no industry, and no institution of learning that Sapir had not been involved in and had not helped. No man got up earlier and worked harder or with more consistency and more devotion. He was indefatigable, and economic progress in Israel was his main concern. He was a great fund-raiser, and people had confidence in him.

It is very difficult to be critical now, so soon after he died in harness. But without analyzing the influence he had on the country, it will be impossible to understand many things that have happened here and even more difficult to repair them. For a long time even before his death, Sapir had been a controversial figure, and during the last few months of his life much of the disastrous economic situation and low morale was blamed on him. There were accusations against the "Sapir system" and the "Sapir Fund" and many other facets of the economy. My own relationship with Sapir was an ambivalent one. I had the greatest admiration for his work capacity and for his ability to cut through red tape, make quick decisions, and make them stick, so that his officials could not revoke them. But I did not feel this qualified him to set the direction for the workings of Israel's economy. And while Sapir's practical achievements were noteworthy, the legal, orderly, and moral basis of his transactions was regrettably lacking.

I criticized Sapir openly on various occasions, frequently in his presence. (I must say that this did not affect the personal relationship between us, and even when he was most occupied, I had free access to him.) My argument with Sapir was not personal; it was over the "Sapir system." He judged many matters not on their merits but by who had brought the problem before him and how it had been presented. Thus an important matter might be pushed aside because the "wrong" person advocated it; a poor policy may have found favor because it was advocated by someone who was close to Sapir and willing to call on him in his modest home and implant the idea over a glass of tea on a holiday afternoon. It was also a method by which Sapir personally made decisions on an ad hoc basis, and the Ministry of Commerce and Industry and the Ministry of Finance lacked clear guidelines and standards for dealing with big business. Thus industrialists had far more to gain by currying the favor of ministry officials, or of Sapir himself, than by trying to improve their production or cutting down on their labor costs. It was easier to make a profit this way than to work hard and achieve increased sales or lower costs.

This same attitude also led to some give and take in connection with the "Sapir Fund," which must inevitably have led to some abuses—though I was sure that as far as Sapir personally was concerned, it was absolutely aboveboard.

Sapir was linked with some unsavory incidents, although he himself was of the highest personal integrity. There is not a soul, not even among his most violent critics—most of whom have halted their criticism since his death—who believed that he stood to gain personally in these dealings. But that is not the point. The issue was not the man, but the system. And the system is not restricted to the minister himself.

Basically I always believed in approaching people to donate money for a specific educational or civic project. That would allow the donors to see the results of their generosity. Under Sapir, however, government officials dealt with people who were investing and building in Israel, so that the very same people were offering gifts and applying for certain concessions. When you combined donations and the Sapir method of conducting business, disaster was inevitable. It was impossible to establish priorities when the methods befitted the small-town leader who knew everybody's problem and could conduct business out of his waistcoat pocket. A minister of finance, even in a small country like Israel, must be a statesman.

As to Jerusalem, Sapir supported many of its institutions but not the city itself. Whenever I claimed that Jerusalem was not getting its share, he showed me long lists of industrial and educational institutions that had been showered with funds. He had no understanding of the fact that when you invest hundreds of millions of pounds in a university, for example, you also have to invest an appropriate amount at least in building the roads leading to it. The same surely is true about the new suburbs going up around the city and a parallel strengthening of the central city. We have not yet entirely overcome this negative tradition. It

was very difficult to fight Sapir, and it is astonishing that we did make progress in getting some governmental support, in spite of his attitude.

Perhaps the gravest danger of all, however, was not to recognize immediately after the Yom Kippur War that the time had come to bring home to the people the need to lower sharply our standard of living. Sapir saw the solution in going out and collecting more donations from the Jews all over the world, rather than in changing policy at home. I am perfectly convinced that in a few years' time nobody will be able to understand how we survived for years and years under Sapir's shortsighted economic dictatorship.

It was principles of this kind that played a major role in the Lavon Affair, the battle Ben-Gurion undertook and lost. When he resigned in June 1963, Levi Eshkol was Ben-Gurion's choice to succeed him, and naturally Ben-Gurion's friends wanted him to be successful. I had known Eshkol a long time and had worked closely with him while he was minister of finance. I usually called on him on Saturday mornings to discuss the affairs of the week and bring about some coordination between Ben-Gurion and his chief lieutenant in the Cabinet. We had many talks during the Lavon Affair. He felt that Ben-Gurion was exaggerating its importance but supported him because of a sense of loyalty that came naturally. He knew it would be tough for anyone to follow Ben-Gurion, and those of us inside the Prime Minister's Office tried hard to adjust to Eshkol and help him. Yizhak Navon, Ben-Gurion's personal secretary, had gone to Latin America on a mission when Ben-Gurion resigned. Uri Lubrani, who had been working on Arab affairs in the Prime Minister's Office, had temporarily replaced Navon and continued to act as Eshkol's private secretary during his first few weeks in office. But soon it became clear that Eshkol had to have people of his own choice.

Eshkol brought in some people recommended by Yaakov Arnon, the director-general of the Finance Ministry, and I remained with my vague and many-sided role as director-general of the Prime Minister's Office. But the whole style of things was completely different. As the months went by, Eshkol began to take a much greater interest in the details pouring into the Prime Minister's Office than Ben-Gurion ever had. His interest went beyond deciding on policy or principle; he intervened in the smallest decisions. Moreover, you might arrive at a decision with him and the next morning, having talked to someone else, he had changed his mind. Sometimes he even forgot to tell you so. Still, it was impossible to dislike Eshkol, and we remained on good personal terms for the rest of his life.

After he became prime minister, Eshkol remarried (he had been a widower). There were quite a few candidates, but Miriam [Zelikovitz] was the lucky one. It was a sudden marriage ceremony squeezed into an overburdened schedule, as Eshkol had become a very busy man. A rabbi was provided for the wedding on a few hours' notice. I remember that at the last moment Eshkol said jokingly, "Maybe we should postpone it?" He always hated making crucial decisions. "You'll have to decide one day," we said almost in unison. Finally, at eleven o'clock, it was decided to hold the wedding at noon. I rushed home, Tamar grabbed half a cake and a bottle of champagne, and we rushed off to what was a very small and pleasant wedding party at Eshkol's home. It became a happy marriage indeed.

Miriam had a strong influence on Eshkol, and I think she directed him on to the wrong course in his rift with Ben-Gurion. She apparently felt that Eshkol should assert himself and be a strong prime minister and that this was the only way he could demonstrate leadership to the country. It may have been a legitimate attitude on her part, but left to his own devices, Eshkol might have found ways to compromise with Ben-Gurion. Such accommodation might have lessened the tensions that eventually led to the split in Mapai, which had a long-term negative influence on Israel's affairs. Even though the party was reunited a few years later, the wound was not entirely healed. Sometimes a little stone on the tracks can derail a large train.

My final break with the Prime Minister's Office resulted mainly from the continuing argument about secret, absolutely personal reports from the head of Intelligence to the prime minister. Eshkol appointed Meir Amit, a former general and deputy chief of staff and an extremely intelligent and capable person, to head the Mossad.[7] I tried to persuade the prime minister to implement the Yadin-Sharef committee's recommendations by appointing a permanent liaison in the Prime Minister's Office.[8] I even wanted him to make this a condition of Amit's appointment. But Amit opposed the idea as not being in the tradition of the service, and Eshkol gave in.

I believed that this situation might one day cause disastrous results, as it had in the past. Although I had no direct connection or responsibility in this sphere, I did not want to remain in the Prime Minister's Office if the loose arrangements of the past were perpetuated. I finally decided to leave. Eshkol made several attempts to persuade me to stay (in general he didn't like upheavals), but I felt that my usefulness had come to an end.

Some time after the changeover from Ben-Gurion to Eshkol, I had a long conversation with Isaiah Berlin[9] on the difference between the two regimes. Isaiah tried to explain to me that it was time to bring the "heroic period" to a close. We could not go on demanding heroism from the people all the time, as Ben-Gurion did. The country should be able to relax a little, and whatever our personal feelings were, we should be happy that a shift toward relaxation had taken place. I tried to convince him that our roots were in many ways still very shallow, and another four years with Ben-Gurion as prime minister would have been tremendously advantageous. Now, many years later, I still believe that.

NOTES

1. Uri Lubrani (b. 1926), senior official in the Israeli Foreign Ministry and Prime Minister's Office since the early 1950s. Lubrani has served as head of the Eastern Europe Department; political secretary to the Prime Minister, 1952–53; adviser on Arab affairs, 1960–63; head of the Prime Minister's Office, 1963–65; ambassador to Ethiopia; and ambassador to Iran, 1973–78.

2. Yizhak Navon (b. 1921), president of Israel, 1978–83. During the course of his public and political career, Navon has served as a diplomat in the Israeli Foreign Ministry, Ben-Gurion's secretary, a member of the Knesset, and chairman of the Knesset's Committee on Foreign and Security Affairs. Navon joined Rafi when it split from Mapai and rejoined the Labor party when the factions reunited. In September 1982, following the Phalange massacre of Palestinians in the Sabra and Shatila neighborhoods in that part of Beirut under Israeli occupation, President Navon publicly called for the establishment of an Israeli Commission of Inquiry. Soon thereafter he announced that he would not seek a second term as president but would reenter Labor party politics. This aroused speculation, and hopes among many, that he would challenge Shimon Peres for leadership of the Labor party.

3. Pinhas Sapir (1909–75), leader of Mapai and the Labor party. When Eshkol became prime minister in 1963, Sapir inherited Eshkol's position as finance minister and was thus in charge of the country's economic policies. In addition, he domi- nated Mapai (and subsequently, but to a lesser extent, the Labor party) either formally as secretary general or by virtue of his actual power. Sapir died in 1975 while serving as head of the Jewish Agency.

4. Zalman Aranne (Aronowicz) (1899–1970), leader of Mapai and its secretary general, 1948–51. Aranne entered the cabinet for the first time in 1954 and twice served as minister of education and culture—1955–60, 1963–69.

5. Shtetl (Yiddish, small town), small, predominantly Jewish towns in which the majority of Eastern European Jews lived.

6. Kojak, shaved-headed hero of an American television program popular in Israel in the early 1970s.

7. Mossad, Israel's agency for intelligence and special operations.

8. Yadin-Sharef Committee, committee consisting of Yigael Yadin and Zeev Sharef appointed by Ben-Gurion to investigate lines of command and responsibility in Israel's intelligence services—the IDF's Intelligence Branch and the Mossad. The committee's report, recommending that a special adviser to the prime minister be appointed for intelligence affairs, was submitted in mid-1963, after Ben-Gurion had left office, and his successor, Levi Eshkol, did not take action.

9. Isaiah Berlin (b. 1909), noted British historian and philosopher who has been active in public life and Jewish affairs.

YOHANAN BADER
28. The Formation of a Center–Right-Wing Bloc

While the conflicts within Mapai contributed to the eventual weakening of the Labor parties, their historic rivals—the center and right-wing parties—were laying the groundwork for the formation of a center–right-wing bloc.

Yohanan Bader was a leader of the Herut movement and an active member of the Knesset for more than two decades. His memoirs are an indispensable source for the history of the Herut movement as well as

Source: Yohanan Bader, *Haknesset Veani* (The Knesset and I) (Jerusalem: Edanim, 1979), pp. 170–73. Reprinted by permission of Yohanan Bader.

Israeli parliamentary and political history in general. In this excerpt, Bader, a close associate of Menahem Begin, describes in detail the negotiations that led to the establishment of Gahal (the Herut-Liberal bloc) in 1965.

What was the matter with the Liberals, that they reacted negatively to Begin's attempt to establish a joint bloc in the Knesset in August 1961, and then in the beginning of 1965 they themselves suggested the establishment of Gahal?[1] One difference must have influenced the change: in the beginning of the Fifth Knesset they wanted to be accepted in the coalition, and in 1965 they awaited the outcome of the elections. But they also had additional reasons. At the time the Liberal party was established in 1961, the Progressives convinced the General Zionists that it would be necessary to invite some new forces into the partnership, and so they introduced into the list of candidates and into the Knesset list Baruch Uziel as a "new force," as well as Professor [Yizhak] Hans Klinghoffer and Mrs. Rachel Kagan who, according to their own outlook, were much closer to the Progressives than to the General Zionists. At the head of the list they placed Pinhas Rosen (and not [Perez, or Fritz] Bernstein), and he was elected head of the party after Dr. Nahum Goldmann examined the situation and found that his participation [in the election] would not secure for him the foreign portfolio in the government. Another Progressive was elected as head of the faction: Yizhar Harari. Thus the General Zionists became the secondary partner in the framework of the united party, quite in contrast to their relative strength among the supporters of the partnership.

The Progressives were not so happy either. It was to be expected that some Mapai followers would be in the coalition and candidates for any office that Mapai, for reasons of its own, preferred not to yield to its own members (e.g., Dr. Yeshayahu Foerder as director general of the Bank Leumi LeIsrael)[2]. And thus, because of the partnership with the General Zionists, they became a large, oversized faction. In this role they had to demand a high price for the coalition, but for Mapai the partnership of Ahdut Haavodah (eight Knesset members) was enough to assure them a majority in the Knesset. Both of the coalition partners complain about their bitter lot as the second largest opposition faction. They sense in this a constant frustration and debasement. And it is true that in the parliamentary system there really is no position less comfortable than to be a second opposition and to have to rehash in most of the debates the words of the spokesman of the first and large opposition.

And so, after Begin had once again called for the establishment of the Gush [bloc] in the convention of the Herut movement, the Liberals discussed it all over. Harari gave us a speech that was full of contempt. In his opinion the Herut movement was nearing bankruptcy. The public did not like it, on the other hand the chances of the Liberals were excellent. Only Bernstein and [Yosef] Serlin, who had opposed the Ihud [unification] in 1957, expressed their support for the establishment of the Gush.

Begin's proposal came for a vote and was turned down 42 to 8. Avraham Krinitzi, head of the Ramat Gan municipality, and his deputy Shalom Zisman, announced that they would continue to work for a partnership with us. I held lengthy and friendly sessions with Krinitzi, but without results.

After Mapai had decided to establish a common front (Maarakh)[3] with Ahdut Haavoda (in November 1964), Begin turned to the Liberals again, and this time the reaction of the erstwhile General Zionists was positive. Only Simhah Ehrlich[4] was bitterly opposed to a partnership with Begin and with Herut. The leadership of the Liberals decided (20 to 15) on their readiness in principle to ally themselves with us in the forthcoming elections. In this decision I found a confirmation of my suspicions that they were planning to enjoy the partnership with us in the elections but that they would, once the elections were over, prefer a coalition with Mapai. I warned Begin, but he was more optimistic than I. Moshe Kol,[5] Dr. Foerder and even Nahum Goldmann also participated in the internal arguments among the Liberals. All of them opposed the creation of a close tie; the General Zionists, on the other hand, met in the home of an American Zionist to establish the bloc. Actively participating in this meeting were Yosef Sapir, Dr. Elimelech Rimalt, Shalom Zisman, and Aryeh Dulzhin, all of them General Zionists, and also a number of former Progressives. In the meeting they decided to establish a bloc with us, and a joint faction in the coming Knesset. A number of important personalities in the Liberal party, such as the industrialists Dr. Mossberg, Kalir, and also Gershom Schocken (*Haarez*),[6] tried to salvage the unity of the party, but they did not succeed in convincing Pinhas Rosen to agree on the establishment of a bloc with the Herut movement.

At the end of January 1965, Krinitzi invited the leaders of the Liberals and us to his home. Of the Liberals, there appeared Yosef Sapir, Elimelech Rimalt, Aryeh Dulzhin, and Yosef Tamir; from our side Begin, [Aryeh] Ben-Eliezer, [Yosef] Shofman, [Nahum] Levin and myself, as well as the secretary of the faction, Yehiel Kadishai. We did not talk about problems of principle or the actual proposal; we knew that we had plenty of material on hand from the old negotiations in 1957–58 and that we would somehow be able to "arrange things." The Liberals proceeded at once to practical questions: they demanded that the list of candidates for the Knesset and the entire relationship between us be on a basis of parity, or fifty-fifty, because in this Knesset the number of seats was equal for each of the two parties. Begin and Ben-Eliezer replied to them: All of you here are only General Zionists, without so much as one Progres-

sive, and we know very well that you find yourselves on the threshold of a split in your party, and according to our information, only a small majority of the members of your faction will go with you, and how can we then agree to parity? They replied with absolute self-confidence—for which they deserve credit—that the General Zionists are the only serious force in their party, and that if the Progressives would split off, they would at most capture two seats in the Knesset. They did not convince us. We had no trouble remembering that at the time they were unified, the General Zionists had eight seats in the Knesset and the Progressives six, and on that basis they created their unified group (Ihud). The Liberals (one or two among those present) responded that the most important thing is to establish the bloc, but at the same time they demanded parity. I saw that we had arrived at a dead end, and I drafted for myself and read the text of a final proposition according to the system used by Mapai, namely point-counterpoint: they demand parity and we could not agree to that for good reasons. We all resolved to start negotiations about the establishment of a joint bloc. This summary was accepted (the slip of paper is still with Kadishai).

The negotiations were conducted at a speedy tempo. Only practical matters were discussed. In the beginning they met in my house: from our side Levin, Shofman, and myself; from their side Rimalt and Zvi Zimmerman. They spoke of parity and hinted at a small change in our favor. We want to know: How many will they be after the split? My associates and they even exchanged assessments about our mutual strength and about the chances in the elections. I notified Begin: There is no real progress.

We actually broke off contact. After a number of days, Aryeh Dulzhin appeared in the Knesset building to talk with me and then to Begin. They agreed among themselves that the negotiations should start again. Begin invited me to a discussion and brought up his own proposal. He agreed to distribute the first ten seats on the list according to parity, one for one—the first seat for us. He thought that six of the seats (21–26) [slot numbers on the party list] belonged entirely to us and that the rest of them should be distributed again on the basis of parity. Likewise we had to demand that if the bloc obtained thirty seats in the coming Knesset, we should get at least one seat on top of the seventeen that would be ours. It was not likely that the group of Liberals going with us, representing hardly more than nine Knesset members, would obtain twelve seats and that we would have only sixteen or seventeen.

I thought he went out of his way to accommodate the Liberals. But he was interested in the establishment of the bloc and optimistic as to its success (although at the same time careful).

We met again in the King David Hotel. From our side: Nahum Levin and myself, from their side Rimalt and Zimmerman. He spoke at length and profusely. We made a little bit of progress. We set up another meeting. Again I consulted with Begin; he was ready for giving up more . . . we met again with Rimalt and Zimmerman—we made progress—but there was still a gap between our positions, one seat this way or that. I reported to Begin by telephone, and he came to the King David Hotel. I explained the situation to him. He agreed to give up more. We finished our work (I with a heavy heart), and we signed the agreement (2/28/65).

After the agreement concerning the composition of the Knesset list was reached, we proceeded to negotiate officially and openly. A meeting between the two delegations was arranged—each consisting of twelve members—and speeches were made. There was great optimism. Two committees were set up. Begin was at the head of our delegation to the Political Committee, which was to prepare the Gahal agreement and the statement of principles. I was at the head of our delegation to the Municipal Committee,

whose task was to determine the order of candidates on the list of the Gahal candidates for the municipal elections that would take place on the day of the Knesset elections. The basis was the prevailing situation (in the 1959 elections the Liberal party did not exist). Our members in the municipalities argued, and rightly so, that in a general way our strength as a party had grown and their strength had also risen in different locations (since 1955), but that the strength of the General Zionists had dropped. However there was no possibility of determining a different basis. We also agreed to make some special arrangements. In place of a seat in Jerusalem (where heretofore not one single General Zionist had been elected), we were to get "compensation" in Ramat Gan. On the basis of the "status quo," the Liberals will get the first seat in Tel Aviv. I tried to obtain a change at least with respect to Tel Aviv, but without success.

The negotiations in the municipal committee were difficult and drawn out. Simhah Ehrlich, the head of the Liberal delegation, was quite headstrong, and I had a few members who were quick to suggest compromises. But I saw to it that we would not yield to the Liberals more than necessary.

The agreement for the establishment of Gahal was signed on April 25. On May 25 the Knesset committee confirmed the establishment of the Gahal faction, comprising twenty-seven members, seventeen from the Herut faction, eight General Zionists, and two from the "new force," Uziel and Professor Klinghoffer.

The Progressives set in motion their "protection" channels to Mapai in order that their new faction may carry the designation the "Liberal party." I talked about that with Baruch Azaniah of Mapai, chairman of the Knesset Committee. He finally agreed that on the basis of the rules and regulations this title belongs to the larger splinter group, i.e. to our own Liberals. Contrary to this, I agreed (with the consent of my friends) that the smaller splinter group be called the "Independent Liberals." We also agreed that the letter "L" belongs to our Liberals and that the Independent Liberals would use the letters "LI".[7] This arrangement was part of the arrangement of the change in election laws, and I shall talk about it later.

In the negotiations surrounding the establishment of Gahal I had a task to fulfill as representative of the faction, but I had my doubts as to the conditions about its formation, and in particular about the part of the Liberals on the combined list. Krinitzi and Shalom Zisman, the initiators of the talks, emphasized over and over again that the formation of the Gush was only a first step toward the full unity of both parties. The rest of their members, too, used to speak of their readiness to unite both parties after the elections to the Sixth Knesset. If it had not been for those hopes I would certainly have been opposed to the "key" (the order of the list) according to which we surrendered to the Liberals quite a few Herut seats. In the course of the negotiations, my doubts concerning the chances for a unification increased, and in the Central Committee of the movement I voted against the establishment of a Gahal executive in addition to the executive of the Knesset faction that was already in existence. These doubts of mine appeared to have been justified during the subsequent years. The chances for a unification of both parties evaporated, and more than once I proposed to break up Gahal.

There are those who think that the formation of Gahal, and afterward also the formation of the Likud,[8] paved the way toward the Likud government in 1977. As far as I am concerned, the process leading to the decline in strength of the Left in Israel and to the downfall of the Maarakh in the elections was inevitable, and the Herut movement would have achieved what it did even without the formation of Gahal, and by its own strength, in cooperation with the other parties, on the basis of a coalition. But the fact is that Menahem Begin came to power not as the head of the Herut movement but as the candidate of the Likud. The internal difficulties of this government also stem from this situation.

NOTES

1. Liberal party, formed in 1961 through a union of the Progressive party and the General Zionists. The General Zionists appealed primarily to the middle classes and businessmen. Unlike the Revisionists, they had not rejected the WZO or the Jewish Agency; unlike the Progressives, they were generally not willing to cooperate with Mapai. In 1965 the Liberal party joined with Herut to form Gahal, but a significant faction, comprised primarily of former Progressive party members, seceded to form the Independent Liberal party (IL), which failed to win a Knesset seat in the 1981 elections. In October 1982 the Independent Liberals joined the Labor alignment as a faction.

Gahal (acronym for Gush Herut-Liberalim; lit., Herut-Liberal bloc), 1965 coalition of the Liberal party and Herut. Gahal later incorporated several very small parties to form the Likud, which came to power in 1977.

2. Bank Leumi LeIsrael, B.M. (lit., National Bank of Israel, Ltd.), Israel's largest commercial bank. Established in 1902 as the Anglo-Palestine Bank, Ltd., it was reincorporated in 1951 as Bank Leumi. From 1948 until the creation of the Bank of Israel in December 1954, Bank Leumi was the government banker and bank of issue.

3. Maarakh, the Labor alignment of Mapai and Ahdut Haavodah formally approved by both parties in 1965 after Prime Minister Eshkol and Ahdut Haavodah leader Israel Galili reached agreement on November 15, 1964. At the same time Ben-Gurion split from Mapai and formed a new party, Rafi. Shortly after the June 1967 War, in January 1968, Mapai, Rafi, and Ahdut Haavodah united to form the Israel Labor party (ILP; frequently referred to as the Labor party). In January 1969 the Labor party reached an agreement with Mapam and formed a new electoral and parliamentary Labor alignment. Thus the term Maarakh (lit., alignment) actually refers to two separate electoral and parliamentary alliances: the alignment of Mapai and Ahdut Haavodah, 1965–68, and the alignment of the Labor party and Mapam, 1969–present.

4. Simhah Ehrlich (1915–83), leader of the Liberal party and later of Gahal, especially of the centrist Liberal faction within Gahal and, later, the Likud. In 1977, with the election victory of the Likud, Ehrlich became minister of finance. He was influenced by the advice of the American economist Milton Friedman in his economic policies, and he attempted to change the structure of Israel's economy by allowing market forces a greater role, promoting private enterprise in all spheres, removing controls on foreign exchange, and severely reducing or eliminating government subsidies on basic foodstuffs and fuel. Eventually, however, his centrist politics and unresolved economic problems brought him into a clash with Begin, and Ehrlich was forced to give up his portfolio although he remained in the cabinet. In August 1981 Ehrlich became deputy prime minister and minister of agriculture and chairman of the government's Settlement Committee. Just prior to his death in June 1983, he led the ministerial faction within the Likud that challenged Ariel Sharon's version of events surrounding the beginning of the War in Lebanon.

5. Moshe Kol (Kolodny) (b. 1911), leader of the Progressive party and the Independent Liberal party. Kol was a member of the Provisional government and the Independent Liberal representative in the Labor governments, 1965–77. Kol is now a member of the Independent Liberal faction of the Labor party.

6. *Haarez*, one of Israel's leading independent daily newspapers, published by the Schocken Publishing Company.

7. Political parties in Israel are represented at the polls by a letter or series of letters.

8. Likud (lit., Union), right-wing electoral and parliamentary alliance formed in late 1973 by Gahal with the Free Center (which had earlier split from Gahal), the State list (formed in 1969 by Ben-Gurion and members of Rafi who refused to join the Labor party), and a part of the Greater Land of Israel movement. In 1977 the Likud gained a plurality and formed a new government led by Menahem Begin.

J. L. TALMON
29. The Lavon Affair

In the early 1960s the Lavon affair (Haparashah; lit., Affair) became a central issue in Israeli politics. The affair involved Ben-Gurion's drive to depose Pinhas Lavon, secretary general of the Histadrut, for his alleged role in the 1954 Mishap in Egypt (see doc. 11). Immediately after the Mishap, Prime Minister Sharett appointed Isaac Olshan, president of the Supreme Court, and Yaakov Dori (Dostrovsky) (b. 1899), president of the Technion, to investigate what happened and who was responsible. Besides holding responsible and respected positions at the time, both had backgrounds in the military and in Mapai. Olshan's military career be-

gan during World War I when he was a member of the Jewish Legion attached to the British army. He was active in the Whitechapel branch of Poalei Zion while in England as a student and served as liaison officer between Labor leaders in Palestine and the British Labour party. He was also a former commander of the Tel Aviv district of the Haganah. Dori was commander of the Haifa District of the Haganah, 1931–39, and then the Haganah's first chief of staff, 1939–45, 1947–48. He was chief of staff of the Israel Defense Forces through the First Arab-Israeli War.

The Olshan-Dori Committee report, sub-

Source: J. L. Talmon, "The Lavon Affair: Israeli Democracy at the Crossroads," *New Outlook* 4, no. 5 (1961): 23–30. Reprinted by permission.

mitted December 12, 1955, did not present clear-cut answers. The government approved the report, Ben-Gurion's partisans (i.e., Ben-Gurion, Dayan, Eban, Josephtal, and Shitrit) abstaining. The issue remained dormant, but not dead, until suddenly in a 1959 trial *in camera* of an army officer convicted of disclosing secret information to enemy agents (unrelated to the Mishap), the court stated, in passing, that the accused had been persuaded by the officer in charge of Unit 131 to perjure himself before the Olshan-Dori Committee. This renewed the debate. Lavon demanded that his name be cleared once and for all. When Ben-Gurion refused to do so, the debate was continued within the party and in Knesset committees. Eventually the Committee of Seven, chaired by Pinhas Rosen, minister of justice, was formed to look into the matter once again. This committee reported that Lavon did not give the order that resulted in the Mishap. Although this report was endorsed by the government and the Knesset, Ben-Gurion rejected it and attacked the committee mem-

bers. The controversy moved once again to the inner circles of Mapai. Finally, on February 4, 1961, Minister of Finance Levi Eshkol, apparently acting under pressure from Ben-Gurion, introduced a motion in the Mapai Central Committee that Lavon be removed from leadership of the Histadrut. The motion was approved by a vote of 159 to 76. But Ben-Gurion continued to demand another inquiry into the Mishap, thus widening the rift that the affair had caused in Mapai. In 1964 supporters of Lavon formed the Min Hayesod (lit., Back to Basics) faction in Mapai, and in 1965 Ben-Gurion and many of his supporters (e.g., Dayan and Peres) left Mapai to form a new party, Rafi.

Jacob Leib Talmon (1916–80), one of Israel's foremost historians, joined other intellectuals in challenging the moral basis of Ben-Gurion's conduct. He published the following article in *New Outlook,* an English-language journal reflecting Socialist Zionist viewpoints and edited by some of Israel's most prominent left-oriented intellectuals.

Is the tempest over the Lavon Affair—the greatest public scandal since the founding of the State—only the result of the Lavon Affair itself, or is it rather an explosion of pent-up forces, an accumulation of festering frustrations?

Mr. Lavon had every right to try to clear his name, nor can there be any complaint because he was not more moderate or deliberate in his attempts. He was certainly straining things when he attacked what he called the arrangements in the Defence Ministry and in the defence forces as responsible for his dismissal from the post of Minister of Defence. Anyone is justified in objecting to bad management. But by mingling personal with public factors, Lavon became guilty, in the opinion of many, of rationalizing a private grievance. He lost some of the support naturally his as a man wronged, and also raised doubt as to the justice of his fundamental arguments altogether.

Furthermore, if army officers and officials of his own ministry really did conspire against him, one is tempted to conclude that a minister whose subordinates act thus lacks the authority necessary to inspire respect and discipline, like an incompetent schoolmaster whose students misbehave during class. There was considerable naivete in his complaint that the Director of his Ministry—when he was summoned to do so by the committee appointed by the Prime Minister of that time—testified "behind his back." It is naive to expect that in the Ministries or in human relations in general, people will behave like robots without impulses of their own, or to be shocked at acts of intrigue, maneuver or competition.

Certainly it is a sacred principle that the army should always be subservient to the civil authority. In England the situation from this point of view is almost ideal, but nevertheless, in 1940, British generals delivered an ultimatum to Neville Chamberlain, then Prime Minister, that he either fire Hore-Belisha, the Minister of War, or accept their own resignations. Theoretically, the Prime Minister should have chased them out of his office, but he did not. Instead, to the surprise of the whole world, he dismissed Leslie Hore-Belisha, and this put an end to the ministerial career of the brilliant man whom many considered a new Disraeli.

Lavon's position as Minister of Defence was difficult and uncomfortable. His predecessor had been the idol of the army, acclaimed the architect of the forces and victor in the War of Independence. Lavon's past, on the other hand, was not only civilian but also pacificist. Nor was he blessed with the quality of supreme leadership which inspires loyalty, enthusiasm, and the willingness to obey which is the portion of Mr. Ben-Gurion. It is no wonder that in those difficult circumstances Lavon failed to develop the needed self-confidence: his work showed nervousness and instability.

In the course of his efforts to clear his name, Lavon often fell short of good taste, and he was tactless toward both foe and friend. However, when Mr. Ben-Gurion started his counterattack, he went immeasurably further than Lavon. Lavon represented nothing but himself—not even the Histadrut. Whereas the Prime Minister stood for the State, its policies and self-respect.

Pinhas Lavon can hardly be classed among the saints, but the minute he was brought up before the forum of Mapai, to account for his behavior in the "Affair" (while Mr. Ben-Gurion was not required to give any accounting) he became a symbol of the struggle for justice, decency and liberal ideals. It is the way of History, with her fondness for Mephistophelian irony, to choose as symbols of higher values men who are not exactly charming. Dreyfus was hardly an enchanting personality, not even likeable.[1] In eighteenth-century England, John Wilkes, according to all opinion an evil man, became for many years the symbol of justice.[2] His affair was the touchstone of the struggle against strong government, and the democratic uprising against the dictates of those in power and the selfishness of the oligarchy ruling Parliament.

What happened to Mr. Ben-Gurion, who at first declared that he was not a party to the affair, since he had neither charged Lavon nor was he the one to acquit him? He suddenly attacked and did not desist until he had achieved Lavon's immediate dismissal from his job as Secretary of the Histadrut under pressure of the ultimatum "either he or I," and not because of anything that Lavon had done or not done in this post.

It is said that Ben-Gurion as Minister of Defence had refused in 1955 or 1956 to promote the "High Ranking Officer" [Benyamin Givli], who had meanwhile been transferred to another post, on the ground that a trace of suspicion clung to him. But in 1960, Ben-Gurion identified this officer completely with the status and honor of the Israel Defence Forces, and thus began a series of events and circumstances without solution. The worst thing of all is the deterioration or degeneration of the best. The Prime Minister deserves admiration for his deep feeling of responsibility for the good name of the Army. However, it is very dangerous when someone in these circumstances develops a the-army-and-I-are-the-same, or I-am-Defence complex such as King Louis XIV's "L'Etat, c'est moi." A thin line divides a deep sense of responsibility from self-glorification, a feeling of mission from the arrogance of the tyrant. Who can say where deep loyalty ends and idol worship begins? Where is the boundary between fiery devotion and the Machiavellian theory that the end justifies the means? These are things which cannot be measured, nor can subjective "feeling" help much. Personal sincerity is no guide either, but rather, and here we are talking about statesmen, the way the things look in the eyes of the people.

In Mr. Ben-Gurion's letter of resignation, as in the arguments of his partisans, there is heard only one objection on matters of principle: the matter of the judiciary committee, which—so we have been told with much emphasis—is a matter of conscience for Ben-Gurion. Justice must be done to the High Ranking Officer through the courts, for the Committee of Ministers confounded authorities (executive and judicial) and produced a verdict without resort to judicial procedure. Lavon's deposition from his post as secretary of the Histadrut, on the other hand, is attributed to "new circumstances." Thus at this stage the problem came up for political decision according to the rules of power politics and not as a moral question, or a matter of principle or ideology.

One of the most astonishing things in the whole affair is the behavior of the High Ranking Officer, in opposition to all the rules of chivalry. What kept this officer from dropping his cloak of anonymity and publishing a letter to Mr. Pinhas Lavon in something like this fashion: My name is thus-and-so. You have libelled me and made me one of the central figures in a national and even international crisis. This you have done as a member of the Knesset before a body (the Committee for Security and Foreign Affairs) which guarantees you immunity. I hereby challenge you to repeat those same accusations in circumstances which will permit me to take legal action against

you.—If a man is quite sure of the justice of his case, and if the matter is not simply a private affair but one that has set fire to the whole country, then he has no reason to take shelter, like any common criminal, in procedural technicalities. Why does he hide behind a statute of limitations which would be exceedingly difficult to change ex post facto without doing violence to the due process of law?

There was no possibility of holding the government together after the words that passed between the Prime Minister and the Committee of Seven, or rather, the members of the Cabinet who by a large majority endorsed the findings of that Committee. The question here is not whether the Committee was right in its findings or its methods of work, for who can say whether we shall ever know the whole truth? It seems that there will always be things unrevealed about how Lavon tried to come to an agreement with the High Ranking Officer on a joint version of the "sorry business." How could the Prime Minister invite Lavon to head a public committee for national security on the eve of the Sinai Campaign when he already knew about the "capriciousness" of his former Minister of Defence during this time in office?

NOTES

1. Alfred Dreyfus (1853–1935), Jewish captain in the French army convicted and jailed for an act of treason he did not commit. When it was revealed to the French public that he was convicted solely because, as a Jew, blame could be easily placed upon him, one of France's major political scandals erupted; it is still referred to in France as "the Affair." While covering Dreyfus's trial, Theodor Herzl became aware of the nature and severity of European anti-Semitism.

2. John Wilkes (1727–97), popular hero in England who continued to publish criticisms of the king and government even after he was jailed for this offense. The cry of "Wilkes and Liberty" was a popular slogan among eighteenth-century English advocates of freedom of the press and representative government.

SHABTAI TEVETH
30. Dayan and the Conflict between Veterans and Youngsters

Shabtai Teveth is an Israeli journalist and historian. His biography of Moshe Dayan preceded the publication of Dayan's autobiography. The following excerpts examine the generational conflict within the Labor parties and other aspects of their history. They also shed light on the role of the Lavon Affair (see doc. 29) in this conflict and the political demise of Ben-Gurion.

In the elections for the Fourth Knesset, Ben-Gurion won his greatest victory. Out of the 120 seats in the House, Mapai won forty-seven, seven more than in the previous Knesset. It was an impressive achievement by Israeli standards. Mapai entered the Fourth Knesset with renewed vigor and eleven new Knesset members. Among those in the Knesset for the first time with Dayan and Pinhas Sapir were Abba Eban and Shimon Peres. . . .

Disappointed at not having gained sixty-one seats in the house, Ben-Gurion again had to form a coalition government. It should have been child's play after his party's resounding victory in the elections. But forming Israel's ninth government was no simple task because of strife within the victorious party itself. After the elections the veterans again closed ranks to fight the youngsters. Since Golda Meir had announced that she would not accept any public or party position, Ben-Gurion was left without a Foreign Minister. On the face of it he could have given the post to Dayan or Abba Eban. But he could not—and certainly did not want to—let Mrs. Meir go. To make matters worse, Zalman Aranne followed her lead and declared that he would not accept the Education and Culture portfolio which he had held in the previous government. Furthermore, it was unthinkable that other parties would agree to join a coalition in which Mapai was represented only by Youngsters.

Despite the difficulties he expected from the top ranks of Mapai, Ben-Gurion was not prepared to reverse his decision to bring Dayan into the Cabinet. In lengthy, mostly indirect, negotiations with Golda Meir and Zalman Aranne, Ben-Gurion discovered that the veterans would grudgingly agree to Dayan's appointment as a Cabinet minister, but only to the politically innocuous post of Minister of Agriculture.

On December 16, a month and a half after the elections, Ben-Gurion finally presented his Cabinet to the Knesset. To all intents and purposes, it looked as though Mapai had set its house in order. Both Youngsters and veterans were represented, Golda Meir and Aranne had returned to their previous ministerial posts, and the differences were similarly smoothed over in the Knesset, the Histadrut, and the party institutions. Indeed, everything began functioning smoothly on the surface, with Mapai having the strongest government it had ever formed—ten out of the sixteen Cabinet portfolios were in its hands. However, internal dissension was too deeply rooted, and the suspicions aroused were too strong, to give the veterans any peace. Their fears of a takeover by Ben-Gurion and his Youngsters had increased steadily. And now the "Troika"—which consisted of Golda Meir,

Source: Shabtai Teveth, *Moshe Dayan: The Soldier, the Man, the Legend,* trans. D. Zinder. (Boston: Houghton Mifflin, 1973), pp. 296–316. Reprinted by permission of Shabtai Teveth.

Zalman Aranne, and Pinhas Sapir—hardened into a solid core of resistance that was prepared to challenge Ben-Gurion.

The veterans' fears were not entirely self-generated. A district court that by chance tried a person implicated in the "unfortunate business"—later known as "The Third Man" [the head of Unit 131]—on another charge recommended that investigations be carried out to discover whether one of the officers who had appeared before the court had given false testimony to the Olshan-Dori Committee of Inquiry, which had investigated the "unfortunate business" in January 1955. Rumors of forged documents and false testimonies given by army men to the Olshan-Dori committee sprouted among Mapai leaders. Had it not been for the lies, the rumors had it, Olshan and Dori would have acquitted Lavon of all responsibility for the "unfortunate business," instead of apportioning the blame equally to him and the "Senior Officer." Lavon would then have continued to serve as Minister of Defense, Ben-Gurion would not have been called back from Sdeh Boker, and things would have turned out entirely differently. This was the beginning of the frenzy called the "Lavon Affair," which infected the Israeli public with a fever that was to rage for at least five years.

Ostensibly the "Lavon Affair" centered on the question of whether sufficient evidence had been furnished by the army investigation ordered by Ben-Gurion on August 28, 1960 to justify an official legal inquiry into the "unfortunate business," as Ben-Gurion demanded, or whether it was enough for Ben-Gurion himself, on the basis of the evidence furnished him, to clear Lavon of all responsibility for the order that led to the "unfortunate business," as Lavon demanded. To Lavon's great displeasure, Ben-Gurion refused to acquit him since he claimed that he was not a judge. In the climate of suspicion and distrust of 1960, some felt that by demanding a legal investigation, Ben-Gurion was trying to confuse the issue and place Lavon in an equivocal position, so as to weaken the veterans and strengthen the Youngsters. The supporters of the veterans believed that the rehabilitation of Lavon would discredit the Youngsters and check their "gallop to power."

Ben-Gurion's opponents maneuvered him from one difficult position to another. At seventy-four, the "Old Man" seemed changed—weaker and less agile as infighter. It would seem, though, that his weakness was not the outcome of age, but of a personal crisis that concerned his public image. As Prime Minister he was authorized by law to set up a state commission of inquiry and deal with the "Affair" in any way he saw fit. But he did not take this step because he knew he was in the minority. Had he forced the issue in the government, he would surely have been labeled a tyrant. At that point, it was important for Ben-Gurion—the strong man—to be regarded as a democrat and a liberal. He therefore expected the Minister of Justice, who was equally authorized by law, to set up the commission of inquiry for him.

But the Minister of Justice refused. Instead, the "unfortunate business" was raised before the Knesset committee on Foreign Affairs and Defense. In his appearance before this committee, Lavon stressed that he was not accusing Dayan or Peres of having had anything to do with the forgeries and false testimonies. His complaint was that their testimonies before the committee described him as untrustworthy, as one who gives orders and then denies responsibility for doing so.

Although Ben-Gurion, Dayan and Peres were in no way involved in the "unfortunate business" of 1954 and none of them had anything to do with the relations between Lavon and the "Senior Officer," all three became principal targets of the inflamed public opinion that protested against the alleged injustice dealt Lavon. Several movements sprang up to save democracy from their clutches. One of these, organized by religious university students, even declared that it would continue "to fight for the expulsion of Ben-Gurion, Moshe Dayan, Shimon Peres, and their like from the positions of power in the country." Such declarations were not uncommon at that time.

In the end, no evidence was found to prove that there had been forgeries or that documents had been concealed from the Olshan-Dori committee. As the "Lavon Affair" continued to gain momentum, the "unfortunate business" increasingly took a back seat. What concerned the public most was the claim insinuated by Lavon and inflated by opponents of Mapai and the Youngsters that under Ben-Gurion as Minister of Defense, and Dayan as Chief of Staff, and Peres as Director-General of the Ministry of Defense, a phenomenon called "Defensism" developed in the country, that is, a political bias which served its own interests disguised as "the holy cause of national security." Overnight, Ben-Gurion—a universally admired statesman, the guardian and savior of Israel, the leader who won the largest victory in Israeli election history—became a vindictive tyrant, an old man past his prime. Worse still, many began to believe that he had conjured up the notion of Israel's dire security position merely to reinforce his own rule.

This turnabout in public opinion was manna to the opponents of Mapai and the Youngsters. It was Levi Eshkol's hour. Employing his talent for compromise, he stepped in to save Mapai from itself. Instead of a commission of inquiry, he proposed a ministerial committee which, he believed, would satisfy both Ben-Gurion—for it would be government sponsored, if not actually judicial—and Lavon—for it would be a public, rather than a legal body. Eshkol proposed establishing a committee of seven ministers to function as a Cabinet subcommittee, read the material touching on the "unfortunate business," and decide whether or not the appointment of a state commission of inquiry was warranted. In short, he meant to end the "Lavon Affair" once and for all.

Under Eshkol's guidance, the Committee of Seven broke every known rule of procedure, and it is difficult to imagine a greater hodgepodge of powers and jurisdiction. It inquired, interrogated, examined, judged, debated, chose to hear some witnesses and not others, and finally reached conclusions that were masterpieces of Eshkolian compromise. On the one hand, the seven ministers ruled that "Lavon did not give the order upon which the 'Senior Officer' acted, and the 'unfortunate business' was carried out without his knowledge." On the other hand, they failed to mention who did give the order. Against the credit side of Lavon's account, they posted a debit as well: their conclusions implied that as Minister of Defense, Lavon did not manage the affairs of the army in the best manner possible and his term was characterized by shortcomings "that stemmed from a lack of clearly defined limits of responsibility and authority on the highest level." In other words, even if Lavon were not to blame for the "unfortunate business," there was still reason enough to have him dismissed as a Minister of Defense.

Ten ministers, including Eshkol, Golda Meir, and Pinhas Sapir, voted in favor of the committee's conclusions. Dayan and two others abstained. Ben-Gurion was absent from the meeting and another minister was abroad. The results were a personal victory for Lavon. But contrary to Eshkol's calculations, Ben-Gurion was not prepared to lay the issue to rest. On December 25, he announced that he could no longer remain in the government and that he refused to relinquish his principles for the sake of peace within Mapai. He embarked on a campaign that he labeled "the truth above all," aimed at rebutting the conclusion of the Committee of Seven by discrediting the committee's procedure and intended to establish a commission of inquiry to uncover the truth about the "unfortunate business." Ben-Gurion launched a series of moves—all of which failed—to invalidate the Committee of Seven and rebuild his own good name on its demise. On December 31, 1960, only thirteen months after forming the new government, he resigned with the hope that the formation of a new Cabinet would invalidate the findings of the previous Cabinet's Committee of Seven. Eshkol tried to placate him by dismissing Lavon from his position as Secretary-General of the Histadrut on the pretext of an anti-Mapai appearance in the Knesset Committee for Foreign Affairs and Defense and his threat to disclose the contents of a secret dossier. The dismissal meeting, held by the Mapai Executive on February 4, 1961, was in effect a dress rehearsal for the struggle between Ben-Gurion and his opponents in Mapai. Forty per cent of the members voted against the dismissal. This was the largest group ever to oppose Ben-Gurion, and it was a clear sign of his decline.

Ben-Gurion's resignation necessitated new elections. This time Mapai lost five seats in the Knesset. A sharper blow, however, was the demand by Mapai's four former coalition partners that a new government be led by someone other than Ben-Gurion. The task of forming the coalition fell to Eshkol, who saw it as the beginning of his rule within Mapai. He managed to overcome the opposition of two former coalition parties to Ben-Gurion and with their participation formed Israel's tenth government, with Ben-Gurion as Prime Minister. Ben-Gurion's position, however, was very weak. He headed a Cabinet that someone else had formed and he became increasingly bitter about the growing opposition of the Mapai veterans, particularly Golda Meir. Ben-Gurion contemplated retirement for some time. Finally, on June 16, 1963—taking his Cabinet colleagues by complete surprise—he announced that he was resigning for personal reasons. He hoped to be more successful in his struggle against the Committee of Seven outside the government than within it. Ten days after Ben-Gurion's resignation, Eshkol presented his new Cabinet to the Knesset, calling it a "follow-up Cabinet" to the one headed by Ben-Gurion.

. . . During Dayan's tenure as Minister of Agriculture, political developments set off in 1961 went on unabated. After Ben-Gurion announced that he could no longer remain in the government because of the miscarriage of justice perpetrated by the Committee of Seven, he sent a letter to the Mapai Secretariat stating that his decision to resign was final. But the Mapai Secretariat, which conferred on December 31 until the early hours of the morning, was not certain whether or not he might still change his mind. The leaders of Mapai understood that Ben-Gurion's implied condition was the establishment of a legally constituted commission of inquiry to investigate the "unfortunate business" of 1954. What he wanted above all was to invalidate the Committee of Seven's conclusions. If the public would see that he had been right from the start, he would regain its faith. On the other hand, such an outcome would amount to a virtual incrimination of Eshkol and the veterans, who had set up the Committee of Seven, participated in it, and supported its conclusions. Consequently, the words "commission of inquiry" and "Committee of Seven" acquired significance above and beyond the dispute between Lavon and the "Senior Officer," and the former Committee of Seven became a strategic stronghold seized by the veterans to ensure their continued hold over the party.

Golda Meir quickly announced that she too was resigning. In so doing, she effectively blocked the way of any of the veterans who might consider giving in to Ben-Gurion. Aranne, who had resigned a short time before, informed the Secretariat that should Golda resign, Sapir would follow suit, and he made it quite clear that these were planned moves against Ben-Gurion. The party would then have to find replacements for them in the Cabinet, meaning that for the first time there would be a government without Mapai. This was obviously unacceptable to the Secretariat.

Because of his association with Ben-Gurion, the pressures on Dayan steadily increased. He had reached a moment of truth in his political life, and found it imperative to make decisions that would define his political identity. Dayan did not approve of Ben-Gurion's moves over this issue. He was convinced that Lavon had not given the order which led to the "unfortunate business," that it had resulted from the initiative of the person who became known as "the Third Man," and that Lavon gave the order to the "Senior Officer" only afterward. In any case, he felt that since Ben-Gurion had appointed Lavon as his successor, he now had no alternative but to stew in his own juice. In principle, therefore, Dayan was in agreement with the Committee of Seven. Furthermore, he was against a legal commission of inquiry and felt that the entire affair should have been ended before it began. By the same token, however, he opposed the Secretariat's decision to appoint Eshkol as "peacemaker" and empowering him to appoint the Committee of Seven. Nor was he overly pleased with the way in which the Committee of Seven had functioned.

Quite apart from all these judgments, Dayan knew that the only way to ensure the perpetuation of a Ben-Gurion line in the government, which he supported without reserve, was by ensuring that Ben-Gurion himself continued to serve as Prime Minister. It was for this reason that he undertook to mediate between the sides. Despite his own objection to a legal inquiry, he proposed amending the Secretariat decision of January 20 stating that the affair of 1954 "must be dealt with in accordance with the demands of law and justice in the appropriate state institutions," and—to satisfy Ben-Gurion—have it read the affair should be investigated "in the appropriate national and legal institutions." The amendment was unanimously approved, but after the meeting Eshkol and the veterans bowed to heavy pressure from Lavon and had the word "legal" deleted again.

Dayan was probably aware of the increase in the veterans' strength and the decline of Ben-Gurion's power. A novice in politics, he had to beware lest his political future be bound up with the future of one man. Actually, more of his lone-wolf disposition than political shrewdness came into play here. . . .

. . . In the middle of 1963, when Ben-Gurion resigned for good, the Youngsters felt he had abandoned them. Some thought that Ben-Gurion himself had advised Eshkol to take the Defense portfolio as well as the Premiership, thus blocking the way for Dayan or Peres to a top-ranking cabinet post. It was quite clear that Dayan was in a far weaker position than he had been before. As far back as the beginning of 1961 the veterans of Mapai began talking of bringing Ahdut Haavodah, which had split from Mapai in 1942, back into the party fold as an effective means of consolidating a new political force to replace Ben-Gurion and his Youngsters. Ahdut Haavodah agreed and joined the Cabinet formed by Eshkol for Ben-Gurion. This was the beginning of the Alignment that in 1968 became the Israel Labor Party.[1] From Dayan's point of view, it was also the germ of a new force that was to oppose him on a political as well as a personal level. For it was in this Cabinet that Yigal Allon returned to a position of national prominence as Minister of Labor, after twelve years in the opposition. There was hardly any question about the fact that he would eventually aim for the positions of Minister of Defense and Prime Minister. And politically—especially where social and economic issues were involved—Dayan was the arch enemy of Ahdut Haavodah.

Dayan's position in Eshkol's first Cabinet was in some respects a come down from his previous political standing. While he remained Minister of Agriculture, on June 24, 1963 Eshkol became Prime Minister and Minister of Defense: Eban, who until then had been Minister of Education, was appointed Deputy Prime Minister; and Golda Meir, Zalman Aranne (who had returned to the post of Minister of Education), and Pinhas Sapir (now holding two portfolios, Treasury and Commerce and Industry) wielded immense power both in Mapai and

Eshkol's government. Dayan was alone, outside—or kept outside—the corridors of power.

At first he fought for a position of influence. For an opener, he submitted his resignation—right after Ben-Gurion had submitted his—at a time when Eshkol was still unsure of himself and needed the widest possible support even from the Youngsters. Certainly that was the best time to extract concessions—to get closer to the decision-making circle—and Dayan was loath to let the opportunity slip. Hidden from the public eye, a political in-fight began. Dayan disclosed to no one the real reasons behind his resignation. The struggle took the form of meetings between Eshkol and Dayan and their intermediaries in which Eshkol proved himself a master tactician and eventually completely outmaneuvered Dayan. As a first step, he asked Dayan to postpone his resignation for a few months to "prevent crises in the government." Dayan agreed, thereby giving Eshkol time to improve his position. Eshkol used the time well and gained widespread party and public support. His attainment of political security was aided by two factors. First, he was Mapai's only candidate for Premiership and therefore indispensable to the party's integrity. Second, the country was permeated by a feeling that in the interests of democracy, Israel must overcome its total dependence on Ben-Gurion and prove to the world, and to itself, that its leadership was not bound to one man. Moreover, the country was beginning to grow tired of Ben-Gurion's powerful, centralized rule and began demanding a more lax, perhaps even collective rule, for which Eshkol seemed the ideal man. The fact that Ben-Gurion supported Eshkol removed the final obstacle—any lingering doubts about his ability to serve as Minister of Defense.

Ben-Gurion did not openly support Dayan when he turned to the public demanding a different Cabinet and challenging Eshkol's definition of his Cabinet as a "continuation" of the one before. When Dayan demanded that Eshkol's Cabinet present its political "identification card," the only support Ben-Gurion offered was a promise from Eshkol and Golda Meir that Dayan and Peres (who stayed on as Deputy Minister of Defense) would retain their status in the new Cabinet. But Eshkol found it as easy to break promises as to make them. It was at that time that his saying "I promised but did not promise to keep my promise" became a byword.

From June 24, the day he presented his Cabinet, Eshkol's power increased steadily while Dayan, rather than gaining support by virtue of his rebelliousness, invoked bitter criticism from top-ranking Mapai members and even his fellow-Youngsters. Shrewd a bargainer as he was, Eshkol did not reject Dayan's demands out of hand, but entered into protracted negotiations, letting time and circumstances be the villains while he continued to play the kind-hearted, amenable Prime Minister. A few well-timed leaks to the newspapers sufficed to create a situation in which Dayan's demands for a say in defense matters became inconceivable. The coalition began clamoring for clarifications and demanding assurances that Dayan would not be given access to or influence over defense matters above and beyond those accorded any member of the ministerial Committee on Defense Affairs and that he would not be, in Aranne's paraphrase, "more equal among equals."

Dayan emerged from his negotiations with lavish pats on the back but empty pockets. Eshkol and Sapir agreed to his demand that a ministerial committee be given control over the Economic Planning Authority. It was a hollow gesture, however, for even had such a committee been set up, Dayan would have been hopelessly overpowered by Eshkol and Sapir, the natural, all-powerful members of any committee on economic affairs. As a further gesture of condescending good will, the two agreed to transfer certain departments of the Ministry of Commerce and Industry to the Ministry of Agriculture, while Eshkol promised "greater coordination" between the Jewish Agency's settlement Department (which he still headed) and Dayan's ministry. They thus dispatched Dayan not ignominiously, but with only a few token sweets to disguise the bitterness of his failure in the power play.

Yet no sooner were the three months Dayan had offered Eshkol over, and no sooner had Dayan declared his intention to remain in the government "after receiving clarifications on a number of issues, especially defense," than Eshkol and Sapir began reneging on the minor concessions they had made. Eshkol backed down from his promise to hold consultations of Mapai ministers on defense matter and Sapir tied so many strings to his offer of transferring a

department from the Ministry of Industry and Commerce to the Ministry of Agriculture that it became a farce. Promises were broken on a matter close to Dayan's heart and one of the mainstays of his agricultural policies—increasing farmers' incomes—for Eshkol and Sapir let it be known that any decision he made regarding prices of agricultural produce would have to be approved by the Sapir-controlled Committee for Economic Affairs. A few months later Eshkol simply ignored his promise of "greater coordination" between the Settlement Department and the Ministry of Agriculture by publishing his own plan for the establishment of settlement and rural centers in the Galilee, without showing Dayan so much as a preliminary draft.

NOTE

1. Israel Labor party (Mifleget Haavodah Ha-Israelit; commonly referred to by its acronym ILP or simply as Labor party), party formed in 1968 by

the merger of Mapai, Rafi, and Ahdut Haavodah. The Independent Liberals became a faction of this party in October 1982.

DAVID BEN-GURION
31. Social and Ethnic Tensions in the Late 1950s

Wadi Salib, a poor neighborhood in the "lower town" of Haifa, was deserted by its Arab inhabitants in 1948–49 and subsequently settled by impoverished immigrants from North Africa. In July 1959 an outburst of violence in Wadi Salib shocked the Israeli

public and alerted it to the explosive potential created by the overlapping of poverty and feelings of communal and ethnic discrimination. The following account is from David Ben-Gurion's memoirs.

About a month after the last recess of the Third Knesset, a sad occurence in Haifa agitated the entire country. On Friday, July 12, 1959 the Minister of Police Behor Shitrit, told the story in the Knesset:

On the night of Wednesday, July 8, and on Thursday July 9, regrettable events took place in Haifa. At 6 P.M. on Wednesday a police sergeant in a patrol car encountered a drunken man obstructing traffic on Shivat Zion Street in Haifa (a

Source: David Ben-Gurion, *Israel: A Personal History* (New York and Tel Aviv: Funk and Wagnalls, Inc. and Sabra Books, 1971), pp. 561–63. Reprinted by permission.

quarter with largely Oriental residents). The policeman persuaded him to leave the street and left him in the hands of local residents who promised to take him home.

A short time later a patrol car came to one of the cafés on that street. The owner of the café stated he had had trouble with a drunk who had caused damage, seized a panful of hot coals, injured one of the customers, and run away. The policeman later found the drunk imbibing alcoholic beverages in one of the nearby cafés. Two policemen asked him to accompany them to the sergeant in the car. He did so but when requested to get into the car refused, ran back into the café, and began throwing bottles at the policemen. At this point policemen fired four or five shots from two revolvers, under circumstances that are now being investigated.

The subject of the complaint, a resident of the Wadi Salib Quarter, was injured by one of the shots and was immediately taken to the hospital by the police. The disturbance and the shooting led to a gathering of local inhabitants. When a car of the Criminal Investigation Department arrived, it and the men in it were attacked by the crowd. A policeman who happened on the scene and saw the policemen in trouble fired one pistol shot in an attempt to rescue them. A local resident who lived on the top floor also fired a pistol, for which he had a permit. Additional police reinforcements arrived, including a Subdivision Commander who expressed his regret at the occurrence, announced that an investigation would be held, and asked the inhabitants to calm down, and they complied.

The next morning there was a procession of some two hundred people carrying black flags and the national flag smeared with blood. The procession reached the area in front of police headquarters and a delegation on its behalf was received by the Subdivision Commander. The Commander expressed his regret at the incident and denied all rumors to the effect that the injured man had died. He provided information regarding his condition and the delegation appeared to calm down. The crowd finally dispersed.

After this demonstration, a number of incidents of hit-and-run vandalism were perpetrated by small groups of inhabitants of the Quarter. In these disturbances a number of shops and cafés in the lower city and in the Quarter itself were damaged and a number of private automobiles were overturned and set on fire. The Mapai club and the Labor Council club in the Quarter were destroyed. In several of these disturbances the participants included young people, children, and even women. The police, quickly arriving on the scene, were stoned. They did their best to soothe tempers and were successful in many cases, while in others they were compelled to use force to disperse the crowd and had to make arrests.

Around 6 o'clock a serious outbreak occured when a small group of youngsters from Wadi Salib ran up the steps of the Quarter and through the main streets of Hadar Hakarmel[1] breaking shop and kiosk windows indiscriminately, injuring anyone in their way and overturning automobiles. This outbreak lasted only a very short time and its perpetrators vanished into the narrow streets out of which they had come. At 8 P.M. demonstrators armed with stones again made their way up to Hadar Hakarmel and began throwing them. The police dispersed them by force before they caused any damage.

A total of thirty-two persons, including two women, were arrested. On Friday, July 10, when things had quieted down, all the arrested persons were released. In the course of the disturbances thirteen policemen were injured; two of them required treatment though their condition is not serious. Two civilians were injured and hospitalized.

At its meeting on July 12 the Cabinet heard a report by the Minister of Police and decided to appoint a committee of inquiry headed by a judge. The other members were the Rabbi of Ramlah, Yizhak Abuhazeira and Knesset member Yizhar Harari. The assignment of the committee was (1) to determine how and under what circumstances the police acted on Wednesday and Thursday, July 8 and 9; (2) what factors and circumstances led bystanders to take part in the incidents; (3) whether any organization was involved in the riots.

In the debate that followed, the first speaker was Aryeh Eliezer: "This is one of the most serious events since the renewal of our political life, and one of the gravest since the arrival of the exiles in the Homeland in which they hoped to become one nation. We must call for an assuagement of tempers, the imposition of order, and the insurance of justice." He proposed that a parliamentary committee be set up instead of the committee the Government had appointed. Israel Rokah suggested that the existing committee be enlarged by the addition of two Knesset members.

Israel Yeshayahu Sharabi said that for many years we had been worried by the possibility of just such a flareup of communal passions as had occurred in Haifa: "The ingathering of the exiles from all corners of the world has revealed a distressing situation, for though we are one nation in our historic awareness and our Jewish religion, we find ourselves after two thousand years of exile a people that not only has been dispersed among the nations but fragmented by sharp differences of language, food, dress, customs, concepts, ways of thinking, and other things. Nor is this the result of any conscious desire but a curse, perhaps the harshest one that has been imposed upon us by exile."

"The way of life developed in Israel before and especially after the rise of the State," he continued, "has generally been directed not only to upbuilding of the country's desolate areas but to the rehabilitation of its people. In actual fact our achievements in this area have exceeded expectations. From my personal experience of thirty years in this country I know that there is no comparison between the relations among the various communities thirty years ago and today. However, in three areas—economic, social, and educational—progress has not been completely satisfactory. I would request that in speaking and writing about this unfortunate incident, we do not implicate an entire community."

After the debate the Herut proposal for a parliamentary committee was rejected and the Knesset adopted the proposal by Hannan Rubin and Akiva Govrin which said: "After hearing the Government's statement, the Knesset refers the matter to the Knesset Interior Committee."[2]

NOTES

1. Hadar Hakarmel, major commercial center in Haifa with shops that cater to middle-income groups.

2. After these events the government officially recognized the problem of the "social gap" and instituted a few programs aimed at alleviating it. In particular, efforts were made to increase the number of Israelis of North African and Asian descent in the higher grades of the educational system. For the next decade and a half, however, there was virtually no social mobility among this group. Protest movements such as the Black Panthers (see doc. 50) were one consequence of this failure of social policy.

EMMANUEL MARX
32. The Development Town

Development towns were built to accommodate the masses of new immigrants who arrived in Israel in the 1950s. In the following document Emmanuel Marx, a professor of anthropology at Tel Aviv University, discusses both the policies of settling new immigrants in these towns and some of the social consequences. Galilah is the code name he chose for the development town in which he conducted his research.

Source: Emmanuel Marx, *The Social Context of Violent Behaviour: A Social Anthropological Study in an Israeli Immigrant Town* (London: Routledge and Kegan Paul, 1976), pp. 19–26. Reprinted by permission.

The little town of Galilah is situated in the mountains of Galilee. It was founded in 1956, and almost all of its 3,000 inhabitants are immigrants from various parts of Morocco. The town lies off a main road leading to the nearest town, Nahariyah, a resort on the Mediterranean seashore. Buses ply the Galilah-Nahariyah route at half-hourly intervals, and there is also a regular taxi shuttle service. A small number of Galilah people are employed in Nahariyah; many others make a weekly trip to Nahariyah for their shopping (or window-shopping) and entertainment.

The town's appearance is that of a neat and moderately prosperous residential suburb. There are various types of new-looking houses, ranging from tiny whitewashed bungalows often surrounded by well-tended gardens, to five-storied grey block of flats, with litter-strewn courtyards. All dwellings are connected to the central water and electricity networks. The house roofs are studded with solar water heaters and the occasional television aerial. The paved streets are maintained in good repair. On all but the main road there is little traffic. The townspeople themselves own only five or six trucks and commercial vehicles, and the only private cars are the mayor's and the anthropologist's, so most of the traffic consists of buses, taxis, and the cars of visitors. The smaller children use the streets at most times for play and expect drivers to watch out for them. In the late afternoon they are joined by the older children back from school, and on summer evenings their elders also come out into the street, men and women gossiping in their separate small clusters.

Most of the public institutions are centred on the pleasant little town square, which is planted with trees and shrubs. The most prominent buildings are the local Council and the Trade Union offices, standing next to each other. On the square one also finds the bank, the post office and the "café," a small snack bar frequented by men only. Then there is the First Aid and ambulance station, the main bus stop and the "kiosk," a soda-fountain. Just off the square are the Sick Fund's[1] clinic, the Jewish Agency, the Labour Exchange, the Housing Corporation and the Welfare Offices, as well as the largest of the town's eleven synagogues and the ritual bath. On top of a hill in the town centre a large modern sports hall has been built. It has not yet been equipped, and is therefore mainly used as an improvised cinema; performances are given once a week. Not far from it is a well-stocked public library. The three schools are housed in modern airy buildings. For a town of this size, Galilah is well provided with public services.

In contrast, there are only fifteen shops, which fall into the following categories: five grocers; four greengrocers (one of whom also sells fish); one butcher; one poulterer; seven shopkeepers selling durable goods (household goods, furniture and electric equipment, tools and building materials, and clothing). The shops selling provisions are usually packed with customers, and their turnover of staple foods is considerable. The grocers and the other shopkeepers selling provisions often extend short-term credits to their regular customers. The other shops keep small stocks and their few customers usually require long-term credits. Therefore their prices are rather higher than in neighbouring towns. Cash-paying customers prefer to shop outside Galilah, where prices are lower and the choice of goods is wider. It appears that the townspeople do not control enough money to provide livelihoods for a larger number of shops selling durable goods. But there could be more grocers' and greengrocers' shops, if there were suitable premises. The town's planners did not take these requirements into account and, in the interest of orderly planning, the Local Council sees to it that traders and artisans set up only in suitable premises. Even if suitable commercial premises were to be constructed, the potential entrepreneurs would not possess the necessary capital to buy them (according to the rules, such premises are only to be sold, not to be let); therefore whoever wishes to set up in business has to do so illegally. One man hawks his wares on the pavement, another sets up a wooden shack next to his house, and all become involved in litigation with the local authority. Only a few have the perseverance to fight it out with the authorities, and these are the men who ultimately obtain permission to stay in business.

Industry too has not developed in Galilah. The authorities laid the groundwork for an industrial estate on the town's outskirts; they built approach roads and a few halls, and then waited for suitable applicants. In spite of official inducements in the form of government loans and tax concessions, few firms moved into the industrial estate. Most of them lacked capital and, after a short and troubled life span, closed down. Only a workshop maintained at a loss by the Trade Unions [Histadrut], and a small private firm producing building materials, some of which were used locally, held out for several years.

The town was planned within the framework of a national settlement policy. Immediately following the establishment of the State of Israel in 1948, large numbers of Jewish immigrants entered the country, increasing the Jewish population from 700,000 in 1948 to 1,400,000 in 1951. The authorities did their best to absorb the immigrants, while taking into account both the available accommodation and national strategic requirements. Many were settled in deserted Arab quarters of the cities and in smaller towns. Others were temporarily housed in tent-towns, and later in tin-shack towns, set up and run by the Jewish Agency. At the same time plans were drawn up to establish a large number of co-operative villages all over the country, and to turn immigrants into small farmers. This scheme sought in particular to settle the strategically sensitive regions along the Egyptian and Jordanian borders. Galilee was more sparsely endowed with new Jewish villages, and these were mostly located in a semi-circle around the western, southern and eastern fringes of Galilee, where plains provided good farmland. In mountainous central Galilee most of the indigenous Arabs and Druzes had stayed on after the Israeli forces occupied the area. Although there was a contiguous Arab population in central Galilee and in southern Lebanon, the Israeli defence authorities felt no urgent need to establish many Jewish settlements in Galilee, as the Lebanese border stayed peaceful. Therefore the local Arab population was left undisturbed, and only a few selected areas were reserved for Jewish settlement. One of these was located near the site on which Galilah was later established. There, within a radius of 7 km (about 4½ miles) from Galilah, eight new settlements were established, in addition to the existing eight villages inhabited by Druzes, Christians and Muslims. Two of the new settlements were communal (kibbutzim), and the other six were co-operative villages (moshavim).

By the mid-fifties agricultural settlement had reached saturation point, and the authorities began to build more new towns. These towns were intended to offset the tendency of an ever-increasing proportion of the population to converge on the three large cities, Jerusalem, Tel Aviv and Haifa. The new towns were to supply services to the surrounding villages, to process farm produce, and to develop other light industries. It was left to the future inhabitants of the towns to attract investments with the help of generous financial concessions offered by the government. At that time the Egyptian government, which had until then been concerned with internal reform, returned to full participation in Middle Eastern politics. One of its chief aims became the military encirclement of Israel. This caused the Israeli authorities to renew their interest in settling central Galilee. Galilah was established in 1956, and the following year a Jewish town was founded on the outskirts of Arab Nazareth. A third town, Karmiel, was set up in 1964 astride the main east-west road of central Galilee.

The town of Galilah was settled by some of the new immigrants who were still arriving in great numbers. The rate of population growth was determined by the number of houses available for occupation. In 1957 there were already 1,000 inhabitants, in 1961 nearly 1,700, and in 1964 about 3,100. Towards the end of 1964 immigration came to a standstill, and Galilah's population has remained stationary since. It attracted none of the immigrants who again began to arrive from 1967 onwards. Most of the immigrants who were settled in the town had undergone a twofold selective process. During Galilah's first years, most of the immigrants to Israel came from Morocco. Many of the professional and skilled Moroccan emigrants settled in France, and a relatively small number of them made their way to Israel.[2] Numerous people in Galilah had close kinsmen in France; among them were doctors and lawyers, technicians and skilled artisans. A second selection took place when the immigrants arrived in Israel. Every immigrant was entitled to subsidized housing and other material privileges, but had to accept a house anywhere if it was vacant. Families with able-bodied members who were willing to become farmers could still in those years join a co-operative farm. They established in their countries of origin contacts with an Israeli emissary, who would then arrange for them to join a settlement affiliated to his political party. People with suitable professional qualifications or with capital insisted on going to places where work could be found or where they could set up profitable businesses. They often dispensed with the Jewish Agency's services, or used force and influence to obtain accommodation where they wanted it. The immigrants who agreed to move to the outlying towns like Galilah were those whose freedom of choice was restricted, and who depended on the accommodation and assistance offered by the authorities. Many of the new arrivals in Galilah were destitute, lacked skills and educational qualifications,

and had large families. A considerable proportion of them were elderly and infirm.

The decision where to send the new immigrants was made at the Jewish Agency head office. There the Absorption Department collated weekly lists of the available accommodation submitted by Amidar Housing Corporation[3] with reports from the Jewish Agency's Immigration Department on the number of immigrants due to arrive. The reports included details on their social characterics and local preferences. But the Department's main concern was to settle immigrants in the available accommodation and it considered other factors only when suitable pressure was applied. The Department was responsible for the immigrant only during his initial three months in the country, and from then on he was formally on his own, and had to deal as best he could with various bureaucratic organizations, although the Department often continued to assist him. As the Jewish Agency officials were not concerned with his long-term problems, they dealt only with those that faced him immediately upon arrival. That meant first and foremost the provision of a roof over his head. The Absorption Department also contributed to the immigrant's maintenance during his first three months and, where required, provided welfare assistance. It issued him with some household equipment, beds, chairs and blankets. The Jewish Agency attended mainly to his immediate needs: the provision of suitable employment was a long term problem, involving re-training, language study and other preparations. The Jewish Agency sent the immigrant to intensive Hebrew language courses, or to vocational training centres, but by the time the training was completed it was no longer responsible for him. It helped him to find work, but was not unduly concerned when he could find only a temporary job or was employed on relief work, as it had solved his short-term problem of employment. A senior official of the Absorption Department made it clear where his Department's primary concern lay when he proudly asserted that "never yet has an immigrant left without a roof over his head." He thus expressed satisfaction that the Department's main task had been properly accomplished.

Galilah is a town only in the administrative sense. While its inhabitants lack the capital and skills to make it economically viable, it is also too small to be able to develop the complex division of labour associated with town life. There is not only very little industry in the town, but few businesses and almost no places of entertainment. Neither is it a village, however, for its inhabitants do not own or cultivate land. There are only limited employment opportunities locally available. Official statistics in 1966 put the number of unemployed, and employed on relief work, at about half of the working population, a figure which understated the reality.

Galilah is located in a region of relative underemployment. The townspeople are worse off than some others living in the region, as they are restricted in their search for work to the area under the jurisdiction of their local Labour Exchange. This is a branch office of the Labour Exchange in the neighbouring town, Nahariyah, a seaside resort of nearly 20,000 inhabitants, which also has some industry. The people of that town are served first by their Labour Exchange, so that hardly any jobs are left for Galilah men, although an exception is made at one industrial plant, where a number of places are reserved for them. The Arab and Druze villagers of the area supplement their incomes from farming by working in towns, and compete successfully for jobs with the men of Galilah. They engage in trade, crafts and clerical work, and have come to occupy an important place in farm work and construction, two branches of the economy which rely largely on seasonal labour. The skilled and semi-skilled work on building sites in the areas is often done by Arabs. Most of the fifty to sixty Galilah men regularly employed in construction, and

even those working in the town itself, are semi-skilled or unskilled workers.

The kibbutzim and moshavim in the area directly employ only two or three persons from Galilah, and altogether contribute very little to the town's economy. Both types of settlement are affiliated to national political and economic organizations based in the main cities. They market their produce and obtain their supplies through central co-operatives, and do not provide much custom to the small towns. Their political regional and national organizations seek to protect sectoral rather than local interests. While they do not adhere strictly to the ideological injunction against employing hired labour, the settlements in the Galilah region are not sufficiently developed to require workers from the town. The links between the town and its hinterland are thus very tenuous.

The Labour Exchange's policy always to prefer local people for local jobs was initially designed to curb the tendency of the population to converge on the main cities. One result was to keep people from depressed areas out of work, unless they moved their domicile to the region in which work was available. Most of the inhabitants of Galilah are not in a position to take such a momentous decision. Few could collect the amount of money needed to acquire a flat or to rent accommodation or to maintain themselves during a transitional period. This applies particularly to large families which, therefore, are seldom able to move away from Galilah and improve their condition.

The economic opportunities in the town are too limited to attract individual settlers from other parts of the country. Only a handful of old-established Israelis have found employment, and only some of them actually live there. For instance, of the sixty teachers employed in Galilah's schools, ten live locally. The others either commute daily or were sent to the town to serve an obligatory period as teachers, either as soldiers or as civilians, and leave at weekends and during vacations.

Against this background, Galilah's present condition can be understood. The town is inhabited mainly by people who have no better economic chances elsewhere, or are unable to leave the town for lack of resources and who do not possess the capital and skills to develop the local economy unaided. They depend largely on material resources provided by governmental and other public organizations. The two most important sources of income available to the inhabitants are relief work and welfare assistance.

Relief work is supplied by the Ministry of Labour, or by the Jewish National Fund (KKL)[4] acting as its agent. The work is allocated mostly to men responsible for households, and only when there are no able-bodied males in the house will a woman be employed. In 1966 there were 342 persons employed on relief work, of whom 287 were men and 55 women. Relief work is often productive and useful, in spite of its welfare connotation. Most of the men are employed in road construction, land reclamation and afforestation, and women usually in afforestation. Physically handicapped men are employed as part-time relief workers, on light menial tasks such as road-sweeping. Land reclamation is physically very demanding work, and some of it semi-skilled. Basic pay equals that of unskilled farm hands, but some of the harder jobs, such as work on a pneumatic drill or blasting, are paid at a slightly higher rate. Gross pay ranges from IL 11.40 to IL 14.80 (£1.35 to £1.75 approximately) per day. While wages of relief workers are relatively low, they are then comparable with those for ordinary unskilled work. Relief work has some important attractions: it is paid regularly, by a monthly or fortnightly cheque; it is available throughout the year, unlike seasonal farm work; and a person can remain on the job as long as no better one is available. Many of the Galilah men have been on relief work since their arrival in the country seven or eight years ago, and they are confident that the government will provide this type of work as long as required.

They feel quite secure in their employment and, in a sense, consider themselves to be employed by the state. Relief work cannot, however, be fully equated with ordinary work because of the manner of its distribution. It is allocated to families according to their requirements. Single men and women were in the past employed between ten to fifteen days monthly, and only family heads were given the full twenty-two days or more. During my field-work period, some of the lighter kinds of relief work were still rationed in this manner. The local Labour Exchange treated relief work as suited only to persons otherwise unemployable; it was considered to be undignified. Only elderly, unskilled heads of large households were thought to be fit for such work, and young men were only reluctantly engaged in it. They came under moral pressure from officials not to degrade themselves by accepting this kind of job. Thus I heard a foreman in charge of relief work remonstrate with a young unmarried worker: "This is no place for someone like you who served in the army. You must help yourself, no one else will. If you cannot find work here, there is nothing left for you but to seek it elsewhere." He felt that the young man had no need to be "supported" by the state. Yet pay in relief work was often as good as, or better than that in local industry. A young carpenter who had been dismissed from his job in a local workshop took to relief work only unwillingly, after several attempts to regain his job had failed. But he admitted that he was now better paid than in the workshop.

Relief work, however exacting and useful, does not give the workers a sense of achievement and satisfaction, for it is categorized as a social welfare benefit handed out by the state. Men thus employed understand that they obtain this work in order to maintain their families on a standard appropriate to their needs. They subscribe to the state's socialist principles, manifested in relief work, welfare assistance and in many other ways. They feel that being new immigrants without resources of their own they have a right to be supported, and do not usually realize that they are providing valuable labour in return.

The income of many relief workers is supplemented by regular welfare assistance. Out of the town's 620 households, 340 are on the lists of the Ministry of Social Welfare, and 240 of these receive regular monthly welfare grants. Some households obtain several types of welfare assistance, and their income from this source may exceed that derived from relief work. There are also some who depend almost entirely on welfare aid. When there is a married adult male in the household, the welfare office considers him to be the provider, and the assistance is given to him. A wife may plead with the welfare officer for aid just as her husband does, but as a rule the monthly welfare cheque is made out in his name. The combined income from these two main sources of income, and the additional services supplied gratis, are just enough to give people a decent standard of living, to allow them to meet demands made upon them and to provide in addition a modicum of security. While most of the industries hitherto established in the town have closed down after a short time, relief work and welfare assistance payments have continued regularly over the years. People realize that, in the balance, dependence on the state may be as good as a job in industry and they express this insight in a frequently-quoted equation: "Welfare and relief work = Isasbest." Individual economic enterprise is at a disadvantage in these conditions, particularly as it is linked with less social security and loss of welfare benefits.

The inhabitants of Galilah depend on a number of officials in a variety of ways. I have already referred to some of these: the officials who allocate relief work and welfare aid, the main sources of income; the housing official, who is the sole landlord of all the real estate; the Jewish Agency representative, who assists immigrants in their first steps in the new country or helps them to move to another locality if they so desire. These are the officials on whom almost everyone depends. There are some others whose resources are valuable only occasionally or for certain sections of the population: one of them is the local doctor who functions like an official, as all the inhabitants are members of his organization, the Trade Unions' Sick Fund, and entitled to free treatment. People who are absent from work because of illness or convenience require medical certificates if they do not wish to lose their pay. Then there is the bank clerk, who decides whether a man is good for a personal loan. A number of Local Council officials can help, or cause obstructions, in such matters as admitting children to schools and nurseries, hygienic inspections in shops, Local Council contracts, or admission to interviews with the mayor. All these officials are supervised by the mayor, appointed by the Minister of the Interior. While funds for relief work, welfare, housing and education are, in this new and economically non-viable town, allocated by the appropriate government office, the mayor bears the overall responsibility for their use. He is very influential—not because the officials are formally subordinated to him, but rather because he has access to their superiors and can cause them inconvenience. Therefore officials do not lightly reject the mayor's demands even when they have doubts about their justification.

NOTES

1. Kupat Holim (lit., Sick Fund, or Fund for the Ill), system of health care provided without charge to all members of the Histadrut (i.e., to about 70 percent of the population of Israel). The Kupat Holim operates clinics and hospitals throughout the country. Recent proposals have sought to abolish the Kupat Holim and provide a state-controlled system of national health care and insurance. The intent of such proposals is, at least in large part, to weaken the strength of the

Histadrut by allowing Israelis to get health care without paying dues to the Histadrut.

2. Citizens of the French colonies in North Africa were French citizens and thereby entitled to emigrate to France.

3. Amidar Housing Corporation, Israeli national immigrant housing company owned by the state (75 percent of all shares) and the Jewish Agency (25 percent). In recent years Amidar's construction activities have been transferred to other companies. It is the proprietor and administrator of public housing.

4. Keren Kayemet LeIsrael (KKL; lit., Jewish National Fund), fund established in 1901 by the World Zionist Organization to purchase land in Palestine for Jewish settlement. Today its activities have shifted to land reclamation and afforestation.

THIRD KNESSET
33. The Basic Law on the Knesset

The basic political structure of the State of Israel evolved from the political institutions of the Yishuv (see docs. 3,4,5). The debate on a constitution (see doc. 7) reveals why a constitution was never adopted. Rather, the Knesset decided to formulate Basic Laws. As the text of the Basic Law on the Knesset demonstrates, in general these laws only formalized what had already become law and practice. This law was passed on February 12, 1958, almost a decade after the Knesset began functioning as the supreme authority of the state.

Although the Knesset formally has supreme legislative powers, the nature of parliamentary coalition politics in Israel and the requirement that all governments formally submit a coalition agreement of principles results in de facto power residing in the government on most crucial issues. This is, of course, true only so long as the parties to the coalition agreement can maintain party discipline. On certain issues, either when party discipline breaks down or when there has been no previous party decision, Knesset debate is crucial.

1. The Knesset is the parliament of the State of Israel.

2. The Knesset shall sit in Jerusalem.

3. The Knesset shall, upon its election, consist of 120 members.

4. The Knesset shall be elected by general, national, direct, equal, secret, and proportional elections, in accordance with the Knesset Elections Law; this section shall not be changed except by a majority of the members of the Knesset.

5. Every Israeli national of or over the age of eighteen years shall have the right to vote in elections to the Knesset unless a court has deprived him of that right by virtue of any law; the Elections Law shall determine the time at which a person shall be considered to be eighteen years of age for the purpose of the exercise of the right to vote in elections to the Knesset.

6. Every Israeli national who on the day of the admission of a candidates' list containing his name is twenty-one years of age or over shall have the right to be elected to the Knesset unless a court has deprived him of that right by virtue of any law.

7. The following shall not be candidates for the Knesset: (a) the president of the state; (b) the two chief rabbis;[1] (c) a judge (*shofet*), so long as he holds office; (d) a judge (*dayan*)

Source: Laws of the State of Israel, 5718—1957–58 (Jerusalem: Government Printer, 1958), 12:85.

of a religious court, so long as he holds office; (e) the state comptroller; (f) the chief of the general staff of the Israel Defence Forces; (g) rabbis and ministers of other religions while holding office for a remuneration; (h) senior state employees and senior army officers of such grades or ranks and in such functions as shall be determined by law.

8. The term of office of the Knesset shall be four years from the day on which it is elected.

NOTE

1. The Chief Rabbinate dates back to the Ottoman rule when a Sephardi chief rabbi (also called harishon le-Zion; lit., First in Zion) had religious and legal authority in the Jewish community. Under the Mandate, a united Chief Rabbinate comprised of a Sephardi chief rabbi, Ashkenazi chief rabbi, and a rabbinical council was established by the British with the encouragement of the Religious Zionists. The independent state has maintained its legal status. It has authority over the religious courts and matters of marriage and divorce.

SUPREME COURT
34. Jewish Religion and Israeli Nationality: The Brother Daniel Case

Persistent religious controversies within Israel have given rise to legal and political problems for the state (see docs. 6,7,9). In what became known as the Brother Daniel case a convert to Christianity applied for Israeli citizenship under the provisions of the Law of Return, and the courts were forced to deal with the problem of defining "who is a Jew." The Supreme Court ruling, excerpted here, was a landmark decision that still stands. It has not, however, ended the controversy. Factions of the religious parties have frequently demanded a Knesset law giving the religious courts sole jurisdiction over defining "who is a Jew" as a condition for their participation in a government coalition. To date these factions have been unsuccessful. Moreover, non-Orthodox religious movements have attempted to pass resolutions in recent Zionist congresses calling on the Israeli government to recognize marriages and conversions performed by their rabbis, thus, in effect, giving them some authority over defining "who is a Jew."

The applicant was born in Poland, in 1922, to Jewish parents and received a Jewish upbringing. In his youth he was active in a Zionist youth movement, spending two years, approximately, in a pioneer training farm in preparation for his immigration to Palestine. With the outbreak of war between Germany and Russia, in June 1941, he was imprisoned by the Gestapo, but fled. After managing to acquire a certificate stating that he was a German Christian, he became secretary and translator for the German

Source: Supreme Court Decision 72/62, *Osvald Rufeisen v. Minister of the Interior*, In the Supreme Court Sitting as a Supreme Court of Justice (March 14, November 19, December 6, 1962).

police station in Mir, the district capital. While in Mir, he used to notify the Jews of German plans for anti-Jewish actions. When he discovered the German intention of destroying the Mir ghetto, he informed the Jews of the city and the surrounding area and provided them with weapons. On the basis of his information, many fled from the ghetto and joined the partisans; most of the survivors now live in Israel. He was denounced, interrogated by the police and jailed, but once again he fled. For a long time he hid in a convent and, at the first opportunity, joined the ranks of the Russian partisans. The Russians suspected him of being a German spy and sentenced him to death, but he was saved thanks to evidence given in his favor by a Jewish survivor of Mir; in the end he received a Russian medal of honor for his partisan activity. In 1942, during his stay in the convent, he converted to Christianity; in 1945 he became a priest, entering the Carmelite order because it would give him the opportunity to join the Carmelite monastery in Israel. During our War of Independence, and many times after, he requested permission from his superiors to immigrate to Israel; his request was granted only in 1958. In all his appeals to the Polish authorities he emphasized that, despite his conversion to Christianity, he had never stopped thinking of himself as a nationalist Jew, tied heart and soul to the Jewish people. The travel certificate issued to him by the authorities was of the kind issued only to Jews immigrating to Israel and leaving Poland forever; as far as his native country was concerned, he came to Israel as a Jew. His request for an immigrant's certificate and to be registered as a Jew on his identity card was refused by the minister of the interior on the basis of a government decision from July 20, 1958, which determines that only a person who declares in good faith that he is a Jew, and has no other religion, will be registered as a Jew.

The applicant's claims were (1) that the concept "nationality" is not identical with the concept "religion" and that a Jew by nationality need not be a Jew by religion; (2) that according to Jewish religious law [halakhah] he is a Jew because he is the son of Jewish parents; (3) that the decision of the government from July 20, 1958, which served as the basis for the minister of the interior's refusal, has no legal basis and is therefore not binding; (4) that the minister of the interior's refusal to grant him rights is arbitrary, that it is based on considerations outside the legal framework, that it is an affront to the law and to the rights of the applicant, and that it constitutes an act of discrimination against him. On the basis of the above claims, the minister of the interior was served with an *order nisi* to come and explain his reasons for not granting the applicant an immigrant's certificate in accordance with paragraph 3(a) of the Law of Return (1950), and an identity card in accordance with paragraph 7 of the Registration of Inhabitants Ordinance (1949), in which it would be registered in the column "Nationality" that the applicant is Jewish.

The question facing the court in simple legal terms is, What is the meaning of the term "Jew" in the Law of Return (1950), and does it also include Jews who have left Judaism and been baptized as Christians, but consider and feel themselves to be Jews in spite of their conversion?

The Supreme Court, nullifying the *order nisi* by a majority decision, ruled:

1. The dominant opinion in Jewish law is that an apostate is a Jew in all regards, with (perhaps) the exception of some peripheral laws that have no essential importance with regard to the question of principle; the laws of Judaism are not merely the laws of Judaism but they are laws that obligate Jews, and if the halakhah applies them to the apostate, then he also is a Jew.

2. (a) The opinion is unacceptable that even according to the religious ruling the apostate is not a total Jew but only a "partial Jew," a half, a third; the evidence for this opinion: he is not considered a Jew in matters of inheritance, interest (usury), and

participation in a quorum [minyan] of ten males required for a communal prayer. (b) First, the opinion is unacceptable on principle. Judaism is a status, and status is indivisible; we have found such an arithmetical division only in the case of a slave who has two masters; the Jewish religion, like every other religion, is total in its essence, comprehensive, exclusive. The Israelite character of the apostate, which finds clear legal expression in laws of marriage, divorce, and levirate marriage, is a status that does not allow for any split or relativity. (c) Second, the opinion is also unacceptable by its very nature. It is absurd to think that an apostate, who believes in another deity, could participate in a religious quorum in which the rest of the members are praying to the God of Israel. (d) Then again, there is a real doubt as to whether one may lend money with interest to an apostate. The question of inheritance is also a matter of dispute among the authorities; in opposition to Rabbi Hai Gaon's opinion, there are other authorities who think that according to the Biblical law [the Torah] an apostate inherits his father, but the court or the elders have the authority to fine him so that he does not inherit. Even if we follow those who ruled that an apostate may be lent money with interest and that he does not inherit his father, these rules in themselves do not turn him into a "non-Jew" in matters of interest and inheritance; if that were the case, his "Gentileness" would work both ways: the very split—i.e., borrower as opposed to lender, inheritor as opposed to testator—is a clear indication that the question is not one of detraction from the Jewishness of the apostate but of whether to deal strictly or leniently, for various reasons that are based not on the status *Rem* but on the possession of that status *in Personam*.

3. (a) Clearly the term "Jew" as used in the Law of Return (1950) does not have the same meaning it does in the Rabbinical Courts Jurisdiction (Marriage and Divorce) Law (1953). The latter is religious in meaning, as prescribed by the laws of Judaism; the former is secular in meaning, in accordance with its ordinary meaning when used in popular language and by Jews. (b) The logic of the matter is that the Rabbinical Courts Jurisdiction Law is meant to increase the authority of the rabbis, and it is common knowledge that this authority was requested and granted in order to broaden the application of Jewish religious law to Jews. (c) It follows that the question of "who is a Jew" must also be solved on the basis of Jewish law, for if any other criterion—external, secular, non-halakhic—becomes the determining factor, then Jewish laws will not be applicable.

4. (a) This is not so in the Law of Return. It is a secular law, the terms of which, having no definition in either law or verdict, we must interpret according to their popular meaning, taking into consideration, so as to avoid stereotyping, the legislative aim that led to the legislator's directive. (b) The Law of Return being an original Israeli law, and not an adapted law, it would seem that the term "Jew" should be interpreted as we, the Jews, understand the content and the essence of the term "Jew." (c) In the light of the popular, Jewish meaning of the term "Jew," a Jew who has converted to Christianity is not called a Jew. (d) For this reason the applicant, despite his many positive qualities and the sincere love of the Jews that he has proved, does not have the right to call himself by the name "Jew."

5. (a) Israel is not a theocratic state, because it is not religion that orders the lives of its citizens but the law. And this present case is evidence of that fact; had we applied the religious categories of Jewish law to the applicant, then he would actually be considered a "Jew." (b) The basic attitude, that "Jew" and "Christian" are two mutually exclusive titles, is shared by all, whether it be the mass of the people or the scholars; none of these can consider an apostate as a member of the Jewish nation.

6. (a) The applicant, Brother Daniel, is not a member of the Jewish nation, nor is he a member of the Polish nation, since he

relinquished that right before leaving Pol-
and. He is a nationless person and will be so
registered in his identity card. (b) The space
above which is written the item "Nationality," according to paragraph 4 (a) of the
Registration of Inhabitants Ordinance, will
remain blank and unfilled. And there is no
anomaly in this, because not every applicant
for an identity card can fill in all of the items
in it, for instance, an atheist.

DAVID BEN-GURION
35. The Capture of Adolf Eichmann

In May 1960, Adolf Eichmann (1906–62),
head of the Gestapo section that dealt with
Jewish affairs in Nazi Germany and the
deportation of Jews to death camps, was
abducted by Israeli security agents from
Argentina, where he had been hiding since
1950. The abduction created diplomatic tensions between Israel and Argentina, which
claimed that its sovereignty and Eichmann's
rights had been violated. The Israeli Supreme Court ruled that Eichmann could be
tried in Israel. He was charged with "crimes
against the Jewish people and humanity," a
charge punishable under Israeli law. The
trial took place before the Jerusalem District
Court, April–December 1961. Eichmann was
found guilty, and in May 1962 he was
hanged in an Israeli prison.

During the trial the grim facts of the Nazi
Holocaust were presented throughout the
world by the news media, and the historical
and moral issues they engendered were
raised. Within Israel a generation that had
experienced the Holocaust used the trial and
the events surrounding it to educate their
children and their non-European cocitizens
about the centrality of this experience, and
European anti-Semitism in general, to their
collective historical memory. Because of the
importance of the Holocaust to Jewish national identity, the Eichmann trial evoked
strong emotions among most of Israel's
Jewish population as it simultaneously reinforced one aspect of this national identity.

This reading includes, first, Ben-Gurion's
announcement in the Knesset of Eichmann's
capture. With these few words Ben-Gurion
set in motion a trial that would remain at the
center of Israeli public life and debate for
two years. Illustrating the kind of controversy the trial aroused is the second section
of this reading, Ben-Gurion's reply to an
article by Nahum Goldmann arguing that
Eichmann ought to be tried by an international tribunal instead of an Israeli court.

Announcement in the Knesset

I have to inform the Knesset that a short
time ago one of the greatest of the Nazi war
criminals, Adolf Eichmann, who was responsible, together with the Nazi leaders,
for what they called "the final solution of the
Jewish question," that is, the extermination
of six million of the Jews of Europe, was
found by the Israel Security Services.

Source: "Eichmann Found by Security Services; To Be Tried Here for Crimes against Jews," *Jerusalem
Post,* May 24, 1960, p. 1. Reprinted by permission. David Ben-Gurion, *Israel: A Personal History* (New
York and Tel Aviv: Funk and Wagnalls, Inc. and Sabra Books, 1971), p. 575. Reprinted by permission.

Adolf Eichmann is already under arrest in Israel, and will shortly be placed on trial in Israel under the terms of the Law for the Punishment of Nazis and Nazi Collaborators, 5710–1950.

Reply to Goldmann

American journalists, who have not suffered from the Nazi atrocities, may be "objective" and deny Israel's right to try one of the greatest Nazi murderers. But the calamity inflicted on the Jewish people is not merely one part of the atrocities the Nazis committed against the world. It is a specific and unparalleled act, an act designed for the complete extermination of the Jewish people, which Hitler and his collaborators did not dare commit against any other people. It is therefore the duty of the State of Israel, the only sovereign authority in Jewry, to see that the whole of this story, in all its horror, is fully exposed—without in any way ignoring the Nazi regime's other crimes against humanity, but as a unique crime without precedent or parallel in the annals of mankind.

It is perhaps the first such episode of historic justice in history when a small nation, beset by many foes, is able on its sovereign territory to try one of its chief enemies for atrocities against hundreds of thousands of its sons and daughters. It is not the penalty to be inflicted on the criminal that is the main thing—no penalty can match the magnitude of the offense—but the full exposure of the Nazi regime's infamous crimes against our people. Eichmann's acts alone are not the main point in this trial. Historic justice and the honor of the Jewish people demand this trial. Historic justice and the honor of the Jewish people demand that this should be done only by an Israeli court in the sovereign Jewish State.

NEW OUTLOOK
36. The Israeli Arab Minority: A Sample of Outlooks

The Arab minority was integrated into the Israeli polity in the 1950s and 1960s in a process that culminated in the abolition of the military government in the Arab sector in 1966. As reflected in the symposium reproduced here, however, the basic problem of a national minority that is part of the Arab world has remained unsolved.

These opinions were published in *New Outlook* in response to an article by Elias Tuma, an Israeli Arab who had migrated to the United States, that advocated emigration as the only solution to the problem of the Arab minority in Israel. They were written by Ibrahim Shbat, a member of Mapam; Boulos Farah, a former leader of the Palestine Communist party; and Mansour Kardosh, a leader of al-Ard, an anti-Zionist group banned by the Israeli government.

Source: New Outlook 9, nos. 3, 4 (1966): 47–50, 42–43, 43–44. Reprinted by permission.

Ibrahim Shbat, "Co-existence and Not Emigration"

"The only acceptable solution to the problem of relations prevailing between the two peoples in the State of Israel is for the Arabs of the country to leave as a group, by agreement, with fair compensation for their property, provided that this be carried out under international supervision." That is the main "logical" conclusion reached by Mr. Elias Tuma, the young Israeli Arab who left his village in Israel more than ten years ago to complete his studies in the United States, and who returned for a five-week visit with his wife a little while ago.

In my view, Mr. Tuma's impressions could be divided into three separate chapters, each of which treats of a different theme. In the first, the writer describes his subjective feelings upon boarding the plane that was to take him to Israel and his impressions of the profound changes that have taken place in various spheres of Arab Israeli life in the ten years of his absence from the country.

In the second chapter, Mr. Tuma tells us that the progress and prosperity enjoyed by the Arabs of Israel today are merely one aspect of their situation, and that the other is of a far more sombre shade—for the prevailing attitude is a combination of deep disappointment and despair over the future.

In the third section, Mr. Tuma enumerates several possibilities which might serve as a basis for the solution to the problem which, in his opinion, is growing daily more serious among the Arab population. In my view Mr. Tuma is correct in some of his analyses but in the others he was not only mistaken but also gravely misleading, as I shall attempt to show.

To begin with, Mr. Tuma asserts that the Arabs of Israel do not know where they belong, that they do not belong to the Arabs of the neighboring countries, but neither do they have any sense of belonging as citizens of the State of Israel. I am convinced that on this point Mr. Tuma is entirely wrong, for the Arabs of this country have never since the state was established, left off stressing that they belong to the Arab nations and are at the same time citizens of Israel—which they share jointly with the Jewish people and in which they have been consistently fighting for full equality.

It is true that a large proportion of the Arab farmers have left agriculture to work as wage earners in other trades, but no one can prove that all those who are engaged as hired laborers outside their home villages were driven to this because of their land being requisitioned. Statistics show that many of those who still have plots of farm land have given up farming to take up jobs in the building trades or in industry. That, it seems to me, is easily understood: individualism is too deeply rooted still in Arab society for the establishment of cooperatives in the Arab village. Many farmers who own small plots of land in different parts of their village cannot afford to purchase agricultural machinery for their own use alone. They have to employ workers to do jobs that might have been partly executed by machines, and wages today are high. The farmer can therefore hope for a much smaller income from his plots today than in the past, and they can earn twice as much when employed as building or industrial workers. This is the reason why many farmers have neglected their plots, leased them to others or sold them, preferring to seek more remunerative work in the cities. The fact that a major proportion of manpower from the Arab sector is today employed in Jewish enterprises should therefore not be attributed to any deliberate policy of humiliating the Arab citizens; in my view this is natural and, under existing circumstances, a positive factor. It is natural because so far the Arab sector has not displayed a proper awareness of economic trends and necessities, and this has meant that no one has taken the initiative to establish any viable productive enterprises in the Arab localities that would be capable of providing employment for the local working population. This lack of local enterprises cannot continue indefinitely and the fact that Arab workers are employed in Jewish enterprises may at some point prompt some of them to take the initiative in establishing enterprises themselves. It is now providing them with an opportunity to gain experience and know-how for the management of such enterprises. Some projects have been set up recently in Nazareth, foremost among them two chemical factories which are run and managed by young Arabs from Nazareth who learned their trade in Jewish plants in Haifa and Tel Aviv. Here is a living example of the kind of initiative one hopes for in the future.

At the same time, there are negative features prominent in the official policies of the authorities towards the Arab citizens—such as the seizure of land at various places, not for development purposes; oppression of Arab citizens through the Military Government; and discrimination against Arabs in work and employment opportunities.

Mr. Tuma also points out that the Arab citizens of the state live without hope for the future and without security or inner stability. For this he blames only government policy. As evidence, he notes that the Arab teachers, social workers and officials whom he approached refrained from making any comments in public but would only open up when he arranged to meet them separately and in private. He says that this was because they feared dismissal from their positions or other forms of persecution for voicing negative opinions. However, it seems to me that Mr. Tuma missed two essential points which have also helped mold the present situation.

The first point lies in the very serious fact that there can be no solution to many of the difficulties that have arisen between the state and its Arab citizens until such time as a final solution is found to the general problem known as the Arab-Israeli dispute in the region, and both the authorities and the Arab citizens are well aware of this. In order to expose the problem entirely frankly, I would like to ask what those who demand absolute equality of rights in all matters would say if they were asked to contribute to that equality by fulfilling all the normal civic duties, foremost among which is the elementary duty of serving in the Israel Defense Forces and of assuming their share of responsibility for the state's security. The reader will have no difficulty in concluding from this that, under existing conditions, there cannot be the kind of absolute internal stability among the Arabs of Israel that is sought by Mr. Tuma.

We might also be led to conclude from Mr. Tuma's article that the authorities are solely to blame for the present situation in which the Israeli Arabs say one thing and believe another. The question is where the Israeli Arabs themselves really stand; what the intellectuals among them have done to bring about a change for the better, to improve the status of the Arab citizens and to preserve their community even when official policy was apparently designed towards driving them out of their country? History tells us that the Jews in Hitler's concentration camps often spared no effort to set up schools for their children even when they knew that they faced death on the morrow. . . . I don't intend to draw any analogy, but it is a constructive approach and initiative that we seek. I would like to ask what the Arab citizens of Israel have done to voice their protest against "official policies" which consistently discriminated against them and which, so it is claimed, endanger their future?

Did they express their anger when they consistently gave mass support to the initiators of that policy and to those who implemented it? It would be instructive for the Arab citizens of Israel to remember how the English once showed what a mass reaction to an undesirable policy could do: when a penny increase in railway fares was announced a mass boycott of the railway was staged and the authorities had no choice but to withdraw the increase in face of this overwhelming protest.

It is unfortunate that Mr. Tuma did not take his investigation of the general problem deep enough, as is shown in the possibilities he mentions as solutions to the problem. With regard to the hopes placed in the possibility that the Arab refugees might return, he questions the belief that "the difficulties faced by the present Israeli Arabs will be shared by a large, and not a small minority, and their situation will therefore be eased." Whatever the effects of the possible return of refugees to Israel, however, any such solution must, in my view, depend first on Arab recognition of the right of the Jewish people to exist here as an integral part of the peoples of the Middle East. The return of the refugees, or some of them, according to agreement between the parties concerned, will complicate matters even further, rather than point the way to a solution, if this fundamental condition is not fulfilled.

Another possibility suggested by Mr. Tuma: assimilation of the Arabs into Israel's Jewish society, is not only unlikely for sociological and historical reasons, but will also lead to an intensification of the entire Arab-Israeli dispute. As for the suggestion of autonomy for the Israeli Arabs, this must be rejected for two reasons. The first lies in the fact that we are all living in a small and young state, in which contacts and meetings between the two communities are an essential part of our lives. Autonomy would undermine these contacts and ties. The second reason lies in the danger that autonomy might, in the special conditions in which both peoples are living today, increase the barriers between the two peoples and might lead to greater clashes than those that have taken place every once in a while in the past.

In view of the above, and in the belief that only co-existence between Jews and Arabs in the state can serve as a basis for future co-existence between Israel and the Arab peoples, we must also reject Mr. Tuma's final suggestion that the Arabs migrate from Israel en masse. For the good of both the peoples, which have in the course of history encountered each other at various times and various places throughout the region—from prehistoric times through the Biblical era, the first centuries of Islam and the Golden Age of Spain, we must all seek for a way to strengthen the historic encounter which has been renewed in the twentieth century. Mr. Tuma was mistaken in claiming that only the Ihud Movement[1] in Israel sincerely seeks Arab-Jewish brotherhood and peace. There are wide democratic circles in the country which seek to further these causes and their numbers among the Jewish population is growing steadily.

Finally, I believe that until peace is established, the following measures must be taken by the state: a clear and constructive official policy should be adopted towards the integration of the Arab citizens in all spheres of life; efforts should be made to foster oriental culture and qualities, in addition to those brought by the Jews from their Diaspora, which are for the most part Western in character; Israel's foreign policy should be one of non-dependence on either the West or the East; it should be neutral and one of identification with the Afro-Asian liberation movements.

With regard to the Arab countries, I believe that once living standards improve there and democratic regimes are set up in those states, there may be but a short way to go before peace can be established between Israel and her neighbours—undoubtedly to the benefit of all the peoples of the region and indeed of the whole world.

Boulos Farah, "There Are Democratic Solutions"

I have read and reread Mr. Tuma's article to find a basis for some comments. Unfortunately, I have found none. His analysis of the status of the Arab national minority in Israel seems artificial and shallow.

According to Mr. Tuma "The Arabs of

Israel . . . are not a community; they are not a nation or part of a nation." What are they then? In his opinion, "they just live." He does not even honor them and raise them to the category of a herd. We Arabs are not a people, we are only the "Arabs of Israel." Mr. Tuma's "sociological sense" teaches him that because we live "in a state of disorganization, distrust, despair and suffer from a high degree of demoralization," therefore, we belong to nowhere and to nobody. He emphasizes that we Arabs are "not one with the Arab states" and that we "live in Israel but do not form an integral part of it."

Why does he call us Arabs if we do not belong to the Arab nationality? Are we simply a nonentity, without history, culture and tradition of our own? Don't we form a part of the Israeli state because we differ from the majority of the populace? Do disorganization and supposed despair, at a certain historical stage, deprive a national minority of its national characteristics? Mr. Tuma's so-called "sociological sense" is entirely senseless.

The Arab national minority is an integral part of the state of Israel, and belongs, nationally, to the great Arab nation. Distrust, despair and persecution do not deprive a people of its national or political

status. On the contrary, they strengthen the feelings of nationality, and emphasize the just struggle for lawful political rights.

The state of Yugoslavia, for example, is formed of different nationalities, but still they are all Yugoslavs.

As for Mr. Tuma's long list of complaints, they are well known and do not need much emphasis; they do not, however justify his so-called solutions. He discusses those solutions academically and avoids the simple democratic practical ones. He does not, for instance, call upon the state to mend the wrongs and desist from discrimination against its national minority. His negative attitude clearly reflects his lack of faith in the democratic development of the state. He wants us to believe in the eternity of oppression and racial discrimination. He sees in Israel a past and a present, as far as her minority is concerned, without any future whatever, and thus he comes to his impasse. The Arabs are here to stay, in their homeland. The majority and its representatives are destined to accept them, sooner or later, as equal partners; and the majority will understand that it is in its own interest, in the long run, to grant their lawful rights, and abolish all vestiges of political, social and economic discrimination.

Mansour Kardosh, "For A Palestinian Arab State"

Mr. Elias Tuma describes the symptoms of the ills but avoids mentioning their origin and causes. He says: "Arabs of Israel . . . are not a nation or part of a nation." Indeed, the Arabs of Israel are not a nation, but they are emphatically and uncontestedly part of a large nation. The Arabs of this land were and will forever remain part of the Arab Palestinian people who are an integral part of the Arab World. Therefore, the starting point of any discussion should begin from this basic and fundamental truth.

Mr. Elias Tuma, no doubt purposely, ignored the imposing problem of the majority of the Palestinian Arab people who are

miserably scattered and whose minority is oppressed and deprived of its freedom of expression. It is forcibly denied its legitimate right to establish the Arab Palestine State. Incessant courage and sacrifices are still needed to fulfill that rightful claim. To ignore the lot of the Arab Palestinian people constitutes a flagrant breach against justice and maintains a constant state of tension all over the area.

As for Mr. Tuma's sophisticated suggestion that ". . . the only way open to them (the Arabs of Israel) is to leave the country as a group, by agreement . . . ," I bitterly reject it and consider it "treason of a soldier on the battle-field." Can we abandon the land of our fathers and forefathers for the sake of "... a high premium of individual freedom, happiness and peace of mind ..." or should we remain to preserve and guard the Arab contact and heritage?

For Mr. Tuma's suggestion won't lead to any peaceful solution of the Palestine tragedy but, on the contrary, will yield bitterness and animosity.

I should mention here the blessed attempts of Ihud and some other factions of the Jewish people, to establish a joint Arab-Jewish front whose main task will be to erase hatred and to consolidate a policy of cooperation and peaceful co-existence.

During the three months of exile in Arad that I endured last year, I met several individuals who support those goals and showed respect for my aspirations.

All efforts channelled in that direction will ultimately destroy the evils that poison our atmosphere—as those witnessed lately in Natanyah—and help to impose a spirit of confidence and common sense. Such forces will bolster the indestructible stand of the *freedom-conscious* Arabs in Israel.

Nevertheless, I can't ignore the tremendously dreadful forces that seek dissension among our communities, tend to widen the abyss and try by all immoral means to provoke hatred and uneasiness.

I conclude by stressing that we can't abandon our lands, we will continue to live on with pride and dignity and for all the generations to come.

NOTE

1. Ihud (lit., Unity), a coalition of leaders of Brit Shalom, Hashomer Hazair, and a small group of Arabs (most of whom were assassinated by Arab extremists) formed in 1942, as Arab-Jewish tensions increased, to press their call for a binational solution for Palestine. Brit Shalom (lit., Covenant of Peace) had been established in the 1920s by Jewish academics at the Hebrew University to advocate a binational state of Arabs and Jews.

1956–67
Foreign Policy Issues

DWIGHT DAVID EISENHOWER
37. The Eisenhower Doctrine

The Eisenhower Doctrine was a policy statement on the Middle East issued by the U.S. president, Dwight David Eisenhower on January 5, 1957; its provisions were authorized by Congress in March. The doctrine was meant to bolster the pro-Western Arab regimes (e.g., Lebanon, Jordan, and Iraq) by granting military and economic assistance to Middle Eastern states requesting aid and promising the use of U.S. military forces to protect the territorial integrity of any state threatened by communist aggression. This doctrine did not prevent the Lebanese Civil War or the fall of the Iraqi monarchy in May and July 1958 respectively. Following the military coup in Iraq and fearing destabilization of the region, both Jordan and Lebanon invoked this clause for direct military intervention. In the summer of 1958 the United States sent troops to Lebanon and Britain sent troops to Jordan.

Israel's response was ambiguous. On the one hand, it wanted to see stabilization and increased Western influence in the area. On the other hand, particularly in light of America's opposition to the Sinai Campaign, Israel feared that the doctrine might lead to the strengthening of its enemies. Nevertheless Ben-Gurion articulated support for the Eisenhower Doctrine despite this slight uneasiness and in the face of opposition from Ahdut Haavodah and Mapam, whose socialist orientations led them to oppose Israeli involvement in the cold war, and from Herut and the General Zionists, who believed that the doctrine did not go far enough in protecting Israel and the region.

The formulation of the Eisenhower Doctrine and the American response to Soviet advances in the Middle East and to the challenge of regional anti-Western forces are described here from the president's personal vantage point.

At 7:50 on the morning of Saturday, January 5 [1957], I arrived at my White House office. It was still dark outside. I dictated an insert for the Special Message to the Congress on the Middle East. At noon, I went up to Capitol Hill to deliver it in person before the legislators assembled in a Joint Session.

Weaknesses in the present situation and the increased danger from International Communism, convince me that basic United States policy should now find expression in joint action by the Congress and the Executive. Furthermore, our joint resolve should be so couched as to make it apparent that if need be our words will be backed by action. . . .

The action which I propose would, . . . first of all, authorize the United States to cooperate with and assist any nation or group of nations in the general area of the Middle East in the development of economic strength dedicated to the maintenance of national independence.

A further purpose was to authorize the President to undertake programs of military assistance and cooperation with any nation desiring them, such programs to include United States military aid when requested, against armed aggression from any nation controlled by international Communism.

The message recommended financial support in reasonable amounts and pledged,

"These measures would have to be consonant with the treaty obligations of the United States, including the Charter of the United Nations."

That same day the administration bill, House Joint Resolution 117, was introduced into the Congress.

The members of the Congress did not move as one man to endorse the administration's proposal. Far from it. Some thought it would confer on the President constitutional authority belonging to the Legislative branch. Others, friends of Israel, did not like helping any Arab nation. Still others feared it would weaken our ties with either Western Europe or the United Nations or both. One suggested the far-fetched possibility that if the Soviet Union did some minor meddling in the Middle East, the Resolution would authorize "an all-out attack" on the Soviet Union.

Speaker [Sam] Rayburn circulated among his colleagues on Capitol Hill a substitute—a thirty-four-word declaration, "The United States regards as vital to her interest the preservation of the independence and integrity of the states of the Middle East and, if necessary, will use her armed force to that end."

When asked, "Would the administration accept this substitute?" Secretary Dulles, with my approval, gave a flat "No." A resolution in these words, he said, would look like an effort to establish an American protectorate over the countries of the Middle East; it would call for a guarantee, by the United States alone, of existing Middle East boundaries; it would violate the U.N. Charter by calling for military action to overthrow any regime which comes under Communist control by peaceful means; and it would ignore the importance of economic aid.

From around the world reports came in of varying responses to the suggested new policy.

Britain and France generally favored the plan. Communist China and the Soviet Union condemned it as a "substitution for British and French imperialism." The Moslem countries divided: Syria was hostile, Iraq and Saudi Arabia were cautiously critical, while Turkey, Pakistan, Lebanon, and Iran saw the doctrine as the best possible guarantee of peace.

Prime Minister Nehru wrote to me of his dislike of a "military approach to these problems"—an approach which, he thought, might excite ". . . passions and create divisions among the Arab countries and thus add to the tension. . . ."

"I do not think that, in existing circumstances," Nehru continued, "there is any danger of aggression in the Middle East from the Soviet Union. The Soviet Union is too much tied up with its difficulties in the Eastern European countries. Even otherwise, nationalism is a far stronger force in the Middle East than any other."

The next day I dictated a reply, assuring him that the United States' purpose was to help stabilize the area and promote the rise of living standards.

We have no thought that any country in the group would want, or indeed could afford, great armaments. When we speak of assisting in a military way, we mean only to help each nation achieve that degree of strength that can give it reasonable assurance of protection against any internal rebellion or subversion and make certain that any external aggression would meet resistance. . . .

. . . It is my belief that this announcement will tend to diminish, if not eliminate, any chance of this kind of aggression. . . .

But we are far more interested in bringing about conditions that will tend to lessen tensions and provide a climate that will bring about the possibility for conciliation even among the Israelis and the Arabs. We stand ready to make considerable sacrifices to bring this about, and in return we want nothing whatsoever except the confidence that these nations are gradually developing their economic strength and living standards and are achieving the ability to live more happily and peacefully among themselves and with the world.

At the first news conference of my second term on the morning of January 23, I was asked whether I had any comment on the Democratic criticism that in asking for advance approval to use the armed forces, I was creating a tradition which might restrict and embarrass future Presidents.

"What we want now," I said, "is an expression of the convictions of the vast portion of the American people without regard to party. . . ."

". . . I would like the nations to know that America is largely one in our readiness to assume burdens and, where necessary, to assume risks to preserve the peace, because this peace is not going to be obtained in any cheap way and it is not going to be maintained in any cheap way."

On January 30 the House passed the Middle East Resolution 355 to 61.

After extensive consideration of the Joint Resolution the Senate, on March 2, voted down 58 to 28 a proposal by Senator Richard Russell to eliminate any funds for economic and military assistance. This rejection came after Senator Knowland read on the floor of the Senate a letter from me opposing this cut and deploring any suggestion that "our country wants only to wage peace in terms of war." For the Russell amendment, which would have cut the heart out of the Resolution, only five Republicans lined up with twenty-three Democrats.

Three days later, the Senate passed the Joint Resolution by a vote of 72 to 19 and on March 9 [1957] the Resolution was signed into law. As in similar cases in the past, the doctrine acquired the name of the President who proposed it and came to be known as the "Eisenhower Doctrine."

With the help of statesmen of both parties, against the grumbling of some opposing congressmen and senators, and against the well-intentioned counter-suggestions of some leading Democratic foreign policy thinkers, we had effectively obtained the consent of the Congress in proclaiming the administration's resolve to block the Soviet Union's march.

The next day Senator J. William Fulbright of Arkansas demanded that Secretary Dulles submit a white paper justifying in detail the conduct of American foreign policy in the Middle East since 1952.

Secretary Dulles made the obvious response: nothing he could think of would do more damage to our relations with England and France than such a rehearsal of events now past, dredging up the painful memories of recent division, and "reopening all the wounds" in the Atlantic Alliance. After modifying his original proposal to take the policy review back to 1946, Fulbright finally abandoned it.

In the course of the Senate's deliberations, I wrote a letter of thanks to former President Truman in appreciation for a syndicated newspaper column urging prompt passage of the Resolution. "I feel that your attitude," I said, "is in the high tradition of non-partisanship on foreign policy matters of grave national concern," to the Mediterranean, to the Suez Canal and the pipelines, and to the underground lakes of oil which fuel the homes and factories of Western Europe.

MICHAEL BAR-ZOHAR
38. Ben-Gurion and the Policy of the Periphery

The years following the Sinai Campaign saw a marked improvement in Israel's international position. The United States, which had opposed that campaign, came to regard Nasser as a Soviet proxy. Hence by the late 1950s Israel was partially emerging from the

Source: Michael Bar-Zohar, Ben-Gurion: A Political Biography (Tel Aviv: Am Oved, 1977), pt. 3, pp. 1321–26. Reprinted by permission.

regional and international isolation that had characterized its position earlier in the decade. It now had the opportunity to find its place within the regional and global policies of the Western powers that were trying to establish a network of regional treaty organ-izations and security alliances committed to resisting Soviet influences. David Ben-Gurion's biographer offers an account of Israel's successful attempt in the late 1950s to develop a semialliance with Iran, Turkey, and Ethiopia.

While Israel was getting more than its fill of bitter pills and frustration from the United States, it was establishing, under cover of darkness, a clandestine pact in the Middle East. Around it, in dead secrecy, rose a ghost organization, which grew and spread until it ringed the entire Arab Middle East. We must be forgiven our picturesque language: in this case, expressions like "under cover of darkness," "in dead secrecy," "ghost organization" are not at all extravagant. Even they pale in the presence of the actual circumstances which formed the backdrop for these events, and which would fire the wildest imagination. For some years, in hidden underground conditions, Israel engaged in very intensive activity throughout the Middle East. Using various disguises, fictitious names, forged passports, night flights, circuitous paths, Ben-Gurion's many messengers took off for and returned from the capitals of the new allies. Special envoys, high officials, ministers and experts were all involved in the complex operation. The secret action encompassed different spheres, most of which have not been revealed to this day. Many of those involved, including some of its initiators and thinkers, will remain anonymous for a long time to come. Only a tiny fraction of these activities have leaked into public knowledge as the years passed, and it is known as the "peripheral pact."

The affair began even before the Sinai Campaign. Secretly, special relations were forming between Israel and two states on the edge of the Middle East: Iran in the north, and Ethiopia in the south. Nasser's subversion and his expansionist aspirations wakened growing concern in Iran and Ethiopia. And not only in those two countries. Other states also shuddered at the thought of the Egyptian lust for power. Moshe Sharett mentioned one in his diary. "Concrete possibilities of joint action with the Ummah party[1] in Sudan have been clarified," he wrote just a few days prior to his resignation, "and one of its leaders is planning a visit to Israel for more serious talks." He later added: "I asked myself, over and over again, what will happen to all these if and when I leave."

Sharett had no cause for worry. The Prime Minister, the new Foreign Minister, and their aides were no less aware of the matter's importance.

The blow dealt to Nasser by Israel in the Sinai Campaign reverberated throughout the Middle East and its periphery with an intensity beyond all expectations. States fearful of Nasser's ambitions suddenly found an element capable of overcoming him. Leaders concerned about Communist infiltration via Egypt realized that there was someone capable of halting the Soviets. Ethiopia, an isolated Christian enclave in Africa, was particularly worried, and observed Nasser's pan-Islamic and pan-African expansionist tendencies with growing anxiety. Shortly after the Sinai Campaign, a high-level Israeli official, who was in charge of an important political sector in the Israeli government, arrived in Ethiopia. He met with Emperor Haile Selassie. The two discussed joint political action against Nasser's subversion, as well as economic and development cooperation. The envoy met with some of the Emperor's senior officials, and procedures and ways of action for a plan of broad scope were established. The plan included the assignment of Israeli experts to Ethiopia, and the sending of Ethiopian trainees to Israel, the establishment of joint

projects, and courses of study. But something additional came of the meeting in
Ethiopia. In the course of time, a secret trip
was planned for Ben Gurion so that he could
meet with the Emperor Haile Selassie. Ben-
Gurion also expressed his willingness for
such a trip, but at the last minute he was
prevented from implementing it. Israel coordinated its actions with France, which had
vital interests in black Africa. Some of the
missions to Ethiopia were carried out by
Yosef Nahmias, who had returned from his
work as head of the Defense Ministry delegation in Paris. But the pact with Ethiopia
expanded and grew, and was expected to be
long-lasting.

Meanwhile, Israel was looking eastward
as well. Widespread activity was begun in
Persia, parallel with the Ethiopian connection. Ben-Gurion's envoys came to Teheran,
and met with the Shah of Iran,[2] with his
Prime Minister and with senior officials of
his retinue. Iran also hoped to halt the
Nasserist and Communist influence in the
Middle East, especially considering its
border with the Soviet Union and its feeling
of being in real danger. Iran was aflutter
with powerful anti-Arab feelings, which
eased the making of contact with Israel. The
state was grappling with serious problems in
the spheres of agriculture, development,
and the exploitation of science. Israel was
prepared to offer assistance in all those
spheres: many Israeli envoys arrived in Iran,
and the ties were gradually strengthened.
On top of all that, came cooperation, the
exchange of information and coordination of
outlooks and actions in the face of developments in the Middle East. In 1958 a letter
was delivered to the Shah from Ben-Gurion,
in which the Old Man mentioned the works
of Cyrus, King of Persia,[3] for the sake of the
Jews. The Shah asked that Ben-Gurion be
told, in his reply, that "the memory of
Cyrus' policy regarding your people is precious to him, and he strives to continue in
the path set by this ancient tradition."

The unwritten pact with Iran became the
basis for the establishment of a "triangle." In

April 1958, a meeting was held between
Ambassador Eliyahu Sasson and [Fatin
Rustu] Zorlu, the Turkish Foreign Minister.
The Turkish Minister expressed his country's concern about the new reality which
was consolidating in the Middle East. Only
months earlier, a revolutionary change had
occurred on Turkey's southern border: some
of the traditional Syrian leaders, fearful of
the rapidity with which Soviet influence was
infiltrating their country, suddenly flew to
Egypt and placed the fate of their country in
Nasser's hands. Egypt's ruler was surprised
and discomfited, but saw only one way out
of the imbroglio: the establishment of a
"United Arab Republic," by uniting Egypt
and Syria into one state, consisting of two
"districts." This event raised a scare in the
pro-Western countries of the Middle East.
Jordan and Iraq, which hoped to block the
Nasserist influence, hurried to establish the
"Arab Unity." A sort of weak blending of
the two states.

The Turkish leaders worriedly followed
events in Syria. During 1957, they sensed a
clear threat to their country's existence when
a treaty was drawn up between their northern neighbour, the Soviet Union, and their
southern neighbour, Syria. Nasser's appearance in Syria quickened their sense of
danger, since he was known for his subversive activities. With the struggle between
Israel and between Syria and Egypt as the
background, they lit on a revolutionary idea
for joint action. Zorlu and Sasson met once
more, and agreed on a timetable and on
topics, with the intention of arranging further meetings on the senior levels. One of
those most active in forming the ties with
the Ankara government was Reuven Shiloah. Israel decided to establish a tie with its
two new friends in the north—Iran and
Turkey. It was aware of the fact that those
two countries were the principle strongholds of American influence in the Middle
East, and its most forward positions against
Russia.

Now, on the backdrop of the promising
connections with states in both north and

south, Israeli political thought turned to the idea of a comprehensive plan for a "peripheral pact": the establishment of a bloc of states situated on the periphery of the Middle East, and connected to Israel in a "triangle," with Turkey and Iran in the north, and Ethiopia in the south. The common denominator of these states was expressed mainly in their political position: sharp opposition to Nasserist expansionism and subversiveness, and the aspiration to halt Soviet influence. The unwritten pact had a clear implication for the West. The United States was most concerned in view of the Soviet penetration of the Middle East: the Eisenhower Doctrine [see doc. 37] did not succed in arresting the deterioration of the situation. For the first time, Israel sensed that it had something to offer the Americans: no longer would it be a small, isolated ally, hated and ostracized by all the Arab countries, but the leader and the connecting link of a bloc of states, one of which was a member of NATO, two—of the "Baghdad Pact," and one—an important African state. Here was a bloc whose population exceeded the number of Arabs in the Middle East, and which was prepared for far-reaching cooperation with the Americans in opposing Soviet ambitions in the area. Israel realized that it was terribly important to win America's political and financial support for the clandestine organization.

The first to propose arousing the United States' interest in the peripheral pact was Moshe Dayan. He came to Ben-Gurion with a suggestion: to "sell" the "pact" idea to Field Marshall Montgomery, who would pass it on to his friend Eisenhower, with whom he had fought side by side in the Second World War. A few months earlier, Dayan, on a visit to Europe, had been invited for a long talk with Montgomery. The experienced warrior had unfolded a plan for the solution of the problems of the Middle East. The programme was naive, and it is doubtful whether it could have been implemented. Montgomery was interested in Ben-Gurion's opinion of the plan, and

intended to present it to President Eisenhower. Ben-Gurion and Dayan had not been enthusiastic about the plan; now, however, with the peripheral pact beginning to take shape, Dayan thought that it might be possible to make use of Montgomery's good services in order to inform Eisenhower of what was happening, in an unconventional way. Ben-Gurion gave his approval, and Dayan flew to Europe and met with the Field Marshall. He described, for Montgomery, the pro-Western pact in the Middle East, the oil pipeline as an alternative to the Suez Canal, and the strength and ties of the north and south countries of the triangle. After the meeting, Montgomery set out for Washington and a visit with Eisenhower. Ben-Gurion, for his part, reported this development to Eban, who was Israel's ambassador in the United States capital. "The proposed plan contains one weak link—Turkey," admitted Ben-Gurion,

because it is a member of NATO, not only of the Baghdad Pact, and is not dependent for its security on the Baghdad Pact. Turkey also receives much more American aid than does Iran. And its hatred of the Arabs is not as great as that of Iran. Turkey's present principal leaders are hypocrites. Nevertheless, the plan has some basis . . . there is an objective reality in the Middle East which provides a slight hope for my plan. Jordan is hanging on a shoestring. Iraq's situation is also shaky.

Should America take over this idea—the connection between Iran, Turkey, Israel—and, we must add, Ethiopia as well—there is a chance that something important might come of it. And we should stand guard during Montgomery's visit.

It seems that Montgomery did not even raise the subject with Eisenhower. And at the same time, Eban expressed doubts as to the pact's chances of success. But Ben-Gurion was very enthusiastic about the subject, and as usual, he kept moving forward; nothing could stop him any more. "Our ties with Iran and Ethiopia are on the highest level," he wrote to Eban. "In Iran—with the Shah, in Ethiopia—with the Emperor."

There is no need to establish a pact immediately. But the development of ties of friendship and cooperation—even if they are secret in the meantime—in the fields of science and in economic affairs as well, particularly if we construct a wider oil pipeline—have much value. . . . The ties with these countries (Ethiopia and Iran) are becoming closer and closer: and if the meeting with the Turks really does take place, and the expected connection is established—it will be a triple thread with many possibilities . . . together with the budding signs in Ghana, Liberia, Nigeria, Burma, these relations are of great significance and may provide many opportunities. The good will of the United States (even without its knowing yet of all our cooperative ventures with Iran and Ethiopia) will move things forward.

The "weak link," as Ben-Gurion pointed out, remained Turkey. After the Sasson-Zorlu meeting, a high-level delegation arrived in Turkey from Israel. The background of the meeting was exotic: the representatives of Israel and Turkey met on board a grand ship, floating on the waters of the enchanting Marmara Sea. Here, at least, they could be sure that no one would see them and that their secret would not be discovered. But this was not the meeting referred to by Ben-Gurion, when he spoke of "the meeting with the Turks." To ensure himself that it was possible to establish the pact, he wanted to hold a high-level discussion with the Turkish government.

It is doubtful whether the meeting would ever have taken place had it not been for the storm which broke out in the Middle East in the summer of 1958, and swept a number of states into a powerful whirlpool. In May, civil war erupted in Lebanon between the Christian groups, gathered around the retiring Lebanese Prime Minister, Camille Chamoun, and the Moslems, working to integrate Lebanon within the Arab Nasserist bloc. The armed uprising, which began as an internal conflict, was fanned by the propaganda of Nasser's agents, and fed by the support of Egypt and Syria in the form of money, weapons and soldiers. The situation in Lebanon deteriorated dramatically; pro-Western elements in the Middle East tried to

provide weapons for the anti-Nasserist elements in Lebanon, but their help was limited. In July, the crisis struck Iraq and Jordan as well. When the situation in Jordan worsened, and the throne was endangered, the Iraqi government sent help in the form of a motorized division under General [Abd al-Karim] Qasim. But half-way, Qasim ordered his troops to turn back, and attacked Baghdad. He, together with his friends in the "Free Generals" action, carried out a speedy military coup and took power. Faisal, King of Iraq was put to death in his palace, while kneeling, still in his nightclothes and begging for his life. The heir to the throne, Abdul Illa, was murdered in his palace. The Prime Minister, Nuri Sa'id, the "strong man" of Iraq for many years, fled for his life, disguised as a woman. But the next day, as he walked through the streets, he was recognized by the crowds; they tore him to bits. Qasim, in his first broadcasts to the people, announced that Iraq was to be a "People's Republic."

When Iraq collapsed, it seemed that all the strongholds of the West in the Middle East were crumbling one after the other. Nuri Sa'id was the confidante of the British; Iraq was the heart of the Baghdad Pact, and the central link in the "Northern Tier," which the West had set up against the Soviet Union. Now it seemed that Iraq would become a Soviet satellite. Iran and Turkey, both of which shared borders with Iraq, sensed, with terror, that the Soviet noose was gradually tightening around them. . . .

. . . The Soviet Union didn't just stand by, either. Nikita Khrushchev advised Nasser, who came to Moscow for a visit, to fly to the Middle East immediately. Nasser flew to Damascus, where he declared his full support for the Iraqi revolution. The Soviet Union, for its part, announced maneuvers involving 24 divisions to be carried out in the Caucasus, along the border with Turkey. The latter, together with Iran, put heavy pressure on the United States to intervene also in Iraq. Ben-Gurion too, urged the American government to "put down the rebels (in Iraq)". The Iraqi coup spurred the Turkish leaders to overcome their remaining hesitations, and to tighten their ties with Israel as quickly as possible. "A," our envoy, was invited to Zorlu in Istanbul," wrote Ben-Gurion excitedly in his diary, five days after the Iraqi coup, "and (Zorlu) told him that they are acting parallel to our actions, and that he will be pleased to see full cooperation between our political activities and theirs. We are in historic times, and the opportunity for this action will not come again. He also notified me of the agreement, in principle, for a meeting between the two Heads of State . . . (but) should this become known, the whole matter will explode and then the Americans will also interfere."

Ben-Gurion did not agree with Zorlu about the possibility of American interference; on the contrary, now that he had Turkey's agreement to strengthen the ties— and to solidify the last layer of the peripheral pact—the Old Man decided to move on to the next stage: to arouse American interest in this pact. The next day, he convened a consultation in Golda's [Meir] house, in order to discuss the "tightening of ties with Iran, Turkey and Ethiopia, with America's help, in other words, by applying pressure to America which would in turn apply pressure and offer aid to those countries." Ben-Gurion believed that if he could interest the United States in the peripheral pact, then the United States would encourage the countries of the periphery to consolidate their ties with Israel; this would in turn help to consolidate the pact. The Middle East conflagration provided a once-in-a-lifetime opportunity for such an appeal. Ben-Gurion immediately formulated an urgent memo to President Eisenhower, in which, for the first time, he revealed the matter of the peripheral pact.

First Ben-Gurion described the gravity of the present situation and the dangers which threatened Jordan, Lebanon and Saudi Arabia. "Nasser's take-over of the Arab Middle East, with the assistance of the tremendous might of the Soviet Union, would have serious implications for the West." Among those implications, he listed: the failure of France's efforts to solve the Algerian problem and to retain its friendly relations with Tunisia and Morocco; the breakdown of Libya's independence and of American and British influence there; the danger of a communist revolt in Iran; Egyptian and Soviet domination of Sudan; the endangering of Ethiopia's independence; a sweeping assault by Nasser on "Black Africa" with the intention of gaining control over that area.

"There is no need for me to emphasize the significance of such a process, for Israel and Turkey," wrote the Old Man, placing the emphasis on Turkey in particular, since he was aware of the special American interest in that country's security.

We have begun to strenthen our ties with neighbouring countries on the outer circle of the Middle East: Iran, Ethiopia and Turkey, with the purpose of creating a powerful dam against the Nasserist-Soviet torrent. We have established friendly relations and an attitude of mutual trust with the government of Iran and the Emperor of Ethiopia. Recently, our ties with the Turkish government have become more intimate, above and beyond our normal diplomatic relations.

Our purpose is the creation of a group of states, not necessarily an official and public pact which . . . will be capable of standing firm against the Soviet expansionism with Nasser as its middleman, and which may be able to save the independence of Lebanon; perhaps, with time, that of Syria as well. This group will include two non-Arab Moslem countries (Iran and Turkey), one Christian country (Ethiopia), and the State of Israel.

Ben-Gurion described Israel's possible role to Eisenhower: "I don't want to exaggerate my estimation of our ability. I am aware of our limitations in material resources and man-power . . . nevertheless I can say that it is within our power to help . . . in those countries." Ben-Gurion made much of the peripheral states' fears of foreign "domination," stating that this fear did not exist regarding Israel. "We are capable of carrying out our mission, which is a vital need for us and also a source of tangible might for the West in this part of the world." He detailed the help which Israel could extend: technical assistance, scientific and research assistance, help in the fields of agriculture and education; he described the importance of laying an oil pipeline between Eilat and the Mediterranean Sea, "to diminish Nasser's extortion power and the chances of Soviet domination in this region."

With the above as background, Ben-Gurion presented Israel's demands: It is vital and urgent to grant Israel full security with regard to the integrity of its borders, its sovereignty and its capability for self-defence.

"I am not speaking of a distant vision. The first stages of this plan are already in the process of implementation. But two things are necessary: political, financial and moral American support, and the instilling, in Iran, Turkey and Ethiopia, of the feeling that our efforts in this direction have the support of the United States."

In concluding, Ben-Gurion emphasized the fact that the group of states in whose name he spoke, could save freedom in the central part of the Middle East and even in some of the North African countries. "When the flanks of the region are guaranteed, it will be easier to develop a resistance to Soviet and Nasserist penetration in the other parts of the Middle East."

A similar memo, worded slightly differently, was sent by Ben-Gurion to the French Prime Minister.

Now came the dread and tension of awaiting the American reaction; and when Eban delayed one day in delivering the memo, he burst out angrily: "We've lost a very precious day in such a critical time . . . instead of rushing off to Washington, Eban stayed an extra day in New York and had a talk with Hammarskjold. . . ."

Late in the evening of July 24th, Eban met with Dulles and handed him Ben-Gurion's memo. Dulles read the message on the spot, and immediately handed it to one of his aides. "Get this to the President at once," he

said, and repeated: "at once!" He turned to Eban, and added: "This is a very important letter. It must be handed to the President immediately."

Eban suggested that the Secretary of State encourage the governments of Turkey and Iran to cooperate with Israel. Dulles replied: "I see no reason why I shouldn't notify Turkey and Iran of our satisfaction with the development of ties between you and these countries."

The next day, the first reaction from Eisenhower reached Ben-Gurion. "I was deeply impressed by your comprehensive perception of the grave problems faced by the free world, both within the Middle East and beyond it . . . since the Middle East includes Israel, you can be assured of the United States' interest in the wholeness and independence of Israel. I discussed your letter with the Secretary of State, who will write to you in more detail, in the near future."

Ben-Gurion was somewhat disappointed by this reply. In his letter to the President, he had hinted of his willingness "to have an urgent discussion with the United States on these questions"; he had hoped to be invited to Washington for official talks. Some of this disappointment was expressed in a conversation with a high-level visitor from the United States. "Why doesn't the President invite me," he complained, "when he invites heads of government from large and small countries?"

Dulles and Eisenhower were still cautious; but finally, when Dulles replied to Ben-Gurion, he expressed a positive opinion and encouraged Ben-Gurion to establish the peripheral pact.

Ben-Gurion gave the green light for intensified action. But not all of his friends favoured the idea—in consultations with "our friends," Eshkol expressed doubts about the operation. There were also some ministers who were critical of the idea, but Ben-Gurion was convinced that the operation would succeed. Contacts with Turkey entered an advanced stage. Golda Meir met with the Turkish Foreign Minister, Zorlu, for two detailed talks, in which it was definitely agreed that the two Prime Ministers should

meet. During the last days of August, Ben-Gurion convened his close aides for decisive counsultations.

NOTES

1. Ummah (lit., Nation), Sudanese political party that took a pro-Western line while Egypt was moving more and more into the Soviet camp. Immediately after Sudanese independence in early 1956, Egypt—Britain's former partner in the Sudanese condominium—began pressing for new borders with Sudan. In part because of this crisis, the Ummah party became the dominant party in a new coalition formed in July 1956.

2. Muhammad Reza Pahlavi (1919–80), shah

of Iran from 1941 until he was overthrown and exiled in the Iranian revolution of January 1979. By the mid-1960s he had established a virtual police state.

3. Cyrus, king of the Persian empire in the sixth century B.C.E. Cyrus promoted the reestablishment of a Jewish community in Judaea, thus ending the first Babylonian Exile, which had begun in the years 597–586 B.C.E..

MICHAEL BAR-ZOHAR
39. Ben-Gurion and Israel's Regional and International Position in 1958

Although under David Ben-Gurion's leadership Israel successfully placed itself as an ally of the Western powers and of the anti-Nasserist, anti-Soviet states in the area (Iran, Turkey, and Ethiopia), it still faced the enmity of many nations and the threat of international isolation from the growing "neutralist" Third World bloc. The following pages from Michael Bar-Zohar's biography of Ben-Gurion, known affectionately, by this time, as The Old Man, are based largely on

Ben-Gurion's own diary. Ben-Gurion's outlook at the time was clearly influenced by the successes of the Nasserist movement in the Arab world, and particularly by the formation of the United Arab Republic (UAR), which formally united Egypt and Syria from February 1958 until September 1961. Of particular interest, in light of the June 1967 War, is Ben-Gurion's assessment of the importance of a modern air force to meet Israel's security needs.

On 4 March 1958, at the beginning of an event-filled year, Ben-Gurion attended a political session of Mapai's Foreign Affairs Committee. In his pocket was the carefully worded agenda he had prepared. But suddenly,

Something happened to me that had happened several times before, but not for a long time: all of

a sudden I saw before me a picture of the world, and I sensed our position in it very clearly; and when it came to my turn to speak, I didn't use one word of what I had prepared but instead described what I had suddenly seen, and I knew that this picture was right even if it was "cruel." And it seemed that those who heard also felt that this was an accurate picture of how we were seen by the Arab world, Russia, China, India, the small

Source: Michael Bar-Zohar, *Ben-Gurion: A Political Biography* (Tel Aviv: Am Oved, 1977), pt. 3, pp. 1359–62. Reprinted by permission.

nations of Asia and Africa—and the countries of America and Europe—and the political line that we must take.

At this same moment of elation, which he himself saw as prophetic, Ben-Gurion turned his attention to each of the political problems facing Israel. The spontaneity with which the words flowed belied his methodic thought as he constructed layer after layer of sober analysis and logical conclusions, each becoming the foundation for the subsequent layer. At the very basis of this structure he placed the Israel-Arab relationship, and described the Land of Israel, "as the Arabs see it."

"To Arab eyes," he claimed,

it seems as if ten years ago or more, people came from Poland, Rumania, Russia, and took over this country, this Arab land. And for them a country inhabited by Arabs for 1500 years is Arab . . . why should they give this country up. It stands as a wedge between the Arab countries. Abba Eban, with his skilful turn of phrase, has called it not a wedge but a bridge. That's from Eban's standpoint. But when I put myself in an Arab's place, I see it as a wedge, . . . but if we put ourselves in the Arabs' place, the conclusion we arrive at is bitter. But a bitter conclusion that is true is preferable to an illusion, however sweet. . . .

Ben-Gurion stated categorically: "I have come to a bitter conclusion, that at the present time there is no prospect of an Arab-Jewish peace.

"Two questions arise: if there is no prospect now, is there no prospect forever? But there is a still graver question. If there is no prospect now, is our existence secure?"

He asked and responded: "The two questions are linked together. . . . There is no possibility, I am deeply convinced, to bring about peace before the Arabs are convinced that it is impossible to destroy us. It's the only road to peace."

At this point he began to review the global factors shaping this reality. He admitted that [the attainment of] this [goal] has become more difficult in recent years because of Russia. He emphasized that the Soviet

Union was hostile to Israel for two reasons: "its interests in the Arab world and the problem of Soviet Jewry. . . ."

Ben-Gurion's conclusion was that Israel will receive no help from Russia, Communist China or Nehru's India; these states will not make it clear to the Arabs that it is impossible to destroy the state of the Jews.

Nor did he find the U.S. very helpful. "Now, America is in a state of ebb. The America of Eisenhower and Dulles is so perceived by the Americans as well as by the whole of Europe. . . ."

"So, who is left?" he asked. There are small nations in Asia and Africa. There is America, North America, the U.S. and Canada and the countries of Latin America. And there is Western Europe. We have hope and prospects in all these countries and only in them. . . .

He then moved to analyze the actual current problem. He reported the information that the UAR might form a Palestinian government in exile in the Gaza Strip, to add it to the UAR and launch a campaign designed to push Israel back to the time of partition. The Old Man recommended that Israel refrain from any reaction at that point. But in view of the growing danger to Israel's existence a rapid build-up was crucial. The major source of weapons, France, was facing serious difficulties due to the Algerian problem. "It cost them money and blood. They need friends and the most important friend for them is Germany." Hence his conclusion that Israel should develop her ties with Germany in order to obtain the aid that France was hard put to provide. "But the aim is not just Germany, though she holds the central position but Germany, France, the Netherlands, Belgium." He also alluded to the alliance that was then taking shape in the Middle East without mentioning the names of the members of the alliance of the periphery [see doc. 38]. "I won't talk about them, we are merely beginning and it should remain unpublicized. . . ." Thus he reached the summing up of his political outlook:

The Arab unions could pose a big danger if Russia is behind them. In view of this we should strive to achieve guarantees for the status quo in the Middle East. It will be a great achievement if Russia could be made part of this guarantee. . . .

. . . And if we can bolster our security with an air-force that cannot be defeated in a surprise attack, then we can face the power of the Arabs themselves even if they are equipped with Soviet weapons. And we should strive for guarantees by global forces that Russia will not and does not want to challenge seriously. . . . [And if] the Arabs realize that Israel cannot be destroyed, then there may be people among the Arabs who would begin to think that this "quarrel" should be stopped and peace should, perhaps be made with Israel.

SHIMON PERES
40. American Arms for Israel

In the early 1960s President John F. Kennedy tried to reopen a dialogue with Nasser's Egypt, and that meant attempting to resolve the Arab-Israeli conflict. Ben-Gurion, however, was skeptical of any fundamental change in the Arab states' stance (see doc. 39). Israel's anxiety that its security might be affected was relieved by major American-Israeli arms deals. In the first of these, announced in September 1962, the United States agreed to sell the short-range defensive Hawk missiles to Israel. This sale was not only the first time that a nation outside of the Western bloc received supersonic weapons and supporting equipment; it was also a reversal of U.S. policy not to be a major source of weapons for any nation in the Middle East. This policy reversal grew out of the U.S. Defense Department's concern that the amount of Soviet military equipment recently furnished to Egypt, Iraq, and Syria would tip the military balance of forces in the Arabs' favor and that such an imbalance might lead either to an Arab attack on Israel or to a "preventive" attack by Israel upon one of the Arab states with offensive military power.

Following the Hawk missiles deal, arms negotiations between Washington and Israel accelerated. Growing Soviet involvement in the Middle East and the failure of the attempt at an American-Egyptian rapprochement led to a reevaluation of Israel's role in American strategic planning. As a result, the United States overcame some of its earlier objections to a close military relationship with Israel. During Lyndon Johnson's presidency American-Egyptian relations deteriorated even further as tension and conflict within the region increased. The following reading presents these processes from the perspective of Shimon Peres, who had been near the center of Israel's defense planning since the early 1950s.

The story of America's refusal, until fairly recently, to help Israel achieve an arms balance seems almost as unreal today as the account of France's generous response to Israel's arms pleas up to the Six Day War. The unreserved friendship of Paris and the restraining hesitations of Washington now read like forgotten chapters of a distant past.

Source: Shimon Peres, *David's Sling* (London: Weidenfeld and Nicolson, 1970), pp. 87–108. Reprinted by permission of Shimon Peres.

Yet, as with many events of the past, they have a relevance for the future: what has happened before *may* happen again. The interests of Israel demand—as they always have and always will—that she not be dependent on a single source of arms supply, for she may find herself the victim of a change in attitude by the supplying country. Such change may occur without any special action on Israel's part. It may be—and most often is—motivated by extraneous factors, notably by changes in relationships with other countries and not necessarily with other countries in the Middle East. The birth of new international relationships, unlike that of humans, cannot always be anticipated; nor is the gestation always apparent. Their death, similarly, is not always, if ever, a function of age or accident. A small State, much affected by international political changes, must therefore always preserve its power of initiative, seek alternative forms of insurance, follow a pluralistic policy in its international associations.

The United States did respond in some measure to Israel's arms requests even before the middle 1960s; but her modest compliance was far outweighed by her reservations. These were due primarily to what in those earlier years was considered to be the relative insignificance of a major political factor powerfully in evidence today—the Soviet presence in the Middle East. Soviet penetration was then thought to be slight, and John Foster Dulles, Secretary of State in President Eisenhower's Government, believed it could be contained. He had high hopes of "rescuing" Nasser from the overtures of Russia, and had no wish to jeopardize his efforts by delivering major arms to Israel. Dulles was further inhibited from so doing by his attachment to the aim of winning the hearts of the "unaligned" States, led by India, Yugoslavia and Egypt. (It proved equally fruitless.) It must also be added that he and his President did not always approve of Israel's policies.

However, neither was completely indifferent to Israel's arms needs, and after a time they enabled her to acquire certain types of defensive weapons—recoilless anti-tank guns, anti-aircraft guns and radar systems. But Dulles specifically demanded a softening of Israel's reactions to the terror and sabotage raids by the Arab States. . . .

Shifts in America's arms policy towards Israel followed major changes not only in the situation in the Middle East but also in the world. By the time Presidents Kennedy and Johnson reached office, the special enterprise of winning over the "unaligned" States was no longer relevant; the India-Yugoslavia-Egypt bloc had crumbled (particularly after the death of Nehru). Also no longer relevant was the design, demonstratively pursued by Dulles, to gain favour with the Arab States by dissociating America from the colonialism of her allies, Britain and France. The departure of France from North Africa, and Britain from her remaining territories in the Middle East, left the United States with no "imperialism" to decry. The principal major change, however, was the increasing penetration of the Soviet Union in the Middle East, which developed deeper and deeper in the years that followed until it ultimately evolved into a full-scale presence. The Russians had operated shrewdly: they were careful not to take unnecessary risks, but they were energetic and alert enough to seize every opportunity to extend the range of their influence.

An important factor, too, was the growing awareness in the United States of the independence-minded qualities of Israel. She had shown that she was able to stand up for herself, and even to withstand Soviet pressures. These qualities, of course, sprang from sources that were wholly Israeli. But Israel's determination not to become a victim of Soviet penetration—nor indeed to become anyone's puppet—was nonetheless congruent with wider American interests.

These international developments and their constant review and reappraisal by America's leaders eventually brought about a revolutionary change in the American response to Israel's requests for arms—from a virtual embargo in the early fifties to the supply of tanks and planes in the middle sixties. . . .

The Hawk missiles, which Ben-Gurion had requested in his first talk with Kennedy as President, were the first major weapons to breach the wall of America's arms embargo. They were to play a valuable part in strengthening the deterrent and defence system of Israel. . . .

My second memorable visit to Washington took place a year later. On the last day of May 1964, I accompanied the late Levi Eshkol, who had followed Ben-Gurion as Prime Minister of Israel, on his first official visit to the American capital. President Johnson, in a special gesture to Mr. Eshkol, had given it the status of a State visit, and Mr. Eshkol was a guest of the President. . . .

Before leaving for Washington, we had reviewed our prospects. We were reasonably certain of getting some of the things we would ask for, hopeful about others. We also thought there might be subtle political pressures on some points. In the event, we found we had exaggerated the danger of pressures, and had been slightly optimistic about securing all we wanted. We had not yet learned that in a visit of a few days, one can do no more than open doors. Practical results take longer.

We felt that the visit would have several useful effects. It would demonstrate to the world the warmth of Israel-American relations. It would enable us to gauge at first hand the Administration's attitude towards Egypt. It would give the Israeli Prime Minister the opportunity to seek directly an American declaration to support Israel if she were attacked. It would also give us the opportunity of trying to break the partial arms embargo which the United States still maintained against us. We were particularly interested in tanks—we were still getting aircraft from France—for disturbing reports had reached us of a new arms deal between Russia and Egypt, as well as information on the development of two types of ground-to-ground missiles

which the Egyptians were carrying out with the aid of German scientists.

There were two other items on which we sought American help. One concerned an idea we had been working on to establish a nuclear desalination plant, and we thought the United States might aid us in a joint project—for lack of water was becoming a problem for some regions of America as well. Finally, we were very worried about the fate of the Jews in Russia, and we hoped the United States might use her good offices to secure an easing of their lot.

As against our requests, we thought we might find ourselves under pressure from the United States Government on two subjects. One was the possible American demand that we take back Arab refugees before any Arab-Israel agreement and without any permanent political arrangement for peace in the region. The other was that we accept an inverted arms balance, namely, a reduction in the quantities of arms in the Middle East, which would leave us woefully short.

On the morning of 1 June 1964, the President's helicopter landed us on the White House lawn, and through the windows of the craft we could see the honour guard already drawn up in the form of three sides of a square, composed of Navy, Marines, Air Force and Infantry detachments. Near them stood two military bands and the official welcoming party. As soon as the door of the helicopter was opened, the President stepped towards us, accompanied by Lady Bird [Johnson's wife], and greeted us warmly. After a short and graceful speech by the President and Mr. Eshkol's response, Mr. Johnson led us into his working office. It seemed much the same as in Kennedy's day, except that the model of the PT-boat was no longer there, and against one wall was a small bust of the assassinated President.

After polite exchanges, Mr. Johnson hinted that he would like to conduct part of the talk with the Prime Minister alone, and we all left them. When we were asked to come in again, Eshkol was beaming. As I took my seat beside him, and while the rest of the party were going to their places, he had time to tell me that the President could not have been more friendly, saying that "the United States stands four-square behind Israel"; that America would "not be idle if Israel is attacked"; and that this undertaking, given by both his predecessor and himself, was a "solemn and serious commitment."

The talks now entered the formal stage, and the President opened by making clear America's position on five points: on water, he said that the United States would support the implementation of the "Johnston Plan"—the plan drawn up by President Eisenhower's special envoy, the late Eric Johnston, on the division of the waters of the Jordan and Yarmuk rivers between Israel and Jordan, on tanks: America would help Israel get them, on the defence of Israel: America stood behind her; on missiles: the United States was against proliferation of nuclear weapons in the world, and she was certainly against their proliferation in the Middle East; on desalination: the United States would extend her help.

The President enlarged on all these points, and he concluded by saying that he regarded Mr. Eshkol's visit as an expression of the friendship that existed between the two peoples. Turning to the Prime Minister, he added, with a smile: "Some say that we're alike. Well, that's not at all bad."

It was now Eshkol's turn to speak. This was certainly one of the most dramatic moments of his life, and one heavy with responsibility. He had come a long way from his father's flour mill in the Ukraine, and from the swamps in the Jordan Valley which he had helped to clear as a young labouring pioneer in Palestine. He was now a guest in the White House, the official representative of his people. He spoke with his usual simplicity, his mind firmly focused on essentials. After outlining the dangers which still encompassed Israel, he said that he certainly appreciated the "American commitment," but he could not go back and tell his people that they could rely on that alone. A nation had to rely on itself, its soldiers and its weapons for its defence. It might be true, as the President had said, that the Egyptian missiles were "primitive" and not very accurate; but they could cause much damage in our populated areas. The balance of forces was in Nasser's favour—or Nasser might think so—and it was impossible to depend only upon "the nice words said about Israel's Defence Forces." Israel wanted tanks. He hoped the President would understand that the defence of Israel had to be a "do it yourself" undertaking. It would be worth helping Nasser only when he agreed to transfer the resources of Egypt from the military to the economic field. He ended by urging the President to do what he could to speed up the joint desalination project.

The opening statements by the two principals were followed by a discussion in which the rest of us took part. This first meeting established the framework of our negotiations, though it did not exhaust the subjects we would be taking up. . . .

The negotiations ended with America's agreement to supply Israel with Patton tanks (which the Jordanians were already getting) and Skyhawk planes. (Jordan preferred the F-104.) This brought to an end the policy of the United States "not to be the major supplier of arms to the Middle East." This, to my mind, became inevitable the moment the Russians took that function upon themselves—but becoming the chief supplier to one side only. This was the side of the Anti-Western Arab States, whose enmity of Israel had brought them to the abandonment of their vaunted "non-alignment" stand in the global conflict and bound them tightly to the policy of Moscow. This policy, for all Moscow's pretensions to be the pioneers of Marxist revolutionary ideology, was but a continuance of the imperialist ambitions of Czarist Russia.

EHUD AVRIEL
41. Israel's Beginnings in Africa

In the early 1950s Israel tried to break out of its partial international isolation by establishing relations with the emerging Asian and African nations. Burma was the first of the developing countries to establish diplomatic relations with Israel and enter into economic cooperation and aid programs. Ghana, in 1957, was the first African state to do so. In the following years, through trade agreements, training programs, and economic cooperation programs run by both the state and the Histadrut, Israel successfully established diplomatic ties with all Black African states except Somalia and Mauritania, which did not recognize Israel. The relationships were mutually beneficial until the aftermath of the October 1973 War, when most African states suspended formal diplomatic relations with Israel. Guinea had severed relations following the June 1967 War, Uganda in 1972.

Ehud Avriel, an early member of the Israeli Foreign Ministry and an aide to Ben-Gurion, was one of the architects of Israel's African policy. His memoirs describe the "golden" era of the African-Israeli relationship.

With joy one remembers how we in Israel threw ourselves, with verve and boundless enthusiasm, into cooperation with the fledgling movement of emerging African nationalism. The latter half of the fifties was not a period of idealistic optimism regarding the future of our planet and society. The cold war was sobering to hopes entertained during the brief euphoria immediately following the victory over Hitler's Axis. Commercialism had replaced the magnanimous expectations engendered by the new beginning after the darkest interlude in human history; the war-time Alliance had disintegrated; European powers were on the verge of decline; the adjustment to life in the shade of the two giant superpowers was beginning to take its awkward shape.

The sound of cheerful drumming from remote Africa, announcing the stirrings of Nkrumah's[1] national liberation movement and its scattered echoes from other parts of the black continent were the one encouraging message in an otherwise most unimaginative world. Israel was among the first to derive courage from these signs on the firmament; we were looking for kindred souls, people in hope for justice, equality, purposeful social development, unorthodox politics, daring foresight, readiness for sacrifice. We had just received an inkling of these from a different source. David Hacohen, Israel's first ambassador to Burma, had evolved unprecedented schemes for practical cooperation. Rather than content himself with the analysis of political trends in the country in which he represented us, he attempted to dig more deeply. His enthusiasm infected the leadership of the Burmese People's party. Soon Israeli technicians, advisers and experts arrived in faraway Burma to help avoid the repetition of mistakes we had made, just recently, when we began to develop our own country with the new elan that came with independence.

Our first encouter with the new Africa

Source: Michael Curtis and Susan Aurelia Gitelson, eds., *Israel in the Third World* (New Brunswick, N.J.: Transaction Books, 1976), pp. 69–74. Copyright © 1976 by Transaction, Inc. Reprinted by permission of Transaction, Inc.

occurred thanks to one of Israel's most stable friends, President [William V.S.] Tubman of Liberia. Ambassador Daniel Lewin went in 1956 to the president's third inauguration to represent Israel. On the late president's pilgrimage to the American Congress in 1935 (for the resumption of relations) he was shunned by most and scorned by many. Congressman Emanuel Celler[2] was the one person who comforted and encouraged President Tubman in his despair. Ever since Tubman remained a true friend of the Jewish people whom he regarded as equal only to Africans (and blacks in America) in terms of suffering and disdain on the part of the "superior races." At that inauguration Lewin met two representatives of the Gold Coast. The Israeli and the Africans spent hours on end telling each other about their respective countries, comparing the underlying philosophies of the Zionist movement and of the Convention People's party, and found that they had much common ground.

In search for new sea routes—in view of the barring of the Suez Canal to Israeli shipping—a representative of the National Shipping Line (Zim) explored the West Coast of Africa at that time for suitable harbors. He found what he had looked for— and more—in Accra. Shalom Klinghofer returned from his search for new outlets for Zim's initiatives with glowing reports about the Convention People's party and their leaders: high-minded, dedicated young men who thought along much the same lines as the Haganah (volunteer defense forces before Israel became a state) and the pioneering movement in Israel.

Ambassador Lewin, then in charge of African and Asian affairs in the Foreign Office, added a file inscribed "Gold Coast" to his lean archives and started to look around for an emissary to the newly discovered territory. As independence was still some way off, the first representative of Israel was to be a consul rather than an ambassador. Luckily, Lewin was able to obtain the most suitable candidate for the mission into the unknown. Hanan Yavor, a kibbutznik without the protocol air but with devotion to the heritage of the pioneering movement that built Israel and love for exciting adventure. He went to Accra and planted the Israeli flag in the center of what was to be for a number of years the Jerusalem of African nationalism; Kwame Nkrumah's capital city, Accra.

During the winter of 1956–57 the Foreign Relations Department of the Histadrut received a telegram from four African trade unionists, who had attended an Asian trade union conference in Bandung. There they had heard so much invective against Israel that their curiousity was aroused: where there was so much smoke there must be some fire. If, they had argued, Arab countries with no free trade union movement whatsoever, inveighed so aggressively against the one country in their area that had a model trade union movement—they would like to have a look for themselves at the object of Arab tirades. Could they spend a few days as guests of the Histadrut on their way home? Barkatt[3] was delighted and cabled immediate acceptance. They came, led by John Tettegah of the Ghana Trade Union Congress (TUC) and at that time a close aide of Kwame Nkrumah's, and stayed not for a few days but for a few weeks. They were overcome with admiration for the achievements of Israel during the short time that had elapsed since the end of "colonial rule" and overwhelmed by the warmth of their comradely reception. Also they were impressed by the fact that they were not exposed to anti-Arab polemics. Instead of hostile instigation against their nonaligned Arab friends, they were led from one serious discussion about the real problems concerning the social and technological development of their territories to another. As they returned to their respective countries (Ghana, Nigeria, Northern Rhodesia [later Zambia] and Upper Volta), human contacts had been established stronger than any vitriolic Arab incitement against the "Zionist imperialists." (Incidentally, one of the issues that remained unexplained during this crucial encounter, and was to remain a moot point throughout most of the ensuing relationship, was the speed of Israeli development; when we insisted that we had begun to lay the foundations for independent statehood right under the nose of the Mandate we were often judged overmodest or exaggerating unavoidable insignificant initiatives. How, the Africans asked, could you begin to build the infrastructure of your educational system, your agriculture, your industry, and moreover your armed services while foreign power is still all-pervasive. The fact that this attitude was the source of their weakness—as ours was the secret of our relative strength—remained clouded to the end.)

The proclamation of Ghana's independence was welcomed by high tides of warm love from all over the world. Delegations of all sovereign countries and of most underground movements still struggling for their freedom congregated in Accra. The emergence of the first black African state from colonial rule was regarded as a momentous event. The fact that this emergence had become possible by mutual consent and compromise between the British and the Ghanaians augured well for future relations. It was generally assumed though, that for quite a while Ghana would be alone. No other British colony and certainly no French dependency would soon follow the path of Ghana to independence.

At the end of the Ghanaian festivities, the Israeli delegation had a private audience with Kwame Nkrumah. He presented them (David Hacohen with his Burmese experience was a member) with exactly the same list of urgent requirements he expected from the older states: a shipping line to transport the countries' exports, mainly cocoa, to overseas markets, advice on modernization of agriculture, technical assistance in the production of import replacements, schools, frameworks for the mobilization of youth in the service of the new state's development.

Under Golda Meir's energetic leadership, the Israeli Foreign Office vastly expanded its technical assistance program that had just been installed. Ambassador Aharon Remez was given the task of coordinating Israeli government agencies, public and private entrepreneurs, universities, the Histadrut, the kibbutz movement and the Israeli Army in an effort to meet Ghana's demands.

Less than one year after Ghana's proclamation of independence, Israel had already installed an embassy in Accra. Before the first year was out, every single requirement on Nkrumah's list had become a subject for intensive cooperation between Ghana and Israel. We provided the top men. We received first-rate Ghanaians to understudy and serve as second-in-command to prepare to take over as soon as possible from our specialists. Ghana, still in possession of vast foreign exchange reserves, provided most of the capital necessary. Over two hundred Israelis were busy on the many schemes. As a matter of policy we very seldom seconded personnel to existing departments in Ghana, and later, as cooperation expanded, in other African countries. We preferred to assist in the creation of new enterprises or new departments of public administration, better suited to the requirements of an independent state than the carry-overs of colonial structures.

India and Israel were at that early stage the countries closest to Nkrumah's mind. He venerated Nehru's continuous neutralism, antiimperialism and nationalistic pride that offered no favors to the technologically more advanced white nations. He admired Israel's tenacity in the face of widespread hostility, its military prowess in the face of more numerous and more heavily equipped, long-established armies, its success in "making the desert bloom" through hard work and the application of unorthodox technical and social devices. Nkrumah shrewdly calculated that his acceptance of our enthusiastically and massively offered aid would have to constitute sufficient reward for a people accustomed to dwell in solitude and unpampered by the support of likeminded power blocs.

It was in this spirit that major strides forward were made in our cooperation with Ghana during the initial period of our friendship. The Black Star Line—the first African shipping line ever—was founded on only a fraction of the investment deemed necessary by older (and more self-centered) seafarers than has Israel; a nautical college was installed to provide officers and engineers for the merchant navy when we discovered, to our consternation, that black Africans had been kept down to the level of unskilled deckhands. Chicken farming was most successfully introduced with negligible capital investment to overcome the trauma left along the West African coast by a grandiose but wholly inexpert scheme the British had tried out and which had left behind the myth that eggs cannot be produced in the tropics and that the few eggs necessary—only whites would need them anyway—would be forever imported from Northern Europe. Alumni of the Israeli pioneering movement, the kibbutz and the paramilitary defense-cum-settlement movement Nahal[4] arrived in Ghana to instil patriotic dedication into the members of the Youth Brigade, established to take unemployed youngsters from idleness to productivity.

These and many other programs deepened the relationship between Israel and Africa's first decolonized model country. A major breakthrough into wider expanses was to occur on this background during the All-African-People's Conference, held in Accra in December 1958. This meeting of the movements of national liberation from all over Africa could have easily been overshadowed by extremist Arab incitement against recognition and cooperation with Israel. The competition between Nasser and Nkrumah for leadership of the oppressed was fierce. While Nasser had the necessary funds and ambition, Nkrumah knew well how to use his kingship and the uniqueness of his constitutional achievement in making Ghana the African symbol of decolonization.

Golda Meir was on a state visit to Ghana just as the conference convened and Accra abounded with resistance fighters from all corners of the continent. George Padmore, venerated father of Pan-Africanism, suggested that Nkrumah's guest, the foreign minister of Israel, meet in special session with the participants of his revolutionary gathering. With the president's blessing Golda Meir entered a conference hall containing mostly people who had little—or utterly negative—information about Israel. George Padmore acted as host and moderator. Mrs. Meir, in her outspoken simplicity, repelled the attack of Algeria, orchestrated by the immensely popular Algerian delegates. As they remonstrated against Israel's involvement with France (still our "friend and ally"), Mrs. Meir patiently and convincingly explained Israel's true philosophy to an increasingly interested and warmly affected audience. Padmore's affirmation of the Israeli position elevated her statements to a level beyond any possible doubt. Within that afternoon Israel had sown the seeds of future attachements with otherwise completely unattainable personalities. The pessimistic timetables of the leaders of decolonization were soon to be overturned by de Gaulle's[5] ruse and by Britain's sudden awareness of "the winds of change." Within less than one year the subversive ringleaders who had congregated at Accra to prepare for a long-drawn struggle found themselves in positions of acknowledged legitimacy as heads of states. Many of those present who had listened to Mrs. Meir's talk, gladly grasped the hand of Israel profferred to initiate cooperation on the Ghana model.

When the lights went out in one Israeli embassy in Africa after another many an Israeli was deeply saddened. Not only those who had actively participated in our cooperative effort; not only the diplomats and commentators whose business is the analysis of political events. The severance of diplomatic relations was—when it came right during the Yom Kippur war—a heavy blow: we felt abandoned by countries we had helped in their own hour of need and rejected by people for whom we felt great warmth.

The African decision to break relations with Israel is partly the result of the self-imposed law of unanimity that prevails at the Organization for African Unity: the Arabs of Northern Africa, shedding all pretense, forced the Middle Eastern conflict upon a forum designed mainly for the purpose of dealing with problems more directly pertinent to Africa's own survival in a troubled world.

Israel has no regrets concerning its role in the emergence of African independence. If we were privileged to add even the tiniest particle to the liberation of the oppressed Africans and to the amelioration of their cruel living conditions, we shall always regard ourselves vastly rewarded for whatever efforts we may have invested in a great human enterprise.

NOTES

1. Kwame Nkrumah (1909–72), head of state of Ghana from its independence in 1951 until he was deposed by a coup in 1966. Nkrumah had been a leader of the Pan-African movement since the 1940s and was a major figure in African and Third World politics.

2. Emanuel Celler (1888–1980), Jewish member of the U.S. House of Representatives from Brooklyn, New York, 1923–73.

3. Reuven Barkatt (Burstein) (1906–72), head of the International Department of the Histadrut, 1950–60; later secretary general of Mapai, 1962–66, and speaker of the Knesset, 1969–72.

4. Nahal (acronym for Noar Haluzi Lohem; lit., Fighting Pioneer Youth), special corps in the Israel Defense Forces that combines military and agricultural training in order to establish new settlements, usually in border areas.

5. Charles de Gaulle (1890–70), leader of the French Resistance during World War II, founder of the Fifth Republic, and president of France, 1959–69. During the last years of the Fourth Republic, de Gaulle remained aloof from the political squabbles and conflicts. Nevertheless he still commanded great influence and loyalty among many French politicians and citizens. After the June 1967 War de Gaulle accused Israel of aggression, criticized Israeli policy, and called for an immediate withdrawal of Israeli troops from the conquered territory.

GAMAL ABDUL NASSER
42. The Arab Summit Conferences

The Sinai Campaign was followed by a lull in the Arab-Israeli conflict. Israel acquired the means for a policy of deterrence, and Egypt was determined not to be dragged into another war without proper preparation. The debate over the issue of the Jordan River waters serves to illustrate both the Egyptian outlook at that time and the interlacing of the Arab-Israeli conflict and inter-Arab rivalries.

Shared usage of the Jordan River waters has been a persistent issue in the Arab-Is-

raeli conflict. Eric Johnston's mission in the early 1950s led to a de facto agreement between Israel and Jordan regarding the distribution and utilization of the waters that allowed Israel to build its National Water Carrier System in stages. In 1964, during the final stages of its completion, Jordan and Syria attempted to divert the Jordan River, the sources of which are primarily in Syria, and thereby deprive Israel of most of these waters.

The First Arab Summit Conference, held

Source: Israeli Foreign Broadcast Information Service, *Daily Report*, no. 55 (June 3, 1965), pp. B5–B7.

in Cairo in January 1964, was called by
Nasser to counter Israel's plans to pump
Jordan River waters to the Negev. At the
meeting the Arab League decided that its
members should proceed with plans to
divert the river waters. The Arab kings and
heads of state also addressed broader issues.
They affirmed that "they will regulate their
political and economic relations with other
countries according to the stands of these
countries towards the Arabs' legitimate
struggle against Zionist designs in the Arab
world." They accused Israel of "continuous
acts of aggression," "practicing racial dis-
crimnation against the Arab minority," having "evicted the Arab Palestine people from
their home," and subjecting Afro-Asian
states to "Zionist, imperialist dangers and
designs—particularly in Africa" (Egyptian
Information Department, *The First Arab Summit Conference, Cairo, [13–17 January 1964]*,
pp. 17–19). To put teeth into these accusations, they placed their armies under a
Unified Arab Command. The conference
also began the discussions that led to the
establishment and support of the Palestine
Liberation Organization, which was pro-

claimed in March 1964 at the Arab Palestinian Congress in (Jordanian) Jerusalem.

With the diversion of the Jordan River
waters thus approved by the Arab League,
Israel responded by artillery and tank fire to
obstruct the project and finally, in November 1964, attacked construction sites by air.
Israel had long maintained that any attempt
to deprive it of its rightful share of the
Jordan River waters would be considered a
casus belli. The Second Arab Summit Conference, held in Alexandria in September 1974,
dealt with essentially the same set of issues,
as did a meeting of Arab heads of state held
in Cairo in May 1965.

The following excerpts are taken from a
speech delivered by President Nasser to the
Palestine National Council on May 31, 1965,
shortly after the meeting of Arab heads of
State in Cairo. It addresses the controversies
among the Arab states, particularly Egypt
and Syria, over implementation of the resolutions of the conferences. The issues at
stake—the diversion of the tributaries of the
Jordan River waters, the Palestinian entity,
the Unified Arab Command—ultimately
produced the crisis of May 1967.

On 23 December [1963] I stood and called
for a conference of the Arab kings and
presidents to discuss the question of Palestine and for a unified Arab action in regard to
Palestine. The question was that Israel had
diverted the Jordan River, that resolutions
had been made in the Arab League since 1960
providing for the diversion of the Jordan
River tributaries, and that some other resolutions had been made at the Arab League since
1960 providing for the setting up of a Unified
Arab Command but that these resolutions
have not been implemented.

For this reason, at the time I felt the great
danger to our action and felt that work
within the framework of the Arab League in
the normal way would not bring us a step
forward toward collective Arab action and
that it was our duty to make another
attempt. Thus I called for the conference of

Arab kings and presidents. This was another
or second course of unified Arab action.

The Arab kings and presidents met. All of
us were aware of the conditions of the Arab
states at the time and of the disputes and
clashes and how imperialism and Zionism
relied on these disputes and clashes and
fanned them. The conference represented a
course of Arab action. In my personal
opinion, it worked for the accomplishment
of one marginal or secondary task (*muhimah
janibiyah aw fariyah*). It tackled one of the
complications of the danger which faced us
at the time, namely, the waste of the unified
Arab effort in the face of the Israeli action.

Again in order to be well informed about
things, we ask ourselves: is this conference,
the first conference of Arab presidents and
kings and the second conference of Arab
presidents and kings, and the conference of

heads of states or the one Arab action which resulted from the summit conference—are they the road to the liberation of Palestine? We ask ourselves this question in order to reply to it and find out what the state of affairs is among Arab nations. There are contradictions among the Arab states. There are problems among the Arab states. There is lack of confidence among the Arab states. There is war among the Arab states. In Yemen, there is a conflict between Yemen and the UAR on the one side and Saudi Arabia on the other, and the British as well.

There are these contradictions. Shall we forget them and shall we close our eyes and say that all the matters have been settled, all the problems have been solved, and that the way is now paved? Shall we say that we have held a conference for the kings and presidents, that some speeches were made at this conference, and that some resolutions were adopted and, therefore, the Palestine problem is solved?

I say that we must view things realistically. . . . Differences could be gradually settled through meetings and conflicts could also be overcome gradually. We can adopt a unanimous attitude on certain things but we will not be able to be unanimous about everything. Everyone has his own interests. Everyone has his apprehensions about the other. This shows that there are suspicions and conflicts. This is evident in not allowing the Arab armies to move from one Arab country to another. This is a reality which we must admit.

There are problems between Syria and Iraq; there are problems between Syria and Egypt; and there are problems between Saudi Arabia and Egypt. There are, of course, suspicions in Lebanon—they do not accept any Arab force. We are experiencing these situations and, therefore, we must accept them and not overlook them. But how could the unified Arab action be of help to us? Unified Arab action which was the result of the conference of kings and presidents had pushed us a step forward from the point where we were before in the Arab League. Therefore, unified Arab action is only one way of Arab action.

Palestine cannot be liberated by holding conferences. When the Arab countries meet, as they met last week, some try to outbid the others; some launch attacks; some write articles and make broadcasts. We read of some Arab countries—that we must open all the Arab fronts against Israel and that a joint Arab action should be taken when Syria is attacked. We also read that the Arab unified command did not take any action when Syria and Jordan were attacked. And every Arab country tries to put the blame on another Arab country claiming that it is carrying out its duties fully while the Unified Arab Command failed to fulfill its task. Such countries hold that the Unified Arab Command should have done this or that. We can do nothing unless air and land protection is provided for us and we cannot divert the Jordan tributaries without land and air protection, and so everyone puts the blame on the other.

SYRIAN BA'ATH PARTY
43. The Conflict with Israel

The Ba'ath (lit., Renaissance) party, founded in Syria in the 1940s, is Pan-Arab and calls itself socialist. It won seats for the first time in the Syrian elections of 1954 and began to spill over into Jordan, Lebanon, and Iraq. After 1958 pressure from Nasser forced it underground, but it reemerged in Syria in 1963 and in Iraq in 1968.

On February 23, 1966, one faction of the Ba'ath party in Syria staged a military coup and ousted its rivals from power. The coup resulted in the emergence of a radical regime that preached and implemented a more militant policy in a number of spheres, including the Arab-Israeli conflict. The new line was clearly articulated in this statement of purpose adopted at the regional (Syrian) congress of the Ba'ath held in March 1966.

The traditional presentation of the campaign for the liberation of Palestine and the resolutions of the summit conferences which were cast into this would in the end lead only to the piling up of arms in the various Arab countries. Military preparations are indeed necessary, but they must be made within the framework of a program which has a time limit. It has become absolutely clear that time in no way favours the Arabs, and that each passing day increases Israel's military and economic strength. The time factor will progressively work in her favour now that she has decided to exploit the atom both for peace and for war. It is therefore necessary to consider decisive revolutionary action, which will deny Israel the benefit of the time factor and frustrate the plans she has based on it. It is essential to begin the campaign; obviously, this presentation of the problem demands a definition of the nature of the struggle, its methods and its instruments. The experiences of the peoples struggling against Imperialism have proved that the only way to make war against superior forces is by means of a people's war of liberation. This war has to take on a certain form, suited to the given Arab reality. This demands an analysis of the problem in revolutionary terms which lays bare the actual possibilities and describes their development and growth in the future: the world powers, both east and west, regard the Middle East in a special way. The traditional policy strives to maintain this region free from war and its accompanying phenomena, since any escalation towards war would endanger the martime passages and the oil lines, a result affecting the whole world. Until now this concern has been directed towards the preservation of Israel's existence, as a consequence of the Arabs' weakness and their surrender to pressure and their reluctance to act. The time has come for us to exploit this concern in our favour, and we will not be able to do this unless we prove that we are stronger than this pressure and that our firm decision to open the campaign will be accompanied by a real readiness to make enormous sacrifices. We must be psychologically prepared to bear the consequences (of beginning the war), however dire they may be, even if the price demanded is the total destruction of all that we have built up within the sphere of civilization, or of all the development proj-

Source: Abraham Ben-Tzur, ed., *The Syrian Ba'ath Party and Israel: Documents from the Internal Party Publications* (Givat Havivah: Center for Arab and Afro-Asian Studies, 1968), pp. 19–21. Reprinted by permission.

ects which we thought of building; because all of these things can be created again after the elimination of Israel, and then we will direct our enormous resources towards economic development and prosperity.

YITZHAK RABIN
44. The Last Stages of the Crisis

Tensions between Israel and the neighboring Arab states increased in the spring of 1967. Egypt, Syria, and Jordan were mobilizing their troops and preparing for a possible military confrontation. When Nasser declared on May 22 that the Straits of Tiran (see map 3) were closed to Israeli shipping, he committed a belligerent act that Israel had long maintained would be a *casus belli*.

Yitzhak Rabin, Israel's prime minister in the years 1974–77, was chief of staff of the Israel Defense Forces when war broke out in June. In the preceding years, when Levi Eshkol was prime minister and minister of defense, Rabin had played a crucial role in shaping Israel's defense policies. The following is a brief account by Rabin of the development of the May Crisis that led to the June 1967 War.

The Syrian government passed the information on to Egypt[1] and requested an urgent consultation with the Egyptian chief of staff. Eager to prove that he was capable of deterring Israel from carrying out her "aggressive designs," Nasser began to undertake a series of steps. On 14 May I received the first report—vague and laconic—that something was afoot in Egypt. The chariots of war were beginning to roll.

The following day, as I stood in the reviewing stand in Jerusalem watching the IDF's Independence Day parade, firm reports of Egyptian troop movements were whispered into my ear. The Egyptian army was moving through the streets of Cairo on its way eastward toward the Suez Canal. I immediately instructed Southern Command to step up its reconnaissance activities and Northern Command to refrain from superfluous troop movements (so as not to foster the impression that we were planning to attack). The next day our government also took a political step by notifying the American and French ambassadors that the reports of Israeli troop concentrations on the northern border were unfounded. What, then, was going on?

GHQ's Intelligence Branch submitted its assessment that we were facing a repetition of Operation Rotem[2] and that the Egyptians would withdraw their forces to the west of the Suez Canal after a time. Nevertheless over the next few days we continued to take precautions: heightening the alert of our forces, deploying regular armoured units in the south, placing reserved armoured brigades on mobilization alert, and laying minefields at vulnerable spots along the Egyptian border. At the same time, standing orders were to refrain from overt movements to avoid an escalation of tension. It was a very delicate situation. We had to react to the military moves in Egypt, both to

---

Source: Yitzhak Rabin, *The Rabin Memoirs* (Jerusalem and London: Weidenfeld and Nicolson, 1979), pp. 133–139. Reprinted by permission of Yitzhak Rabin and Weidenfeld and Nicolson.

protect our security and keep up our deterrent posture. Had we failed to react—giving the Egyptians the impression that we were either unaware of their moves or complacent about them—we might be inviting attack on grounds of vulnerability. On the other hand, an overreaction on our part might nourish the Arabs' fears that we had aggressive intentions and thus provoke a totally unwanted war.

As we constantly monitored Egypt's moves, events moved slowly but steadily toward a more alarming situation. As early as the evening of 16 May, I spoke to the prime minister about the option of beginning to mobilize reserves. The Egyptian 4th (Armoured) Division—whose movements were considered highly indicative of Egypt's intentions—had not yet left its camps near Cairo. But if it were to move into Sinai, I felt there was no way of postponing partial mobilization. Eshkol was understanding of my position and approved the call-up of a reserve armoured brigade.

The next day, 17 May, we learned that the Egyptians had stepped matters up another notch by demanding that the U.N. forces stationed along the Sinai border be removed from their positions and transferred to Gaza and Sharm el-Sheikh. This move was a radical departure from the pattern of Operation Rotem and sufficient reason for alarm. Still, it was a calculated step and did not necessarily call for an immediate, belligerent response. First of all, as many people throughout the world expected, rather than respond to Nasser's dictates the U.N. might categorically refuse to remove the UNEF force. At the very least it would take time for the General Assembly or Security Council to meet and debate the matter, which would slow down the momentum of developments. On the other hand, by focusing world attention on his martial posturing, Nasser might only be using the U.N. as a tool to impress his point on Syria and other Arab states: he was not hiding behind the UNEF force. On the contrary, he was trying to remove it and, by doing so, was sufficiently intimidating Israel

to defer any warlike actions on her part. Seen in this light, Nasser might even have been banking on the assumption that the U.N. would turn down his request.

But even if the U.N. let him have his way, Nasser assumed that as long as he did not order the UNEF to leave the Gaza Strip and Sharm el-Sheikh (guarding the sea lane through the Straits of Tiran), he would not be confronting Israel with a *casus belli*. Instead, he would be manoeuvring us into the uncomfortable position of having to deal with a potentially explosive situation that none the less fell short of being a clear-cut pretext for war, while he would remain free to dictate all the moves. Or so he thought.

The one possibility that Nasser overlooked was that the U.N. would not necessarily play the game by his rules. Commentators and historians have spent much ink on speculations about what would have happened if Secretary-General U Thant[3] had agreed to Nasser's demand for a limited withdrawal of U.N. forces. But on 17 May we learned that U Thant had presented Nasser with only two options: either the U.N. troops remained in all their positions or they withdrew from the Middle East entirely. Given that choice, Nasser was left with the problem of saving face. His reply was quick in coming: the U.N. force was to withdraw from all its positions. In the chain of events that drew Nasser into war—perhaps contrary to his original intention—U Thant's action proved to be a vital link.

Our response was no less unequivocal. A GHQ order placed all land, sea and air units on top alert. On the evening of 17 May, Aharon Yariv,[4] the head of Intelligence Branch, reported that the Egyptian forces in Sinai were equipped with ammunition containing poison gas. At that time we were unprepared for chemical warfare and our anxiety deepened. Moreover, for the first time in the current train of events, Yariv altered his basic assessment: if Nasser were to order all the U.N. units to withdraw, we should regard the move as a clear indication of Egypt's aggressive intentions.

Early on the afternoon of 18 May our final uncertainties about the U.N. forces were dispelled. The Egyptian foreign minister officially demanded the total withdrawal of all U.N. units from Egyptian territory. I asked the prime minister to approve the mobilization of additional reserves primarily for the defence of our border with the Gaza Strip, where a Palestinian division with forty-four tanks was stationed. I also notified Eshkol that the entire Syrian army was now on emergency footing, and he consented to the mobilization of one battalion in Upper Galilee. Yet we still felt bound to act cautiously since any mobilization exceeding our vital needs was liable to lead to further escalation, which we were anxious to prevent.

I held a further conference with the prime minister at eleven o'clock that night and submitted my assessment that the Egyptians were liable to close the Straits of Tiran within two or three days, placing Israel in a situation that would oblige her to go to war. I added, however, that even if the Egyptians refrained from blockading the straits, our situation would be no less difficult. We simply could not keep our reserves mobilized for long, as demanded by the presence of large Egyptian forces in Sinai. Whether or not the Egyptians were bent on leading the situation to war at present, we were inevitably moving in that direction.

By that evening, 19 May, the U.N. forces had been withdrawn and we faced the imposing order of Egypt's forces in Sinai. Yariv's new assessment was that the Egyptians would continue their build-up and choose one of four options: (1) undertaking no further action but reaping the fruits of victory by declaring that Egypt had deterred Israel from carrying out her "aggressive designs;" (2) instigating a provocation in order to bait us into striking back; (3) initiating an attack without prior provocation, to make the most of surprise; or (4) opting for a long period of tension—thereby forcing us to keep our reserves mobilized— and then choosing a comfortable opportunity to attack.

It was clear to me that whichever option Egypt adopted, Israel would stand alone in its forthcoming struggle. I ordered all commanding officers to make it clear to their men that we were heading for war. Without doubt we now faced the gravest situation Israel had known since the War of Independence. Yet any immediate action on our part was bound by a severe political drawback: the Egyptians had still not presented us with a concrete *casus belli* to justify launching a full-scale war. I agreed with our political leadership that we must not attack as long as the Egyptians had not undertaken some blatantly warlike act—such as blockading the Straits of Tiran or attacking targets in Israel. But deep inside I was convinced that this was only a matter of time; and I naturally assumed that, given a *casus belli*, the IDF would be ordered to attack. In the meanwhile, however, Nasser was still dictating the moves, and the delicate balance had to be maintained.

NOTES

1. The Soviet Union fed the Syrian government false information that the IDF had mobilized between eleven and thirteen brigades on the northern border and was about to launch a full-scale attack.

2. Operation Rotem, Israel's code name for its deployment of troops in early 1960 after Egypt began to deploy troops in the Sinai. No shots were fired, and a "minicrisis" (Rabin's term) was avoided. Rabin was chief of operations at the time.

3. U Thant (1909–74), Burmese diplomat who was secretary general of the United Nations, 1961–71.

4. Aharon Yariv (b. 1920), leader in the Labor party and presently head of the Center for Strategic Studies at Tel Aviv University. Yariv's military career began in the prestate years and culminated in his appointment as military attaché to the United States, 1957–60, and director of military intelligence, 1963–72. During the 1970s he served in Labor governments.

ZAYD AL-RIFA'I
45. The Nasser-Hussein Reconciliation

Zayd al-Rifa'i (b.1936) is from one of the few Palestinian families who became fully integrated into the Jordanian political elite. He is a member of king's entourage and served as prime minister, 1973–76. His account of

Jordan's drift into an alliance with Egypt just before the June 1967 War illuminates the relationship between inter-Arab relations and the Arab-Israeli conflict.

When Abdul Nasser closed the Straits of Tiran, the king[1] became convinced that war was inevitable. Just as with the withdrawal of the U.N. Emergency Force, Jordan was not consulted and not given warning. We gathered these two important pieces of information by listening to radio broadcasts from Cairo, just like the rest of the Arab world and Egypt's Soviet allies—a fact about which Moscow complained bitterly.

This is the sequence of events:

On the morning of Monday, May 22 [1967], I was sitting, as usual, at my desk in the palace when I received a telephone call from Radio Amman. I was informed that Cairo Radio had just announced the closing of the Gulf of Aqaba [Gulf of Eilat to the Israelis].

At one o'clock the king arrived at his office and called me in. He had already heard the news and was most disturbed.

"This is very serious," he said. "I feel that war is now inevitable." But we contented ourselves with noting the event and nothing more.

The truth is that for the past year, Jordan had been isolated in the Arab world and had to accept abuse and vilification from Egypt. We therefore refused to get in touch with Egypt in order to hear her explanation. We were tired of always being the ones to make the first move. Since the withdrawal of the U.N. forces from Gaza, the king—who

certainly derived no satisfaction from the events—had made several moves toward Cairo. We wanted to revive the machinery of Arab unity, which was more important than ever when we were confronted with this peril. All these moves had been of no avail, for Cairo kept silent.

For a few days nothing happened. After the initial moment of shock had subsided life returned to normal. The tension abated. We followed the diplomatic feelers that were put out after the "Gulf affair."

Meanwhile, forty-eight hours after the closing of the gulf we requested reinforcements from Saudi Arabia and Iraq through diplomatic channels. This was a cautious step in view of the deteriorating circumstances, a step that was entirely in accord with the principle of the collective defense pact that the Arab states had signed in Cairo in 1964 [see doc. 42]. The reinforcements took their time to arrive. To be more specific, the Saudi forces arrived after everything was over and done with. The Iraqis responded with a downright refusal.

On May 28 another stage was reached in the process of escalation: President Abdul Nasser stated in Cairo at a press conference for three hundred reporters: "If Israel wants war then I say 'welcome.' " In other words, "Gentlemen, you will fire the first shot!"

With my ear attuned to the radio on my desk, I followed Abdul Nasser's press con-

Source: Zayd al-Rifa'i, *Hussein Holekh la-Milhamah* (Hussein Goes to War), ed. A. Kam (Tel Aviv: Maarak-hot, 1974), pp. 46–48. Reprinted by permission.

ference from beginning to end. Then I realized that His Majesty's fears were well founded. After all this, there could be no doubt that war would ensue.

The king also heard the Egyptian president's speech and immediately decided to send the chief of staff of the Jordanian army, Major General Amar Hamash, to Cairo. General Hamash's task was to contact the Unified Arab Command, whose headquarters had been in Egypt ever since the first summit meeting. He was to find out from the heads of the command their plans for withstanding a possible Israeli attack.

Upon his return from Cairo, Hamash informed the king that the end was looming over the Unified Arab Command as a result of disagreements between Egypt and the other Arab countries. These disputes caused a complete breakdown in all the command's activities.

Hamash also discovered that the command had played no role whatsoever in the present events. Egypt was acting according to a bilateral accord with Syria in these matters.

On the same day the Egyptian parliament invested Abdul Nasser with full authority and declared a state of emergency in all Egyptian airfields.

Faced with a clear deterioration in the situation, the king decided to make one last attempt to achieve a reconciliation with Egypt. He invited the Egyptian ambassador in Amman, Othman Nuri, to a meeting and informed him of his desire to meet with Nasser as soon as possible. The king stressed the importance of the meeting for coordinating our defense systems against the Israeli threat.

This desire to meet with Abdul Nasser may appear strange in the light of the insults broadcast on Cairo Radio over the preceding year, but there was no rhyme or reason at all for evading an issue in which clearly the whole Arab world was to become involved.

Cairo's response was received late at night on May 29. It was Sa'ad Juma'a, the Jordanian prime minister, who let the king know immediately by phone: Abdul Nasser welcomes the king's initiative.

On the morning of Tuesday, May 30, at sunrise, the king ordered a Caravel airplane from the Jordanian airlines Alia (named after the king's eldest daughter). At seven in the morning the plane took off from Amman airport. It carried a full crew, but, as usual, the king took the cockpit. King Hussein is too active a man to allow others to take the wheel, whether he is in a car or a plane. He himself said, "Flying a plane soothes me and gives me great pleasure." One interesting detail: the king wore a khaki combat uniform and a beret bearing the emblem of the crown and his rank of supreme commander. He was armed with an American Magnum 357 revolver in a cloth holster attached to his belt above his left hip. Since the dispute broke out, the king had been in uniform like all of us.

Not a single bodyguard or member of the secret service or even a policeman accompanied him: this was one of the king's characteristic acts of bravery.

Before takeoff His Majesty said, "I shall probably be back for lunch," which in Jordan is at about 1:30 P.M.

The discussion with Abdul Nasser took longer than the king thought. He did not return at the time he had stated but ate with Nasser at the Kubbeh Palace, which had once been the residence of King Farouk.

The king's trip to Egypt had been kept secret, and so here at the palace in Amman the whole staff listened to the radio. This was a habit we had developed over the past fifteen days. Since Cairo had adopted her independent path, this had become the only means at our disposal for keeping up-to-date with the latest developments.

In my office, adjacent to the king's, I was also glued to my transistor.

At 3:30 P.M. Radio Cairo interrupted its broadcast with a news flash: "King Hussein and President Abdul Nasser are about to sign a mutual defense pact. The ceremony will be broadcast over the radio."

We all heaved a sigh of relief.

NOTE

1. Hussein (b. 1935), king of Jordan, 1953 to the present. Hussein was born in Amman and educated in Egypt and England. He assumed the throne after his grandfather (Abdullah) was assassinated in 1951 and his father (Talal) declared mentally unfit to rule.

III

1967–73
Domestic Issues

46. The Domestic Impact of the June 1967 War

When the Israeli government became convinced that war was inevitable, it launched a preemptive strike on June 5, 1967, which immediately devastated the air forces of Egypt, Syria, and Jordan. The June 1967 War (also called the Six-Day War) began. By the third day of the war Israel had taken control over most of the West Bank of Jordan and began its capture of the Old City of Jerusalem. On the fourth day Israeli forces had reached the Suez Canal. On the fifth and sixth days Israel took the Golan Heights, and its forces were in a position to attack Damascus. On the sixth day, June 10, the war ended with a cease-fire on all fronts (see map 3).

The crisis that preceded the war, the swift military victory, the occupation of the West Bank and Gaza with their Palestinian population, and the lack of progress toward peace, all had a profound impact on Israeli society and generated a sustained debate. The discussion among reserve and regular soldiers at the Givat Haim Kibbutz immediately after the war reflects the ambivalent feelings and moral questions that followed on Israel's impressive military victory.

AMRAM: Did you feel any hatred when you were in Jordan?

PETER: No, there wasn't any hatred in us. I did come across a sort of general hatred on the Syrian heights, but not in Jordan. It was all a matter of fighting and advancing, work and fatigue. The enemy was anonymous. But in Syria I did notice signs of a general outbreak of hatred.

AMRAM: What do you suppose was behind it? The Syrians themselves or something they'd done?

PETER: Yes . . . the things they'd done recently. But apart from that, mass psychosis is catching, you know. You see three or four people infected, and suddenly the atmosphere's full of it.

AMRAM: Were any of your unit fighting for the first time?

PETER: Yes, lots of them.

AMRAM: How did they react to it?

PETER: Just like all the others, they weren't any different.

SHIMON: There's a big difference between the men who're married and have kids and the younger ones who aren't married yet, who don't have their own families. I remember once when we were under heavy fire, I was behind some cover and I caught myself thinking at that very moment that I ought to watch out. We weren't on the move, just waiting under cover, we didn't have to advance and I thought I ought to try to improve my own position a bit, get some better cover so that I'd manage to make it home again, because I had a wife and kids waiting for me there. I remember thinking about it.

AMRAM: Didn't you think that way when you were younger?

SHIMON: It certainly bothered me far less. I don't remember worrying about myself so much. But I must add that I also had a feeling, and I think the others shared it, too, that I was ready to give anything, to do anything. . . . I remember that when I was sheltering behind that rock waiting to move forward any minute, I didn't want to get hit.

Source: Henry Near and Avraham Shapira, eds., *The Seventh Day: Soldiers Talk about the Six Day War* (Middlesex, England: Penguin Books, 1974), pp. 93–97. Copyright © 1970 by Henry Near (New York: Charles Scribner's Sons, 1970). Reprinted by permission of Charles Scribner's Sons.

But I knew the minute the order to advance was given, I'd have to get up and run, and that then it wouldn't matter at all what happened. It was the same later on, as we continued to advance. I remember that on the one hand I was conscious of the fact that I had a wife and kids at home, and on the other hand, I knew that the whole war was really being fought for their sakes, and if I didn't come back that was for their sake, too. All these things which seem like platitudes, subjects for books and stories, kept flashing through my mind as we came under fire that night. I remember thinking that there wasn't any point in getting hurt for no good reason. But the minute it really became necessary— you had to do it. I'd have done it at any price, and so would the others. I'd have jumped from behind cover to save someone else, and I knew the others would have done the same for me.

AMRAM: You really felt there was some special link between you and the others?

SHIMON: A very strong link. I'd no doubt about it. Take the matter of evacuating the wounded for example: just think how all the boys rushed around and dragged each other to safety. I remember it so clearly. That mutual trust that had grown up between us through the years of reserve training was very clearly felt right through the unit.

AMRAM: If we're discussing that point, Peter said that in his unit it was almost like a kibbutz—all the boys made up a team, linked to each other, explaining things to each other. I should think the atmosphere in your crowd was something like that.

SHIMON: Yes, very similar, so much so that I remember the CO once saying, "I want to hear orders. When you give an order, that's that. But when you say, 'Come on, boys, let's do such and such a thing,' then it's friends you're talking to and you can't be so sure things will get done." I think that shows just how close we were.

PETER: The CO got the whole battalion together and gave us a talk. He really did a good job. He spoke about a relative of his who'd been in the Ezion bloc during the war

in 1948 and had been taken prisoner, along with some of the others. He kept emphasizing the point that these boys had been taken into the home of one of the Arab Mukhtars [village leaders] so that they could later be turned over to the Arab Legion. Then along came some of the irregulars who wanted to finish them off. They told the Mukhtar to bring them out and hand them over—and he went outside with his gun and stood up to them and said: "They're my guests, under my roof, and I shall deliver them over to the Legion. Anyone who wants to do anything about it will have to finish me off first." He really saved their lives. The CO kept repeating this story, at every possible opportunity, and when the boys started cursing the Arabs, he used to say, "Okay, you're right up to a point, but there are good Arabs, too. There are Arabs who do know what honour and honesty mean, who do know how to behave." He used to explain to them, "We're going to have to live with the Arabs—if not now, then in another ten years' time. It's inevitable. Any cruelty we show now will simply arouse more hatred. Some people claim that if we behave properly to them, see to their wounded, give them water, cigarettes, and treat them fairly it doesn't have results. But I think it can have results." And he convinced them. The boys believed in him. Once he'd talked to them, the problem was over. There wasn't any cruelty. A couple of them had some extreme views on the subject, and he felt it. He got hold of them and discussed it with them personally, very quietly and convincingly. And they accepted his point of view.

SIMON: Soldiers of all ranks used to spend hours talking about this question. In our crowd there were two boys—one from Givat Brenner and another from Tivon—who'd managed to crystallize two quite different attitudes to the war, and it was they who used to lead the discussions.

PETER: There was a man in the brigade who was once our CO. They didn't call him up, but he showed up all the same and went to HQ. A really exceptional man who's been secretary of Kibbutz Yagur three times. He used to go from unit to unit explaining his point and seeing to it that there wasn't any doubt whatever. When he got to our lot, he could see that there wasn't any need to explain, we were all quite clear about it. But among some of the men in the rear, in the workshops and so on—they really had whole lectures on the subject. It was taken good care of.

AMRAM: The question is, how far do people who've been through a war lose their humanitarian standards, stop treating people as people, and begin behaving towards them as if they were some *Arabush* [derogatory term] or as if they'd ceased to see them as human beings? . . .

PETER: I take a very serious view of things like this. I've got very clear ideas about hatred. You know, I've got a lot of experience in this business of hatred because of my own past experiences, and I've come to the conclusion that hatred is a matter of individual personality.

SHIMON: Do you mean hatred in general, or hating particular people?

PETER: Real hatred, like any real and deep emotion such as love, has to have some definite focus. Someone who's done something to you, someone you've got an account to settle with—that's the sort of person you can strangle or do in. Someone who's done something to you, or someone who's close to you—a friend, a relative, someone there's some sort of personal connection with—that's the sort of person you can hate, too. But to say you hate Arabs, that's just talk. I can understand justifiable hate. Do you want to know why I'm so certain about the whole question? It's because I went into it myself with the Germans, only a short while after the Second World War. I found I couldn't hate. I didn't want to talk to them, I didn't want to have

anything to do with them: but it was still a long way from hatred. And even if I did use the word hatred then, I was quite certain that what I meant wasn't hatred. Hatred's far stronger. I wasn't at all sorry when they punished the Germans. "Fair enough," I said. But that's still not hatred. Whatever bestial qualities there are in man—the more primitive a man is, the more powerful they are.

SHIMON: You could really see these things in the weeks before the war, because at that stage we weren't yet on a war footing, we didn't even know if there would or wouldn't be a war. You could see then, in the way people talked, exactly how they approached the whole question of war, just how they reacted to the Arabs. There were differences in how they felt about Jordanians, Egyptians and Syrians.

I don't think there is any difference here between people from the towns and those from the kibbutzim, or between people from kibbutzim of different political outlooks. I know boys from Hashomer Hazair kibbutzim who've been educated on the concept of love for humanity and so on—yet some of them said that the only way they could see the Arab question was through a gun-sight.

AMRAM: It seems to me, from various stories I've heard, that this business bothered some of the boys from the kibbutz, but that they didn't have the moral strength to stand up for their own views, to withstand the pressures. . . .

PETER: As far as all that's concerned, I haven't got the slightest shadow of doubt what my duty is and what I've got to do. Apart from this, I didn't have any doubt about the opinions of all the old crowd in the battalion, from the CO right down through all the officers and men, just no doubt at all.

AMRAM: It's a question of about a tenth of a second in which you've to decide.

47. Administering the West Bank

At the end of the June 1967 War, the Israelis found themselves in control of territories containing about one million Arabs and other non-Jews (see map 3). At the end of 1967 the estimated population of the West Bank was 585,700; the estimated population of Gaza and northern Sinai was 380,700. The population of the Golan Heights—comprised almost totally of Druze, a sect that broke away from Islam centuries earlier and does not consider itself Arab—was unknown. One of the first steps taken to facilitate the transition from wartime control to peacetime governance of these territories was to declare them "nonenemy" areas and to place them under a combination of military and civilian administration. (Eastern Jerusalem was incorporated into the municipal administration of Jerusalem, and the city soon became administered as a unified city.) In the following account Shabtai Teveth, one of Israel's leading journalists and political analysts, examines this transitional process as it occurred in the West Bank.

Moshe Dayan did not place himself personally in the governing apparatus handling the occupied territories. First Colonel Yehuda Nizan and afterwards Colonel Dan Hiram functioned with his deputy, Zvi Zur, as coordinators of the Committee of Director-Generals, which was responsible to the Ministerial Committee headed by Finance Minister Pinhas Sapir. In August he established a coordinating committee and put Brigadier-General (then Colonel) Shlomo Gazit in charge. But this committee too was not given official status. Shlomo Gazit himself was subordinate to the Army General Staff. Thus, Dayan functioned through bodies responsible to other Ministers or directly subordinate to the General Staff.

Lack of a special apparatus in his own office created a situation whereby Zahal alone was responsible for the Military Government. Perhaps the real reason was that Dayan did not wish to create a new structure and fragment responsibility for the handling of the occupied territories. Absence of such machinery in his office brought about direct contact between Dayan and the military commanders in the various districts. This method of action not only put Dayan in the driver's seat of the government machine in the territories, but also made him the engine behind it. There were obvious inherent disadvantages in this method, as well as the advantages of daring and speedy action and maximal use of Dayan's talents and personality.

Initially, Herzog's[1] command functioned in Jerusalem and the West Bank and Dayan maintained direct contact. While Herzog's HQ was in process of organization Dayan was still engaged in directing the war. On Friday 9 June the battle for Ramat Hagolan commenced and was ended the following day, Saturday 10 June, with the cease-fire order of the Security Council. During the battle in Ramat Hagolan Dayan visited the front, arriving there by air from Tel Aviv. In the week commencing Sunday 11 June and ending the following Friday he was still occupied with war problems and Army and Government meetings which laid down the principles of administration in the occupied

Source: Shabtai Teveth, *The Cursed Blessing: The Story of Israel's Occupation of the West Bank* (London: Weidenfeld and Nicolson, 1970), pp. 96–105. Reprinted by permission of Shabtai Teveth and Weidenfeld and Nicolson.

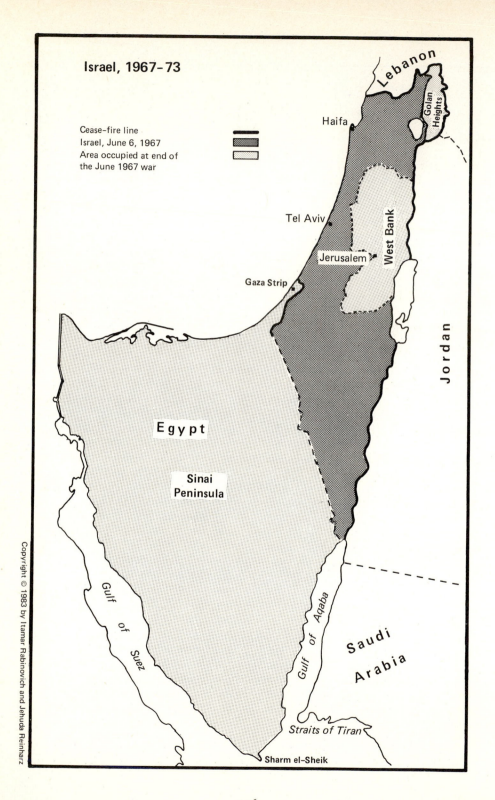

Israel, 1967–73

Cease-fire line
Israel, June 6, 1967
Area occupied at end of
the June 1967 war

Lebanon

Golan Heights

Haifa

Tel Aviv

West Bank

Jerusalem

Gaza Strip

Jordan

Egypt

Sinai
Peninsula

Gulf of Suez

Gulf of Aqaba

Saudi
Arabia

Straits of Tiran

Sharm el-Sheik

territories. It was only on Saturday 17 June that he managed to pay a visit to the West Bank, Jerusalem, Nablus and Jenin.

It was a busy week even for someone who delegated authority in every aspect of his work. For Dayan, who wanted to personally get the feel of every problem and to set the administrative machine in motion by both steering and propelling the wheels, it was a particularly crowded week. During this week he was able to lay down only the most general of principles for Herzog's Command, which were to concentrate on Jerusalem and to return services to normal as speedily as possible.

However, for the first week of its existence absolute confusion reigned in Herzog's Command. His staff officers were personally the finest of their kind—and each, by virtue of his personality and his high position in the managerial and economic life of Israel, was entitled, at least in his own opinion, to participate in the supreme forum of the Command. Since no prior format for orderly staff work had been devised, General Herzog was forced to preside over large meetings where everyone was given the right to air his views as if it were some home circle for the clarification of questions of universal moment. The Command did not function through channels of bureaucracy, handing down of reports, executive functions and supervision. In addition the Command lacked an administrative base. In the first few days there was no one to prepare food for the scores of Command personnel crowded in the Ambassador Hotel.

A regular soldier like Brigadier-General—then Colonel—Vardi was concerned not with the shortcomings of the Command in dealing with civil matters, but with the fact that this was a command of Zahal forces supposed to be in charge of all units in the area, and, as a military command its main deficiency was that it lacked the means of communication with its own units.

Herzog, who was aware of these defects, agreed that the only way out of the confusion was to return matters to their previous state, namely, that the Central Command serve as both Army command and civil administration. The Central Command had an efficient headquarters, and means of communications with all units which had proved efficient during the war. One week after his appointment as Commander of Zahal Forces in the West Bank General Herzog returned the authority vested in him to General Narkis. From 15 June General [Uzi] Narkis was both General of the Central Command and the Commander of Zahal Forces on the West Bank and, in everyday language, Military Governor. The military section of Herzog's HQ was annulled, there being no need for it, while the civil section was reorganized and added to the Central Command as a fourth branch. General Narkis had two chiefs of staff, his regular military chief of staff and a chief of staff for civil affairs, Colonel Raphael Vardi.

The timing of the annulment of General Herzog's command coincided with the Cabinet meeting at which it was decided to set up the Committee of Director-Generals. Government offices began sending their representatives to the West Bank Command and they replaced the various reserve officers and volunteers. The civil administration under Narkis and Vardi was divided into three departments—economic, services and special affairs.

During his week as OC Zahal Forces in the West Bank, Herzog put a stop to the looting of shops and houses, order was established in the eastern section of Jerusalem and the services got moving. On Friday 9 June water and electricity supplies were resumed. Herzog even took upon himself responsibility for clearing the square in front of the Western Wall.

On Thursday 8 June at 4 P.M. Herzog called a meeting of the heads of religions in the Ambassador Hotel. About thirty priests were present, among them heads of the Christian Churches, the Greeks, Armenian, Syrian, Latin Lutheran, Anglican, Coptic, the Apostolic Representative of the Vatican and others. As General Herzog entered the hall the heads of the clergy rose to their feet. After thanking them for the honour showed him, he informed them that he had come to assure them in the name of the Israeli Government that there would be freedom of religious worship in the holy city. Despite the fact that for the nineteen years of Jordanian rule Jews from Israel had been forbidden access to holy places or to worship in the eastern city, Israel would act not in accordance with the precept of an eye for an eye but according to the rules of liberty and fraternity.

General Herzog spoke in a very personal vein. He knew many of the leaders of the clergy from the house of his father, the late Chief Rabbi of Palestine, Rabbi Yizhak Halevi Herzog. On opening his talk he mentioned this fact. "I know many of you from my father's house and I regard it as a great privilege that it has fallen to me to represent the Government of Israel before you and to be the person authorized to pledge full freedom of religion and rites to all denominations and sects." On the day of the meeting Legionnaires who had discarded their uniforms but retained their arms were still hiding in Christian religious institutions, many of whose religious officials were Arabs. General Herzog promised that no harm would befall these soldiers if they were handed over to Zahal. But while guaranteeing freedom of religion and worship, he announced that he would take strong measures against violators of law and order.

The Greek Patriarch, His Highness Gregorianus, replied in the name of those assembled there. Speaking in Greek, which was translated into English by one of the bishops accompanying him, he thanked the Government of Israel in the name of his colleagues for the polite and humane attitude displayed by the conquering Zahal soldiers. He then said that representatives of Christianity were not politicians and that their desire for freedom of religion and worship was very strong. Accordingly, he welcomed General Herzog's announcement assuring full freedom of religious worship. He concluded on

a personal note. He personally regarded it as a sign from heaven that it should be the son of Rabbi Herzog who was given the task of passing on the tidings of freedom of religion in Jerusalem in the name of the Government of Israel, because he knew that the son of Rabbi Herzog understood the full significance of this promise.

The speakers following the Patriarch also warmly recalled the late Rabbi Herzog. After the head of the Lutheran Church had spoken in Arabic, Bishop McReas spoke in the name of the Anglican Church. He particularly stressed the significance of the fact that Rabbi Herzog's son was the harbinger of the communication from the Government of Israel and he regarded the fact that the Rabbi's son was the Governor as God's will. The Anglican commended Zahal for the fact that even at the cost of the lives of its soldiers it had made every effort not to damage the holy places in the heat of war. History would credit Zahal with this fact.

The representative of the Lutheran Church asked, "Why are our friends, the shepherds of the Moslem Community, absent from this gathering?" This was said as if he wished to assure their welfare. Herzog replied that he had intended to invite the Moslem priests but had been unable to locate them. He solemnly vowed that he would meet with the heads of the Moslem religion and decree their freedom of religion just as he had done with the leaders of the Christian sects. At the conclusion of the meeting champagne goblets were filled and everyone toasted the President of Israel.

General Herzog did not manage to meet the Moslem leaders and a meeting was held in special circumstances by Dayan. But on Friday afternoon 9 June Herzog called the Jordanian Commissioner of the Jerusalem District, Mr. Anuar El Khatib, to meet him. The Jordanian Commissioner was in a state of shock, a fact noted by Herzog himself. "Only on Tuesday afternoon, I was speaking to King Hussein and he told us: 'Hold out—we are coming to your aid,' and then on Wednesday morning I had to meet

Colonel Mordekhai Gur[2] and inform him that all resistance had ceased." El Khatib told Herzog that he had appealed to the Legion not to fight from the Temple Mount, but they had paid him no heed and had stationed snipers in the Al-Aqsa Mosque.[3] He was touched by the humane attitude of the Zahal soldiers and admitted: "I never dreamed it would be this way." He too, like many Arabs, imagined that an Israeli victory would mean slaughter. Anuar El Khatib explained the set-up of the Jordanian administration in Jerusalem and offered his services getting the regional services functioning again and in returning life to normal. Herzog, however, had no reply for him since no policy on activation of Jordanian Government departments in the West Bank had as yet been decided upon.

At the end of the meeting Anuar El Khatib made a request which quite unintentionally was to be of political significance. He asked that the families of consuls from Arab states in Jerusalem, who had been stranded with no source of livelihood, be permitted to cross to the East Bank. He requested this specially for those among them who were his personal friends, for humane reasons. General Herzog promised him his full cooperation and even decided on an arrangement whereby on an appointed day, buses would be waiting at Nablus Gate to provide transport for whoever wished to get to the Jordan crossings. From there they could go to Jordan and the East Bank. El Khatib found it difficult to believe him.

"Whoever wants to go?" he asked.

"Whoever wants to go. We won't ask questions. We only want those who leave to sign that they are doing so of their own free will and not under duress."

Anuar El Khatib agreed and in this way he and General Herzog started an exit service to the East Bank. Herzog's Command issued an order stating that commencing on Thursday 15 June special arrangements would be made for the transport of Jordanian citizens wishing to cross from East Jerusalem to Jordan. They would be taken from the Nablus Gate to Jericho in special buses and from there would cross the Jordan on foot to the East Bank. Following this arrangement similar ones were made in other West Bank cities. In this way organized emigrant traffic from the West Bank to the East was being carried on in addition to that which had taken place before and during the war. Many others reached the river independently, by vehicle or on foot, and from there crossed to the East Bank. In all about 200,000 Arabs emigrated from the West Bank during and after the Six-Day War.

In spite of its deficiencies General Herzog's command instituted a series of measures which were later to be of great help to the Military Government. It was his command that decided to make a census of the population and before this was executed, gathered statistical data from Jordanian Government records. An inspiring example of quick Israeli action under impromptu circumstances was the survey on employment in the West Bank, including East Jerusalem, carried out by Hanoch Smith. This report was presented to the West Bank Command on Friday 9 June. The data was based on reports received from governors of various regions and on observations. Smith's report was interesting in that it estimated the population on the entire West Bank up to Thursday 7 June at under 800,000 persons. In the census run by the Central Bureau of Statistics on 11 July 1967, just under 600,000 inhabitants were counted on the West Bank (excluding East Jerusalem, which was then included in Israeli territory). A registration of inhabitants carried out by the Ministry of the Interior on 26 June 1967 put the population of East Jerusalem at just under 60,000 inhabitants. Taking into account the emigration, which was at its height in June, and which was estimated at 150,000 persons for that month, the final number comes to exactly Hanoch Smith's estimate.

In the reorganization of the West Bank Command, there was a portent of the general character of the future administration. General Narkis did not appoint Colonel

Yehoshua Werbin as chief of his HQ Staff, but Colonel Raphael Vardi. Werbin had been a Military Government man in Israel and afterwards headed the GHQ department which had inherited the responsibilities of the Military Government in the Arab-populated areas of Israel, which had been annulled by Eshkol before the Six-Day War. Narkis dubbed him a *moshlan,* that is to say a professional governor, and many copied the term. Since Dayan's method was to function through regular Army units in all matters pertaining to administration, General Narkis also thought that what he needed was a Regular Army man like Vardi as chief of staff, and not a specialist in government. Dayan had objected to the ways of the former Military Government in Israel and had no desire to repeat them on the West Bank. Also, Narkis felt more at home with field soldiers. This step subsequently led to the appointment of field officers as governors in various areas.

The first decision by Narkis and Herzog on the West Bank was routinely military in nature. Permits and check-points were strictly controlled both within and on the outside. The first thing the Zahal spokesman announced on 8 June was that a strip of land fifty metres wide along the length of the borders of the occupied territories was closed by the military authorities and any trespasser endangered his life. Since there had been no time for the West Bank administration to make advance preparations and Herzog's Command lacked communication with the units in the area, even this regime of permits and barriers lacked uniformity. Each commander issued his own permits and decided on his own checkpoints. The West Bank Command did not manage either to control the situation or to issue a uniform licence form. Entry permits were issued by GHQ, by Herzog's Command, by brigade commanders, battalion commanders and company commanders.

NOTES

1. Chaim Herzog (b. 1918), president of Israel since May 1983. Herzog was the first military governor of the West Bank, June 1967. His military career has included service as chief of staff of the Southern Command, 1957–59; director of military intelligence, 1959–62; and military attaché to the United States, 1950–54. Subsequently he entered private practice as a lawyer but remained an influential military commentator. He has been active in the Labor party and was Israel's ambassador to the United Nations, 1975–78. He is the son of Rabbi Yizhak Halevi Herzog and the brother of Yaacov Herzog.

2. Mordekhai (Mota) Gur (b. 1930), Israeli military leader who has served as a commander of the paratroopers (his brigade fought in Jerusalem in 1967), military attaché to the United States during the October 1967 War, and chief of staff, 1974–78. Gur is now active in the Labor party.

3. Al-Aqsa Mosque, part of the Haram al-Sharif (in Arabic, lit., Noble Sanctuary), a complex of religious buildings on the Temple Mount in Jerusalem considered the most sacred place to Muslims after Mecca and Medina. The Al-Aqsa Mosque and the Qubat al-Sakhra (Dome of the Rock) are the two most important buildings in the complex.

48. The Nationalist, Clericalist, and Business Elites

The Lavon affair and internal dissension brought about the decline of the Labor parties in the 1960s at the same time that the center–right-wing bloc increased in strength (see docs. 28–30). The formation of the National Unity government on the eve of the June 1967 War, which brought Gahal into the government for the next three years, further contributed to the Labor movement's loss of hegemony and the center's and right wing's progress toward electoral victory. Aspects of these developments, and particularly the evolution of the religious parties—a key element in all Israeli government coalitions—are analyzed here by Yuval Elizur and Eliahu Salpeter, two of Israel's leading political correspondents, who offer a portrait of the Israeli elite in the early 1970s.

The split in the leadership of the National Religious party (which was formed following the merger of Mizrahi and Hapoel Hamizrahi,[1] both Religious Zionist parties) came after the 1970 death of party leader Haim Moshe Shapira, who was a unifying factor not only in his own party but also in the government. For example, Shapira was instrumental in May, 1967, in convincing Prime Minister Levi Eshkol to bring Moshe Dayan into the government and make him Minister of Defense. Today at least five factions are jousting for power within the NRP. One group is headed by Cabinet Ministers Yosef Burg and Michael Hazani, another by Minister Zerah Warhaftig, a third represents the religious kibbutz movement, and yet another group represents young party activists. One of the largest groups within the party is headed by Yitzhak Raphael, who considers himself the heir of Haim Moshe Shapira.

Yitzhak Raphael (Werfel), born in Poland in 1914, married the daughter of Rabbi Yehuda Leib Maimon, the late leader of Mizrahi. His family background, Hebrew University education and boundless energy soon helped his rise within the party. His ambitious drive for a ministerial post was almost fulfilled in 1961 when he became Deputy Minister of Health. Even his numerous opponents admit that Raphael showed talent in running the Ministry, which for many years had been completely passive, leaving initiative in the health-care field to Kupat Holim, the Histadrut sick fund, and other institutions. Yet Raphael became indirectly involved in a bribery scandal in the planning of a new hospital and was forced to resign.

His controversial reputation probably harmed him in 1970 when the party secretariat decided by a margin of one vote to select Michael Hazani and not Raphael for a government post after the death of Haim Moshe Shapira. After his defeat, Yitzhak Raphael concentrated on foreign affairs and became one of the NRP's most outspoken hawks, objecting to any cut in the defense budget and any withdrawal from the West Bank, and demanding larger investments in the Jewish settlement at Hebron.[2] Raphael often has voiced criticism of his own party's role within the Cabinet.

Yitzhak Raphael's hawkish ideas are similar to positions taken by young leaders of the

Source: Yuval Elizur and Eliahu Salpeter, *Who Rules Israel?* (New York: Harper and Row, 1973), pp. 138–42, 223–27. Reprinted by permission of Yuval Elizur and Eliahu Salpeter.

NRP, among them Chicago-born Dr. Ye-huda Ben-Meir[3] and the articulate sabra[4] Zevulon Hammer, who have become the most outspoken representatives of the young members of the party.

Hammer, who was born in [1936] in Haifa, studied at Bar-Ilan University, served as a tank officer during the Six-Day War, and was instrumental in organizing the young members of the party, many of whom are graduates of the Bnei Akiva[5] youth move-ment, into a powerful political faction.

Hammer, who entered the Knesset in 1969, became a real threat to the party leadership early in 1973, when his faction won 23 percent of the seats at the party convention and succeeded in passing a number of resolutions that embarrassed the old leadership. Among these resolutions was one that objected to withdrawal from any part of the West Bank and another that would prevent the party from joining a coalition cabinet, unless the Law of Return [doc. 6] is changed so that only those who are born Jews or are converted by Orthodox rabbis are recognized as Jews (the existing law does not specify that only Orthodox conversion is accepted).

Although the wording of the resolutions was later somewhat softened, it is generally believed that because of the obstinate stand taken by Zevulon Hammer and his young hawks, the National Religious party may not join the coalition cabinet after the 1978 elections. At the very least it may demand a much higher price for its support of Labor policies.[6]

One of the major disputes in the National Religious party in 1972 was over the position of the Chief Rabbinate and the party's interference in the election of the Chief Rabbis. Traditionally there are two Chief Rabbis in Israel, one representing the Se-phardi community and the other the Ashke-nazi. At the time of the Turkish rule over Palestine and later during the British Man-date, the Chief Rabbis had a special position as "religious dignitaries" representing the Jewish community. Since the establishment

of the State, their position has been more controversial, especially because some of the more extreme Orthodox groups, such as Agudat Israel,[7] have always challenged the religious authority of the men who served as Chief Rabbis. For Agudat Israel the Moezet Gedolei Hatorah (Council of Torah Sages)[8] is the supreme authority for religious and even political decisions.

The National Religious party, however, not only saw the need for the Chief Rabbi-nate but was actively involved in the selec-tion of candidates, seeing the positions as one of the party's traditional centers of power. Many Israelis believe that the con-stant disputes over the Chief Rabbinate, the petty infighting between the rabbis them-selves, and the close association between political-clerical issues and religious-moral issues have all but destroyed the authority of the Rabbinate in the eyes of most Israelis. Only in the Hasidic sects,[9] each of which has its hereditary Rebbe whom its members admire and whose authority they accept unquestioningly, do rabbis still wield the influence they traditionally held in Jewish communities before the establishment of the State of Israel.

Rabbi Shlomo Goren, who was elected to the Chief Rabbinate of the Ashkenazi com-munity in October, 1972, is a product of this prolonged infighting. Yet, at the same time, his supporters believe that he will gradually acquire enough moral authority as well as the necessary political backing to restore some of the traditional glory to the position of Chief Rabbi. Shlomo Goren, former Chief Army Chaplain and later Chief Ashkenazi Rabbi of Tel Aviv, has an unquestioned ability to synthesize the old traditional ordi-nances of the halakhah (religious law) with the needs of modern reality.

Goren, of medium height, with a long gray beard, showed a knack for the dramatic during his long service in the Army (where he held the rank of major-general) as when he blew the shofar (the ceremonial ram's horn) on top of Mount Sinai after it was captured by Israeli troops in June, 1967, as well as good feeling for publicity when he saw to it that photographers were present when he prayed at the sacred Western Wall when the Old City of Jerusalem fell to the Israelis on June 7, 1967.

He is given credit for his unyielding efforts to provide all Israeli war casualties with Jewish burial and, at an earlier stage, for causing the abandonment of a plan to form special Army units of Orthodox soldiers. Instead, Goren saw to it that kosher food was supplied to all Army units. At the same time he helped to find ways of adjusting religious regulations to Army routine and needs. He also showed flexibility in enabling widows of fallen soldiers to remarry even if the death of their husbands had not been established as required by Jewish law.

Goren, born in Poland in 1917, arrived in Palestine in 1925. He studied at the Hebron Yeshiva and at the Hebrew University in Jerusalem. He was among the founders of Kfar Hasidim, an Orthodox agricultural settlement near Haifa, and wrote a number of research studies in Jewish law. (Following the Apollo moon landing he organized a special symposium to study the question whether the traditional monthly blessing of the new moon should be said by persons on the moon.)

Goren's first bid for the position of Chief Rabbi was in 1966, following the death of the late Chief Rabbi, Yizhak Halevi Herzog. However, at that time he lost by a narrow margin to Tel Aviv Chief Rabbi Isser Yehudah Unterman. Goren ran again against the octogenarian Unterman in 1972 after a dramatic struggle within the Orthodox camp.

One of Goren's first moves upon becoming Chief Rabbi was to appoint a special tribunal which enabled a brother and sister to marry their chosen partners, even though they had been declared "bastards" [mamzerim], who, according to Jewish law, are children of a married woman by someone other than her husband, and are not allowed to marry "eligible" Jews.

The case, which was a tragic result of the Holocaust (the mother of the "bastards" did not know her first husband was still alive), created bitter feelings in Israel against the Rabbinate and religion in general. Yet, in solving this case, Goren diminished some of the laws which no longer fit present circumstances. He also bitterly antagonized the extreme Orthodox circles, who refuse to accept his authority.

Goren believes that, given time, he can modernize religion and at the same time impose the rule of halakhah, the religious law, on the broad masses of the Israeli public. At the same time he may be tempted to try his hand at wielding secular authority as well. His influence on the National Religious party was said to be growing even after his election to the Chief Rabbinate. . . .

Central Trade was not the only Israeli concern to go into the banking business at a certain point in its development. Almost every group of companies in Israel became the proud owner of a bank of its own in the early 1960's. During the same period there was also a development in the opposite direction: banks which had started their operations in conventional fashion, taking deposits and offering loans, became active in other fields as well, investing in industry, shipping, real estate and even in the import of computers.

The large and small banks which went into business in those years in the name of diversification did so to a large extent in imitation of the Israel Discount Bank, which already by the early 1960's was a multinational company based in Israel, active in many fields in various countries. The story of the Discount Bank, established in 1935 by Leon Recanati, who started as a teacher in Salonika and after immigrating to Israel, invested 60,000 Palestine pounds in his Tel Aviv bank, which in less than thirty years developed into a formidable economic empire, is a success story of international scale.

Of the four sons of Leon Recanati—who succeeded in mobilizing the support of old Sephardi families living in Palestine—two,

Daniel and Raphael, today share control over the firm's shipping business, Cargo Ships El Yam, and the oldest brother, Harry, who lives in Europe, recently left the family business. Like the Rothschild brothers before them, Daniel, who lives in Tel Aviv, and Raphael, who for many years has lived in New York, utilize the distance between them to act separately, but in carefully coordinated fashion, in order to effect a constant expansion of the family empire. Daniel and Raphael Recanati divide between themselves a management fee of 5 percent of hundreds of thousands of Israel pounds for each of them.

In Israel the influence of Daniel Recanati, who is respectfully called "Mr. Dani" by employees of the bank, is obviously stronger. He was born in Salonika in 1921. After graduating from high school in Tel Aviv he studied at the London School of Economics, but returned soon after the outbreak of World War II, and later joined the British Army, serving in Egypt and Italy. He also served in the Israeli Army in 1948 but at that time was already involved in the activities of the Discount Bank, whose general manager he became in 1954.

Daniel Recanati is thin, his face narrow and his hair graying. He is always elegantly dressed, mostly in dark suits. When he receives someone in his office he is relaxed and never looks at his watch, the telephone does not ring, and the secretary never interrupts to bring letters for his signature. His behavior is conservative to the nth degree. The bank has no public-relations consultant, and Mr. Recanati personally signs the invitations to the yearly press conference (invariably held on a Tuesday), on the occasion of the publication of the bank's financial report. He once told a journalist, "My aspirations are the aspirations of the bank. I grew up in the Israel Discount Bank, and I identify with it."

Daniel Recanati knows that in order to live by his conservative, capitalist beliefs, he must compromise with the unique reality of Israel, and with the people who grew up with a different background. The Discount group has learned through the years to walk a tightrope suspended over the difficult reality of doing business in Israel. When asked how he, as a private businessman, adjusts himself to government intervention in business, Daniel Recanati reportedly replied: "When you are in a vineyard, you have to decide if you want to eat the grapes or antagonize the watchman."

The representative of the South American group in the Discount Bank family is Benno Gitter, who joined the group in 1958, after a group of investors from Argentina sold its holding in the Accadia Hotel and established a mortgage bank, together with the Discount Bank, with the sums that were realized.

Gitter, born in Holland in 1919 to a family involved in the tanning business, escaped in 1942 from Holland to Argentina, where he rejoined his relatives, whose business had already begun to flourish on the new continent. Young Gitter, who in his youth had planned to immigrate to Palestine, after 1948 began to devote his energies to developing business connections with the young State of Israel. In Argentina he founded an Argentine-Israel trading company and headed a group of investors in a number of Israeli enterprises.

In the Discount Bank group, his influence grew fast. He was appointed vice-chairman of its holding company and of its industrial-investment company, as well as to the board of half a dozen other companies. He is an ideal board member, a type almost unknown on the Israeli scene. He is quick, thoroughly at home with complicated financial reports. He speaks many languages (with a Dutch accent), and makes friends easily. Like someone who has always been well-to-do, money to him is not an object in itself. He gladly undertakes public responsibilities, and serves on the board of governors of the Hebrew University of Jerusalem, as well as of the Tel Aviv University, the Israel Philharmonic Orchestra and the Cameri Theater.

Gitter served for two and a half years as

Clal's[10] first managing director (a job for which he earned one dollar for the whole period). In December, 1970, he went so far as to resign from all his functions in the Discount Bank and accept an economic mission abroad. However, when his expectations did not materialize, he returned a year later to business in Israel. Despite his close relations with the government and especially with Finance Minister Sapir, he did not hesitate to write a letter to the editor of the *Haarez* daily newspaper in May, 1972, bitterly condemning some well-publicized early-morning raids by income-tax inspectors at homes of private citizens.

In recent years the management of the Discount Bank group absorbed a number of retiring senior Army officers, who play a growing role, especially in running the company's industrial enterprises. The first and senior member of this group is General (Res.) Dan Tolkowsky, a one-time Commander of the Israeli Air Force, whose influence on the thinking behind Israel's industrial development goes beyond his specific position in the Israel Discount Bank industrial complex. He is today one of the ideologists of Israel's technological progress.

Dan Tolkowsky, short, thin, with light hair, does not look at all like a sabra who was born in Tel Aviv in 1912. His blond mustache, mannerisms and even his accent in Hebrew show the clear impact of four years of studying mechanical engineering in London and four years of service in the Royal Air Force during World War II. He was trained as a pilot in South Africa and served as a fighter pilot in Italy and France and later in Crete and Greece. For ten years he served in the Israel Air Force and was its commander in 1956 Sinai Campaign, which was one of its finest hours. It was during his service as Air Force Commander that it became an all-jet air force, and the foundations were laid for this technological transition.

As managing director of the Israel Discount Bank Investment Company, Dan Tolkowsky is loyal to the conservative line of the firm. However, as an industrialist, more than a financier, he does not hesitate to recommend investing relatively large sums in fields which he thinks have a future in Israel, such as electronics and chemicals—although the final decision, as is usual in the Discount concern, is not made by him alone.

Dan Tolkowsky initiated the investment of his firm in Elron when the company, now a leading electronics complex, was still a struggling workshop founded by a number of instructors from the Haifa Technion. Some of Tolkowsky's efforts are directed to increasing cooperation between Israel's private industry and the defense effort. He is convinced that industry must participate in the application of the new technologies needed by Israel's defense; at the same time, he thinks industry will benefit from the spin-off of the huge investments in the country's defense.

NOTES

1. Mizrahi (abbreviation for Merkaz Ruhani; lit., Spiritual Center), Religious Zionist party, founded in Vilna in 1902, dedicated to the establishment of the people of Israel in the Land of Israel in accordance with the precepts of the Torah.

Hapoel Hamizrahi, Labor-oriented Religious Zionist organization in Palestine, established in 1922 "to build the country in accordance with the teachings of Torah and tradition through labor. Its aim is to put its members on a firm material and spiritual footing, to develop and strengthen religious sentiments among workers, and to make it possible for them to live as religious workers" (*Encyclopedia of Zionism and Israel*, 2:794). Hakibbutz Hadati, the Religious Kibbutz Federation, emerged from Hapoel Hamizrahi. Although Hapoel Hamizrahi and Mizrahi were separate organizations until their merger in 1956, they have run on the same election list since prestate years. Yosef Burg's roots are in Hapoel Hamizrahi.

2. Kiryat Arba, Jewish quarter in Hebron established by members of the Greater Land of Israel movement shortly after the June 1967 War

despite opposition of the Labor government. It eventually won grudging support from that government and more enthusiastic support from the Likud government when it came to power.

3. Yehuda Ben-Meir (Rosenberg) (b. 1939), leader of the National Religious party. Ben-Meir is a rabbi with a doctorate in psychology. He is currently deputy minister of foreign affairs.

4. Sabra (in Heb. zabar; pl. zabarim; a cactus with thorny hard skin and sweet fruit), a Jew born in Israel.

5. Bnei Akiva (lit., Sons of Akiva), youth movement of Hapoel Hamizrahi, established in 1929.

6. Since the publication of Elizur and Salpeter's *Who Rules Israel?* conditions have changed. Elections were held in May 1977 and the Likud formed a coalition with the NRP and other parties. Zevulon Hammer (b. 1936) became minister of education and culture and has slowly been gaining power within the NRP. Moreover, following the 1982 War in Lebanon, Hammer has moderated his position regarding a territorial compromise involving the West Bank.

7. Agudat Israel (lit., Union of Israel), world organization of Orthodox Jewry founded in Germany in 1912 by Orthodox Jews who feared that their secular and assimilated brethren of the World Zionist Organization would assume the mantle of Jewish leadership and the exclusive right to represent Jewry before the world. These Orthodox Jews recognized that modern organizational strategies were allowing the Zionists and other non-Orthodox groups to influence Jewish communal and cultural life, and when the 1912 Zionist Congress endorsed the cultural program of secular Zionism, they founded Agudat Israel. Its first convention reaffirmed the unimpeachable authority of Torah and halakhah. As a group,

Agudat Israel opposed the Zionist program as a profanation of Judaism because it attempted to revive Jewish patrimony in Erez Israel through human agency and promoted a secular Jewish society there. On the other hand, Agudat Israel, particularly since the Holocaust, regards the Land of Israel as the center—both spiritual and physical—of "Torah-true" Jewry. Just prior to independence in 1948, Ben-Gurion and Agudat Israel reached an agreement that led to its participation in the Provisional State Council. In the elections to the First Knesset, Agudat Israel and its Labor wing, Poalei Agudat Israel (lit., Agudat Israel Workers), formed an electoral alliance with the National Religious front (i.e. Hamizrahi and Hapoel Hamizrahi) called the United Religious front. Even after the 1953 Education Law went into effect, Agudat Israel continued to run its own independent school system, supervised (but not controlled) and heavily subsidized by the state.

8. Moezet Gedolei Torah (lit., Council of Torah Sages), rabbinical court established by Agudat Israel, which viewed the combined Chief Rabbinate as a Zionist organ and refused to recognize its authority. Agudat Israel recognizes Moezet Gedolei Torah and considers its decisions are binding on the party.

9. Hasidism (lit., Pietism), diverse movement within Judaism with roots in late eighteenth-century Eastern Europe. Originally the Hasidic movement challenged the traditional institutions of Rabbinic Judaism and created its own leaders. The movement also served to reinforce traditional Judaism in the modern period by creating institutions to fight assimilation and acculturation.

10. Clal (Israel) Ltd. (formerly Clal Israel Investment Corporation), one of Israel's largest corporations in the private sector.

AMNON RUBINSTEIN
49. The Israeli Left

Israel's military victory in June 1967 did not bring about the hoped-for political solution to the Arab-Israeli conflict. As it became clear that peace would not automatically follow the war, public debate centered increasingly around the political and diplo-

Source: Amnon Rubinstein, "And Now in Israel a Fluttering of Doves", *New York Times Magazine*, July 26, 1970, pp. 8–9, 44–45, 47–48. Reprinted by permission of Amnon Rubinstein.

matic policies that Israel should be willing to pursue. A relatively small but vocal and well-organized network of left-wing groups emerged in opposition to the policies of the Labor-dominated National Unity government. In general these organizations believed that in any peace settlement Israel should be willing to return all territories captured during the war and recognize the legitimate national rights of the Palestinians; therefore Israel should not establish permanent civilian settlements in the captured territories.

Amnon Rubinstein (b. 1931), dean of the Tel Aviv University Law School and later a leader of the nonsocialist left-wing opposition in the Knesset (the Democratic Movement for Change and then Shinui), discusses the emergence of this left-wing dissent in an article, excerpted here, published in the *New York Times Magazine*.

A wave of public disagreement with Government policy was brought about by the Goldmann affair. Dr. Nahum Goldmann, the 75-year old president of the World Jewish Congress, has voiced growing dissatisfaction with what he regards as the Israeli Government's rigid policy, but until recently few Israelis paid any attention to him. The old-time Zionist leader has never been a popular figure in Israel. His Swiss passport, his departure from Israel before the June war, and his private diplomacy have not endeared him to the public. When, on April 2, *Haarez*, Tel Aviv's independent daily, began publishing a series of articles in which Goldmann expounded his credo, his seemed an ancient voice in a new reality. Three days later, in an ironic twist of public mood, Goldmann, who had long felt rejected and forgotten, became the newly acclaimed hero of an angry opposition, a campus idol overnight. This change was brought about by a short communiqué on April 5, in which the Israeli Government announced that it had declined to sanction a Goldmann mission to Cairo to meet President Nasser.

The communiqué reflected the Israeli Government's notorious talent for ruinous public relations. The pompous language used was characteristic of Israeli bureaucracy. The Government failed to give reasons for its rejection and also omitted to add that it had no objection to Goldmann visiting Cairo on his own and not as a representative of Israel.

Many Israelis were astounded by the Government's announcement. Most Israelis believe that every possible crack in the wall of Arab enmity ought to be explored, and many felt that the alleged invitation to Goldmann constituted such a crack. At Tel Aviv University, a student assembly voted— by a clear majority—for the Goldmann visit, and against the Government. Newspaper columnists denounced the Government in unprecedented terms. *Haarez* threw its weight into an all-out campaign against the Cabinet's policies in general and its handling of the Goldmann affair in particular; a random poll by that paper showed 63 percent against the Government on this issue. Even *Davar*,[1] Labor's own newspaper, demanded a more satsifactory explanation of the Cabinet's refusal to sanction the visit.

Fifty-six Jerusalem high-school pupils, including the son of a Cabinet minister, signed a letter addressed to Mrs. Meir in which they bluntly questioned whether their forthcoming military service was justified in the light of the Government's decision. In Jerusalem, about 100 demonstrators tried to break into Mrs. Meir's house [Ed. note: actually into the courtyard] and were repulsed by the police. Demonstrators sat down at three major road junctions and stopped traffic for an hour until they were forcibly removed by the police. For Israeli radicals, the Goldmann affair had at least one virtue: it removed the "stigma" of national consensus. They can now wear a "we, too" badge and look their Western colleagues straight in the eye.

The new voices of dissent emerged not out of any organized opposition to the

Government, but spontaneously from amorphous groups. In Israel's centrist politics, this is a welcome innovation all the more surprising since it comes while the country is fighting a brutal war under siege conditions. Part of the explanation for this expression of nonconformist moods actually may be found in the united front and wide-coalition Government itself.

The Government commands a majority of 102 out of the 120 seats in the Knesset. Friction inside the Cabinet is not uncommon and the rule of collective government responsibility is honored more in its breach than in its observance. Yet, the very existence of this wall-to-wall coalition and the virtual disappearance of a real opposition have produced an atmosphere of political tranquillity. A minority of Israelis find this consensus stifling and almost instinctively rebel against it. "Someone," said a high school student on a recent radio program, "has to say 'no,' otherwise we may forget what democracy is all about."

The nay-sayers comprise a number of small, divergent groups. The original nucleus came from the Hebrew University of Jerusalem, where, after the Six-Day War, a group of professors founded the Movement for Peace and Security.[2] Among the members and supporters of this movement are some of the university's leading names: Yehoshua Bar Hillel (philosophy), Yaakov Talmon and Yehoshua Arieli (history), and Avigdor Levontin (law). The movement, which has a substantial following among younger faculty members and the student body, was formed as an antidote to the Greater Israel Movement.[3] It has pleaded, at meetings and through newspaper advertisements, against annexation of Israeli-occupied areas and the creation of *faits accomplis* in the new territories, and for a moderate policy which would leave open every option for a peaceful settlement.

Out of the Jerusalem campus sprang the Peace List which, in November, 1969, ran in the Knesset elections. It was headed by two young professors: Gadi Yatziv, a sociologist,

and Saul Fogel, a mathematician, and failed to win even one seat. The beating at the polls weakened the movement and dulled its edge. Yet the nucleus of dissenting professors is still there and their peace offensive has gathered momentum as a result of the Goldmann storm.

The Jerusalem group has recently initiated a public campaign against the Government's plan to build 250 houses for Jewish settlers in Hebron [see doc. 48]. The campaign began with an advertisement which said the project would "antagonize the Palestinian Arabs and hinder peace efforts"; the public was invited to pay for and sign further advertisements. The results were impressive: seven long ads and hundreds of signatures. Among the signatories were artists, authors, journalists, scientists and prominent Israelis from all walks of life. Surprisingly, the list included names of persons highly placed in the establishment, such as the Inspector of Banks and the former Director of the Treasury.

The Hebron ads are part of an almost daily press war fought between doves and hawks. They include petitions for and against annexation, direct talks, and Government rigidity; eccentric, far-fetched peace solutions spelled out by a Jerusalem doctor; cartoons against administrative arrests of suspected fedayeen; farmers lashing out in Agnewish[4] terms against the loud minority of professors and journalists; peace poems lamenting the dead, denouncing annexationists, glorifying peace. All these quite expensive ads are paid for by individuals—often from their meager funds—and testify to the Israelis' inherent need to speak out, not despite the war, but because of it.

Siah,[5] a new radical-left group, does not participate in this ad war. It has been involved in noisy demonstrations and occasional clashes with the police. The members of this group have taken much of their terminology and some of their tactics from the New Left in Europe or America. Protesting against the planned settlement in Hebron, a number of Siah members carried a coffin which bore the slogan: "Here lies the last chance of peace," and buried it next to Government offices. Because of its noisy carryings-on, Siah has been accused of anti-Israeli sympathies and has even been equated with the Mazpen,[6] the extreme pro-Fatah,[7] anti-Zionist group. Yet Siah's philosophy is Zionist and its only quarrel is with the Government's policy.

Siah has no ordinary membership. About 500 people participate in its activities and another 500 are regarded as supporters. They come from three sectors: members of left-wing (Mapam) kibbutzim, who are disillusioned with their party's participation in the coalition Government; ex-Communists who frown upon their leadership's return to the fold; intellectuals and artists who associate themselves with the New Left. Prominent members are two students at Tel Aviv University: Ran Cohen, 31 (economics), member of Kibbutz Gan Shmuel and a reserve officer in the paratroop corps, and Yossi Amitai, 33 (Middle Eastern Studies), member of Kibbutz Gvulot.

Says Ran Cohen:

We regard ourselves as Zionists and radicals. Our philosophy is based on self-determination within Palestine, for Arabs and Jews. We regard the Six-Day War as a justified defensive war, but because (it was this), we are against any annexation and any Jewish settlement in the occupied territories. We believe in the possibility of a peaceful settlement which will give the Palestinians their inherent right to self-determination and will, at the same time, insure Israel's security. We are also committed to the radical left—not in its Soviet perversion—but in its true meaning. Yet we are different from the New Left in the West. First, we, unlike them, have to insure our national existence. Secondly, our whole background and society are different from theirs. But we have things in common: a belief in direct action, a rejection of the old dogmatic left, a burning need to change the present reality.

Though tiny, Siah has played an important role in the new dissent. It has, in some ways, saved the radical tradition in Israel. With the traditional left in Government, and

the Israeli (Jewish) Communist party[8] domesticated and respectable, Siah remains the bearer of Israeli radicalism. By its acceptance of basic Zionist tenets, Siah has demonstrated that the ideas of the New Left do not necessarily lead to a rejection of Israel as a Jewish state. The facts that almost all of Siah's members are recruited from the younger generation and that its leaders play their part in the defense of the country, have made its role significant. Unlike Mazpen, Siah has managed to be virulently anti-Government without associating itself with the Arab cause. On the contrary, Siah criticizes the Arab left for denying the Jewish people the inherent right to self-determination.

Haolam Hazeh[9] is another advocate of nonconformist ideas. This small party has two members of Knesset, and its leader, Uri Avnery, was the first political figure to wave the flag of Palestinian entity and to draw public attention to the growing role the Palestinians play in the Arab world.

All these groups make up a small part of the Israeli public. The reason the new dissent has the impact that it does is that it occasionally appeals to a broader section of public opinion. This broad section encompasses people from most political parties: they are united not by any definitive ideology but by an almost instinctive rejection of nationalist myths and annexationist creeds. They believe that some compromise solution must be found to bring an end to the tragic conflict between Arabs and Jews.

This mood is tested daily by the brutal fedayeen attacks on civilians and the venomous anti-Jewish propaganda emanating from Arab radio stations and press. Yet the mood persists; its motto is: "If the Arabs are ready for real peace, we would be ready to give up a lot." In other words, these dissenters believe, the national consensus is being kept in existence by the continuous Arab "no."

The Goldmann affair and its aftermath indicate how deeply divided public opinion in Israel would have been had there been any positive Arab response. For a moment, when it seemed that there was a faint rumor of an Arab voice whispering "yes," the whole country seemed to have been rent asunder.

It is this phenomenon and not the noise emanating from small radical groups which is indicative of the strength of the peace lobby in Israel. The great majority of Israelis would give up territory, dispense with diplomatic paraphernalia and go out of their way to put an end to the war. At the same time, they are ready to fight with the courage and valor which have made them famous, provided they know that there is *ein breirah*, that there is "no alternative," and that war and death are forced upon them.

Mrs. Meir and her Government are impressed by the new sounds of protest, not because of their volume but because, for a time, they seemed to have shaken the solid rock of *ein breirah* on which national consensus has been built. Mrs. Meir has sensed that in this case the qualms of the young and the question marks of the journalists have to be tackled and answered immediately.

It is no secret that Mrs. Meir and some of her colleagues were alarmed specifically by the outcry against the Government's rigidity. As a senior Cabinet minister admitted off the record, Mrs. Meir's recent statement in the Knesset in which she accepted the Security Council's settlement-terms resolution of Nov. 22, 1967, should be ascribed not only to external factors—mainly American prodding—but also to internal pressure: the Government wanted to appease the determined minority which was unhappy about Israeli *nyets*. It was this anxiety which, at least partly, was responsible for the Government's relatively moderate reaction to the recent American initiative [the Rogers Plan, described below].

This sensitivity to under-current moods of public opinion is not characteristic of Israeli politics. On the contrary, because of the completely proportional electoral system, under which members of the Knesset are picked by party nomination committees, there is a tendency to disregard minority groups. Only a few months before the Goldmann fiasco, the Government had disregarded strong secular feelings on the "Who-is-a-Jew" issue and highhandedly pushed a quasi-orthodox definition through the Knesset. This new response to public mood does not usher in a new atmosphere; it merely attests to the magnitude of the issue involved. On this issue of *ein breirah*, of no alternative, even a small minority of nay-sayers succeeds in shaking the political establishment.

How strong are the moderates? In a public-opinion poll conducted last May, 22 percent of Israelis defined themselves as doves and 31 percent stated that they had not yet decided, and 15 percent gave a "don't know" answer. This poll explains the dilemma of the liberal, moderate Israeli. Most Israelis would trade almost all of the new territories in return for peaceful relations with neighboring countries. But nobody offers Israel such a peace. Not even friendly intermediaries talk of the type of peace which would allow Israel to reduce its armaments and live in security. Nobody offers Israelis the kind of peace they aspire to, that which Abba Eban calls a "Benelux peace": diplomatic relations and trade agreements with neighbors and, above all, open borders. In the utopian image of a peaceful Middle East harbored by Israelis there are Israeli tourists in Cairo and Beirut. This image, still clung to in the popular songs, is nowadays further from reality than ever before.

All the American peace plans mapped out since the Six-Day War exclude diplomatic relations and do not insure open borders between Israel and her neighbors. The "contractual peace" provided for by Secretary of State Rogers's formula[10] seeks to squeeze out of the Arabs hardly anything more than a legal recognition of Israel and its borders. Israeli withdrawal from the west bank of the Jordan River, under present circumstances, would restore the pre-1967 closed borders and would bring the fedayeen from the Jordan Valley to the outskirts of Tel Aviv.

It is this reality which explains why so many Israelis cannot define themselves as either doves or hawks. Not that they cannot make up their minds, but rather that they lack the facts which would enable them to decide. It is generally assumed that this silent majority—silent, not out of apathy but because of the bewildering reality—is mostly made up of "tentative doves" who would give up almost everything in return for that which, at present, seems unattainable. The strength of the radical peace groups stems from their blaring appeals to the wishful thought of the great majority of Israelis.

The Arab governments could easily exploit the prevailing Israeli mood to sow dissension and disruption inside the country. They could, without giving up any real point of advantage, encourage opposition to the Meir Government by speaking softly in Israeli ears. The fact that they have not done so, and that they continue their incessant barrage of anti-Semitic propaganda, indicate the depth of their unfathomable hatred of Israel. Every time a powder keg of dissent builds up inside Israel, the Arabs douse it with a cold shower of curses and abuse. Radio Cairo was not content with denying the alleged Egyptian invitation to Goldmann, but declared emphatically that the Arabs would never deal with any Jew who had Zionist aspirations.

And after Goldmann met King Hassan of Morocco, a new campaign followed. Aksan Abdul Kadus, one of the leading Egyptian columnists, writing in *Akhbar El-Yom*, the Cairo daily, compared the earnest president of the World Jewish Congress with Rudolf Hess: "He attempts to fulfill the same task as that performed by Hitler's envoy, who flew to Britain in World War II in order to negotiate an end to war." And he goes on to accuse Goldmann of supporting a "racist" (i.e., Jewish) state in Palestine.

Jordanian press and radio outdo Cairo. Yacob-al-Salti wrote in the reputable Amman daily, *A Difa*, last April: "It is a serious mistake to link Nazism with Zionism and its activities. The Zionists and their followers claim that Nazism used modern methods to liquidate the Jews, burning them alive and killing them in masses. If Nazism had only completed this humanitarian task and had it carried out this social service, in other words, had it done what it is accused of doing by the Zionists, the universe would have been purged of the Zionist existence and the nightmare of plotting and evil would have been removed from the face of the earth." Such statements do not exactly encourage Israelis to believe that moderation will be met with moderation from the other side. . . .

But the deepest and most significant expression of dissent is to be found not in the mass media, but in contemporary Israeli literature. There one can find the most stirring, controversial and soul-searching words written on the Arab-Jewish conflict. The young generation of authors has, almost without exception, expressed an empathy for the Arab side which comes as a shock to the uninitiated. In their novels, poems and short stories the Arab appears not as an enemy, never as a villain but as the innocent victim of a tragic conflict. *Khirbet Hizeh* and *The Prisoner of War* by S. Yizhar, *The Swimming Match* by Benjamin Tammuz and *The Acrophile* by Yoram Kanyuk are four pieces representative of the period after the 1948 war. When these authors write of the Israeli war of independence they do not neglect to portray the Arab fellahin [village peasants] uprooted, displaced and killed in the war. . . .

A younger group of authors, bewildered by the apparent endlessness of the war, continued this tradition in a more dramatic fashion. Amos Oz in *My Michael*, perhaps his most mature novel, writes of a deranged Jewish woman in Jerusalem who cherishes the memory of Arab twins who grew up with her in Mandated Jerusalem: the woman imagines the twins across the border . . . the playful children of yesteryear have turned into menacing figures, desperate marauders, and the book ends with an apocalyptic scene in which the twins sneak across the border and blow up a Jewish settlement. A.B. Yehoshua, 34-year-old novelist and playwright, has another symbolical ending in *Facing the Forests:* the hero, a student employed as a forest guard, watches an Arab peasant set fire to a forest planted by the Jewish National Fund on a site which had once been an Arab village.

The feeling of guilt toward the Arab is the theme which dominates the latest Israeli literature. Yehoshua says that the "feeling of guilt is there and it would be dangerous to repress it.". . .

This inherent empathy for the Arab, this amazing understanding for a brutal enemy, has perhaps no immediate practical relevance. Yet poets and writers often echo a palpable sense of reality, which looms above and beyond the world of current events and newspaper headlines. . . .

And, above all, they provide spiritual and philosophical justification for the Israeli dove: a compromise between Arab and Jew is needed not only because war is hateful, but also because a compromise is a just and moral solution to a tragic conflict between two types of "justice"—the Jewish justice and the Arab justice. Yet, as Amos Oz has pointed out, the conflict is asymmetrical: while the Israelis are ready for compromise and coexistence, the Arabs seek to annihilate Israel. As long as this asymmetry persists, this inherent understanding for the Arabs will not be translated into action. But no one will deny that this understanding represents a powerful force in Israel society and culture.

What are the specific issues on which dissent is centered? Practically all Israelis agree that there should be no withdrawal without a peace agreement with neighboring Arab states. Almost all Israelis agree that Jerusalem must remain united and under some measure of Israeli control. From this point onward consensus gives way to divergence.

Attacks against the Government's rigidity—and again it should be emphasized that we are dealing with a minority, sometimes a very small minority—have been aimed at different issues. Since Golda Meir's latest speeches in the Knesset, the voices of critics have been lowered. But they still aim their arrows at the Government's failure to do anything about the Palestinians; its intention to build the Jewish settlement near Hebron; its rejection of the limited cease-fire proposed by Rogers; its insistence on contractual peace and the Rhodes formula; its failure to formulate a positive peace plan which could be presented to the Arabs and to world public opinion.

The dissenters' case is often encumbered by the very fault which they ascribe to the Government. The dissenters criticize the Government but rarely point to a constructive way which would lead to peace or even to a state of nonwar. Their strongest point is their emphasis on the need for a direct rapprochement with the Palestinians, but even here they are hampered by the lack of any real response from the Palestinians. Their arguments seem to be somewhat academic and are often founded upon wishful thinking—of an expected *volte face* in the Arab world, a naive belief that moderation will be countered by moderation, a rational analysis of an irrational hatred.

Their greatest frustration is the total absence of any corresponding voice of dissent from the other side. The only voice for Arab moderation is that of Cecil Hourani, a Westernized Arab, who opposes Arab war tactics against Israel. But even this courageous and lonely voice in the wilderness rejects the idea of a Jewish state in Palestine and sees Arab moderation as a means toward diluting and then eliminating Israel. Yet the existence of Israel as an independent Jewish nation, the right of Jews to self-determination, is a condition *sine qua non* to all dissenting groups, excepting Mazpen.

Often the peace dissenters themselves admit that, in the present circumstances, nothing Israel can do unilaterally will help. Occasionally, they concede that their alternative policy is aimed not at a foreseeable solution but at a slow, gradual process which may eventually produce a corresponding mood in the Arab countries. Some go even further and regard their activities as of essentially psychological importance. Listen to this *cri de couer* by Gadi Yatziv, who headed the Peace List [and is, in 1983, secretary of Mapam] and who figures prominently in the camp of no-sayers:

"A reality in which the best political alternative left in the hands of the Government is to send its sons to death is not a reality to which a mentally healthy people can acquiesce. Anyone who does not understand this truth shows that he is unable to fathom the monstrous dimension of our life. This refusal to accept the present reality does not necessarily have political implications and is not always reflected in political solutions. This nonacceptance is not a sign of defeatism: it is one of the healthy instincts of a life-loving social organism. This type of protest is an important element in our capacity to hold our own. This protest against the present reality is the real 'realism.' " Protest is needed not as a means to immediate political action but as an almost symbolic rejection of deadlock.

Moreover, the Soviet menace has overshadowed the internal argument. The intervention of the Soviet empire with its tradition of ruthlessness and anti-Semitism has given a new dimension to the conflict. The Russian bear, casting an ominous shadow across the canal, dwarfs the Arab masses shouting for revenge. The Soviet intervention has diminished the debate inside Israel. The issue now is not what to do about the west bank or the Palestinians but how to insure the survival of the Jewish state. The Soviet danger looms, like some monstrous evil, over the whole Middle East.

Some observers tend to regard the emergence of dissenting groups in Israel as a sign of weakness and the result of the war of attrition. There is some indication that both the Arabs and the Soviets see the recent outbursts as symptoms of disintegration, the beginnings of a disruptive process inside Israel. It is perhaps understandable that governments which rule by repression, censorship and police-state methods should misinterpret the sounds of clogs and brakes in a democratic machine. It was a similar kind of miscalculation which led the Soviets to misjudge Israel's strength on the eve of the Six-Day War, when the country was plagued by an economic recession and public morale under the nonleadership of a nongovernment seemed to have reached its lowest ebb. Actually, the rise of dissent in Israel is proof that the war of attrition waged upon Israel by the Arabs and the Soviet Union has failed at least in one respect. Against all odds, Israel at war retains all the features of a peaceful democracy.

The visual image of Israeli democracy is the frank, often even wild, debate heard through the sounds of war. It is the image of Ran Cohen, who returns from army duty on the canal to join in a demonstration against the Government's policy, or of the author, Yizhak Orpaz, a reserve lieutenant colonel, who in his recent novel, *Daniel's Dream*, describes the plight of the questioning Israeli and the tragedy of his enemy. It is the image of Prof. Don Patinkin, who volunteered to serve as a private in an infantry reserve unit and who opposes the Government's policy in the press and on television. It is the image of *Keshet*, a literary magazine, which devoted its last issue to an academic and objective examination of postwar Arab literature and poetry. It is the image of Capt. Israel Guttman, killed on the Suez front on May 19, three days after he had written a letter to a class of Beersheba pupils, in which he assured them that "the Egyptians on the other side of the canal are human beings who want to live like us—and to return safely home to their wives and children," and urged them not to hate the Arabs. It is the image of a tiny, odd, occasionally exasperating, always intriguing people attempting, in peace and war, to do the seemingly impossible.

NOTES

1. *Davar*, daily newspaper of the Histadrut. *Davar* was established by Berl Katznelson, who was its first editor, in 1925. As Mapai gained control over the Jewish Agency Executive, it also became the unofficial newspaper of the Jewish semiautonomous government.

2. Movement for Peace and Security, organization of liberal and leftist academics who believed that peace could be obtained only by recognizing the Palestinian rights for national self-determination and by territorial compromise on the part of the Israeli government. Established shortly after the June 1967 War, the Movement for Peace and Security seemed to draw on the same network from which the Brit Shalom had drawn earlier and from which the Peace List, which ran in the 1969 elections.

3. Movement for Greater Israel (also called Greater Land of Israel movement, Greater Israel movement, and Land of Israel movement), organization devoted to preventing territorial compromise out of the belief that all of Erez Israel should be under Israeli sovereignty. It also emerged after the June 1967 War. Its leaders included Israel Eldad and Eliezer Livneh.

4. Spiro T. Agnew (b. 1918), vice-president of the United States, 1969–73, who was known for his invective attacks on the press, liberals, and intellectuals. He was forced to resign because of a graft scandal.

5. Siah (acronym for Smol Israeli Hadash; lit. Israeli New Left), leftist organization that emerged from two separate, unrelated groups which happened to choose the same name. Shortly after the June 1967 War, a group of students at the Tel Aviv University who were unhappy with Mapam's joining the Labor alignment, formed a new organization around the consensus that Israel had to recognize Palestinian national rights and had to be willing to withdraw from all or most of the conquered territories. Most of these students were members of Hakibbutz Haarzi, and they defined themselves as Zionist. Simultaneously, students of the Hebrew University campus in Jerusalem, many of whom had belonged to Mazpen, Maki, or other nonmainstream socialist organizations, also formed a group they called Siah. This organization was unable to reach a consensus regarding whether it was Zionist, anti-Zionist, or a-Zionist. It did, however, reach a consensus regarding its commitment to socialist ideology and to the necessity of Israeli recognition of Palestinian national rights and withdrawal from all the conquered territories. In the summer of 1970 the two groups merged into one national organization. Throughout the 1970s Siah, like the rest of the Israeli Left, split into factions that reunited in new coalitions. Moked, Shelli, and Shasi received most of Siah's members at various times (see nn. 8, 9 below).

6. Mazpen (lit., Compass), publication of the Israeli Socialist organization and the name by which the organization is commonly known. The Israeli Socialist organization originated as a faction of Maki that was expelled in 1962 and became a small anti-Zionist, anti-imperialist faction of the Israeli Left. It criticized Maki for its lack of commitment to revolutionary socialism. Similarly it refused to give its unqualified support to the PLO because of its "petit bourgeois" leadership. Mazpen does not run in national elections; it urges its members and supporters to vote for Rakah (or, in recent years, the Democratic Front for Peace and Equality) as the best alternative.

7. Al-Fatah (reverse acronym for Harakat Tahrir Filastin; lit., Palestine Liberation Movement; the acronym also forms the Arabic word for Conquest), oldest and largest political and military organization of Palestinians, formed in the late 1950s. Since 1969 al-Fatah has been the dominant member of the Palestine Liberation Organization, and its chairman, Yasir Arafat, has been PLO chairman.

8. Maki (acronym for Miflagah Kommunistit Israelit; lit., Israeli Communist Party), re-formation of the Palestine Communist party (PKP) in 1948. In 1954 Moshe Sneh's Mifleget Hasmol Hasozialisti joined Maki.

In 1919 the Mifleget Poalim Sozialistim (lit., Socialist Workers' Party) was formed by Socialist Zionists who refused to join Ahdut Haavodah. They rapidly moved away from Zionism in order to be granted membership in the Comintern and formed the PKP, which was recognized by the Comintern in 1924 and expelled from the Histadrut. During the 1940s the PKP was plagued with factionalism and schisms, generally over the nationalist issue. In May 1943 many Arabs left the party to form the Arab League of National Liberation; other schisms occurred as well. In 1944 the reduced (and largely Jewish) PKP was reinstated into the Histadrut. In 1948 most of the factions reunited to form Maki.

In 1965 Maki split into two separate parties.

One faction, led by Moshe Sneh and Shmuel Mikunis, was primarily Jewish and retained the name Maki. The other faction, led by Meir Vilner and Toufiq Toubi, was primarily Arab and formed Rakah (Reshimah Kommunistit Hadashah; lit., New Communist List). At first both parties were recognized by Moscow, but soon only Rakah had that distinction. In the 1973 elections Maki combined with the Tkhelet Adom (lit., Blue-Red) faction of Siah to form Moked (lit., Focus). In 1977 Maki joined the Shelli coalition.

9. Haolam Hazeh–Koah Hadash (lit., This World-New Force), nonsocialist leftist party in Israel led by Uri Avnery, editor of the weekly magazine *Haolam Hazeh*. The party, generally referred to simply as Haolam Hazeh, ran in the 1965 and 1969 elections. In 1973 it split into two factions—Meri (acronym for Mahaneh Radikali; lit., Radical Camp) and the Israel Democrats. Meri, led by Avnery, attracted support from parts of Maki and Siah. The Israel Democrats, led by Shalom Cohen, a long-time assistant to Avnery, gained support from most of the Black Panthers (see doc. 50). In 1977 Meri joined Shelli.

10. William Pierce Rogers (b. 1913), U.S. secretary of state, 1969–73. Rogers was the author of the plan that led to a cease-fire in the War of Attrition.

LEA BEN-DOR
50. The Black Panthers

The years following the June 1967 War saw an exacerbation of sociopolitical tensions in Israel that derived from the government's preoccupation with foreign and defense affiars, accelerated economic activity, and the reaction of underprivileged social groups to the privileges extended to new immigrants from the West and the Soviet Union. The absorption of the latter group has not been free of problems, but it was an irritant that induced young, non-Western Jews, mostly of North African descent, to articulate their grievances through the formation of a protest movement, the Black Panthers,[1] in 1971. The Black Panthers tried to focus attention on what they regarded as systematic discrimination against non-Western Jews by the European establishment in areas such as housing,[2] employment, and education. Lea Ben-Dor, a senior journalist and commentator for Israel's English-language daily newspaper, the *Jerusalem Post*, analyzes this phenomenon.

"So you see the Panthers are real; they aren't just an invention of the press," said a sympathiser in a radio discussion of the Panther riot on Wednesday evening.

They are real. But they are not black, and "Panther" is no more than wishful thinking. The ones I have met, or seen, are mostly undersized, even rather underfed looking. They are no match for husky policemen, with or without batons. The grievance of many, after all, started with the fact that they were rejected by the army. Their school attendance was sketchy in most cases. Some were ill, others were caught out in petty crimes and drifted into delinquency; for others, hashish provided solace against the hardships of poverty.

Their battle-cry, not very loud but increasingly persistent, has been "discrimination." Who runs the country, who has the good

Source: Lea Ben-Dor, "A Dream of Panthers," *Jerusalem Post Week-End Magazine*, May 21, 1971, p. 7. Reprinted by permission.

jobs? The Ashkenazim. Who lives in over-crowded housing, who does the poorly paid work? The children of the Oriental families. The answer seems close to hand and has long lurked around the corner.

Except that it is just not true and those of the Panthers who think about their situation—and not a few of them do—know that is so. The Black Panthers of Detroit or Chicago had no difficulty in pinning down the exact points at which there is discrimination. Their namesakes in Jerusalem have now been able to claim a specific grievance, which is that immigrants of today get incomparably better housing than their parents did in the early years of the state. But other young Israelis, or old Israelis for that matter, do not get cheap housing any more than do the Panthers.

What has really emerged is a terribly deep sense of frustration that here they are, an Israel-born generation, and little better equipped for a competitive society than their fathers were in the confusing years after their arrival here; less well off possibly than their grandfathers, who suffered varying degrees of discrimination in Arab countries but had learned how to live in that world. It is worse than discrimination: it is failure.

Little is heard today of A. D. Gordon[3] and the healing dignity of manual labour, except in kibbutzim that still constitute isolated communities, and it was always a concept that could appeal only to those who had a choice in the matter. There is unskilled work to be had, but its acceptance has become more difficult in a place like Jerusalem where the shortage of manual labour had been solved by Arabs from East Jerusalem and beyond. The Panther's relationship to an Arab fellow-worker is likely to be both closer and far more problematical than that of a European Jew, rather as European Jews who lived through the Holocaust find contacts with today's Germans more difficult than does a Yemenite or a South American.

The Panthers are kids who not only know that they have not got a proper job now, a job with what they call "status," but that they are never going to have one, because they have neither the training nor the habit of work; that not only do they still have to share a bed with another brother in a cramped flat full of squabbling people, but that they are never going to be able to get a proper home of their own, or not the way things are at the moment.

Casual jobs provide enough money for a few jazzy clothes and the cinema. But for marriage and a home? Nor is the situation made any easier by the fact that plenty of boys of their own communities have made good, learned a trade, carried on with it in the army, became foremen in a factory; sweated their way through high school, to head a department in the post office; or struggled into university and escaped altogether into a different world.

The Panthers blame others for their troubles, and they are right. The basic, original trouble was not discrimination, but the lack of it. All over the Western world, but specifically in Eastern Europe, the Jews have been mobile. They have escaped persecution and, scarcely arrived in their new country, fought for security. Fathers in factories pushed their children through school and into university, to arm them with knowledge, to make them secure. Nobody really gave much thought to whether the large and disorganized families from Arab countries who arrived here after 1948 were equally ready to pull themselves up by their own bootstraps.

The remnants from the camps in Europe made this effort. In the Orient, fathers take precedence over sons, they do not slave and scrape to send them to college. In any case a small family is no credit to anyone, there was never enough room for the large families in the small flats we provided, and the children drifted out into the street and fell behind at school. In the early years of the state, with a small population and mass immigration, there was a simplistic assumption that merely being in Israel, where a school was provided, would create equal learning conditions for the ten children of an illiterate and the two of a professor. Belatedly, an attempt was made to even things up with long school days in some of the schools, with extra tuition, special classes in summer and easier admission to high school. But only lucky ones, or the capable ones, escaped the trap of overcrowding, which prevented children from making use of the education they were offered. . . .

If there is one single thing we could do to reduce the gap between those who can make a living and those who see nothing but odd jobs in their future it is to provide public housing for rent, quickly, on an emergency basis, like we build armies or roads or industries. The fact that a man cannot get a place to live without a down payment that is astronomical for the unskilled labourer is destructive of his sense of independence and self-confidence. If flats are rented, a man can move to a new job, an unproductive factory can be closed down, older couples can move to a smaller flat when the children have grown up. Flats that must be bought become straitjackets.

Today the Panthers are not a political movement but a group that has banded together, more or less, in the hope of getting unspecified satisfaction for the fact they are not equipped to get anywhere, even into the army. They are already split on whether they should press the issue of "discrimination" or poverty.

They are equally split on whether to accept political and financial help from the left-wing groups, Mazpen and Siah. Some money is handy for any organization, but these donors are the privileged, students, professors even, very few of them of Oriental background. The Panthers may seek to be a revolutionary group, but most have no left-wing ideology, nor socialist or Maoist,

that is for intellectuals. Their would be friends put out stencilled broadsheets signed "Solidarity Committee for the Black Panthers," because the Panthers do not want to be identified with any of the existing political groups. Perhaps the Panthers have a healthy suspicion that their wealthier friends are only enjoying the pleasures of slumming. The friendship is one-sided.

As a group looking for help the Panthers have made many mistakes. The name itself, borrowed from a bitterly anti-Semitic organization, is an affront. Their first target seemed to be immigrants from Russia who have themselves barely escaped from danger and genuine discrimination—but they hurried to the Wall now to tell the demonstrators there that this is not what they meant. Their next target in Tuesday's demonstration, was the police, the great majority of which consists of the sons of other Oriental immigrants whose living conditions are removed a bare half step, if that much, from that of the Panthers themselves. Fighting the police is the fashion in America, it seeps in like pop music and nudity.

Because of their real grievances, the Panthers in fact received a great deal of public interest and attention. One result is that they have developed a hunger for continuous publicity and excitement. Talking to the press and ringing up the police has the missing "status." Can you feel equally important talking about job training?

They are going to have to struggle hard for their identity, or else they will be swallowed up by busy leftists looking for a cause, or anyone ill-disposed towards Israel. Even flats are easier to conjure up out of nothing than the dream of status that hides in the name "Panthers."

NOTES

1. Black Panthers (no connection, other than choice of name, with the American Black Panthers of the 1960s), protest movement of young Sephardim from poor urban neighborhoods in Tel Aviv and Jerusalem that emerged in early 1971. By 1973 the movement had split. One faction, led by Charlie Biton, joined with Rakah to form the Democratic Front for Peace and Equality. Most of

the Panthers, however, joined the Israel Democrats. In 1977, a faction led by Saadiah Marciano
joined Shelli, and another faction led by Eddie
Malkah formed the Blue and White Panthers. In
1981 the former Panthers were split even further.
Biton's group stayed with the Democratic Front
for Peace and Equality led by Rakah. A new
election list, Ihud (lit., Unity) was formed by
Saadiah Marciano and Mordekhai Elgrably, who
in 1977 was elected to the Knesset on the
Democratic Movement for Change list. Some
former Panthers were included on Tami's list.
Finally, Amha (lit., Your People), led by Victor
Tayar, also ran in the 1981 elections.

2. The provision of public housing to new
immigrants from the West and the Soviet Union,
while housing in Sephardi neighborhoods still
frequently reflects the conditions of the early
1950s (see doc. 8), has been continuously and

vigorously protested by the Black Panthers and
their various factions from their earliest demonstrations. It was expressed as recently as March
1981 by MK Charlie Biton in a political demonstration outside of a Knesset reception for Joseph
Mendelevich, former "Prisoner of Zion" (i.e.,
Soviet Jew persecuted for Jewish activism—or
merely desiring to emigrate). In addition, during
the housing shortage of the early 1970s organizations of newly married couples frequently demonstrated, demanding that their needs for housing
be given precedence over new immigrants.

3. Aharon David Gordon (1856–1922), early
leader of the Labor Zionist movement who advocated labor as a means of personal self-fulfillment
as well as national renaissance. Gordon stressed
in particular the importance of "natural" agricultural labor.

1967–73
Foreign Policy Issues

ALEXEI KOSYGIN
51. The Soviet Union and the June 1967 War

The diplomatic barrage against Israel, led by the Soviet Union and the Arab states, began almost simultaneously with the June 1967 War itself. Alexei Kosygin, premier of the Soviet Union from 1964 until his death in 1980, presented the Soviet line in a speech, excerpted here, before the United Nations General Assembly on June 19, 1967.

Representatives of almost all States of the world have gathered for this special emergency session of the United Nations General Assembly to consider the grave and dangerous situation which has developed in recent days in the Near East, a situation which arouses deep concern everywhere.

True, no hostilities are under way there at this moment. The fact that a cease-fire has been brought about is a definite success for the peace-loving forces. This is in no small way due to the Security Council, although it failed to discharge fully its obligation under the United Nations Charter. The aggression is continuing. The armed forces of Israel are occupying territories in the United Arab Republic, Syria and Jordan.

As long as Israeli troops continue to occupy the territories seized by them, and urgent measures are not taken to eliminate the consequences of aggression, a military conflict can flare up with renewed force at any minute.

That is exactly why the Soviet Union took the initiative in convening an emergency session of the General Assembly. We are pleased to note that many States supported our proposal. They have displayed their awareness of the dangers with which the situation is fraught and manifested their concern for the consolidation of peace.

The General Assembly is confronted with the primary task of adopting decisions that would clear the way for a restoration of peace in the Middle East. This task concerns all States irrespective of differences in social or political systems and philosophical outlook, irrespective of geography and alignment with this or that grouping. It can be solved only if the multiple and complex nature of today's world does not relegate to the background the common bond that joins States and peoples together, and above all the need to prevent a military disaster. . . .

Not a single people wants war. Nowadays no one doubts that a new world war, if it started, would inevitably be a nuclear war. Its consequences would be disastrous for many countries and peoples of the world. . . .

The nuclear age has created a new reality in questions of war and peace. It has laid upon States an immeasurably greater responsibility in all that pertains to these problems. . . .

However, the practice of international relations abounds in facts which show that certain States take quite a different approach. Continuous attempts are made to interfere in the internal affairs of independent countries and peoples, to impose upon them from outside political concepts and alien views on social order. Everything is done to breathe new life into military blocs. A network of military bases, the strong points of aggression, flung far and wide all over the world, is being refurbished and perfected. Naval fleets are plying the seas thousands of miles from their own shores

Source: Yaacov Roi, ed., *From Encroachment to Involvement: A Documentary Study of Soviet Policy in the Middle East, 1945–1973* (Tel Aviv: Shiloah Center, 1974), pp. 450–55. Reprinted by permission.

and threaten the security of States over entire regions.

Even in those cases when the aggravation of tension or the emergence of hotbeds of war danger is connected with conflicts involving relatively small States, not infrequently big Powers are behind them. This applies not only to the Middle East, where aggression has been committed by Israel, backed by bigger imperialist Powers, but also to other areas of the world. . . .

If we analyze the events in the Middle East, we are bound to conclude that the war between Israel and the Arab States did not result from some kind of disagreement or inadequate understanding of one side by the other. Nor is this just a local conflict. The events that recently took place in the Middle East in connection with the armed conflict between Israel and the Arab States should be considered squarely in the context of the over-all international situation in the world. . . .

We should note that the main features in the relations between Israel and the Arab States during the past year were the ever-increasing tension and the mounting scale of attacks by Israel troops on one or another of Israel's neighbor States. . . .

On 7 April last, Israel troops staged an attack against the territory of the Syrian Arab Republic. . . .

. . . Israel was warned by a number of States about its responsibility for the consequences of the policy it was pursuing. But even after that the Israeli Government did not reconsider its course. Its political leaders openly threatened "wider military actions against Arab countries.". . . On 9 May 1967 the Israeli Parliament authorized the Government of Israel to carry out military operations against Syria. The Israeli troops began concentrating at the Syrian borders, and mobilization was carried out.

At that time the Soviet Government, and I believe others too, began receiving information to the effect that the Israeli Government had chosen the end of May as the time for a swift strike at Syria in order to crush it and then planned to carry the fighting over into the territory of the United Arab Republic [see doc. 44].

When the preparations for war had entered the final stage, the Government of Israel suddenly began to spread, both confidentially and publicly, profuse assurances of its peaceful intentions. It declared that it was not going to start hostilities and was not seeking conflicts with its neighbors. Literally a few hours before the attack on the Arab States, the Defence Minister of Israel swore his Government was seeking peaceful solutions. "Let diplomacy be put to work," the Minister was saying at the very moment when Israel pilots had already received orders to bomb the cities of the United Arab Republic, Syria and Jordan. This is indeed unprecedented perfidy.

On 5 June, Israel started war against the United Arab Republic, Syria and Jordan. . . .

What followed is well known.

Here, within the United Nations, I shall only recall the arrogance with which the unbridled aggressor ignored the demands of the Security Council for an immediate cease-fire.

On 6 June the Security Council proposed (Resolution 233 [1967]) an end to all hostilities as a first step towards the restoration of peace. Israel expanded operations on all fronts.

On 7 June the Security Council (Resolution 234 [1967]) fixed a time limit for the cessation of hostilities. Israel troops continued their offensive, and Israel aircraft bombed peaceful Arab towns and villages.

On 9 June the Security Council (Resolution 235 [1967]) issued a new categorical demand providing for a cease-fire. Israel ignored that too. The Israel army mounted an attack against the defensive lines of Syria with the purpose of breaking through to the capital of that State, Damascus.

The Security Council had to adopt yet another, fourth, decision (Resolution 236 [1967]); a number of States had to sever diplomatic relations with Israel, and a firm warning was given that sanctions might be applied, before Israel troops halted their military activities. A large part of the territory of Arab countries now actually occupied by Israel was seized after the Security Council had taken the decision on the immediate cessation of hostilities.

FOURTH ARAB SUMMIT CONFERENCE
52. The Khartoum Resolutions

The Khartoum Conference, convened in September 1967, was the first Arab summit to be held after the June 1967 War. It formulated the Arab consensus that underlay the policies of most Arab states participating in the conflict until the early 1970s. The following is an excerpt from a summary of the summit prepared for the U.S. Senate Committee on Foreign Relations.

The Arab heads of state have agreed to unite their political efforts on the international and diplomatic level to eliminate the effects of the aggression and to ensure the withdrawal of the aggressive Israeli forces from the Arab lands which have been occupied since the 5 June aggression. This will be done within the framework of the main principles to which the Arab states adhere, namely: no peace with Israel, no recognition of Israel, no negotiations with it and adherence to the rights of the Palestinian people in their country.

Source: U.S. Senate Committee on Foreign Relations, *A Select Chronology and Background Documents relating to the Middle East,* 2d rev. ed. (Washington, D.C.: Government Printing Office, February 1975), p. 249.

U.N. SECURITY COUNCIL
53. Resolution 242

With hindsight, it is easy to see the cycle that led from the June 1967 War to the October 1973 War. By the end of 1967 the euphoric hopes of the Israelis for a quickly negotiated peace settlement were dashed, and it was clear that a stalemate between Israel and the Arab states would prevail (see doc. 52). The U.N. Security Council Resolution 242, No-

Source: U.S. Senate Committee on Foreign Relations, *A Select Chronology and Background Documents relating to the Middle East,* 2d rev. ed. (Washington, D.C.: Government Printing Office, February 1975), pp. 249-50.

vember 22, 1967, terminated efforts to legislate a solution to the Arab-Israeli conflict in
the United Nations in the aftermath of the
June 1967 War. The general nature of the
resolution and the ambiguity of language
that made the resolution acceptable also
made it largely inoperative.

The Security Council

Expressing its continuing concern with the grave situation in the Middle East,

Emphasizing the inadmissibility of the acquisition of territory by war and the need to work for a just and lasting peace in which every State in the area can live in security,

Emphasizing further that all Member States in their acceptance of the Charter of the United Nations have undertaken a commitment to act in accordance with Article 2 of the Charter,

1. *Affirms* that the fulfillment of Charter principles requires the establishment of a just and lasting peace in the Middle East which should include the application of both the following principles: (a) withdrawal of Israeli armed forces from territories occupied in the recent conflict; (b) termination of all claims or states of belligerency and respect for and acknowledgement of the sovereignty, territorial integrity and political independence of every State in the area and their right to live in peace within secure and recognized boundaries free from threats or acts of force;

2. *Affirms further* the necessity (a) for guaranteeing freedom of navigation through international waterways in the area; (b) for achieving a just settlement of the refugee problem; (c) for guaranteeing the territorial inviolability and political independence of every state in the area, through measures including the establishment of demilitarized zones;

3. *Requests* the Secretary-General to designate a Special Representative to proceed to the Middle East to establish and maintain contacts with the States concerned in order to promote agreement and assist efforts to achieve a peaceful and accepted settlement in accordance with the provisions and principles in this resolution;[1]

4. *Requests* the Secretary-General to report to the Security Council on the progress of the efforts of the Special Representative as soon as possible.

NOTE

1. Gunnar Jarring (b. 1907), former Swedish ambassador to Moscow appointed by U Thant to be his special representative to the Middle East, as specified in this resolution. Jarring's mission began in November 1967. At first Israel opposed the format of his mission because it desired direct negotiations. Eventually, however, Israel accepted his "shuttle diplomacy" (which served as a model for Henry Kissinger's missions after the October 1973 War) as a form of indirect negotiations following the precedent set by Ralph Bunche in 1949. Jarring's mission led to temporary cessations of fighting.

EZER WEIZMAN
54. The War of Attrition

In the fall of 1968 Egypt began bombarding Israeli positions on the Suez Canal. This led to an escalation of hostilities known as the War of Attrition and to an arms race as Egypt introduced new Soviet ground-to-air missiles and Soviet personnel.

During this period Ezer Weizman (b. 1924) was chief of operations of the Israeli General Staff. He had served in the British Royal Air Force in World War II and then helped establish the Israel Air Force, in which he held numerous commands. He also rose to become one of the leaders of the Herut faction of Gahal, and in 1969 he entered the National Unity cabinet. His political influence grew when the Likud came to power in 1977, and he was named defense minister, but his personal and political conflict with Menahem Begin forced him to resign his position and leave the Likud.

These excerpts from Weizman's autobiography echo the debate that took place in Israel over the strategy employed by the government during the War of Attrition with Egypt from 1969 to 1970.

In August and September 1968, while we were battling with the guerillas and building up our army, the new Skyhawks [missiles from the United States] arrived, and our hearts felt a little lighter. We re-organized the armoured units and the paratroopers. Although there was no telephone call from down there, the Egyptian border was quiet. And then, in October, the blow landed. Fourteen soldiers were killed in an Egyptian bombardment at Kantara on the Suez Canal. We sensed that a new era had begun. It didn't have a name yet; later it was called the War of Attrition. Fortunately, we did not fall into the snare of thinking that the Egyptians had struck once and would not do so again. After the bombardment in October, there was an interval of a few months before the static battle was renewed, but, all the same, we took matters in hand. The first thing was to erect fortifications. A number of officers, headed by Elhanan Klein, the chief engineering officer, brought up an idea: "It's a long affair to pour concrete into fortifications so that they can stand up to bombardments. Let's strip down the Egyptian railway line in Sinai and use its rails as steel shields."

Haim Bar-Lev[1] hesitated. We didn't know if it would stand up to bombardment. We built a wall like the one they proposed and conducted experiments on it. We fired 120-mm and 160-mm mortar shells straight at it, as well as 105-mm, 130-mm and 155-mm cannon shells, and the Russian 122-mm, and the wall didn't collapse. The detonating layer held out. We stripped down the railway line, ordered used rails from abroad and built the first fortresses. Between March 1969 and 1 August 1970, we lost 250 dead and about 1,000 wounded on the Canal. Only a few were killed inside the fortresses, all the rest were hit when they were outside them or on their way to or from the line.

March 1969 is usually regarded as the beginning of the War of Attrition. I was in my second year as head of General Staff Division. There were two things troubling

Source: Ezer Weizman, *On Eagles' Wings: A Personal Story of the Leading Commander of the Israeli Air Force* (London: Weidenfeld and Nicolson, 1976), pp. 269–75, 280–82. Reprinted by permission of Ezer Weizman.

me. First, never having conducted a static war, our ground forces were unaccustomed to it and could not bring their full potential to bear, as they weren't storming forward to put a stop to Egyptian provocations. Second, our magnificent air force was sitting back; other than photographic missions and intercepting enemy planes, it wasn't doing a thing. It was forfeiting its image as the arm whose absolute superiority could decide every war.

During the months of March–June 1969, 20,000 Soviet advisers poured into Egypt, penetrating into the lowest command echelons of Egyptian armour, artillery and infantry battalions. Soviet planes, with Russian pilots, were stationed in Egypt. Our soldiers were being killed daily. The Egyptians were growing more and more arrogant. We were faced by an army with 1,000 tanks and as many artillery pieces, and, yet, Israeli forces weren't doing what they should and could do. Even when they did act, it was often too little, too late. They made the grievous error of reverting to outdated methods, which may have been good enough for attacks on Jordan or Gaza during the fedayeen raids preceding the Sinai Campaign but were hardly suitable now. "Deep penetration" was the slogan. The army carried out demolition atacks: destroying a transformer station deep inside Egypt; blowing up a bridge; a deep penetration raid with armour. These showed a great deal of courage, daring and resourcefulness, but all this was no more than tickling the Egyptian army. Such actions earned the Israeli army world-wide renown and threw tasty morsels to Israeli public opinion, but they didn't decide the war; they didn't bring it to an end, nor even dampen it.

Whether I was listened to or not, I repeated, over and over again, "A war like this can't be won by commando raids! It won't work! The Israeli army has to be employed in full and overwhelming force, not only to put an end to the War of Attrition—important enough unto itself— but also to check the Egyptian army before it

launches more dangerous offensives!" But mine was a lonely voice. A state with a strong standing army that has just defeated its enemies in a brilliant lightning campaign and yet chooses to conduct commando raids instead of making full use of its strength does so either because it doesn't believe in its ability to employ that strength to the utmost or because of the illusion that some commando raid can solve the problem. The facts proved that the problem wasn't solved until the air force went into action on a large scale.

My efforts to convince my General Staff colleagues to give up these commando pricks and prods and to deploy the army in earnest, so as to put an end to the War of Attrition, were not successful. Another prod and another prick, and the next day, there'd be 1,000 Egyptian shells, 2,000, 5,000, 10,000. Soldiers were getting killed, and the mood in the streets was swaying between grim and grotesque.

If I didn't succeed in conveying to my colleagues how essential it was to employ the army's full strength and to desist from commando raids—and events proved that I did not—I tried to persuade them at least to use the air force effectively, to strike such painful blows at the Egyptians that they would cease to regard the War of Attrition as profitable. Here, too, I encountered opposition. For the first time in the history of Israel, the air force commanders said that, because of the Egyptian SAM anti-aircraft system, they could not conduct operations unless the United States supplied us with some missile or other. I regarded this view as extremely dangerous. Never before had such a contention been put forward. When there had been nothing better, the Pipers of the War of Independence were good enough for the aerial missions required at the time, and no one ever contended that we could not cope because the Egyptian air force had better planes. The Israeli soldier—with his daring, his skills, his devotion, his patriotism, his inner motivation, his readiness to sacrifice his life—was the guarantee of our ability to survive. To trade this mighty treasure for the contention that we lacked some contraption or missile and that as long as we didn't acquire them from our friends or manufactured them ourselves we were powerless to defend Israel's security was, without any exaggeration, acquiescing to a death sentence on the Jewish state. . . .

Finally, on 20 July, we carried out the operation; we sent the air force in for a powerful surprise strike along the whole Egyptian line. We also had sixteen helicopters on stand-by, with 150 paratroopers awaiting permission to cross over to the other side and demolish a considerable portion of the Egyptian line. The plan was ready, and we were fully convinced of its prospects of success, but permission was not received. From one of the air force bases, the deputy commander called me up on the telephone: "Sir, it's just like the Six Day War. They're fleeing their dugouts like mice, we can take the whole line!" Indeed we could have. I was sure of that.

Despite the great success of the air operation, when we discussed it that night there were still some officers who opposed continuation of the bombings. I pressed for further attacks, contending that we should exploit our success and continue to strike at the Egyptians. Permission was given for bombing to be resumed the next day. But I didn't get much satisfaction from my success. Systematic recourse to the air force involved great difficulties and the loss of planes and pilots. After the air force succeeded in knocking out the ten missile batteries along the Canal, Russian involvement increased, and so did the number of batteries. Instead of regarding the air force as one of the components of the war against the Egyptians, instead of committing ground forces and armour on a large scale to pulverize the Egyptian line, with its artillery and missiles, the whole task devolved upon the air force, which came to be considered the sole solution, while the ground forces continued digging in. The Egyptians got used to living under bombing and did not give up their campaign of attrition. They were also reassured by the success of their attempts to lay ambushes in between our fortified positions. It was here they learnt the lesson they were to apply so successfully in the Yom Kippur War: leave the fortified positions alone and establish footholds in between.

Throughout the War of Attrition, there were apprehensions about the Russians, which was why the ground forces were not used for any decisive purpose, and also why the air force attacked here and there, causing the Egyptians—and itself—casualties and damage, but without employing its full strength.

As the war dragged on, without any army finding a way to put a stop to it, I, unlike others, became gradually convinced that this was the first time we were not winning. I said so countless times: we failed in this war. We did not comprehend it correctly. When the Egyptians agreed to a cease-fire, in August 1970, we interpreted it as an admission on their part that they couldn't stand our bombing any more. Without detracting from the great suffering inflicted on them by our air force, I don't have a shadow of a doubt that the Egyptians wanted a cease-fire in order to move their missile system forward to the Canal, so that it could neutralize our air force when their units crossed the waterway. All this backs up both of my contentions. First, the War of Attrition, in which our best soldiers shed their blood, resulted in the Egyptians gaining a free hand, over a period of three years, to prepare for the great war of October 1973; if so, it is no more than foolishness to claim that we won the War of Attrition. On the contrary, for all their casualties, it was the Egyptians who got the best of it. Second, by our errors between March 1969 and August 1970, and, subsequently, by our tragic acquiescence when the Egyptians violated the cease-fire and moved their missiles ahead, we, with our own hands, smoothed Egypt's path to the Yom Kippur War. When our blindness caused us to misread Egyptian intentions and prevented us from applying an accurate interpretation—or taking action to forestall the enemy—it was then that the Yom Kippur War began, with all its ensuing results. . . .

In 1948 and 1967, and during all the difficult times up to 1970, we never budged from the concept, without which Israel's existence would have been inconceivable, that our safety would be ensured not by parity of armament, but by the quality of the Israeli soldier; that it wasn't technological superiority which made us stronger than our enemies, but our great spiritual pre-eminence; that it wasn't arsenals crammed with the weapons and missiles which maintained us in the Middle East, but resourcefulness and cunning and brains, following the precept, "By ruses shall you make war." All through the War of Attrition, there wasn't a day when we didn't talk of our moral preponderance, but we contented ourselves with talk; without being convinced of these truths, all this was mere lip-service. Of the great conviction that we could overcome the Arabs, even if we didn't have some weapon or missile—ground, air or naval—nothing was left but words whose meaning had vanished. Either we got the Shrike [missile]—or what? Indecision. Lack of initiative. Acquiescence. Thus, the War of Attrition was the first one in which we gave in to technological limitations.

To use the terms of ground warfare, our Phantoms hacked through the barbed-wire fences of missiles and broke through the aerial fortifications, despite the losses they suffered; but they weren't backed up by the force that should have swept the objectives, demolishing the Egyptian positions and hurling them back from their footholds on the west bank of the Canal. The Egyptian surface-to-air missile system, which was the cause of our air losses and glumness, could have been eliminated in 1970. It would have required sending in infantry and armour, in addition to the air force. Whoever came to the conclusion that we lacked the strength to do so decreed that for the first time in her history, Israel would back down before the superior weapons possessed by the Arabs, thereby condemning the state to face the Yom Kippur War and concede its political positions, until it stood in real peril. And those who did so committed a further sin: in the course of the years 1970–3, they cultivated the delusion that we had won the War of Attrition, thus lulling our senses. Instead of saying: "We have failed to destroy the missiles system. Let's prepare for the eventuality that this system will fulfil a decisive role in the next war, and let's find ways of eliminating it!" we said: "Once again, we've won, once again, the Egyptians have had to rely on American favours to get them out of trouble" (and they were, indeed, in trouble). Thus, we created a myth, instead of dealing with the facts. We may have improved public morale, but we did so at a high price.

The results were not long in coming. Two or three weeks after the cease-fire ending the War of Attrition went into effect, in August 1970, the Egyptians took a meaningful and highly important step towards the Yom Kippur War: they moved their missile bases right up to the edge of the Canal, under cover of the agreement and in express defiance of it. The Israeli leadership did not have the courage to order a full-scale attack to annihilate the missile system, because they didn't believe it could be done. Then, by appealing to the Americans, they sowed the seed of total dependence on U.S. wishes.

NOTE

1. Haim Bar-Lev (b. 1924), deputy chief of staff during the June 1967 War and chief of staff, 1968–72. Like two of his predecessors in the IDF's top position—Dayan and Rabin—Bar-Lev began his military career in the Palmah. After his tenure as chief of staff, Bar-Lev entered the cabinet and was later secretary general of the Labor party.

55. The Palestinian National Charter

In addition to launching the War of Attrition (see doc. 54), the Arab states put their collective weight behind the Palestine Liberation Organization in order to break the deadlock in Arab-Israeli relations. Frequently these states sought to further their own competing policies and approaches by manipulating factions of the PLO—or even by organizing new factions.

After drafting the original Palestinian National Charter in 1964, the PLO underwent several important changes. Ahmad Shuqeiri, the first chairman, was replaced in 1967 by Yahya Hamuden, who was in turn replaced in 1969 by Yasir Arafat,[1] head of al-Fatah. During the transitional period that followed the June 1967 War, the PLO became increasingly independent of the Arab states and served as an umbrella organization of semiautonomous Palestinian groups. Fatah, the largest of these, has continued to dominate it. Following the May 1983 Lebanese-Israeli agreement, Arafat's leadership of Fatah was seriously challenged for the first time.

The Popular Front for the Liberation of Palestine (PFLP), headed by George Habash, was organized in December 1967. In 1968 Nayef Hawatmeh and his followers seceded from the PFLP to form the Popular Democratic Front for the Liberation of Palestine. The Palestine Liberation front was reorganized by Ahmad Jibril into the Palestine Front for the Liberation of Palestine—General Command. In 1968 the Syrian Ba'ath party established Al-Saiqa—Vanguard of the People's War of Liberation—and in 1969 the Iraqi Ba'aths established the Arab Liberation front, which later also gained the support of Libya.

To accommodate the changes occurring in the PLO, new institutions were established and a new charter was formulated. The charter adopted by the Fourth Palestine National Council, meeting in Cairo, on July 17, 1968, is reproduced here.

This Charter shall be known as "the Palestine National Charter."

Articles of the Charter:

1. Palestine, the homeland of the Palestinian Arab people, is an inseparable part of the greater Arab homeland, and the Palestinian people are a part of the Arab Nation.

2. Palestine, within the frontiers that existed under the British Mandate, is an indivisible territorial unit.

3. The Palestinian Arab people alone have legitimate rights to their homeland, and shall exercise the right of self-determination after the liberation of their homeland, in keeping with their wishes and entirely of their own accord.

4. The Palestinian identity is an authentic, intrinsic and indissoluble quality that is transmitted from father to son. Neither the Zionist occupation nor the dispersal of the Palestinian Arab people as a result of the afflictions they have suffered can efface this Palestinian identity.

5. Palestinians are Arab citizens who were normally resident in Palestine until 1947. This includes both those who were forced to leave or who stayed in Palestine.

Source: Yehoshafat Harkabi, *The Palestinian Covenant and Its Meaning* (London: Vallentine, Mitchell and Co., 1979), pp. 119–24. Reprinted by permission of Yehoshafat Harkabi.

Anyone born to a Palestinian father after that date, whether inside or outside Palestine, is a Palestinian.

6. Jews who were normally resident in Palestine up to the beginning of the Zionist invasion are Palestinians.

7. Palestinian identity, and material, spiritual and historical links with Palestine are immutable realities. It is a national obligation to provide every Palestinian with a revolutionary Arab upbringing, and to instill in him a profound spiritual and material familiarity with his homeland and a readiness for armed struggle and for the sacrifice of his material possessions and his life, for the recovery of his homeland. All available educational means and means of guidance must be enlisted to that end, until liberation is achieved.

8. The Palestinian people is at the stage of national struggle for the liberation of its homeland. For that reason, differences between Palestinian national forces must give way to the fundamental difference that exists betwen Zionism and imperialism on the one hand and the Palestinian Arab people on the other. On that basis, the Palestinian masses, both as organizations and as individuals, whether in the homeland or in such places as they now live as refugees, constitute a single national front working for the recovery and liberation of Palestine through armed struggle.

9. Armed struggle is the only way of liberating Palestine, and is thus strategic, not tactical. The Palestinian Arab people hereby affirm their unwavering determination to carry on the armed struggle and to press on towards popular revolution for the liberation of and return to their homeland. They also affirm their right to a normal life in their homeland, to the exercise of their right of self-determination therein and to sovereignty over it.

10. Commando action constitutes the nucleus of the Palestinian popular war of liberation. This requires that commando action should be escalated, expanded and protected, and that all the resources of the Palestinian masses and all scientific potentials available to them should be mobilised and organised to play their part in the armed Palestinian revolution. It also requires solidarity in national struggle among the different groups within the Palestinian people and between that people and the Arab masses, to ensure the continuity of the escalation and victory of the revolution.

11. Palestinians shall have three slogans: national unity, national mobilisation and liberation.

12. The Palestinian Arab people believe in Arab unity. To fulfill their role in the achievement of that objective, they must, at the present stage in their national struggle, retain their Palestinian identity and all that it involves, work for increased awareness of it and oppose all measures liable to weaken or dissolve it.

13. Arab unity and the liberation of Palestine are complementary objectives; each leads to the achievement of the other. Arab unity will lead to the liberation of Palestine, and the liberation of Palestine will lead to Arab unity. To work for one is to work for both.

14. The destiny of the Arab nation, indeed the continued existence of the Arabs, depends on the fate of the Palestinian cause. This interrelationship is the point of departure of the Arab endeavour to liberate Palestine. The Palestinian people are the vanguard of the movement to achieve this sacred national objective.

15. The liberation of Palestine is a national obligation for the Arabs. It is their duty to repel the Zionist and imperialist invasion of the greater Arab homeland and to liquidate the Zionist presence in Palestine. The full responsibility for this belongs to the peoples and governments of the Arab nation and to the Palestinian people first and foremost. For this reason, the task of the Arab nation is to enlist all the military, human, moral and material resources at its command to play an effective part, along with the Palestinian people, in the liberation of Palestine. Moreover, it is the task of the

Arab nation, particularly at the present stage of the Palestinian armed revolution, to offer the Palestinian people all possible aid, material and manpower support and to place at their disposal all the means and opportunities that will enable them to continue to peform their role as the vanguard of their armed revolution until the liberation of their homeland is achieved.

16. On the spiritual plane, the liberation of Palestine will establish in the Holy Land an atmosphere of peace and tranquility in which all religious institutions will be safeguarded and freedom of worship and the right of visit guaranteed to all without discrimination or distinction of race, colour, language or creed. For this reason the people of Palestine look to all spiritual forces in the world for support.

17. On the human plane, the liberation of Palestine will restore to the Palestinians their dignity, integrity and freedom. For this reason, the Palestinian Arab people look to all those who believe in the dignity and freedom of man for support.

18. On the international plane, the liberation of Palestine is a defensive measure dictated by the requirements of self-defence. This is why the Palestinian people, who seek to win the friendship of all peoples, look for the support of all freedom, justice and peace-loving countries in restoring the legitimate state of affairs in Palestine, establishing security and peace in it and enabling its people to exercise national sovereignty and freedom.

19. The partition of Palestine, which took place in 1947, and the establishment of Israel, are fundamentally invalid, however long they last, for they contravene the will of the people of Palestine and their natural right to their homeland and contradict the principles of the United Nations Charter, foremost among which is the right of self-determination.

20. The Balfour Declaration, the Mandate Instrument, and all their consequences, are hereby declared null and void. The claim of historical or spiritual links between the Jews and Palestine is neither in conformity with historical fact nor does it satisfy the requirements for statehood. Judaism is a revealed religion; it is not a separate nationality, nor are the Jews a single people with a separate identity; they are citizens of their respective countries.

21. The Palestinian Arab people, expressing themselves through the Palestinian armed revolution, reject all alternatives to the total liberation of Palestine. They also reject all proposals for the liquidation of internationalisation of the Palestine problem.

22. Zionism is a political movement that is organically linked with world imperialism and is opposed to all liberation movements or movements for progress in the world. The Zionist movement is essentially fanatical and racialist; its objectives involve aggression, expansion and the establishment of colonial settlements, and its methods are those of the Fascists and the Nazis. Israel acts as cat's paw for the Zionist movement, a geographic and manpower base for world imperialism and a springboard for its thrust into the Arab homeland to frustrate the aspirations of the Arab nation to liberation, unity and progress. Israel is a constant threat to peace in the Middle East and the whole world. Inasmuch as the liberation of Palestine will eliminate the Zionist and imperialist presence in that country and bring peace to the Middle East, the Palestinian people look for support to all liberals and to all forces of good, peace and progress in the world, and call on them, whatever their political convictions, for all possible aid and support in their just and legitimate struggle to liberate their homeland.

23. The demands of peace and security and the exigencies of right and justice require that all nations should regard Zionism as an illegal movement and outlaw it and its activities, out of consideration for the ties of friendship between peoples and for the loyalty of citizens of their homelands.

24. The Palestinian Arab people believe in justice, freedom, sovereignty, self-determi-

nation, human dignity and the right of peoples to enjoy them.

25. In pursuance of the objectives set out in this charter, the Palestine Liberation Organisation shall perform its proper role in the liberation of Palestine to the full.

26. The Palestine Liberation Organisation, as the representative of the forces of the Palestinian revolution, is responsible for the struggle of the Palestinian Arab people to regain, liberate and return to their homeland and to exercise the right of self-determination in that homeland, in the military, political and financial fields, and for all else that the Palestinian cause may demand, both at Arab and international levels.

27. The Palestine Liberation Organisation shall cooperate with all Arab countries, each according to its means, maintaining a neutral attitude vis-a-vis these countries in accordance with the requirements of the battle of liberation, and on the basis of that factor. The Organisation shall not interfere in the internal affairs of any Arab country.

28. The Palestinian Arab people hereby affirm the authenticity and independence of their national revolution and reject all forms of interference, tutelage or dependency.

29. The Palestinian Arab people have the legitimate and prior right to liberate and recover their homeland, and shall define their attitude to all countries and forces in accordance with the attitude adopted by such countries and forces to the cause of the Palestinian people and with the extent of their support for that people in their revolution to achieve their objectives.

30. Those who fight or bear arms in the battle of liberation form the nucleus of the popular army which will shield the achievements of the Palestinian Arab people.

31. The Organisation shall have a flag, an oath of allegiance and an anthem, to be decided in accordance with appropriate regulations.

32. Regulations, to be known as Basic Regulations for the Palestine Liberation Organisation, shall be appended to this Charter. These regulations shall define the structure of the Organisation, its bodies nad institutions, and the powers, duties and obligations of each of them, in accordance with this Charter.

33. This Charter may only be amended with a majority of two thirds of the total number of members of the National Council of the Palestine Liberation Organisation at a special meeting called for that purpose.

NOTE

1. Yasir Arafat (b. 1929 in Cairo or Gaza), chairman of al-Fatah, 1968–present, and of the Palestine Liberation Organization, 1969–present. An engineer by profession, Arafat served as a reserve officer in the Egyptian army in the late 1950s and was chairman of the Palestinian Student Union in Gaza, 1957. By 1958 he had emerged as one of the foremost leaders of al-Fatah and became its spokesman in February 1968. When the following year Palestinian groups led by al-Fatah took over the PLO, Arafat assumed its chairmanship as well. In September 1970 he became commander in chief of all Palestinian guerrilla forces.

YITZHAK RABIN
56. The Jordanian Crisis of September 1970

Israel was hard put to devise a solution to the Palestinian problem, both in strategic terms and to the challenge of terror. But the Palestinian problem has plagued several of the Arab states as well. As the Palestine Liberation Organization grew in strength—diplomatically and militarily—it tried to establish a territorial base for itself, first unsuccessfully in Jordan and then with limited success in Lebanon. During the late 1960s and the Lebanese civil wars of the 1970s the PLO achieved virtual sovereignty over large areas of Lebanon.

In September 1970 the Palestinian organizations attempted first to assassinate King Hussein, then to overthrow him by waging war against him. During the first week of September there were sporadic attacks and hijackings, by mid-September Jordan was torn by a full-scale civil war. On September 18, Syrian forces tried to intervene on the side of the Palestinian oganizations. This development alarmed Israel, which threatened to intervene in Jordan against the Syrian forces. Moreover the United States acted quickly to deter the involvement of Moscow on behalf of its client-state Syria. In the end Syria's attempt to intervene proved abortive, and Hussein's army dealt a crushing blow to Palestinian organizations in Jordan, who called this clash with Jordan their Black September.

The Jordanian crisis of September 1970 was an important turning point. The diplomatic maneuvering is described here by Yitzhak Rabin, who was Israeli ambassador in Washington and, together with the U.S. secretary of state, Henry Kissinger,[1] played a major role in coordinating American and Israeli policies during the crisis.

Ever since the guns fell silent along the Suez Canal, a grave crisis had been brewing in Jordan. The Palestinian terrorist organizations based there were at the peak of their strength and conducted themselves like a state within a state. As control progressively slipped out of his hands, King Hussein realized that the hour of decision was drawing near, and in September he launched a life-or-death battle against the terrorists. It was a cruel conflict, with the army using tanks and artillery against Palestinian refugee camps. Official casualty figures have never been published, but they are estimated to run into the thousands. With the terrorists on the defensive during what they called their "Black September," Syria saw an opportunity to send armoured units across the borders—ostensibly to aid the terrorists, but actually to gain effective control of Jordan. The Jordanian army deployed for defence, but it was pathetically inferior to the Syrians in armour and air power.

By that time Golda Meir had completed her visit to Washington and on her last evening in the United States was scheduled to address a large United Jewish Appeal dinner at the New York Hilton. It was there, at eight in the evening, that I was asked to call Henry Kissinger immediately at his Washington office. When the call was put through, he spoke with a ring of urgency in his voice: "King Hussein has approached us, describing the situation of his forces, and

Source: Yitzhak Rabin, The Rabin Memoirs (Jerusalem and London: Weidenfeld and Nicolson, 1979), pp. 146–48. Reprinted by permission of Yitzhak Rabin and Weidenfeld and Nicolson.

asked us to transmit his request that your air force attack the Syrians in northern Jordan. I need an immediate reply."

"I'm surprised to hear the United States passing on messages of this kind like some sort of mailman," I told Kissinger. "I will not even submit the request to Mrs. Meir before I know what your government thinks. Are you recommending that we respond to the Jordanian request?"

"You place me in a difficult position," Kissinger begged off. "I can't answer you on the spot. Perhaps in another half-hour."

After we rang off, I stole Golda away from the cocktail party in progress, moved off into another room, and told her of my conversation with Kissinger. We decided to notify Acting Prime Minister Yigal Allon of this latest development and ask for his opinion. In the meantime, minutes were ticking by and Kissinger had not called back. Golda spoke with both Allon and Dayan and found that opinions back home were split down the middle: the former inclined toward fulfilling the request, while the latter was far more reserved. I suggested that reconnaissance flights be made over the combat zone in northern Jordan and asked our people to explore the feasibility of establishing direct contact between the IDF and the Jordanian command. Battles unfold swiftly, and it would be absurd to have to communicate via Washington.

Over an hour later Kissinger finally called back: "The request is approved and supported by the United States government," he said.

"Do *you* advise Israel to do it?" I pressed.

"Yes," he said, "subject to your own considerations."

That the Americans were eager to ensure our intervention in the Syrian-Jordanian conflict was underscored by the fact that Kissinger arranged for a special White House plane to fly me back to Washington that same night. I accompanied Mrs. Meir to Kennedy Airport for her own flight back to Israel, and at 2 A.M. a plane was waiting at La Guardia to take me to Andrews Air Force Base near Washington, where I was picked up by a White House limousine and taken home. I called Kissinger again, even though it was already three-thirty in the morning, and while talking to him I had the impression that someone was listening in on our converstation. I later learned that it was the president [Richard Nixon].

When I met Kissinger at nine the next morning, the American reports on the military situation were still sketchy. But the reports from Israel were encouraging, and I now became the major source of intelligence on the conflict. Although the Syrians had penetrated northern Jordan, Hussein's armoured units were holding on to the two routes leading south and had inflicted losses on the invasion force. In response, the Syrians were massing further armoured units near the border, but they had refrained from using their air power.

Although Golda had not yet arrived in Israel, the government had worked out its general lines of approach to the United States. I was notified that Israel was prepared to take action, but (one of the few times that I could address this word to the Americans) should our intervention in Jordan lead to a renewal of fighting along the Suez Canal, we wanted the United States to back our response. I also told Kissinger and Sisco[2] that we wanted a written undertaking to provide us with an American "umbrella" vis-à-vis the Russians if the Soviet Union threatened Israel directly and that we wanted additional arms. Their response was affirmative on the arms, but when it came to the "umbrella" they were in a predicament.

As we were bargaining, events in the Jordanian-Syrian conflict continued to unfold, as with the IDF reinforcing its forces in the Golan Heights, the Jordanians succeeded in halting the 300 Syrian tanks and the American moves bore fruit. Israeli-U.S. co-operation in planning the IDF intervention, together with the Israeli troop concentrations near the Syrian border convinced the Russians and the Syrians that they should halt the advance into Jordan. In weighing up their options, the Russians could not have been oblivious to the fact that the Sixth Fleet's[3] aircraft carriers were moving eastward in the Mediterranean and that a group of American officers took off from one of the carriers and came to Israel to discuss operational coordination. "Hints" of that nature may or may not have been subtle, but they were certainly effective, for soon afterward the Syrians withdrew from Jordan and the risk of a broader war was averted. At the same time, these events had a far-reaching impact on U.S.-Israeli relations. Israel's willingness to co-operate closely with the United States in protecting American interests in the region altered her image in the eyes of many officials in Washington. We were considered as a partner—not equal to the United States, but nevertheless a valuable ally in a vital region during times of crisis.

On 25 September Kissinger phoned me and asked me, on behalf of the president, to convey a message to our prime minister: "The president will never forget Israel's role in preventing the deterioration in Jordan and in blocking the attempt to overturn the regime there. He said that the United States is fortunate in having an ally like Israel in the Middle East. These events will be taken into account in all future developments." This was probably the most far-reaching statement every made by a president of the United States on the mutuality of the alliance between the two countries. I had never heard anything like it and still look back on that pronouncement with nostalgia. Now we waited to see how the sentiment would be translated into concrete policy.

NOTES

1. Henry Alfred Kissinger (b. 1923), national security adviser to President Nixon, 1969–74, and U.S. secretary of state under presidents Nixon and Ford, 1973–77. Kissinger was born in Germany to Jewish parents who fled to the United States after the Nazis came to power. Before entering government service he taught international relations at Harvard University. As secretary of state he became particularly concerned with U.S. policy in the Middle East and orchestrated the various policies and diplomatic efforts during and after the October 1973 War. His style

of conducting foreign relations by personal visits to the principals involved allowed him both to carry out indirect negotiations and to pursue U.S. interests in the area. In 1973 Kissinger won the Nobel Peace Prize.

2. Joseph John Sisco (b. 1919), U.S. assistant undersecretary of state in charge of the Near East and South Asia, 1969–74, and undersecretary of state for political affairs, 1974–76.

3. Sixth Fleet, U.S. naval forces stationed in the Mediterranean.

PALESTINE LIBERATION ORGANIZATION
57. Political Program, 1973

This political program of the Palestine Liberation Organization, written in late 1972–early 1973, is interesting in several respects. It reflects the political outlook of the PLO leadership after Black September, at a period of an apparent Israeli success before the

Source: Yehoshafat Harkabi, The Palestinian Covenant and Its Meaning (London: Vallentine, Mitchell and Co., 1979), pp. 132–39, 141–44, 145–46. Reprinted by permission of Yehoshafat Harkabi.

changes that the October 1973 War introduced. Yet there were already signs that the collective power of the Arab world was rising and that the PLO was to be a major beneficiary of that trend.

Prologue

Throughout its glorious struggle for liberation, democracy and unity, our Arab people has been persistently subject to conspiracies from the colonialist and imperialist forces and their lackey local reactionaries. These colonialist and imperialist forces see in our Arab homeland ample opportunity for imperialist plunder of its unlimited natural resources. They regard it, also, as an important strategic take-off point, owing to its unique central position amidst the three continents of Asia, Africa and Europe, and to its control over vital air and sea routes, especially the Mediterranean Sea, the Suez Canal, the Red Sea, the Arabian Gulf and the Indian Ocean. They also view it as a center of gravity for whoever dominates it in international politics.

In their invasion of our Arab homeland, the colonialist and imperialist powers feared that the rising patriotic and national struggle would stand in the way of their schemes. Neither were they confident of the ability of their local reactionary mainstays to hold out against the rising national tide. Hence, using the world Zionist movement, they plotted the usurpation of Palestine, intending to create therein a colonialist racist entity which would constitute both an outpost for the protection of colonialist and Zionist domination over our Arab homeland and a heavy club to be raised by world imperialism in the face of the ever-growing Arab struggle for liberation.

In collusion with the reactionary forces which ruled the whole area—except Syria where a nationalist regime existed—the colonialist and imperialist forces succeeded in planting the colonialist Zionist entity in Palestine arbitrarily and forcibly. They also succeeded in uprooting the Palestinians from their land. The Palestinian Arab people, however, did not submit. On the basis of its right to defend its homeland and its existence, and in view of the responsibility it bears as a forward defense line against the imperialist-Zionist assault on the Arab nation, the Palestinian Arab people, for thirty years, put up a heroic and relentless struggle. In each of its revolutionary uprisings, which culminated in the 1936 and 1947 revolts, the reactionary and lackey forces played a role in undermining the Palestinian struggle and bolstering the position of its enemies and the enemies of the Arab nation.

This was the situation on January 1, 1965, when the vanguard of our Palestinian people initiated the contemporary armed national revolution against the Zionist entity, which exists on Palestinian soil through aggression and the force of arms, and which has never desisted from using violence to expel our people and to finalize the realization of its schemes for the usurpation of the whole of our land. In this revolution, which erupted on that glorious first day of 1965, the vanguard of our people embodied the noble revolutionary traditions of our people and of our Arab nation. They also raised anew the flag of the struggle for liberation against imperialism and Zionism, the flag in whose defense tens of thousands of martyrs have fallen everywhere in the Arab homeland.

This vanguard (with it the Palestinian people, the Arab masses and the free of the world) believed that armed struggle is the correct, the inevitable and the main method of liberating Palestine. For such an antagonistic contradiction with the Zionist enemy cannot be resolved except through revolutionary violence.

When the Palestinian revolutionary vanguard resorted to armed struggle, it aroused the Palestinian and Arab masses, filling them with the will to fight. This led to a violent transformation of Arab realities in the direction of insistence upon rejecting the

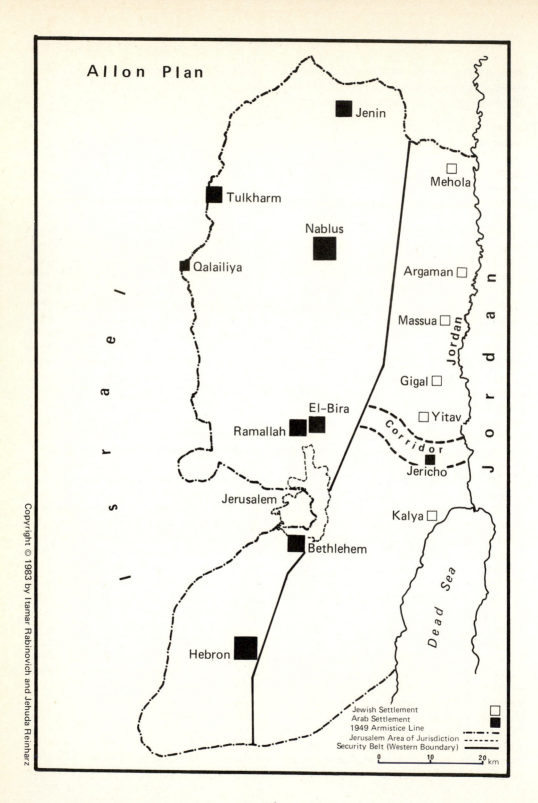

Allon Plan

Jenin

Mehola

Tulkharm

Nablus

Argaman

Qalailiya

Massua

Gigal

Yitav

El-Bira

Ramallah

Corridor

Jericho

Jerusalem

Kalya

Bethlehem

Hebron

I s r a e l

J o r d a n

Jordan

Dead Sea

Jewish Settlement
Arab Settlement
1949 Armistice Line
Jerusalem Area of Jurisdiction
Security Belt (Western Boundary)

0   10   20
km

defeat and determination to take the offensive against the Zionist enemy and to defeat the American imperialist plots. Consequently, Jordan became a base for armed struggle and a take-off point for both the escalation of armed struggle and its protection on Palestinian soil. In addition, extended battle fronts were opened against the enemy which included the Suez Canal and the whole of the Palestinian frontier with Transjordan, Lebanon and Syria. Armed popular resistance was escalated in the West Bank and in the Palestinian territory occupied prior to June 1967. The Gaza Strip witnessed heroic deeds of armed struggle to the point where semi-liberated neighbourhoods in Gaza itself were created.

The Palestinian revolution moved from one victory to another and grew quickly, in spite of all the imperialist and Zionist plots and notwithstanding all difficulties. It was able to emerge victorious from all the battles in which it confronted imperialist conspiracies and counter-revolutionary forces in Jordan and Lebanon from November 1968 up to June 1970. The Zionist enemy, too, failed in the extermination campaigns which it conducted against the bases of the revolution. The revolution was able to turn these campaigns of the enemy into victories, as witnessed at Al-Karameh and Al-Arqub.[1]

However, the revolution began to face an extremely difficult situation due to the American initiatives and the plans they spawned (such as the Rogers Plan [see doc. 49]). These initiatives were accompanied by large scale encirclement of the revolution and the spread of the spirit of defeatism. This situation provided the counter-revolutionary forces in Jordan with a valuable opportunity to exploit some of the negative features that characterized the course of the revolution in order to implement the American-Zionist-Hashemite schemes. These schemes aimed at administering a harsh blow to the Palestinian revolution as a preliminary step towards its elimination and towards the liquidation of the Palestine problem. The Palestinian revolution and the Palestinian-Jordanian masses

fought gloriously in Jordan in September 1970, in defense of the principle of armed struggle and for the Palestinian and Arab cause. Their battle shall forever remain an epic of incredible heroism and historic resistance under the harshest of conditions. But in July 1971, the lackey Jordanian regime eliminated the public presence of the Palestinian revolution in Jordan and began to follow policies which carried the threat of (a) an official capitulation to the enemy concerning the West Bank and Jerusalem, (b) the liquidation of the unity of the Palestinian presence, (c) the encouragement of dissension among the ranks of the Palestinian people and of divisions between Palestinian and Jordanian, between soldier and fedayi, (d) the conversion of the East Bank into a buffer favoring the Zionist entity and into a military, political and economic sphere of influence for Israel, which means transforming it into an American, West German and British backyard where imperialist influence dominates, (e) the repression, pillage and impoverishment of the Jordanian masses, the suppression of their democratic freedoms, in addition to the wrecking of the national economy. It is no secret that the American schemes aim at rebuilding the Jordanian army so it can be directed against Syria and Iraq also. These circumstances presented the Zionist enemy with the golden opportunity for making its occupation more secure by concentrating its efforts on trying to wipe out the armed resistance in the Gaza Strip and pacify the situation in the occupied territories. Thus the Gaza Strip was subjected to the harshest forms of repression and population expulsions; while in the West Bank local municipal elections were imposed to create favorable conditions for the occupation, divide the Palestinian people and attempt at promoting phony political leaders to substitute for the Palestinian revolutionary leadership. This went simultaneously with King Hussein's plan for the establishment of a so-called United Arab Kingdom with goals identical to those of the Zionist plot.

On the other hand, American imperialism intensified its assault according to a broad plan to securely contain and liquidate both the Palestinian revolution and the Arab liberation movement. For this purpose, American imperialism resorted to numerous manoeuvres and plots under such signboards as the so-called American initiative, peace proposals, interim settlements and United Nations Security Council resolutions. In this they were abetted by active defeatist forces, bound by strong economic and political ties to the imperialists.

The blow that was administered to the Palestinian revolution in Amman in mid-1971, the intensification of the American and Zionist imperialist assault against the Palestinian revolution and the Palestinian masses in the occupied territories and outside, and finally the growing deterioration in the official Arab situation in favor of capitulation, have all continued to generate a crisis for the Palestinian revolution and the Palestinian and Arab masses. This general crisis has, on the one hand, captivated the whole Arab nation throughout the greater Arab homeland and, on the other, produced a series of conspiratorial schemes aiming at the liquidation of the Palestinian revolution, of the Palestinian people's unified national existence and of its patriotic cause. These conspiracies have taken such forms as the Allon Plan,[2] the proposed Palestinian state on the West Bank and the Gaza Strip, annexation, judaization, as well as the absorption and assimilation of the Palestinians in the societies where they lived in the diaspora.

In this atmosphere of crisis, we find our Palestinian Arab people moving with firmness and determination to defend its armed revolution, its unified national existence and its right to liberate its entire homeland. Our people will allow neither the liquidation of this just cause, nor of its revolution, both of which constitute a central point from which military and revolution radiate onto an area over which the imperialists and the Zionists want to extend their full domination. . . .

In these new and dangerous circumstances and in the face of the responsibilities which the Palestinian revolution bears, the Palestine Liberation Organization, with all its groups and forces, has agreed to an interim political program based on four principal strategic axioms:

1. The continuation of the mobilization and organization of all our people's potentials, both within and without the homeland, for a protracted people's war in pursuit of total liberation, and the creation of a democratic state in accordance with the aspirations of the Arab nation for comprehensive unity and national liberation.

2. The tight linking of our people's struggle with that of our brothers the Jordanian people in a Jordanian-Palestinian liberation front to be entrusted (in addition to its tasks in Palestine) with the conduct of the struggle for the liberation of Jordan from the lackey reactionary royalist regime, which acts both to mask actual Zionist domination over the East Bank and to guard fiercely the said Zionist occupation of Palestine.

3. The linking of the Palestinian struggle with the overall Arab struggle via a front of all the national and progressive forces hostile to imperialism, Zionism and neo-colonialism.

4. Solidarity with the world struggle against imperialism, Zionism and reaction, and for national liberation.

The Palestine Liberation Organization defines its tasks as follows:

First: On the Palestine Scene

1. To continue the struggle, particularly armed struggle, for the liberation of the entire Palestine national territory and for the establishment of a Palestinian democratic society which guarantees the right to work and to a decent life for all citizens so they can live in equality, justice and fraternity, a democratic society opposed to all forms of prejudice due to race, color or creed. This society will guarantee the freedoms of thought, expression and assembly, freedom to demonstrate, strike and form national political and labor organizations, freedom of

worship for all creeds; such that this democratic Palestinian sociey will constitute a part
of the entire united Arab democratic society.

2. To militate against the compromising
mentality and the plans it spawns which are
either contrary to our people's cause of
national liberation, or aim to liquidate this
cause through "proposed Palestinian en-
tities" or through *a Palestinian state on part of
the Palestinian national soil*. Also to oppose
these plans through armed struggle and
political struggle of the masses connected to
it.

3. To reinforce the bonds of national
unity and joint struggle between our compatriots in the territory occupied in 1948 and
those in the West Bank, the Gaza Strip and
beyond the occupied homeland. . . .

Second: On the Jordanian-Palestinian Scene

The Jordanian-Palestinian national front is
called upon to direct the struggle of the two
peoples towards the following strategic
aims:

1. The establishment of a national democratic regime in Jordan which shall: create
the appropriate atmosphere for the continuation of the struggle for the liberation of the
whole of Palestine; guarantee the national
sovereignty of both Jordanian and Palestinian peoples; guarantee the renewal of the
union of the two banks on the correct basis
of the complete national equality between
the two peoples, so that the full historical
national rights of the Palestinian people and
the present national rights of the two
peoples are safeguarded; ensure common
national development economically, socially
and culturally; strengthen the ties of
brotherhood and equality between the two
peoples by means of equal legal constitutional, cultural and economic rights and by
means of placing the human and economic
resources of each people in the service of
their common development.

2. The consolidation of the struggles of
both the Palestinian and Jordanian peoples
with that of the Arab nation so as to: complete
national liberation; oppose imperialist plans
aiming at imposing solutions and conditions
in the Arab homeland that mean surrender to
the enemy; eradicate all forms of Zionist and
imperialist presence (economic, military and
cultural), as well as all the forces connected
with them which act as mediators for neo-colonialism and its policies.

NOTES

1. Al-Karameh, Palestinian base located in
Jordan that was attacked by Israel on March 21,
1968, in the largest such Israeli attack at that time.
A joint Palestinian-Jordanian defense inflicted
relatively heavy losses on the Israeli forces,
heavier than the damage the Israelis inflicted.

Al-Arqub, area in southeast Lebanon, near the
Syrian and Israeli borders, that was taken over by
the Palestinians in the late 1960s and controlled by
them since then. Israelis commonly refer to the
area as Fatahland.

2. Allon Plan, plan developed in 1968 by Yigal
Allon in the wake of the October 1967 War to
retain Israeli military control over the West Bank
through strategically placed military and para-
military bases while returning most of the populated territory to Jordan (see map 4).

58. The Eve of the October 1973 War

Israel's intelligence failure—the assessment that, numerous reports notwithstanding, Egypt was not going to launch war—was a crucial fact underlying the developments of October 1973. Hanoch Bartov, an Israeli writer and journalist, illuminates this failure through his biography of General David (Dado) Elazar (1925–75), the IDF's chief of staff from January 1973 until April 1974. Elazar was forced to resign on April 2, 1974, because of the findings of the Agranat Commission of Inquiry established to investigate the intelligence failure (see doc. 60). Elazar came out of the Labor movement and began his military career in the Palmah. He was Northern Area commander during the June 1967 War. After the October 1973 War he represented Israel in signing the Egyptian-Israeli separation-of-forces agreement on January 18, 1974 at Kilometer 101 (see doc. 74).

This excerpt deals with the outlook of the Israeli political and military elite in the spring and summer before the war.

A week after Sadat[1] put together his new government and took over as its head, Arnaud de Borchgrave published an interview with him in *Newsweek* (on April 2) whose purpose was to reinforce the impression that Egypt was indeed preparing for an all-out confrontation with Israel. Sadat warned the United States that the evolving situation in the Middle East would prove worse for America than the "national trauma" of Vietnam, from which she had recently emerged. The picture of stalemate in the region would change radically when Egypt renewed the fighting, Sadat told the *Newsweek* correspondent. Official sources deliberately leaked word of Egypt's intentions; a military exercise was publicized; and civil defense exercises were held. By April 8 the *Sunday Times* correspondent in Cairo was moved to write that there were signs that Sadat really intended to land a limited military blow against Israel. He was not aiming for the defeat of Israel—which Egyptian generals did not believe they could achieve—but a move to break the deadlock in the Middle East, which could be accomplished with Syrian and Libyan aid. The scenario called for capturing part of the Sinai Peninsula and fielding as much weaponry as possible in order to inflict considerable damage on the Israelis. Presumably this action would open up new political options for Egypt, which undoubtedly meant the intervention of the superpowers to impose a solution on Israel.

The background to this burst of activity in Egypt was Leonid Brezhnev's[2] forthcoming visit to the United States, which was heralded by a flurry of diplomatic activity on the part of the superpowers. The third round of talks in Helsinki, laying the groundwork for the Foreign Ministers' Conference on European Security, was coming to a close at about that time, and the conference itself was scheduled to open in June. Thus the Israeli chief of staff viewed the *Newsweek* interview and Sadat's speech upon unveiling his new government as part of an Egyptian political offensive. Sadat's remarks were addressed to two audiences. Domestically, they were

Source: Hanoch Bartov, *Dado: 48 Shanah Veod 20 Yom* (Dado: 48 Years and 20 More Days) (Tel Aviv: Maariv Book Guild, 1981), pp. 188–96.

meant to draw attention away from the country's economic and social problems, which were growing worse every day. Outside Egypt, they hinted at developments that would be undesirable to the United States and other countries, so that the recipients of the message would pressure Israel to give in to the Arab position.

Yet conflicting reports on a state of alert also began to come in from Egypt at that time. On the one hand, there was talk of Russian military advisers returning to Egypt and considerable amounts of military equipment arriving from Libya by airlift. In contrast, Jim Holland of the *Washington Post*, for one, reported an "expert's" opinion that the Egyptian air-defense network had been destroyed and the little that had been redeemed in the meanwhile was merely "first aid." He likewise reported that the maintenance of the army's equipment was worse than ever, civil defense was in a bad state, and that the consistent weakness of the Egyptian military machine made it obvious that renewing the war would be the equivalent of "suicide."

Dado believed that there was a good deal of exaggeration in the reports of the total inefficacy of Egypt's anti-aircraft and missile networks and warned that "we shouldn't regard it as an inoperative system." Moreover, despite the fact that there were no concrete signs of a war-footing in Egypt, the chief of staff cautioned against ignoring the risk that matters would deteriorate, so that "our readiness remains high." Yet his assessment of the situation did not fill Dado with any sense of apprehension, and he was confident of the IDF's ability to overcome the missile system, regardless of its degree of efficacy on any given day.

We have already described the general mood in Israel during this period, placing special emphasis on the political and military outlook of the minister of defense. We have also noted that Dayan's influence over the military establishment was considerable, by virtue of both his formal status and the senior command's admiration for him. That influence extended to the interface of political and military evaluations—meaning such questions as the probability vs. intent—as well as such purely military subjects as the acquisition of certain types of hardware and operational decisions. At the beginning of April, Dayan aired his assessment of the situation publicly, and it proved to run contrary to Dado's view that in the absence of political progress Israel could expect hostilities to be renewed. "Until recently I wasn't sure," Dayan stated at a convention of paratroopers in Jerusalem, "but now I believe that we are on the threshold of the crowning era of the Return to Zion." This feeling had been roused not only by the Six Day War itself but by the cease-fire on the Bar-Lev Line,[3] the collapse of the eastern front and the terrorist organizations, and the expulsion of the Russians from Egypt, "which has ensured stability without war." In a speech delivered atop Massadah[4] before members of the Israel Exploration Society, he characterized the times as being blessed by a constellation of circumstances "the likes of which our people has probably never witnessed in the past, and certainly not since the modern Return to Zion." The first of these factors was the power of Israel's army, "the superiority of our forces over our enemies, which holds promise of peace for us and our neighbors." The second feature was "the jurisdiction of the Israeli government from the Jordan to Suez."

Speaking more explicitly in closed sessions with the senior command of the army at the beginning of April, Dayan was more specific: Israel was now at the end of war. The Russians had gone home, and he didn't have the impression that the region was on the brink of an explosion. The cuts in expenditures for equipment—meaning the latest reductions in the five-year plan "Ofek A"—were not the last, for the nation had more pressing priorities. Everything had to be planned with an eye to the needs of the next war, which was not expected before 1976—if at all. Israel would not start a war, for it was not in her interest to do so, and the

Arabs knew that they hadn't a chance of defeating Israel. Therefore, Dayan concluded, Israel would continue to man the present lines for at least another three years—or slightly different lines if an interim agreement was concluded in the meantime.

This assessment was also reflected in the decision about purchasing fording equipment. Dayan believed that it was preferable to postpone ordering such equipment for a year, in view of his assessment of the situation, budgetary considerations, and the fact that it was an election year. But the chief of staff opposed him on the question of amphibious craft, arguing that what you put off today won't be available tomorrow. And Dado would not give in on that point, even if it had to be brought before the prime minister, though he wanted to settle the matter then and there.

Moreover, as if to belie Dayan's unqualified confidence and optimism, Dado's attention was taken up with the insistent reports that Egypt was preparing to renew hositilities in the near future. Sadat had paid a visit to Libya and proclaimed the inauguration of "the stage of total confrontation." Libya's Qaddafi[5] had visited Boumedienne[6] in Algeria. A sqaudron of sixteen Iraqi Hunter fighter planes and their pilots had reached Egypt on April 7. And following the Libyan airlift, on April 10 sixteen Mirage fighter planes that France had sold to Libya were transferred on to Egypt. Undercover sources suddenly began to supply very specific information that was not made public, even though it was remarkably similar to the reports published in the *Sunday Times* on April 8. The gist of the information was that Sadat had decided to go to war on May 15. His plan was to have five infantry divisions cross the Canal while helicopters landed commandos deep inside Sinai and attacked Sharm el-Sheikh. Once the infantry divisions had made it across the Canal, armored formations would follow into Sinai. This is essentially the plan that was carried out on Yom Kippur afternoon. But it was back on

April 8, when everything was still tinged by the effect of the Beirut raid,[7] that the "countdown" began. From mid-April into the summer of 1973, the possibility that Egypt would opt for a surprise attack preoccupied the IDF and the Israeli government. And for weeks there would be ups and downs, endless discussions and operational planning sessions, the institution of measures to bolster the IDF's fighting ability, until slowly but surely the idea would take hold that it was all a false alarm. In mid-August, seven weeks before the outbreak of the Yom Kippur War, this alert footing in anticipation of an Egyptian attack—code named Blue-White—was finally and formally cancelled.

Was Sadat really capable of pulling off a war in 1973, or were the circumstances that led to Blue-White merely posturing with an empty gun? This was the problem that faced the General Staff and the government in the spring of 1973. Despite the detailed intelligence reports—including the basic outline of the Egyptian war plan, the forces that were to cross the canal, their targets and the timetable of the two-stage assault—the probability of an Egyptian-initiated war remained an open question. And though that question would be kicked around by many people during the long wait from the middle of April onward, the three main characters in this drama-before-the-drama were the chief of intelligence, the chief of staff, and the minister of defense.

Before we follow the development of Blue-White, however, a word or two about procedure. If we were to construct a flow-chart for the Intelligence Branch, it would show the raw intelligence data moving toward the chief of intelligence and his aides, each of whom was an expert in his field. These are the men responsible for the final sifting of the data and for transforming it into concentrated summaries that include both the relevant information and an assessment of its reliability, significance, and implications. At the time, the Intelligence Branch was Israel's only broad-based, experienced, and efficient apparatus for constructing a comprehensive political-military intelligence picture. What's more, even though the purpose of the branch was primarily to aid the army's various command levels in making the best possible "command decision" by providing them with data and assessments, its influence did not stop at the chief of staff's office.

This state of affairs had come in for sharp criticism from the Yadin-Sharef Committee, which had submitted its conclusions in mid-1963. But in essence nothing had changed over the next ten years. The Research Department of the Foreign Ministry had not been upgraded, and it was totally incapable of providing the prime minister with independent political appraisals. The Mossad [at this time under the direction of the Prime Minister's Office] had not been elevated to a status that would enable it not only to gather information but submit its own political-military assessments to the government. Although the head of the Mossad had a standing invitation to General Staff meetings, and in the period under discussion Maj. Gen. Zvi Zamir also had easy access to both the prime minister and the chief of staff, everyone's attention naturally gravitated toward the body that had the tools to effect a solid job of evaluation. After all, in making its assessments the Intelligence Branch availed itself of the data collected by the entire "intelligence community."

Finally, the need for selectivity in drawing up an intelligence report is inevitable, since it is impossible to imagine a situation in which all the "raw data" is regularly passed on to the chief of staff, the minister of defense, and the prime minister as the summary accompanying the assessments is. The reliability of intelligence evaluations depends to no small degree upon the good judgment of the men and women responsible for sifting and evaluating the data all along its treacherous path to the top and the degree of confidence they enjoy from the recipients of the final product.

It is at the end of this mine-strewn path that the chief of intelligence comes together with the chief of staff and the minister of defense. The meeting that took place between them on April 13, 1973, three days before Passover, was not between three "incumbents" but three very singular men. Maj. Gen. Eli Zeira drew his authority from both his formal standing at the apex of the intelligence pyramid and his reputation for a sharp mind, articulate tongue, and forceful views. Everyone has remarked upon his direct and close relationship with the minister of defense, and the two men were known to share a long acquaintanceship and remarkably similar political outlooks. Dado also placed great faith in Zeira, even though throughout that summer they continued to differ in their appraisals of the probability of war—and all that followed therefrom. Suffice it to say here that all evidence leads to the impression that there was direct contact between each of the three vertices of the Dayan-Elazar-Zeira triangle, and a triangle—rather than a linear heirarchy—is precisely how this relationsip should be understood.

As in November 1972, Zeira again concluded that nothing in the new intelligence data merited a change in his fundamental assessment—namely, that the Egyptians could not possibly be as foolish as their war plans made them appear. Hafez Ismail[8] was to meet with Henry Kissinger on May 19. Brezhnev was scheduled to visit the United States in June. An all-out war at this point would mean a resounding military defeat for Egypt, and there was no reason to believe that Sadat had revised his own assessment that he was incapable of waging a war on such a scale. Thus the inescapable conclusion was that Sadat merely wanted to create a menacing atmosphere in order to boost the Arab bargaining position before the talks scheduled for May and June.

The situation also called for certain conclusions to be drawn vis-à-vis the United States. Despite reports of Egypt's martial intentions, Israel must beware of pressing the panic button and leading the Americans to believe that she is alarmed by the threats of war emanating from "the great Sadat." Any sign of squeamishness would probably invite negative political consequences, for in order to head off a military crisis the Americans would undoubtedly be quick to advance their own proposals for a political settlement; and if precedent were any guide, their proposals would most likely be unacceptable to the Israeli government.

Dayan's assessment of the situation that spring was much more circumspect than Zeira's. He too believed that Sadat was merely putting on a show of muscle-flexing before the series of political meetings, but could anyone be absolutely sure that the latest threats were merely bluster? The Egyptians might open fire precisely in order to spur some progress on the political front, and the detailed intelligence data did appear to be reliable. There was no doubt that the odds of a war breaking out were higher than they had been at the end of 1972. But the question remained whether by "war" Sadat meant a full-scale attack or a more modest and manageable undertaking. One way or the other, Dayan agreed with Zeira that "crying wolf" to the Americans would only invite pressure to return to the path of negotiations. So although the intelligence must be passed on to the United States, Israel should refrain from appending any definitive assessment of its significance.

Dado, for his part, basically accepted Zeira's analysis, but he could not get away from the political factor: the very passage of time and perpetuation of the stalemate in themselves constituted a motive for Egypt to go to war. He confessed that he had not yet seen the data upon which Zeira had based his evaluation, so that he could not judge whether "it is certain that they will open fire." But he believed that "there's a very good chance it can happen" because he could see the beginning of an erosion in the situation and preparations for war. "Instinctively I feel that this time it's more serious than the previous warnings," he remarked. But since there was at least a month before fighting would break out, the IDF would

have time to prepare for war, and that included the adoption of deterrent or preemptive measures.

Dayan advised that any plans should take into account the Arab brand of logic, which is likely to dictate that if they've lost planes anyway, they might as well have a full-blown war. Sadat, for example, maintains an army of half a million soldiers on salary; why shouldn't they do something productive to earn their keep?

Three days later, on the eve of Passover (April 16), when Dado convened a General Staff meeting, Eli Zeira reiterated his assessment that Egypt's strength had not changed in any significant way since the end of 1972, and the additional Libyan Mirages and Iraqi Hunters did not create a new balance of power in the air. The probability of war was low, Zeira concluded—perhaps even very low—but it did exist. And if Egypt wished to create the impression that she might resort to an act of desperation on the eve of the Nixon-Brezhnev summit, Israel must not let it be thought that she was susceptible to the threats, had put her forces on alert, or was asking the world to deflect the Egyptians from their resolve to make war. An overreaction on Israel's part would only contribute to the making of a war scare, which would be exploited by whomever wants to exert pressure.

Many of the participants in the discussion shared Zeira's feelings. The commander of the Southern Area, Ariel Sharon, believed that southern front was prepared for the contingency of war and was generally in good shape insofar as control systems, communications, command posts, and access roads were concerned. A special road was in the process of being paved for the roller bridge, but even if it were not completed, the troops could get along without it. What's more, all combat plans had recently been reviewed and updated. Sharon also aired his standard view on reducing the number of strongholds: only the absolutely necessary minimum should be maintained along the waterline in areas where it was in Israel's interest to maintain a presence for the purpose of effecting a quick crossing. Incidentally, Sharon viewed the crossing itself as a very attractive operation but believed its importance to be marginal and felt that it could definitely be waived. He was not concerned with the appraised strength of the Arabs' armor; another 1,000 Egyptian tanks and 500 Syrian tanks would not endanger the existence of the State of Israel or challenge its defensive capability as long as the IDF occupied its present lines, he felt.

Contrary to Sharon, the chief of Training Division, Maj. Gen. Shmuel Gonen, felt that the IDF must not treat the information it had recently received as though nothing had changed. Quite the opposite, serious preparations should be made for war. Essentially he too believed that nothing would come of it all; but in case something did happen, he reasoned, we would never be able to explain to ourselves or anyone else that we simply didn't believe a war would break out. Obviously the army should not adopt tactics that would create a war scare—e.g., mobilizing reserves or making changes in troop deployments and scheduled maneuvers. But plans should be reviewed, the level of alert upgraded to anticipate the opening artillery barrage, and the units slated to cross the canal should be given special training. Gonen was concerned by the rise in the number of tanks at the disposal of the confrontation states. He therefore concluded that changes should be made in the long-range armament programs to increase the tank force at the expense of equipment for the other ground forces. But not only was Gonen's voice a lonely one in that room, it sounded oddly out of tune.

Before bringing the meeting to a close, the chief of staff went into a lengthy analysis of the components that made up the present situation. Although he again granted the logic of the intelligence assessment that an Egyptian decision to go to war immediately was unlikely, he also explored the antithetical logic, citing Egypt's frustration over the continuing deadlock and the passage of time, which added up to "a feature, politically speaking, that worries the Egyptians." Hafez Ismail's more recent visit to Washington had been fruitless, whereas Golda's [Meir] visit had brought Israel assurances of continued weapons supplies. Egyptian hopes of renewed Soviet support were also disappointed. Added together, all this clearly aggravated the dilemma facing President Sadat and explained his preoccupation with planning for war.

In all likelihood, Dado stressed, the latest flurry of Egyptian activity was merely meant to raise Sadat's political capital in the eyes of the superpowers and Israel. But it was impossible to predict whether or not he would cross the Rubicon that separates threats from acts. Perhaps he had another aim in mind. Perhaps Sadat hoped "that there will be a brief round of fighting, and even if it ends in a draw—without any tragedy befalling Egypt—within a few days, the Egyptians will again be a fighting nation, and the war will have launched the entire problem back into the headlines and onto the negotiating table." Illogical as that may sound, it was possible to imagine the Egyptians harboring such illusions, "for that is essentially the only thing that would really solve Egypt's problem for a few years," Dado summed up. "And the subjective temptation, desire, and ambition are so strong that despite the great risk, Sadat might try it. It's illogical. The risks are much greater than the prospects, and I presume that in the end he will be dissuaded. But I can't be fully confident of that."

The more Dado went into his analysis, the greater the political element took precedence over the military and heightened his feelng that his latest warning should be treated more seriously: "A war can be tempting to Egypt today, as we come to the end of the sixth year since the Six Day War and the years of stalemate create a more established situation." Yes, a war might indeed break out.

Did Israel have any reason to allow such a war to break out? "My answer is unequivocal," Dado pronounced. "We are not interested in a war. And if it's possible to go on for another five, six, seven years without a war, that would be best for the people of Israel . . . from both a strategic viewpoint and the standpoint of Israeli domestic affairs. Israel fought very well in the Six Day War because it felt that it had been forced into a war that it did not want and did not instigate."

So it was clear the Egyptian and Israeli interests were diametrically opposed on this point. But the question remained whether Egypt really would initiate a war. And if so, how could Israel make the best of it?

Dado did not believe that any kind of war would bring about peace, but a serious Egyptian defeat could change the situation in the region for a few years and postpone for five years or so the pressures to arrive at a settlement that might well be unpalatable to Israel. If that kind of war broke out, Israel's aim must be not to solve the conflict but to win a military decision as quickly as possible while causing maximum damage to the enemy and securing long-range military and political benefits. That being the case, the warning that Israel received should be taken very seriously, and the coming month should be devoted to feverish preparations. First priority immediately after the Passover holiday should go to speeding up the construction of bridging equipment, updating operative plans, upgrading the level of alert, and the like. "And if war breaks out in another month or month and a half, we'll have the maximal means to carry on a war with optimal effect."

Many things that were said and done in anticipation of that war appear in retro-spect—after the Yom Kippur War—to assume a tragic dimension on both personal and national plane. During Passover 1973 and the weeks following, Israel's political and military leadership "knew no sleep," and despite the differing assessments on the question of probability, the chief of staff directed the General Staff to act as if war were a certainty.

A number of questions that arose during that Passover eve meetng were destined to crop up again during the containment phase of the Yom Kippur War. Should the strongholds on the waterline be held, for example, or would the troops retreat into the interior of Sinai and wage the decisive battle with the Egyptian armor there? Dado reasserted his decision of the previous year—expressed during the discussion on the defensive system in Sinai—that the strongholds must be manned and held. However,

if I know that they are going to attack in the morning, we could say—as an intellectual exercise—that under certain circumstances 30 kilometers in Sinai could be completely evacuated. We let them move five divisions into Sinai, and then we slam the door on them. Such a battle implies a number of political risks, but it's a beauty, and I'm sure it will make it into the military history books. . . . We must be completely free to choose a modus operandi and decide on a last-minute plan, and I'm open to any plan. I am not committed to anything. I have no biases. We may hold down a fortification here and evacuate another one there. . . . We have no interest in war, but if one breaks out in 1973 it's a historic opportunity to deal a crushing military and political blow that will last for a very long time to come.

NOTES

1. Muhammed Anwar al-Sadat (1919–81), president of Egypt from September 1970 until he was assassinated on October 6, 1981. Sadat was a co-conspirator with Nasser and Naguib in the Officers' Revolt that overthrew King Farouk in 1952. In the years following he was in and out of the inner circles around Nasser and was vice-president just before succeeding Nasser. After the October 1973 War Sadat oriented Egyptian foreign policy toward the United States and abandoned Nasser's Pan-Arabism—as evidenced, for example, in the change of Egypt's official name from the United Arab Republic to the Arab Republic of Egypt. Following his trip to Jerusalem in 1977 and

the Camp David Agreements in 1978, Sadat shared the Nobel Peace Prize with Menahem Begin.

2. Leonid Brezhnev (1906–82), secretary general of the Communist party of the Soviet Union. In 1964 Brezhnev and Kosygin replaced Khrushchev as head of the Soviet government and Communist party. Brezhnev was succeeded by Yuri Andropov.

3. Bar-Lev Line, Israeli fortifications—a series of hardened concrete and steel-reinforced bunkers—built along the east bank of the Suez Canal between October 1968 and March 1969.

4. Massadah, fortress in the Judaean desert built by King Herod abut two-thousand years ago, where a small sect of Zealots—the last of the Jewish rebels—made their futile stand against the Romans after the destruction of the Second Temple in 70 C.E. In the spring of 73 C.E. it became clear that the Roman army would breach the walls of the mountain fortress; rather than be killed by the enemy, the Zealots killed each other. Massadah thus came to be a symbol of Jewish resistance and bravery. Since the completion of the archaeological excavations directed by Yigael Yadin, the site has become a popular spot for IDF ceremonies.

5. Muamar Qaddafi (b. 1941), Libyan military and political leader. Qaddafi studied history and military science at Ghazi University and in Britain. In 1969 he participated in the coup in Libya that overthrew the monarchy and was promoted to commander in chief of the army. In January 1970 he became prime minister and minister of defense.

6. Houari Boumedienne (pseud. of Muhammed Ben Brahim Boukharrouba) (1923–78),

president of Algeria, 1965–78. Colonel Boumedienne joined forces with Ahmed Ben-Bella to stage the civilian-military coup of 1962, then became commander of the National People's Army and, in late September 1962, sovereign Algeria's first minister of defense. For almost three years Ben-Bella and Boumedienne shared power, until Boumedienne led a coup d'etat in May 1965.

7. On April 10, 1973, Israeli intervention in Lebanon again inflamed the Lebanese-Palestinian conflict. An Israeli commando unit, landing by night on a Beirut beach, rendezvoused with seven Israeli secret agents who had arrived earlier with European passports. These agents, passing themselves off as tourists, rented cars to transport the Israeli hit-team to their objectives in four Beirut neighborhoods. They killed three Fatah leaders—Kamal Nasser, Abu Yussouf, and Kamal Radwan—in their apartments. Several innocent bystanders and two military police were killed or wounded. In addition, an office building of the Popular Democratic Front for the Liberation of Palestine was blown up.

The Israelis met no interference from the Lebanese army, and the Lebanese premier then resigned over a dispute with the president about the army's reluctance to defend the country. This resulted in increased tensions between the presidency and the Muslim communities that were critical of the appointment of weak premiers and thus solidified the centralization of power in the hands of the Maronite rightist president.

8. Muhammed Hafez Ismail (b. 1918), Sadat's special adviser for national security, 1971–74.

HANOCH BARTOV
59. The Turning Point in the October 1973 War

Despite advance intelligence information, Israel was caught unprepared when it was attacked by Egypt and Syria on October 6, 1973. That day was Yom Kippur (Day of Atonement), the holiest day of the year in the Jewish religious calendar and a national holiday in Israel. In several of his writings and speeches on the October 1973 War (also

Source: Hanoch Bartov, 48 Shanah Veod 20 Yom (48 Years and 20 More Days) (Tel Aviv: Maariv Book Guild, 1981), pp. 482–89. Reprinted by permission.

called the Yom Kippur War), Chaim Herzog has suggested that the Arabs made a mistake in choosing this day, when virtually all Israelis were at home or in synagogues and could therefore be immediately contacted and mobilized.

Nevertheless, during the first days of the war Israel suffered heavy casualties as its positions in Sinai and the Golan Heights were overrun by the Arab armies. The turning point occurred on October 16. On October 22 a cease-fire with Syria took effect, and two days later, on October 24, fighting with Egypt ended (although the cease-fire agreement was not signed until November 11). Hanoch Bartov's biography of David Elazar, based on the Israeli chief of staff's war diaries, provides a detailed description of the developments of October 16 when an Israeli expeditionary force crossed the Suez Canal and established itself on its western bank.

01:32

Back at midnight, when he discovered that the pontoons were not making it through the traffic jams, Arik Sharon ordered his men to hurry the Gilois rafts[1] up to the crossing site. At about the same time, the paratroops began to move out from Tasa in the direction of the [Suez] Canal.

Right now the paratroops are beginning to cross the canal silently in rubber dinghies and are clambering onto the waterway's western bank completely unnoticed. The following report immediately reaches the senior command waiting in Southern Command's war room: the paratroops are past the waterline to the west of the canal.

03:00

Sharon's forward headquarters reaches the Compound.[2] All together he has ten tanks with him there.

The chief of staff contacts Col. Dani Matt, the commander of the paratroop brigade, who is now with the advance forces across the canal, and congratulates him.

04:00

The Gilois rafts reach the Compound along with ten more tanks. So do two bulldozers, which immediately begin to create a breach in the section of the embankment specially preconstructed so that such a breakthrough would be quick and easy.

At the High Command—for all intents and purposes, now ensconced in Southern Command headquarters—a decision is tak-

ing shape to have Bren's [Avraham Adan] division cross the canal first.

06:00

Only now does the overall picture come into focus for the senior command: the paratroops have made it across the canal; the Gilois rafts are assembled alongside the embankment ready to cross; a passage is being dug through the embankment; and finally a battle continued to rage against an Egyptian antitank position at the Tirtur-Lexicon[3] crossroad. Evidently the IDF is in for a hard time and heavy casualties. Moreover, Arik Sharon is asking for help in opening up Tirtur, and he wants one brigade from Bren's division.

Despite the snags, however, the High Command decides against retrieving the paratroops from the west bank and in favor of pursuing the plan. If they manage to get the brigades up before the day is out, fine; if not, tomorrow is another day. This not an easy decision to make, for up to now nothing has gone according to the original schedule, and no essay has been consummated.

06:15

Dayan talks with the prime minister [Golda Meir], assuring her he is not concerned about the paratroops being cut off on the west bank. "I am convinced that what we need more than anything else is a victory over the Egyptian army. And the way to achieve that victory is to cross the canal," he tells her.

06:52

The first Israeli tank reaches the west bank of the canal. Following it on Gilois rafts come additional tanks, but the real problem is still the antitank position at the Nahala-Tirtur crossroads and the fact that the bridges are being held up. Only now does the High Command realize that there's been another hitch with the roller bridge: one of its hinges has broken and will take some time to repair.

It also becomes evident now that Bren's division must join the battle for the bridgehead to stave off the Egyptian assaults that are both blocking Tirtur and preventing the flow of traffic along Akavish.[4] From now on Bren's division will also assume responsibility for transporting the pontoons to the Compound so that the first bridge can be assembled.

09:00

The chief of staff decides to return to the Pit.[5] His colleagues will be let in on his grim mood during the meeting that takes place upon his return.

10:00

A whole day—brimming with expectations, enormous tension, anxiety, and anger—has passed since the chief of staff was last in the Pit. But even though the review he now conveys to his colleagues is as clear and orderly as ever, he is exhausted and unable to suppress his anger over a number of slipups that occurred during the night: the lack of a realistic time estimate, the manner in which the battle was being conducted, and more than anything else, the sloppy reports coming in from the crossing site, "in a vein I never heard before, in all my years of warfare, coming over the communications network all night long!" Dado would subsequently recall his impressions of that night as follows:

Our plan was a very good one, except for one flaw I noticed at the very beginning of the night: the whole thing was built around having Arik capture a bridgehead and cross the canal. Early on in the night I said to Haim and Shmulik:[6] "Listen, things will go much faster around here if Arik's forces stick to extending the bridgehead." The operation was going all right and you couldn't have expected more than that. The Egyptians didn't understand what was happening. They didn't read the attack correctly; they thought it was some kind of a raid, so they didn't call for reinforcements to dam up the breach. And when we finally got Dani Matt's paratroops across, there were no Egyptians there. The shore was absolutely deserted, and that's the way it went on for hours. At first light we began to send tank after tank across, and they still did not hinder us. There was no deployment of any kind facing us.

In the midst of all that tumult, however, an obstacle emerged. At first it was referred to as an "ambush," then an "antitank position," "something we've gotten messed up in." To this moment I don't know how extensive it was, because the boys got stuck in the mess at night, and when they began to unravel it in the morning it turned out to be more formidable than we thought: antitank weapons, missiles, and tanks all in one. So first it was necessary to sort out the imbroglio before they could penetrate and attack.

By then, Dado went on to explain, it had become clear to him that Sharon's division alone would not be able to mop up and secure the crossing zone and cross the canal in strength. When Sharon was asked whether he would be able to accomplish both, he asked for a brigade from Bren's division to help in the battle for the bridgehead. But when he was ordered to clear a corridor to the canal, so that Bren's division could begin to cross in the meantime—since at that stage it was hardly involved in the fighting—Sharon replied that he had sufficient forces to cross as well. "Fortunately," Dado now explains to hs colleagues in the Pit, "it took the enemy until nine in the morning to catch onto what was happening—and perhaps he still doesn't realize it and hasn't closed off the sector. When I left, we already had a bridgehead on the west bank—paratroops plus twelve tanks."

In the meantime, someone remarks, the number of tanks on the west bank has grown to twenty-eight and some half-tracks and APCs [armored personnel carriers] have also been sent across.

But the chief of staff is far more worried about the east bank and that "little snag" that still hasn't been overcome and is blocking Tirtur, so that all traffic must flow on a single axis along the shore of the Great Bitter Lake. "There are two bridges here that can be there by the afternoon." Dado points to the map. "And the advance force is screaming that the Egyptians still haven't grasped what's going on. Here it's still empty; here it's still wide open. We're already in, at the sweet-water canal and we're waiting! In short, that was the situation. And it hurts like hell, because that whole business is wide open. If the bridge had been up by ten, Bren could have gone in and wreaked havoc!"

"He'll do it yet," Talik [Israel Tal] consoles him.

"Hold on. I haven't lost the war yet. It's just that it makes your heart ache. If ever there was a golden opportunity, this is it."

In a little while it will be eleven o'clock, and the element of complete surprise— which could have been exploited to the hilt if a large force had penetrated the deserted area of the "seam" between the two Egyptian armies that night—is rapidly being lost. Had a tank force from Bren's brigade sped futher west toward the screen of anti-aircraft missiles immediately after crossing and attacked it with tanks and artillery, then "everything would have been wide open for the air force, all our hopes would have been fulfilled.". . .

The men in the Pit are monitoring Southern Command's communcation networks, and there, too, the command is waiting expectantly for the armor to deal with that "little snag" and hoping that by afternoon two bridges will be spanning the canal. It is highly doubtful whether Southern Command or the General Staff has any idea of the scope of the losses or the fierceness of the fighting in the bridgehead. And they certainly don't even begin to envision the kind of battle awaiting the IDF in the next twenty-

four hours for the roads leading to the crossing site. By that hour, it would later come out, 200 men had already fallen and fifty tanks had been lost in this battle. And certainly no one imagined that the fortified localities menacing the bridgehead from the north—Missouri and Televiziah—would not be overcome before the cease-fire, though much blood would be shed over them.

All in all, the men in the Pit are expecting a dramatic turn in events—and within a few hours, at that. But the roller bridge is still stuck on the road linking Akavish and Tirtur, and the latest estimate is that its repair will take another twenty-four hours. What's more, while flying back from Sinai this morning, Dado was stung by anxiety at the sight of columns of vehicles jammed along the few arteries—an easy target for enemy planes—so he ordered his helicopter to land, summoned the commanders in charge, and ordered them to spread out as much as possible to forestall a catastrophe. And stuck somewhere in the midst of this "mess" that extends for miles are the pontoons, still not making any headway.

As Dado is relating all this in the Pit, Gonen had reached Bren's forward headquarters and continued by jeep (together with the division's second in command, Col. Dovik Tamari) to see for himself how matters stood with the roller bridge. On the one hand, he was relieved to hear that the repair would be completed in another half hour. But he also discovered that the entire area was under tank fire. As Gonen and Tamari strode westward, they found that countless Egyptians were dug in all around the Chinese Farm[7] (Amir) and that the Akavish axis was also blocked by fire now. While they were still standing there peering westward, a solitary tank headed toward them. Its turret had been knocked off by a direct hit, two of its crew were dead, and a third was wounded. The driver told them that he had just been hit by an antitank missile on Akavish.

All of this brought Gonen to the conclusion that Bren's division should be sent in to reopen Akavish and assume responsibility for transporting the pontoons to the "yard" without further delay. Upon his return to Southern Command headquarters. Gonen relayed his impressions to Bar-Lev, and as a result Sharon was ordered not to float any more tanks across the canal on rafts until further notice. The divisional commander was also informed that from now on Bren's division would take over the fight to open the two blocked axes and see to it that the pontoons were brought forward to the waterline.

Sharon greeted this order—which he received at 11:00 [A.M.]—with a shower of bitter criticism, for he viewed it as a cardinal military error—and had no intention of keeping his opinion to himself. That same evening, for example, when he returned to the Pit from the south, Ezer Weizman told the chief of staff that junior officers in Sharon's division had complained that hundreds of tanks could have crossed the canal on the rafts but were being held back. The outspoken rivalry and friction that Israelis refer to as "the wars of the Jews" are not even tempered in time of war and will grow even sharper during the coming days.

NOTES

1. Ariel Sharon, frustrated by high command decisions to delay the crossing of the Suez Canal since October 9 and convinced that once under way the operation should proceed rapidly, decided to cross the canal on rafts before bridges could be built to provide logistical and tactical support.

2. Preparations for crossing the Suez Canal began after the June 1967 War while Sharon was commander of the Southern Area. Plans included the construction of a leveled area (approx 150 × 400 yds.) surrounded by a high earthen rampart that could be easily breached by Israeli equipment. Located at the juncture of the canal and the north end of the Great Bitter Lake, the Compound was the staging area for crossing the canal.

3. Tirtur, east-west dirt road about 6 m wide that links the Compound with more easterly positions. Lexicon is a road that runs parallel to the east bank of the canal.

4. Akavish, main road south of and parallel to Tirtur. Troops and supplies for the crossing operation were to be delivered via the Tirtur and Akavish roads.

5. Pit, war room of Israeli General Headquarters in Tel Aviv.

6. Elazar is referring to Haim Bar-Lev who, on October 10, was asked to be Elazar's "special representative" at the Southern Command, and to Shmuel Gonen, commander of the Southern Area, who three months earlier had been Sharon's subordinate and was now—with the arrival of Bar-Lev—again de facto second in command.

7. Chinese Farm, former Japanese-operated agricultural station near the Tirtur-Lexicon crossroad.

IV

1973–83
Domestic Issues

AGRANAT COMMISSION
60. Interim Report

On the eve of the October 1973 War Israel's intelligence services provided the Israel Defense Forces and the Israeli government with information about Egypt's and Syria's intention to launch a war (see doc. 58). The military and civilian leadership accepted the evaluation of the IDF's Intelligence Branch that the threat of war was not serious. This evaluation was changed at the last moment, and Israel entered the war unprepared, its reserve army only partially mobilized. This intelligence failure largely accounted for the military reverses sustained during the initial phases of the war (see doc. 59). At the end of the war a commission headed by Shimon Agranat, president of the Supreme Court was appointed to investigate the chain of events that preceded the war and the army's performance. Members of the commission also included Moshe Landau, Yizhak Nebenzahl, Yigael Yadin, and Haim Laskov. They decided to restrict the investigation to the military level and not to deal with the cabinet's performance. The following document is a summary of the commission's interim report, together with Chief of Staff Elazar's reply, prepared for the Foreign Broadcast Information Service. The full text of the final report remains classified.

The committee investigating the Yom Kippur events this evening published an interim report containing conclusions and recommendations on instutional and individual affairs.

The committee is recommending that the chief of staff, Lt. Gen. David Elazar end his service, that Maj. Gen. Shmuel Gonen not fulfill an active role in the IDF until the committee completes its investigation of matters connected with the continuation of the fighting; that Maj. Gen. Eliahu Zeira not continue to serve as chief of intelligence in the General Staff; and that the services of Brig. Gen. Aryeh Shalev, Lt. Col. Yonah Bandman, and Lt. Col. David Gedalyah in intelligence duties end.

The committee, headed by the president of the Supreme Court, Judge Shimon Agranat, rules that the defense minister, Moshe Dayan, was not obliged to order additional precautionary measures or precautionary measures different from those ordered by the IDF General Staff according to joint evaluation and consultations between the chief of intelligence and the chief of staff.

The committee also notes that on May 21 the defense minister issued a directive to the General Staff in which he predicted that the war would break out in the second half of last summer. The defense minister, the committee rules, was not responsible for the operational details of the deployment of forces and that this was under the jurisdiction of the chief of staff. Also, no request or proposal was submitted to the defense minister to mobilize the reserves before Yom Kippur.

The committee says that in view of Mr. Dayan's special abilities in army affairs it was possible to reach a conclusion different from that which was proposed to him unanimously by his technical experts, but a matter of this kind does not come under the jurisdiction of the committee. . . .

Source: Israeli Foreign Broadcast Information Service, *Daily Report: Middle East and North Africa 5*, no. 65 (April 3, 1974): N1–N7.

The committee says that it questioned the defense minister and the prime minister as to whether their decision on the mobilization of the reserve forces was influenced by the fact that the elections for the Knesset were scheduled to take place at the end of October. The two emphatically denied this, and the committee believes that Mrs. Meir and Mr. Dayan did not think of letting party considerations take preference over their obligations to the state on this matter.

It was right for the prime minister to give information about the situation on the borders during the cabinet meeting convened two days before the war broke out, the committee says. The prime minister was also not expected to know of the [absence?] of ministers who were not in Tel Aviv on the eve of Yom Kippur.

At the same time, the committee is convinced that the activities of the prime minister in the decisive days which preceded the war indicate an approach appropriate to the heavy responsibility which the prime minister shouldered.

The committee points out that the prime minister had the great right [of decision making] and that she made correct use of the right of decision making on the morning of Yom Kippur. Mrs. Meir adopted a decision with wisdom, good sense, and speed in favor of mobilizing the reserves despite weighty political considerations, and thus carried out a very important act for the defense of the state.

The committee rules that with the passage of time, confusion has taken place in regard to the duty the government has to fulfill in discussions and adoption of decisions on defense matters at the highest level. This confusion is connected with the absence of the ministerial committee for security affairs in its original framework and the fact that the cabinet has turned into a ministerial committee for security affairs. The leaks from cabinet discussions made it difficult to bring information to cabinet sessions, and the investigating committee recommends the setting up of a ministerial committee

with a limited number of members and adherence to the implementation of the law and government regulations which ensure secret discussions on security matters. The investigating committee says in this way there will be no excuse for transferring the center of gravity of the discussion of security matters to an ad hoc body outside the cabinet.

Regarding the personal responsibility of Lt. Gen. David Elazar, the investigating committee says the following: "We reached a unanimous decision that the chief of staff bears personal responsibility for what happened on the eve of the war, both with regard to the evaluation of the situation and to the preparedness of the IDF." The committee says this with particular regret because the person in question is a soldier who has served the state for many years with dedication and distinction and has accomplished glorious achievements.

The committee also regrets the fact that the interim report does not deal with the subject of fighting after the firing broke out, because it is known that despite the grave crisis in the first stages of the fighting, the chief of staff led the IDF in the fighting to check the enemy at our gates. However, even if it is found that in later stages the chief of staff carried out great deeds, this does not obliterate the impressions of the initial mistakes.

The committee says the chief of staff should have recommended a partial mobilization of the reserves on October 1 and by October 5 at the latest. The committee rules that it did not accept Lt. Gen. David Elazar's explanation that he did more than necessary when he ordered an alert in the regular army. The chief of staff also erred in his excessive confidence that there would always be sufficient warning to mobilize the reserves and that the IDF would always and under all circumstances be able to repulse a general offensive by the enemy on both fronts through the use of regular forces alone.

The committee rules that the chief of staff

did not use the means at his disposal to evaluate the situation correctly on the eve of the war. He did not tour the front lines to receive impressions from the warning signs which were discovered through observation or to consult commanders in the field. The chief of staff was content with information that lacked operational clarity—information that he received from the Southern Area commander—and thus in the difficult circumstances which occurred our forces were denied the measure of preparedness and deployment that they could have achieved. The result was that when the war broke out the armored force in the south was caught in improper deployment and the enemy gained an initial advantage. However, in the emergency situation that prevailed on the morning of Yom Kippur the chief of staff should have seen to it that his intentions were translated into clear operational orders.

The committee ends this chapter with the following: "In view of the above facts, we view it as our obligation to recommend the ending of the services of Lt. Gen. Elazar as chief of staff."

Maj. Gen. Shmuel Gonen, who was the Southern Area commander during the war, the committee says, did not carry out his duties properly when the war broke out and in the days that preceded it. Maj. Gen. Shmuel Gonen is also partially responsible for the dangerous situation in which our forces were caught on Yom Kippur. What has been found out about his activities and failures regarding the evaluation of the situation and the preparedness of his command in the days which preceded the war and on the day it broke out is sufficient for adopting the serious conclusion that the committee has reached regarding him.

The committee points out that Maj. Gen. Gonen's command received enough information to arouse grave concern in the heart of a commander. But two days before the war, Maj. Gen. Gonen was outside his area of command on a private visit. During the entire week that preceded the war he ac-cepted the chief of intelligence's evaluation that what was taking place in Egypt was only an exercise. But his main failure was on Yom Kippur itself. While he should have deployed the Armored Corps with two-thirds of that corps near the canal and the other third in the rear, Maj. Gen. Gonen kept the corps in a contrary arrangement. He told the committee that he ordered the implementation of the correct deployment two hours before the hour of the expected attack. But the operational documents of that day do not contain such an order, and when the enemy opened fire, no force from the rear began to move forward to the front line. Not only that, but according to the command orders, the forward force did not deploy near the canal at the right time, and when the armor began to move forward it was confronted with an Egyptian ambush east of the canal. Artillery and tank fire was opened on these armored forces, and its functioning was thus disrupted and it was seriously hit.

The committee rules that the order not to deploy the Armored Corps in time was an unfortunate order. Maj. Gen. Gonen gave as a reason for that action that he did not want to cause nervousness among the enemy, but the committee says it is not clear what source Gonen [word indistinct] this limitation and his fears [about arousing the enemy] did not justify the failure.

The committee rules that Maj. Gen. Gonen did not act in accordance with his ability to use the force he had at his disposal to break the surprise thrust of the enemy forces.

The committee says that at this stage it is not making a final recommendation regarding the ability of Gonen to carry out duties in the IDF, but it recommends that he not continue on active duty until the investigation regarding the stage of the war to check the enemy is completed.

Regarding the chief of intelligence, Maj. Gen. Eliahu Zeira, the committee says that he is respected at higher political levels, but that he adopted a concept with such inflexibility that it prevented him from maintaining the flexibility necessary to tackle the information which flows into the Intelligence Branch, and Maj. Gen. Zeira even strengthened this concept. Zeira tended to view himself as the decisive factor in the state on intelligence matters. The committee rules that in view of his serious failure, Maj. Gen. Zeira cannot continue his duties as chief of intelligence in the General Staff.

The committee also criticizes and places personal responsibility on three other officers whom it recommends should end their services in the intelligence Branch.

The committee rules that there were three reasons for the failure to evaluate the situation before the war. These are the clinging of certain elements to the idea that Egypt would not go to war until it had assured aerial capability to attack deep inside Israel and paralyze the Israel Air Force. A second reason was Maj. Gen. Zeira's assurance to the IDF that intelligence would give advance warning regarding enemy intentions to launch an all-out war and the fact that this assurance was the mainstay of the IDF's defensive operations. The committee rules that there was no basis for giving such an assurance. A third reason for the failure was the readiness . . . to justify the enemy's preparations on the front line on the assumption that the matter did not go beyond defense preparations in Syria and exercises in Egypt. This was the result of the theory detailed above.

The chief of intelligence failed to adopt other measures that could have been adopted and which could have revealed important complementary information. Thus, the enemy was able to mislead and surprise the IDF.

The committee points out that two weeks before the war broke out the Northern Area Commander expressed concern over the limitations of receiving sufficient warning in view of the dangerous situation that developed in the Golan Heights following the reinforcement of the Syrian deployment. The defense minister was impressed by the concern of Maj. Gen. [Yizhak] Hofi. He visited the area and voiced a warning to the Syrians. It was decided then to strengthen the armor and artillery on the Golan Heights.

When the prime minister returned from her trip to Europe she convened, on the initiative of the defense minister, a military and political meeting in which Ministers Allon, Galili, and Dayan participated three days before the war. The chief of staff and Brig. Gen. Shalev also took part. In that meeting, Brig. Gen. Shalev presented the Intelligence Branch's evaluation that war was not a likely possibility and none of the participants questioned his evaluation. It was then decided to hold a cabinet meeting on Sunday, October 7. On Friday, the defense minister and the chief of staff met, and then there were consultations at the prime minister's office with the defense minister, the chief of staff, and the chief of intelligence. The chief of staff announced that on Yom Kippur there would be a very high alert in the army. The prime minister decided to call a meeting of the ministers present in Tel Aviv that day. The chief of staff and the chief of intelligence said in that meeting that war was not a likely possibility although there was no proof that the enemy did not intend to attack. The chief of staff said that for the time being there was no need for a call-up. The participating ministers authorized the prime minister and the defense minister to decide on the mobilization of the reserves if the need arose.

On Saturday morning news was received of the enemy's plan to go to war. The chief of staff recommended to the defense minister that all reserve units be mobilized in preparation for a counterattack. The defense minister was of the opinion that the largest number of forces that the chief of staff thought would be necessary for defensive duties should be mobilized, but there was a delay of about two hours in calling up these forces because the chief of staff was waiting for the prime minister's decision regarding the mobilization.

At 0905 the prime minister approved the call-up. The defense minister was convinced that it was convenient to limit the mobilization to defense needs so that no friendly state could accuse Israel of causing an escalation of the war. The defense minister's reasoning was connected with arms purchases. The committee says that this was a political stand that can be disregarded as a justification that was rejected. The prime minister did not agree to this contention. In the discussion at the prime minister's office, the chief of staff suggested launching a deterrent attack but it was decided not to launch an attack for political reasons.

The committee concludes its interim report by saying that in the Yom Kippur War, the IDF was faced with a task that was one of the most difficult that any army could face. The IDF came out of this war with the upper hand despite the dangerous circumstances under which the war began and despite the mistakes committed in that stage. Moreover, the IDF was able to mobilize large and complex reserve units with unprecedented speed. While mobilizing its forces, it also halted a massive invasion carried out by the enemy's armies after preparing and training on this invasion plan for years.

The victory of the IDF was achieved through many dear sacrifices and thanks to the supreme heroism of its troops of all ranks, and thanks to the presence of mind of its commanders and the stability of its structure.

These facts strengthen the committee's opinion that the IDF cannot only stand up against criticism and draw the painful conclusions, but also that it will be able to increase its strength. . . .

Lt. Gen. Elazer's Reply, Read to the Cabinet

Madame Prime Minister: I have just read for the first time the report of the [investigating] committee. I am convinced that I do not agree with a number of the committee's rulings which are not in my favor. I shall here give examples of some of them. The committee ruled that according to information which the chief of staff had in his possession he should have recommended a partial call-up of the reserve units of the land forces at the beginning of the week preceding the war in order to establish the right balance between the enemy forces, who were in a full state of alert and who were prepared against us, and our forces. I state that during my service as a chief of staff, and before that, the IDF has never had the right balance between the prepared enemy forces and our forces for a number of basic reasons which are known to all responsible elements. Among these reasons was our reliance on intelligence warning. This time, there was no such warning, and the committee rules that I was not to blame for that.

I reject the committee's ruling that no proper defense plan was prepared for the eventuality that the regular army would have to halt by itself a general enemy attack on both the Egyptian and Syrian fronts at one and the same time. The truth is that there was such a plan in the Northern and Southern commands. The plan was known and trained for, even in the lower ranks.

I reject the ruling that on that morning no clear directions were given to the Southern Area commander. The truth is that in addition to the operational plan that was prepared in advance, I gave directions to the area commanders on the morning of October 6 and I even invited them to a meeting at noon to make sure of their readiness for the fighting. The committee itself does not say anything about the directions which were given to the two area commanders in the same way.

It is not the duty of the Chief of Staff and it is not within his ability to go into minor tactical details. I testify that during my service as Northern Area commander in 1967 I submitted general plans to the then chief of staff, but I did not receive detailed directions either for defense or for attack.

I reject the committee's ruling that the difference between me and the defense minister on the morning of October 6, 1973, was in connection with the forces needed for defense as though I requested additional forces only for a counterattack. My demand for the mobilization of the entire reserve force emanated from a general concept regarding the need for forces for war when counterattacks are an organic part of a useful defense plan.

My request proves that I did not have excessive confidence in the IDF's ability to stand up against a general enemy attack on two fronts with the regular forces alone. This is an unfounded claim. I never said or thought so. I said the opposite. I do not know what the committee bases this assumption on. My request to mobilize reserves on a larger scale was approved by the Prime Minister, proved to be justified and decisive in the course of war. Had it not been adopted, undoubtedly there would have been a disaster at least in the Northern Area Command.

There is no truth in the claim that the chief of staff awaited the prime minister's decision regarding the mobilization of all the reserves. The defense minister did not approve my mobilization of reserves that morning. The approval for the mobilization was given afterwards during a discussion with the prime minister and on the basis of my proposal.

I reject the basic approach that the committee adopted regarding the authority of the defense minister and the chief of staff. This incorrect approach has misled the committee.

According to the standing authority, the defense minister is the operative authority above the chief of staff, and all operational plans and questions were brought to him for approval before the war. Only during the war itself did the defense minister cease in practice to constitute an operational authority.

I do not accept the committee's ruling that the chief of staff did not make a genuine effort to evaluate [word indistinct] on his own. According to information that I had in my possession I could not reach an evaluation different from that of the Intelligence Branch. Only through the investigating committee did I learn of intelligence information of warning value that I did not know about. Had I known of that, perhaps I would have made a different evaluation, as happened in April and May 1973.

I reject the committee's ruling that I engaged in planning counterattacks instead of concentrating on [word indistinct] the warning. I acted in the two spheres and it was my duty to lead the IDF a number of stages forward. I did so throughout the war.

Why does the committee believe that I should have reached the conclusion that reserves should be mobilized on October 5, 1973, when the defense minister was unable to reach the same conclusion, although both of us had the same information, and when no one in the General Staff thought of or suggested mobilizing the reserves? This can only be explained by saying that the committee did not treat both of us equally.[1]

NOTE

1. Elazar ended his letter by saying that he did not see any possibility of continuing his duties and that until further notice they should be carried out by the head of the General Staff, Maj. Gen. Yizhak Hofi. Mordekhai Gur was appointed to succeed Elazar as chief of staff.

MOTTI ASHKENAZI
61. The Protest Movements in the Aftermath of the October 1973 War

The recommendations of the Agranat Commission did not satisfy the Israeli public, who felt that the failure on the eve of the October 1973 War could not be ascribed to just a group of officers. Several protest movements arose spontaneously and demanded far-reaching change in Israeli society and the political system. The pressure of these movements was an important part of Golda Meir's decision to resign the premiership in early April 1974 despite her electoral victory a few months earlier. Motti Ashkenazi, a reserve officer, was a leader in the protest movements and wrote the following article for *Haarez*.

If one wants to understand what have been commonly known as the "protest movements" (in actuality they are nonconformist movements), one would err by seeking their roots in the Yom Kippur War. That war—which was and is a catalyst for a new type of social unrest in Israeli society, lying quite deep beneath the surface—can be seen as outstanding characteristic of Israeli society in its entirety, as well as a mirror of its state of affairs.

On the one hand, this society has magnificent potentials, qualities, and abilities of a personal and social nature that enabled us, in times of crisis, to wrestle successfully, even under the most gruesome conditions, with a situation that made other societies totter, even if only temporarily. On the other hand, this society unwisely and wastefully uses those resources. This exacts from us a bloody price, in more than one sense, far beyond what is necessary given the reality in which we live. This situation has led to a frustrated society that is able to utilize only a part of its latent potential and that drowns in a destructive process of debilitating apathy.

The Yom Kippur War shocked many of those for whom social indifference served as a refuge from this frustration, and it also served as a catalyst arousing those who had even before found it difficult to make peace with the direction and deterioration of the society in which we live. Those who were among the first to give expression to the speed of this social nonconformism were precisely the people who formed themselves into groups and called themselves, in the communications media, "protest movements." The role of those groups was to act as a catalyst in the process of deep social change, on whose threshold we find ourselves.

The public's lack of understanding of the ongoing change makes it likewise difficult for those groups to fulfill the roles for which they were destined, because they now feel themselves urged more and more by public expectation to carry out a task they are not at all fit for at this moment—namely the establishment of alternative leadership that could utilize the national potential and could find the best possible solutions to the national challenges we are facing.

The task I see for the nonconformist movements is based on my belief and judgement that after decades of mistaken

Source: Motti Ashkenazi, "Tafkidei Tnuot I-ha-Hashlamah," (The Tasks of the Nonconformist Movements), *Haarez*, June 7, 1974, p. 17. Reprinted by permission.

groping and lack of understanding of the era in which we live and the geostrategic arena in which we function—an era during which Israeli society placed at its head men whose outlook and understanding were anchored in a world and an environment that had long since disappeared—we find ourselves in the process of building a leadership that is the product of the environment and the era in which we live today, and in which we shall be living in the immediate future.

There is a reciprocal relationship between a leadership and the society it leads. A healthy society knows how to place at its head a leadership able to utilize a given situation for future achievement and to utilize all the potential of society in order to arrive at those achievements.

Israeli society is not a healthy society, at least in this sense, but in my view it finds itself at the beginning of a recuperative process. In each and every society such a process is prolonged and erratic even with regard to the social framework in which it takes place. A revolutionary change occurs because a different human being has to be created, who has different personal and social needs that the new society, different from its predecessor, has to learn to adopt. That is a slow process which takes its time. It is difficult to accomplish it in one leap.

In a society laboring under enormous internal and external pressures such as Israeli society, care should be taken so that this process is accomplished as quickly as possible without leading in the wrong direction. Here, in my view, lies the role of the nonconformist movements; they must be a strong and forward-pushing stimulant that does not mistakenly create processes of self-destruction and needless waste of social energies, processes that very often render social changes ineffective. If we are able to understand and recognize this role we shall ourselves, as individuals as well as a society, be in a position to prevent exaggerated expectations that can only lead to frustration.

We see our task in the following areas:

• Building public awareness of the de-structive processes and shortcomings in the structure and the function of society, and a public struggle to prevent them from occurring. In that light we have to see the political fight we are now waging to establish such basic social values as the sharing of public responsiblity, the accountability of publicly elected officials to their constituencies, the placing of national interests over narrow group interests, and the setting of a personal example of leadership, the closing of "social gaps," and so forth.

• The search for, discovery of, and presentation of better and more up-to-date solutions to social problems, with the aim of enhancing the quality of life. Toward this end we must increase the involvement of those individuals who are part of these networks but for some reason—conservatism, bureaucracy, or whatever—are unable to utilize their abilities. In this light we must applaud the attempts to forge a group of activists from among social workers, community workers, and the underprivileged strata who will dare challenge rote bureaucratic methods, suggest unconventional ideas, put experimental models into practice, and through public debate teach the Establishment how to implement the lessons.

• Educating the individual toward personal involvement in society and a firm understanding of the meaning of "quality of life," as well as fostering the social standards that will lead to these goals. In this light we have to see and understand the demonstrations and the discussions of social and political problems among young people and adults in civil service, schools, and meetings.

• Formation of a political "pressure group" that will activate its members toward a struggle for content and for values within the framework that now exists among parties and other sociopolitical configurations. And all this—in order to hasten the social change so necessary for our survival. In this light we have to see the building of contacts and the creation of common ground among all the different groups included in the nonconformist movement. It may be assumed that this process will find a political and parliamentary expression if and when it becomes clear to these groups that the current establishment actually prevents, and not merely hampers, that process of change.

In this case it seems to me necessary to get a wide agreement on the following three basic principles: (1) a revision of the operating procedures of the existing system in the direction of an open and much closer relationship between the voters and those elected; (2) heightened efforts to narrow the social gap, even if this should lead to a freezing of the present standard of living of large classes of people and to its decline among the elite; (3) an active wrestling with the Palestinian problem, and that means acknowledging that this problem is at the center of the Arab-Israeli conflict and that there is room for a sovereign Palestinian state on the soil of historical Erez Israel.

If we learn to appreciate this task correctly, and to work toward its realization along democratic lines, we shall succeed in building a mature society that knows how to solve its national problems in such a fashion that the citizen who lives in it will utilize his own potential within its framework and will be proud to belong to it. Such a society will be a social and economic focal point in the Middle East and will, at the same time, realize the values of Zionism.

It is worthwhile to remember that one should not judge the achievements of the nonconformist movement from moment to moment but rather in terms of its contribution to the process described above. The contribution during these first four months of its existence has been far beyond expectations, but it is still not enough compared to what must be achieved in the near and distant future.

MENAHEM BEGIN
62. Prospects for the New Government

The shock caused by the initial Israeli reverses during the October 1973 War was a catalyst for profound changes in Israeli politics. The Agranat Commission report (doc. 60) blamed professional army officers for the intelligence and military failures during the first days of the war. But public reaction (see doc. 61) forced Golda Meir to resign despite her recent electoral victory. Her replacement by Yitzhak Rabin was insufficient to preserve the Labor party's rule. In the May 1977 elections the Likud, under Menahem Begin, gained a plurality and formed a new government.

The Likud's victory was significant in several ways. It resulted in the first transfer of power from one wing of the Israeli political system to the other. The new government has been trying to implement a different social and economic philosophy affecting both domestic and foreign policies. This interview with Menahem Begin on May 19–20, 1977–immediately after his electoral victory and before he assumed office– reveals his ideas and frame of mind before his actual encounter with the realities of power.

Source: Israeli Foreign Broadcast Information Service, *Daily Report: Middle East and North America* 5, no. 99 (May 23, 1977): N2–N6.

May 19

Two hours with Menahem Begin, the next prime minister. The time: yesterday morning. A new reality. Bodyguards and policeman stationed at the entrance to the small apartment in Tel Aviv, symbolically making real the change which has occurred in Israel's political world. No longer the opposition leader, but the one who will shortly form the cabinet and lead it.

"Reb [a traditional Yiddish term of respect] Simhah (on the telephone to his friend in the Likud leadership, Simhah Ehrlich, of the Liberal party), listen Reb Simhah, if you agree, I want to send (here comes the name of a man which I was asked not to publish at this stage) [Shmuel Katz] to the United States at once. Yes, yes, at once, even today or tomorrow . . . he will meet with senators, congressmen, famous journalists and will appear on coast-to-coast television programs. Yes . . . it is important and urgent . . . we must explain . . . we must speak to the American people. . . . Fine, I'll let him know at once that he should be set off. . . . Thank you Reb Simhah."

MK Zevulon Hammer is proposing that the National Unity cabinet be established without any basic policy lines and that it should debate each question separately. Is this possible?

No. Definitely not. My dear friend Hammer was wrong. It is a legal commitment binding the whole cabinet to bring agreed basic policy lines to the Knesset for authorization—as well as to present itself to the Knesset and request the confidence of the house. This is demanded by Clause 15 of the Basic Law for the cabinet, as follows: "As soon as the cabinet has been formed it will present itself before the Knesset, announce the basic lines of its policy, its composition and the division of tasks among the ministers and ask for an expression of confidence."

What are you prepared to offer the [Labor] alignment?

What is demanded by the law . . . exactly: Negotiations over the basic policy lines of

the cabinet and over the division of tasks among the ministers.

What will you offer them on the personal level?

We can reach understanding on the personal level too. . . . It is possible, . . . it is still too soon to determine things. It was only last night that I managed to get some normal sleep. I slept wonderfully. First I had a nice doze in the armchair and then went quietly to bed. It was wonderful. If the alignment agrees—we will begin negotiations seriously, both on the basic policy lines and on the manning of government ministries with ministers.

And the negotiations with the Mafdal, the Democratic Movement for Change,[1] Agudat Israel, and Poalei Agudat Israel?

Everything in its proper time. We will certainly discuss things with everyone and we will look for ways to reach understanding and agreement for the sake of a cabinet which enjoys the confidence of the nation, a cabinet which initiates, thinks, does things. Of course . . .

What improvements will you make in the government ministries?

There will be ministries which we will eliminate completely. For example, the Ministry of Police will cease to exist. It will become a branch of the Ministry of the Interior. We will establish a ministry of social betterment, which will include the ministries of welfare and labor. A new ministry will be established—a ministry of publicity abroad. The emphasis, please, on the word abroad. Not internal publicity. It was a mistake to establish such a ministry. This is an institution only befitting a totalitarian country. In a democratic country such as ours there is no need for a ministry of internal publicity. The citizens explain to themselves what they see with their own eyes, how they must behave and how they should judge the acts of their government. But a ministry for publicity abroad—this is definitely needed from the political point of

view. We must speak not only with governments, but to the people as well. I have the
most talented candidate for this task, but I
will not say his name until I consult both
with my colleagues and with him. . . .

*Is that the man you are sending to the United
States now?*

Exactly! That's the man! A wonderful man!

*Is the rumor correct that says that you intend to
appoint as ministers experts in their professions,
who have not been members of any of the Likud
factions, but that you are meeting with opposition
on the part of powerful men from among the
Likud parties?*

I deny this completely! Public honesty demands that the important tasks be given to
people who must be talented and capable,
but who have toiled and labored diligently,
even suffered, for many years, and when
the time comes . . . they must prove themselves in senior tasks. As against this I am
sure that all the members of the Likud
leadership and of the factions will agree that
a talented man who is not in one of the
Likud factions can certainly serve as a
cabinet member. I will give you an example,
just to illustrate, since there has not yet been
any consultation and we have not yet received the agreement of the man himself—
but to me Prof Yuval Neeman[2] is certainly
suitable to be a cabinet member.

And Ariel Sharon?

Certainly! Ariel Sharon and his friends will
support the Likud cabinet and he certainly
could and should be one of its members.

*Do you intend to man the senior posts in the
cabinet with your people? To change the senior
ambassadors in the different capitals and appoint
people beneath them who are loyal to you?*

We have a great rule and that is of "civil
service." Civil servants can rest easy. There
will be no dismissals in the civil service.
Those with political and economic views
different from those of the Likud from
among the civil servants can be sure that this
will under no circumstances be an obstacle
to the continuation of their work. I call on
them to continue doing their jobs.

There will undoubtedly be a number of
central jobs where there will be changes. But
the reference is to a very few jobs. We came
to serve and not to set traps. And this
applies to ambassadors. Only in a few
embassies will there be changes.

And in senior IDF appointments?

Even more so: All the commanders will
continue to serve in their jobs and it is not to
be imagined that because of any views
whatsoever there will be a change in the
status of a commander in the IDF, neither in
relation to his promotion or in relation to
holding up his promotion. There will be no
such thing!

*President Carter's[3] announcement that the change
of rule in Israel will not influence relations between
the two countries and will not detract from the
U.S. commitments to Israel's security . . .*

The announcements by President Carter and
the new American ambassador to Israel, Mr.
[Samuel] Lewis, made us rejoice. I will tell
you a secret: Before I felt ill I was about to
write an article for a paper in which you and
I are partners, under the heading: "An Open
Letter to President Carter." However, because of the illness I did not finish it. In one
sentence I expressed my view that if there is
a change of power in Israel as a result of the
elections, that fact would increase the honor
of Israel in the eyes of the U.S. president—
since he himself is used to this and knows
from experience what is the real sign of a
democratic regime: changes in power. I was
happy to hear the president's words and I
am sure that Israel's honor will indeed
increase in his eyes.

I was also happy to hear that he will send
me an invitation to visit him after the
formation of the cabinet. It will be an honor
to exchange views, information and evaluations with him—as two free men.

When do you assume your meeting will be held?

Not before the beginning of July. And I will have enough time to prepare myself, to prepare myself most exactly.

You will no doubt also talk about the Bible . . .

Oh, certainly. There is reason to assume that we will discuss the Bible very much indeed, since both of us know it. And allow me also to welcome the new American ambassador. His first announcement in the country and his warm words about democracy were wonderful, really. I will call him today and bless him for his words.

Will the Likud cabinet really try to fight inflation by creating controlled unemployment?

There will be no unemployment under the Likud cabinet: there will not! The alignment people again slandered my friend Simhah Ehrlich and accused him of causing unemployment. Unemployment is inconceivable. I remember, and none of us have forgotten, the slump and the unemployment under the alignment regime. That was a national tragedy, which principally harmed the development towns. We will not go back to those dark days.

How, then, will you fight inflation?

We can certainly curb inflation by up to 15 percent a year. We will do this through a tripartite agreement between the cabinet, the Histadrut and the employers. For a period of two years there will be no increase in taxes, prices will not go up and the workers will refrain from any demand to increase their wages. Thus we will succeed in curbing inflation, we will bring back stability to the currency, we will increase output and production. After the first two years we will check on what can be done to add to the real wages of the worker. We will seek with all our strength to enable the worker to support himself on his wages with confidence and honor.

Will the Likud cabinet remove the controls on foreign currency or at least appreciably increase the allocation to travelers abroad, so that citizens will not be currency smugglers and criminals against their wishes?

Yes. Definitely! We will very seriously and urgently consider completely eliminating controls over foreign currency. It is well known that where there is control, the black market flourishes. We learned this in the days of Dov Joseph, when control over food brought out a flourishing black market in food commodities. Control over foreign currency is also one of the obstacles to foreign investments and from this aspect as well it is harmful. . . .

May 20

Mr. Begin, in the political sphere, we hear of concern in Washington in view of the establishment of a Likud government headed by you. Do you think that Israel now faces the choice between confrontation with the United States and a territorial compromise that is unacceptable to you?

No, I do not think we are going toward a confrontation with the United States. Of course, I do not determine Washington's policy. Yet, I am convinced that we, Israel and the United States, have a mutual interest and that we can explain it in the United States. I am certainly doing so now. I have heard various announcements. This morning, for example, we heard that the *New York Times* published an article by Mr. Reston[4]— he is well known to you, he is one of the most important commentators in America— to the effect that it may ultimately be desirable to have such a government. Well, then, if this is desirable, this is certainly good. At any rate, I want to correct the term territorial compromise, as Mr. Peres and Mr. Allon say for example, what is actually said? We say that we are giving part of Judaea and Samaria[5] and keeping part to ourselves. I want everyone to remember that the Arabs answered with an absolute no to this. Allon's plan was presented to King Hussein three times. He said: Totally unacceptable. I think that it is exactly those using this deceptive term who have blocked the path toward the agreement with the Arabs.

I am not claiming that the Arabs will accept our plan. They do not agree to any Israeli plan. The difference is that those who say that they will give up Judaea and Samaria, while they do not and really cannot reach an agreement with the Arabs, only invite pressure—from America as well. That is to say, we are told: You are not prepared to withdraw enough, withdraw a little more. The proof is President Carter's announcement before the elections. He made the announcement concerning the withdrawal to the 1967 borders with slight modifications, which is in fact the famous Rogers Plan, a few weeks before May 17. This term is totally deceptive. It has a certain sound. How did the late Eshkol put it: "Everyone is fond of his own compromises." However, we are not discussing love here but a policy. Therefore, I wish not to use this deceptive and misleading term. I think that we will act to explain this mutual interest between Israel and the United States. There does not have to be a confrontation, there does not have to be American pressure.

But your policy is unacceptable in Washington, Mr. Begin. From my experience I know that there is no single senator, no administration official in the United States who is prepared to put up with a policy that will impose Israeli law on Judaea and Samaria.

The problem of imposing the law is a problem involving a discussion, a special decision of the Knesset. I would like to ask you: Has any Israeli representative ever told a senator that Judaea and Samaria should, by law, justice, and right, be an integral part of Israeli politics? What can you or any other Israeli expect from these senators when you tell me that they are not prepared to accept the policy according to which Judaea and Samaria should be an integral part of Israel? Should they be more Israeli than the Israelis themselves? They received lessons from Mr. Allon, Mr. Peres, Mr. Rabin and Mrs. Golda Meir to the effect that we are prepared to give up Judaea and Samaria. Thus they have come to believe that this is in fact a just policy since the Israelis themselves preach it.

Now, I hope, we will start to explain it properly for the first time in ten years, we will begin to explain that this is not so, that the retention by Israel of Judaea and Samaria is the thing that guarantees the chance for peace. If we give up Judaea and Samaria, there will not be any chance for peace. We have not started yet; that is, we have just started. I have not yet visited President Carter. I have not yet spoken before the Congress. Let us have the possibility of carrying out this task. For ten years all Israeli representatives said that we are withdrawing, that we will leave Judaea and Samaria. Mr. Allon presented his own plan before the American representatives. They do not accept it. The American representatives have never said that they favor Allon's plan. On the contrary, I know that in Washington King Hussein's words were said again—totally unacceptable. What is the difference then? I think that the Israeli policy and information campaign were totally wrong. We should now turn over a new leaf.

NOTES

1. Democratic Movement for Change (DMC; also called by its acronym, Dash), movement and political party formed in 1976 when the Shinui (lit., Change) movement (a liberal protest movement arising after the October 1973 War and led by Tel Aviv University law professor Amnon Rubinstein) merged with Yigael Yadin's Demo-cratic list. Later that year the DMC also attracted the Zionist Panthers (a faction of the former Black Panthers) and Shmuel Tamir's faction of the Merkaz Hofshi. It thus expanded its base, but also sowed the seeds of its own destruction. In the 1977 elections the DMC won fifteen seats and became the third largest party. Apparently it

attracted many intellectuals and middle-class Ashkenazim who were disgruntled with the Labor party. Following the elections it joined the Likud government, and Yadin became the deputy prime minister after some protracted negotiations that split the party. In 1981 Shinui ran as a separate party and won two seats; the Yadin-Tamir faction joined the Likud, forming (along with members of the former State list) the Laam faction. In December 1981 this faction left the Likud.

Merkaz Hofshi (lit., Free Center) is a political party and faction that believes Israel should not withdraw from territories conquerred in 1967, especially from the West Bank. In early 1967 Shmuel Tamir led a secession of a number of Herut members from Gahal and formed the Free Center, which won two seats in the 1969 elections. In 1973 the party joined the Likud. During the Eighth Knesset the Free Center allied itself with the State list and Greater Land of Israel movement to form the Laam faction within the Likud. In October 1967 a faction led by Tamir joined the Democratic Movement for Change.

2. In 1979 Neeman and Geulah Cohen (b. 1925) led a faction out of the Likud and formed the Hatehiyah (lit., Revival) party, which opposed the withdrawal of Israeli forces from the Sinai. Many members of the Gush Emunim (who opposed any territorial compromise on the West Bank) also joined Hatehiyah. It won three seats in the 1981 elections. After the return of the Sinai had become a *fait accompli* Hatehiyah joined the Likud coalition as a separate party, and Neeman was given a portfolio in August 1982.

3. James (Jimmy) Earl Carter (b. 1924), president of the United States, 1977–81. In the early years of his presidency Carter seemed to favor improving U.S. relations with the PLO and (in order to promote a U.S.-Soviet detente) including the Soviet Union in peace negotiations. Following Anwar Sadat's visit to Jerusalem in 1977, however, Carter dropped these policies and was instrumental in achieving the Camp David Agreements.

4. James Reston, "Israel: Second Thoughts," *New York Times*, May 20, 1977, p. A25.

5. Judaea, Biblical name of the area around Jerusalem and Bethelhem; Samaria is the Biblical name of the Central Hills region north of Judaea. In modern Hebrew these names are used to designate these historically significant geographic regions. One of the early symbolic acts of Begin's government, revealing his attitude toward the land conquered from Jordanian rule in 1967, was to instruct all government personnel (including ambassadors abroad) to use these terms to designate the political entity previously called the West Bank.

GUSH EMUNIM
63. Opinion Paper

The cardinal issue in Israel's domestic politics in the late 1970s has remained the debate over the fate of the territories captured in 1967, particularly the West Bank and Gaza. The signing of a peace treaty with Egypt and the return of the Sinai only served to exacerbate the debate on the Palestinian issue inside Israel.

On one side of this issue is Gush Emunim (lit., Bloc of the Faithful), a group of ultra-right-wing religious nationalists who believe that Jews have a holy obligation to retain soveriegnty over Western Palestine. The group is led by Rabbi Moshe Levinger and Hanan Porat; many of its followers are recent immigrants from Western countries. Before the formation of a sympathetic government in 1977, Gush Emunim established settlements on the West Bank illegally, forcing the Labor governments either to compromise and allow the settlement to remain or to use military force to remove the illegal settlers.

Source: Ohadei Gush Emunim (Friends of Gush Emunim), January 1978, pp. 2–5.

The Labor governments usually compromised. The Likud governments have been more openly supportive of such settlements.

The following opinion paper was published in Gush Emunim's newsletter.

The hope for peace has captured the people of Israel of all ages. The people of Israel—its blessing is peace, the end of its prayers is for peace, and even upon leaving for battle it calls out to its enemies for peace.

But just because of our strong desire for peace, we need great strengths of wisdom and courage not to mistake a deceitful peace for a real peace, a weak peace for a peace of honor and strength, a peace of crisis and retreat for a peace of renewal and creation. We must painfully conclude that the peace plan proposed by the government of Israel has no truth, no honor and strength, no redemptive power. The basis of this plan is a deceitful peace; its spirit, one of breakdown and weakness; and its results, crisis and retreat.

This "peace plan" is based on three main points of distortion:

1. Readiness for complete withdrawal down to the last centimeter, to the borders before the Six-Day War. This withdrawal would signify acknowledgment of the Arab claim that the "obliteration of the traces of Israeli aggression" is a condition for peace. This claim is false and deceitful, and willingness to accept it as a basis for a peace plan, and to retreat indiscriminately now from all of Sinai and the Golan Heights, is an unethical step lacking the propriety in which the prime minister prides himself.

2. Readiness to remove all the Jewish settlements from the Rafiah Salient[1] and Sharm el-Sheikh from Israeli sovereignty and to transfer them to Egyptian sovereignty. This readiness reflects an approach lacking in national responsibility and represents not only a mortal blow to the ability of these settlements to exist but also a basic undermining of the ideological foundation of Zionist fulfillment, which determined from its beginnings that settlement of the land is the basis for sovereignty. A blow to

the practical and ideological roots of settlement undermines the motivation to settle, and therefore whoever thinks that it is possible to call upon the people of Israel to become pioneers and go out to settle the land in great numbers on the basis of this plan is mistaken and deceiving.

3. The idea of administrative autonomy for the Arabs of Judaea and Samaria and the Gaza District.[2] The autonomy as it is proposed is not limited to the regional municipal framework but represents a basis for Arab national institutions to be elected in general democratic elections. One would be completely blind not to realize that this autonomy will lead directly to the establishment of a Palestinian state that will enjoy—despite Israel's opposition—recognition by the overwhelming majority of the countries of the world. There is not one Arab leader, not even the "most moderate of the moderates," who will not see autonomy as the basis for a Palestinian state and who will not do everything to bring this about. This proposal does not bring a solution to the Palestinian question any closer. On the contrary, it exacerbates the question and will force the question that much sooner. Therefore, it not only does not contribute to peace and tranquility but actually brings closer the time at which the War of Palestinian Liberation is likely to set off a war in the entire Middle East.

In conclusion, we reject this plan from the start and call for a public struggle for its abolition. This is not a personal struggle against the prime minister. It is a deep moral struggle against the spirit of deceit, the weakness inherent in the very basis of the plan; it is a struggle for the spirit of the great renaissance.

Our sages have said, "A bit of light pushes much of the darkness aside," and we will proceed likewise. We will raise the light of revival, we will arouse the power of Israel through great public outcries of honor and strength; we will rejoice in the land with settlements and waves of immigration; we will, through education and information, open our eyes to see what is this peace we are yearning for, and what the difference is between true peace and a deceitful peace. Rav Kook,[3] of Blessed Memory, said, "The truth is not shy or cowardly." We shall follow in his footsteps and not be deterred from stating loudly the truth of renaissance, even if it is not the kind of peace that can be attained from one day to the next, one that is all lies and illusion.

We believe that the people will yet awaken from the illusion of this imaginary peace and will strengthen itself in its onward struggle.

We pray that this awakening will not be accompanied by the sufferings of despair and as a result the hope for true peace, of strength, brotherhood, honor, and light will not be lost.

God will grant His people strength
God will bless His people with peace!

Come, let us go up and settle the land!

Shiloh

Shiloh, at which the members of Gush Emunim intend to lay the cornerstone for a new city today, has been the target for settlers since the middle of 1974.[4]

Shiloh has great significance and holds a special place in the history of the Jewish people. According to tradition, Shiloh is one of the holy places for the people in which the Divine Presence abided. Here the land was divided up among the tribes, and the Tabernacle and Ark of the Covenant arrived here. It is said that the graves of Eli the Kohen and his two sons are here.[5]

The site, at which archeological excavations have long been held, is near the Arab village of Turmus-Aya in Samaria, about two miles east of the Ramallah-Nablus road, about fourteen miles north of Ramallah. At the mound itself, remnants have been found of buildings, walls, burial caves, and more—remnants of an Israelite city that existed before Jebusite Jerusalem was conquered and reached the height of its development in the tenth century. When the renowned Jewish traveller Ishtorai Hafarhi visited it in 1322, he saw ruins, among them a mosque. Its remains can be found in the area today.

Next to the mound is the Valley of Shiloh, which is intended to serve the city the settlers plan to establish. In Arabic the valley is called Marg-el-eid (lit., Valley of the Holy Day), in which, it seems, large public gatherings were held in the days of its glory. Among the vineyards of the valley, the tribe of Benjamin laid in ambush for the daughters of Shiloh, in order to kidnap them and take them for wives, as told in the Bible.

NOTES

1. Rafiah Salient, area in the northern part of the Sinai immediately south of the Gaza Strip.

2. Autonomy Plan, proposal for "administrative autonomy" for the West Bank and Gaza first developed by the Begin government in late 1977 and presented as a twenty-six-point plan to Sadat in December of that year (see doc. 76). The plan agreed to at Camp David used the term "full autonomy," and autonomy talks began in May 1979 but made no real progress.

3. Abraham Isaac Kook (1865–1935), early religious Zionist leader and the first Ashkenazi chief rabbi of Mandatory Palestine, 1921–35. Kook established his own religious academy, later named Merkaz Harav, which became a training center for religious Zionist youth movements, especially Bnei Akiva. His son Rabbi Zvi Yehudah Kook (1891–1982) was head of the Yeshivat Merkaz Harav.

4. Shiloh, Gush Emunim settlement established in January 1978 and officially classified as an archaeological site despite Gush Emunim's public statement that it intended a permanent settlement. By March 1979 Shiloh was officially included in the list of settlements under the jurisdiction of the Settlement Section of the Jewish Agency.

Elon Moreh is another Gush Emunim settlement that created controversy. Members of Gush

Emunim originally tried to establish a settlement near Nablus in 1972, but the government forcibly removed them. In June 1979 Elon Moreh was established with the government's support. In October 1979, however, the Supreme Court ruled that civilian settlement on land privately owned by Arab residents was illegal, rejecting the government's argument that the land was appropriated for security reasons and stating that no such justification existed in this instance. The court ordered that the settlement be evacuated by November 18, 1979. Both the settlers and the government ignored this deadline at first, but the settlement was finally evacuated in 1980.

5. Eli the Kohen (lit., priest), priest at Shiloh in central Samaria, one of the major religious centers of the Israelites before the Temple was built. Eli trained Samuel. See 1 Sam. 1–3.

YEHUDA BEN-MEIR
64. The Ideology of the NRP

The victory of the Likud alignment in 1977 had an impact on the role of the religious parties in the government. For the first time Agudat Israel was included in the coalition along with the National Religious party (NRP). Moreover, the 1977 coalition agreement accorded the religious parties a larger role than they had been given by the Labor governments.

Dr. Yehuda Ben-Meir, MK, is one of the leaders of the NRP and currently deputy minister of foreign affairs. This ideological profile of the party addresses both domestic and foreign policy issues.

The National Religious party (NRP) is a direct offspring of the Religious Zionist movement established over seventy-five years ago. As such, and in common with other parties whose ideological and organizational roots lie in the Zionist movement of prestate days, the NRP's ideology is an expression of its unique concept and particular brand of Zionism. Indeed, the original name of the Religious Zionists was Mizrahi, which stood for Merkaz Ruhani (lit., Spiritual Center), thus expressing the religious-spiritual approach to Zionism and to the Zionist ideal.

The NRP, as its Mizrahi forerunner, has always been part and parcel of the Zionist movement and participated actively in all its activities and endeavors, perceiving it as the movement of and for Jewish National Liberation. At the same time, the NRP championed, most vehemently, the idea that in order for Zionism to be a truly *Jewish* movement for National Liberation, and for it to succeed, it must be rooted in Jewish tradition, which is synonmous with Jewish religion. Thus the NRP advocated, consistently and strongly, that Zionism must and should reflect, in its outward expression, Jewish religious values, norms, practices, and institutions. The NRP saw as its goal and purpose the guaranteeing of the traditional Jewish character of Zionism, of the State-in-Being, and eventually of the Jewish state itself.

Central to NRP ideology throughout the years was the close relationship between nationalism and religion. This *duality*, combining nationalistic fervor with religious belief, can be traced throughout Jewish history, emerging at key periods of that history as a factor of paramount importance, exercising a key influence on the Jews of that day. The nationalist-religious relationship—even symbiosis—is rooted in the unique

Source: Written specifically for this volume by Yehuda Ben-Meir.

self-definition of the Jew and of the Jewish people, as being at one and the same time a nation and a religion. No less a secularist than David Ben-Gurion always stressed that for a Jew, being a member of the Jewish nation and of the Jewish religion was one and the same, totally indivisible and inseparable. And it was the Israeli secular Supreme Court that ruled that the state could not recognize someone as being a Christian Jew, because such a definition is self-contradictory and goes against the universally accepted definition of a Jew [see doc. 34]. For the NRP the concept of the *unity* of nationhood and religion, and the total indivisibility of the two, is the very cornerstone of its ideology and system of belief.

A prime example of the close relationship between Jewish nationalism and religion can be found in the person of Rabbi Akiva. Rabbi Akiva, who lived in Israel a generation after the destruction of the Second Temple (70 C.E.), is considered one of the greatest Torah scholars and sages of all times. He is the symbol of religious learning and scholarship and was compared by the rabbis to Moses himself. And it was the same Rabbi Akiva who was the spiritual and political leader of the great Bar-Kokhba rebellion against Roman rule over Israel.[1] It was Rabbi Akiva, the great religious luminary, who was also the fierce freedom fighter, willing to risk all in order to liberate the Jewish people and the Land of Israel from foreign domination, from the yoke of Roman rule and subjugation. Interestingly enough, the NRP's youth movement—considered by many to be the most successful one in Israel and indeed throughout the Jewish world—is called Bnei Akiva (lit., Sons of Akiva) after the same Rabbi Akiva. Indeed, no better a symbol of the NRP's ideology could be found than Rabbi Akiva.

The twin pillars of nationalism and religion, which form the basis and heart of Religious Zionism, are clearly and explicitly expressed in the very name given to the political arm of the movement in Israel, namely the National Religious party. The

same idea was clearly enunciated, close to eighty years ago by Rabbi [Yizhak Yaakov] Reines, the founder of the Religious Zionist movement, when he coined the famous phrase, "The Land of Israel for the People of Israel by the Torah of Israel" and determined that this objective is the goal and purpose, the raison d'être of the Mizrahi movement. During the past eighty years the emphasis has moved, back and forth, from the national to the religious, from the Land and People of Israel to the Torah, but the essential synthesis has remained the core belief of the Religious Zionist movement as a whole, and of the NRP in particular, and has been the guiding factor in forming its policies and approaches to the various issues facing Israel.

The overall ideology and the specific policies of the NRP are the result not only of the joint effect of these two forces or values but also of the interacting effects of one on the other—both the reinforcing effects as well as the tempering effects. It should be clear that Jewish nationalism and Jewish religion can and do reinforce one another, but no less significant is the tempering effect of these two forces each on the other. Indeed, it is only through an awareness and realization of these far-reaching tempering effects that one can understand how and why the NRP evolved as a center party and as a centrist force of the political spectrum. It was the deep sense of Jewish nationalism, of the unity of the Jewish people, of the need for national liberation that tempered the religious fervor of the Religious Zionist, countering the trend to isolationism and preventing the creation of a closed caste and the erection of a wall between the religious and the nonreligious Jew. Herein lies the basic difference between Religious Zionism, between the Mizrahi, and the Agudah movement [i.e., Agudat Israel]. The ultraorthodox Agudah saw secularism as the prime danger to the Jewish people, a danger that must be met and fought at all costs and with which there could be no cooperation and no truce. Thus the Agudah was vehemently anti-Zionist. The Mizrahi was no less religiously committed than the Agudah, and no less opposed to secularism than the Agudah, but its strong sense of nationalism led it to be willing to cooperate—within the framework of the Zionist movement, within a framework dedicated to the national liberation of the Jewish people—with the nonreligious and even with the antireligious. The NRP fought Agudah isolationism, claiming that for the sake and in the cause of the Land of Israel and Jewish liberation all Jews, regardless of their religious convictions or behavior, must stand together and work together.

To the same degree it was the pragmatism, the worldliness, the practicality of Jewish religion that tempered the nationalistic fervor of the religious Zionist, preventing nationalism from turning into chauvinism, guaranteeing moderation and countering extremism. Thus, although sympathizing with the Revisionists and supporting many of their positions, the Religious Zionist movement refused to follow Zeev Jabotinsky[2] out of the Zionist movement, rejecting separatism, and chose to remain an integral and active part of the World Zionist movement. The NRP sympathized deeply with many of the political positions of the Revisionists, including, to a large degree, rejection of the Partition Plan; yet it chose to ally itself with the Practical Zionism[3] of the Labor movement. Ben-Gurion's Practical Zionism, which stressed practical activity and the upbuilding of the Land of Israel through a "step-by-step" (or, as it was called in Hebrew, "dunam after dunam") process, appealed to the religious side of the Religious Zionist because it struck a responding chord and a common vein with the pragmatism, worldliness, and down-to-earthness so characteristic of the precepts, values, and norms of the Jewish religion.

Having laid the basic ideological foundation, we can try to follow the development and formation of NRP policy during the past thirteen years—from the June 1967 War to the signing of the Egyptian-Israeli Peace Treaty. In so doing, we must never forget that these policies are deeply rooted in an overall ideological framework—an ideology that is part of a total way of life and world approach, an ideology at whose heart lies a synthesis between religion and nationalism and an attempt to reach a synthesis between a deep commitment to basic values and a recognition and acceptance of political realities of our world.

Thus the NRP has consistently *differentiated* between its approach to Judaea, Samaria, and Gaza on the one hand, and toward the Sinai and Golan Heights on the other. The NRP has maintained, steadfastly, since 1967 that Israel's position regarding Sinai and the Golan Heights should be determined *solely* by security considerations, although, such security considerations can, of course, lead to radically different results regarding the two different areas. But the main point always was and remains that the *sole* criterion in determining the final boundaries for the area should be Israel's security—in the broadest sense of the word. To the same degree the NRP has maintained, with the same tenacity and consistency, that Israel's position on Judaea, Samaria, and Gaza must be based on *national-religious* considerations and sentiments side by side with the security criterion. The inalienable right of the Jewish people to their ancient homeland—the Land of Israel—the heart of which, by both geography and history, is Judaea and Samaria, is a basic and undeniable tenet of faith of both Jewish nationalism and Jewish religion.

The NRP supported the position that the Sinai Penisula was not essential for Israel's security and that in the context of a genuine and permanent peace with Egypt the Israeli military presence could be replaced and substituted by a demilitarization of Sinai and that specific and guaranteed arrangements on the ground, such as demilitarized zones and buffer zones, could effectively maintain Israel's security. For this reason the NRP supported the resolution of the National Unity government taken in June 1967 and transmitted to the American government—namely, that Israel would be willing to conclude a peace agreement with Egypt on the basis of the international boundary in Sinai. Based on the same logic, the NRP in March 1979 supported the peace treaty between Israel and Egypt on the basis of the Camp David Agreements. The NRP's opposition to the removal of the settlements in the Rafiah Salient was based on security considerations and on the national-religious significance attached to Jewish settlement once already established and inhabited. One should remember that the settlements were established for security reasons and on the basis of a strategic-security concept and not as a result of religious significance attached to the area itself. In this respect, the NRP always rejected the Greater Israel movement's claim that an active Israeli military presence in Sinai is vital for Israeli security.

The NRP's approach to the Golan Heights is also based on security criterion. One need not be a military strategist to realize the vital significance of the Golan Heights for the defense of Israel. One need only to stand on the top of the heights, and to see the entire Galilee in the palm of his hand, to realize that a strong military and civilian presence on the Golan Heights is absolutely essential for the defense of the entire North and for the very security of Israel. Thus the NRP is part of the national consensus which holds that Israel will never go down from the Golan Heights. Yet, since the basis for Israel's adamant stand on the Golan Heights is security, the NRP supports the government's position that while Israel remains on the Golan she is willing to negotiate with Syria—in the context of a permanent peace treaty—on the final borders of the Golan, which need not be identical to the present lines.

Judaea, Samaria, and Gaza present an entirely different picture. The NRP's attachment to these areas is founded *both* on security grounds and on their national-religious significance as an integral part of Erez Israel, the Land of Israel. The NRP has always refrained from determining the *relative* importance of each of these two factors, stressing the vital importance and centrality of each one in its own right and the fact that each complements and reinforces the other—both jointly leading to the same conclusion and both forming the joint basis for the NRP's position. Thus, the NRP firmly rejects a territorial compromise in Judaea and Samaria, claiming that such a compromise does not meet either the requirements of Israel's security or of the maintenance of her national right.

The NRP's position is that while the Allon Plan *might* be an answer to the external threat to Israel's security, it leaves the question of internal security and terrorism wide open. The presence of Israeli forces on the Jordan River, as envisaged by the Allon Plan, *might* deter Arab aggression from the East, although the need for such a force to be maintained and reinforced through narrow corridors in hostile territory could seriously impair its effectiveness and its deterrent capability. But the creation of a sovereign Arab entity—be it Jordanian or Palestinian—inhabited by close to a million Arabs, raised and educated on hatred and on a dream of revenge, adjacent to Israel's population centers, would mean a hotbed of irredentism and terrorism that would be uncontrollable and make life in Israel unbearable and unlivable. The only answer to such a possible nightmare in the future is a strong Israeli presence in these areas, with Israel enjoying the prime responsibility for internal security for the entire area west of the Jordan River.

Similarly the NRP believes that once Israel returned to parts of its historic homeland—as a result of an aggressive war waged against it by Jordan—it cannot permit itself to sever these areas from any relationship or contact with the Jewish people. The NRP's position is that there must be some relationship and some contact between the Jewish people and Israel and between these areas.

Nevertheless, the NRP supports a compromise solution for Judaea, Samaria, and

Gaza, a compromise that falls far short of meeting the just national aspirations of the Jewish people. For this reason, the NRP has *not* demanded the annexation of Judaea and Samaria. On the contrary, it has opposed legislation calling for the annexation of Judaea, Samaria, and Gaza or parts of these areas, as for instance, has been proposed by Gush Emunim. The NRP supports the Autonomy Plan of the present government and is actively involved in the autonomy nego-

tiations. In fact, the NRP is not demanding Israeli sovereignty in Judaea and Samaria but is willing to support a *functional compromise*, by which authority, government, and effective sovereignty would be shared by the Palestinian Arabs and Israel. This is the essence of the Autonomy Plan, and the NRP sees in this plan, or in a similar approach, the only viable compromise with which both sides can live.

NOTES

1. Bar Kokhba (d. 135 C.E.), leader of the Jewish revolt against the Romans, 132–135 C.E. The great rabbinic leader of the period, Akiva, considered Bar-Kokhba to be the Messiah. The revolt was put down, and both leaders were killed.

2. Zeev Yonah (Vladimir Yevgenievich) Jabotinsky (1880–1940), leader of the Revisionist movement. Like Theodor Herzl, Jabotinsky regarded the Jewish question as preeminently the problem of anti-Semitism and Jewish suffering. Dissatisfied with the accommodation of the World Zionist Organization to the policies of the Palestine Mandatory administration, Jabotinsky resigned from the Zionist Executive in 1923 and founded the World Union of Zionist Revisionists in Paris in 1925.

3. The First Zionist Congress endorsed Political Zionism as espoused by Theodor Herzl. According to Herzl, the Jewish problem could be solved only by large-scale migration and settlement of Palestine, which could be attained only through the political assistance and consent of the community of nations. On the other hand, many Eastern European Zionists advocated practical Zionism—i.e., the building of the Jewish state through acquisition of land, settlement, and the creation of an economic infrastructure. Chaim Weizmann's program of Synthetic Zionism maintained that both kinds of activities should go on simultaneously to complement each other.

PEACE NOW
65. Platform

Peace Now is an unstructured political movement that emerged as a dovish pressure group during the Egyptian-Israeli negotiations resulting in the Camp David Agreements (see doc. 76). It seeks to counterbalance the activities of the Gush Emunim and other right-wing and religious move-

ments that advocate militaristic or hawkish policies and the further expansion of Israeli settlements on the West Bank. Its leadership includes reserve officers. In the 1981 elections many former Peace Now activists supported the Civil Rights movement. The 1980 platform of Peace Now is excerpted here.

Source: Leaflet distributed by Peace Now, 1980.

1. The Peace Now movement was founded and exists out of a deep concern for the peace and security of the State of Israel.

The movement acts with the cognizance that *peace* is the basis for attaining the goals of the State of Israel.

The movement is opposed to government policy since it believes that it will lead neither to peace nor to security.

The movement has a broad, comprehensive perception of the concept "security" that is not confined to territorial superiority alone but has additional components: the strength of the Israel Defense Forces and its soldiers' conviction that they are following the right path; the quantity of arms that Israel receives; assistance from and liaison with the United States and other countries of the world; security arrangements that are determined by negotiation; preparedness of the other party for peace; demilitarization of evacuated territories; the time factor in the peace settlements; mutual confidence between the two parties willing to find a peaceful solution; the success of the peace processes; the moral, social, and economic vigor of the State of Israel. All these, not just a single factor, are the components of security. Without these and without their perpetual reassessment, no peace will be established, nor will there be security.

The Peace Now movement will use democratic means to oppose any government in Israel that does not take into account these broad aspects of security and peace and is not open to options which might lead to a solution by negotiation. The movement does not deny the existence of historical and religious ties in themselves but believes that Israel's peace and security take precedence.

The movement demands from any government in Israel that it view the subject of security in its broadest sense, taking all its components into account, and that it be prepared for any negotiations which are not damaging to broader considerations of security. The movement opposes any extreme positions that might further postpone negotiations.

The movement demands from any government in Israel that it maintain the traditional aims of Zionism that work toward a Jewish state, and not one that negates the rights of some of its inhabitants; that does not rule over another nation, just as it would not allow another nation to rule over it; and exists by virtue of its own labor. It encourages *genuine settlement* but not expansion at the expense of others. . . .

3. The Autonomy Plan is merely an interim plan that should be implemented only with the cognizance that Israel has no rightful claim of sovereignty over the West Bank and the Gaza Strip.

Israel will express willingness to withdraw to secure boundaries that will be agreed upon in comprehensive negotiations and according to security considerations alone. The lack of real progress in the negotiations about the future of the autonomy is liable to affect the stability of the peace with Egypt.

4. Israel must halt its settlement activity on the West Bank and Gaza Strip, and cease all attempts at legislation intended to alter the status quo, because: (a) The settlements constitute a precondition before negotiations; and just as we require the Arabs to sit down around the discussion table without prior conditions, so we must demand from ourselves a cessation of the settlements in the area under discussion in the negotiations. (b) The settlements are intended to create established facts, but they do not guarantee a better bargaining position; quite the reverse, they goad the other side into adopting even more extreme positions. (c) The settlements have an adverse effect on the peace process and on the stability of the peace with Egypt, and they testify to the Israeli government's intention to perpetuate Israeli sovereignty over the West Bank and to continue to exercise control over one and one-half million Arabs. (d) The settlements cause unrest among the inhabitants of the West Bank and the Gaza Strip and increase animosity. (e) The settlements cost billions of Israel pounds, an investment that dam-

ages Israel's security and its image instead of buttressing the society, the economy, and the army. A state with a shaky economy cannot maintain a modern army, and a state with a discontented population will also witness destructive trends in the army. (f) The settlements display haughtiness, immorality, and a lack of integrity. (g) The settlements keep world Jewry aloof from Israel, cause a deterioration in Israel's foreign relations, and divide the nation.

5. The State of Israel paid a high price for the peace with Egypt. The Palestinian problem is the next stage in the process of creating peace, a stage during which lack of progress is liable to do harm to the stability of the existing peace with Egypt.

The Peace Now Movement has never demanded a return to the 1967 borders or the establishment of a Palestinian state. Since the chief consideration of the movement is the security of the State of Israel, we demanded and continue to demand that the government of Israel keep open any option for peace that does not negate Israel's security.

The government must investigate the following options: (a) the Jordanian option, which must be based on Resolution 242 [see doc. 53], on the Camp David Agreements [see doc. 76], and on the principle of not endangering Israel's security; (b) a combination of the Jordanian option and the Palestinian option; (c) the Palestinian option, according to which the State of Israel must initiate a step that will break through the vicious circle of Israeli-Palestinian hostility and will advance the possibility of a solution. The State of Israel will hold negotiations with the Palestinians who will recognize the method of negotiation as the only way to find a solution to the conflict in the Middle East.

These negotiations must be based upon the following principles: (a) The Palestinians will recognize Israel's sovereign right to exist as a Jewish state within secure borders, and they will abandon the path of terror. For its part, Israel will recognize the rights of the Palestinians to a national existence, so long as this is not at odds with the security of the State of Israel. (b) Both parties will enter into negotiations with full cognizance of the fact that only by each side giving way on some of the political claims, based upon the historical rights of both nations, is there any likelihood of directing the region toward peace. (c) Israel will give way on its fundamental claims for sovereignty in the West Bank and the Gaza Strip, and will base her claims solely on considerations of security. During the course of the negotiations all settlement activity will come to a halt and also all legislation liable adversely to affect the peace process. Palestinian representatives will be given a status equal to that of the representatives of the other nations participating in finding a solution for their problem and the problem of the West Bank and the Gaza Strip.

The autonomy proposed in the Camp David Agreements is simply an interim step on the way to a comprehensive solution for the Arab-Israeli conflict. The autonomy is linked to the peace-building process with Egypt and should be enforced in all the territories of the West Bank and the Gaza Strip. The negotiations between all parties who participate in the peace process will be conducted upon the basis of the Camp David Agreements and Security Council Resolution 242. Israel will view the Palestinian question as the problem of a nationally distinct group and not merely as a question of refugees.

6. Jerusalem, the capital of Israel, will not be divided. Any proposal for a settlement will be discussed in detail in the framework of comprehensive negotiations.

7. The status of existing settlements will be discussed in the framework of negotiations for a permanent settlement regarding the West Bank and the Gaza Strip.

YIGAL ALLON

66. The West Bank and Gaza within the Framework of a Middle East Peace Settlement

Yigal Allon, who died in 1980, held during his political career such positions as deputy prime minister and minister of foreign affairs. At the end of the June 1967 War he constructed the Allon Plan for a territorial compromise in the West Bank. In 1976, while minister of foreign affairs, Allon utilized the prestigious journal *Foreign Affairs* to present his own personal perspective regarding the Arab-Israeli conflict and preferred paths toward its settlement. In the following article he reanalyzes the conflict and discusses the Camp David Agreements (see doc. 76) in light of competing peace proposals.

Now that a peace treaty has been signed between Egypt and Israel and the reality of peace between the two peoples is slowly evolving, the unraveling of the remainder of the Middle East knot depends, to a very large extent, on a judicious settlement for Samaria, Judaea and the Gaza District.

These three regions, which had formed part of the Palestine Mandate were, for various reasons, not regions of intensive Jewish settlement prior to the departure of the British from the country, except for the Gush Ezion area (which fell into Arab hands in the 1948 fighting). Due to their predominantly Arab populations these regions were allotted to the Arab Palestinian state which was supposed to emerge following the U.N. Partition Plan of November 29th, 1947. However, the Palestinian Arabs rejected the opportunity offered them to establish their own state in 1948. Following the British evacuation of Palestine on May 15th, 1948, Samaria and Judaea were occupied and later annexed by Jordan, and came to be known as the West Bank within the Hashemite Kingdom of Jordan, while the Gaza Strip was occupied by Egypt.

Many Israelis, myself included, found it difficult to come to terms with the partition of Palestine in 1948, believing as we did in the absolute historical right of the People of Israel to the Land of Israel. In the course of the 1948–49 Israeli War of Independence I had also become concerned with the problem of defensible boundaries and in particular with the "soft underbelly" of Israel's defense system that resulted from the fact that Samaria and Judaea remained in the hostile hands of the Jordanian Arab Legion.

The outcome of the Six Day War, the third war imposed upon the State of Israel in twenty years, appeared, on the surface, to have made our dreams of an undivided Erez Israel come true. Yet, even while the guns were still roaring doubts began to creep into my mind as to the wisdom of fulfilling the dream and utilizing our right.

Until the establishment of the State of Israel in 1948, I had believed that once the gates of the country were opened to free Jewish immigration the ancient messianic dream of a mass return by the dispersed Jewish people would materialize. I believed that if the majority of the Jewish people would return to the western half of the Land of Israel there would be no reason why a

Source: Yigal Allon, "The West Bank and Gaza within the Framework of a Middle East Peace Settlement," *Middle East Review*, 12, no. 2 (Winter 1979–80): 15–18. Reprinted by permission.

substantial Arab minority could not continue to live in our midst, with full minority rights and its own cultural heritage, religion and traditions fully respected.

However, the rate of Jewish immigration which followed the establishment of the State of Israel proved to be much lower than expected and the Jewish birth rate in the country did not exceed that of the indigenous Arab population, or even keep up with it for that matter, and so the dream of the Jewish people rapidly becoming a solid majority within an undivided Erez Israel, *without* an exodus of the Palestinian Arab population, vanished into thin air. The military victory of 1967 did not change an iota of this basic demographic reality despite a temporary rise in Jewish immigration figures which followed the Six Day War.

Though the outcome of the War seemed to open up many new possibilities for resolving the Middle East tangle in a manner favorable to Israel, actually the situation in 1967 was less favorable, from an Israeli point of view, than that which had existed in 1949. For one thing, the Palestinian problem had become more acute after twenty years of festering without any real effort having been made to resolve it and the political exploitation of the plight of the refugees by the Arab States and extremist Palestinian elements. Secondly, the international atmosphere was less sympathetic than it had been when the Holocaust was still fresh in peoples' minds and the Zionist enterprise was the object of great admiration as demonstrating both the vitality of the wounded Jewish people and the development possibilities of a land which had suffered the ravages of centuries of neglect. In 1948 both Superpowers had given their blessing to the newly born Jewish State, and there was as yet no independent Third World emotionally inclined towards the Arab position in the Middle East conflict. By 1967 the international arena had become much less congenial.

Since Israel wished to preserve her Jewish, democratic and progressive character and avoid complete international isolation both demographic and international realities dictated Israeli withdrawal from *most* of the territories occupied in the West Bank and Gaza in the course of the War. However, though the repartitioning of Erez Israel seemed inevitable, it became of great importance for Israel to use the military gains made during the War to ensure that two major issues be confronted and tackled *before* her withdrawal: (a) Israel's security would have to be protected more effectively than under the 1949 Armistice Lines; (b) the various aspects of the problem of the Arab Palestinians would have to be satisfactorily resolved once and for all.

In the plan which eventually came to bear my name I attempted to offer practical and just solutions to both problems. I proposed to return the densely populated territories of the West Bank and Gaza to Arab sovereignty while ensuring that certain desolate and unpopulated zones vital for Israel's security—particularly the Jordan Valley Rift, the first mountain range west of it and several other locations of strategic importance to Israel in the deserts of Judaea and Samaria—should remain under Israeli control.

This plan advocated that those areas of the West Bank and Gaza which were to be returned to Arab sovereignty should not be constituted into a separate state but should merge with the Kingdom of Jordan either in the form of a federation or some other constitutional arrangement that would enable the population of either side of the River Jordan to maintain their separate identities that had evolved after 1922.

The proposal of uniting the West Bank and Gaza with Jordan is not as far-fetched as some observers might protest, and for the following reasons: (a) The West Bank and Gaza are territorially too small to form a viable state capable of offering homes, land and jobs to all the Arab Palestinians who might wish to live in a Palestinian Arab state. (b) Transjordan is part of historical Palestine which was arbitrarily cut off from the rest of the country by the British in order to provide the Emir Abdullah with a realm.

(c) The Arab population on either side of the River Jordan forms part of the same ethnic group.

Though this plan was never adopted as the official policy of the Israel Labor Party when it was in power, successive Labor Governments saw to it that Jewish settlement in the Administered Territories took place within the parameters of the plan, and with the exception of East Jerusalem which was reunited with its western half, refrained from extending Israeli sovereignty to the Administered Territories.

In fact all options were left open. The West Bank and Gaza remained under an Israeli Military Government, enforcing the Jordanian and British Mandatory laws respectively, while their economy was allowed to develop with a dual orientation: one towards the Israeli economy which allowed for the free movement of labor and goods across the "Green Line" [Israel's pre-1967 borders] and the other towards Jordan and beyond by means of the "open bridges" policy which encouraged the maintenance of trade and personal contacts between the populations of the two banks of the Jordan River.

In the latter part of 1974, following the signature of disengagement agreements between Israel, Egypt and Syria, there was a real chance for a partial interim agreement between Israel and Jordan on the basis of the "Jericho Plan"[1] which might well have acted as a first step towards the realization of peace on the basis of the plan outlined above. Unfortunately, the Rabat Conference [see doc. 71] prevented Jordan from taking this positive step by unequivocally stating that the PLO alone could act as the representative of the Palestinian people to negotiate the future of the West Bank and Gaza.

The "political unheaval" of May 1977 brought the Likud Party to power in Israel, and with it a concept that maintained that Samaria, Judaea and Gaza, as part of the ancient homeland of the Jewish people, should never pass from Israeli sovereignty. Though Mr. Begin's Government has so far taken no legal steps to annex the West Bank and Gaza to Israel, its settlement policy in the Administered Territories and its official declarations, not least of all in regard to the proposed Autonomy Plan now being negotiated, point in this direction.

The Labor Alignment rejects this policy of the Likud Government not because there is no link between the Jewish people and the whole of Erez Israel, not because there is no legal basis for a continued Israeli presence in the West Bank and Gaza, not because there are no security reasons for Israel's occupation of the Administered Territories, but despite these considerations. We reject this policy because we want Israel to remain a democratic, progressive Jewish state following a realistic policy, and because we want to see the Palestinian issue satisfactorily resolved.

At the outset I stated that now that a peace treaty had been signed between Egypt and Israel the next problem on the peace agenda was working out a settlement concerning the status of the West Bank and Gaza. In fact, Egypt made the signing of the Peace Treaty conditional on progress on the Palestinian issue; the Camp David Agreements of September 1978 unfolded a basic plan for the establishment of autonomy for the inhabitants of the West Bank and Gaza as an interim arrangement towards the negotiation of a permanent settlement—a settlement that would determine the status of these territories, the future of the Palestinian Arabs, the nature of the peace between Israel and her eastern neighbor and provisions for the security needs of Israel.

The Likud Government has viewed the whole autonomy concept as presented in the Camp David Agreements as a means for perpetuating Israeli control over the West Bank and Gaza while giving their Arab inhabitants a measure of self-rule in the form of *personal* autonomy.

The Labor Alignment, on the other hand, true to the letter and spirit of the Camp David Agreements, sees Autonomy, a *territorially* based autonomy, as an interim arrangement paving the way for a permanent settlement. Such a settlement must *prevent* the establishment of a third state in addition to Israel and Jordan in the territory of historical Palestine, should not include the continuation of Israeli control over the territories inhabited by Arabs in the West Bank and Gaza and must ensure that Israel would remain in control of certain locations and zones vital for her long run security. In conformity with this concept the Labor Party Center decided that Autonomy must apply to the territories densely inhabited by Arabs in the West Bank and Gaza while the Israel Defense Forces should be redeployed into the Jordan Valley Rift, the Gush Ezion area, a minute buffer zone in the southern tip of the Gaza Strip, and several other minor locations of vital importance.

Though the Camp David Agreements deliberately left many details concerning the proposed Autonomy Plan vague, in order to paper-over some fundamental differences of approach between the Egyptian and Israeli Governments, and thus left much to be desired with regard to the basic frame of reference for the Autonomy's establishment, the Labor Party accepted it as a constructive step in the direction of a comprehensive peace settlement in the Middle East.

In particular the plan makes the following three important contributions towards attaining this goal by providing for: (a) the election of an Administrative Council which will form the first democratically elected representation of the Arab Palestinian community in the West Bank and Gaza. This Administrative Council will gain five years of experience in self-government within the Autonomy Plan and will be able to partici-

pate alongside with Egypt, Jordan and Israel in working out a permanent settlement: (b) the involvement of Jordan in the process of establishing the Autonomy Plan and the negotiations which are to follow its establishment; (c) the determination of security locations into which the Israel Defense Forces are to withdraw once the Autonomy Plan is established—security locations which should be designed to take into account Israel's long run security needs.

Though the Jordanian Government and the Palestinian Arab community in the West Bank and Gaza have so far opted not to be involved in the Autonomy negotiations, whether due to pressure from the Arab Rejectionist Front or because of concrete objections to the Camp David formula, at present the Autonomy Plan is the *only* key to opening further gates on the path leading to an overall peace. Unless the Jordanians and representatives of the Palestinian Arabs from the West Bank and Gaza join the negotiations this key may be lost. Such a situation would lead to a dangerous stalemate which would not only prevent further progress on the road to peace but would endanger the stability of the peace between Egypt and Israel.

On the basis of informal and unpublished discussions which I have had with various important personalities from the Administered Territories I can state that I am not pessimistic with regard to the prospect of Palestinian spokesmen from the Territories and of Jordanian representatives joining the Autonomy negotiations, if not while the Likud is in power then once it is replaced by a Labor government.

NOTE

1. Jericho Plan (Jericho Corridor Plan), plan outlined in 1974 for an initial Jordanian settlement based on the return of the Jericho region to Jordanian control. It was integrated into the Allon Plan (see map 4).

NATIONAL COMMITTEE FOR THE DEFENSE OF ARAB LANDS
67. Manifesto

The June 1967 War and the October 1973 War generated processes that radicalized Israel's Arab citizens and fostered the development of political groups to the left of the Communist party, such as the National Committee for the Defense of Arab Lands.[1]

One government policy contributing to this radicalization was the expropriation of Arab-owned land. On March 30, 1976, a general strike was planned in the Arab sector to protest such expropriations. In the attempt by the authorities to suppress the general strike and in the accompanying antigovernment riots, six Arabs were killed and many more were wounded. Since then Land Day has been commemorated with rallies and demonstrations by Israeli Arab nationalists and the Jewish Left. The following manifesto was published by the National Committee for the Defense of Arab Lands on the third anniversary of Land Day.

Few days separate us from the 30th of March, the third anniversary of Land Day, the day the Arab minority in Israel commemorates as a symbol of its struggle to defend Arab-owned land and as an act of protest against the policy of land expropriation and the demolition of Arab houses. The decisions adopted in the conference held in Nazareth by the National Committee for the Defense of Arab Lands on February 17, 1979, form the basis for this anniversary. These decisions are as follows:

1. The Arab masses in Israel, joined by democratic forces in Israel, will commemorate the Land Day by holding four mass rallies on March 30 in the following places: Dir-Hanna village, Kfar Kanna village (Galilee), Taibeh village (Triangle), and Tel El-Sabi' (Negev). At these rallies representatives of the committee, local councils, and public figures—both Jews and Arabs—will speak.

2. This anniversary takes place while the impetuous policy and actions of land expropriations and the expulsion of Arabs from the land continue, especially in the Negev where Bedouins are forced out of the houses and lands on which they have lived for hundreds of years. The criminal acts perpetuated by the Green Patrol[2] against the Bedouin livestock should move people of conscience, Jews and Arabs alike, to demand an end to these brutal measures that are in violation of law and justice and are fundamentally opposed to basic human rights. These actions are threatening the mere existence and fate of those unprotected citizens in their own homeland.

3. The Arabs in Israel express their resolve to continue their just struggle relentlessly against all acts of land confiscation and the demolition of Arab houses and for safeguarding their rights for full equality as citizens and as human beings.

4. It is naturally expected that any peace policy should begin at home by guaranteeing equality for the Arab citizens and by recognizing their right to ownership of their lands. Peace policy should mean the banning of all manifestations of national oppression and discrimination that are being carried out against the Arabs, including the

Source: Press release distributed by the National Committee for the Defense of Arab Lands, March 25, 1979.

policy of dispossessing them of their lands and homes. The National Committee for the Defense of Arab Lands calls for the withdrawal of all court cases against Arabs who were charged since 1976 of disturbing law and order on the eve of the Land Day.

5. The committee will intensify its propaganda campaign to mobilize public opinion in Israel and elsewhere toward solidarity with the just demands of the Arabs in Israel. In addition the committee has appealed in a letter to the president of the state that its efforts toward a genuine solution to the suffering of the Arab masses be given a hearing.

6. The committee wishes to make it known that if all appeals fall on deaf ears, it will find itself bound to step up its struggle by using all legitimate means including strikes and demonstrations in order to win justice, equality, and democratic rights.

7. The Arab masses in Israel consider their struggle for full equality, for the abolition of national oppression and discrimination expressed first and foremost by dispossession, as part and parcel of the general democratic struggle for a just peace and for ensuring democratic rights and coexistence among the peoples of the region. This peace is what all of us desire and seek.

NOTES

1. In the elections of June 30, 1981, it appears that a significant number of Israeli Arabs who had previously been voting for Rakah (or rather the electoral list it formed and led, the Democratic Front for Peace and Equality) voted for the Labor alignment.

2. Green Patrol, police force established in the Ministry of Agriculture during Ariel Sharon's tenure in order to guard state lands, especially in areas contested by Bedouins.

SIMON MARKISH
68. A Soviet Jewish Intellectual Abroad

The 1970s witnessed a large emigration of Jews from the Soviet Union, and in the early part of that decade many went to Israel. By the mid-1970s it was clear that Soviet Jewish immigrants were encountering serious problems in Israel, and many chose other destinations. The nature of these problems, especially for the class of intellectuals, is explained by a Soviet Jewish emigrant who chose not to settle in Israel.

Simon Markish (b. 1921), son of the Yiddish writer Peretz Markish, was trained in classical philology. He left the Soviet Union in 1970 and has been living in Geneva, where he teaches at the university, since 1974. The article excerpted here appeared in *Commentary*, the intellectual journal published by the American Jewish Committee.

Source: Simon Markish, "Passers-by: The Soviet Jew as Intellectual," *Commentary* 66, no. 6 (December 1978): 34–38. Reprinted from *Commentary* by permission. © 1978 by the American Jewish Committee. Also by permission of Simon Markish.

Once an intellectual is abroad, and has passed through the period of shock which every emigrant from the USSR must inevitably experience—it is largely a mixture of alarm and rapture—he begins to adapt psychologically. His mind, and especially his emotions formulate a set of responses to his new situation. Whether the response will be predominantly gloomy or bright depends as much on physical circumstances as on mental baggage, though possibly the latter is more important. With all the difficulties of life in Israel, material conditions there are, with rare exceptions, greatly more favorable than in the USSR. But neither Israel nor the West is like the preconception of them which the future émigré has before his departure, and that is because his preconceptions are made up of Soviet components. It might be said that this is not more true of the present-day émigré than it was of the Jewish émigrés from Russia at the turn of the century, and that the real America was sharply different from the Realm of Gold dreamed of in the shtetl. But the mental baggage of Jews was different then, the disparity between ideal and real was experienced differently.

The very departure from the USSR is felt by the émigré to be something of a feat, and in many cases it is just that: months and even years of "refusal" status, letters of protest, arrest, prison, and so on. But even if everything has gone smoothly, the émigré has had to overcome his terror of the all-powerful state and authorities, a feeling which is incomprehensible to anyone in a free society. Every émigré, moreover, has to tolerate all manner of humiliation and loss to the very last, at the various customs checkpoints—and not only in the USSR; if he goes by train, he is openly robbed by the Poles and the Czechs—and his sufferings acquire the nature of virtues in his mind. He is a hero and a martyr, and therefore has a legitimate claim to retribution.

Judging as he does by Soviet standards, he is not capable of understanding that his retribution begins from the moment he steps off the train or the plane in Vienna. Everything that comes his way he accepts as his just desert. This is not only because he is a hero and a martyr, but because everything has already been paid for by the American Jews. And Israel has nothing to do with it, he owes nothing to Israel. Hence the fierce aggressiveness of some émigrés in their very first moments on Israeli soil, in the immigration hall at the airport. Hence the frank discussions in Vienna. The immigration official from the Jewish Agency asks one of those who have announced their intention to go straight to the U.S., Canada, or Australia, "But what if you could only have gone to Israel; would you have emigrated?" And without any hesitation the "straighter" answers, "No."[1]

Judging as he does by Soviet standards, he is not capable of understanding that the country he has come to has its own laws and customs, its own difficulties, and that it is trying to overcome then in its own way. He does not understand that the only way to get used to the place and to feel at home is to accept the rules of the game, and not to stand on the doorstep and demand that they be abolished or fundamentally altered. This is not to say that the rules are ideal; many of them are no good at all. But if you want to tidy up the house, you might at least wait until you are inside. The "noisy minority," however, do not go beyond the doorstep; their sense of superiority does not allow it. We have suffered more than anybody else, they seem to say, we know better than anybody else, we will explain everything and teach everything.

The passion for preaching overcomes new émigrés from Russia, regardless of their origin, Jew and non-Jew alike. In essence there is no difference between the repatriate, hardly able to express himself in kitchen Hebrew but already discoursing on the poverty of spiritual life in Israel, and the professional émigrés traveling around different countries and answering all questions without hesitation, settling any problem without the least difficulty. Though there is one important distinction. The émigré knows his place after all, he knows he is a stranger whom nobody has asked or especially invited, and so he knows how far he may go in his attacks and exposures. It is one thing to hear the view expressed at dinner in a private home that Harvard University is worse than Elets Teachers' Training Institute; this is hardly a view to put into a newspaper or to pronounce from the lecture platform. The repatriate, however, knows no such limitations or inhibitions.

Coming to the concrete reasons for dissatisfaction and disillusionment, we should exclude the obvious and well-known ones like the hard climate in Israel or the rude civil servants. All new arrivals suffer from these, whatever country they come from. The former Soviet Jewish intellectual, especially if he belonged to, or numbered himself among, the so-called creative intelligentsia, is shaken, apart from everything else (and sometimes above all else), by the change in his accepted scale of values. He is no longer in an elite, or at any rate not in the only elite, and not the most important of elites. To be a writer is no more honorable than to be an engineer or a doctor. Poverty and lack of success are no longer evidence of a proud and independent talent, but more likely the result of hopes that have been dashed. The accepted scale of values is overturned, and there remains only the choice between adopting a new one and living in a fantasy world of old and hurriedly renovated values—or repudiating any scale of values altogether.

The first course represents, strictly speaking, a completely different subject of discussion: namely, the successful adaptation and integration of immigrants. It is worth pointing out that the quickest to adapt are those who have inner resources, people with convictions and ideas. For example, and above all, believers or new believers. Or old-school Zionists, although even they are not immune from disillusionment, irritation, and straightforward rebellion. We need not dwell on the loud protests made by Geor-

gian Jews about religious life in Israel, since their psychology is a mystery to many besides myself; complaints about inadequate piety of the state of Israel and of its scandalous godlessness are clearly not the monopoly of the old Hasidic inhabitants of Meah Shearim.[2] The point is, however, that the first course, the course of adaption, is most accessible to those who bring with them or quickly acquire some positive spiritual equipment: to put it simply, a love of God, of freedom, of the Jews, of Israel, but only the real Israel, and not the one dreamed up in the Soviet vacuum, bathed in tears of humiliation or drunkenness. These people grow quickly in their new soil, put down roots, forget the discrimination of their Soviet existence, forget even their existence itself, the land of the Soviets, Russia, and their past hatred for it, once so fierce as to serve virtually as the chief content of their lives.

The second course is the most interesting to the outside observer and, most likely, the most bitter to those who follow it. It is a course taken by many a Soviet intellectual in Israel. He who felt himself to be a Jew in Russia, and for that very reason "returned to the historic homeland," finds himself once there to be a Russian, not because of Israeli phraseology, not because it is generally accepted that immigrants from Russia are called Russians, but because he suddenly feels for certain that he is a Russian. In Russia, being a Jew was the most important mark of self-identification, whether personal or social; it was the main motive and factor in any interpretation of one's destiny; it marked the conscious or subconscious frontier between one's own and what was not one's own, between "ours" and "not ours." This is perhaps natural in any diaspora, and almost inevitable in the process of reidentification in the new environment, Israel.

If the mind recoils from the new circumstances, once so desired when they were a dream and a goal, and if the mind does not want to harbor this new feeling of hostility but cannot overcome it, and also cannot or does not want to change the circumstances, then in order to avoid self-destruction it will return to the past, reshape it, shifting the emphasis, reassessing evaluations. All the old forms, standards, and patterns are preserved. We are not like the others, we are better, we know more; but they do not value us, they envy us, they don't want to help. Everything around us is alien; we are not interested in "their" petty concerns and primitive pleasures; we are aristocrats of the mind, we live our own internal lives, we are intellectuals, we are members of the Russian intelligentsia, we are the third wave of the Russian emigration. We are in Israel by chance, just as we could be in Canada or in France, by chance.

Passers-by were they there, passers-by are they now here.

NOTES

1. A conflict with world Jewry regarding the settlement of Soviet Jewish émigrés has arisen over the last decade. The Israeli government has argued that Jewish philanthropic funds should be given only to those Soviet Jews emigrating to Israel, with the exception of those uniting with their families elsewhere.

2. Meah Shearim (lit., One Hundred Gates), Orthodox neighborhood in Jerusalem with a large concentration of militantly Orthodox organizations.

ASHER ARIAN
69. Elections 1981

The elections of 1981, resulting in the second Likud government despite the Labor party's improved performance over 1977, reflected the increasing polarization of Israeli politics. In the following article, Asher Arian, a professor of political science at Tel Aviv University who specializes in Israeli electoral politics, analyzes the processes that led to the Likud's second victory and the consequences of these elections for Israeli politics. The article appeared immediately after the elections in the *Jerusalem Quarterly*, published in Jerusalem by the Middle East Institute.

Israel's most bitter, violent and unsavory campaign ended on June 30, 1981, with the election of the Tenth Knesset, but it settled very little. It created a virtual tie between the two largest political groupings in the country—the Likud with 48 of the 120 Knesset seats and the Labor-Mapam Alignment with 47—and underscored the observation that the country was divided in an unprecedented manner.[1] The close elections retained for the religious parties the balance of political power which they had come to expect, although the National Religious Party (NRP), the largest component among them, lost half its previous strength by falling from twelve to six seats.

Source: Asher Arian, "Elections 1981: Competitiveness and Polarization," *Jerusalem Quarterly,* no. 21 (Fall 1981): pp. 3–27. Reprinted by permission.

Elections determine the division of power in a political community and as such have far-reaching influence on the body politic. But the election results themselves are conditioned by a series of political, social, and economic factors, some objective and other subjective. The most striking characteristic to emerge from the 1981 elections was evidence of polarization in Israel along ethnic, social and political lines. These features were noted in the past; it was the degree of their intensity and the fact that these polarities tended to overlap which made the 1981 election campaign unique and its results disquieting.

Never before had the country been divided so evenly and so massively by the two major parties. Never before had the electorate of the two parties been so homogeneous in its ethnic composition. Never before had ethnicity been exploited as a campaign theme in such a barely implicit manner. Never before had violence in the campaign seemed so threatening and so immediate.

Competitiveness: Away from Dominance
The major party of the labor movement (first called Ahdut Haavodah, then Mapai, now Labor) had been dominant in Israeli politics for the first 29 years of independence and for a couple of decades before independence as well. In 1977 the pattern of dominance was broken when the Likud won the largest number of Knesset seats. The 1981 elections determined beyond any doubt that the era of Labor dominance had ended, and not only temporarily suspended as some had thought. The system had become competitive, the former dominant party no longer being able to count on plurality support from most social groups of the electorate.

Never before in Israel's history had a more competitive election occurred, for this was the first time that both major parties considered the possibility that the other party might win. In the past, including the turnabout 1977 elections, the leaders of the Herut/Liberal parties and coalitions (Gahal in 1969, the Likud since 1973) had been

pretenders to victory but the Labor/Mapam leadership had always been confident—and correct until 1977—about remaining the biggest party and therefore the major component in the formation of the government coalition. The electorate was swept into the drama of a two-party race and many voters disappointed smaller contenders on the left, right and center by being sucked into the ranks of the two large parties.

The portion of the two-party vote was unprecedented, reaching 95 of the 120-member Knesset, or almost 80 percent. The previous high for the vote of the two largest parties was in 1973, when the Alignment and the Likud split 90 seats between them, 51 and 39 respectively. In 1981 the race was extremely close, the Likud winning 48 seats, the Alignment 47; between them they won almost a million and a half votes of the almost two million cast, but only 10,405 votes was the difference between them. Within the Jewish population the Likud was an even bigger winner, since Arabs accounted for 47,300 of the Alignment total.

There was a general feeling of disappointment with the election results within the two big parties. Inevitably, politicians deal with the relative and not the absolute. Therefore, objective indications of major achievements by both parties were overshadowed by the knowledge that the competitor did almost as well, or better. The Likud continued its steady growth and added more than 100,000 votes to its 1977 total. The Alignment was somewhat heartened by its 1981 showing since it bounced back from its 1977 trauma and grew by 50 percent. But comparing the 1981 results to the Alignment's more glorious past leads to the inevitable conclusion that it remains a party in decline despite the good 1981 showing. The difference between the 1969 and 1981 votes for the Alignment, for example, was a mere 75,000 votes, whereas the Likud in the same period added more than 375,000 votes to its total. The number of voting Israelis grew in that same period by more than half a million.

When looked at in terms of the two major

parties, the growth of the Likud is clear. If present trends are projected into the future the Likud will continue to grow and the polarization of 1981 will be remembered as a momentary—and random—meeting of curves.

The size of the two-party vote in 1981 was unique; it is usually helpful in Israeli politics to think in terms of party blocs. Looked at in this way, it is also clear that political fortunes in Israel are steadily moving to the right. In 1981 Israeli politics was divided into two large camps, but over time the parties of the center and right grew and the parties left-of-center declined. Adding together the seats won by adjacent parties during the last four elections (1969, 1973, 1977 and 1981) provides the following breakdown for the center and right: 32, 39, 45, 51. For the left-of-center parties (including the Democratic Movement for Change [DMC] and the Arab parties affiliated with the Alignment) the trend line is 66, 62, 52 and 50. (Dayan's Telem was not included since he is hard to categorize.)

Images and Ideology

Images played a central role in the 1981 elections: the image of the Likud as an anti-establishment party representing the underprivileged in Israeli society, willing to use the "big lie" in portraying its policies in order to be re-elected; the image of the Alignment as the party of the bosses, anxious to return to the government to which their establishment status seemed to entitle them; the image of Begin as a self-confident leader expressing some of the deepest doubts of the Jewish people regarding the degree to which non-Jews could be trusted and the Israeli penchant for assertiveness even if cooler minds thought it dangerous at best, suicidal at worst; the image of Peres as an indecisive politician who would do almost anything to further his own career, whose smooth tongue sometimes appeared slick, and who was set on not missing the opportunity to be prime minister. Ideological differences between the parties were

much less crucial in determining the election results. In a basic sense, this was a non-ideological election.

While emotions ran high and many found fault with both of the major contestants, this was not an "anti" election. Many voted for the party of their choice because they thought it was better, not only because the other was worse. There was no evidence of alienation from the political system or withdrawal from the election. The participation rate—78.5 percent in 1981—was similar to past elections.

Party Images

A social myth is a convenient way of ordering reality. While reality is usually complex, myths have a simplifying quality about them. They are easily grasped, widely accepted, able to convert masses of detail into an understandable whole.

Similarly, the image that a party or a leader has is no less important than his real opinion or personality. If Peres is thought of as insincere, or Begin as unstable, conflicting evidence can easily be put aside in favor of the popular image which allows us to grasp the essence of the man more easily.

In the 1981 election campaign the Alignment was perceived to be the establishment party even though it had been in opposition to the government for four years. The Alignment's negative image is also evidenced in that it was perceived to be the party more concerned about its own interests than those of the citizens', and not very honest. The Likud was closer to the ideal party image, perceived as a slightly stronger party, honest, one that could be trusted and a party more concerned with the citizens than with itself.

In politics, perceptions are as important, or more so, than reality. It may be that the sample's perceptions reflect reality, but it is certainly noteworthy that a party in opposition for four years still retains in the public mind many characteristics of an establishment, governing party. The Likud still benefited from its image of newness, of innocence, and was given credit for its efforts in undoing many of the difficult legacies it had inherited from the Alignment. In fact, 41 percent of a national sample reported that they thought that the argument "four years are not sufficient for the Likud to undo what the Alignment had destroyed in thirty years" was a convincing reason to vote for the Likud.

On other dimensions there were differences in the parties' images as well. For example, the Alignment was the opposite of the ideal on the young/old dimension, the ideal being young, the Alignment perceived as old. The Likud also had an older image, but much less extreme than that of the Alignment. While the ideal called for a progressive party, both parties were perceived as old-fashioned, but the Alignment more so than the Likud. A strong party was called for, and the Likud was perceived as slightly stronger than the Alignment. In fact, on almost every dimension, the Likud was closer to the ideal than the Alignment.

On class and ethnic dimensions the differences between the parties and their images were striking. The ideal party was almost evenly divided among those who preferred a middle-class party, those who preferred a working-class party and those in between. The Alignment was perceived to be close to that ideal, although more working-class, while the Likud was very far from the ideal with a high preponderance of middle-class responses. As we have seen, the workers tended to support the Likud and not the Alignment even though the Alignment is the labor party associated with the socialist movement.

The ethnic dimension also fits the pattern. The socialist label gave the Alignment claim to being the worker's party, but the Alignment was also overwhelmingly Ashkenazi, or European. As such, the Alignment had negative appeal for the Sephardi who tended to have lower education and lower status occupations. Both the Likud and the Alignment were led by Ashkenazi politicians, but the rejection of the Alignment was

indicated by the fact that it was perceived to be so overwhelmingly Ashkenazi when in fact its leadership was no more Ashkenazi than the Likud's.

In the 1981 campaign, the Alignment was broadly perceived to be the party of the European, upper-middle-class bosses and the Likud the party of the Sephardi, lower-class workers. This image was heightened by a campaign which featured expressions of violence and political intolerance especially at Alignment rallies by individuals popularly portrayed as young Sephardi toughs inspired by Likud rhetoric. The ethnic tension was brought to a head during a huge Alignment rally held in Tel Aviv three days before the election, when a popular entertainer indulged in ethnic slurs against the Likud electorate, even evoking their relatively low army ranks in the supposedly egalitarian Israel Defence Forces. The polarization of the two parties and their respective ethnic supporters fortified the images which were already prevalent: the Alignment as the party of the bosses, running the Histadrut, the kibbutzim and other economic institutions which oversaw the dependency relations with which many of these individuals lived since arriving in Israel in the early fifties.

The images of the kibbutz had undergone a radical change since the years of independence when kibbutz membership was an ideal and the kibbutz member a folk-hero. The image of the kibbutz was now bifurcated: for the Alignment supporter, it was a preserve of socialist and idealist values and an example of economic success and social equality as well. The kibbutz member was seen as the Israeli landed gentry, loyal, affluent, and entitled to rule. For the Likud supporter, the kibbutz epitomized values perverted. In the name of non-exploitation, exploitation; in the name of equality, inequality. How else explain the kibbutz factories in outlying regions in which the kibbutz members were bosses and the workers Jews (and Arabs) from surrounding settlements? The most successful workers could never

reach manager level since that was preserved for kibbutz members. The explanation was basic: since it was kibbutz capital
which built the factory, it was only right for
kibbutz members to manage the collective's
property. Along with the disregard of socialist values, the tensions also overlapped the
basic social data that the kibbutz members
tended to be Ashkenazi, that they supported
the Alignment overwhelmingly and had
achieved positions of power and leadership
in the Alignment, and hence in the country,
above their proportion in the population,
and that the workers in kibbutz factories
were often Sephardi and Likud supporters.

The Likud was perceived as the party of
the "Second Israel," the Jews from more
"primitive" cultures, exotic music and spicy
foods. They had been given so much by the
state—education, housing, jobs—and yet
they were basically ungrateful and, more
than that, presented a serious threat to the
continued strength of the state. Efforts at
integration meant lower levels of schooling
for the whole population. This brought
about the popularization of mass culture and
the weakening of the more ideological values of the past. Their social problems were
associated with unruly behavior in the
schools, on the buses and in the movie
theaters, and now this was being expressed
in the election campaign.

As in most social myths, there was some
truth to these perceptions. Social problems
were growing in Israel, the introduction of
Sephardi at the highest level of social and
economic élite groups was proceding more
slowly than full integration would require.
Expressing the connection between myth
and party almost openly accelerated the
identification of the Ashkenazi with the
Alignment and the Sephardi with the Likud.
Yes, was the implication, Sephardi are violent, undemocratic, unsuited for governing.
They must be defeated. Or, the other way:
No! They have not learned the lesson, they
have not changed. There, they are deciding
who should be in which ministry, taking us
for granted again. They'll use and exploit us

as they always have. Besides, they can't
even get along with each other.

The polarization was most evident in the
campaign's rallies. The bases of support for
Begin and the Likud overlapped: the young,
Israeli-born, especially those of Asian and
African origin, lower income and lower
education groups supported him overwhelmingly. Peres and Alignment (—and
Rabin) support was centered in older, European, higher education and higher status
groups. There was no important difference
in the patterns of support between Peres
and Rabin when running against Begin.

Begin's appeal to the crowd—some called
it demagoguery—was as great as it had been
during his fighting days in the opposition
during the late forties and fifties. Calls of
"Begin King of Israel" were widespread
during the campaign, his supporters edging
toward the frenzy of mass-hysteria frequent
in other Middle Eastern settings. Peres'
crowds were more polite, subdued—and
smaller. Peres lacked the personal appeal
which Begin enjoyed; an extra-party organization named Alef (Citizens for Peres) was
set up to ensure his nomination and election
by trying to improve his public image.

The tomatoes thrown at Peres during a
Passover folk-festival of Morroccan Jews in
Jerusalem was the first sign of violence in
the campaign. It became fashionable to bait
Peres among certain groups, almost like a
seasonal sport. Whether the Likud actually
had a hand in organizing the anti-Peres
demonstrations (as the Alignment asserted)
or not is beside the point; what is important
is that the expression of anti-Peres feeling
fed on deeply-held animosities and could
easily be expanded much beyond the scope
of the original group which began interfer-
ing at his rallies.

The reaction to the violence was immediate. It accelerated the "verbal violence"
between the two parties which had already
escalated in the campaign and it polarized
the electorate along ethnic lines as never
before. It made support for the small parties
a luxury which many felt they could not

afford since the elections were between two large forces. The stigmatization of the supporters of the Likud by the Alignment as unruly antidemocrats forced many—especially Sephardi—who had voted Likud in 1977, but were disappointed with its performance, to reconsider their decision. They saw in it a manifestation of the lengths to which the Alignment would go to regain (and by implication, to retain) power. They were offended by Peres' reference to "two cultures" (repeated by him in his stillborn victory speech on election night) which they took in an ethnic sense while he meant it in a political one.

The fear of being an embattled minority losing to the Sephardi hordes undoubtedly worked in the Alignment's favor. If the issue lost it some Sephardi votes, it won the Alignment many more Ashkenazi ones. It was also the first time in the long campaign that the Likud's momentum was broken. Everything had worked in the Likud's favor, from Aridor's[2] economics to foreign policy crises such as the Syrian missiles in Lebanon,[3] Begin's verbal attacks on West Germany's Helmut Schmidt and the Israeli attack on the nuclear power installation in Baghdad. The Alignment floundered: its economic attacks were impotent and they were forced to play to Begin's strength in the field of foreign and security affairs. When the violent nature of the campaign became an issue working for the Alignment, its leaders exploited it to the full.

Israel had known violent political campaigns in the past and those familiar with Israel's education system, with the cases tried in its courts or even with Israel's soccer fans, know that violence is not unknown to this society. But instead of being an unpleasant feature of everyday life, in the 1981 campaign it became a focal issue. Partly because television is prohibited from showing candidates on the screen for the month prior to the elections, the television crews began covering the crowds. June was a hot month—and not only because it was summer.

Political Ideology

The heat of the campaign produced more noise than light. Policy questions were raised but the dominant tones of the election were the emotionally charged issues of Begin vs. Peres, democracy vs. fascism, political violence vs. political tolerance, continued progress with the Likud as opposed to going back to the old ways of the Alignment: the growers of the tomatoes against the throwers of tomatoes.

Because the positive pull of one party and the negative push of the other were so central to the 1981 elections, ideological differences between the parties were relegated to a secondary role. Of course, there is a basic sense in which all politics in Israel are ideological. Messages are packaged in ideological containers, code-words are frequently attached. The generation of political leadership active in the 1981 election campaign had grown up during the period when issues and phrases such as fascism, socialism, Revisionism and the basic values of the labor movement had intellectual content and emotional impact. For many of the voters in 1981, however, the ability of these words to evoke images of great events, men or battles or to arouse feelings of deep admiration or hatred, was limited. Yet the leadership persisted in its patterns of communication, talking of these things which meant little to most, as well as of the Holocaust and Zionism, which meant more to many.

The Israeli political system has the reputation of being ideological in character and indeed political communication is often presented in ideological terms. Policies are seen to flow from an overview of society and the nature of the Jewish state and it is important for political communicators to show how this action-oriented program fits in a general pattern of behavior and governing. Upon closer examination, however, it is clear that the style of political communication has overshadowed the importance of the substance. The public is conditioned to hear politicians explain, attack, plead or defend in ideological terms. One does not try to extend military control over parts of Lebanon or destroy Iraqi nuclear capacity, one prevents a holocaust for the Christians of Lebanon and the Jews of Israel, respectively. One does not merely oppose the Likud or try to win the elections, one tries to save the country from Revisionism and Beginism (a Peres phrase which seemed to be a cross between Khoumeinism and Fascism).

If ideology means a master-plan, a system of ideas based on social goals and phrased in terms of social and political action, then the campaign was non-ideological. In a campaign which saw the parties more competitive and the ethnic groups more polarized than ever before, it was not easy to mistake the elections as an ideological struggle over the nation's future. The 1981 elections centered on images and candidates, the frustrations of one ethnic group and the fears of the other.

There was no great debate in Israel over the future of the country or its policies in 1981. There was broad agreement—"national consensus" in the language of Israeli politics—regarding the continued existence of Israel as a Jewish state and with borders reaching from the Mediterranean to the Jordan. Only marginal groups consider pulling back to the pre-1967 borders or annexing all of them outright. In practical politics, the subtle variations between policies make all the difference, and it is basically on the tactics of holding on that the parties are divided. The Likud is now committed to the Camp David accords which provide for autonomy for the West Bank and Gaza populations, the Alignment to territorial concessions while the Jordan River is retained as a "defence border." Reality has forced the leaders of both parties to concentrate less on ideology and more on the tactics of continued security and existence.

There is no doubt about the fact that the country is moving to the right. When asked with which political tendency do you identify, more than a third say "right" today compared with 16 percent in 1969 and 8 percent in 1962. The "right" has become the largest single response category. But we must be careful not to mistake this with political ideology. While the "left-right" distinction is meaningful to most of the sample and widely used within the system, it is not a measure of ideology. What has happened in Israel is that the cues generated by the parties have become central in determining the left-right distribution, quite unrelated to attitudes or political ideology.

The literature on the subject would lead us to expect that as a society's ideological orientation shifts, so too should its positions on political issues. The fascinating finding about Israel is that, although the country has moved to the right politically, the distribution of attitudes on important matters has remained constant. Hardline stands on returning the territories are about as prevalent today as they were in 1969.

The picture is less static than it appears since changes have been taking place in the political context in which the question was asked. The 1973 question was asked before the Yom Kippur War, the 1981 question after most of Sinai had been returned. The samples are different and the distribution of responses is not identical. Still, what is striking is the relative stability of the attitude over time in the society. Ninety percent or more in both 1969 and 1981 favor returning none of the territories or only a small part.

This attitudinal stability even as the political continuum is moving to the right is even more astonishing since the population has not become more capitalistic in economic matters, as might be expected from the "right" label. Almost 60 percent favored socialism throughout the period. Government intervention is often decried and the economy has been liberalized, yet the movement to the right is not reflected in this important attitude. The stability of these attitudes over time forces us to consider the sense in which the system has changed.

What we have witnessed in Israel over the last few decades is a process of political change, not ideological change. The stability of attitudes and the shift of political power to the right has been made possible because ideology is not central to Israeli political life. The growth of the Likud and of the "right" must be understood as a reaction to the years of dominance of the Alignment and the "left." The terms are important as labels but not necessarily as instructors of ideological content. Likud means not only "right"— it also means non-Alignment and hence non-"left." High levels of response to the "left-right" question are artifacts of the passing of dominance and the emergence of competitiveness. The "right" and the Likud are increasing in strength over time and the "left" and Alignment are in decline. But when we look at the responses of only those who reported that they intend to vote for one of the two parties, the picture changes. Then the "right" and the Likud grow, but only the percentage of those who report they will vote Alignment is in decline. The portion of the Alignment voters who identify themselves as "left" is constant. The shrinkage of the "left" is a result of the decline of the Alignment; the growth of the "right" stems from the greater legitimacy and increasing power of the Likud.

That political labels should fill a function of veto by pointing out whom we want to avoid is not surprising to observers who know the nature of political communication in Israel. This function was filled by the "left" in the pre-state and early state era— the period of dominance—when the left was widely considered as the appropriate legitimate authority in the system. Now as that basic understanding is being overturned, the term "right" fills the role of identifying the bad guys (the "left") as much as it does of identifying the group with which one might wish to identify (the "right"). The prime motivator is the identification with one of the political parties; from that flows identification with one of the political labels. This in turn has been facilitated by the fact that the party system has become more competitive and less dominant.

The explanation for this topsy-turvy phenomenon is to be sought in Israel's political and social history. It was the parties of the left, and predominantly Ahdut Haavodah, and later Mapai, which developed the political institutions of the country and were instrumental in absorbing the immigrants who came later. If in Europe the leaders of socialism had to struggle to unite the workers to battle with the establishment of the right, in Israel the pattern was reversed. The establishment was of the left—and operated in the name of the workers. The newcomers were to be absorbed in existing socialist organizations; those who balked and tried to express their opposition to the establishment found a ready ally in the rightist Herut movement and the more centrist Liberal party. The real proletariat of Israel was increasingly rejected by the establishment socialists and as their frustrations grew so too did their search for political outlets for their perceived deprivation.

That the growth of the "right" is a reaction to the "left" can be understood by contrasting the Israeli experience to that of Europe. In Europe, since the beginning of the century, the "left" worked and organized to replace the forces of the "right"— the establishment—in power. Now suppose that it is the "left" which is in power, which has privileged positions, which is associated with the faults of the existing system. The focus of identification for the out-group in this case would be the "right" and not the "left." If we recall that these terms are relative, Israeli politics make much more sense. On May 5, 1789, the "left" emerged because the nobility took the place of honor to the King's right at the first joint meeting of the States-General in France, and the Third Estate was on the King's left. On July 20, 1981, the Likud was on the left of the Knesset chairman, because that provided better exposure to the television cameras covering the opening session of the Tenth Knesset. The Alignment, although members of the Socialist international, were on the chairman's right because the Likud had the majority in the committee that decided on such arrangements. Left and right in Israel are a product of the political party system and achieve their meaning by virtue of the parties and not from the ideological direction which they might provide.

Two factors which are closely related to the rise of the "right" are the political and demographic changes which have occured in Israel since independence. Until 1967, Herut and Begin were ostracized by the Mapai establishment as being outside the system of consensus prior to the formation of the state. In 1967, in the period before the Six-Day War, Gahal (a combination of the Herut movement and the Liberal party) joined the National Unity Government and Begin became a minister in the government of Israel. This legitimacy was enhanced by the fact that Gahal left the National Unity Government well before the 1973 Yom Kippur War which highlighted the process of decline of dominance of the Alignment. Not only were the political fortunes of the Likud and Begin picking up because the political fortunes of the Alignment were turning down, time was working in the Likud's favor. Twenty-five years after independence, a sizable portion of the electorate did not know of the stigma which Begin carried, let alone why. The inter-group fights of the past generation occupied older people and scholars but not the man on the street. His conceptual world of politics was different and with it the role of the "right' and the Likud.

The ascent of the right could be seen in the organizations of *both* parties. It was the Herut in the Likud and Rafi[4] in the Alignment that were becoming dominant. The Liberal party and the other components of Likud were hardly visible and certainly unimportant ideologically. In the Alignment, the dominant role of *Mapai* crumbled and the younger Rafi leaders (Peres, Dayan, Navon) became more influential. The ideological differences within the parties were often greater than those between parties.

Ethnic Polarization

The 1981 elections witnessed an unprecedented crystallization of ethnic differences in Israeli politics. There had always been undercurrents of ethnic politics in Israel's cacophonic symphony, but rather than remaining the counterpoint, in 1981 it became the dominant melody.

Every group develops rules of selection and rejection of members. Often-used criteria include race, religion, sex and—in the modern world—nationality. A group is partially defined by those who are excluded from its ranks. In the broadest sense, the most important ethnic difference in the Middle East as far as Israel is concerned is that between Jews and non-Jews. Jews are a small minority in the region, a majority in the state. Within the state, the non-Jewish groups (predominantly Arabs and Druse) are known in Israel as the "minorities"—a good example of a Hebrew concept with ideological loading. It is true that the Arabs and Druse are a numerical minority within the boundaries of pre-Six-Day War Israel of 1967; referring to them as minorities carries the clear political message that a Jewish state means a Jewish majority. Sometimes, though, it appears that this usage restricts the ability of the language to portray adequately their religious and cultural affinity to Arabs and Druse in the territories and in the neighboring countries.

When ethnic differences are discussed in Israel today, the likely connotation is to differences among Jewish groups and not between Jews and non-Jews. The major distinction among Jews is between Ashkenazi, who came to Israel from Europe and America, and Sephardi, who immigrated from countries of Asia and Africa. Scholars would find this distinction too simplistic and they would demand that finer distinctions be introduced. But for our purposes this basic distinction will suffice; it is popularly used in Israel and the Central Bureau of Statistics reports data based on place of birth and father's place of birth. There is a very high correlation between the European-America born and Ashkenazi and the Asian-African born and Sephardi. The original distinction between the groups relates to the patterns of sojourning of the various communities following different expulsions throughout history, but a useful gauge is the indigenous language once spoken in the community—Yiddish in the case of the Ashkenazi, Ladino by the Sephardi. This measure is only approximate since southern European Jews often spoke Ladino and not Yiddish and the Yemenites spoke neither.

Demographics
As our concern is with politics in Israel today and not with a definitive delineation of the various ethnic groups in Israel, we will not delve into the fascinating topic of intra-ethnic differences within the Jewish community. Suffice it to say that the differences between Iraqi and Moroccan Jews (both Separdi) are as great or greater than the differences between Russian and German Jews (both Ashkenazi). The more recent interaction of these Jews with their host country varied their common heritage as Sephardi or Ashkenazi just as a more distant history varied the common heritage shared by all Jews as they were developing the rituals, traditions and language shared only by Ashkenazi or Sephardi.

For our discussion, these basic data are needed:

1. Jews comprise about eighty-four percent of Israel's population, Arabs and Druse living within the pre-1967 borders and in Jerusalem—but excluding those living in areas under Israeli military jurisdiction—make up the other 16 percent.

2. Of the fourteen and a half million Jews in the world, some 22 percent live in Israel. About 85 percent of the world's Jews are Ashkenazi, the other 15 percent Sephardi. About 10 percent of the world's Ashkenazi live in Israel compared with about two-thirds of the Sephardi. The Sephardi, however, make up about 55 percent of Israel's Jewish population, and the Ashkenazi about 45 percent.

3. The composition of the two ethnic groups in terms of place of birth is different. Of Israel's 3.2 million Jews at the beginning of 1981, more than 800,000 were born in Europe and America, almost 650,000 in Asia and Africa. The number of Israeli-born whose fathers were born in Europe and America was a little over 525,000, whereas the Israeli-born of Asian and African-born fathers numbered more than 800,000. An additional half million were born in Israel of fathers who were also born in Israel. At this stage of Israel's development—but not in fifteen or twenty years—it is safe to conclude that most of the last group are Ashkenazi, reflecting their earlier arrival in the country.

4. The reproduction rates of the various ethnic groups are also different, although increasingly less so. The gross reproduction rate of Jewish mothers born in Asia and Africa was 1.48 in 1979 compared with 2.04 in 1969; for European and American born Jewish mothers it was 1.30 in 1979 compared with 1.32 in 1969. Part of this change is caused by the fact that the foreign-born population of both ethnic groups is aging and the largest fertile group now tends to be the Israeli-born. That group's rate has fallen too, from 1.43 in 1969 to 1.33 in 1979.[5]

5. Because the age structure and the growth rates of the groups differ, the impact on the political system through the composition of the electorate is not identical. European-American-born voters and their Israeli-born children comprised a majority of the electorate in 1981, as they did in past elections, but it is clear that they will soon be smaller in number than the Asian-African voters and their Israeli-born voting children. We have seen that the latter group is already a majority of the Jewish population and that their growth rates are higher than the Europeans'. In the 1981 elections the Ashkenazi had a voting potential of 52 Knesset seats, the Sephardi 48. The shrinking of the Ashkenazi base is evident when compared with their potential in the 1969 elections; 59 for the Ashkenazi, 43 for the Sephardi. The potential of the Sephardi will be more fully realized when their children who are under voting age (53.7 percent of the Asian-African children, 35.8 percent for the European-

American children) begin voting, and when the Ashkenazi, who tend to be older and who have fewer children, make up an increasingly smaller percentage of the electorate. (Arabs and Druse constitute 10 percent of the electorate.)

6. Projecting these figures into the future and thereby calculating the composition of the electorate is risky since the population of Israel has known great fluctuations in the past and is likely to do so in the future. Israel is a country whose past was largely determined by immigrants and whose ideology is still based on the central concept of gathering in the exiled Jews of the world. The Jewish population in 1948 was made up of a little more than a third Israel-born; in 1980, about 55 percent were Israel-born. Population change in Israel is not simply a matter of fertility rates and life expectancies but is also determined directly by immigration—and of course by emigration.

7. Although we have stressed the importance of ethnic polarization in the 1981 elections, the impression that this will be an important factor in future elections must be avoided. Much of Israel's future political life will turn on this very factor. At this point in the analysis it is important to stress that there is no deterministic force at work making it inevitable that ethnic differences will again be as salient in the future as they were in the 1981 elections. Things may be very different when the "desert generation" of Jews who immigrated to the country will no longer be dominant numerically, culturally and politically, and a new Israel-born generation emerges. The language gauge used before probably allows us a glimpse of the future: the young Israel-born generation speaks neither Yiddish nor Ladino (or Arabic)—all speak Hebrew.

Measures of ethnic integration abound but one will suffice. The rates of Jews marrying across ethnic lines rose from 12 percent in 1955 to 20 percent in 1978. Not only that, but the social acceptability of the behavior increased in the sense that the rates of inter-ethnic marriage of both grooms and brides became more nearly equal. In 1955 a little over a third of the marriages were between a groom from Asia-Africa and a European-American bride, with two-thirds the reverse pattern. In 1978 the Asian-African groom and the European-American bride combination accounted for almost half of the marriages, the reverse combination the other half. The fact that the two types of marriage are equally prevalent points to the increasing social acceptability of inter-ethnic Jewish marriages in Israel since, while both types of marriage are on the rise, it is the marriage of the high-status bride (European-American) with the lower-status groom (Asian-African) which is increasing faster.

The Political Dimension

The 1981 elections witnessed the two major parties clearly identified with ethnic groups—the Alignment with the Ashkenazi and the Likud with the Sephardi. This correlation with electoral behavior became more pronounced than in the past, although the general pattern was not a new one.

The Alignment had enjoyed the role of dominant party in the political system which it had founded and shaped. It was the major political force in the 1920s, in those early formative years of the British Mandate, when the major political institutions of the country, such as the Histadrut (the General Federation of Labor), were developed. Its leadership spoke for the young pioneers, newly arrived from Eastern Europe, anxious to fulfill the Zionist dream under very difficult economic and physical conditions. By the time the larger waves of immigration began coming in the period before the Second World War and immediately after the proclamation of independence, the forebears of the Labor party were firmly in position as leaders of the state soon to be proclaimed.

During this period Mapai (later Labor) and the Histadrut which it controlled, filled many functions and provided many services generally provided for by the modern state. Defense, education, housing, employment, culture, health, manufacturing and sport, among others, were activities which were sponsored and/or controlled by the party. It is no wonder then that new immigrants were often caught up in the web of the party. There may be no similar experience in a normal adult's life parallel to the dependency encountered after immigration to a foreign country. Certain features may ameliorate that dependency: for example, if the same language is spoken as in the home country or if one intermingles exclusively with compatriots from the country of origin. To be sure, some immigrants to Israel continued to speak German, Yiddish, English or Arabic and avoided some of the culture-shock of the new society. But for those who were forced to deal with the new reality, some special footing in the system was always helpful. Being affiliated with one of the parties was often such a footing and, since it was the biggest and most powerful of the parties, Mapai was successful in recruiting the largest number of immigrants.

Recruiting meant winning voters. The leaders of the labor movement realized that the ultimate test of their appeal was at the polls. The legitimacy accorded them by independence and sovereignty aided them mightily and some new immigrants could not easily distinguish between the state, the army, the party and Ben-Gurion.

The Irgun Zvai Leumi, the militia headed by Begin which later formed the core of the Herut Movement, was stigmatized as being an underground organization, outside the structure of the national institutions headed by Mapai. This was ironic since the activities of the Haganah and Palmah were equally illegal from the British point of view, but the power to define legitimate and illegitimate was held by the leaders of Mapai. Ben-Gurion placed them in the company of the other ostracized group when he declared that all parties were candidates for his coalition government except the Communists and Herut.

Mapai proved itself a model "party of democratic integration" by being flexible enough to attract large groups of voters and their leaders through changes in government and party policy and by revising ideological planks in its platform. It carried a large number of European votes since many of them had been oriented in youth groups abroad to the leadership and institutional arrangements which Mapai developed. Many of the new immigrant groups from non-European countries also supported Mapai for organizational, ideological and pragmatic reasons.

The important point to stress is that while an increasingly large share of the electorate was of Sephardi origin, Mapai maintained its dominant role as the largest plurality party and the leader of every government coalition. More than that, attempts to appeal to the Sephardi population at election time by lists set up by Sephardi themselves, largely failed. It was only before the mass immigration of the early fifties that representation to the Knesset was achieved by lists manifestly linking themselves with the Sephardi and Yemenites.

The point that must be clearly made was that neither of Israel's major political parties in 1981 was ethnic in the sense that neither had organized politically in order to further specific ethnic ends. The electoral support of both parties was largely ethnic-related, but that is another matter entirely. Both the Alignment and the Likud were run by Ashkenazi, as had always been the case with most parties in Israel. While the appeal to the ethnic vote characterized the 1981 elections, and the social bases of political support were more closely related to ethnicity than ever, the parties themselves were not ethnic.

In fact, the Alignment tried to deal with its problem of lacking appeal among Sephardi voters by placing Sephardi in places assured of election on its list. By any mechanical measure of representation, the Alignment did this more successfully than did the Likud. Of the members of Knesset elected by the two parties, the Alignment had fourteen Sephardi, the Likud nine. Both parties were led by men born in Poland, but both put Sephardi in the number-two slot. The Alignment had a Sephardi woman, Shoshanah Arbeli-Almozlino, as its number two on its list. She was born in Iraq and had been a very effective parliamentarian in the out-going Knesset. The Likud made David Levi number-two. Minister of Housing and Immigrant Absorption and the Likud's candidate to head the Histadrut, Levi was born in Morocco and lived in Beit-Shean, a development town in northern Israel which is beset by many of the social and economic problems with which the underprivileged population must contend.

The Alignment may have been helped by having Arbeli-Almozlino in second place; the Likud was certainly not harmed by making Levi prominent. Everyone knows that the second place on the list has symbolic value only and no one thought that it promised anything about power or succession. In general, representation was not the issue. When asked what group you wanted to see better represented in the party list for which you intend to vote, only 11 percent mentioned an ethnic group while 34 percent wanted younger people, fresh faces. The Likud enjoyed the more favorable image; the number of its Sephardi candidates was irrelevant to the issue.

In the 1981 elections the term "ethnic party" was used often. It was supposed to portray the support of the Jews from Asian and African countries and their children for the Likud. The fact is that the Alignment was closer to being an "ethnic party" than was the Likud. The larger concentration of voters by ethnicity was to be found in the Alignment, with some 70 percent of its voters Ashkenazi. The percentage of the Likud voters who were Sephardi was 65. This had not always been the case. When dominant, the Alignment was heavily supported by Ashkenazi, but Sephardi also often voted for the Alignment. The bulk of the Likud's support also came from Ashkenazi in the past; after all, the Ashkenazi comprised a majority of the electorate. The

Likud was set up in the seventies; its constituent parties in the fifties and sixties, the Herut Movement and the Liberal party, drew from either end of the social and ethnic spectrum. Herut was heavily supported by lower-class Sephardi, the Liberals by upper-class Ashkenazi.

Polls going back to the late 1960s indicate that then too about 70 percent of the Alignment vote was from Ashkenazi. What has been changing on the political map of Israel is the ethnic composition of the Likud vote and the relative size of the two parties. In the late sixties both parties were predominantly Ashkenazi; by 1981 the Alignment had stayed that way and the Likud had become predominantly Sephardi. The turning point seems to have occurred in 1977 when a majority of the Likud vote was Sephardi for the first time. Couple this with the growth of the Sephardi electorate and the abandonment of the Alignment by many Ashkenazi in favor of the DMC in 1977, and the enormity of the Alignment's problem becomes clearer. The period of incubation of the bitterness and frustrations felt against the ruling Alignment ended before the 1977 elections and expressed itself in the vote. In 1981 the Sephardi continued in their alienation from the Alignment; many Ashkenazi who had deserted in 1977 returned.

We have described the contribution of each ethnic group to the two parties, and have found that the portion of the Ashkenazi in the Alignment electorate had been high and consistent regardless of the fluctuations in the size of the Alignment vote, and that the Sephardi as a portion of the Likud vote has been growing and was, in 1981, slightly lower than the Ashkenazi portion of the Alignment vote. By turning the question around and asking how members of the two ethnic groups divided their votes in 1981 between the two large parties we get a mirror-image answer. About 60 percent of Ashkenazi voted Alignment, about 30 percent Likud. About 60 percent Sephardi voted Likud, about 30 percent Alignment.

The fortunes of the Likud and the misfortunes of the Alignment are evident along generation lines as well as the ethnic and demographic ones. The Likud does even better among the second generation of Sephardi than it does in the first. The Alignment's support is greater among Ashkenazi who immigrated than among their children who were born in Israel. The Likud has gained most in those groups which are youngest and growing fastest; the Alignment—gradually losing support within all groups—does best in that group which is oldest and shrinking most rapidly.

Neither the Likud nor the Alignment were "ethnic parties" in 1981. Neither of them organized along ethnic lines or carried an overt ethnic message. Almost a third of the "wrong" ethnic group voted for each party.

The Tami Phenomenon

There was one ethnic list in 1981 that was successful. That was Tami, former Minister of Religions Aharon Abuhazeira's[6] party, which won three Knesset seats. Abuhazeira had been cleared of charges of bribery soon before the election and split from the National Religious Party on the grounds that Sephardi were not adequately represented in the NRP and the other political parties. Abuhazeira managed to recruit a former Agriculture Minister from the Alignment, Aharon Uzan,[7] who relinquished his place on the Alignment list in order to run on Tami's. Together with other leaders, they presented a Sephardi list with special appeal to Moroccan voters. The Moroccan Jews are the largest Sephardi group in the country and are unproportionally concentrated in its lower classes. The Moroccans who arrived in Israel in the early 1950s did not come as a complete community since many of the leadership preferred to emigrate to France. Unlike the Iraqi community which arrived with its political, economic and cultural leadership intact, the Moroccans were the slowest in achieving higher status and positions of influence. Lacking any other identifiable leadership, and with lower levels of skill, education and resources than other groups, some voters were receptive to Tami's arguments. Abuhazeira also capitalized on his being a scion of a prominent rabbinical family in Morocco and so for some his political plea turned into a religious appeal as well.

The emergence of lists trying to tap ethnic resentment is not new; what was special was its partial success in 1981 and its appearance during a campaign charged with ethnic tension. Tami's 45,000 votes were the clearest, most authentic expression of ethnic political organization to have appeared in these elections. But its appeal must also be measured against previous efforts. In the past two elections, ethnic lists had competed and, while they did not win representation, they came close. In 1973, the Black Panthers and Avner Shaki's[8] list, which split from the NRP, received almost 25,000 votes between them and in 1977, Ben-Porat's[9] list (an Iraqi who was number two on Dayan's list in 1981) won almost 15,000 votes. With ethnic representation becoming more prevalent in the major parties, the likelihood of great success for ethnic lists in the future seems small. Despite Tami's gains, the rule remains that most voters—both Sephardi and Ashkenazi—tend to support the mainstream national lists.

Conclusion

The 1981 election results reflected deeper social processes. One of the most important of these was the clear emergence of social class politics in Israel. Ethnic polarization was the outward expression of the unrealized expectations of many Sephardi who had aspired to, and reached, the middle class but were stymied in their mobility, and the reaction of the Ashkenazi who were fearful that their privileged status was in jeopardy. It is fashionable to discuss the ethnic problem as if its focus was in the development towns of Israel and the underprivileged neighbourhoods of the big cities, but the statistical fact is that the Jews living in these places constitute a minority of the

Sephardi community. Their problems are most acute and therefore most visible, but the bulk of the Sephardi voters have achieved middle to high levels of education and income to an extent greater than the stereotype of the slum-dweller permits. The feeling that the Alignment's vision of society meant the continued domination of Ashkenazi and the continued relegation of Sephardi to secondary levels of management, status and power, was as important a reason as any other for the massive support of the Likud by the Sephardi.

Another pressing issue, barely mentioned in the campaign, is the fundamental justification and goal of the State of Israel. Many Ashkenazi tend to accept the vision of Israel as a modern, liberal, Western state. The continued domination over a vast Arab population in the territories presents a problem for holders of this view. Another way of conceiving the Jewish state is that its legitimacy stems from basically religious sources. Whether God-given or not, the ties between the people, its history and the land are ultimately a matter of belief and therefore differ basically from the rationalist model of the modern state. Many Sephardi, who tend to be more traditional, respond to the logic of the religion-sanctioned state. Begin utilizes the symbols and language of religion masterfully; the Alignment, while attacking the religious parties and their disproportionate gains through coalition bargaining, appeared at times to be anti-religious.

Ethnicity is an extremely important factor in Israeli political life today, but its centrality is likely to prove transitory. Much more crucial in the long run are social cleavages based on class differences and divisions concerned with religion and religiosity. One of the reasons that the 1981 elections were so violent and polarized was that these cleavages overlapped. The upper-class secularist—who also tended to be Ashkenazi—voted Alignment. The lower-class traditionalist—who also tended to be Sephardi—voted Likud. The fact that these dimensions laced together accelerated the

effect of each of them. Ethnicity will remain a central issue as long as the overlapping exists. But if the Alignment's practices and image change, and significant groups of the Sephardi community perceive it to be open to Sephardi leaders, aspirations and demands, the tension of the ethnic element will lessen in Israeli politics. But if the growing Sephardi population does not perceive such a change on the part of the Alignment, the Likud's fortunes are likely to continue to grow. It is useless to speculate here what effects changes of leadership in either party, international crises, massive immigration—to name but a few—might have on the equation. What is important to stress is that ethnic polarization is the symptom of a more fundamental cleavage within the Israeli society and polity.

There is an ideological consensus within Israeli society clearly establishing the norm of equality for all Jews as a direct extension of the notion of "gathering in the exiles." Ethnic political organization does not conform to this norm. There is of course no similar consensus regarding religion. That religious groups have organized politically and have always been successful in gaining at least some of their demands by being partners in the government coalitions has meant that the religious cleavage has been cushioned by being part of the legitimized struggle for power through the electoral and coalition processes. Organizing politically over ethnic differences, in contrast, has never been legitimized in the sense that most efforts have been unsuccessful. The norm being unity, the evidence of ethnic polarization in the 1981 elections was shocking. The unsettling—and even dangerous—features of the emergence of ethnicity is that it correlates so strongly with other indicators of social mobility. As long as the Alignment is perceived as denying opportunities for continued social advancement, the growing Sephardi community is unlikely to vote for it.

The Alignment did not use the power bases in its control—the Histadrut, the kibbutzim, the Sick Fund, the workers' councils—to restore its image as a worker's party. On the contrary, its elitist, Ashkenazi image was augmented over the years. The Likud benefited from the Alignment's stagnation, in part because of its popular policies, in part because of Begin's appeal.

The Likud capitalized on the Alignment's internal divisions and establishment image. As it becomes more comfortable in government power, the demands made on it are likely to grow. Simply castigating the Alignment's failures will no longer be enough. It must develop policies and a second generation of leadership equal to the expectations of the growing Sephardi electorate without alienating the large number of Ashkenazi who support it. The Likud will enjoy many of the advantages—and be exposed to the political dangers—which they won at the polls.

NOTES

1. Soon after the elections, Shulamit Aloni joined the Alignment, making the size of the Knesset delegations of the two largest groups equal (Arian's note).

2. Yoram Aridor (b. 1933), Israeli minister of finance, 1981–1983. Aridor, a member of Herut, originally entered the Likud government as minister of communications in January 1981, but in less than three weeks also acquired the finance portfolio when Yigal Hurvitz resigned over economic policy differences. (Hurvitz's resignation was accompanied by the defection of former Rafi members from the Likud.) With Aridor's appointment, the government implemented controversial economic policies designed to buy votes by reducing taxes on major appliances and luxury goods. The new measures were supposed to be temporary but two years later still have not been rescinded. The economic crisis of early 1983 again focused public debate on Aridor's controversial policies. As the economic crisis worsened, Aridor announced his resignation on October 12—only two days after the formation of the Shamir government—following a controversial proposal to link consumer prices to the dollar.

3. In the spring of 1981 Syria placed sophisticated Soviet missiles in Lebanon. Israel considered this move provocative and a danger to its security and threatened a preemptive strike against these sites if Syria did not unilaterally remove the missiles. The United States restrained Israel from this move. Nevertheless, the situation in Lebanon deteriorated (see doc. 79).

4. Rafi (acronym for Reshimat Poalei Israel; lit., Israel Workers' List), originally a faction, led by Ben-Gurion, within Mapai but wishing to submit a separate list for the elections. After faction members were expelled from Mapai, Rafi became a separate party. The leaders were David Ben-Gurion, Shimon Peres, Yosef Almogi (a cabinet member and secretary general of Mapai, 1959–62), and later Moshe Dayan. Most of Rafi united with Mapai (and Ahdut Haavodah) in January 1968 to form the Israel Labor party, but another faction, the Reshimah Mamlakhtit (lit., State List, or National List) remained independent only to later join the Likud alignment. The State list, much of the Greater Land of Israel movement, and the faction of the Free Center that had remained in the Likud formed the Laam (lit., For the People) faction within the Likud. The former Rafi members left the Likud on January 12, 1981.

5. The gross reproduction rates of the non-Jews is much higher but it too is falling. For Muslim mothers it was 4.36 in 1969 and 3.22 in 1979; for Druze 3.59 in 1969 and 3.14 in 1979 (Arian's note). The gross reproduction rate is the number of females born, per woman, given the age-specific fertility rates of the population. It is thus a measure of the extent to which a population reproduces itself.

6. Aharon Abuhazeira (b. 1938), former minister in both Begin cabinets and mayor of Ramlah, 1971–77. Abuhazeira first entered the government in 1977 as minister of religious affairs and as a member of the National Religious party. Prior to the 1981 elections he was implicated in a scandal involving bribes and the misuse of public funds while mayor of Ramlah. The affair shook the NRP and affected Abuhazeira's status in the government and party. In mid-May 1981, following the second indictment against him, the Knesset forced Abuhazeira to leave the cabinet. (About a week later he was acquitted of the bribery charges.) In the summer of 1981 he formed the Tami party and, following the establishment of

the second Likud government in August 1981, he was again given a portfolio—minister of labor and social affairs and of immigrants' absorption. However, on November 22, 1981, he took a leave of absence and finally submitted his resignation on April 30, 1982 (which, by law, took effect forty-eight hours later). He was eventually convicted in early 1982 on another charge, connected to the abuse of funds while mayor, and began serving his sentence in October 1983.

7. Aharon Uzan (b. 1924), successor to Abu-hazeira as minister of labor, social affairs, and immigrants' absorption. Uzan, who was born in Tunisia, is a former member of the Labor party secretariat and a former general secretary of the Tnuat Hamoshavim (Moshav movement). In 1975 he became minister of immigrants' absorption before inheriting Abuhazeira's portfolio.

8. Avner Shaki, former member of the NRP. In 1972 Shlomo Lorincz of Agudat Israel introduced a bill into the Knesset that would have amended the Law of Return (see doc. 6) so that a Jew would be defined as someone born to a Jewish mother or converted according to the Orthodox interpretation of Jewish law. Hence the Lorincz Bill would have had the effect of overturn-ing the Supreme Court decision in the "Brother Daniel" case (see doc. 34). Shaki was deputy minister of education at the time and voted for the bill despite the fact that the NRP—which was a member of the coalition and had pledged not to change the status quo regarding religious affairs—abstained in the Knesset vote. Shaki then resigned his post and his membership in the NRP. In 1973 he led the Social Equality movement list, which received 10,202 votes but no seats.

9. Moredekhai Ben-Porat (b. 1923), minister without portfolio in the second and third Likud cabinets. Ben-Porat, who was a member of Mapai, Rafi, and the Labor party, left the Labor party to lead the Zionist and Social Renewal party in 1977. In the 1981 elections he joined Moshe Dayan's Telem. With the death of Dayan the party ceased to be a coherent political organization, and in the summer of 1982 the remnants of Telem joined the Likud coalition in return for Ben-Porat's ministerial appointment, which was confirmed by the Knesset on July 5, 1982. During the First Arab-Israeli War, Ben-Porat was sent back to his birthplace, Iraq, to organize Operation Ezra and Nehemiah, the underground organization of immigration to Israel.

1973–83
Foreign Policy Issues

70. Ending the October 1973 War

Israel's foreign relations following 1973 were dominated by the impact and consequences of the October 1973 War, primarily by the inauguration of the "peace process"—the efforts to settle the Arab-Israeli conflict through political means. Negotiations began with the agreements terminating the war itself. The following series of documents records the transition from the military hostilities to the process of peace-making.

On October 22, 1973, the United Nations Security Council adopted Resolution 338, which was based on the joint U.S.-Soviet draft proposal. Israel immediately accepted the proposal, and later that day the U.S. secretary of state, Henry Kissinger, conferred with the Israeli prime minister and senior ministers, explaining the background for the resolution. It resulted in the cease-fires of October 22 and 24 with Syria and Egypt respectively. The first document in this series is the Israeli cabinet decision of October 22, which includes the text of Resolution 338.

The cease-fire with Egypt left the Egyptian Third Army in the Sinai Peninsula completely surrounded by Israeli troops, and Israeli troops on the western bank of the Suez Canal. The Six-Point Agreement of November 11, 1973, reached through Kissinger's mediation, was signed by Israeli and Egyptian military officers at Kilometer 101 on the Cairo-Suez road. It regulated some of the immediate problems threatening to undermine the fragile cease-fire.

The Sixth Arab Summit Conference, which met in Algiers in November 1973, formulated the new Arab consensus on the terms for a settlement of the Arab-Israeli conflict. This enabled Egypt and Syria to sign the disengagement agreements of 1974, which led to troop withdrawals from the borders. Included with the official published text of the November 1973 summit meeting of the Arab League are the unpublished "secret" resolutions as they were reported in the Arabic-language Beirut newspaper, *Al-Nahar*.

Israeli Cabinet Decision, October 22, 1973

At its meeting this morning (Monday), the cabinet decided unanimously to accept the proposal of the U.S. government and President Nixon and to announce its readiness to agree to a cease-fire in accordance with the Security Council resolution following the joint U.S.-Soviet draft proposal.

Under the terms of this proposed resolution, the military forces will remain in the positions they occupy upon the coming into effect of the cease-fire. Israel will insist on an exchange of prisoners.

The implementation of the cease-fire is conditional upon reciprocity.

The cabinet decision will be brought to the notice of the Foreign Affairs and Defense Committee and of the Knesset.

The proposed U.S.-Soviet resolution submitted to the Security Council [and passed as Resolution 338] reads as follows:

The Security Council:

1. Calls upon all parties to the present fighting to cease all firing and terminate all military activity immediately, not later than twelve hours after the

Source: Meron Medzini, ed., *Israel's Foreign Relations: Selected Documents, 1947–74* (Jerusalem: Ministry of Foreign Affairs, 1976), 2:1052–53, 1067, 1074–77. Reprinted by permission of the director general, Ministry of Foreign Affairs, Jerusalem.

moment of the adoption of this decision, in the positions they now occupy.

2. Calls upon the parties concerned to start immediately after the cease-fire the implementation of Security Council Resolution 242 (1967) [see doc. 53] in all its parts.

3. Decides that immediately and concurrently with the cease-fire, negotiations start between the parties concerned under appropriate auspices aimed at establishing a just and durable peace in the Middle East.

With regard to paragraph 2 of the proposed resolution, the cabinet has decided to instruct Israel's representative at the United Nations to include in his address to the Security Council a passage clarifying that Israel's agreement to this paragraph is given in the meaning defined by Israel when she decided, in August 1970, to accept the initiative of the U.S. government regarding the cease-fire as notified to the United Nations on August 4, 1970, and as announced by the prime minister, Mrs. Golda Meir, in the Knesset on the same date.

The minister of defense and the chief of staff reported on the situation on the battlefronts.

At 4 P.M. the government issued the following statement:

The Government of Israel has been informed that the Government of Egypt has instructed the armed forces of Egypt to cease hostilities in accordance with the Security Council Resolution concerning the cease-fire.

Following upon this, the Government of Israel has issued orders to the Israel Defense Forces on the Egyptian front to stop firing at 1850 hours Israel time today, October 22, provided it is confirmed that the Egyptians have indeed ceased hostilities.

The Six-Point Agreement, November 11, 1973

1. Egypt and Israel agree to observe scrupulously the cease-fire called for by the U.N. Security Council.

2. Both sides agree that discussions between them will begin immediately to settle the question of the return to the October 22 positions in the framework of agreement on the disengagement and separation of forces under the auspices of the United Nations.

3. The town of Suez will receive daily supplies of food, water, and medicines. All wounded civilians in the town of Suez will be evacuated.

4. There shall be no impediment to the movement of nonmilitary supplies to the east bank of the Suez Canal.

5. The Israeli check-points on the Cairo-Suez road will be replaced by U.N. checkpoints. At the Suez end of the road, Israeli officers can participate with the U.N. in supervising the nonmilitary nature of the cargo at the bank of the Canal.

6. As soon as the U.N. checkpoints are established on the Cairo-Suez road, there will be an exchange of all prisoners of war, including wounded.

Sixth Arab Summit Conference, Algiers, November 28, 1973

The Arab world is passing through a decisive stage in its history. The struggle against Zionist invasion is a long-term historic responsibility which will require still further trials and sacrifices.

While the war of October 1973 showed the Arab nation's determination to liberate its occupied territories at all cost, the cease-fire in the field means in no way that the struggle has ended and that there can be imposed upon the Arab nation a solution not meeting its just goals.

So long as the causes of the war of agression and expansion, which put the world on the edge of a generalised conflict, are not eliminated, there will be in the

Middle East neither a lasting peace nor true security.

The October War, like those that took place earlier, is an unavoidable consequence of the policy of aggression and *fait accompli* pursued by Israel in defiance of principles and decisions by international organizations and of the law of nations. Since the spoliation of the Palestinian people and its expulsion from its fatherland, Israel has not ceased expanding, taking advantage of the active complicity and economic, technological and military support of the imperialist countries and above all of the United States.

This collusion came to light recently in the mobilization of unprecedented financial and material means, a massive use of specialized mercenaries and the unleashing of a political campaign pursued in union by all the enemies of the Third World's emancipation.

Beyond its policy of war and territorial expansion, Israel also aims, in the framework of the imperialist strategy, at destroying all the possibilities of development by the peoples in the area. At this juncture, marked by the rise of the movements of national liberation and decolonization, Zionism thus appears as a serious resurgence of the colonial system and its methods of domination and economic exploitation.

In spite of the complicity binding Israel and international imperialism, which puts at its disposal the most refined means for the pursuit of its aggressive designs, the Arab nation has never abandoned its national goals nor has it backed down before the imperatives of its struggle. Far from weakening its national will, the setback and trials have only stimulated and strengthened it.

In October 1973, the Egyptian and Syrian armed forces, together with the Palestinian resistance supported by other Arab forces, inflicted severe blows on the Israeli aggressors.

The Arab peoples and their governments gained in this fight a sharp awareness of their responsibilities and their material and human means. This awareness resulted in practical solidarity which showed its efficiency and which forms a new dimension in the process of Arab liberation.

The expansionist character of Israel policy has become clear to all. Israel's alleged friendship with the African peoples has been unmasked and alone in Africa, the colonialist and racist regimes of South Africa, Rhodesia, and Portugal lend it their support.

Israel's policy has likewise been openly condemned by other nonaligned nations.

The diplomatic isolation of Israel has today become a reality. It is signicant in this respect that certain European governments, which traditionally have been won over to the Israeli viewpoint, are beginning to wonder about the foundations of an adventurous policy which has raised grave risks for international peace and cooperation.

The cease-fire, put into force more than a month ago, still keeps running into the Israeli side's manoeuvres and obstruction.

The cease-fire is not yet peace and peace presupposes, if it is to be achieved, a certain number of conditions. Among these are two which are paramount and unchangeable: (1) Evacuation by Israel of the occupied Arab territories and first of all Jerusalem; (2) reestablishment of full national rights for the Palestinian people.

So long as these two conditions have not been met, it will be illusory to expect in the Middle East anything but a continuation of unstable and explosive situations and new confrontations.

There is no doubt that the Arab nation will never agree to engage its future in an equivocal way with the sole basis being vague promises and secret dealings. . . .

Peace can be achieved only in full light, far from all manoeuvres and scheming and on the basis of the principles spelled out in this declaration. Thus the Arab countries, kings and chiefs of state believe that any serious and constructive coordination of their policies must take place on this basis.

If the conditions of a just peace are not available and if the Arab efforts in favour of peace run into refusal from Israel and its allies, the Arab countries will be forced to draw all the consequences and to continue, in the long-term perspective, their liberation struggle by all means and in all fields.

Determined to accomplish its duty, ready for sacrifices and abnegation, the Arab nation will not cease intensifying its struggle.

Secret Resolutions of the Algiers Summit Conference

The Current Goals of the Arab Nation

The conference resolves that the goals of the current phase of the common Arab struggle are:

1. The complete liberation of all the Arab territories conquered during the aggression of June 1967, with no concession or abandonment of any part of them, or detriment to national sovereignty over them.

2. Liberation of the Arab city of Jerusalem, and rejection of any situation that may be harmful to complete Arab sovereignty over the Holy City.

3. Commitment to restoration of the national rights of the Palestinian people, according to the decisions of the Palestine Liberation Organization, as the sole representative of the Palestine nation. (The Hashemite Kingdom of Jordan expressed reservations.)

4. The Palestine problem is the affair of all the Arabs, and no Arab party can possibly dissociate itself from this commitment, in the light of the resolutions of previous summit conferences.

Military

In view of continuation of the struggle against the enemy until the goals of our nation are attained, the liberation of the occupied territories and the restoration of the national rights of the Palestinian people, the conference resolves:

1. Solidarity of all the Arab States with Egypt, Syria and the Palestinian nation, in the common struggle for attainment of the just goals of the Arabs.

2. Provision of all means of military and financial support to both fronts—Egyptian and Syrian—to strengthen their military capacity for embarking on the liberation campaign and standing fast in face of the tremendous amount of supplies and unlimited aid received by the enemy.

3. Support of Palestinian resistance by all possible measures, to ensure its active role in the campaign.

Economic

Considering the significance of the economy in the campaign against the enemy and the need to use every weapon at the disposal of the Arabs, as well as to concentrate all resources to enhance fighting capacity, the conference resolves:

1. To strengthen economic ties among the Arab states, and empower the Arab Economic Council to set up a plan of operations to that end.

2. To continue the use of oil as a weapon in the campaign, in view of the resolutions of the oil ministers and the link between the revocation of the ban on oil exports to any country and the commitment of that country to support the just cause of the Arabs. To establish a committee, subordinate to the oil Ministers, which will follow up the implementation of these resolutions and those of the oil ministers with regard to the percentage of the cut in oil supply, so as to arrive at coordination between this committee and the committee of Foreign ministers of the oil-producing countries in respect of the development of the positions of other countries vis-à-vis the Arab cause.

3. To strengthen, as is vital, the steadfast attitude within the occupied territories, and assure it.

4. To make good war-damages of the Arab states, and to heighten the spirit of struggle and the combat capacity of the countries involved in the confrontation.

Political

Political activity complements the military campaign, and is regarded as its continuation, all as part of our struggle against the enemy. As a direct result of the positions of foreign states toward the just struggle of the Arabs, the Conference resolves:

1. In Africa (a) to strengthen Arab-African cooperation in political affairs and enlarge Arab diplomatic representation in Africa; (b) to sever all the diplomatic, consular, economic, cultural and other relations with South Africa, Portugal and Rhodesia of those Arab states which have not yet done so.

SEVENTH ARAB SUMMIT CONFERENCE
71. Resolutions at Rabat

The new Arab consensus in the wake of the October 1973 War was formulated at the Algiers Summit Conference in November 1973. A year later the Arab position was reviewed and amended at Rabat. The most important resolution at Rabat installed the Palestine Liberation Organization as "the sole legitimate representative of the Palestinian people" and disqualified all others (namely Jordan) from reclaiming the West Bank, or parts of it, from Israel. The resolutions of the Seventh Arab Summit Conference were adopted on October 29, 1974. A summary, from the Lebanese newspaper *Al-Safir*, is reprinted below.

The Seventh Arab Summit Conference—having reviewed the resolutions of the Sixth Arab Summit Conference in Algiers, the developments in the Arab and international situations, and the achievements of the combined Arab action in all fields, and after the discussion of the general situation in all its aspects and having noted the report of the Foreign Minister's Council and the reports of the director general of the Arab League, resolves as follows:

The Goal of the Arab Nation
The meeting confirms the following resolutions of the Sixth Arab Summit Conference:

1. Complete liberation of all Arab territories conquered in the aggressive action of June 1967, without surrendering or disregarding any part of the territories of the injury to the national sovereignty over them.

2. Liberation of the Arab city of Jerusalem and nonacceptance of any situation containing elements that adversely affect complete Arab sovereignty over the Holy City.

3. An undertaking to restore the national rights of the Palestinain people in accordance with the resolutions taken by the PLO as the sole representative of the Palestinian people.

4. The problem of Palestine is the problem of all the Arabs, and no Arab party should give up this obligation as approved in the resolutions of the last Arab Summit conference.

Principles upon Which Combined Arab Action Will be Based
1. Strengthening the might of the Arab states, militarily, economically, and politically and continuing to build up the military

Source: Al-Safir, November 30, 1977; reprinted in Hezev, January 2, 1978, pp. 1–3.

strength of the forces for confrontation, and guaranteeing the means for this buildup.

2. Realizing the aim of efficient Arab political, military, and economic coordination that will effect the realization of Arab unity on all levels.

3. Nonacceptance of any attempt to obtain partial political settlements—this being based on the pan-Arab nature of the problem and its comprehensiveness.

4. Unswervingly maintaining the aim of all the Arab states of liberating all the conquered Arab territories and restoring the national rights of the Palestinian people.

5. Implementing a policy that will bring about Israel's isolation politically and economically and a cessation of the political, military, and economic aid she gets from any source in the world.

6. Refraining from Arab battles and contradictions, which are not central issues, so as to concentrate efforts against the Zionist enemy.

The Seventh Arab Summit Conference, following the detailed and exhaustive discussions held by the kings, presidents, and princes on the subject of the Arab situation, in general, and the Palestinian question, in particular, in its national and international senses; and having heard the announcements of King Hussein and Yasir Arafat and the pronouncements of the kings, presidents, and princes in a spirit of frankness, sincerity and full responsibility; and on the basis of the Arab leaders' assessment of the combined national responsibility that the present situation places upon them with regard to withstanding aggression and their obligations to liberate, which are a corollary of the oneness of the Arab problem and the oneness of the struggle for it; and because all understand the Zionists' attempts and plans that continue to be directed at negating the existence of a Palestinian entity and obliterating the Palestinian national entity; and because of a belief that these plans and attempts must be frustrated and reacted against by supporting this entity and that we must stand firm on our obligation to fulfill the requirements of its development and to increase its ability to restore the full rights of the Palestinian people and to shoulder its responsibility within the framework of the collective Arab commitment through close cooperation with their brothers; and basing itself upon the victories achieved by the Palestinian struggle against the Zionist enemy and on the Arab and international levels and in the United Nations, and owing to the necessity for a continuation of the combined Arab action to develop these victories and to put them into practical operation; and since everyone is convinced of all the above and of the conference's success in putting an end to the disputes between brothers by strengthening *Arab solidarity;* the Arab Summit Conference resolves as follows:

1. To confirm the right of the Palestinian people to return to its homeland and to dream of its future.

2. To confirm the right of the Palestinian people to establish an independent, national government under the leadership of the PLO as the sole legitimate representative of the Palestinian people, on all liberated Palestinian territory. The Arab states will assist this government when it is established in all fields and on all levels.

3. To assist the PLO to carry out its responsibility on the national and international levels within the framework of the Arab commitment.

4. To call upon Jordan, Syria, Egypt, and the PLO to decide upon a formula to improve the relations between them in the light of these resolutions and in order to implement them.

5. All the Arab States undertake to guard the Palestinian national unity and not to interfere in the internal affairs of Palestinian action. (The Iraqi delegation had reservations with respect to paragraphs 1–3 above.)

On the Political Level
Basing itself on the aims and principles determined by the Sixth Arab Summit Con-

ference in Algiers, and persevering with political action that will serve the defined goals of the Arab struggle, and will direct the development of our foreign relations with the various world powers, the conference resolves as follows:

1. On the level of organizations and the international arena: (a) to make use of the United Nations and its bodies to expose Israel; to obtain further resolutions on the Palestinian issue and the Middle East that will isolate Israel, politically and propaganda-wise, in world opinion, to try to achieve more effective steps to expose Israel's maneuvers and her refusal to carry out the resolutions of international organizations and to make this apparent to the world and to lay at Israel's door the blame for frustrating the attempts to establish a just peace; (b) to consolidate the cooperation with the nonaligned nations and to take action to implement the resolutions of the Fourth Summit Conference of Nonaligned

Nations and to raise the question of the introduction of sanctions mentioned in the seventh article of the U.N. Declaration against Israel and to demand that she be expelled from the United Nations. All this should take place at the Conference of Foreign Ministers of the Nonaligned Nations that will convene in summer 1975, prior to raising the issue at the 30th session of the U.N. General Assembly [see doc. 72]; (c) to continue activity intended to consolidate the Arab cooperation with Islamic governments and peoples and to make further efforts among the Islamic nations having relations with Israel to persuade them to break off these relations and to make more effective efforts to increase the role played by the Islamic world in supporting the just Arab cause in the Arab-Zionist struggle; (d) to consolidate the cooperation between the Arab League and the Organization of African Unity in all areas of activity.

72. The Anti-Zionist Resolution at the United Nations

Emboldened by the Rabat Summit (see doc. 71) and the initial success of the oil embargo, in the summer of 1975 the Arab states and the Palestine Liberation Organization launched a diplomatic offensive to condemn Israel and Zionism in international forums. The culmination of this effort occurred on November 10, 1975, when the U.N. General Assembly passed Resolution 3379 (XXX) on the elimination on all forms of racial discrimination. The text of this resolution, and Chaim Herzog's reply of the same day, are reprinted here.

Chaim Herzog, brother of Yaacov Herzog, became president of the State of Israel in May 1983. A former general in the Israeli army, Herzog served as ambassador to the United Nations during a period of growing Israeli isolation as Arab, Muslim, and Third World states, often in alliance with the Soviet bloc, joined forces on Middle Eastern issues.

Sources: United Nations Organization, General Assembly, *Resolutions of the Thirtieth Session*, pp. 83–84. Chaim Herzog, *Who Stands Accused? Israel Answers Its Critics* (New York: Random House, 1978), pp. 3–7. Reprinted by permission.

U.N. General Assembly Resolution 3379

The General Assembly,

Recalling its resolution 1904 (XVIII) of 20 November 1963, proclaiming the United Nations Declaration on the Elimination of All Forms of Racial Discrimination, and in particular its affirmation that "any doctrine of racial differentiation or superiority is scientifically false, morally condemnable, socially unjust and dangerous" and its expression of alarm at "the manifestation of racial discrimination still in evidence in some areas in the world, some of which are imposed by certain Governments by means of legislative, administrative or other measures,"

Recalling also that, in its resolution 3151 G (XXVIII) of 14 December 1973, the General Assembly condemned, *inter alia*, the unholy alliance between South African racism and zionism,

Taking note of the Declaration of Mexico on the Equality of Women and Their Contribution to Development and Peace, 1975, proclaimed by the World Conference of the International Women's Year, held at Mexico City from 19 June to 2 July 1975, which promulgated the principle that "international co-operation and peace require the achievement of national liberation and independence, the elimination of colonialism and neo-colonialism, foreign occupation, zionism, *apartheid* and racial discrimination in all its forms, as well as the recognition of the dignity of peoples and their right to self-determination,"

Taking note also of resolution 77 (XII) adopted by the Assembly of Heads of State and Government of the Organization of African Unity at its twelfth ordinary session, held at Kampala from 28 July to 1 August 1975, which considered "that the racist regime in occupied Palestine and the racist regimes in Zimbabwe and South Africa have a common imperialist origin, forming a whole and having the same racist structure and being organically linked in their policy aimed at repression of the dignity and integrity of the human being,"

Taking note also of the Political Declaration and Strategy To Strengthen International Peace and Security and To Intensify Solidarity and Mutual Assistance among Non-Aligned Countries, adopted at the Conference of Ministers for Foreign Affairs of Non-Aligned Countries held at Lima from 25 to 30 August 1975, which most severely condemned zionism as a threat to world peace and security and called upon all countries to oppose this racist and imperialist ideology,

Determines that zionism is a form of racism and racial discrimination.

Chaim Herzog, Speech to the General Assembly

It is symbolic that this debate, which may well prove to be a turning point in the fortunes of the United Nations and a decisive factor in the possible continued existence of this organization, should take place on November 10. Tonight, thirty-seven years ago, has gone down in history as Kristallnacht, the Night of the Crystals. This was the night in 1938 when Hitler's Nazi storm-troopers launched a coordinated attack on the Jewish community in Germany, burned the synagogues in all its cities and made bonfires in the streets of the Holy Books and the Scrolls of the Holy Law and Bible. It was the night when Jewish homes were attacked and heads of families taken away, many of them never to return. It was the night when the windows of all Jewish businesses and stores were smashed, covering the streets in the cities of Germany with a film of broken glass which dissolved into the millions of crystals which gave that night its name. It was the night which led eventually to the crematoria and the gas chambers,

Auschwitz, Birkenau, Dachau, Buchenwald, Teresienstadt and others. It was the night which led to the most terrifying holocaust in the history of man.

It is indeed befitting, Mr. President, that this debate, conceived in the desire to deflect the Middle East from its moves towards peace and born of a deep pervading feeling of anti-Semitism, should take place on the anniversary of this day. It is indeed befitting, Mr. President, that the United Nations, which began its life as an anti-Nazi alliance, should thirty years later find itself on its way to becoming the world center of anti-Semitism. Hitler would have felt at home on a number of occasions during the past year, listening to the proceedings in this forum, and above all to the proceedings during the debate on Zionism.

It is sobering to consider to what level this body has been dragged down if we are obliged today to contemplate an attack on Zionism. For this attack constitutes not only an anti-Israeli attack of the foulest type, but also an assault in the United Nations on Judaism—one of the oldest established religions in the world, a religion which has given the world the human values of the Bible, and from which two other great religions, Christianity and Islam, sprang. Is it not tragic to consider that we here at this meeting in the year 1975 are contemplating what is a scurrilous attack on a great and established religion which has given to the world the Bible with its Ten Commandments, the great prophets of old, Moses, Isaiah, Amos; the great thinkers of history, Maimonides, Spinoza, Marx, Einstein, many of the masters of the arts and as high a percentage of the Nobel Prize-winners in the world, in sciences, in the arts and in the humanities as has been achieved by any people on earth? . . .

The resolution against Zionism was originally one condemning racism and colonialism, a subject on which we could have achieved consensus, a consensus which is of great importance to all of us and to our African colleagues in particular. However,

instead of permitting this to happen, a group of countries, drunk with the feeling of power inherent in the automatic majority and without regard to the importance of achieving a consensus on this issue, railroaded the U.N. in a contemptuous maneuver by the use of the automatic majority into bracketing Zionism with the subject under discussion.

I do not come to this rostrum to defend the moral and historical values of the Jewish people. They do not need to be defended. They speak for themselves. They have given to mankind much of what is great and eternal. They have done for the spirit of man more than can readily be appreciated by a forum such as this one.

I come here to denounce the two great evils which menace society in general and a society of nations in particular. These two evils are hatred and ignorance. These two evils are the motivating force behind the proponents of this resolution and their supporters. These two evils characterize those who would drag this world organization, the ideals of which were first conceived by the prophets of Israel, to the depths to which it has been dragged today.

The key to understanding Zionism is in its name. The eastern-most of the two hills of ancient Jerusalem during the tenth century B.C.E. was called Zion. In fact, the name Zion, referring to Jerusalem, appears 152 times in the Old Testament. The name is overwhelmingly a poetic and prophetic designation. The religious and emotional qualities of the name arise from the importance of Jerusalem as the Royal City and the City of the Temple. "Mount Zion" is the place where God dwells. Jersualem, or Zion, is a place where the Lord is King, and where He has installed His King, David.

King David made Jerusalem the capital of Israel almost three thousand years ago, and Jerusalem has remained the capital ever since. During the centuries the term "Zion" grew and expanded to mean the whole of Israel. The Israelites in exile could not forget Zion. The Hebrew Psalmist sat by the waters of Babylon and swore: "If I forget thee, O

Jerusalem, let my right hand forget her cunning." This oath has been repeated for thousands of years by Jews throughout the world. It is an oath which was made over seven hundred years before the advent of Christianity and over twelve hundred years before the advent of Islam, and Zion came to mean the Jewish homeland, symbolic of Judaism, of Jewish national aspirations.

While praying to his God every Jew, wherever he is in the world, faces towards Jerusalem. For over two thousand years of exile these prayers have expressed the yearning of the Jewish people to return to their ancient homeland, Israel. In fact, a continuous Jewish presence, in larger or smaller numbers, has been maintained in the country over the centuries.

Zionism is the name of the national movement of the Jewish people and is the modern expression of the ancient Jewish heritage. The Zionist ideal, as set out in the Bible, has been, and is, an integral part of the Jewish religion.

Zionism is to the Jewish people what the liberaton movements of Africa and Asia have been to their own people.

Zionism is one of the most dynamic and vibrant national movements in human history. Historically it is based on a unique and unbroken connection, extending some four thousand years, between the People of the Book and the Land of the Bible.

In modern times, in the late nineteenth century, spurred by the twin forces of anti-Semitic persecution and of nationalism, the Jewish people organized the Zionist movement in order to transform their dream into reality. Zionism as a political movement was the revolt of an oppressed nation against the depredation and wicked discrimination and oppression of the countries in which anti-Semitism flourished. It is no coincidence that the co-sponsors and supporters of this resolution include countries who are guilty of the horrible crimes of anti-Semitism and discrimination to this very day.

Support for the aim of Zionism was written into the League of Nations Mandate for Palestine and was again endorsed by the United Nations in 1947, when the General Assembly voted by overwhelming majority for the restoration of Jewish independence in our ancient land.

The re-establishment of Jewish independence in Israel, after centuries of struggle to overcome foreign conquest and exile, is a vindication of the fundamental concepts of the equality of nations and of self-determination. To question the Jewish people's right to national existence and freedom is not only to deny to the Jewish people the right accorded to every other people on this globe, but it is also to deny the central precepts of the United Nations.

PALESTINE LIBERATION ORGANIZATION
73. Political Program, 1974

The diplomatic offensive of the Palestine Liberation Organization and the Arab states (see docs. 71, 72) had its echo within the PLO itself. The political program adopted by the Palestine National Council on June 9, 1974, reflects the hard line that it could now take, having gained the support of much of the international community and established a "ministate" in Lebanon.

Source: Yehoshafat Harkabi, *The Palestinian Covenant and Its Meaning* (London: Vallentine, Mitchell and Co., 1979), pp. 147–48. Reprinted by permission of Yehoshafat Harkabi.

The Palestinian National Council:

On the basis of Palestinian National Charter and the Political Programme drawn up at the Eleventh Session, held from January 6–12, 1973 [see doc. 57]; and from its belief that it is impossible for a permanent and just peace to be established in the area unless our Palestinian people recover all their national rights and, first and foremost, their rights to return and to self-determination on the whole of the soil of their homeland; and in the light of a study of the new political circumstances that have come into existence in the period between the Council's last and present sessions, resolves the following:

1. To reaffirm the Palestine Liberation Organization's previous attitude to Resolution 242 [see doc. 53], which obliterates the national right of our people and deals with the cause of our people as a problem of refugees. The Council therefore refuses to have anything to do with this resolution at any level, Arab or international, including the Geneva Conference.

2. The Liberation Organization will employ all means, and first and foremost armed struggle, to liberate Palestinian territory and to establish the independent combatant national authority for the people over every part of Palestinian territory that is liberated. This will require further changes being effected in the balance of power in favour of our people and their struggle.

3. The Liberation Organization will struggle against any proposal for a Palestinian entity the price of which is recognition, peace, secure frontiers, renunciation of national rights and the deprival of our people of their right to return and their right to self-determination on the soil of their homeland.

4. Any step taken towards liberation is a step toward the realisation of the Liberation Organization's strategy of establishing the democratic Palestinian state specified in the resolutions of previous Palestinian National Councils.

5. Struggle along with the Jordanian national forces to establish a Jordanian-Palestinian national front whose aim will be to set up in Jordan a democratic national authority in close contact with the Palestinian entity that is established through the struggle.

6. The Liberation Organization will struggle to establish unity in struggle between the two peoples and between all the forces of the Arab liberation movement that are in agreement on this programme.

7. In the light of this programme, the Liberation Organization will struggle to strengthen national unity and to raise it to the level where it will be able to perform its national duties and tasks.

8. Once it is established, the Palestinian national authority will strive to achieve a union of the confrontation countries, with the aim of completing the liberation of all Palestinian territory, and as a step along the road to comprehensive Arab unity.

9. The Liberation Organization will strive to strengthen its solidarity with the socialist countries, and with forces of liberation and progress throughout the world, with the aim of frustrating all the schemes of Zionism, reaction and imperialism.

10. In the light of this programme the leadership of the revolution will determine the tactics which will serve and make possible the realization of these objectives.

The Executive Committee of the Palestine Liberation Organization will make every effort to implement this programme, and should a situation arise affecting the destiny and the future of the Palestinian people, the National Council will be convened in extraordinary session.

74. The Egyptian-Israeli Disengagement Agreement, September 1975

The cease-fires arranged by the United Nations and U.S. mediation and the direct negotiations between military officers at Kilometer 101—sixty-three miles from Cairo in Israeli-occupied territory—that resulted in the Six-Point Agreement (see doc. 70) were only temporary steps to end the immediate problems of military hostilities in the October 1973 War. The United States and the Soviet Union, seeking a comprehensive settlement in the Middle East that would also maximize their own foreign policy goals, convened the Geneva Peace Conference with the United States, Soviet Union, Israel, Egypt, and Jordan as members; Syria was a member but did not attend. The conference met once, in December 1973, and failed to produce any results. On several occasions since then initiatives have been taken to reconvene it.

The talks at Kilometer 101, which were suspended in early December, resumed to produce an interim separation-of-forces agreement on January 18, 1974. Israel left the west bank of the Suez Canal and pulled back about twelve miles from its positions on the east bank. Three narrow corridors were established on the east bank—an Egyptian and an Israeli limited force zone separated by a U.N. buffer zone. Egyptian forces along the entire eastern bank thereby controlled the canal itself. In a separate letter Egypt agreed to allow nonmilitary cargoes going to and from Israel to pass through the Suez Canal.

Meanwhile U.S. mediators were negotiating terms for a similar separation-of-forces agreement between Syria and Israel. On May 31, 1974, an agreement was reached—again establishing two limited force zones separated by a U.N. buffer zone. Israel withdrew to positions slightly west of the Purple Line, the pre-October 1973 cease-fire line. The disengagement of troops was completed three weeks after the agreement was signed in Geneva.

Following these agreements between Egypt and Israel and between Syria and Israel, Henry Kissinger sought to move to the next phase of the settlement process, but it proved extremely difficult to effect a second Egyptian-Israeli agreement. After a year of crisis-ridden negotiations what was in effect a trilateral American-Egyptian-Israeli agreement was reached. Again it established limited force zones separated by a U.N. buffer zone. Egyptian forces moved further eastward into the Sinai, and Israeli forces moved back to the strategic Mitla Pass. This second separation-of-forces agreement, signed in September 1975, was secured by U.S. guarantees to Israel to provide for observation of Egyptian military activity to compensate for Israel's loss of early warning stations in the territory it evacuated. The September 1975 agreement resolved issues that had been outstanding since the October 1973 War, particularly the untenable position of Israeli and Egyptian troops near the canal. Hence it was also a step toward a resolution of the more fundamental conflict between the two states and set the stage for the 1979 Camp David Agreements (see doc. 76).

Source: "New Agreement between Egypt and Israel Negotiated through Secretary Kissinger during His Trip from August 20 to September 3," U.S. *Department of State Bulletin* 73, 1892 (September 29, 1975): 466–68.

The Government of the Arab Republic of Egypt and the Government of Israel have agreed that:

Article 1

The conflict between them and in the Middle East shall not be resolved by military force but by peaceful means.

The agreement concluded by the Parties on January 18, 1974, within the framework of the Geneva Peace Conference, constituted a first step towards a just and durable peace according to the provisions of Security Council Resolution 338 of October 22, 1973 [see doc. 70].

They are determined to reach a final and just peace settlement by means of negotiations called for by Security Council Resolution 338, this Agreement being a significant step towards that end.

Article 2

The Parties hereby undertake not to resort to the threat or use of force or military blockade against each other.

Article 3

The Parties shall continue scrupulously to observe the cease-fire on land, sea and air and to refrain from all military or para-military actions against each other.

The Parties also confirm that the obligations contained in the Annex and, when concluded, the Protocol shall be an integral part of this Agreement.

Article 4

1. The military forces of the Parties shall be deployed in accordance with the following principles [delineation of troop withdrawals].

2. The details concerning the new lines, the re-deployment of the forces and its timing, the limitation on armaments and forces, aerial reconnaissance, the operation of the early warning and surveillance installations and the use of the roads, the United Nations functions and other arrangements will all be in accordance with the provisions of the Annex and map which are an integral part of this Agreement and of the Protocol which is to result from negotiations pursuant to the Annex and which, when concluded, shall become an integral part of this Agreement.

Article 5

The United Nations Emergency Force is essential and shall continue its functions and its mandate shall be extended annually.

Article 6

The Parties hereby establish a Joint Commission for the duration of this Agreement. It will function under the aegis of the Chief Coordinator of the United Nations Peacekeeping Missions in the Middle East in order to consider any problem arising from this Agreement and to assist the United Nations Emergency Force in the execution of its mandate. The Joint Commission shall function in accordance with procedures established in the Protocol.

Article 7

Nonmilitary cargoes destined for or coming from Israel shall be permitted through the Suez Canal.

Article 8

This Agreement is regarded by the Parties as a significant step towards a just and lasting peace. It is not a final peace agreement.

The Parties shall continue their efforts to negotiate a final peace agreement within the framework of the Geneva Peace Conference in accordance with Security Council Resolution 338.

Article 9

This Agreement shall enter into force upon signature of the Protocol and remain in force until superseded by a new agreement.

HAROLD H. SAUNDERS
75. The United States and the Palestinian Issue

Following the signing of the Egyptian-Israeli Disengagement Agreement on the Sinai in September 1975 (see doc. 74), it became clear that Henry Kissinger's step-by-step approach to a Middle East settlement had exhausted itself. Kissinger began to contemplate what his critics had suggested—a comprehensive solution that would address the Palestinian issue as well.

Harold H. Saunders (b. 1930), a U.S. intelligence and foreign service officer, is a specialist in the Middle East. As deputy assistant secretary of state for Near Eastern and South Asia Affairs, he accompanied secretaries of state Kissinger and Cyrus Vance on all of their Middle Eastern trips. Saunder's testimony before a subcommittee of the U.S. House of Representatives Committee on International Relations in November 1975 was an important signal of the imminent change in U.S. policy.

A just and durable peace in the Middle East is a central objective of the United States. Both President Ford[1] and Secretary Kissinger have stated firmly on numerous occasions that the United States is determined to make every feasible effort to maintain the momentum of practical progress toward a peaceful settlement of the Arab-Israeli conflict.

We have also repeatedly stated that the legitimate interests of the Palestinian Arabs must be taken into account in the negotiation of an Arab-Israeli peace. In many ways, the Palestinian dimension of the Arab-Israeli conflict is the heart of that conflict. Final resolution of the problems arising from the partition of Palestine, the establishment of the State of Israel, and Arab opposition to those events will not be possible until agreement is reached defining a just and permanent status for the Arab peoples who consider themselves Palestinians.

The total number of Palestinian Arabs is estimated at a little more than 3 million. Of these, about 450,000 live in the area of Israel's pre-1967 borders; about 1 million are in the Israeli-occupied West Bank, East Jerusalem, and Gaza; something less than a million—about 900,000—are in Jordan; half a million are in Syria and Lebanon; and somewhat more than 200,000 or so are elsewhere, primarily in the gulf states.

Those in Israel are Israeli nationals. The great majority of those in the West Bank, East Jerusalem, and Jordan are Jordanian nationals. Palestinian refugees, who live outside of pre-1967 Israel and number 1.6 million, are eligible for food and/or services from the U.N. Relief and Works Agency (UNRWA); more than 650,000 of these live in camps.

The problem of the Palestinians was initially dealt with essentially as one involving displaced persons. The United States and other nations responded to the immediate humanitarian task of caring for a large number of refugees and trying to provide them with some hope in life.

In later years, there has been considerable attention given to the programs of UNRWA

Source: "Statement by Harold H. Saunders, Deputy Assistant Secretary of State for Near Eastern and South Asian Affairs Made before the Special Subcommittee on Investigations of the House Committee on International Relations on November 12," U.S. *Department of State Bulletin* 73, no. 1901 (December 1, 1975): 797–802.

that help not only to sustain those people's lives but to lift the young people out of the refugee camps and to train them and give them an opportunity to lead productive lives. Many have taken advantage of this opportunity, and an unusually large number of them have completed secondary and university education. One finds Palestinians occupying leading positions throughout the Arab world as professionals and skilled workers in all fields.

The United States has provided some $620 million in assistance—about 62 percent of the total international support ($1 billion) for the Palestinian refugees over the past quarter of a century.

Today, however, we recognize that, in addition to meeting the human needs and responding to legitimate personal claims of the refugees, there is another interest that must be taken into account. It is a fact that many of the 3 million or so people who call themselves Palestinians today increasingly regard themselves as having their own identity as a people and desire a voice in determining their political status. As with any people in this situation, they have differences among themselves, but the Palestinians collectively are a political factor which must be dealt with if there is to be a peace between Israel and its neighbors.

The statement is often made in the Arab world that there will not be peace until the "rights of the Palestinians" are fulfilled; but there is no agreed definition of what is meant, and a variety of viewpoints have been expressed on what the legitimate objectives of the Palestinians are:

• Some Palestinian elements hold to the objective of a binational secular state in the area of the former mandate of Palestine. Realization of this objective would mean the end of the present State of Israel—a member of the United Nations—and its submergence in some larger entity. Some would be willing to accept merely as a first step toward this goal the establishment of a Palestinian state comprising the West Bank of the Jordan River and Gaza.

• Other elements of Palestinian opinion appear willing to accept an independent Palestinian state comprising the West Bank and Gaza, based on acceptance of Israel's right to exist as an independent state within roughly its pre-1967 borders.

• Some Palestinians and other Arabs envisage as a possible solution a unification of the West Bank and Gaza with Jordan. A variation of this which has been suggested would be the reconstitution of the country as a federated state, with the West Bank becoming an autonomous Palestinian province.

• Still others, including many Israelis, feel that with the West Bank returned to Jordan, and with the resulting existence of two communities—Palestinian and Jordanian—within Jordan, opportunities would be created thereby for the Palestinians to find self-expression.

• In the case of a solution which would rejoin the West Bank to Jordan or a solution involving a West Bank–Gaza state, there would still arise the property claims of those Palestinians who before 1948 resided in areas that became the State of Israel. These claims have been acknowledged as a serious problem by the international community ever since the adoption by the United Nations of Resolution 194 on this subject in 1948 [see doc. 14], a resolution which the United Nations has repeatedly reaffirmed and which the United States has supported. A solution will be further complicated by the property claims against Arab states of the many Jews from those states who moved to Israel in its early years after achieving statehood.[2]

• In addition to property claims, some believe they should have the option of returning to their original homes under any settlement.

• Other Arab leaders, while pressing the importance of Palestinian involvement in a settlement, have taken the position that the definition of Palestinian interests is something for the Palestinian people themselves to sort out, and the view has been expressed by responsible Arab leaders that realization of Palestinian rights need not be inconsistent with the existence of Israel.

No one, therefore, seems in a position today to say exactly what Palestinian objectives are. Even the Palestine Liberation Organization (PLO), which is recognized by the Arab League and the U.N. General Assembly as the representative of the Palestinian people, has been ambivalent. Officially and publicly, its objective is described as a binational secular state, but there are some indications that coexistence between separate Palestinian and Israeli states might be considered.

When there is greater precision about those objectives, there can be clearer understanding about how to relate them to negotiations. There is the aspect of the future of the West Bank and Gaza—how those areas are to be defined and how they are to be governed. There is the aspect of the relationship between Palestinians in the West Bank and Gaza to those Palestinians who are not living in those areas, in the context of a settlement.

What is needed as a first step is a diplomatic process which will help bring forth a reasonable definition of Palestinian interests—a position from which negotiations on a solution of the Palestinian aspects of the problem might begin. The issue is not whether Palestinian interests should be expressed in a final settlement, but how. There will be no peace unless an answer is found.

Another requirement is the development of a framework for negotiations—a statement of the objectives and the terms of reference. The framework for the negotiations that have taken place thus far and the agreements they have produced involving Israel, Syria, and Egypt has been provided by U.N. Security Council Resolutions 242 and 338 [see docs. 53, 70]. In accepting that framework, all of the parties to the negotiations have accepted that the objective of the negotiations is peace between them based on mutual recognition, territorial integrity, political independence, the right to live in peace within secure and recognized borders, and the resolution of the specific issues which comprise the Arab-Israeli conflict.

The major problem that must be resolved in establishing a framework for bringing issues of concern to the Palestinians into negotiation, therefore, is to find a common basis for the negotiation that Palestinians and Israelis can both accept. This could be achieved by common acceptance of the above-mentioned Security Council resolutions, although they do not deal with the political aspect of the Palestinian problem.

A particularly difficult aspect of the problem is the question of who negotiates for the Palestinians. It has been our belief that Jordan would be a logical negotiator for the Palestinian-related issues. The Rabat summit, however, recognized the Palestine Liberation Organization as the "sole legitimate representative of the Palestinian people" [see doc. 71].

The PLO was formed in 1964, when 400 delegates from Palestinian communities throughout the Arab world met in Jerusalem to create an organization to represent and speak for the Palestinian people. Its leadership was originally middle-class and relatively conservative, but by 1969 control had passed into the hands of the Palestinian fedayeen, or commando, movement, which had existed since the mid-1950's but had come into prominence only after the 1967 war. The PLO became an umbrella organization for six separate fedayeen groups: Fatah; the Syrian-backed Saiqa; the Popular Democratic Front for the Liberation of Palestine; the Popular Front for the Liberation of Palestine; the General Command, a subgroup of the PFLP; and the Iraqi-backed Arab Liberation Front. Affiliated with the PLO are a number of "popular organizations"—labor and professional unions, student groups, women's groups, and so on. Fatah, the largest fedayeen group, also has a welfare apparatus to care for widows and orphans of deceased Fatah members.

However, the PLO does not accept the U.N. Security Council resolutions, does not recognize the existence of Israel, and has not stated its readiness to negotiate peace with Israel; Israel does not recognize the PLO or the idea of a separate Palestinian entity. Thus we do not at this point have the framework for a negotiation involving the PLO. We cannot envision or urge a negotiation between two parties as long as one professes to hold the objective of eliminating the other—rather than the objective of negotiating peace with it.

There is one other aspect to this problem. Elements of the PLO have used terrorism to gain attention for their cause. Some Americans as well as many Israelis and others have been killed by Palestinian terrorists. The international community cannot condone such practices, and it seems to us that there must be some assurance if Palestinians are drawn into the negotiating process that these practices will be curbed.

This is the problem which we now face. If the progress toward peace which has now begun is to continue, a solution to this question must be found. We have not devised an "American" solution, nor would it be appropriate for us to do so. This is the responsibility of the parties and the purpose of the negotiating process. But we have not closed our minds to any reasonable solution which can contribute to progress toward our overriding objective in the Middle East—an Arab-Israeli peace. The step-by-step approach to negotiations which we have pursued has been based partly on the understanding that issues in the Arab-Israeli conflict take time to mature. It is obvious that thinking on the Palestinian aspects of the problem must evolve on all sides. As it does, what is not possible today may become possible.

Our consultations on how to move the peace negotiations forward will recognize the need to deal with this subject. As Secretary Kissinger has said: "We are prepared to work with all the parties toward a solution of all the issues yet remaining—including the issue of the future of the Palestinians."

We will do so because the issues of concern to the Palestinians are important in themselves and because the Arab governments participating in the negotiations have made clear that progress in the overall negotiations will depend in part on progress on issues of concern to the Palestinians. We are prepared to consider any reasonable proposal from any quarter, and we will expect other parties to the negotiation to be equally open-minded.

NOTES

1. Gerald R. Ford (b. 1913) president of the United States, 1974–76. Ford, who had spent a generation in the U.S. House of Representatives, became Vice-President when Agnew was forced to resign in 1973. He then became president when Nixon resigned in August 1974.

2. While Israel has acknowledged the legitimacy of property claims by Palestinian refugees from the First Arab-Israeli War, and in fact released blocked bank accounts held by these refugees, it has always insisted that the final settlement take into account the property claims of Jews forced to flee Arab states in the aftermath of the war. Over 360,000 Jews went to Israel from Arab countries in these years, a large proportion of whom were forced to leave behind property. (Immigration figures, 1948–53, refer to all Jewish immigration from Asia and Africa; from Moshe Sicron, "Haaliyah LeIsrael, 1948–53" [The Immigration to Israel, 1948–1953], in *Olim BeIsrael: Mikraah* [Immigrants in Israel: A Reader], ed. Moshe Lissak, Beverly Mizrahi, and Ofra Ben-David [Jerusalem: Akademon, 1969], p. 115).

76. The Egyptian-Israeli Negotiations, 1977–78

In November 1977 Egyptian president Anwar Sadat, speaking before the Egyptian People's Assembly, declared that he was willing to travel to Jerusalem if necessary to find a solution to the Arab-Israeli conflict. The Israeli government immediately picked up on this cue and sent Sadat an invitation to come to Jerusalem and address the Knesset. Sadat received the invitation on November 17, arrived in Israel on November 19, and on Sunday afternoon, November 20, spoke to the Israeli people. This special session of the Knesset was televised live throughout the world. Sadat spoke in Arabic, one of Israel's official languages. Israeli prime minister Menahem Begin replied in Hebrew and appeared to be speaking extemporaneously without a prepared text. Shimon Peres, leader of the Labor party opposition, also spoke on that occasion.

Simultaneously, the U.S. president, Jimmy Carter, was trying to reconvene the Geneva Peace Conference and bring the Soviet Union into the peace process. But the conference never reconvened, and Sadat's gambit effectively kept the Soviet Union out of the picture while beginning the first direct negotiations between belligerents in the Arab-Israeli conflict. The ultimate results were the Camp David Agreements of September 1978, implemented by an Egyptian-Israeli peace treaty in 1979.

Following Sadat's historic trip to Jerusalem, Begin and Sadat met together in Ismailia on December 26, 1977. In early January 1978 Carter and Sadat met at Aswan. On February 2, 1978, representatives of Algeria, Libya, Yemen (Aden), Syria, and the Palestine Liberation Organization met in Algiers to frustrate the peace negotiations. Iraq refused to attend this meeting, accusing the participants of not being radical enough.

Sadat visited the United States, February 3–8, and from February 9 to 13 he met with the leaders in Great Britain, Germany, Austria, Rumania, France, and Italy. Begin was in Washington, March 21–22. At this point the peace negotiations began to reach an impasse. Israel had invaded southern Lebanon in March. Moreover, the Israelis were pursuing a hard line and articulating little readiness for hard compromises. The negotiating position Begin took while in Washington was approved by the Israeli cabinet on March 29. On July 13 Ezer Weizman and Sadat met near Salzburg, Austria. On July 19 the Egyptian and Israeli foreign ministers met in England. Egypt then stated that further talks were futile. Israel recalled its ten-man mission from Alexandria.

As the Egyptian-Israeli negotiations came to a standstill, Carter engaged in "personal diplomacy" and arranged for a summit meeting at Camp David, a presidents' retreat near Washington, D.C. On August 8, 1978, the White House announced the two heads of state accepted the president's offer for a meeting that would "seek a framework for peace in the Middle East." The meeting opened on September 5, 1978, without a specified time limit.

Following are some of the key documents of the Egyptian-Israeli negotiations, beginning with Sadat's visit to Jerusalem in November 1977 and ending with the Camp David Agreements of September 1978.

Sources: Colin Legum and Haim Shaked, eds., *Middle East Contemporary Survey, 1978–79* (New York: Holmes and Meier Publishers, 1980), app. 1, pp. 134–42, 144–54. Reprinted by permission. U.S. Department of State, *The Camp David Summit, September 1978*, Department of State publication 8954, Near East and South Asia ser. 88 (Washington, D.C.: Government Printing Office, September 1978), pp. 6–15.

Sadat's Speech to the Knesset, November 20, 1977

In the name of God, Mr. Speaker of the Knesset, ladies and gentlemen. Allow me first to thank the Speaker of the Knesset deeply for affording me this opportunity so that I may address you. And as I begin my address, I wish to say peace and the mercy of God Almighty be upon you, and may peace be for us all, God willing. Peace for us all, all the Arab lands and in Israel, as well as in every part of this big world, this world which is so complexed [sic] by its sanguinary conflicts, disturbed by its sharp contradictions, menaced now and then by costly wars launched by man to annihilate his fellow men. Amidst the ruins of what man has built, and the remains of the victims of mankind, there emerges neither victor nor vanquished. The only vanquished remains always a man—man, God's most sublime creation, man whom God has created as Gandhi,[1] the apostle of peace, put it, to forge ahead, to mould a way of life, and to worship God Almighty.

I come to you today on solid ground to shape a new life and prepare a peace. Well, on this land, the land of God, we all—Muslims, Christians and Jews—we all worship God and no one but God. God's teaching and commandments are love, sincerity, purity and peace.

I do not blame all those who received my decision when I announced it to the entire world before the Egyptian People's Assembly—I say I do not blame them. I do not blame all those who received my decision with surprise and even with amazement. Some even, struck by violent surprise, believed that my decision was no more than verbal juggling to cater for world public opinion. Others still interpreted it as political tactics to camouflage my intention to launch a new war.

I would go as far as to tell you that one of my aides in the Presidential Office contacted me at the late hour following my return home from the People's Assembly and sounded worried as he asked me: "Mr. President, what would be our reaction if Israel should actually extend an invitation to you?" I replied calmly: "I will accept it immediately." I have declared that I would go to the end of the world. I would go to Israel, for I want to put before the people of Israel all the facts.

I can see the point of all those who were astounded by my decision, all those who had any doubts as to the sincerity of the intention behind the declaration of my decision. No one would ever have conceived that the President of the biggest Arab state, which bears the heaviest burden and the main responsibility pertaining to the cause of war and peace in the Middle East, could declare his readiness to go to the land of the adversary while we were still in a state of war. Rather we all are still bearing the consequences of four fierce wars waged within ten years [sic]. All this at a time when the families of the 1973 October War are still suffering the cruel pain of widowhood and bereavement of sons, fathers and brothers.

As I have already declared, I have not consulted, as far as this decision is concerned, with any of my colleagues or brothers, the Arab Heads of State, or the confrontation states. Those of them who contacted me following the declaration of this decision spoke of their objection because the feeling of opposite mission and absolute lack of confidence between the Arab states and the Palestinian people on the one hand, and Israel on the other, still surges in us all.

It is sufficient to say that many months within which peace could have been brought about have been wasted over differences and fruitless discussions on the procedure for the convocation of the Geneva conference, all showing utter suspicion and absolute lack of confidence. But, to be absolutely frank with you, I took this decision after long thinking, knowing that it constitutes a grave risk for, if God Almighty has made it my fate to assume the responsi-

bility on behalf of the Egyptian people and
to share in the fate-determining responsibility of the Arab nation, the main duty
dictated by this responsibility, is to exhaust
every means in a bid to save my Arab people
and the entire Arab nation the horrors of
new, shocking and destructive wars, the
dimensions of which are foreseen by no
other than God Himself.

After long thinking, I was convinced that
the obligation of responsibility before God
and before the people makes it incumbent
upon me that I should go to the farthest
corners of the world, even to Jerusalem, to
address members of the Knesset, the representatives of the people of Israel, and ac-
quaint them with all the facts surging in me.
Then I would leave you to decide for
yourselves. Following this, may God Almighty determine our fate.

There are moments in the life of nations
and peoples when it is incumbent for those
known for their wisdom and clarity of vision
to overlook the past with all its complexities
and weighing memories in a bold drive
towards new horizons. Those who, like us,
are shouldering the same responsibilities
entrusted to us, are the first who should
have the courage to take fate-determining
decisions which are in consonance with the
circumstances. We must all rise above all
forms of fanaticism, above all forms of
self-deception and above all forms of obsolete theories of superiority. The most important thing is never to forget infallibility is the
prerogative of God alone.

If I said that I wanted to avert from all the
Arab people the horrors of shocking and
destructive wars, I must sincerely declare
before you that I have the same feelings and
bear the same responsibility towards all and
every man on earth, and certainly towards
the Israel people. . . .

In light of these facts—which I've placed
before you the way I see them—I would also
wish, in all sincerity, *to warn you*. I warn you
against some thought which could cross
your minds. Frankness makes it incumbent
upon me to tell you the following.

First, *I have not come here for a separate
agreement between Egypt and Israel*. This is not
part of the policy of Egypt. The problem is
not that of Egypt and Israel. Any separate
peace between Egypt and Israel, or between
Arab confrontation states and Israel, will not
bring permanent peace, based on justice, in
the entire region. Rather, even if peace
between all the confrontation states and
Israel were achieved, in the absence of a just
solution to the Palestinian problem, there
would never be the durable and just peace
upon which the entire world today insists.

Second, *I have not come to you to seek a
partial peace*—namely, to terminate the state
of belligerency at this stage, and put off the
entire problem to a subsequent stage. This is
not the radical solution that would steer us
to permanent peace.

Equally, *I have not come to you for a third
disengagement agreement in Sinai, or in the
Golan and the West Bank*, for this would mean
that we are merely delaying the ignition of
the fuse. Rather, it would also mean that we
are lacking the courage to face peace, that
we are too weak to shoulder the burdens
and responsibilities of a durable peace based
on justice. I have *come to you so that together
we can build* a durable peace based on justice,
to avoid the shedding of one single drop of
blood from either of the two parties.

It is for this reason that I have proclaimed
my readiness to go to the farthest corner of
the world. *Here I would go back to the big
question: How can we achieve a durable peace
based on justice?* In my opinion, and I declare
it to the whole world from this forum, the
answer is neither difficult, nor is it impossible, despite long years of feuds, vengeance,
spite and hatred, and breeding generations
on concepts of deep-rooted animosity. The
answer is not difficult, nor is it impossible—
if we sincerely and faithfully follow a
straight line.

We used to reject you. We had our reasons
and our claims, yes. We refused to meet
with you anywhere, yes. We used to brand
you as "so-called Israel," yes. We were
together in international conferences and

organizations and our representatives did not—and still do not—exchange greetings with you, yes. This has happened and is still happening.

It is also true that we used to set, as a pre-condition for any negotiations with you, a mediator who would meet separately with each party, by this procedure the talks for the first and second disengagement agreements took place. Our delegates met in the first Geneva conference without exchanging a direct word, yes. This has happened.

Yet today *I tell you, and I declare it to the whole world, that we accept living with you in permanent peace based on justice.* We do not want to encircle you, or be encircled ourselves, by destructive missiles ready for launching, nor by the shells of grudges and hatred. *I have announced on more than one occasion that Israel has become a fait accompli, recognized by the world,* and that the two super-powers have undertaken the reponsibility of its security and the defense of its existence.

As we really and truly seek peace, we really and truly welcome you to live among us in peace and security. There was a huge wall between us which you tried to build up over a quarter of a century, but it was destroyed in 1973. It was a wall of a continuously inflammable and escalating psychological warfare. It was a wall of fear of the force that could sweep the entire Arab nation. It was a wall of propaganda that we were a nation reduced to a motionless corpse. Some of you had gone as far as to say that even after 50 years the Arabs would not regain their strength. It was a wall that threatened always, with a long arm that could reach and strike anywhere. It was a wall that warned us against extermination and annihilation if we tried to use our legitimate right to liberate the occupied territories. Together we have to admit that the wall fell and collapsed in 1973.

Yet there remains another wall. This wall constitutes a psychological barrier between us. A barrier of suspicion. A barrier of rejection. A barrier of fear of deception. A barrier of hallucinations around any action, deed or decision. A barrier of cautious and erroneous interpretation of all and every event or statement. It is this psychological barrier which I described in official statements as constituting 70 percent of the whole problem. . . .

As I have told you, there is no happiness to the detriment of others. Direct confrontation and straight-forwardness are the short cuts, and the most successful way to reach a clear objective. Direct confrontation concerning the Palestinian problem and tackling it in one single language with a view to achieving a durable and just peace lie in the establishment of their state. With all the guarantees you demand, there should be no fear of a newly born state that needs the assistance of all countries of the world when the bells of peace ring, there will be no hands to beat the drums of war. Even if they existed, they would be soundless.

Conceive with me a peace agreement in Geneva that we would herald to a world thirsty for peace. A peace agreement based on the following points: (1) ending the Israeli occupation of the Arab territories occupied in 1967; (2) achievement of the fundamental right of the Palestinian people and their right to self-determination, including their right to establish their own state; (3) the right of all states in the area to live in peace, within their boundaries, their secure boundaries, which will be secured and guaranteed through procedures to be agreed upon, providing appropriate security for international boundaries, in additon to appropriate international guarantees; (4) commitment of all states in the region to administer the relations among them in accordance with the objectives and principles of the U.N. Charter, particularly the principles concerning the non-resort to force and the solutions to differences among them by peaceful means; (5) ending the state of belligerency in the region.

Peace is not a mere endorsement of written lines. Rather it is a rewriting of history. Peace is not a game of calling for peace to defend certain whims, or hide certain ambitions. Peace, in its essence, is a joint struggle against all and every ambition and whim. Perhaps the examples and experience taken from ancient and modern history teach us all that missiles, warships and nuclear weapons cannot establish security. Rather, they destroy what peace and secur-

ity build, for the sake of our peoples, and for the sake of the civilization made by man, we have to defend men everywhere against the rule of the force of arms, so that we may endow the rule of humanity with all the power of the values and principles that promote the sublime position of mankind.

Begin's Speech to the Knesset, November 20, 1977

Mr. Speaker, Mr. President of the State of Israel, Mr. President of the Arab Republic of Egypt, ladies and gentlemen, members of the Knesset: We send our greetings to the President, to all the people of the Islamic religion in our country, and wherever they may be, on this occasion of the feast of the festival of the sacrifice 'Id al-Adha. This feast reminds us of the binding of Isaac. This was the way in which the Creator of the World tested our forefather Abraham, our common forefather, to test his faith, and Abraham passed this test. However, from the moral aspect and the advancement of humanity, it was forbidden to sacrifice human beings. Our two peoples in their ancient traditions know and taught what the Lord, blessed be He, taught while peoples around us still sacrificed human beings to their gods. Thus, we contributed, the people of Israel and the Arab people, to the progress of mankind, and thus we are continuing to contribute to human culture to this day.

I greet and welcome the President of Egypt for coming to our country and on participating in the Knesset session. The flight time between Cairo and Jerusalem is short, but the distance between Cairo and Jerusalem was until last night almost endless. President Sadat crossed this distance courageously. We, the Jews, know how to appreciate such courage, and we know how to appreciate it in our guest, because it is with courage that we are here, and this is how we continue to exist, and we shall continue to exist.

Mr. Speaker, this small nation, the re-

maining refuge of the Jewish people who returned to their historic homeland, has always wanted peace, and since the dawn of our independence, on 14 May 1948 (5 Iyar Tashah), in the declaration of independence in the founding scroll of our national freedom [see doc. 1], David Ben-Gurion said: "We offer peace and amity to all the neighbouring states and their peoples and invite them to cooperate with the independent Jewish nation for the common good of all." One year earlier, even from the underground, when we were in the midst of the fateful struggle for the liberation of the country and the redemption of the people, we called on our neighbours in these terms: "In this country we will live together and we will live lives of freedom and happiness. Our Arab neighbours, do not reject the hand stretched out to you in peace."

But it is my bounden duty, Mr. Speaker, and not only my right, not to pass over the truth that our hand outstretched for peace was not grasped and one day after we had renewed our independence, as was our right, our eternal right, which cannot be disputed, we were attacked on three fronts, and we stood almost without arms, the few against many, the weak against the strong, while an attempt was made, one day after the declaration of independence, to strangle it at birth, to put an end to the last hope of the Jewish people, the yearning renewed after the years of destruction and holocaust. No, we do not believe in might and we have never based our attitude toward the Arab people on might. Quite the contrary, force was used against us. Over all the years of this generation we have never stopped being attacked by might, of the strong arm stretched out to exterminate our people, to destroy our independence, to deny our rights. We defended ourselves, it is true. We defended our rights, our existence, our honour, our women, and our children, against these repeated and recurring attempts to crush us through the force of arms, and not only on one front. That, too is true. With the help of God Almighty, we overcame the forces of aggression, and we have guaranteed existence for our nation. Not only for this generation, but for the coming generations. Yet we do not believe in might, we believe only in right. And therefore our aspiration, from the bottom of our hearts, has always been to this very day, for peace.

Mr. President, Mr. President of Egypt, the commanders of the underground Hebrew fighting organizations are sitting in this democratic house. They had to conduct a campaign of the few against the many, against a huge, a world power. Here are sitting the veteran commanders and captains who had to go forth into battle because it was forced upon them and forward to victory, which was unavoidable because they were defending their rights. They belong to different parties. They have different views, but I am sure, Mr. President, that I am expressing the views of everyone, with no exceptions, that we have one aspiration in our hearts, one desire in our souls, and all of us are united in these aspirations and desires—to bring peace, peace for our nation, which has not known peace for even one day since we started returning to Zion, and peace for our neighbours, whom we wish all the best, and we believe that if we make peace, real peace we will be able to help our neighbours, in all walks of life, and a new era will open in the Middle East, an era of blossoming and growth, development and expansion of the economy, its growth as it was in the past.

Therefore, permit me today to set forth the peace programme as we understand it. We want full, real peace with complete reconciliation between the Jews and the Arab peoples. I do not wish to dwell on the memories of the past, but there have been wars: there has been blood split: wonderful young people have been killed on both sides. We will live all our life with the memories of our heroes who gave their lives so this day would arrive, this day, too, would come, and we respect the bravery of a rival, and we honour all the members of the younger generation among the Arab people who also fell.

I do not wish to dwell on memories of the past, although they be bitter memories. We will bury them; we will worry about the future, about our people, our children, our joint and common future. For it is true indeed that we will have to live in this area, all of us together will live here, for generations upon generations: The great Arab people in their various states and countries, and the Jewish people in their country, Erez Israel. Therefore, we must determine what peace means.

Let us conduct negotiations, Mr. President, as free negotiating partners for a peace treaty, and, with the aid of the Lord, we fully believe the day will come when we can sign it with mutual respect, and we will then know that the era of wars is over, that hands have been extended between friends, that each has shaken the hand of his brother and the future will be shining for all the peoples of this area. The beginning of wisdom in a peace treaty is the abolition of the state of war. I agree, Mr. President, that you did not come here, we did not invite you to our country in order, as has been said in recent days, to divide the Arab peoples. Somebody quoted an ancient Roman saying, Divide and rule. Israel does not want to rule and therefore does not need to divide. We want peace with all our neighbours: with Egypt, with Jordan, with Syria and with Lebanon. We would like to negotiate peace treaties. . . .

And there is no need to distinguish between a peace treaty and an abolition of the state of war. Quite the contrary, we are not proposing this nor are we asking for it. The first clause of a peace treaty is cessation of the state of war, forever. We want to establish normal relations between us, as they exist between all nations, even after wars. We have learned from history, Mr. President, that war is avoidable, peace is unavoidable. Many nations have waged war among themselves, and sometimes they used the tragic term perennial enemy. There are no perennial enemies. And after all the wars, the inevitable comes—peace. And so we want to establish, in a peace treaty, diplomatic relations as is the custom among civilized nations.

Today two flags are flying over Jerusalem: the Egyptian flag and the Israeli flag. And we saw together, Mr. President, little children waving both the flags. Let us sign a peace treaty and let us establish this situation forever, both in Jerusalem and in Cairo, and I hope the day will come when the Egyptian children wave the Israeli flag and the Egyptian flag, just as the children of Israel waved both these flags in Jerusalem.

And you, Mr. President, will have a loyal ambassador in Jerusalem and we will have an ambassador in Cairo. And even if differences of opinion arise between us, we will clarify them like civilized peoples through our authorized envoys.

We are proposing economic co-operation for the development of our countries. There are wonderful countries in the Middle East. The Lord created it thus: oases in the deserts as well and we can make them flourish. Let us co-operate in this field. Let us develop our countries. Let us eliminate poverty, hunger, the lack of shelter. Let us raise our peoples to the level of developed countries and let them not call us "developing countries."

And with all due respect, I am willing to confirm the words of his majesty the King of Morocco, who said—in public too—that if peace arises in the Middle East, the combination of Arab genius and Jewish genius together can turn this area into a paradise on earth.

Let us open our countries to free traffic. You come to our country and we will visit yours. I am ready to announce, Mr. Speaker, this day that our country is open to the citizens of Egypt and I make no conditions on our part. I think it is only proper and just that there should be a joint announcement on this matter. But, just as there are Egyptian flags in our streets, and there is also an honoured delegation from Egypt in our capital and in our country, let the number of visitors increase; our border will be open to you, and also all the other borders.

And as I pointed out, we want this in the south and in the north and in the east. And so I am renewing my invitation to the President of Syria to follow in your footsteps, Mr. President, and come to us to open negotiations for achieving peace between Israel and Syria and to sign a peace treaty between us. I am sorry to say but there is not justification for the mourning they have declared beyond our northern border. Quite the contrary such visits, such links, such clarifications can and must be days of joy, days of lifting spirits for all peoples. I invite King Hussein to come to us to discuss all the problems which need to be discussed between us, and also genuine representatives of the Arabs of Erez Israel, I invite them to come and hold talks with us to clarify our common future, to guarantee the freedom of man, social justice, peace, mutual respect. And if they invite us to go to their capitals, we will go to those capitals in order to hold negotiations with them there. We do not want to divide. We want real peace with all our neighbours, to be expressed in peace treaties whose contents I have already made clear.

Mr. Speaker, it is my duty today to tell our guest and the peoples watching us and listening to our words about the link between our people and this country. The President recalled the Balfour Declaration. No, sir, we did not take over any strange land; we returned to our homeland. The link between our people and this country is eternal. It arose in the earliest days of the history of humanity and has never been disrupted. In this country we developed our civilization, we had our prophets here, and their sacred words stand to this day. Here the kings of Judah and Israel knelt before their gods. This is where we became a people; here we established our kingdom. And when we were expelled from our land because of force which was used against us, the farther we went from our land, we never forgot this country for even a single day. We prayed for it, we longed for it, we believed in our return to it from the day the words were spoken: "When the Lord restores the fortunes of Zion, we will be like dreamers. Our mouths will be filled with laughter, and our tongues will speak with shouts of joy." These verses apply to all our exiles and our sufferings, giving the consolation that the return to Zion would come.

This, our right, was recognized. The Balfour Declaration was included in the mandate laid down by the nations of the world, including the United States, and the preface to this recognized international document says: "Whereas recognition has the Bible given to the historical connection of the Jewish people with Palestine and to the grounds for reconstituting their national home in that country"—the historic connection between the Jewish people and Palestine—or, in Hebrew, Erez Israel, was given reconfirmation, reconfirmation as the national homeland in that country, that is, in Erez Israel. . . .

Israel's Autonomy Plan, December 28, 1977

1. The administration of the Military Government in Judaea, Samaria and the Gaza district will be abolished.

2. In Judaea, Samaria and the Gaza district, administrative autonomy of the residents, by and for them, will be established.

3. The residents of Judaea, Samaria and the Gaza district will elect an Administrative Council composed of eleven members. The Administrative Council will operate in accordance with the principles laid down in this paper.

4. Any resident, eighteen years old and above, without distinction of citizenship, or if stateless, will be entitled to vote in the elections to the Administrative Council.

5. Any resident whose name is included in the list of candidates for the Administrative Council and who, on the day the list is submitted, is 25 years old or above, will be entitled to be elected to the Council.

6. The Administrative Council will be elected by general, direct, personal, equal and secret ballot.

7. The period of office of the Administrative Council will be four years from the day of its election.

8. The Administrative Council will sit in Bethlehem.

9. All the administrative affairs relating to the Arab residents of the areas of Judea, Samaria, and the Gaza district will be under the direction and within the competence of the Administrative Council.

10. The Administrative Council will operate the following Departments: education; religious affairs; finance; transportation; construction and housing; industry, commerce and tourism; agriculture; health, labour and social welfare; rehabilitation of refugees; and the administration of justice and the supervision of local police forces; and promulgate regulations relating to the operation of these Departments.

11. Security and public order in the areas of Judaea, Samaria and the Gaza district will be the responsibility of the Israeli authorities.

12. The Administrative Council will elect its own chairman.

13. The first session of the Administrative Council will be convened thirty days after the publication of the election results.

14. Residents of Judaea, Samaria and the Gaza district, without distinction of citizen-

ship, or if stateless, will be granted free choice (option) of either Israeli or Jordanian citizenship.

15. A resident of the areas of Judaea, Samaria and the Gaza district who requests Israeli citizenship will be granted such citizenship in accordance with the citizenship law of the state.

16. Residents of Judaea, Samaria and the Gaza district who, in accordance with the right of free option, choose Israeli citizenship, will be entitled to vote for, and be elected to, the Knesset in accordance with the election law.

17. Residents of Judaea, Samaria and the Gaza district who are citizens of Jordan or who, in accordance with the right of free option will become citizens of Jordan, will elect and be eligible for election to the Parliament of the Hashemite Kingdom of Jordan in accordance with the election law of that country.

18. Questions arising from the vote to the Jordanian Parliament by residents of Judaea, Samaria and the Gaza district will be clarified in negotiations between Israel and Jordan.

19. A committee will be established of representatives of Israel, Jordan, and the Administrative Council to examine existing legislation in Judaea, Samaria and the Gaza district, and to determine which legislation will continue in force, which will be abolished, and what will be the competence of the Administrative Council to promulgate regulations. The rulings of the committee will be adopted by unanimous decision.

20. Residents of Israel will be entitled to accquire land and settle in the areas of Judaea, Samaria and the Gaza district. Arabs, residents of Judaea, Samaria and the

Gaza district who, in accordance with the free option granted them, will become Israeli citizens, will be entitled to acquire land and settle in Israel.

21. A committee will be established of representatives of Israel, Jordan and the Administrative Council to determine norms of immigration to the areas of Judaea, Samaria and the Gaza district. The committee will determine the norms whereby Arab refugees residing outside Judaea, Samaria and the Gaza district will be permitted to immigrate to these areas in reasonable numbers. The rulings of the committee will be adopted by unanimous decision.

22. Residents of Israel and residents of Judaea, Samaria and the Gaza district will be assured freedom of movement and freedom of economic activity in Israel, Judaea, Samaria and the Gaza district.

23. The Administrative Council will appoint one of its members to represent the Council before the Government of Israel for deliberation on matters of common interest, and one of its member to represent the Council before the Government of Jordan for deliberation on matters of common interest.

24. Israel stands by its right and its claim of sovereignty to Judaea, Samaria and the Gaza district. In the knowledge that other claims exist, it proposes, for the sake of the agreement and the peace, that the question of sovereignty in these areas be left open.

25. With regard to the administration of the holy places of the three religions in Jerusalem, a special proposal will be drawn up and submitted that will include the guarantee of freedom of access to members of all the faiths to the shrines holy to them.

26. These principles will be subject to review after a five-year period.

The American Position: Reaffirmation of the Carter-Sadat Summit at Aswan, February 1978

The United States will remain faithful to its historic commitments to the security of Israel and to the right of every state in the area to live in peace within secure and recognized boundaries.

Helping the parties achieve a negotiated

comprehensive settlement of Middle East conflict remains of highest importance in American policy, and President Carter will spare no effort in seeking ways to move the peace process forward.

A peace settlement must go beyond the mere termination of belligerency. It must provide for the establishment of normal peaceful relations between Israel and its neighbours.

The peace settlement should be comprehensive and should be embodied in the Peace Treaties between Israel and its neighbors. The settlement must be based on all the principles of Security Council Resolution 242 [see doc. 53], including withdrawal of Israel armed forces from territories occupied in 1967, and the right of every state in the area to live in peace within secure and recognized boundaries. Resolution 242 is applicable to all fronts of the conflict.

There can be no just and lasting peace without resolution of the Palestinian problem

The President reaffirmed what he said at his meeting with President Sadat in Aswan on 4 January. There must be a resolution of the Palestinian problem in all its aspects; it must recognize the legitimate rights of the Palestinian people and enable the Palestinians to participate in the determination of their own future.

President Carter also reaffirmed the long-standing U.S. view that Israeli settlements in occupied territory are contrary to international law and an obstacle to peace and that further settlement activity would be inconsistent with the effort to reach a peace settlement.

The Egyptian Position: The Peace Plan Published by the Egyptian Foreign Ministry, July 5, 1978

1. The establishment of a just and lasting peace in the Middle East necessitates a just solution of the Palestinian question in all its aspects on the basis of the legitimate rights of the Palestinian people and taking into consideration the legitimate security concerns of all the parties.

2. In order to ensure a peaceful and orderly transfer of authority there shall be a transitional period not exceeding five years at the end of which the Palestinian people will be able to determine their own future.

3. Talks shall take place between Egypt, Jordan, Israel and representatives of the Palestinian people, with the participation of the United Nations with a view to agreeing upon: (a) details of the transitional regime; (b) timetable for the Israeli withdrawal; (c) mutual security arrangements for all the parties concerned during and following the transitional period; (d) modalities for the implementation of relevant U.N. resolutions

on Palestinian refugees; (e) other issues considered appropriate by parties.

4. Israel shall withdraw from the West Bank (including Jerusalem) and the Gaza Strip, occupied since June 1967. The Israeli withdrawal applies to the settlements established in the occupied territories.

5. The Israeli military government in the West Bank and the Gaza Strip shall be abolished at the outset of the transitional period. Supervision over the administration of the West Bank shall become the responsibility of Jordan. Supervision over the administration of the Gaza Strip shall be the responsibility of Egypt. Jordan and Egypt shall carry out their responsibility in cooperation with freely elected representatives of the Palestinian people who shall exercise direct authority over the administration of the West Bank and Gaza. The United Nations shall supervise and facilitate the Israeli withdrawal and the restoration of Arab authority.

6. Egypt and Jordan shall guarantee that the security arrangements to be agreed upon will continue to be respected in the West Bank and Gaza.

Camp David Agreements, September 17, 1978

A Framework for Peace in the Middle East

Muhammed Anwar al-Sadat, President of the Arab Republic of Egypt, and Menahem Begin, Prime Minister of Israel met with Jimmy Carter, President of the United States of America, at Camp David from September 5 to September 17, 1978, and have agreed on the following framework for peace in the Middle East. They invite other parties to the Arab-Israeli conflict to adhere to it.

Preamble

The search for peace in the Middle East must be guided by the following:

The agreed basis for a peaceful settlement of the conflict between Israel and its neighbors is United Nations Security Council Resolution 242, in all its parts.

After four wars during thirty years, despite intensive human efforts, the Middle East, which is the cradle of civilization and the birthplace of three great religions, does not yet enjoy the blessings of peace. The people of the Middle East yearn for peace, so that the vast human and natural resources of the region can be turned to the pursuits of peace and so that this area can become a model for coexistence and cooperation among nations. . . .

The provisions of the Charter of the United Nations and the other accepted norms of international law and legitimacy now provide accepted standards for the conduct of relations among all states.

To achieve a relationship of peace, in the spirit of Article 2 of the United Nations Charter,[2] future negotiations between Israel and any neighbor prepared to negotiate peace and security with it, are necessary for the purpose of carrying out all the provisions and principles of Resolutions 242 and 338.

Peace requires respect for the sovereignty, territorial integrity and political independence of every state in the area and their right to live in peace within secure and recognized boundaries free from threats or acts of force. Progress toward that goal can accelerate movement toward a new era of reconciliation in the Middle East marked by cooperation in promoting economic development, in maintaining stability and in assuring security.

Security is enhanced by a relationship of peace and by cooperation between nations which enjoy normal relations. In addition, under the terms of peace treaties, the parties can, on the basis of reciprocity, agree to special security arrangements such as demilitarized zones, limited armaments areas, early warning stations, the presence of international forces, liaison, agreed measures for monitoring, and other arrangements that they agree are useful.

Framework

Taking these factors into account, the parties are determined to reach a just, comprehensive, and durable settlement of the Middle East conflict through the conclusion of peace treaties based on Security Council Resolutions 242 and 338 in all their parts. Their purpose is to achieve peace and good neighborly relations. They recognize that, for peace to endure, it must involve all those who have been most deeply affected by the conflict. They therefore agree that this framework as appropriate is intended by them to constitute a basis for peace not only between Egypt and Israel, but also between Israel and each of its other neighbors which is prepared to negotiate peace with Israel on this basis. With that objective in mind, they have agreed to proceed as follows:

A. West Bank and Gaza

1. Egypt, Israel, Jordan and the represen-

tatives of the Palestinian people should participate in negotiations on the resolution of the Palestinian problem in all its aspects. To achieve that objective, negotiations relating to the West Bank and Gaza should proceed in three stages:

(a) Egypt and Israel agree that, in order to ensure a peaceful and orderly transfer of authority, and taking into account the security concerns of all the parties, there should be transitional arrangements for the West Bank and Gaza for a period not exceeding five years. In order to provide full autonomy to the inhabitants, under these arrangements the Israeli military government and its civilian administration will be withdrawn as soon as a self-governing authority has been freely elected by the inhabitants of these areas to replace the existing military government. To negotiate the details of a transitional arrangement, the government of Jordan will be invited to join the negotiations on the basis of this framework. These new arrangements should give due consideration both to the principle of self-government by the inhabitants of these territories and to the legitimate security concerns of the parties involved.

(b) Egypt, Israel, and Jordan will agree on the modalities for establishing the elected self-governing authority in the West Bank and Gaza. The delegations of Egypt and Jordan may include Palestinians from the West Bank and Gaza or other Palestinians as mutually agreed. The parties will negotiate an agreement which will define the powers and responsibilities of the self-governing authority to be exercised in the West Bank and Gaza. A withdrawal of Israeli armed forces will take place and there will be a redeployment of the remaining Israeli forces into specified security locations. The agreement will also include arrangements for assuring internal and external security and public order. A strong local police force will be established, which may include Jordanian citizens. In addition, Israeli and Jordanian forces will participate in joint patrols and in the manning of control posts to assure the security of the borders.

(c) When the self-governing authority (administrative council) in the West Bank and Gaza is established and inaugurated, the transitional period of five years will begin. As soon as possible, but not later than the third year after the beginning of the transitional period, negotiations will take place to determine the final status of the West Bank and Gaza and its relationship with its neighbors, and to conclude a peace treaty between Israel and Jordan by the end of the transitional period. These negotiations will be conducted among Egypt, Israel, Jordan, and the elected representatives of the inhabitants of the West Bank and Gaza. Two separate but related committees will be convened, one committee, consisting of representatives of the four parties which will negotiate and agree on the final status of the West Bank and Gaza, and its relationship with its neighbors, and the second committee, consisting of representatives of Israel and representatives of Jordan to be joined by the elected representatives of the inhabitants of the West Bank and Gaza, to negotiate the peace treaty between Israel and Jordan, taking into account the agreement reached on the final status of the West Bank and Gaza. The negotiations shall be based on all the provisions and principles of U.N. Security Council Resolution 242. The negotiation will resolve, among other matters, the location of the boundaries and the nature of the security arrangements. The solution from the negotiations must also recognize the legitimate rights of the Palestinian people and their just requirements. In this way, the Palestinians will participate in the determination of their own future through: (i) the negotiations among Egypt, Israel, Jordan and the representatives of the inhabitants of the West Bank and Gaza to agree on the final status of the West Bank and Gaza and other outstanding issues by the end of the transitional period; (ii) submitting their agreement to a vote by the elected representatives of the inhabitants of the West Bank and Gaza; (iii) providing for the elected representatives of the inhabitants of the West Bank and

Gaza to decide how they shall govern themselves consistent with the provisions of their agreement; (iv) participating as stated above in the work of the committee negotiating the peace treaty between Israel and Jordan.

2. All necessary measures will be taken and provisions made to assure the security of Israel and its neighbors during the transitional period and beyond. To assist in providing such security, a strong local police force will be constituted by the self-governing authority. It will be composed of inhabitants of the West Bank and Gaza. The police will maintain continuing liaison on internal security matters with the designated Israeli, Jordanian, and Egyptian officers.

3. During the transitional period, representatives of Egypt, Israel, Jordan, and the self-governing authority will constitute a continuing committee to decide by agreement on the modalities of admission of persons displaced from the West Bank and Gaza in 1967, together with necessary measures to prevent disruption and disorder. Other matters of common concern may also be dealt with by this committee.

4. Egypt and Israel will work with each other and with other interested parties to establish agreed procedures for a prompt, just and permanent implementation of the resolution of the refugee problem.

B. Egypt-Israel

1. Egypt and Israel undertake not to resort to the threat or the use of force to settle disputes. Any disputes shall be settled by peaceful means in accordance with the provisions of Article 33 of the Charter of the United Nations.[3]

2. In order to achieve peace between them, the parties agree to negotiate in good faith with a goal of concluding within three months from the signing of this Framework a peace treaty between them, while inviting the other parties to the conflict to proceed simultaneously to negotiate and conclude similar peace treaties with a view to achieving a comprehensive peace in the area. The Framework for the Conclusion of a Peace Treaty between Egypt and Israel will govern the peace negotiations between them. The parties will agree on the modalities and the timetable for the implementation of their obligations under the treaty.

C. Associated Principles

1. Egypt and Israel state that the principles and provisions described below should apply to peace treaties between Israel and each of its neighbors—Egypt, Jordan, Syria and Lebanon.

2. Signatories shall establish among themselves relationships normal to states at peace with one another. To this end, they should undertake to abide by all the provisions of the Charter of the United Nations. Steps to be taken in this report include: (a) full recognition; (b) abolishing economic boycotts; (c) guaranteeing that under their jurisdiction the citizens of the other parties shall enjoy the protection of the due process of law.

3. Signatories should explore possibilities for economic development in the context of final peace treaties, with the objective of contributing to the atmosphere of peace, cooperation and friendship which is their common goal.

4. Claims Commissions may be established for the mutual settlement of all financial claims.

5. The United States shall be invited to participate in the talks on matters related to the modalities of the implementation of the agreements and working out the timetable for the carrying out of the obligations of the parties.

6. The United Nations Security Council shall be requested to endorse the peace treaties and ensure that their provisions shall not be violated. The permanent members of the Security Council shall be requested to underwrite the peace treaties and ensure respect for their provisions. They shall also be requested to conform their policies and actions with the undertakings contained in this Framework.

Framework for the Conclusion of a Peace Treaty between Egypt and Israel

In order to achieve peace between them, Israel and Egypt agree to negotiate in good faith with a goal of concluding within three months of the signing of this framework a peace treaty between them:

It is agreed that:

The site of the negotiations will be under a United Nations flag at a location or locations to be mutually agreed.

All of the principles of U.N. Resolution 242 will apply in this resolution of the dispute between Israel and Egypt.

Unless otherwise mutually agreed, terms of the peace treaty will be implemented between two and three years after the peace treaty is signed.

The following matters are agreed between the parties: (1) the full exercise of Egyptian sovereignty up to the internationally recognized border between Egypt and mandated Palestine; (2) the withdrawal of Israeli armed forces from the Sinai; (3) the use of airfields left by the Israelis near al-Arish, Rafah, Ras en-Naqb, and Sharm el-Sheikh for civilian purposes only, including possible commercial use by all nations; (4) the right of free passage by ships of Israel through the Gulf of Suez and the Suez Canal on the basis of the Constantinople Convention of 1888[4] applying to all nations; the Strait of Tiran and the Gulf of Aqaba are international waterways to be open to all nations for unimpeded and nonsuspendable freedom of navigation and overflight; (5) the construction of a highway between the Sinai and Jordan near Eilat with guaranteed free and peaceful passage by Egypt and Jordan; and (6) the stationing of military forces listed below.

Stationing of Forces

No more than one division (mechanized or infantry) of Egyptian armed forces will be stationed within an area lying approximately 50 km [30 miles] east of the Gulf of Suez and the Suez Canal.

Only United Nations forces and civil police equipped with light weapons to perform normal police functions will be stationed within an area lying west of the international border and the Gulf of Aqaba, varying in width from 20 km [12 miles] to 40 km [24 miles].

In the area within 3 km [1.8 miles] east of the international border there will be Israeli limited military forces not to exceed four infantry battalions and United Nations observers.

Border patrol units, not to exceed three battalions, will supplement the civil police in maintaining order in the area not included above.

The exact demarcation of the above areas will be as decided during the peace negotiations.

Early warning stations may exist to insure compliance with the terms of the agreement.

United Nations forces will be stationed: (1) in part of the area in the Sinai lying within about 20 km of the Mediterranean Sea and adjacent to the international border, and (2) in the Sharm el-Sheikh area to ensure freedom of passage through the Strait of Tiran; and these forces will not be removed unless such removal is approved by the Security Council of the United Nations with a unanimous vote of the five permanent members.

After a peace treaty is signed, and after the interim withdrawal is complete, normal relations will be established between Egypt and Israel, including full recognition, including diplomatic, economic and cultural relations; termination of economic boycotts and barriers to the free movement of goods and people; and mutual protection of citizens by the due process of law.

Interim Withdrawal

Between three months and nine months after the signing of the peace treaty, all Israeli forces will withdraw east of a line extending from a point east of al-'Arish to Ras Muhammad, the exact location of this line to be determined by mutual agreement.

Exchange of Letters accompanying the Camp David Agreements

To President Carter from Prime Minister Begin,
September 17, 1978
I have the honor to inform you that during two weeks after my return home, I will submit a motion before Israel's parliament (the Knesset) to decide on the following question: "If during the negotiations to conclude a peace treaty between Israel and Egypt all outstanding issues are agreed upon, 'are you in favour of the removal of the Israeli settlers from the northern and southern Sinai areas or are you in favour of keeping the aforementioned settlers in those areas?' "

The vote, Mr. President, on this issue will be completely free from the usual parliamentary party discipline to the effect that although the coalition is being now supported by 70 members out of 120, every member of the Knesset, as I believe, both of the government and the opposition benches will be enabled to vote in accordance with his own conscience.

To President Sadat from President Carter,
September 22, 1978
I transmit herewith a copy of a letter to me from Prime Minister Begin setting forth how he proposes to present the issue of the Sinai settlements to the Knesset for the latter's decision.

In this connection, I understand from your letter that Knesset approval to withdraw all Israeli settlers from Sinai according to a timetable within the period specified for the implementation of the peace treaty is a prerequisite to any negotiations on a peace treaty between Egypt and Israel.

To President Carter from President Sadat,
September 17, 1978
In connection with the "Framework for a Settlement in Sinai" to be signed tonight, I would like to reaffirm the position of the Arab Republic of Egypt with respect to the settlements:
1. All Israeli settlers must be withdrawn from Sinai according to a timetable within the period specified for the implementation of the peace treaty.

2. Agreement by the Israeli Government and its constitutional insitutions to this basic principle is therefore a prerequisite to starting peace negotiations for concluding a peace treaty.

3. If Israel fails to meet this commitment, the "framework" shall be void and invalid.

To President Carter from President Sadat,
September 17, 1978
I am writing you to reaffirm the position of the Arab Republic of Egypt with respect to Jerusalem:

1. Arab Jerusalem is an integral part of the West Bank. Legal and historical Arab rights in the city must be respected and restored.

2. Arab Jerusalem should be under Arab sovereignty.

3. The Palestinian inhabitants of Arab Jerusalem are entitled to exercise their legitimate national rights, being part of the Palestinian People in the West Bank.

4. Relevant Security Council Resolutions, particularly Resolutions 242 and 267,[5] must be applied with regard to Jerusalem. All the measures taken by Israel to alter the status of the city are null and void and should be rescinded.

5. All peoples must have free access to the City and enjoy the free exercise of worship and the right to visit and transit to the holy places without distinction or discrimination.

6. The holy places of each faith may be placed under the administration and control of their representatives.

7. Essential functions in the city should be undivided and a joint municipal council composed of an equal number of Arab and Israeli members can supervise the carrying out of these functions. In this way, the city shall be undivided.

*To President Carter from Prime Minister Begin,
September 17, 1978*
I have the honor to inform you, Mr. President, that on 28 June 1967, Israel's parliament (the Knesset) promulgated and adopted a law to the effect: "The Government is empowered by a decree to apply the law, the jurisdiction and administration of the State to any part of the Erez Israel (land of Israel—Palestine), as stated in that decree."

On the basis of this law, the Government of Israel decreed in July 1967 that Jerusalem is one city indivisible, the Capital of the State of Israel.

*To President Sadat from President Carter,
September 17, 1978*
I have received your letter of 17 September 1978, setting forth the Egyptian position on Jerusalem. I am transmitting a copy of that letter to Prime Minister Begin for his information.

The position of the United States on Jerusalem remains as stated by [U.S.] Ambassador [Arthur] Goldberg in the United Nations General Assembly on July 14, 1967, and subsequently by Ambassador [Charles] Yost in the United Nations Security Council on July 1, 1969.

*To President Carter from President Sadat,
September 17, 1978*
In connection with the "Framework for Peace in the Middle East," I am writing you this letter to inform you of the position of the Arab Republic of Egypt, with respect to the implementation of the comprehensive settlement.

To ensure the implementation of the provisions related to the West Bank and Gaza and in order to safeguard the legitimate rights of the Palestinian people, Egypt will be prepared to assume the Arab role emanating from these provisions, following consultations with Jordan and the representatives of the Palestinian people.

*To Prime Minister Begin from President Carter,
September 22, 1978*
I hereby acknowledge that you have informed me as follows:

1. In each paragraph of the Agreed Framework Document the expressions "Palestinians" or "Palestinian People" are being and will be construed and understood by you as "Palestinian Arabs."

2. In each paragraph in which the expression "West Bank" appears, it is being, and will be, understood by the Government of Israel as Judaea and Samaria.

*Harold Brown, U.S. Secretary of Defense, to
Ezer Weizman, Israeli Defense Minister,
September 29, 1978*
The United States understands that, in connection with carrying out the agreements reached at Camp David, Israel intends to build two military airbases at appropriate sites in the Negev to replace the airbases at Eitam and Ezion which will be evacuated by Israel in accordance with the peace treaty to be concluded between Egypt and Israel. We also understand the special urgency and priority which Israel attaches to preparing the new bases in light of its conviction that it cannot safely leave the Sinai airbases until the new ones are operational.

I suggest that our two governments consult on the scope and costs of the two new airbases as well as on related forms of assistance which the United States might appropriately provide in light of the special problems which might be presented by carrying out such a project on an urgent basis.

The President is prepared to seek the necessary Congressional approvals for such assistance as may be agreed upon by the U.S. side as a result of such consultations.

NOTES

1. Mohandas Gandhi (1869–1948), spiritual leader of the Indian nationalist and anticolonial movement. Gandhi's philosophy of militant passive resistance and nonviolence has had a great impact on political movements throughout the world. His followers called him Mahatma (Great Soul).

2. Article 2 of the U.N. Charter reads:

The Organization and its Members, in pursuit of the Purposes stated in Article 1, shall act in accordance with the following Principles.

1. The Organization in based on the principle of the sovereign equality of all its Members.

2. All Members, in order to ensure to all of them the rights and benefits resulting from membership, shall fulfil in good faith the obligations assumed by them in accordance with the present Charter.

3. All Members shall settle their international disputes by peaceful means in such a manner that international peace and security, and justice, are not endangered.

4. All Members shall refrain in their international relations from the threat or use of force against the territorial integrity or political independence of any state, or in any other manner inconsistent with the Purposes of the United Nations.

5. All Members shall give the United Nations every assistance in any action it takes in accordance with the present Charter, and shall refrain from giving assistance to any state against which the United Nations is taking preventive or enforcement action.

6. The Organization shall ensure that states which are not Members of the United Nations act in accordance with these Principles so far as may be necessary for the maintenance of international peace and security.

7. Nothing contained in the present Charter shall authorize the United Nations to intervene in matters which are essentially within the domestic jurisdiction of any state or shall require the Members to submit such matters to settlement under the present Charter; but this principle shall not prejudice the application of enforcement measures under Chapter VII.

3. Article 33 of the U.N. Charter reads:

1. The parties to any dispute, the continuance of which is likely to endanger the maintenance of international peace and security, shall, first of all, seek a solution by negotiation, enquiry, mediation, conciliation, arbitration, judicial settlement, resort to regional agencies or arrangements, or other peaceful means of their own choice.

2. The Security Council shall, when it deems necessary, call upon the parties to settle their dispute by such means.

4. The convention between Great Britian, Austria-Hungary, France, Germany, Italy, the Netherlands, Russia, Spain, and Turkey, respecting the free navigation of the Suez Maritime Canal, signed in Constantinople, October 29, 1888, has guided public international law ever since. Article 1 reads: "The Suez Maritime Canal shall always be free and open, in time of war as in time of peace, to every vessel of commerce or of war, without distinction of flag. Consequently the High Contracting Parties agree not in any way to interfere with the free use of the Canal, in time of war as in time of Peace. The Canal shall never be subject to the exercise of the blockade." Following the nationalization of the canal and the Sinai Campaign, Egypt issued the Declaration on the Suez Canal and the Arrangements for Its Operation on April 24, 1957, in which it reaffirmed its commitment "to respect the terms and the spirit of the Constantinople Convention of 1888 and the rights and obligations arising therefrom" (R. R. Baxter, *The Law of International Waterways, With Particular Regard to Interoceanic Canals* [Cambridge: Harvard University Press, 1964], pp. 119–23).

5. Resolution 267, July 3, 1969, the Security Council said that it: "censures in the strongest terms all measures taken to change the status of the City of Jerusalem; confirms that all legislative and administrative measures and actions taken by Israel with purport to alter the status of Jerusalem, including expropriation of land and properties thereon, are invalid and cannot change that status."

MOSHE ZAK
77. A Survey of Israel's Contacts with Jordan

Israel has always viewed relations with Jordan as a key toward a permanent peace, and its contacts with Jordan and King Hussein were a well-known but unadvertised secret (see docs. 5, 15). In 1980, as part of the debate in Israel over the feasibility of a Jordanian-Israeli settlement in the West Bank, many details concerning these contacts were revealed. Prime Minister Begin's public reference to past contacts served to embarrass Hussein in the Arab world, which had proclaimed the Palestine Liberation Organization to be the only legitimate voice regarding any such negotiations. In the following article, Moshe Zak, the editor of the Israeli independent daily newspaper *Maariv*, surveys Israel's contacts with Hussein on the basis of the newly revealed information.

"Relations in our region are cyclical," said King Hussein during one of his meetings "somewhere in Israel." "We build and develop," his deep voice continued, "and then comes the war and destroys our achievements. Again we turn to development, rehabilitation, and again there is war. How long will we be caught up in this vicious cycle?"

His emotional appeal came in the middle of a discussion of Israeli proposals to Jordan for cooperative irrigation and transportation development projects. In one of the meetings, Israel offered Hussein a "free area" in the Kishon port. Israel went even further, suggesting that Jordan might keep a battalion of soldiers to guard this free area in the vicinity of Haifa, as well as guarantee the road for the transfer of merchandise to and from Jordan via the port.

Israel's offers were very generous, but when the time for decisions came, Hussein explained that he could not sign any agreement that granted him less than a complete Israeli withdrawal to the June 4, 1967, lines. "If you want to give less, go to the PLO. They can agree to less, I can't. I'm ready to sign a full peace agreement, without reservations—but only in return for full withdrawal."

The talks with Hussein began in September 1960, a few days after the murder of Jordan's premier, Haz'a al-Majali. The Syrians had planted explosives in the parliament of the Jordanian government, and the prime minister and several of this cabinet were killed. At first Hussein had considered a reprisal action in Syria, but the Syrians were quicker and concentrated troops on the Jordanian border. At that time, Hussein turned to Israel for guarantees of quiet on his "back" border, while his army was busy on the Syrian front.

Exactly ten years later, in September 1970, Hussein appealed to Israel, via the Americans, to enlist its support in resisting the Syrian invasion of Jordan; that time the initiative was Syria's. But in September 1960, when he planned his acts of reprisal in Syria, he did not want to involve the Americans. He simply requested guarantees that Israel would not take advantage of the situation, and that the Israel Defense Forces would not take action even if border skirmishes should occur.

Source: Moshe Zak, "Kol Ha-Pgishot Im Hussein" (All the Meetings with Hussein), *Maariv*, April 25, 1980, pp. 13–14. Reprinted by permission of Moshe Zak.

And so the cyclical pattern was established. In September 1960, as in September 1970, Hussein turned to Israel in connection with the Jordanian-Syrian dispute. Anyone troubling to search for signs of the cyclical pattern need only recall that in September 1950 the American Embassy reported to the State Department in Washington that David Ben-Gurion and Moshe Sharett were "adamant in their determination not to allow the incident to prevent the planned meeting" (between Israeli representatives and King Abdullah).

The incident referred to was a serious one, in which four Israeli soldiers were killed by a mine planted in the vicinity of Beit Guvrin by terrorists who had come from Jordan. In a meeting between Dr. Walter Eytan and the king, Abdullah announced "that he intended to dismiss the existing Jordanian cabinet and appoint another, which would renew relations with Israel which had been severed some months earlier, and also, perhaps, to sign a nonaggression treaty for five years."

That was in 1950. Hussein's request in 1960 was more modest: not an agreement, but silent consent. He sent the head of his office to confer with an Israeli representative. The request was referred via the Israeli officer to the Armistice Committee. The government sent General Chaim Herzog to the meeting; the head of the king's office delivered to Herzog the king's request that Israel should not harm Jordan while the Jordanian army was involved on the Syrian front. Israel's promise was given.

Later this meeting aroused a debate in the top levels. One person felt that Chaim Herzog should not have met with the head of the king's office, lest this meeting lead to the cancellation of another meeting he had planned—between David Ben-Gurion and King Hussein, in Teheran, at the shah's invitation.

This plan was nearing realization, but meanwhile Hussein was under pressure to guarantee quiet on his "back" border with Israel, while he was busy on the Syrian border.

Anyone who examines all the links of the Israeli-Jordanian dialogue can't help but be impressed by the extent to which the Syrian question provided a bridge upon which the talks between Hussein and Israel developed.

This was in 1960, in the wake of the attempt to instigate a revolution in Jordan. The Syrian bomb planted in the parliament of the Jordanian government was intended as a sign for revolt; actually, even when Hussein forsook the line of talks with Israel, at the time when he aligned himself with Hafez al-Asad,[1] the Syrian question continued to be brought up on the Jordanian-Israeli talks.

Although the Jordanian front was not active in the 1973 War, the Jordanian army was beaten in that war: the Jordanian division which Hussein had no choice but to dispatch to the Golan front, in order to assist the Syrians, suffered heavy losses (as Jordan did when Hussein was drawn by the enthusiasm of May 1967 into the Six-Day War). Hussein learned from his own experience that any military confrontation in the region drags both him and his army with it; therefore he feared a Syrian-Israeli confrontation in Lebanon.

The rapprochement between Hussein and Asad is based on their shared opposition to Sadat's policies. Hussein considered himself tricked by Sadat at the Rabat Conference in 1974 [see doc. 71], and Asad considered himself tricked by Sadat at the time of the signing of the Sinai Agreement in 1975 [see doc. 74]. But while Hussein continued to meet and discuss with Israeli representatives, Asad talked of "Sadat's betrayal." Yet, though Asad knew of the "hidden connection" between the king of Jordan and Israel, he did not sever ties with him.

At that time both Kissinger and Hussein thought that the Syrian involvement in Lebanon might lead directly to the beginning of a Syrian-Israeli rapprochement. The military necessity for a Red Line[2] to prevent confrontation might, in Kissinger's opinion, lead to the achievement of other partial arrangements. The Red Line would merely be the first step. But Operation Litani cancelled the need for Syrian-Israeli talks about the Red Line because the Red Line was replaced by UNIFIL.[3]

Hussein's first change of attitude toward Syria after his bitter experiences with that neighbor in 1960 and 1970 occurred, as a matter of fact, on the eve of the Yom Kippur War. Shortly before the war, Amman renewed its diplomatic relations with Damascus, and this in itself should have been sufficient warning to Israel that the reconciliation between Jordan and Syria was similar to that which took place between Amman and Cairo just before the Six-Day War [see doc. 45].

Only later was it understood that the renewal of diplomatic relations was merely an external sign of a much broader understanding. Even Kissinger did not read the signs from Amman; the day before the outbreak of the Yom Kippur War, when Israel notified him that war was imminent, he turned to Hussein (and to Faisal),[4] and asked them to exert their influence on Egypt and Syria to refrain from war. The two kings didn't even bother to answer him. The war broke out before there was time for answers.

Today it is clear that Hussein was not happy about this war either. He was dragged into it. Damascus asked him to open up a "third front," but since he had been so badly burned in the Six-Day War, he did all in his power to avoid becoming embroiled in another war, or more correctly, to avoid exposing himself to IDF actions on his border.

In the past, when the need arose to move soldiers from the Jordanian-Israeli border, Hussein tried to make contact with Israel so that it would not "take advantage of the situation." So it was in 1960, and again in 1970, when he planned his army's offensive against the Fatah strongholds. In both cases he appealed to Israel not to attack him at this opportune moment, when his forces were thinned.

In October 1973, when the Syrians demanded that he send Jordanian army units to fight Israel on the Golan front, the situation was not quite the same. The problem was more an Israeli one; the IDF had its hands full with two fronts—the Egyptian and the Syrian—and it was Israel that wanted to know how much strength it had to allot for the "quiet front" on the Jordan. The chief of staff, Commanding General David Elazar, estimated correctly that Hussein would not open up a "third front," while Defense Minister Moshe Dayan, who had until then avoided meeting with Hussein, was concerned—he had been mistaken in his estimate of Amman just prior to the outbreak of the war—and now tried to be overly careful.

Elazar took the chance, and only afterwards did confirmation come that Jordan was sending an armed force to the Golan front. By some trick of fate it was the Jordanian division, which advanced slowly, not rushing into battle, that was most heavily beaten by the IDF.

After the war, when the meetings between Hussein and the Israeli representatives were resumed, the king did not spare his criticism of the government of Israel for not relating correctly to his estimates on the eve of the war. Hussein returned to this subject in five meetings, and warned the Israeli ministers not to be deaf to his estimations, as they had been prior to the Yom Kippur War.

Hussein kept returning to this subject, hoping to reap benefits. Why not a "separation agreement" between Israel and Jordan, like the one between Israel and Egypt, and between Israel and Syria, he asked. "Is it because I didn't open fire during the war, and didn't tie your troops up on the Jordanian front?"

Hussein's suggestion was very simple: he asked for a 12 km-wide Israeli withdrawal along the whole length of the Jordan. The Israeli government could not agreed to this, because such a separation agreement would have meant the uprooting of the Jordan Valley settlements and denial of the government program that regarded the Jordan River as Israel's security border.

Israel suggested a political interim agreement: the transfer of civil government in some parts of Judaea and Samaria, even without being granted, in return, the end of the state of war. But Hussein was not prepared for any partial political agreement and simply repeated over and over again that he was ready to sign a full peace treaty in return for full withdrawal, but he was also prepared to accept the model of a "separation agreement" like that between Israel and Egypt and between Israel and Syria; in other words, a military withdrawal without any salient political components.

This was the background on which Yigal Allon thought up the Jericho Corridor Plan [see doc. 66]. It was an interim period, and there were no National Religious party ministers in the government; therefore there was no need to uphold the obligation not to withdraw under any circumstances from Judaea and Samaria without first asking the nation.

In any case, Yigal Allon was prepared to take a chance on new elections on this issue while Yitzhak Rabin preferred that the elections be centered on a real agreement with Jordan, and not on a "separation agreement" with no political components. But the two didn't argue the matter for long, because both Kissinger and Hussein feared that the Jericho Corridor Plan, with its hint of the Allon Plan, might create problems for Hussein at the Rabat Conference.

Shulamit Aloni,[5] who in October was still a member of Yitzhak Rabin's government, wrote to me that she remembers Rabin rejecting Kissinger's suggestion regarding the Jericho Corridor. But Rabin vehemently denies that the American or Hussein presented Israel with such a plan.

There are others who were ministers in Yitzhak Rabin's government who confirm that there was no discussion of an American proposal for a Jericho Corridor. What some of the [Labor] Alignment ministers do recall is a discussion among a team of ministers about Yigal Allon's suggestion, and that Yitzhak Rabin said that it was not worth calling new elections on the question of Jericho. But, as mentioned above, this plan wasn't given a chance because Kissinger was afraid to jeopardize Hussein's position in Rabat by any sort of agreement between him and Israel. Kissinger was worried that the PLO might use such an agreement to pull the rug out from under Hussein's feet, whereas if Hussein himself went to Rabat, an agreement with Sadat in his hand, Hussein was sure that the Arab Summit Conference would accept the formula of a Jordanian-Palestinian Federation under his leadership just as he was certain of Sadat's support against the PLO stand. This explains Hussein's disappointment after Rabat, and this is the reason he abandoned Sadat and joined with Asad.

Unlike the situation during the days of Rusk[6] and Rogers, Kissinger requested reports about the Hussein-Israel meetings from both sides as soon as he took over the position of secretary of state. He followed every detail of the long talks carefully. Once, when Israel was one day late in sending a report on a meeting with Hussein, Kissinger unhesitatingly remarked, "What happened to the Israelis? Hussein has already reported, and no word from them."

This was why Kissinger did not make a fuss about Hussein befriending Asad after Sadat signed the Sinai Agreement. He knew Hussein's position and considered that in this way he was preserving a connection with Asad for the United States. Kissinger learned the "Hussein subject" from the detailed reports he received from both Hussein and Rabin about their eight meetings, and also from face-to-face meetings with Hussein. He knew, as did the Israeli ministers, to respect Hussein's analytical ability and not simply his courage. For that reason, at the last stage, during President Ford's leadership, Kissinger approached Israel with the suggestion of a partial agreement in return for a conclusion of the state of war; he was aware that Hussein had told the Israelis he could not make full peace without full withdrawal and that Israel could never agree to such a withdrawal.

Meanwhile, however, there was a change of power in Washington. Ford and Kissinger stepped down, and were replaced by Carter and Brzezinski.[7] And not only Israel but Hussein as well immediately noticed President Carter's new coin—"the Palestinian homeland." . . . The new administration did not encourage the continuation of talks between the Israelis and Hussein.

At the time of the Camp David talks, Washington left the job of inviting Hussein to the conference, or even to a postconference report meeting, up to Sadat. Carter did not show any sensitivity to Hussein's lack of trust in Sadat. And when Hussein later requested an audience with Carter, the president of the United States gave a reception at the White House for Hussein to meet with Robert Strauss, at that time the special ambassador to the autonomy talks.

Hussein, insulted, did not come to Washington. . . .

The long-term talks between the Israelis and Hussein raised many ideas, and examined many possibilities, though no agreement was reached.

And yet the talks created an atmosphere which was useful for both sides. Pinhas Sapir was able to meet with the heir to the Jordanian throne, the king's brother, and arrange practical matters with him, but this same brother of Hussein refused to meet with Yigael Yadin, even when the Americans initiated such a move because Moshe Dayan had no patience for the dialogue. When Hussein came and told him that nothing less than full withdrawal would do, Dayan backed out of the talks. Dayan had no time for "symposiums"; he rushed to the practical negotiations with Egypt, but because of that there was no way to hold the Yadin-Hussein talk, and for that reason contact was entirely cut off.

NOTES

1. Hafez al-Asad (b. 1928), leader of the Syrian Ba'ath party and Syrian head of state since 1970. Asad was minister of defense and commander of the Syrian Air Force, 1966–70. In October 1970 he led a coup and became prime minister and minister of defense. He was elected president in 1971 and has held that title since.

2. Red Line, a line Israel drew in Southern Lebanon, roughly parallel to the Litani River, below which it would not accept the presence of Syrian or PLO troops. In 1978 Israeli troops engaged in Operation Litani to enforce this policy and remove the military threat growing on its border (see doc. 79).

3. United Nations International Force in Lebanon (UNIFIL), U.N. peacekeeping force created by Security Council Resolutions 425 and 426, passed on March 19, 1978.

4. Faisal Ibn Abd al-Aziz (b. 1905), ruler of Saudi Arabia, 1964–75. The second son of Abd al-Aziz, first monarch of Saudi Arabia, Faisal was kept from power by his brother until 1958. Faisal's ability to establish order and good fiscal management eventually led to his rise to power. In March

1964 the ministerial committee stripped his brother, King Saud (r. 1953–64), of power in the midst of the crisis caused by the Yemen civil war and conflict with Egypt, and Faisal became King. He was assassinated by a nephew in March 1975 and was immediately succeeded by his half-brother, crown prince and deputy prime minister Khalid Ibn Abd-al-Aziz Al Saud (b. 1913).

5. Shulamit Aloni (b. 1929), Israeli lawyer who left the Labor party in 1973 to form the Civil Rights movement (CRM). Aloni was minister without portfolio in the Rabin government until November 1974, when her party joined the opposition.

The Civil Rights movement advocates the separation of church and state, and thus, for example, favors civil marriages and legal abortions on demand. It serves as a consumers' advocate, aligns itself with the feminist movement, and tends to be dovish on the Palestinian issue. From May to December 1975 the CRM merged with Aryeh Eliav's faction to form the Yaad party, which broke up on December 31, 1975. At the present time, the CRM has one seat in the Knesset.

6. Dean David Rusk (b. 1909), U.S. secretary of state, 1961–69, under presidents Kennedy and Johnson.

7. Zbigniew Brzezinski (b. 1928), national security adviser to President Carter, 1977–81, who like his predecessor, Henry Kissinger, had an academic career.

URI LUBRANI
78. The Iranian-Israeli Relationship

Until the Iranian revolution of late 1978 and early 1979 Israel had good diplomatic relations with Iran, which included the sale of Iranian oil to Israel. When the shah was deposed and the Ayatollah Khomeini rose to power, Iran severed diplomatic relations with Israel and openly articulated support for the Palestine Liberation Organization. One consequence of the Iranian monarchy's fall has been a series of revelations on the Iranian-Israeli relationship during the shah's reign. Uri Lubrani, former Israeli ambassador in Teheran, published this article in *Davar*, the daily newspaper of the Histadrut.

Since the last group of Israelis left Iran in January last year [1979], much has been written about our special relations with this country.

Many Israeli leaders, in fact all the top political echelons of Israel since the establishment of the state, visited Teheran at one time or another. Among them were Ben-Gurion, Golda Meir, Eban, Rabin, and Allon, and after the government changeover, Begin and Dayan too.

Each visit had its story. And this time I shall devote these lines to Yigal Allon's visit to Teheran in August 1976.

At the time Allon was deputy prime minister and foreign minister, and the main purpose of his visit was to meet with the shah, Muhammad Reza Pahlavi.

I viewed the meetings between the Israeli leaders and the shah as important. In the first years of my service in Teheran, I was not given the opportunity of meeting him face to face. Only three and a half years after my arrival in Teheran, was the dam opened and I given the opportunity to meet him. Because of the centralized regime in the country and the many powers vested in the shah, it was important that he meet with Israeli leaders frequently in order to hear from them directly those things I was able to convey to him only through intermediaries. The latter included five or six of the persons closest to the shah. But I was never sure that what I wanted brought to the shah's notice was really conveyed to him accurately, just as I was never sure whether his reactions were faithfully relayed to me, without additional interpretations tacked on by the intermediaries. For this reason, the shah's meetings with Israeli leaders, which took place every few months, were important.

The Iranians agreed to these meetings only on condition—promised in advance—that they would not be publicized. For their part, the hosts took care of the physical safety of the guests from Israel, for it was clear that if an Israeli personality were injured, an international scandal would en-

Source: Uri Lubrani, "Allon be-Armon Hashah" (Allon in the Palace of the Shah), *Davar*, April 20, 1980, pp. 3–4. Reprinted by permission.

sue and all efforts to preserve the secrecy of the visits would be foiled. From the Israeli point of view, there was no need to keep these visits secret. We were careful about this only because we knew that if one visit became public knowledge, the Iranians would be hesitant about allowing another. Arrangements were, therefore, made in Israel so that the absence of the Israeli leader would not be noticed and invite guesses. This was the reason why the visits usually took place on the Sabbath or festivals.

When the prime minister used to visit Iran, the pressures of security and the secrecy instructions were particularly stringent, and it was difficult to break through them. They made it necessary to minimize the length of the visit and the number of meetings. Allon's visit, too, had of course to be kept secret. But, at the same time, I was eager for Allon to meet not only with the Shah but also with some of his chief aides. . . .

. . . The visits of the Israeli leaders to Iran were usually planned with some matter of importance as the topic of discussion. The main subject on the agenda for this visit of Allon's was the character of the relations between Iran and Israel with respect to the supply of oil. In addition, the agenda included such subjects as a report on Israel's current political positions and particularly its attempts to find a way to a settlement with the Arab countries.

When the date of Allon's visit had been finalized, the detailed, practical planning of the visit began. For reasons of secrecy, only a handful of people in Israel knew about it. Even the top officials in the Foreign Ministry, except for the director general and the minister's closest aides, did not know about it. This made the staff work and preparation of the material more difficult, since I was not able to get assistance from the Foreign Ministry in Jerusalem. It meant that we had to make arrangments to brief the visitor from Israel upon his arrival in Teheran, before his visits with the Iranian leadership began.

The prime minister and other persons visiting Iran used to come on a special plane for reasons of secrecy and also because the El Al flight timetable would have introduced many restrictions. On this visit, Yigal Allon decided to make an effort to reduce expenses and to come on an El Al flight. In order to prevent recognition by the passengers, the foreign minister and his entourage were well made up. When I met him at Teheran airport between ten and eleven o'clock at night, I almost didn't recognize him. His hair was hidden under a wig. He was wearing strange glasses and a Tyrolean hat with a feather. Allon was accompanied by the head of his bureau, Haim Bar-On, who was also disguised, and a security man.

The Iranian services made sure that Allon did not have to go through a check, and he was taken to a guest room specially installed for visits like these. The official Iranian host who was waiting for him was the deputy prime minister, Ne'matollah Nasiri [executed after the revolution], who also headed the Savak, the Iranian Secret Service. The reception was very warm; we joked about the makeup and the disguise and without further delay we left for the guest house of the Prime Minister's Office. This guest house is situated in the northeastern part of Teheran, and, in order to reach it, we had to drive through the huge city of five million inhabitants for some forty-five minutes.

The absence of the Iranian foreign minister from the reception committee at the airport was not accidental. The foreign minister, ['Abbas 'Ali] Khal'atbari, was well known, and it was not desirable for questions to be asked about his presence at the airport. Furthermore, Nasiri was always the host for Israeli personalities. He had sole responsibility for their security, and since internal political considerations also played a role, he laid down rules that enabled him to be the first to meet important visitors from Israel. This gave him a special status in everything concerning relations with us, and he usually preferred to be the only one to receive the guest. Allon's other visits (he visited three times while I was in office) were not brought to the knowledge of the foreign minister, and it was my unpleasant task to inform Khal'atbari that his Israeli counterpart had visited Teheran and even met with the shah. I feared that the Iranian foreign minister would be insulted and suspect me of being involved in a plot against him. But eventually it was explained to me that, since every visit of an Israeli leader and all the arrangements are given the explicit approval of the shah, everyone accepted it as an unshakable command and even the foreign minister did not view it as a reason to feel insulted. But, this time, the Iranian foreign minister was included in the schedule of meetings with Allon, and he was waiting for us at the guest house of the Prime Minister's Office.

Khal'atbari was an experienced diplomat of the old school, educated and brought up in the West, a graduate of French universities, who had climbed up through the ranks of the Foreign Ministry. At the time, he had already been foreign minister for six or seven years. He was not garrulous, and it would be best to describe him as the shah's faithful retainer in the sphere of foreign policy. Khal'atbari did not initiate; he only carried out the shah's wishes with absolute loyalty. At the same time, he displayed a measure of politeness toward Israel as contrasted with the previous foreign minister, Ardashir Zahedi, the close friend of the shah and for a certain period even his son-in-law, who subsequently was the Iranian ambassador to Washington and was hostile to us, both as foreign minister and as ambassador.

Later that evening we reached the guest house where a few members of the embassy were waiting—the minister who is the ambassador's substitute and one or two of the senior staff. The others were not privy to the secret. After a few polite words, the foreign minister took his leave and Nasiri and the Israeli group were left alone with the guest house staff at our service.

This guest house is one of the most modern and luxurious buildings in Teheran. Much work had been put into designing it in a typical Iranian architectural style. Around the central building are auxiliary structures, and all the buildings are surrounded by a garden that stretches over tens of dunams, with lawns and trees, large pools, fountains, and artistic lighting, all of which create the feeling that the visitor is not in a real world but has suddenly found himself in the setting of an eastern fable.

It was the custom for the senior guest to be given a whole floor to himself in the central building which he and his bodyguard occupied. On the floor above, the ambassador and the guest's aides were housed. In this case, Haim Bar-On and the other members of the entourage resided in one of the adjacent buildings that are part of the guest house complex.

At first I thought that on that same evening we would hold a preparatory discussion for the meetings Allon was to have the next day. But I saw that Yigal was already tired, and I decided that it would be better to let him rest and to start the discussion on the morrow. The meeting with the shah was scheduled for 11 A.M., and Yigal had to leave the guest house at 10:35. The discussion was postponed until the morning.

In this discussion, we reviewed the topics we were interested in having brought to the shah's attention. We also discussed Allon's possible reactions if the shah responded in this or that manner to the things he was told. During these talks we had to take into account the fact that the house had been equipped with the latest listening devices, and we, therefore, used to switch on a radio so as to prevent our talks from being recorded. As always, Yigal was a good listener, and he welcomed any idea or advice that gave him "ammunition" for his talk with the shah, which was always shrouded in tension. It must be recalled that, at that time, the shah was at the height of his power and influence in the international arena. Since the oil crisis following the Yom Kippur War, oil prices had risen dramatically and Iran had begun to enjoy royalties she had not dreamed of. Iran became a focal point of political and economic influence, and all the countries of Europe wished to cultivate her. The shah realized this and exploited it. He began to exhibit an aggressive stand toward the countries of the West and explained to them that he had no intention of continuing the old system whereby Iran supplied oil and the Western countries supplied her with equipment and services and thus the money they paid out for oil returned to them. The shah declared that it was his intention to turn Iran into a strong regional military and industrial power within fifteen years, a power that would not be dependent on the good will of countries or world blocs. In light of this, the delicate position of the Israelis on this visit to the shah must be understood, for our relationship with Iran was more complex and complicated than that of other states.

The main subject for this meeting between Allon and the shah was the attempt on the part of Iranian officials to change the relationship between the two countries with respect to the oil supply. Allon's intention was to persuade the shah to continue supplying oil, despite the proposals of his aides. Yigal digested the topic thoroughly in our talks before the meeting with the shah. It must be remembered that Allon was never very involved in the oil situation in Israel, while the shah was very informed about everything concerning the Iranian oil setup. The confrontation with him was, therefore, no easy matter, particularly since the person facing him was not an oil man. But Yigal Allon was blessed with a flair for learning things quickly and thoroughly, and I was amazed that not only did he absorb the central issue but he developed a set of arguments to justify our position that had a touch of originality.

Yigal Allon also had to use this meeting with the shah to discuss, thoroughly, the political developments in the Middle East. For example, if my memory serves me, just prior to the date of the meeting we had discovered disturbing signs of a rapproche-ment between Syria and Iran, and Yigal wanted to investigate the nature of this development and also to get from the shah information and reactions to a wide variety of topics.

About half an hour before it was time to set out for the shah's palace, the Iranian foreign minister came to the guest house to hold a short meeting and to accompany Yigal Allon to the palace. We said farewell to Allon, who went with Khal'atbari in a car placed at his disposal by the Iranian authorities and accompanied by a guard. Allon went to the Niavaran Palace, the shah's new palace in northern Teheran where he resided most of the year and in which he had his private offices.

Visitors to the palace followed a fixed routine, and Allon did so too. He reached the central gate of the wall around the palace. The car was stopped, and the guards peered closely at the occupants even though they knew about the visit in advance and despite the fact that one of the occupants was the Iranian foreign minister. After this examination, an Iranian security officer entered Allon's car and rode with them for the few hundred meters to the palace entrance where the deputy chief of protocol of the palace awaited them. He was in charge of secret visits of this type and led Allon to a waiting room on the second floor of the building. On their way to the waiting room, the visitors passed objets d'art, priceless statues, and breathtaking carpets. After drinking the traditional glass of Persian tea, the moment came for Allon to enter the presence of the shah for a private conversation. According to the custom in the shah's court, the Iranian foreign minister had to remain outside, and it was an embarrassing moment when the Israeli guest went in to the meeting while his Iranian counterpart was forced to wait outside the door like an errand boy. I remember that Yigal Allon did not understand this arrangement and was distressed at the insult his colleague suffered. This custom of the shah's court epitomized the centralistic, authoritarian character of the regime. The shah, alone, was at the top, and subordinate to him were officials who received instructions from him and carried out his orders without really being part of the decision-making process.

Allon put all his powers of persuasion into this meeting with the shah in order to ensure that the relations between the two countries in regard to oil would continue along the same lines. Whoever meets the shah has to try to find the middle road between a cordial atmosphere that includes a desire to please the shah and an unwillingness to be obsequious and the necessity to bargain and argue convincingly against the claims and considerations of Iran, which we did not always find pleasant. Allon's argument was that a fundamental identity of interests between Iran and Israel made it essential to maintain the existing relationship. Allon explained that he would not allow the oil supply arrangement that had proved most convenient for Iran in the past to be interrupted at the recommendation of officials who took only economic considerations into account and were, perhaps, not always sufficiently aware of the real essence of common interests. To this end Yigal gave a well-informed lecture on the important role that, in his opinion, the cooperation between Iran and Israel had to play in the international arena. Allon even implied— and one must know how to hint to Orientals without insulting them—that the continuation of relations with Israel might be a bother to Iran now, but tomorrow the tables might be turned and so it was as well to base the relations between the two countries on firm principles rather than on a passing inference of events.

Since the conversation was held in private, we only learned about the dialogue later when, after the meeting was over, Allon reported what had taken place almost verbatim. There is no doubt that the entire conversation was recorded by the devices in the shah's palace. From Allon we learned that he had achieved his main objective: the shah told him that he did not intend to

change the existing relations between the two countries with regard to the oil supply. This decision of the shah gave Yigal much personal satisfaction.

In meetings of this nature, it was customary for the shah to recite a monologue in which he presented his up-to-date interpretation of events in the international arena. In the conversation he would talk with some frankness about various aspects of Iran's foreign policy. Sometimes he would express serious complaints against the United States, which he felt, did not understand the processes taking place on the international scene in general, and in the Middle East in particular. The shah would even express his evaluation of various statesmen, knowing that his words would not reach the wrong ears. During his talks with Allon, the shah made him privy to his worries about Iran's internal troubles, including her pace of development, but, at the same time, there was no hint that the shah sensed the signs of the earthquake that was to shake the foundations of his regime. The shah's talks with his Israeli visitors usually lasted sixty to seventy-five minutes, but the meeting with Allon took over two hours. As was customary, Allon presented the shah with a gift at the end of the meeting. It was usual to give the shah some antique object from the time of the Persian conquest of the Land of Israel. This time Allon had decided to give him something more modern—a statue of a Galilee leopard about to pounce, made by an artist from Safed. . . .

Allon returned to the guest house and after a short break continued on to the foreign minister's house where a luncheon was being given in his honor. A small group of senior Iranian officials was present at the meal. Allon had the opportunity to exert all his charm and talent for rhetoric. The people present were charmed by Allon's simple manner and his direct approach and by his experience and knowledge of international affairs. In his free, flowing style, Allon told about Israel's difficulties and about his home on [Kibbutz] Ginosar. I remember that the

Iranian foreign minister was very impressed by his words and said that he very much wanted to visit Israel and see things for himself. And, indeed, he did come to Israel on a secret visit in March 1977 and was Yigal Allon's guest at Ginosar. Khal'atbari was accompanied by his wife and daughter, and he was the most senior Iranian representative to visit Israel while I was ambassador. A friendship sprang up between the two foreign ministers, and this later made my contact with Khal'atbari easier, for he paid closer attention to any message or request I brought him from Yigal Allon.

The conversation at the foreign minister's house was cut short because Allon was due at a meeting with the prime minister. This meeting took place due to the endeavors of Khal'atbari, who had a close relationship with Prime Minister ['Abbas] Hoveyda. We rushed off to the meeting at the Prime Minister's Office on Kakh Street in central Teheran. This time, we were driving in broad daylight in the court limousine with the companion car close to us. It was at the peak period of traffic, and we had to drive crazily and, at times, break the traffic regulations. I was afraid that someone would identify Allon, who was not disguised. We passed through bustling streets, and we sometimes stopped at junctions despite ourselves, and anyone could have looked in and seen who was sitting in the car. But I felt that Yigal Allon enjoyed this opportunity of rushing through the streets of Teheran and seeing something of the city and the human side of things. Perhaps he also enjoyed the drama in the situation, but for me, it was almost a traumatic experience.

Prime Minister Hoveyda was waiting for Allon in his luxurious office. He had already managed to fill himself in on the talks Allon had held with the shah and the foreign minister. Hoveyda was the most senior official in the Iranian government, and the meeting with him was important, not because I expected there to be any practical outcome but because I wanted Allon to have the opportunity to hear Hoveyda's views.

Furthermore, it was obvious that this conversation would be reported to the shah, and it therefore gave Allon an opportunity to convey to the shah his complimentary impressions of the meeting with him.

Right from the very outset of the meeting, a feeling of intimacy was created—what is today called "chemistry"—between Allon and the prime minister. Amir 'Abbas Hoveyda, the scion of a Bahai family, was born in Acre. He moved up through the ranks of the Iranian bureaucracy after he began his service in the Foreign Ministry. He was then appointed to a senior post in the national oil company of Iran and finally became prime minister. Hoveyda was a highly educated man and at home with Western culture. He had a good command of English, French, German, and Arabic and was one of the few Iranian personalities who read widely. His well-endowed library was like that of a very highly cultured Western person. Hoveyda would follow events in the world not only in the political and economic sectors but was also conversant with trends in English, American, and French literature. During an evening at his home, one could also meet Iranian men of culture who were not part of the establishment. The conversation between Hoveyda and Allon ranged over a variety of topics. Hoveyda was not an Arab sympathizer. He told of meetings with prime ministers of foreign countries at which the issues of Israel and the Middle East were discussed. The talk moved on to affairs of culture and economics, and there was a feeling that it could have gone on and on. But Allon had to leave on the El Al plane, and it was clear that he and Hoveyda regretted having to part.

Once again, we rushed with Allon in the car from the Prime Minister's Office to the guest house in the north of the city and there we found the gifts from the shah and the prime minister, in reciprocation for the presents Allon had made them. Suitcases were hastily packed, and Allon once again looked like a tourist who had visited Teheran on a pleasure trip.

On the way to the airport, Allon was accompanied by his official host, Nasiri. The El Al passengers had already been on the plane for some time when the "strange tourist" and his two companions took their seats. The plane took off, and I heaved a sigh of relief that everything had gone off all right.

KAHAN COMMISSION
79. Final Report

The 1982 War in Lebanon was the most important development in Israel's Middle Eastern policies since the Camp David Agreements and the signing of the Egyptian-Israeli peace treaty in 1979. Prior to the 1975–76 civil war in Lebanon, Israel had a comfortable relationship with a state only marginally involved in the Arab-Israeli conflict. Israel had abandoned earlier hopes that Lebanon's Christian communities would make peace with it and viewed the status quo in Lebanon as a desirable but precarious state of affairs. The civil war changed all that and confronted Israel with a choice between radical alternatives—acceptance of Syrian or another form of Arab domination of Lebanon, or acceptance of the request-cum-offer by leaders of the Maronite Christian[1] community to intervene militarily on their behalf with a prospect of a Christian Lebanon allied to Israel.

The Rabin government opted for a middle-of-the-road solution. Israel agreed to a limited Syrian intervention in Lebanon (the Red Line agreement), extended limited help to the Maronite militias in central and northern Lebanon, and established a direct link with the population of the border area. Gradually that link developed into cultivation of Major Saad Haddad's militias as a *cordon sanitaire* to protect the Israeli border from raids by the Palestine Liberation Organization.

In October 1976 the Lebanese civil war was brought to an end,[2] but the Lebanese crisis went on. The underlying conflict between two rival camps in Lebanon over the nature of the Lebanese state and the distribution of power in it continued. So did the involvement by foreign powers, primarily Syria, the PLO, and Israel.

Israel's involvement in the Lebanese crisis grew deeper in the late 1970s as a result of several developments—the growth of a proto-Palestinian state in the southern half of Lebanon, the consolidation of Syria's grip over the country, the disappointment of the Begin government with Egyptian-Israeli peace, and the exacerbation of Israel's conflict with the PLO in southern Lebanon and across the Lebanese-Israeli border.[3] Israel continued to cultivate the militias of Major Haddad and developed its relations with the Maronite militias and parties in the center of the state into an actual alliance with Bashir Jumayyil,[4] the leader of the Phalanges[5] and of the broader Lebanese Front.

In 1981 a series of developments occurred that a year later led to the launching of a full-fledged war: (1) the introduction of Syrian ground-to-air missiles in Lebanon; (2) the Palestinian-Israeli artillery duel of July 1981, which demonstrated the PLO's ability to shell most of northern Israel from southern Lebanon; (3) the Likud's electoral victory of June 1981 and the formation of the second

---

Source: Commission of Inquiry into the Events at the Refugee Camps in Beirut, 1983, *Final Report* (Jerusalem: Government Printer, February 8, 1983).

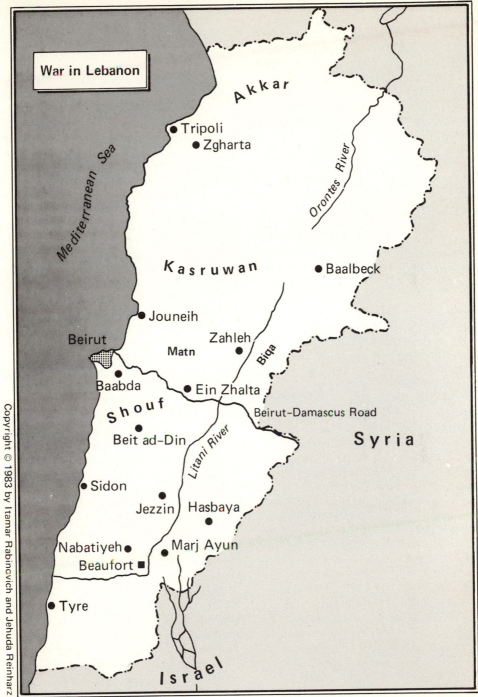

War in Lebanon

Mediterranean Sea

Akkar

● Tripoli
● Zgharta

Orontes River

Kasruwan

● Baalbeck

● Jouneih

Zahleh

Beirut

Matn

Biqa

Baabda

● Ein Zhalta

Beirut–Damascus Road

Shouf

● Beit ad–Din

Litani River

Syria

● Sidon

● Jezzin

● Hasbaya

Nabatiyeh ●

● Marj Ayun

Beaufort ■

● Tyre

Israel

Begin government with Ariel Sharon as defense minister; (4) the preparations for a new phase in the Arab-Israeli settlement process, focusing this time on the West Bank and the Gaza Strip, following the completion of Israel's withdrawal from the Sinai in April 1982; (5) the change in the U.S. outlook on the Lebanese crisis as the Reagan administration[6] decided to support a solution based on the reconstruction of the Lebanese state and a reduction of Syria's and the PLO's roles.[7]

In 1982 the Begin government formulated a plan that, through a large-scale military operation, sought to achieve four aims: (1) to destroy the PLO's military infrastructure and presence in southern Lebanon and to create an effective security zone there; (2) to diminish—if not eliminate—the hold of Syria and the PLO over the Lebanese state and to facilitate its reconstruction under the presidency of Bashir Jumayyil; (3) to preempt the possibility of a Syrian-Israeli war; (4) to guarantee a better bargaining position for Israel in the new phase of negotiations on the continuation of the settlement process.

The expected clash finally erupted in June 1982 (see map 5). The world's attention was focused on the guerrilla warfare in Central America, the Falklands crisis (involving Britain and Argentina) and the Iraqi-Iranian war in the Middle East. Officially, Israel stated that when it launched Operation Peace for Galilee it was retaliating against the assassination attempt on its ambassador in London. The initial thrust into Lebanon and the military campaigns against the PLO and the Syrian forces and missile system were conducted swiftly and successfully. But the alliance and coordination with the Phalange were disappointing. The Phalange did not capture West Beirut as planned and the Israeli government and military command refused to storm a densely populated Arab capital. After a few days of confusion, Israel opted for the siege of Beirut, which lasted ten weeks. The PLO finally evacuated Beirut but the lengthy siege and bombardment of

parts of the city were the principal factors in turning the War in Lebanon into Israel's most controversial war, at home and abroad.

Israel's ally, Bashir Jumayyil, was elected president of Lebanon in August, and in the first half of September it looked like most of the war's aims had been accomplished. But Jumayyil was assassinated, and it seemed that Israel's position would be undone. The assassination prompted the Israeli government to dispatch the Israel Defense Forces into West Beirut. It was in this context that the Israeli army authorized and facilitated the entry of Phalange militiamen into Beirut to "mop up" the Palestinian camps, or neighborhoods of Sabra and Shatila, where, according to its information, PLO combatants were still positioned.

Israel sought to employ the Lebanese militiamen for two main reasons: to minimize its own losses and to involve the Phalanges in a more active role in the liberation of their own capital. As the judicial commission of inquiry later determined, the Israeli officials who had made the decision were not sufficiently sensitive to the possibility that the militiamen might seek to revenge the death of Jumayyil or to generate a Palestinian exodus from Beirut. The result was a massacre that, aside from its tragic human dimensions, had important bearings on Israel's domestic politics and on its standing in Lebanon.

The public outcry in Israel forced the government to form a judicial commission of inquiry on September 28, 1982, despite Prime Minister Begin's initial vehement opposition. It was chaired by Yizhak Kahan, president of the Supreme Court. The two other appointees were Aharon Barak, justice of the Supreme Court and Maj. Gen. (Res.) Yonah Efrat. Although most of the Kahan Commission's hearings were closed, due to the security and national defense information that was scrutinized, many hearings were open. Similarly, when the commission completed its work in February 1983, a portion of its report was not published. The most important immediate outcome of the report was the resignation of Defense Minister Ariel Sharon, the architect of the war in Lebanon. But it also sheds an important light on the War in Lebanon and its broader context.

_____

Introduction

The commission's task, as stipulated by the cabinet's resolution [of September 28, 1982] is "to investigate all the facts and factors connected with the atrocity which was carried out by a unit of the Lebanese Forces against the civilian population of the Shatila and Sabra camps." These acts were perpetrated between Thursday, September 16, 1982, and Saturday, September 18, 1982. The establishment of the facts and the conclusions in this report relate only to the facts and factors connected with the acts perpetrated in the aforementioned time frame, and the commission did not deliberate or investigate matters whose connection with the aforementioned acts is indirect or remote. The commission refrained, therefore, from drawing conclusions with regard to various issues connected with activities during the war that took place in Lebanon from June 6, 1982, onward or with regard to policy decisions taken by the government before or after the war, unless these activities or decisions were directly related to the events that are the subject of this investigation. . . .

In one area we have found it necessary to deviate somewhat from the stipulation of the cabinet's resolution, which represents the commission's terms of reference. The resolution speaks of atrocities carried out by "a unit of the Lebanese Forces." The expression "Lebanese Forces" refers to an armed force known by the name "Phalanges" or "Keta'ib." It is our opinion that we would not be properly fulfilling our task if we did not look into the question of whether the atrocities spoken of in the cabinet's resolution were indeed perpetrated by the Phalanges, and this question will indeed be treated in the course of this report.

The commission's deliberations can be divided into two stages. In the first stage, the commission heard witnesses who had been summoned by it as well as witnesses who had expressed the desire to appear before it.[8] . . . When this stage terminated, the commission issued a resolution in accordance with [the Commissions of Inquiry Law of 1968], concerning the harm that might be caused certain people as a result of the investigation or its results; this was done in order to enable these people to study the material to appear before the commission and to testify. . . . The chairman of the commission sent notices to nine people; the notices detailed how each one of them might be harmed.[9] The material in the commission's possession was placed at the disposal of those receiving the notices and of the attorneys representing them. During the second stage of the deliberations we heard witnesses who had been summoned at the request of the lawyers, and thus some of the witnesses who had testified during the first stage were cross-examined.

Afterwards, written summations were submitted, and the opportunity to supplement these summations by presenting oral arguments was given. . . .

When we resolved to issue . . . notices about harm to the nine people, we were not oblivious to the fact that during the course of the investigation, facts were uncovered that could be the _prima facie_ basis for results that might cause harm to other persons as well. Our consideration in limiting the notices about possible harm to only nine persons was based on (the conception) that it is our duty as a public judicial commission dealing with an extremely important issue—one which had raised a furor among the general public in Israel and other nations—to deliberate and reach findings and conclusions with regard to the major and important things connected with the aforementioned events, and to the question of the responsibility of those persons whose decisions and actions could have decisively influenced the course of events. We felt that with regard to the other people who were involved in one way or another in the events we are investigating, but whose role was secondary, it would be better that the clarification or investigation, if deemed necessary, be carried out in another manner, and not before this commission, viz., before the military authorities, in accordance with the relevant stipulations of the military legal code and other legislation. We chose this path so that the matters under investigation would not expand and become overly complicated and so that we could complete our task in not too long a time.

In the course of the investigation, not a few contradictions came out regarding various facts about which we had heard testimony. In those cases where the contradictions referred to facts important for establishing findings and drawing subsequent conclusions, we shall decide between the variant versions in accordance with the usual criteria in judicial and quasi-judicial tribunals. Our procedures are not those of a criminal court; and therefore the criterion of criminal courts that stipulates that in order to convict someone his guilt must be proven beyond a reasonable doubt, does not apply in this case. Nevertheless, since we are aware that our findings and conclusions are liable to be of significant influence from a social and ethical standpoint, and to harm also in other ways persons involved in our deliberations, no finding of significant harm was established with regard to any one of those to whom notices were sent, unless convincing evidence on which to base such a finding was found, and we shall not be satisfied with evidence that leaves room for real doubt. We shall not pretend to find a solution to all the contradictions in testimony. . . .

A Description of the Events: The Period before the Events in Beirut

In 1975, civil war broke out in Lebanon. This war began with clashes in Sidon between the Christians and Palestinian terrorists and subsequently widened in a manner to encompass many diverse armed forces—under the auspices of ethnic groups, political parties, and various organizations—that were active in Lebanon. In its early stages, this war was waged primarily between the Christian organizations on the one hand, and Palestinian terrorists, Lebanese leftist organizations, and Muslim and Druze organizations of various factions on the other. In the course of the civil war, Syrian army forces entered Lebanon and took part in the war, for a certain period of time on the side of the Christian forces, and subsequently on the side of the terrorists and the Lebanese leftist organizations. During the early years of the war, massacres on a large scale were perpetrated by the fighting forces against the civilian population. The Christian city of Damour was captured and destroyed by Palestinian terrorists in January 1976. The Christian residents fled the city and the conquering forces carried out acts of slaughter that cost the lives of many Christians. In August 1976, the Christian forces captured the Tel Za'atar refugee camp in Beirut, where Palestinian terrorists had dug in, and thousands of Palestinian refugees were massacred. Each massacre brought in its wake acts of revenge of a similar nature. The number of victims of the civil war has been estimated at close to 100,000 killed, including a large number of civilians, among them women and children.

The Palestinians' armed forces organized in camps inhabited by refugees who had arrived in Lebanon in various waves, beginning in 1948. There are various estimates as to the number of Palestinian refugees who were living in Lebanon in 1982. According to the figures of UNRWA (the United National Relief and Works Agency), the Palestinian refugees numbered approximately, 270,000. On the other hand, the leaders of the Christian armed forces estimated the number of Palestinian refugees at approximately 500,00 or more. This estimate is probably exaggerated, and the more realistic estimate is the one that puts the number of Palestinian refugees at approximately 300,000—and in any case, not more than 400,000.

The main Christian armed force that took part in the civil war consisted mainly of Maronite Christians, though a small number of Shi'ites[10] joined them. This force comprised several armed Christian organizations, the largest among them being the organizations under the leadership of the Chamoun family and of the Jemayyil family. The head of the Jemayyil family, Mr. Pierre Jemayyil, founded the Phalange; and the leader of this organization in recent years was Pierre's son, Bashir Jemayyil. In the course of time, the Phalange became the central element in the Christian forces; in 1982, the Phalange ruled the Chrisian armed forces. Even though the "Lebanese Forces" formally comprised several Christian organizations, the dominant and primary force in this organization at the time under our scrutiny, was the Phalange led by the Jemayyil family.

When the war broke out in Lebanon in June 1982, the Phalange force included a nucleus of approximately 2,000 full-time recruited soldiers. In addition, the Phalange had a reserve armed force—that is, men who served part time in their free hours or when they were called up for special service. When fully mobilized the number of Phalange soldiers reached 5,000. Similarly, the Phalange had militias in the villages. There were not ranks in this military force, but it was organized along military lines with Bashir Jemayyil as the military and political leader who enjoyed unimpeachable authority. The Phalange had a general staff comprised of several commanders. At the head of this general staff was a commander named Fadi Frem; at the head of the Phalange's intelligence division was a commander by the name of Elie Hobeika.

The link between the Christian forces and the State of Israel was formed shortly after the start of the civil war. In the course of time, this link grew stronger, from both political and military standpoints. The Christian forces were promised that if their existence were to become endangered, Israel would come to their aid. Israel extended significant aid to the Christian armed forces, supplying arms, uniforms, etc. and also training and instruction. Over the course of time, a considerable number of meetings were held between leaders of the Phalange and representatives of the Government of Israel and the IDF. In the course of these meetings, the ties between the leaders of the two sides grew stronger. The Institute for Intelligence and Special Assignments (henceforth, the Mossad) was made responsible for the link with the Phalange; and representatives of the Mossad maintained—at various times, and in various ways—a rather close connection with the Phalange leadership. In the course of these meetings, the Phalange leaders brought up varous plans for strengthening the Christian forces' position as well as various ways of bringing about the end of the civil war in Lebanon and restoring the independence of that nation, while (simultaneously) buttressing the status of the Phalange and those allied with it in a regime that would be established in Lebanon. Israel's representatives expressed reservations with regard to these plans and Israel's involvement in their realization.

A separate armed force is the military force in southern Lebanon—the Army of Free Lebanon under the command of Major Haddad. This force comprises several hundred full-time soldiers. In addition, there is in southern Lebanon a National Guard, which, under the command of local officers, does guard duty in the villages. Relations between the Phalange and Haddad's men are not particularly close, for various reasons, and there were points of tension between these two forces. In 1982, soldiers of both Major Haddad and the Phalange wore uniforms provided by Israel—and similar to those worn by the IDF. The Phalange's uniforms bore an emblem consisting of the inscription "Keta'ib Lubnaniyeh" and the drawing of a cedar, embroidered over the shirt pocket. Major Haddad's soldiers had an emblem on the epaulet inscribed with the words "Army of Free Lebanon" in Arabic and the drawing of a cedar. During the war, Haddad's force advanced and reached the Awali River. Pursuant to IDF orders, Haddad's army did not proceed north of the Awali River.

The subject of the Palestinian population in Lebanon, from among whom the terrorist organizations sprang up and in the midst of whom their military infrastructure was entrenched, came up more than once in meetings between Phalange leaders and Israeli representatives. The position of the Phalange leaders, as reflected in various pronouncements of these leaders, was, in general, that no unified and independent Lebanese state could be established without a solution being found to the problem of the Palestinian refugees, who, according to the Phalange's estimates, numbered half a million people. In the opinion of the Phalange, that number of refugees, for the most part Muslims, endangered (both) the demographic balance between the Christians and Muslims in Lebanon and (from other standpoints as well) the stability of the State of Lebanon and the status of the Christians in that country. Therefore, Phalange leaders proposed removing a large portion of the Palestinian refugees from Lebanese soil, whether by methods of persuasion or other means of pressure. They did not conceal their opinion that it would be necessary to resort to acts of violence in order to cause the exodus of many Palestinian refugees from Lebanon.

As we have said, the Mossad was the organization that actually handled the relations between the Phalange and Israel, and its representatives maintained close contacts with Phalange leadership. In addition, the Intelligence Branch of the IDF (henceforth Military Intelligence) participated, albeit in a more limited capacity, in the contacts with the Phalangists; and it, by virtue of its job, was to issue a not insignificant number of evaluation papers on the Phalange, its leaders, aims, fighting ability, etc. The division of labor between the Mossad and Military Intelligence with regard to the Phalange was spelled out in a document. While this division of duties left room for misunderstandings and also duplication in various areas, there is no room for doubt that both the Mossad and Military Intelligence specifically dealt with drawing up evaluations on the Phalange, and each one of them was obligated to bring these evaluations to the attention of all interested parties. Neither the head of the Mossad nor the director of Military Intelligence disagreed with this in his testimony before us.

From the documents submitted to us and the testimony we heard, it emerges that there were differences of opinion between the Mossad and Military Intelligence with regard to the relations with the Phalange. The Mossad, to a not inconsiderable extent under the influence of constant and close contact with Phalange elite, felt positively about strengthening relations with that organization, though not ignoring its faults and weaknesses. This approach of the Mossad came out clearly in the testimony we heard from the person who was in charge of the Mossad's contacts with the Phalange. The head of the Mossad, in his testimony before us on December 27, 1982, said, *inter alia*, that "the Mossad tried, to the best of its ability, throughout this period, to present and approach the subject as objectively as possible; but since it was in charge of the contacts, I accept as an assumption that subjective, and not only objective, relations also emerged. I must accept that in contacts, when you talk to people, relationships are formed." In contrast, Military Intelligence was to emphasize in its evaluations the danger in the link with the Phalange, primarily because of this organization's lack of reliability, its military weakness, and other reasons we need not specify here. A characteristic expression of the difference in approach between these two agencies, whose reponsibility it was to provide evaluations on the Phalange and the desirability of relations with them, can be found in the exchange of documents when one of the intelligence officers who served as a liaison officer on behalf of Military Intelligence in the Mossad's representation at Phalangist headquarters at the beginning of the war submitted an assessment on cooperation with the Phalange. The Military Intelligence officer rendered a negative evaluation, from Israel's standpoint, of the Phalange's policy during the war and its aims for the future. This criticism was vigorously rejected by the Mossad.

The "Peace for the Galilee" War (henceforth, the war) began on June 6, 1982. On June 12–14, IDF forces took over the suburbs of Beirut and linked up with the Christian forces who controlled East Beirut. On June 25 the encirclement of West Beirut was completed, and IDF forces were in control of the Beirut-Damascus road. There followed a period of approximately one and a half months of negotiations on the evacuation of the terrorists and the Syrian forces from West Beirut, and during this time various targets in West Beirut were occasionally shelled and bombed by the IDF's Air Force and artillery. On August 19, 1982, the negotiations on the evacuation of the terrorists and the Syrian forces from West Beirut were completed. On August 23, 1982, Bashir Jemayyil was elected president of Lebanon. His term of office was supposed to begin on September 23, 1982.

On August 21–26, a multi-national force arrived in Beirut, and the evacuation of the terrorists and the Syrian forces began. The evacuation was completed on September 1; however, according to information from various sources, the terrorists did not fulfill their obligation to evacuate all their forces from West Beirut and hand their weapons over to the Lebanese army but left in West Beirut, according to various estimates, approximately 2,000 fighters, as well as many arms caches, some of which were handed over by the terrorists to the Lebanese leftist militia Mourabitoun. This militia numbered approximately 7,000 men in West Beirut,

and it cooperated with the terrorists. After the evacuation was completed, the multinational force left Lebanon (September 10–12, 1982).

At the beginning of the war, the chief of staff [Lt. Gen. Rafael Eitan][11] told the Phalange that it should refrain from all fighting. This order was issued because of the fear that if the Phalange force got into trouble while fighting, the IDF would be forced to come to its aid, thereby disrupting the IDF's plan of action. Even after IDF forces reached the Damour-Shouf line, the IDF's orders were that the Phalangists would not participate in fighting. After IDF forces reached the area under Christian control, the Phalangist commanders suggested that a company of theirs of approximately three hundred men set up a training base at a place called Beit ad-Din, a site of historical importance in Lebanon. The chief of staff agreed to this, but made his agreement conditional on the Phalange forces' exercising restraint and discipline, as the area was Druze. At first this condition was honored; afterwards there were outbursts of hostilities between the Phalange and the Druze in Beit ad-Din. The Druze committed some murders, and the Phalange took revenge; a small IDF force was stationed in the area in order to prevent such actions. In the early stages of the war there were also some acts of revenge and looting on the part of the Christians in Sidon; these were stopped by the IDF.

When IDF forces were fighting in the suburbs of Beirut and along the Beirut-Damascus road, the Phalange was asked to cooperate with the IDF's actions by identifying terrorists, a task at which the Phalange's expertise was greater than that of the Israeli security forces. During these actions there were generally no acts of vengeance or violence against the Palestinian civilian population by the Phalanges who were operating with the IDF. Another action of the Phalange's military force was the capture of the technical college in Reihan, a large building in Beirut not located in a built-up area. The Phalangists captured this place from the armed Shi'ite organization Amal. One day after the place was taken, the Phalange turned the building over to the IDF and left the site.

The fighting actions of the Phalangists during that time were few, and in effect the fighting was all done by IDF forces alone. This state of affairs aroused criticism and negative reactions from the Israeli public, and among IDF soldiers as well. This dissatisfaction was expressed in various ways; and in the political echelon, as well as in the media, there was amazement that the Phalange was not participating in the fighting, even though the war was its battle as well, and it was only right that it should be taking part in it. The feeling among the Israeli public was that the IDF was "pulling the chestnuts out of the fire" for the Phalange. As the number of IDF casualties mounted, public pressure for the Phalange to participate in real fighting increased. The plan formulated in mid-June 1982, when it was

still uncertain whether the terrorists would agree to leave West Beirut, was that the Christian forces would fight to take control of West Beirut; the IDF would not take part in that operation; and only in the event that it became necessary would the IDF help out the Phalange with long-range artillery fire. This plan was discussed in the cabinet meeting of June 15, 1982, where it was proposed by the Prime Minister, and his proposal was adopted by the cabinet, namely, that IDF forces would not enter West Beirut, and this job was to be done by other forces (meaning the Phalange) with help it would be given by the IDF. Even after his resolution, no real fighting was done by the Phalange for the purpose of extending control over West Beirut; and, as we have said, eventually the terrorists were evacuated as the result of a political agreement, after the IDF had shelled various targets in West Beirut.

NOTES

1. Maronites, largest Christian community in Lebanon, constituting about 25 percent of the total population or roughly the same size as the Sunni Muslim community. The Maronites are a Uniate church, i.e., tied to the Vatican.

2. On October 17–18, 1976, a meeting of the leaders of Syria, Egypt, Lebanon, Kuwait, and the PLO met in Riyadh. This meeting endorsed the actions of Syrian forces in the 1976 civil war, increased the force to 30,000, and arranged for a cease-fire. These positions were later reaffirmed by the full Arab League meeting in Cairo a week later.

3. The situation in southern Lebanon was radically altered in the second week of March 1978 following the massacre of Israeli bus passengers and other civilians by a Palestinian terrorist squad on March 11. The government felt that the severity and central location of the massacre called for a massive retaliation. Rather than retaliating for the sake of retaliating, however, it was thought better to solve or at least to alleviate Israel's "problem of southern Lebanon" by eliminating the PLO's presence and infrastructure in

the area. After deliberating three days on how to respond to this attack, Israel launched Operation Litani, a massive military offensive resulting in Israel's occupying the region south of the Litani River, with the exception of the area around Tyre. The size of the operation, and the casualties and dislocation it caused, generated sharp international criticism. Israel's presence in Lebanon lasted three months, the phased withdrawal of Israeli forces being completed on June 13. They were replaced by units of UNIFIL.

4. Bashir Jumayyil (1947–82), Lebanese Phalange leader elected as president in 1982 but assassinated before his term of office began. Before the election, Jumayyil was president of the Ashrafiyah sector of the Phalange and commander in chief of the United Lebanese Forces; he was friendly to Israel. Following his assassination, his brother Amine Jumayyil (b. 1942) became president of Lebanon. Both are sons of Pierre Jumayyil (b. 1905), a founder of the Phalange in 1936.

5. Phalange (or Keta'ib party), dominant Christian force in Lebanon today. The followers of

Chamoun are a second political group with a more uncompromising stand against a Syrian presence in Lebanon.

6. Ronald Reagan (b. 1911), president of the United States, 1981–present.

7. In the spring and summer of 1981 events in southern Lebanon again captured the headlines of the world press. Syria had placed sophisticated Soviet missiles in Lebanon. The United States restrained Israel from engaging in a preemptive strike against the missile sites. Nevertheless, hostilities escalated as the PLO factions increased the frequency and intensity of terrorist atacks and Israel retaliated with land, sea, and air forces. In July 1981, after Israeli planes attacked Fatah headquarters in Beirut, an agreement by the PLO and Israel to refrain from military attacks across the Lebanese border was negotiated by special U.S. ambassador Philip Habib. Between the time of this agreement and the outbreak of the 1982 war, no Israeli lives were lost due to PLO attacks from Lebanon.

8. The commission had previously published notices in the press and other media inviting anyone who wished to testify or to submit material in any form to do so. A special effort was made to collect testimony from foreigners, including provision of transportation, etc. There was little response from abroad.

9. Prime Minister Begin was chastised for his lack of involvement in the decisions regarding using the Phalange, and his indirect responsibility was noted.

Defense Minister Sharon was chastised for having disregarded the danger of using the Phalange and for not ordering measures to prevent or reduce the danger of a massacre. The commission recommended that he resign or be removed from his position. (The cabinet subsequently forced him to resign as defense minister and appointed him minister without portfolio.)

Foreign Minister Yizhak Shamir's indirect responsibility was noted. He erred in not immediately reporting information he received from Communications Minister Mordekhai Zippori regarding the Phalange's actions.

The chief of staff, Gen. Rafael Eitan (see n. 11

below), was chastised for his inaction in preventing the massacre and for issuing an order to provide the Phalange with a tractor. The commission noted that since he was due to retire in April and would not be reappointed, no purpose would be served in recommending his dismissal.

The commission recommended the dismissal of the director of military intelligence, Major General Yehoshuah Saguy.

The commission noted that the inaction by the head of the Mossad was not serious. (For security reasons, the name of the head of the Mossad is never revealed publicly.)

The commission noted the indirect responsibility of general operations commander of the Northern Area, Major General Amir Drori.

The commission recommended that division commander Brig. Gen. Amos Yaron not serve as a field commander for at least three years.

The commission was unable to determine whether the personal aide to the defense minister, Avi Dudai, had failed to pass on information in a timely manner.

10. Shi'ites, nominally the second largest Muslim community in Lebanon but in fact the largest. Shii Muslims are part of the sect of the Matawilah who believe that only Muhammad's son-in-law, Ali, and his descendants, are true successors to the Prophet Muhammad.

11. Rafael (Raful) Eitan (b. 1929), Israeli chief of staff, 1978–83. Eitan began his military career as an officer in the Palmah and held high-ranking positions in the Paratroop Brigade, was operations commander of the Northern Area, 1974–77, and chief of the General Staff Branch, 1977–1978. In April 1983 he was succeeded by Moshe Levy, (b. 1936), who had also held various positions in the Paratroop Brigade during the early part of his military career. Levy gained the nickname "Moishe Vehezi" (lit., Moshe-and-a-half) because of his height (over two meters). In 1974 he moved up into the General Staff becoming chief of operations and subsequently commander of a tank division, chief of the Central Command, and deputy chief of staff and head of operations. During the 1982 War in Lebanon, Levy was responsible for coordinating units and logistics.

APPENDIX

Demography and Government in Israel

The Presidents of the State of Israel

Name	Term
Chaim Weizmann	February 1949–November 1952[a]
Yizhak Ben-Zvi	December 1952–April 1963[a]
Zalman Shazar	May 1963–May 1973
Efraim Kazir	May 1973–May 1978
Yizhak Navon	May 1978–May 1983
Chaim Herzog	May 1983–

[a] Indicates died in office. See text for exact dates of death.

Chiefs of Staff of the Israel Defense Forces

Name	Term
Yaakov Dori	1939–1945, 1947–1948 (Haganah), 1948–1949
Yigael Yadin	1949–1952
Mordekhai Makleff	1952–1953
Moshe Dayan	1953–1957
Haim Laskov	1958–1961
Zvi Zur	1961–1964
Yitzhak Rabin	1964–1968
Haim Bar-Lev	1968–1972
David Elazar	1973–1974
Mordecai Gur	1974–1978
Rafael Eytan	1978–1983
Moshe Levy	1983–

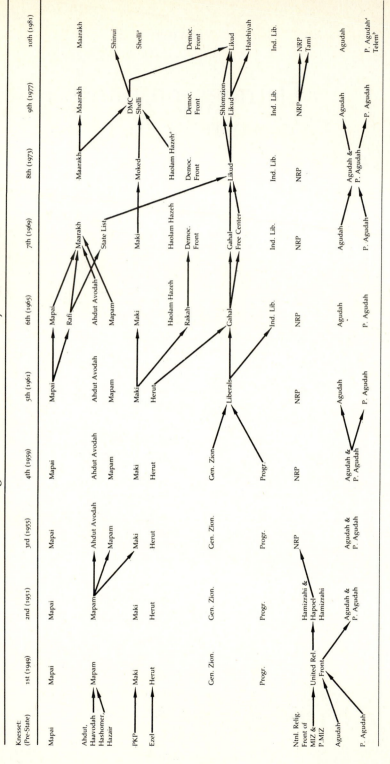

Changes in Political Alliances of Major Israeli Parties

Results of Knesset Elections, 1949–81, by List (in Absolute Numbers, in Percentages, and Knesset Seats Obtained)

Knesset / Date of Election		First 25 Jan. 49	Second 30 July 51	Third 26 July 55	Fourth 3 Nov. 59	Fifth 15 Aug. 61	Sixth 2 Nov. 65	Seventh 28 Oct. 69	Eighth 31 Dec. 73	Ninth 17 May 77	Tenth 30 June 81
Eligible voters		506,567	924,885	1,057,795	1,218,483	1,271,285	1,499,709	1,748,710	2,037,478	2,236,293	2,490,014
Voters		440,095	695,007	876,085	994,306	1,037,030	1,244,706	1,427,981	1,601,098	1,771,726	1,954,609
Valid votes cast		434,684	687,492	853,219	969,337	1,006,964	1,206,728	1,367,743	1,566,855	1,747,820	1,937,366
Turnout (%)		86.9	75.1	82.8	81.6	81.6	83.0	81.7	78.6	79.2	78.5
Mapai[a]	Votes	155,274	256,456	274,735	370,585	349,330	443,379	632,035	621,183	430,023	708,536
	Seats	46	45	40	47	42	45	56	51	32	47
	%	35.7	37.3	32.2	38.2	34.7	36.7	46.2	39.6	24.6	36.6
Rafi	Votes						95,323				
	Seats						10				
	%						7.9				
Mapam	Votes	64,018	86,095	62,401	69,468	75,654	79,985				
	Seats	19	15	9	9	9	8				
	%	14.71	12.5	7.3	7.2	7.5	6.6				
Ahdut Haavodah[b]	Votes	—	—	69,475	58,043	66,170					
	Seats	—	—	10	7	8					
	%	—	—	8.2	6.0	6.6					
Minorities' lists connected with Alignment[c]	Votes	13,413	32,288	37,777	37,782	35,376	39,894	47,989	48,961	24,185	11,590
	Seats	2	5	5	5	4	4	4	3	1	0
	%	3.0	4.7	4.4	3.9	3.5	3.3	3.5	3.1	1.4	0.6
National Religious Party[d]	Votes	52,982	56,730	77,936	95,581	98,786	107,966	133,238	130,349	160,787	95,232
	Seats	16	10	11	12	12	11	12	10	12	6
	%	12.2	8.3	9.1	9.9	9.8	8.9	9.8	8.3	9.2	4.9
Agudat Israel[e]	Votes	—	13,799	39,836	45,569	37,178	39,795	44,002	60,012	58,652	72,312
	Seats	—	3	6	6	4	4	4	5	4	4
	%	—	2.0	4.7	4.7	3.7	3.3	3.2	3.8	3.4	3.7
Poalei Agudat Israel[e]	Votes	—	11,194	—	—	19,428	22,066	24,968	—	23,571	17,090
	Seats	—	2	—	—	2	2	2	—	1	0
	%	—	1.6	—	—	1.9	1.8	1.8	—	1.3	0.9

Knesset Date of Election		First 25 Jan. 49	Second 30 July 51	Third 26 July 55	Fourth 3 Nov. 59	Fifth 15 Aug. 61	Sixth 2 Nov. 65	Seventh 28 Oct. 69	Eighth 31 Dec. 73	Ninth 17 May 77	Tenth 30 June 81
Sefardi Party	Votes	15,287	12,002								
	Seats	4	2								
	%	3.5	1.7								
Fighters' List	Votes	5,363									
	Seats	1									
	%	1.2									
Herut (& Gahal & Likud)[f]	Votes	49,782	45,651	107,190	130,515	138,599	256,957	296,294	473,309	583,968	718,941
	Seats	14	8	15	17	17	26	26	39	43	48
	%	11.5	6.6	12.6	13.5	13.8	21.3	21.7	30.2	33.4	37.1
Democratic Movement for Change	Votes									202,265	
	Seats									15	
	%									11.6	
Free Center	Votes							16,393			
	Seats							2			
	%							1.2			
Shlomzion	Votes									33,947	
	Seats									2	
	%									1.9	
State list	Votes							42,654			
	Seats							4			
	%							3.1			
General Zionists	Votes	22,661	111,394	87,099	59,700						
	Seats	7	20	13	8						
	%	5.2	16.2	10.2	6.2						
Liberal Party	Votes					137,255					
	Seats					17					
	%					13.6					
Independent Liberals[g]	Votes	17,786	22,171	37,661	44,889	—	45,299	43,933	56,560	20,384	11,764
	Seats	5	4	5	6	—	5	4	4	1	0
	%	4.1	3.2	4.4	4.6	—	3.8	3.2	3.6	1.2	0.6

Party		1	2	3	4	5	6	7	8	9	10
Citizens' Rights Movement	Votes								35,023	20,621	27,921
	Seats								3	1	1
	%								2.2	1.2	1.4
Shelli	Votes									27,281	8,691
	Seats									2	0
	%									1.6	0.4
Moked	Votes								22,147		
	Seats								1		
	%								1.4		
Maki	Votes	15,148	27,334	38,492	27,374	42,111	13,617	15,712			
	Seats	4	5	6	3	5	1	1			
	%	3.5	4.0	4.5	2.8	4.2	1.1	1.2			
Haolam Hazeh—Koah Hadash[h]	Votes						14,124	16,853	10,469		
	Seats						1	2	0		
	%						1.2	1.2	0.7		
Rakah[i] (Dem. list for Peace & Equal.)	Votes						27,413	38,827	53,353	79,733	64,918
	Seats						3	3	4	5	4
	%						2.3	2.8	3.4	4.6	3.4
Flatto Sharon	Votes									35,049	10,823
	Seats									1	0
	%									2.0	0.6
Hatehiyah	Votes										44,700
	Seats										3
	%										2.3
Tami	Votes										44,466
	Seats										3
	%										2.3
Telem	Votes										30,600
	Seats										2
	%										1.6
Shinui	Votes										29,837
	Seats										2
	%										1.5

Knesset Date of Election		First 25 Jan. 49	Second 30 July 51	Third 26 July 55	Fourth 3 Nov. 59	Fifth 15 Aug. 61	Sixth 2 Nov. 65	Seventh 28 Oct. 69	Eighth 31 Dec. 73	Ninth 17 May 77	Tenth 30 June 81
Other minorities' lists	Votes			4,484	8,469	3,896	5,541		3,269	6,780.	10,900
	Seats			0	0	0	0		0	0	0
	%			0.5	0.9	0.4	0.5		0.2	0.4	0.6
Other lists	Votes	22,970	12,378	16,133	21,422	3,181	15,369	14,845	52,220	40,189	29,045
	Seats	2	1	0	0	0	0		0	0	0
	%	5.3	1.8	1.9	2.2	0.3	1.3	1.1	3.3	2.2	1.5

SOURCES: *Statistical Abstract of Israel,* 1978, Table XXI, 1972, Table XX/1; *ibid.,* 1972, Table XX/1; *Encyclopaedia Judaica,* vol. 9. p. 326; *Encyclopaedia Judaica Yearbook, 1974.* p. 326; State of Israel, Government Press Office, *(Daily) Press Bulletin* (July 9, 1981); *Israleft,* 190 (July 16, 1981); Asher Zidon, *Knesset: The Parliament of Israel* (New York: Herzl Press, 1967); Peretz Merhav, *The Israeli Left: History, Problems, Documents* (New York, A.S. Barnes, 1980); *The Jerusalem Post* (International Edition), No. 1080 (July 12–18, 1981); Inspector General of Elections, *Results of Elections to the Ninth Knesset 17.5.1977* (Jerusalem: Central Bureau of Statistics, 1977). Where sources differed, the last source generally proved to be the most reliable.

[a] Includes the Maarakh (Labor Alignment) of Mapai and Ahdut Haavodah, 1965; also includes the Maarakh of the Israel Labor Party and Mapam, 1968 to the present.

[b] In the first two elections, Ahdut Haavodah was part of Mapam.

[c] Includes Arab lists connected with the Labor parties and, since the Seventh Knesset, both Labor alignments.

[d] Includes votes of the United Religious Front (First Knesset) and of the electoral alignment of Hamizrahi and Hapoel Hamizrahi before their formal merger.

[e] The four religious parties comprising the United Religious Front (i.e., Hamizrahi, Hapoel Hamizrahi, Agudat Israel, and Poalei Agudat Israel) ran together in the first election as the United Religious Front. In the third, fourth, and eighth elections Agudat Israel and Poalei Agudat Israel ran on the same list.

[f] Includes Herut, Gahal, and the Likud.

[g] Through the fourth Knesset, these figures refer to the Progressive Party. In the fifth Knesset, the Progressives merged with the General Zionists to form the Liberal Party. From the sixth Knesset the Progressive faction ran as the Independent Liberals.

[h] In the eighth Knesset, Haoloam Hazeh and other leftist groups ran under the name "Meri" (acronym for Israel Radical Camp).

[i] From the seventh Knesset on, Rakah was the major faction within the Democratic Front for Peace and Equality.

Governments of Israel, 1948–55

Portfolio	First Knesset				Second Knesset		
	(Prov. Govt.) 14 May 1948	7 Mar. 1949	1 Nov. 1950	8 Oct. 1951	22 Dec. 1952	26 Jan. 1954	29 June 1955
Prime Minister	MAPAI Ben-Gurion	MAPAI Ben-Gurion	MAPAI Ben-Gurion	MAPAI Ben-Gurion	MAPAI Ben-Gurion	MAPAI Sharett	MAPAI Sharett
Defense	MAPAI Ben-Gurion	MAPAI Ben-Gurion	MAPAI Ben-Gurion	MAPAI Ben-Gurion	MAPAI Ben-Gurion	MAPAI Lavon (-2.55) Ben-Gurion (fr. 2.55)	MAPAI Ben-Gurion (fr. 2.55)
Deputy PM				MAPAI Kaplan (25.6.52–d.14.7.52)			
Agriculture	MAPAM Zisling	MAPAI Joseph	MAPAI Lavon	MAPAI Eshkol (-6.52)[3] Naftali[3] (fr. 25.6.52)	MAPAI Naftali	MAPAI Naftali	MAPAI Naftali
Commerce & Industry	GEN ZION Bernstein[4]	MAPAI Kaplan	NON-PARTY Geri	MAPAI Joseph	GEN ZION Bernstein	GEN ZION Bernstein	MAPAI Naftali
Transportation	MAPAI Remez[1]	MAPAI Remez	MAPAI Joseph	MIZRAHI Pinhas (d.14.8.52)	GEN ZION Y. Sapir	GEN ZION Y. Sapir	MAPAI Aranne
Posts				MAPAI Remez (-11.52) MIZRAHI Nurok (fr. 11.52)	P.MIZ Burg	P.MIZ Burg	P.MIZ Burg
Development					MAPAI Joseph (fr. 6.53)	MAPAI Joseph	MAPAI Joseph
Education and Culture		MAPAI Shazar	MAPAI Remez	MAPAI Dinur	MAPAI Dinur	MAPAI Dinur	MAPAI Dinur
Finance	MAPAI Kaplan	MAPAI Kaplan	MAPAI Kaplan	MAPAI Kaplan (-6.52) Eshkol (fr. 6.52)	MAPAI Eshkol	MAPAI Eshkol	MAPAI Eshkol
Foreign Affairs	MAPAI Sharett	MAPAI Sharett	MAPAI Sharett	MAPAI Sharett	MAPAI Sharett	MAPAI Sharett	MAPAI Sharett

| | (Prov. Govt.) | First Knesset | | | Second Knesset | | |
Portfolio	14 May 1948	7 Mar. 1949	1 Nov. 1950	8 Oct. 1951	22 Dec. 1952	26 Jan. 1954	29 June 1955
Health	P.MIZ H.M. Shapira	P.MIZ H.M. Shapira	P.MIZ H.M. Shapira	P.MIZ Burg	P.MIZ Burg (-10.53) Serlin	GEN ZION Serlin	MAPAI Joseph
Immigration (Absorption)	P.MIZ H.M. Shapira	P.MIZ H.M. Shapira	P.MIZ H.M. Shapira				
Interior	GEN ZION Gruenbaum	P.MIZ H.M. Shapira	P.MIZ H.M. Shapira	P.MIZ H.M. Shapira	GEN ZION Rokah	GEN ZION Rokah	NRP H.M. Shapira
Justice	PROGR Rosen	PROGR Rosen	PROGR Rosen	MAPAI Joseph (-6.52) NON-PARTY Cohn	PROGR Rosen	PROGR Rosen	PROGR Rosen
Labor MAPAI	MAPAM Bentov[5]	MAPAI Meyerson[6,7]	MAPAI Meyerson[6]	MAPAI Meyerson[6]	MAPAI Meyerson[6]	MAPAI Meyerson[6]	MAPAI Meyerson[6]
Police	SEFARADIM Shitrit	MAPAI Shitrit	MAPAI Shitrit	MAPAI Shitrit	MAPAI Shitrit	MAPAI Shitrit	MAPAI Shitrit
Religious Affairs	MIZRAHI Maimon[8]	MIZRAHI Maimon	MIZRAHI Maimon	P.MIZ H.M. Shapira[9]	P.MIZ H.M. Shapira[9]	NRP H.M. Shapira	NRP H.M. Shapira
Social Welfare	AGUDAH Levin	AGUDAH Levin	AGUDAH Levin	AGUDAH Levin (-9.52)[9]	P.MIZ H.M. Shapira[9]	NRP H.M. Shapira	NRP H.M. Shapira
Supply & Rationing	MAPAI Joseph	MAPAI Joseph					
Without Portfolio				MAPAI Naftali (-6.52) Lavon (fr. 8.52)	MAPAI Joseph (-6.53) Lavon	MAPAI Aranne	

Governments of Israel, 1955–69

Portfolio	Third Knesset		Fourth Knesset	Fifth Knesset			Sixth Knesset
	3 Nov. 1955	7 Jan. 1958	17 Dec. 1959	2 Nov. 1961	24 June 1963	22 Dec. 1964	12 Jan. 1966
Prime Minister	MAPAI Ben-Gurion	MAPAI Ben-Gurion	MAPAI Ben-Gurion	MAPAI Ben-Gurion	MAPAI Eshkol	MAPAI Eshkol	MAPAI Eshkol (d. 26.2.69) Allon (Acting PM fr. 26.2.69)
Defense	MAPAI Ben-Gurion	MAPAI Ben-Gurion	MAPAI Ben-Gurion	MAPAI Ben-Gurion	MAPAI Eshkol	MAPAI Eshkol	MAPAI Eshkol (5.6.67) RAFI Dayan (fr. 5.6.67)
Deputy PM					MAPAI Eban	MAPAI Eban	ILP Allon (fr. 1.7.68)
Agriculture	MAPAI Luz	MAPAI Luz	MAPAI Dayan	MAPAI Dayan	MAPAI Dayan (-10.64) Gvati (fr. 9.11.64)	MAPAI Gvati	MAPAI Gvati
Commerce & Industry	MAPAI P. Sapir	MAPAI P. Sapir	MAPAI P. Sapir	MAPAI P. Sapir	MAPAI P. Sapir	MAPAI P. Sapir (-31.5.65) Zadok (fr. 31.5.65)	MAPAI Zadok (-11.66) Sharef (fr. 22.11.66)
Transportation	AHDUT AVODAH Karmel[1]	AHDUT AVODAH Karmel	AHDUT AVODAH Ben-Aharon	AHDUT AVODAH Ben-Aharon (-5.62) Bar-Yehudah (fr. 28.5.62)	AHDUT AVODAH Bar-Yehudah	AHDUT AVODAH Bar-Yehudah (-5.65) Karmel	AHDUT AVODAH Karmel[1]
Posts	NRP Burg	NRP Burg (-6.58)	P. AGUDAH Mintz (7.60– d. 30.5.61)	MAPAI Sasson	MAPAI Sasson	MAPAI Sasson	MAPAI Sasson (-2.1.67) Yeshayahu (fr. 2.1.67)
Development	MAPAM Bentov	MAPAM Bentov	MAPAM Bentov	MAPAI Josephtal[10] (d. 22.8.62) Almogi (fr. 29.8.62)[10]	MAPAI Almogi	MAPAI Almogi (-4.5.65)[10] Zadok (fr. 31.5.65)	IND LIB Kol[11]
Education and Culture	MAPAI Aranne	MAPAI Aranne	MAPAI Aranne (-5.60) Eban (fr. 8.60)	MAPAI Eban	MAPAI Aranne	MAPAI Aranne	MAPAI Aranne

Portfolio	Third Knesset		Fourth Knesset		Fifth Knesset		Sixth Knesset
	3 Nov. 1955	7 Jan. 1958	17 Dec. 1959	2 Nov. 1961	24 June 1963	22 Dec. 1964	12 Jan. 1966
Finance	MAPAI Eshkol	MAPAI Eshkol	MAPAI Eshkol	MAPAI Eshkol	MAPAI P. Sapir	MAPAI P. Sapir	MAPAI P. Sapir (-5.8.68) ILP Sharef (fr. 5.8.68)
Foreign Affairs	MAPAI Sharett (-6.56) Meir (fr. 6.56)	MAPAI Meir	MAPAI Meir	MAPAI Meir	MAPAI Meir	MAPAI Meir	MAPAI Eban
Health	MAPAM Barzilai	MAPAM Barzilai	MAPAM Barzilai	NRP M. Shapira	NRP M. Shapira	NRP M. Shapira	MAPAM Barzilai
Housing							MAPAM Bentov
Immigration (Absorption)							ILP Allon (fr. 1.7.68)
Interior	AHDUT AVODAH Bar-Yehudah	AHDUT AVODAH Bar-Yehudah	NRP H.M. Shapira	NRP H.M. Shapira	NRP H.M. Shapira	NRP H.M. Shapira	NRP H.M. Shapira
Justice	PROGR Rosen	PROGR Rosen	PROGR Rosen	MAPAI Joseph	MAPAI Joseph	MAPAI Joseph	MAPAI Y.S. Shapiro
Labor	MAPAI Meir (-6.56) Namir (fr. 6.56)	MAPAI Namir	MAPAI Josephtal	AHDUT AVODAH Allon	AHDUT AVODAH Allon	AHDUT AVODAH Allon	AHDUT AVODAH Allon (-1.7.68) ILP Almogi (fr. 1.7.68)
Police	MAPAI Shitrit	MAPAI Shitrit	MAPAI Shitrit	MAPAI Shitrit	MAPAI Shitrit	MAPAI Shitrit	MAPAI Shitrit (-12.66) Sasson (fr. 2.1.67)

Religious Affairs	NRP H.M. Shapira	NRP H.M. Shapira (-7.58) NON-PARTY Toledano (fr. 12.58)	NON-PARTY Toledano (d. 15.10.60)	NRP Warhaftig	NRP Warhaftig	NRP Warhaftig	NRP Warhaftig
Social Welfare	NRP H.M. Shapira	NRP H.M. Shapira (-6.58) MAPAI Naftali (fr. 11.58)	NRP Burg	NRP Burg	NRP Burg	NRP Burg	NRP Burg
Tourism						MAPAI Govrin	
Without Portfolio	MAPAI Naftali	MAPAI Naftali	MAPAI Eban (-8.60)	MAPAI Almogi (-29.8.62)	MAPAI Govrin (fr. 4.12.63)		AHDUT AVODAH Galili[12] ILP P. Sapir (fr. 5.8.68) GAHAL Begin (fr. 5.6.67) Y. Sapir (fr. 5.6.67)

Governments of Israel, 1969–83

Portfolio	Sixth Knesset	Seventh Knesset	Eighth Knesset		Ninth Knesset	Tenth Knesset	
	17 Mar. 1969	15 Dec. 1969	10 Mar. 1974	3 June 1974	20 June 1977	7 Aug. 1981	10 Oct. 1983
Prime Minister	ILP Meir	ILP Meir	ILP Meir	ILP Rabin	LIK-HERUT Begin	LIK-HERUT Begin	LIK-HERUT Shamir
Defense	ILP Dayan	ILP Dayan	ILP Dayan	ILP Peres	LIK-HERUT Weizman (-27.5.80) Begin (fr. 2.6.80)	LIK-HERUT Sharon (-14.2.83) Arens (fr. 23.2.83)	LIK-HERUT Zipori
Deputy PM	ILP Allon	ILP Allon	ILP Allon	ILP Allon	DMC Yadin (fr. 24.10.77) LIK-LIB Ehrlich (fr. 7.11.79)	LIK-LIB Ehrlich (d. 19.6.83) LIK-HERUT Levy (fr. 3.11.81)	LIK-HERUT Levy
Agriculture	ILP Gvati	ILP Gvati	ILP Gvati	ILP Uzan	SHLOMZION Sharon	LIK-LIB Ehrlich (d. 19.6.83)	LIK-LIB Gruper
Commerce & Industry	ILP Sharef	GAHAL Y. Sapir (-8.70) ILP P. Sapir (8.70) Bar-Lev (fr. 6.3.72)	ILP Sharef	ILP Bar-Lev	DMC Hurvitz[13] (24.10.77–1.10.78) LIK-LIB Patt (fr. 15.1.79)[13]	LIK-LIB Patt	LIK-LIB Patt
Transportation	ILP Karmel	GAHAL Weizman (-4.8.70) ILP Peres[1] (fr. 9.70)	ILP Karmel	ILP Yaakobi	DMC Amit (24.10.77–15.9.78)[1] LIK-HERUT Landau (fr. 15.1.79)	LIK-HERUT Corfu	LIK-HERUT Corfu
Posts	ILP Yeshayahu	GAHAL Rimalt (-8.70)	ILP Yeshayahu	ILP Rabin (pro-temp.) (-9.3.75) Uzan (fr. 9.3.75)	LIK-LIB Modai[2] (15.1.79–5.1.81) LIK-HERUT Aridor (fr. 5.1.81)	LIK-HERUT Zipori[2]	

Portfolio							
Development	IND LIB Kol[11]	GAHAL Landau (-4.8.70) ILP Gvati (fr. 9.70)				HATEHIYAH Neeman[18] (fr. 27.8.82)	HATEHIYAH Neeman[18]
Economic Coordinator							LIK-HERUT Meridor[19]
Education & Culture	ILP Aranne	ILP Allon	ILP Allon	ILP Yadlin	NRP Hammer	NRP Hammer	NRP Hammer
Finance	ILP Sharef	ILP P. Sapir	ILP P. Sapir	ILP Rabinowitz	LIK-LIB Ehrlich (-7.11.79) DMC Hurvitz (7.11.79–11.1.81) LIK-HERUT Aridor (fr. 20.1.81)	LIK-HERUT Aridor	LIK-HERUT Aridor (-15.10.83) Cohen-Orgad (fr. 17.10.83)
Foreign Affairs	ILP Eban	ILP Eban	ILP Eban	ILP Allon	INDEPENDENT Dayan (-21.10.79) LIK-HERUT Begin (23.10.79–10.3.80) Shamir (fr. 10.3.80)	LIK-HERUT Shamir	LIK-HERUT Shamir
Health	MAPAM Barzilai	ILP Gvati (pro-temp. -7.70) MAPAM Shemtov (fr. 7.70)	MAPAM Shemtov	MAPAM Shemtov	LIK-LAAM Shostak	LIK-LAAM Shostak	LIK-LAAM Shostak
Housing	MAPAM Bentov	ILP Sharef	ILP Rabinowitz	ILP Ofer (d. 3.1.77) MAPAM S. Rozen (fr. 17.1.77)	LIK-LIB Patt (-15.1.79)[14] LIK-HERUT Levy[14]	LIK-HERUT Levy[14]	LIK-HERUT Levy[14]

Portfolio	Sixth Knesset 17 Mar. 1969	Seventh Knesset 15 Dec. 1969	Eighth Knesset 10 Mar. 1974	Eighth Knesset 3 June 1974	Ninth Knesset 20 June 1977	Tenth Knesset 7 Aug. 1981	Tenth Knesset 10 Oct. 1983
Immigration & Absorption	ILP Allon	ILP Peres (pro-temp. -7.70) MAPAM Peled	MAPAM S. Rozen	MAPAM S. Rozen	LIK-HERUT Levy[20]	TAMI Abuhazeira[20] (-2.5.82) Uzan[20] (fr. 4.5.82)	TAMI Uzan[20]
Interior	NRP H.M. Shapira	NRP H.M. Shapira (-7.70) Burg (fr. 9.70)	NRP Burg	ILP Hillel (pro-temp. 28.5.74–29.10.74) NRP Burg (31.10.74–21.12.76)	NRP Burg	NRP Burg[15]	NRP Burg
Justice	ILP Y.S. Shapiro	ILP Y.S. Shapiro (-11.6.72) Meir (7.–9.72) Y.S. Shapiro (12.9.72–10.73)	ILP Zadok	ILP Zadok	DMC Tamir (24.10.77–2.8.80) LIK-LIB Nissim (fr. 13.8.80)	LIK-LIB Nissim	LIK-LIB Nissim
Labor	ILP Almogi	ILP Almogi	ILP Rabin	ILP Bar-Am	DMC Katz[17] (fr. 24.10.77)	TAMI Abuhazeira[17] (-2.5.82) Uzan[17] (fr. 4.5.82)	TAMI Uzan[17]
Police	ILP Sasson	ILP Hillel	ILP Hillel	ILP Hillel			
Religious Affairs	NRP Warhaftig	NRP Warhaftig	NRP Rafael	ILP Zadok (pro-temp. 28.5.74–29.10.74) NRP Rafael (-21.12.76)	NRP Abuhazeira (-18.5.81)	NRP Burg	NRP Burg
Social Welfare	NRP Burg	NRP Burg (-8.70) Hazani (fr. 9.70)	NRP Hazani	NRP Rafael MAPAM Shemtov (pro-temp.– 31.10.74) NRP			

Tourism	IND LIB Kol	IND LIB Kol	IND LIB Kol	Hazani (fr. 31.10.74– d.2.7.75) Burg (29.6.5– 11.75) Hammer (5.11.75– 21.12.76) ILP Bar-Am (pro-temp.)		LIK-LIB Sharir[16]	LIK-LIB Sharir[16]
Information		ILP Peres	IND LIB Kol ILP Yariv (-4.2.75)				
Energy & Infrastructure				LIK-LIB Modai	LIK-LIB Modai	LIK-LIB Berman (-24.9.82) Modai (fr. 19.10.82)	LIK-LIB Modai
Without Portfolio	ILP Galili[12] P. Sapir GAHAL Y. Sapir Begin	ILP Peres (-4.8.70) MAPAM Barzilai (d. 6.70) Shemtov GAHAL Begin (-4.8.70) Dulzin (-4.8.70)	ILP Galili IND LIB Hausner	ILP Galili IND LIB Hausner CRM Aloni (-5.11.74)	LIK-LIB Nissim (fr. 10.1.78–4.8.80) LIK-HERUT Landau (10.1.78– 15.1.79)	LIK-LIB Modai (-19.10.82) TELEM Ben-Porat (fr. 5.7.82) LIK-HERUT Sharon (fr. 14.2.83)	LIK-HERUT Sharon LIK-LIB Doron INDEPENDENT Ben-Porat

General Notes and Key to Tables on Israeli Governments

[a]Sources: *Israel Government Year Book*, 1950–1965, 1968–1972, 1978, 1981, 1982; *Who's Who In Israel*, 1976, 1978, 1981; *Encyclopaedia Judaica*, *Divrei Knesset* (*Knesset Minutes*), selected volumes; Michael Brecher, *The Foreign Policy System of Israel: Setting, Images, Process* (New Haven: Yale University Press, 1972), and *Decisions in Israel's Foreign Policy* (London: Oxford University Press, 1974); Colin Legum (ed.), *Middle East Contemporary Survey*, vol. 1 (1976–1977); and, for after August 1981, the daily Israeli press. Also, some information was supplied by the research staff of the Shiloah Institute at Tel-Aviv University and the Israeli Consulates in Chicago and New York.

[b]In general, when an office becomes vacant the Prime Minister assumes responsibility for that portfolio. In some cases, a Minister pro-tempore is appointed. This is indicated by the abbreviation "pro-temp."

[c]When a minister holds a portfolio for only part of the duration of a cabinet, this is indicated in parentheses. Dates given in parentheses follow the European notation—i.e., day, month, year. Thus 31.10.74 means 31 October 1974. Similarly 11.74 means November 1974.

The following notation is used to designate duration of tenure:

(- date): From formation of cabinet until date given.
(fr. date): From date given until new cabinet is formed.
(d. date): Indicates that minister died on that date.

Sources used were inconsistent in dates. We assume that discrepancies between sources are due to differences between, for example, when the appointment is announced and when the appointment is actually confirmed by the Knesset or, for example, when a minister announces the intention to resign and when the minister formally leaves office. We have, where possible, attempted to provide the formal dates of tenure.

General Notes and Key to Tables on Israeli Governments (*continued*)

[d]We have used the following abbreviations for party names:

GEN. ZION	General Zionists
MIZRAHI	Hamizrahi
P. MIZ	Hapoel Hamizrahi
NRP	National Religious Party (Mafdal)
PROGR	Progressive Party
AGUDAH	Agudat Israel
ILP	Israel Labor Party
AHDUT AVODAH	Ahudt Haavodah
P. AGUDAH	Poalei Agudat Israel
IND LIB	Independent Liberals
LIK-HERUT	Herut faction of the Likud
LIK-LIB	Liberal faction of the Likud
LIK-LAAM	Laam faction of the Likud
DMC	Democratic Movement for Change
CRM	Civil Rights Movement
TAMI	Tnuah Mesortit Israelit (Israeli Traditional Movement)

Footnotes to Tables on Israeli Governments

[1]Portfolio defined as Minister of Transport and Communications. The responsibility for posts is included in this portfolio whenever a Minister of Posts is not appointed.
[2]Portfolio defined as Communications.
[3]Portfolio defined as Agriculture and Development.
[4]Portfolio defined as Commerce, Industry, and Supply.
[5]Portfolio defined as Labor and Construction.
[6]Golda Meyerson later changed her name to Meir.
[7]Portfolio defined as Labor and National Insurance.
[8]Portfolio defined as Religious Affairs and War Victims.
[9]After Levin left office Shapira's portfolio was defined as Religious Affairs and Social Welfare. In the next cabinet these were again defined as two separate portfolios, although both were still held by Shapira.
[10]Portfolio defined as Development and Housing.
[11]Portfolio defined as Development and Tourism.
[12]Galili, as Minister Without Portfolio, was given the special responsibility of being in charge of Information.
[13]Portfolio defined as Industry, Commerce, and Tourism.[20]
[14]Portfolio defined as Construction and Housing.
[15]Burg has special responsibility for the Autonomy Talks.
[16]Portfolio defined as Tourism and Trade.
[17]Portfolio defined as Labor and Social Affairs.
[18]Portfolio defined as Science and Development.
[19]Portfolio defined as Economics and Interministerial Coordination.
[20]Portfolio defined as Immigrants' Absorption.

Immigration to Israel, 1948–82

Year	Number of Immigrants[a]
1948–1982	1,721,424
1948[b]	101,819
1949	239,576
1950	170,215
1951	175,129
1952	24,369
1953	11,326
1954	18,370
1955	37,478
1956	56,234
1957	71,224
1958	27,082
1959	23,895
1960	24,510
1961	47,638
1962	61,328
1963	64,364
1964	54,716
1965	30,736
1966	15,730
1967	14,327
1968	20,544
1969	37,804
1970	36,750
1971	41,930
1972	55,888
1973	54,886
1974	31,979
1975	20,028
1976	19,754
1977	21,429
1978	26,394
1979	37,222
1980	20,428
1981	12,599
1982	13,723

SOURCES: *Israel Statistical Abstract*, 1980; and *Monthly Bulletin of Statistics*, 32:2 (February 1981), and 34:6 (June 1983).

[a] Includes tourists who changed their status and potential immigrants (from 1969) but excludes immigrating citizens.

[b] From May 15, 1948.

Jewish Refugees from Arab Countries

Number of Jews Residing in Arab Countries in 1948 and 1980		Number of Jewish Emigrants to Israel (May 1948–1972) from Arab Countries	
	1948	1980	
Morocco	235,000	20,000	Morocco
Algiers	140,000	500	Algiers } 330,800
Tunisia	105,000	2,000	Tunisia
Libya	38,000	—	Libya	35,600
Egypt	75,000	200	Egypt	20,500
Iraq	135,000	200	Iraq	130,000
Syria	30,000	4,500	Syria } 10,500
Lebanon	5,000	200	Lebanon
Yemen	55,000	1,000	Yemen	51,000
Aden	8,000	—	
Total	826,000	28,600		578,400

SOURCE: World Organization of Jews from Arab Countries.

American Immigration to Israel,
1948–82[a]

Year	Number of Immigrants
1948–82	61,792
1948–51	1,711
1952–54	428
1955–57	416
1958–60	708
1961–64	2,102
1965–68	2,066
1969	5,738
1970	6,882
1971	7,364
1972	5,515
1973	4,393
1974	3,089
1975	2,803
1976	2,746
1977	2,571
1978	2,921
1979	2,950
1980	2,312
1981	2,384
1982	2,693

SOURCES: *Israel Statistical Abstract*, 1974–75, 1977–79, 1982; *Monthly Bulletin of Statistics*, 32:2 (February 1981), 34:6 (June 1983).

[a]This table refers to all immigrants and potential immigrants whose last country of *residence* was the United States. The figures for 1961–68 include temporary residents. The figures for 1969–82 include the status "potential immigrant" (oleh bekoah) which was chosen by more than 75% of American immigrants, enabling them to postpone the assumption of citizenship for three years.

Jewish Emigration from the USSR to Israel, 1968–82

Year	Number Emigrated to Israel
1968–1982	163,108
1968–1970	4,263
1971	12,819
1972	31,652
1973	33,477
1974	16,816
1975	8,531
1976	7,274
1977	8,348
1978	12,192
1979	17,614
1980	7,570
1981	1,770
1982	782

SOURCES: Ministry for Immigrants' Absorption figures as reported in *Insight* (London), 3:5 (May 1977), p. 2; Yaakov Roi and Yosi Galdshtein, "Tnuat Hayeziah Mibrit Hamoezot—sikumo shel asor" (The emigration movement from the USSR—decennial summary), *Hainteligenziyah Hayehudit Bivrit Hamoezot* (The Jewish Intelligenzia in the USSR), 4 (June 1980), p. 74; and *Monthly Bulletin of Statistics*, 32:2 (February 1981) and 34:6 (June 1983).

The Extent of Real Immigration and Emigration, 1969–1982.

Following the 1973 war the number of immigrants coming to Israel each year decreased and the number of Israelis going abroad increased. Thus it has been feared that political and economic developments since the 1973 war have led to unprecedented emigration rates and perhaps even a negative migratory balance. The issue of whether or not Israel has a negative or positive migration balance is important for two reasons: (1) Zionist ideology asserts that Israel is the center of world Jewry and should attract and retain Jews from all over the world. (2) The current debate about settlement policies in the West Bank and Gaza is affected by different projections regarding the relative proportion of Jews and non-Jews in Israel and its territories and by different assessments of the political significance of this "demographic problem."

In the following table we try to make sense of the statistical data published by the Israeli Central Bureau of Statistics (CBS) and to compute rough estimates of the number of Israelis permanently leaving the country and the number of immigrants entering each year to settle permanently.

It would seem that this should be a straightforward calculation of emigrants (*yordim*, sing. *yored*) and immigrants (*olim*, sing. *oleh*). However, the CBS provides data only on the number of legal exits and entries through its ports by visa type and registration category. Thus, we know the number of exits by permanent Israeli residents each year (but not the actual number of permanent residents exiting) and the length of their stay abroad. But we do not know how many of these people go abroad as tourists, for extended stays as students or emissaries, etc. Moreover, permanent residents who settle abroad and then return (e.g., after four years, or even after seven or eight years) as tourists may still be registered as returning residents.

In the following table we have tried to estimate the number of people entering the country each year since 1969 who can be expected to remain permanently and also the number of permanent residents leaving each year who can be expected to remain abroad permanently. Our calculations are only estimates.

The first problem is to estimate the number of people entering the country each year who will permanently settle (column 4). In column 1 we have assumed that 80% of the people who take out immigrant visas will in fact become permanent residents. (Because our calculations are only rough estimates of the general magnitude of the immigration balance, we have not attempted to estimate a retention rate that would vary by year according to differences in the economic conditions of Israel and the places of origin of the immigrants. To have done so would be methodologically elegant but misleading as to the rough nature of our estimates.) Column 2 is the number of people entering as "potential immigrants" (*olim bekoah*) who later changed their status and became permanent residents (or who are projected as becoming permanent residents). Column 3 gives the number of children born to Israeli citizens abroad who immigrate. We have assumed that all people registered in this category came to settle. While this is probably untrue, (1) some people probably entered the country under foreign passports, and (2) the numbers involved are not large enough to significantly affect the rough estimates in columns 4, 7, and 8.

The next problem is to estimate the number of permanent residents leaving each year who will in fact never return (except perhaps for brief visits). We have used the following rule of thumb to arrive at the figures in column 5: permanent residents who leave Israel and stay abroad for over four years are *yordim*. The underlying (untested) assumption is that the number of emigrants returning as tourists within four years of their departure approximately equals the number of Israelis permanently returning after four years abroad. Column 5 thus provides an estimate of the number of Israelis leaving each year who will permanently reside abroad.

However, the underlying assumption is probably false. The number of real emigrants returning as tourists within four years of their departure is probably greater than the number of "false" emigrants (i.e., Israelis returning permanently after four years). If this is the case, then the assumption underlying the "four year" rule is

false and, consequently, the figures in column 5 are too low an estimate of the number of permanent emigrants. We attempt to rectify this problem by making a second estimate based on the "three year" rule—i.e., the number of permanent residents who stay abroad for over three years. Column 6 gives the numbers of permanent residents who left Israel in a given year and stayed abroad over three years. The assumption underlying columns 6 and 8 is the same as that underlying columns 5 and 7.

(Demographers and statisticians will note that we should, ideally, subtract exiting new immigrants from columns 5 and 6. However, we have no basis on which to estimate the rate of exit over time—i.e., from which rows should we subtract such and such number of emigrants. Moreover, because of our overestimates in column 1, we are confident in the range of the migratory balance we present in columns 7 and 8.)

Thus the figures given in columns 7 and 8 present our best estimate of the range of the immigration balance for each of the fourteen years.

Our estimates (in columns 7 and 8) are vastly different from those of Yizhak Berman in *Do"h Hevrati al Israel (1969–1979)* (*Report on the Israeli Social Scene 1969–1979*), (Information Department of the Israeli Ministry of Labor and Welfare, July 1981). He states: "From 1969–1979 there has been a negative emigration balance of Israeli residents . . . of 126,464" (p. 12). Our figures, however, show an estimated positive balance of between 149,482 and 171,182 for the same period when all permanent immigration and migration are accounted for. Thus our analysis supports Ya'akov Amead's reaction to Berman's report and his assertion that "having examined the facts of the case we see that Jewish emigration is not the cause for alarm that it has been made out to be." (See Ya'akov Amead, "Emigration—The Non-Issue" [manuscript dated 21 August 1981]) On the other hand, our analysis raises serious questions about the prospects for continued population growth based on continued high—or even medium—levels of net immigration. Therefore, for the years 1969–1978, we estimate a migratory balance of 60,000 to 80,000 less than the estimate in the *Encyclopaedia Judaica Decennial Book, 1973–1982*. Our calculations also suggest that the official CBS population projections are based on a false optimism of high migration balances.

Number of Olim and Yordim, 1969–1982: Estimates of the Number of People Entering Israel with the Intention of Permanently Settling and of the Number of Israeli Residents Permanently Leaving the Country, by Year of Passage through a Legal Port

Year	(1)[a]	(2)[b]	(3)[c]	(4)[d]	(5)[e]	(6)[f]	(7)[g]	(8)[h]
1969	21,374	7,569	—	28,943	6,200	7,800	22,743	21,143
1970	19,670	6,871	1,082	27,623	7,100	8,500	20,523	19,123
1971	23,097	7,296	873	31,266	9,000	10,600	22,266	20,666
1972	36,141	6,346	789	43,276	7,900	9,900	35,376	33,376
1973	36,943	4,698	763	42,404	14,800	17,200	27,604	25,204
1974	20,191	3,831	509	24,531	16,400	18,900	8,131	5,631
1975	11,476	3,182	604	15,262	13,200	15,600	2,062	−338
1976	10,472	3,536	680	14,688	16,000	18,000	−1,312	−3,312
1977	10,874	4,017	752	15,643	14,700	16,600	943	−957
1978	14,218	4,480	711	19,409	(10,000)	11,900	9,409	7,509
1979	20,044	6,778	615	27,437	(4,000)	(6,000)	23,437	21,437
1980	10,296	3,888	514	14,698	(25,500)	(28,000)	−10,802	−13,302
1981	4,619	3,032	471	8,122	(15,000)	(17,500)	−6,878	−9,378
1982	4,715	3,487	542	8,744	(16,000)	(17,300)	−7,256	−8,556
Total	244,130	69,011	8,905	322,046	175,800	203,800	146,246	118,246

The analysis and the table were prepared specially for this volume by Benjamin Mordecai Ben-Baruch.

[a]Column 1 represents 80% of the number of immigrants (including tourists who changed their visa status to "immigrant") and is thus our estimate of the number of immigrants who entered Israel in each of these years and have (or will) in fact remain permanently. Based on *Israel Statistical Abstract*, 1982, Table V/13, between 82.5% and 89.9% of immigrants surveyed after one year in Israel (beginning in 1973–74) indicated that they were "sure to stay." However, the actual number who would in fact remain is probably lower than this. (If we compare *ISA*, 1982, Tables V/3 and V/13 we see that the percentage of potential immigrants who said they were "sure to stay" is 20 to 30% above the actual number who stayed.) We therefore feel that 80% is a somewhat high estimate of the total number of immigrants who will stay permanently. (See text for reason we present a high estimate.) Sources: *ISA*, 1982, Table V/2; and *Monthly Bulletin of Statistics*, 34:1 (January 1983), Table E/2. The figure for 1982 is a projection based on data for 11 months.

[b]Column 2 gives the number of people who obtained a "potential immigrant" visa and who later became immigrants. For years 1969–76, figures were derived from the percentage of those who settled permanently by 1981. For years 1977–82, the assumption was made that 45% would settle permanently. Again, the 1982 figure is projected, based on data for the first 11 months. Sources: *MBS Supplement*, 31:8 (August 1980), Table 10; *ISA*, 1982, Table V/3; *MBS*, 34:1 (January 1983), Table E/2.

[c]Column 3 provides the number of "returning citizens," i.e., individuals born to Israeli citizens living abroad who returned to Israel. Source: *MBS*, 34:1 (January 1983), Table E/2.

[d]Total of columns 1, 2, and 3. It is an estimate of the total number of people who entered the country and have (or will) remain permanently.

[e]Column 5 gives the number of permanent residents who left the country and stayed abroad for over four years. Figures in parentheses are estimates. For 1982 we assumed that 2.5% of those leaving the country would remain abroad for more than four years. Sources: *ISA*, 1982, Table IV/5; and *MBS*, 34:1 (January 1983), Table E/1.

[f]Column 6 presents the number of permanent residents who left the country and stayed abroad for over three years. Figures in parentheses are estimates. For 1982 we assumed that 2.7% of those leaving Israel would remain abroad for more than three years. Sources: Same as those for column 5.

[g]Column 7 is the estimated migration balance based on the "four-year rule." Column 7 = column 5 − column 4.

[h]Column 8 is the estimated migration balance based on the "three-year rule." Column 8 = column 6 − column 4.

Population by District and Population Group in Absolute Numbers and Percentages

District		1948	1961	1972	1981
		Jews			
Jerusalem	(000s)	84.2	187.7	261.1	336.0
District	(%)	12.0	9.7	9.7	10.1
Northern	(000s)	53.4	194.3	255.7	321.9
District	(%)	7.6	10.0	9.5	9.7
Haifa	(000s)	147.7	322.3	408.8	464.7
District	(%)	21.1	16.7	15.2	14.0
Central	(000s)	106.2	380.1	535.3	743.4
District	(%)	15.2	19.7	19.9	22.3
Tel Aviv	(000s)	302.1	692.6	899.9	1,004.0
District	(%)	43.2	35.9	33.5	30.1
Southern	(000s)	6.0	155.3	323.8	433.4
District	(%)	0.9	8.0	12.1	13.0
Administered	(000s)	—	—	2.1	27.2
Territories[a]	(%)	—	—	0.1	0.8
Total	(000s)	716.7[b]	1,932.3	2,686.7	3,330.6
	(%)	100.0	100.0	100.0	100.0
		Non-Jews			
Jerusalem	(000s)	2.9	4.2	86.3	121.1
District	(%)	1.8	1.7	18.7	18.4
Northern	(000s)	90.6	142.8	217.6	304.5
District	(%)	58.1	57.7	47.2	46.3
Haifa	(000s)	27.4	48.0	75.0	105.2
District	(%)	17.6	19.4	16.3	16.0
Central	(000s)	16.1	26.9	44.4	63.9
District	(%)	10.3	10.9	9.6	9.7
Tel Aviv	(000s)	3.6	6.7	7.3	10.5
District	(%)	2.3	2.8	1.6	1.6
Southern	(000s)	15.4	18.6	30.4	52.2
District	(%)	9.9	7.5	6.6	7.9
Total	(000s)	156.0	247.2	461.0	657.4
	(%)	100.0	100.0	100.0	99.9
West Bank[c]	(000s)				703.1
Gaza and Northern					
Sinai[c]	(000s)				442.0
Golan Heights[d]	(000s)				12.0

SOURCE: *Israel Statistical Abstract*, 1980, Table II/4, and 1982, Table II/7; *Monthly Bulletin of Statistics*, 34:6 (June 1983), Table B/1.

[a]Israeli residents who live there.

[b]Including not known.

[c]Source: *Israel Statistical Abstract*, 1982, Table XXVII/1. These figures are estimates of the total population (including Jews). Since it is not known how many of the 27,200 Jews living in the administered territories live in the West Bank and how many in Gaza, we have made no attempt to adjust these figures. However, it can be safely assumed that the vast majority of Jews in the administered territories live in the West Bank.

[d]Estimate of population in January 1982.

Introduction to Tables on Jewish Settlement

The following three tables are presented to provide a statistical overview of several aspects of Jewish settlement in Israel—from the pre-state years until the present. Settlement policy has, from the very beginnings of the Zionist movement, been intertwined with the ideologies, security and defense concerns, and economic and social policies of various Zionist organizations, political parties, and Israeli governments.

The first table, which looks at Jewish settlements in Palestine, Israel, and the administered territories, shows the growth of Jewish settlements and how their geographic concentration (in terms of number of settlements) has varied over time. The second table, focusing on cooperative settlements by type and affiliation, shows the number, population, and type(s) of cooperative settlements established by the various ideologically oriented cooperative settlements movements. Finally, the third table, Jewish settlements, in the West Bank and Gaza, shows which movements are establishing particular kinds of settlements in the territories captured in 1967 and 1973 (and, by implication, which settlement movement is not settling in these areas). As made clear in the text, settlement in these territories has become, both domestically and diplomatically, one of Israel's most controversial policies in recent years.

Jewish Settlements Established in Palestine, Israel, and the Administered Territories by Region and Period of Settlement (Measured in Terms of Service of World Zionist Congresses), as of July 1982

From Congress –to Congress	Period	Total	Galilee Mountains	Northern Region	Central Region	Negev & Arava	West Bank	Jordan Valley	Golan Heights	Gaza Region
Old Settlement										
Up to 1st Congress	Established before1870	8	1	3	3	1	—	—	—	—
1st Congress	1870–1896	14	—	6	8	—	—	—	—	—
1–5	1897–1900	—	—	—	—	—	—	—	—	—
5–8	1901–1906	7	—	6	1	—	—	—	—	—
8–11	1907–1912	8	—	6	2	—	—	—	—	—
11–14	1913–1924	32	—	22	10	—	—	—	—	—
14–17	1925–1930	28	—	13	15	—	—	—	—	—
17–20	1931–1936	64	1	20	43	—	—	—	—	—
20–22	1937–1947	125	7	65	36	17	—	—	—	—
22–23	1948–1950	261	27	62	130	42	—	—	—	—
23–24	1951–1955	122	4	22	51	45	—	—	—	—
24–25	1956–1960	41	6	9	11	15	—	—	—	—
25–26	1961–1963	9	1	3	1	4	—	—	—	—
26–27	1964–1966	13	5	—	5	3	—	—	—	—
27–28	1967–1971	33	—	—	4	3	4	9	12	1
28–29	1972–1976	32	—	2	2	7	6	5	9	1
29–30	1977–1982	205	64	4	6	29	62	17	14	9
Grand Total		1002	116	243	328	166	72	31	35	11

SOURCE: "Map of Settlement of Eretz Israel," presented by the Settlement Division of the Jewish Agency and the Settlement Division of the Zionist Organization, July 1982.

Note: This table includes the following types of settlements: *kibbutzim; moshavim; moshavim shitufim; moshavim; villages; moshavot* (farm communities); rural/industrial centers; *nahal* settlements intended for conversion into civilian settlements; community villages/settlements (planned housing projects in the West Bank, usually for about 300 families, with closed membership and nominally cooperative structures for the provision of municipal, welfare, and cultural services and economic activity); agricultural institutions and schools; and urban settlements.

Settlements that have undergone ideological schisms subsequent to their initial establishment and hence have divided into two settlements affiliated with different movements are treated according to the initial date of settlement. Similarly, settlements that have been abandoned and subsequently resettled are treated according to the date of original settlement of the site.

Cooperative Settlements by Type and Affiliation (as of December 31, 1981)

Cooperative Movement	Affiliation	Number of Settlements	Total Population
Moshavim and Collective Moshavim—total		447	153,100
Moshavim—total		409	144,600
Tnuat Hamoshavim	Formerly Mapai, now Labor Party	248	89,500
Hapoel Hamizrahi	Formerly Hapoel Hamizrahi, now NRP	65	28,500
Haihud Hahaklai	None	46	12,700
Haoved Haziyoni	Independent Liberals	17	4,900
Poalei Agudat Israel	Poalei Agudat Israel	8	2,700
Herut	Formerly Herut, then Gahal, now the Likud	15	2,700
Hitahdut Haikarim	None	5	1,600
No affiliation	—	5	1,900
Moshavim Shitufim—total		38	8,400
Tnuat Hamoshavim	As above	5	1,200
Hapoel Hamizrahi	As above	9	2,800
Hatnuah Hakibbuzit Hameuhedet[a]	Formerly Mapai, now Labor Party	6	1,200
Haoved Haziyoni	As above	8	1,200
Herut	As above	4	800
Poalei Agudat Israel	As above	4	800
Haihud Hahaklai	As above	1	400
Kibbutzim—total		259	113,700
Hakibbutz Haarzi	Formerly Hashomer Hazair, now Mapam	79	37,900
Hatnuah Hakibbuzit Hameuhedet[a]	Now Labor Party	156	66,200
Hakibbutz Hadati	Hapoel Hamizrahi, now the NRP	15	6,500
Haoved Haziyoni	Independent Liberals	5	1,800
Poalei Agudat Israel	Poalei Agudat Israel	2	1,200
Nonaffiliated	—	1	100

SOURCE: *Israel Statistical Abstract*, 1982, Table II/12.

Note: A moshav is an agriculturally based settlement in which property is privately owned but marketing is done collectively. A moshav shitufi (collective moshav) is an agriculturally based settlement in which production and marketing are done collectively but consumption expenditures are decided privately. A kibbutz is a settlement in which all economic activity is collective. All three types of settlements were originally agricultural settlements. Today, especially among the kibbutzim, these settlements frequently have industrial enterprises as well.

[a]Hatnuah Hakibbuzit Hameuhedet was formed by an amalgamation (begun in 1980 and completed in 1981) of Ihud Hakvuzot Vehakibbutzim and Hakibbutz Hameuhad. The former had been affiliated with Mapai. The latter had been affiliated with Ahdut Haavoah (1919–1930), then Mapai and Faction B within Mapai (1930–1944), then Ahdut Haavodah (1944–1948), then Mapam (1949–1954), then Ahdut Haavodah (1954–1968).

As of December 31, 1980, Ihud Hakvuzot Vehakibbutzim had 6 moshavim shitufim with a combined population of 1,200 and 88 kibbutzim with a combined population of 35,300. Hakibbutz Hameuhad had 65 kibbutzim with a combined population of 29,300.

Jewish Settlements in the West Bank and Gaza by Movement and Type of Settlement (January 1983)

Movement and Settlement Type	Number of Settlements
	West Bank
Amanah (*Gush Emunim*)	26
Community	23
Moshav shitufi	3
Herut	10
Community	7
Moshav	2
Moshav shitufi	1
Haoved Haziyoni	2
Moshav	1
Moshav shitufi	1
Haoved Haleumi (*Likud-Laam*)	2
Community	1
Village	1
Haihud Hahaklai	5
Community	1
Moshav	3
Village	1
Tnuat Hamoshavim	5
Community	1
Moshav	4
Poalei Agudat Israel	2
Moshav shitufi	2
Hapoel Hamizrahi	3
Moshav	1
Moshav shitufi	2
Hakibbutz Hadati	3
Kibbutz	3
Ihud Hakvuzot Vehakibbutzim[a]	4
Moshav	1
Kibbutz	3
Hakibbutz Hameuhad[a]	3
Kibbutz	3
Nahal Settlements[b]	10
Nonaffiliated	24
Urban	16
Rural-Industrial	4
Community	3
Unknown Affiliation	16
Community	5
New	2
Pending Approval	2
Recently were Nahal	7

Movement and Settlement Type	Number of Settlements
	Gaza
Hapoel Hamizrahi	6
Moshav	6
Tnuat Hamoshavim	1
Moshav	1
Nahal[b]	1
Nonaffiliated	2
Village	2
Unknown	1
Total	126

SOURCE: "Map of Settlement of Eretz Israel," presented by the Settlement Division of the Jewish Agency and the Settlement Division of the Zionist Organization, July 1982. Figures for the West Bank were updated by David Peiffer, University of Michigan, from Jewish Agency and World Zionist Organization sources.

[a]Ihud Hakvuzot Vehakibbutzim and Hakibbutz Hameuhad merged to form Hatnuah Hakibbutzit Hamehedet.

[b]Nahal settlements are established by the military, often to be converted at some future date into permanent civilian settlements.

Real Wages in Israel since 1948: A Comparison of the Consumer Price Index and Average Monthly Wages per Employee's Post

	Consumer Price Index (Ann. Ave.) Index: Sept. 1951 = 100 (1)[a]	Average Monthly Wages per Employee's Post (IL.) (2)[b]	Percent Change of CPI from Previous Year (3)[c]	Percent Change of Average Wages per Employee's Post from Prev. Year (4)[d]	Percent Change of Real Wages from Previous Year (5)[e]
1948	89	—	—	—	—
1949	91	—	2.2	—	—
1950	85	—	−6.6	—	—
1951	97	—	14.1	—	—
1952	153	—	57.7	—	—
1953	196	—	28.1	—	—
1954	220	—	12.2	—	—
1955	233	—	5.9	—	—
1956	248	—	6.4	—	—
1957	264	—	6.5	—	—
1958	273	—	4.9	—	—
1959	277	—	1.5	—	—
1960	283	—	2.3	—	—
1961	302	275	6.7	—	—
1962	331	317	9.4	15.3	5.3
1963	348	354	5.1	11.7	6.3
1964	371	398	6.6	12.4	5.4
1965	399	477	7.7	17.5	9.1
1966	431	568	8.0	19.1	10.2
1967	438	570	1.6	0.4	−1.2
1968	448	595	2.1	4.4	1.1
1969	459	631	2.5	6.1	3.5
1970	487	688	6.1	9.0	2.7
1971	545	801	12.0	16.4	4.0
1972	615	912	12.9	13.9	0.9
1973	738	1,163	20.0	27.5	6.3
1974	1,031	1,584	39.7	36.2	−2.3
1975	1,436	2,205	39.3	36.7	−2.2
1976	1,886	2,920	31.3	32.7	1.3
1977	2,539	4,342	34.6	48.7	10.8
1978	3,823	6,693	50.6	54.1	1.6

	Consumer Price Index (Ann. Ave.) Index: Sept. 1951 = 100 (1)[a]	Average Monthly Wages per Employee's Post (IL.) (2)[b]	Percent Change of CPI from Previous Year (3)[c]	Percent Change of Average Wages per Employee's Post from Prev. Year (4)[d]	Percent Change of Real Wages from Previous Year (5)[e]
1979	6,817	12,730	78.3	93.0	9.6
1980	15,748	28,730	131.0	125.5	−3.3
1981	34,141	68,710	116.8	139.1	10.4
1982	75,236	150,100	120.4	118.4	−1.0

[a]Sources: *Israel Statistical Abstract*, 1980, Table X/2, and 1982, Table X/2; *Monthly Bulletin of Statistics*, 32:2 (February 1981), Table J/1, and 34:1 (January 1983), Table J/1.

[b]Sources: *ISA*, 1980, Table XII/26; *MBS* 32:5 (May 1981), and 34:6 (June 1983), Table K/4. Data from 1968 exclude workers from the administered territories.

Note that wages are given in Israeli Lira, not in the present currency, Israeli Shekels. IL. 10 = IS. 1. Also note that because of changes in sampling methods, data bases, and tax laws these data should not be manipulated without consulting the original sources. Using the exchange rates of IL./$ (from the *ISA*, 1982, Tables IX/11–12 and from *MBS*, 34:6 [June 1983], Table I/13), we have computed the following average monthly wages in U.S. dollars in order to provide an indication of wage rates in a more stable and universally recognized currency: 1961—$153; 1963—$118; 1968—$170; 1970—$197; 1972—$217; 1973—$277; 1980—$563; 1981—$602; 1982—$456 [sic].

[c]Source: *ISA*, 1982, Table X/I. The *ISA* reversed the proper figures for the years 1963 and 1964. The correct figures are presented here.

[d]Sources: *ISA*, 1982, Table XII/36; and *MBS*, 34:6 (June 1983), Table K/4. Since the figures given for 1968 compare workers, *including* workers in the administered territories, the official figure of 3.2% was revised using the data here.

[e]Source: *ISA*, 1982, Table XII/36. The figures do not exactly correspond to a simple computational procedure of deflating wages by the CPI.

Development of the Educational System since 1948: Number of Institutions and Students

	Jews								Arabs							
	Number of Institutions in Educational System				Number of Students				Number of Institutions in Educational System				Number of Students			
Year	1948/49	1959/60	1969/70	1981/82	1948/49	1959/60	1969/70	1981/82	1948/49	1959/60	1969/70	1981/82	1948/49	1959/60	1969/70	1981/82
Kindergartens	—	—	—	—	25,406	75,699	107,668	248,800	10	120	177	—	1,124	7,274	14,211	18,434
Primary	467	1,501	1,519	1,499	91,133	375,054	394,354	455,431	45	139	219	321	9,991	36,903	85,449	131,398
Intermediate	—	—	32	248	—	—	7,908	81,432	—	—	4	46	—	—	2,457	15,996
Secondary (all)	98	353	544	477	10,218	55,142	129,436	154,193	1	7	35	75	14	1,956	8,050	26,814
General	39	113	219	246	7,168	32,894	63,731	66,155	1	5	18	54	14	1,933	6,198	22,540
Vocational	26	60	258	304	2,002	10,167	49,556	76,361	—	—	16	37	—	—	1,452	3,528
Agricultural	—	30	30	27	—	5,016	7,641	4,284	—	1	1	2	—	23	390	746
Continuation	33	95	109	54	1,048	7,065	8,508	6,853	—	—	—	—	—	—	—	—
Teacher training colleges	—	—	40	44	713	3,077	8,083	11,762	—	1	1	2	—	121	370	411
Other post-secondary	—	—	—	—	583	2,724	6,900	15,937	—	—	—	—	—	—	—	148
Universities	—	—	—	—	1,635	11,300	36,246	60,000	—	—	—	—	—	—	—	—
Other	—	—	—	—	—	10,952	26,300	44,000	—	—	—	—	—	—	—	—
Total	565	1,854	2,104	2,061	129,688	533,948	713,895	1,068,255	46	146	256	366	11,129	46,259	110,537	193,301

sources: *Statistical Abstract of Israel*, 1982, Tables XXII/8,10, and 30; and "Netunim Demografim" ("Demographic Data"), Bureau of the Advisor on Arab Affairs of the Prime Minister's office, March 1980 (unpublished).

Note: Schools in which studies are held at more than one level (such as primary and intermediate, or intermediate and secondary) are counted at each level. But in the "total" they are counted only once.

Institutions defined as "other" include special schools, centers for juvenile offenders, and, in the Jewish sector, certain religious schools with curricula not controlled by the Ministry of Education.

Information for 1981/82 is provisional data.

Enrollment figures for the universities include all students, including non-Jews. Through 1970 over 98% of the university students were Jews. In 1978/79, 96.7% of all university students were Jews (and 94.6% of all students studying for their first degree).

Israeli Casualties from Terrorist Activities, 1967–81

Year	Soliders		Civilians	
	Killed	Wounded	Killed	Wounded
1967[a]	13	57	6	22
1968	52	192	45	275
1969	73	326	24	238
1970	43	253	57	196
1971	12	113	11	52
1972	17	55	45	122
1973[b]	5	30	7	42
1974	16	17	62	196
1975	12	53	33	185
1976	2	8	15	109
1977	3	6	5	155
1978	29	81	57	279
1979	3	12	21	304
1980	9	58	10	77
Total	289	1,261	398	2,252

SOURCE: IDF Spokesman, Information Branch June 29, 1981. No official figures have been released (as of this writing) for 1981. However, the Hebrew language Israeli daily newspaper, *Maariv*, reported that a total of 17 Israelis were killed and 157 Israelis were wounded by terrorist activities during 1981. (*Maariv*, January 1, 1982.)

[a]From June 12, 1967 to December 31, 1967.

[b]Excluding the period of the October 1973 War (October 6–23, 1973).

Index

Italicized page numbers indicate where major figures, events, and organizations are identified.